'This is the book the general public has been waiting for! Positive psy
more fulfilling life – beautifully crafted into a self-development guide that actually works – truly exciting! Lots of content, easy to understand – approved by science – written by a world-renowned expert – what are you waiting for?' – *Robert Isler, PhD, President of the New Zealand Association of Positive Psychology*

'In *Positive Psychology and You: A Self-Development Guide*, drawing from convincing evidence on the effectiveness of positive psychology interventions, Alan Carr offers jargon-free, easy-to-follow exercises which can help you to be physically and mentally healthier and happier and secure your self-development through warm and caring relationships. Unlike other self-help books, apps and diets which lack evidence and oversimplify the complexity and multiplicity of contemporary challenges, *Positive Psychology and You* will give you concrete and constructive strategies and a treasure-trove of resources which you can draw upon, when needed most'. – *Tayyab Rashid, PhD, Inaugural President of the Clinical Division of the International Positive Psychology Association, and author of* Positive Psychotherapy

'For years, Alan Carr's *Positive Psychology* has been my favourite textbook for undergraduate students. *Positive Psychology and You* takes positive psychology one step further by offering a sound, exceptionally clear and well-structured pathway to those interested in applying it in real life. Spanning personal well-being and resilience, couple relationships, parenting and psychological challenges, the book integrates the latest positive psychology with its mainstream cousins, resulting in powerful solutions to apply daily'. – *Professor Ilona Boniwell, PhD, Strategic Leader of MSc in Applied Positive Psychology, Anglia Ruskin University, UK, and CEO of Positran*

'As the author of one of positive psychology's leading textbooks, Professor Carr has once again used his depth of knowledge and expertise to create an accessible and considered book for those wanting to learn more about positive psychology in practice. This book covers a vast array of applied topic areas across both the individual and interpersonal level, whilst embedded within an approachable narrative of real-life examples from his own clinical practice. Readers are also offered the opportunity to undertake personal exercises, reflections, and psychological scales, encouraging deeper learning and engagement with the research presented. This book is a great starting point for those wanting to know more about positive psychology and how to incorporate this fascinating research into their daily life'. – *Kate Hefferon, Head of the Posttraumatic Growth Research University of East London, UK, and author of* Positive Psychology Theory, Research and Applications

'The book *Positive Psychology and You: A Self-Development Guide* by Alan Carr is a true gift to those who want to get the most out of life. The book is full of reliable tools and recommendations based on real science that are easy to follow for those who truly want to enhance their wellbeing and live their life to the fullest. When you read the book you sense that the author knows the topic and has real experience in helping people. Alan has great skill in summarizing various studies like he has done so brilliantly in the past for professionals and students and here he sums up and translates the scientific results and makes them accessible for the public. His background as a clinical psychologist and a researcher is very valuable and makes this book unique. Alan knows that there are no quick-fix solutions to the good life, but that sustainable wellbeing can be achieved through evidence-based positive psychology interventions. I recommend this book to all of those out there who want to live their best life. – ... tir, PhD, President of the European Network for Positive ... minants of Health & Well-Being, Directorate of Health ...

# POSITIVE PSYCHOLOGY AND YOU

This broad and innovative self-development guide shows readers how they can use scientific findings from contemporary positive psychology to enhance their lives. Containing dozens of practical exercises and real-life examples, it helps bring positive psychology findings from the lab into day-to-day life.

Divided into six parts and covering a wide array of themes, this book is designed to help people with or without mental health problems enhance their well-being. It answers questions like: what is well-being? What are the main determinants of well-being, and how can we sustain it? There are also chapters on physical exercise, progressive muscle relaxation and mindfulness meditation, savouring pleasures, creative solution-finding and developing compassionate relationships.

This non-technical and highly accessible book will be of interest to those from all backgrounds with an interest in self-development, as well as mental health workers and related professionals.

**Alan Carr**, PhD, is Professor of Clinical Psychology at University College Dublin, and Couple and Family Therapist at Clanwilliam Institute, Ireland. He has conducted clinical practice in the UK, Canada and Ireland, helping individuals, couples and families with a wide range of problems across the lifespan. He has produced over 25 books and 250 academic papers in the areas of positive psychology, clinical psychology and family therapy.

# POSITIVE PSYCHOLOGY AND YOU

A self-development guide

Alan Carr

Routledge
Taylor & Francis Group

LONDON AND NEW YORK

First published 2020
by Routledge
2 Park Square, Milton Park, Abingdon, Oxon OX14 4RN

and by Routledge
52 Vanderbilt Avenue, New York, NY 10017

*Routledge is an imprint of the Taylor & Francis Group, an informa business*

© 2020 Alan Carr

*British Library Cataloguing-in-Publication Data*
A catalogue record for this book is available from the British Library

*Library of Congress Cataloging-in-Publication Data*
A catalog record has been requested for this book

ISBN: 978-0-367-22434-9 (hbk)
ISBN: 978-0-367-22435-6 (pbk)
ISBN: 978-0-429-27485-5 (ebk)

Typeset in Interstate
by Swales & Willis Ltd, Exeter, Devon, UK

# CONTENTS

# FOREWORD

There has been a lot of hype about positive psychology. You have probably come across it online, in the press, on the TV and on the radio. The message seems to be that you can use positive psychology to be blissfully happy all the time. We would all love this. However, you and I know that permanent bliss is a pipe dream. It's never going to happen. We could all feel a bit happier. But bliss, all day long? That's out of the question.

You read in the blurb on the cover of this book that I'm Irish, a professor of clinical psychology and that my specialist area of clinical practice is couple and family therapy. All of these things inform my view of positive psychology. Being Irish, I'm sceptical of all hype. I'm especially sceptical about hype that promises endless happiness. So as an Irish person, that's where my prejudices lie. I take a sceptical, low-key approach to the whole happiness thing.

As a professor of clinical psychology, I'm a scientist. I have no time for 'pop psychology' that is not grounded in science. I do research on positive psychology and read research on positive psychology conducted by other scientists around the world. I know what science tells us about what can make us happy, for how long and by how much. I also know the limits of this knowledge. That is, I know how much we don't know. So as a scientist, I have access to what is currently known about the science of positive psychology. I teach a course on this at University College Dublin. You might be interested to take a look at my textbook for that course – *Positive Psychology: The Science of Happiness and Human Strengths*.

As a practising clinician and a couple and family therapist, every week at Clanwilliam Institute in Dublin I help people with challenges in their lives. People come to me because they are unhappy, distressed, depressed, anxious, confused or in conflict with themselves and others. My job is to help them understand the factors that are contributing to their distress. I also help them identify their strengths and resources. Then we work together to reduce their distress and help them recover a more satisfying life. I work with individuals, couples and families at all stages of the lifecycle. Some people who come to see me have very severe mental health problems like bipolar disorder, major depressive disorder or obsessive-compulsive disorder. Others have very complicated conflicts within their families, or are facing major life challenges including life-limiting illnesses and disability. These clients help me to keep my feet on the ground. They let me know that a life of endless bliss is a myth. However, they also keep me clued in to just how resourceful and resilient it's possible to be when the chips are down. They let me know that no matter how dark the night is, there is always the possibility of a new dawn.

Another part of my work is training and coaching. I am the founding director of the UCD Doctoral Programme in Clinical Psychology. With a wonderful team of colleagues, for over 20 years, I have been training the next generation of clinical psychologists to work in the Irish public health service. I also provide coaching to a range of health professionals. These experiences keep me in tune with just how challenging it is to work in health services. They also let me know how helpful positive psychology practices can be in managing a demanding job.

This introduction is all by way of saying that if you are looking for a recipe for unending happiness, then you are reading the wrong book. If you want to know how to be a bit happier, and improve your well-being – and if you want to know how to use the science of positive psychology to do this – then this is the book you have been looking for.

Throughout the book, I have distilled what the science of positive psychology has found out about particular issues. I then invite you to try out practical exercises linked to these ideas to enhance your well-being. Where possible, the exercises you are invited to try out are taken from actual scientific studies. I also mention ideas and practices from other fields of psychology that fit well with positive psychology. In particular, I have drawn on scientifically proven practices from the fields of cognitive behaviour therapy and couple and family therapy.

The book is divided into six parts:

- Part 1, Creating resilience, contains chapters on key ideas from positive psychology, valued goals and personal strengths.
- Part 2, Healthy body and mind, has chapters on physical exercise, relaxation and mindfulness meditation.
- Part 3, Enjoying life, includes chapters on savouring, flow and gratitude.
- Part 4, Constructive thought and action, contains chapters on optimism, problem-solving and solution-finding.
- Part 5, Strengthening relationships, has chapters on developing compassionate relationships, as well as on enhancing relationships with long-term partners and children.
- Part 6, Overcoming challenges, includes chapters on grit and perfectionism; courage, fear and posttraumatic growth; assertiveness and anger; and forgiveness.

Parts 1–4, Chapter 11 on developing compassionate relationships in Part 5 and the final Chapter 18 on managing your life are probably relevant to everyone. If you are recovering from any mental health problem, especially depression, then all of the exercises in the first four parts of the book, Chapter 11 on compassionate relationships in Part 5 and the final chapter on managing your life may help with your recovery.

The chapters on couple and parent–child relationships in Part 5 will be relevant to you if you are in a long-term relationship, are married or have children. If you are experiencing relationship distress with your long-term partner, then you may find the exercises in Chapter 12 on couple relationships helpful in improving the quality of your relationship. If you are having difficulties in your relationships with your children, then the exercises in Chapter 13 on parent–child relationship may help you to get along better with your kids.

The chapters in Part 6, which deal with specific life challenges, are not relevant to everyone. If you want to accomplish excellence at work, but find that self-criticism is working against you, then the exercises in Chapter 14 on grit and perfectionism may help you break free from the constraints of problematic perfectionism. If your work is intrinsically danger-ous, if you suffer from anxiety or if you have survived a major trauma, then the exercises in Chapter 15 on courage, fear and posttraumatic growth may be of particular interest to you. These exercises show how you can harness the power of courage to enhance your well-being. If you have difficulty controlling your temper, and would like to find a way to become less aggressive, then the exercises in Chapter 16 on assertiveness and anger control may help you achieve these wishes. If you find that grudges and a desire for revenge are eroding the qual-ity of your life, then you may find the exercises in Chapter 17 help you become more forgiving.

You can dip into this book and read each chapter as a 'stand-alone' unit, or you can read the whole book, one chapter after another. If you decide to read the book cover to cover, there is a note at the end of each chapter inviting you to reflect on what you have learned so far, and letting you know what you will learn in the next chapter.

I wrote this book primarily with a general readership in mind. The ideas and practices in this book are relevant to men and women, of all ages, in all walks of life. I also thought that it might be a useful book for mental health professionals, counsellors and therapists to recom-mend to their service users, clients and patients. Finally, I wrote this book for people who face major mental health challenges in their lives, and bravely strive for recovery.

If, right now, you feel overwhelmed by life's challenges; if everything seems to be too much; then there is the risk that reading this book may make you feel misunderstood. It invites you to try to do new things. If it feels like you have very little fuel left in your tank, and it's taking you your last ounce of oomph to get through each day, then you probably don't want advice on what new things you should do. If you feel too overwhelmed to respond to the invitations in this book, then that's OK. That's how your life is right now. Please consider talking to a clinical psychologist or other mental health professional about your difficulties. When you have done that, and feel more supported and less overwhelmed, then you may wish to come back to this book. You may also wish, at that point, to incorporate some of the positive psychology exercises into your life. In the meantime, please be kind to yourself. I wish you well.

*Alan Carr*
*March 2019*

# ACKNOWLEDGEMENTS

I am grateful to the many colleagues, students and clients who asked me to translate science into practice, and articulate the ideas in this book in an accessible way. Special thanks to Aidan McKiernan for his comments on an early draft of the manuscript. My family have been exceptionally supportive and inspirational while writing this book, so to them I am particularly grateful.

I acknowledge permission from the following authors, publishers or copyright holders listed below to republish or adapt material from the sources specified, for inclusion in the boxes, figures and tables, listed here.

Peggy Kern for Butler, J., & Kern, M.L. (2015). The PERMA Profiler: A brief multidimensional measure of flourishing, available at www.peggykern.org/questionnaires.html or at www.purposeplus.com/survey/perma-profiler, copyright © 2015 by Peggy Kern included in Box 1.1, PERMA profiler.

Ed Deiner for the SPANE on pp. 153-154 of Diener, E., Wirtz, D., Tov, W., Kim-Prieto, C., Choi, D., Oishi, S. & Biswas-Diener, R. (2010). New well-being measures: Short scales to assess flourishing and positive and negative feelings. *Social Indicators Research*, 97(2), 143-156, copyright © 2009 by Ed Diener, included in Box 1.2. Scale of positive and negative experiences for assessing your positivity ratio.

Martin Seligman for the PERMA diagram from www.authentichappiness.sas.upenn.edu/learn, copyright © 2009 by Martin Seligman, included in Figure 1.1, Martin Seligman's PERMA theory of well-being.

Oxford University Press for Figure 3.1 on p. 16 of Cohn, M. & Fredrickson, B. (2009). Positive emotions. In C. R. Snyder & S. Lopez (Eds.), *Handbook of positive psychology* (2nd ed.), copyright © 2009 by Oxford University Press, included in Figure 1.2, Barbara Fredrickson's broaden and build theory of positive emotions.

Penguin Press, an imprint of Penguin Publishing Group, a division of Penguin Random House LLC, and Little Brown/Piatkus for permission to reproduce the diagram on p. 39 of *The how of happiness: a scientific approach to getting the life you want* by Sonja Lyubomirsky, copyright © 2007 by Sonja Lyubomirsky, all rights reserved, included in Figure 1.3, Sonja Lyubomirsky's theory of sustainable happiness.

The American Heart Association for the table at www.heart.org/HEARTORG/Healthy Living/PhysicalActivity/FitnessBasics/Target-Heart-Rates_UCM_434341_Article.jsp#. VuAMIce50y8, copyright © 2015 by American Heart Association Inc., included in Table 4.1, Target heart rates.

Crown copyright © for the diagram on p. 1 of the *Eatwell Guide, Version 4, 2018* published by Public Health England in association with the Welsh Government, Food Standards Scotland and the Food Standards Agency in Northern Ireland, included in Figure 4.1, A balanced diet.

The American Psychological Association for text on p. 318 of Bohlmeijer, E., ten Klooster, P., Fledderus, M., Veehof, M. & Baer., R. (2011). Psychometric properties of the five-facet mindfulness questionnaire in depressed adults and development of a short form. *Assessment, 18*(3), 308–320, copyright © 2011 by American Psychological Association, included in Box 6.1, Five Facets of Mindfulness questionnaire.

Republished with permission of Bantam Books, an imprint of Random House, a division of Penguin Random House LLC, and of Little, Brown/Piatkus from *Full catastrophe living (Revised edition)* (p. 15) by Jon Kabat-Zinn, copyright © 2013 by Jon Kabat-Zinn, all rights reserved, included in Box 6.2, Raisin meditation.

Republished with permission of Bantam Books, an imprint of Random House, a division of Penguin Random House LLC, and of Little, Brown/Piatkus from *Full catastrophe living (Revised edition)* (pp. 95–97) by Jon Kabat-Zinn, copyright © 2013 by Jon Kabat-Zinn, all rights reserved, included in Box 6.4, Body scan meditation.

Republished with permission of Bantam Books, an imprint of Random House, a division of Penguin Random House LLC, and of Little, Brown/Piatkus from *Full catastrophe living (Revised edition)* (pp. 214–216) by Jon Kabat-Zinn, copyright © 2013 by Jon Kabat-Zinn, all rights reserved, included in Box 6.9, Loving kindness meditation.

Guilford Publications for text on pp. 201–202 of *Mindfulness-based cognitive therapy for depression* (Second edition) by Segal, Z., Williams M. & Teasdale, J., copyright © 2013 by Guilford, permission conveyed through Copyright Clearance Centre, Inc., included in Box 6.5, Mindfulness of movement.

Guilford Publications for text on pp. 130–131 of *The mindful way through depression* by Williams M., Teasdale, J., Segal, Z. & Kabat-Zinn, J., copyright © 2007 by Guilford, permission conveyed through Copyright Clearance Centre, Inc., included in Box 6.3, Mindfulness of the breath and body.

Guilford Publications for text on pp. 183–184 of *The mindful way through depression* by Williams M., Teasdale, J., Segal, Z. & Kabat-Zinn, J., copyright © 2007 by Guilford, permission conveyed through Copyright Clearance Centre, Inc., included in Box 6.6, Three-minute breathing space.

Guilford Publications for text on pp. 221–222 of *Mindfulness-based cognitive therapy for depression* (Second edition) by Segal, Z., Williams M. & Teasdale, J., copyright © 2013 by Guilford, permission conveyed through Copyright Clearance Centre, Inc., included in Box 6.7, Mindfulness of sounds and thoughts.

Guilford Publications for text on pp. 151–152 of *The mindful way through depression* by Williams, M., Teasdale, J., Segal, Z. & Kabat-Zinn, J., copyright © 2007 by Guilford, permission conveyed through Copyright Clearance Centre, Inc., included in Box 6.8, Exploring difficulty and practising acceptance.

Madeline Klyne for permission to reproduce and adapt an unpublished work by Madeline Klyne, Core teacher at Cambridge Insight Meditation Centre and co-founder of South Shore Insight Meditation Centre, copyright © by Madeline Klyne in Box 6.10, Daily mindfulness.

Springer Nature Customer Service Centre GmbH for Figure 1 on p. 217 of Tang, Y., Hölzel, B. & Posner, M. (2015). The neuroscience of mindfulness meditation: nature reviews. *Neuroscience,16,*213–225, copyright © 2015, Springer Nature, included in Figure 6.1, Brain regions involved in mindfulness meditation.

Taylor and Francis Group, LLC, a division of Informa plc, for Items 1–27, 29–36 and 45–48 in Table 2.3 on page 49–50 of Bryant, F. & Veroff, J. (2007). *Savouring: A new model of positive experience*, Lawrence Erlbaum, copyright © 2007 by Taylor & Francis, included in Box 7.2, Assess your savouring and dampening strategies.

Springer Nature Customer Service Centre GmbH for text on p. 170 of Engeser, S. & Rheinberg, F. (2008). Flow, performance and moderators of challenge-skill balance. *Motivation and Emotion, 32*(3), 158–172, copyright © 2008 by Springer Nature, included as items 1–10 in Box 7.9, The Short Flow Scale.

The American Psychological Association for text on p. 127 of McCullough, M. E., Emmons, R. A. & Tsang, J. (2002). The grateful disposition: a conceptual and empirical topography. *Journal of Personality and Social Psychology, 82,* 112–127, copyright © 2002 by American Psychological Association, included in Box 8.1, Gratitude questionnaire.

The American Psychological association for text in Table 2, p. 647 of Collins, N. L. & Read, S. J. (1990). Adult attachment, working models, and relationship quality in dating couples. *Journal of Personality and Social Psychology, 58*(4), 644–663, copyright © 1990 by American Psychological Association, included in Box 11.4, Adult attachment scale.

The Gottman Institute Inc. for the diagram at www.gottman.com/blog/the-sound-relationship-house-turn-towards-instead-of-away, copyright © 2019, the Gottman Institute Inc., included in Figure 12.1, Sound relationship house.

Taylor & Francis (www.tandfonline.com) for text in Table 1 on p. 167 of Duckworth, A. L. & Quinn, P. D. (2009). Development and validation of the Short Grit Scale (Grit-S). *Journal of Personality Assessment, 91,* 166–174, copyright © 2009 by Taylor & Francis, included in Box 14.1, Cultivating grit.

Taylor & Francis (www.tandfonline.com) for text in Table 2 on p. 372 of Rice, K. G., Richardson, C. M. E. & Tueller, S. (2014). The short form of the revised almost perfect scale. *Journal of Personality Assessment, 96*(3), 368–379, copyright © 2014 by Taylor & Francis, included in Box 14.2, Perfectionism questionnaire.

Everitt Worthington for Figure 3.1 on p. 38 of Worthington, E. (2001). *Five steps to forgiveness: The art and science of forgiving.* New York, NY: Crown, Copyright © 2001 by Everitt Worthington, included in Figure 17.1, Forgiveness pyramid.

# Part 1
# Creating resilience

# 1   Positive psychology

Positive psychology is about well-being and human strengths. It is about the scientific study of these things. It is also about how to apply this scientific knowledge in clinical settings, schools, organisations and most importantly in our day-to-day lives to help us to thrive.[1] This book will tell you how to apply important findings from positive psychology in your life to improve your well-being. In this first chapter, you will read about some of the most important ideas in positive psychology. You will read about:

- Well-being
- The effects of happiness on physical health and longevity
- The main causes of happiness
- How we adapt to positive and negative life events
- How most of us are poor at judging what will make us happy in future, and
- Positive psychology exercises that have been found to enhance well-being.

You will also have invitations to do exercises to assess your PERMA profile and the ratio of positive to negative emotions in your life. This chapter sets the agenda for the rest of the book, and lets you know about the practical skills you may learn by doing the exercises described in Chapters 2–18.

The idea that psychology can be used by all of us to improve our lives has a long history. In this book, we will be talking mainly about modern positive psychology which began around about the year 2000.[2] Professor Martin Seligman from the University of Pennsylvania in the USA is the founder of modern positive psychology.[3] He was trained originally as a clinical psychologist. He became increasingly disenchanted with the emphasis of clinical psychology on disorders, disability and dysfunction. He reviewed a lot of research on the effectiveness of psychotherapy and medication in helping people overcome mental health problems. He found that they alleviated symptoms in about two out of three cases. However, in most successful cases clients did not feel fulfilled at the end of treatment. Many felt empty. They no longer had symptoms, but they lacked a sense of well-being. As for the one in three cases who did not benefit from psychotherapy and medication, traditional mental health interventions had little to offer these people.[3] Seligman concluded that they required a different kind of intervention that would help them experience well-being rather than emptiness.

It was these considerations that inspired Martin Seligman to develop an approach that focused on what was right with people, rather than on what was wrong with them. He wanted to use the scientific methods of clinical psychology to find out about well-being, human strengths, personal resilience and resourcefulness. The idea was that positive psychology would complement rather than replace traditional clinical psychology. With support from a core group of colleagues, mainly in the USA, he established positive psychology as a rigorous scientific discipline. Since 2000 Martin Seligman has drawn together a network of academics in major universities from all over the world who conduct research in the new field of positive psychology.[4] He has arranged philanthropic funding to support this research.[5] Members of the international positive psychology network publish their scholarly work on this discipline in academic journals and books on positive psychology.[6] Since the year 2000 the number of publications in the field of positive psychology has grown exponentially. Professionals are being trained in positive psychology in the growing number of master's programmes in positive psychology that are being established at universities around the world.

The main thing that distinguishes modern positive psychology from 'pop-psychology' is the bedrock of rigorous science on which it is based. In this book, I will be letting you know about things you can do to improve your well-being. This advice is based on scientific evidence, which I will summarise throughout the book. I will also illustrate how positive psychology has been applied in day-to-day life with stories and case examples.

## The PERMA theory of well-being

According to Martin Seligman's theory, well-being is based on five main elements:

- Positive emotion
- Engagement
- Relationships
- Meaning
- Accomplishment.[7]

Let's look at each element in a bit more detail.

### Positive emotion

Our well-being depends on the extent to which we experience positive emotions like happiness, joy, excitement, contentment and so forth.

### Engagement

Our well-being also depends on the degree to which we are involved in engaging, absorbing activities like sports or skilled work. The experience of being so absorbed in an activity that the sense of self and time is suspended is referred to as being in a state of flow. You will read more about flow in Chapter 7.

### Relationships

Our involvement in supportive relationships with family members and friends also contributes to our well-being. Close relationships provide us with the experiences of attachment, support, being valued and being loved. You will read about enhancing relationships in Chapters 11, 12 and 13.

### Meaning

The extent to which we have a purpose in life and a direction in which we are going also determines our well-being. This often involves pursuing highly valued goals or serving something bigger than ourselves like a sports club, community, charity, work organisation, political party or religion. These things give us the feeling that life is valuable and worth living. You will read more about highly valued goals in Chapter 2.

### Accomplishment

Finally, well-being depends on us having positive accomplishments in our lives. These accomplishments may include completing daily tasks and responsibilities, reaching goals, achieving success and winning. They may be in the domains of work or leisure activities. These accomplishments may give us feelings of mastery and achievement.

This way of thinking about well-being is referred to as PERMA theory. There is a diagram of it in Figure 1.1. PERMA is an acronym based on the first letter of each of the five elements of the theory (**P**ositive emotion, **E**ngagement, **R**elationships, **M**eaning and **A**ccomplishment). In the pursuit of well-being, we may focus on one or more of these elements. Where we focus predominantly on one element, we can be said to be living a particular type of life. For example, if we primarily pursue positive emotion, we may be said to lead 'the pleasant life'. If we mainly seek engagement or the flow state, then we may be said to lead 'the engaged life'. Where we see relationships or serving something greater than ourselves as the most important thing, this leads to 'the meaningful life'. We lead the 'achieving life' if we prioritise accomplishment.

PERMA theory was first presented in 2011. Before and since, within positive psychology, there have been many views on how best to conceptualise well-being. A useful distinction

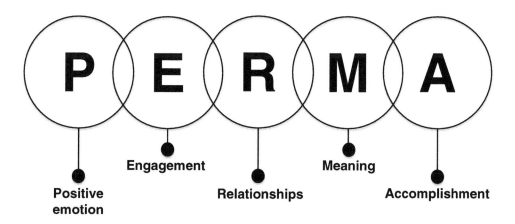

*Figure 1.1* Martin Seligman's PERMA theory of well-being.

may be made between the hedonic and eudaimonic traditions.[8] The hedonic approach defines happiness and the good life in terms of pleasure-seeking and pain-avoidance. The eudaimonic tradition, in contrast, defines happiness and the good life in terms of achieving one's full potential. The hedonic tradition may be traced back to Aristippus and the eudaimonic tradition to Aristotle. Both were Greek philosophers in the fourth century BC. In the eudaimonic tradition it is acknowledged that while the pursuit of pleasure may sometimes lead to well-being, this is not always the case, and in some instances the pursuit of pleasure may prevent well-being. For example, overindulgence in alcohol, drugs and food may lead to addiction, cancer and heart disease. In contrast, the pursuit of virtue may sometimes lead to pleasure, but on other occasions may not. For example, acts of courage, such as saving a person from drowning, or working hard to achieve success at a job that benefits others, may lead to pain rather than pleasure. PERMA theory, to some degree, spans both of these traditions by acknowledging that well-being involves positive emotions and absorption in engaging activities, as advocated by the hedonic approach. However, well-being also involves engagement in meaningful relationships and accomplishing success which is consistent with the eudaimonic tradition. Increasingly positive psychology has become concerned with helping people achieve high levels of well-being. This is referred to as flourishing. Flourishing means living within the optimal range of human functioning.[9] In terms of PERMA theory, it means experiencing high levels of well-being on most PERMA dimensions. So flourishing is not just feeling good. In fact, you could be feeling just OK in terms of positive emotions, but be flourishing because you are excelling by engaging in absorbing activities, relationships, living a meaningful life and achieving highly valued goals.

## PERMA profiler self-assessment exercise

To find out what your PERMA well-being profile is, you may wish to complete the PERMA well-being profiler at www.purposeplus.com/survey/perma-profiler. It takes about five minutes to fill out this questionnaire and there is no cost. The profiler contains three questions about each of the five PERMA dimensions, and other questions on overall well-being, loneliness, physical health and negative emotions. Alternatively, you may complete a short form of the PERMA profiler in Box 1.1. This short form just asks about the five dimensions of PERMA theory.

---

### Box 1.1   PERMA profiler

For each item circle the response that best applies to you.

0 = never, not at all, terrible.

10 = always, completely, excellent.

To get your overall score, sum item scores and divide by 16.

Compare your overall score to the average score for people with high school to postgraduate education which range from 6.6 to 7.1.

Scores above 7.1 indicate that you have a high level of well-being.

Scores below 6.6 indicate a lower level of well-being.

---

*Positive emotion*

| | |
|---|---|
| In general, how often do you feel joyful? | 0 1 2 3 4 5 6 7 8 9 10 |
| In general, how often do you feel positive? | 0 1 2 3 4 5 6 7 8 9 10 |
| In general, to what extent do you feel contented? | 0 1 2 3 4 5 6 7 8 9 10 |

**Engagement**

| | |
|---|---|
| How often do you become absorbed in what you are doing? | 0 1 2 3 4 5 6 7 8 9 10 |
| In general, to what extent do you feel excited and interested in things? | 0 1 2 3 4 5 6 7 8 9 10 |
| How often do you lose track of time while doing something you enjoy? | 0 1 2 3 4 5 6 7 8 9 10 |

**Positive relationships**

| | |
|---|---|
| To what extent do you receive help and support from others when you need it? | 0 1 2 3 4 5 6 7 8 9 10 |
| To what extent have you been feeling loved? | 0 1 2 3 4 5 6 7 8 9 10 |
| How satisfied are you with your personal relationships? | 0 1 2 3 4 5 6 7 8 9 10 |

**Meaning**

| | |
|---|---|
| In general, to what extent do you lead a purposeful and meaningful life? | 0 1 2 3 4 5 6 7 8 9 10 |
| In general, to what extent do you feel that what you do in your life is valuable and worthwhile? | 0 1 2 3 4 5 6 7 8 9 10 |
| To what extent do you generally feel that you have a sense of direction in your life? | 0 1 2 3 4 5 6 7 8 9 10 |

**Accomplishment**

| | |
|---|---|
| How much of the time do you feel you are making progress towards accomplishing your goals? | 0 1 2 3 4 5 6 7 8 9 10 |
| How often do you achieve the important goals you have set for yourself? | 0 1 2 3 4 5 6 7 8 9 10 |
| How often are you able to handle your responsibilities? | 0 1 2 3 4 5 6 7 8 9 10 |

**General well-being**

| | |
|---|---|
| Taking all things together, how happy would you say you are? | 0 1 2 3 4 5 6 7 8 9 10 |

**Note:** Adapted with permission of Peggy Kern from Butler, J., & Kern, M. L. (2015). *The PERMA profiler: A brief multidimensional measure of flourishing.* Copyright © 2015 by Peggy Kern.

---

May I suggest that you complete the PERMA profiler now and when you finish this book and all the exercises in it that are of interest to you. On each occasion, base your answers on 'the past two weeks'. This will allow you to see the extent to which your well-being changed from the two-week period before you started the book, to the two-week period after which you finished the book and all the exercises in it that were of interest to you. By comparing these two scores you will be able to see how much engaging in the positive psychology pro-gramme described in this book improved your well-being.

May I also suggest that today you start a journal to keep track of your responses to the exercises that you will come across throughout this book. You may write this journal in long-hand in a notebook. Alternatively, you may wish to type or audio-record it on your computer, tablet or smartphone. Whatever works best for you. If you wish, the first entry in your journal may be the results of your PERMA profiler exercise, and today's date.

## Benefits of well-being and happiness

By definition, well-being – as conceptualised within PERMA theory – has obvious immediate benefits. These are the experience of positive emotions such as joy and happiness, the experience of being absorbed in engaging skilled work and recreational activities, the experience of satisfying relationships, a sense of meaning and purpose in life, and a sense of achievement. However, research in positive psychology shows that well-being also has a number of long-term benefits. The most important of these are better physical health and longevity.[10] People with high levels of well-being experience better health, mainly because their immune systems work efficiently, and this in turn protects them from illness.

However, there is now evidence from dozens of longitudinal studies that well-being not only improves health, but also increases the lifespan and delays death.[11] The nun study is one of the most widely cited investigations of the effects of happiness on longevity.[12] This remarkable scientific investigation was initiated by Professor David Snowdon at the University of Kentucky in 1986. In this follow-back study of 180 nuns in the USA, his team found that the happiness expressed in essays that the nuns wrote as they entered a religious order in early adulthood was associated with their longevity. This was a carefully controlled study. All of the participants had similar lifestyles. They were all unmarried nuns who worked as teachers and did not smoke or drink and ate a simple balanced diet throughout their adult lives. When they wrote their essays as they entered the order, they gave a biographical sketch and stated their hopes for the future, but had no idea that these essays would be used in a study of happiness and longevity. More than half a century later, the number of positive emotions in the essays was judged by researchers who did not know the age of the participants. Ninety per cent of the happiest quarter lived past the age of 85 compared with only 34% of the least happy quarter.

## Broaden and Build theory

Positive emotion, the first element of well-being in PERMA theory, has the immediate benefit of making us feel good. We have also seen that it affects health and longevity. Does happiness have other benefits? If so, how does happiness lead to better overall adjustment in life? These questions inspired Professor Barbara Fredrickson at the University of North Carolina to develop and test her Broaden and Build theory of positive emotions.[13] She observed that many negative emotions such as anxiety or anger narrow our momentary thought-action repertories, so that we are ready to act in a relatively limited number of self-protective ways. Thought-action repertoires are the collection of thoughts and potential courses of action immediately available to us as possible ways of responding to a situation. For example, if we are frightened, having been awakened by a noise at night, our thought-action repertoire may include relatively few thoughts and potential actions. For example, 'There's a burglar downstairs. This is dangerous. I should keep quiet so he doesn't know where I am. Or I could phone the police. Or I could make a lot of noise and try to frighten him away. Maybe I could surprise him and knock him out'.

While negative emotions narrow our thought-action repertories, positive emotions, in contrast, broaden our momentary thought-action repertories. They lead us to have many new thoughts about a wide variety of possible courses of action that we could potentially take. This broadening of our momentary thought-action repertories creates opportunities for building enduring personal resources; that is, for doing things that will have a long-lasting beneficial effect on our lives. This in turn offers the potential for personal growth and trans-formation by creating positive or adaptive spirals of emotions, thoughts and actions. The process is diagrammed in Figure 1.2.

When we experience intense joy, we may think of a hundred different things we could do on our own, with our families and friends, at work or in leisure activities. If, for example, from all these possibilities, we decide to talk to a friend at work about a new idea to make things in the production area go more smoothly, then this conversation can both strengthen the relationship we have with our colleague and also lead to an improvement in the production area at work. This improved work relationship and increased efficiency in the production area

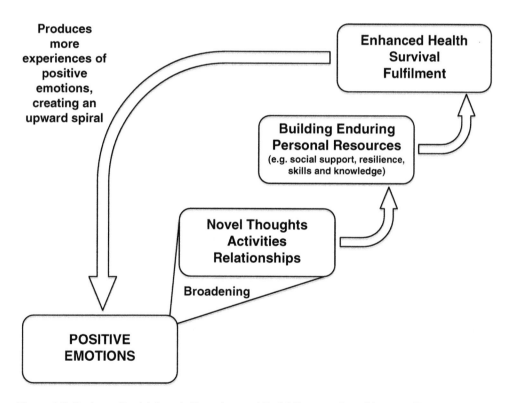

*Figure 1.2* Barbara Fredrickson's Broaden and Build theory of positive emotions.

**Note:** Adapted with permission of Oxford University Press through PL Sclear from Cohn, M., & Fredrickson, B. (2009). Positive emotions. In C. R. Snyder & S. Lopez (Eds.), *Handbook of positive psychology* (Second Edition, p. 16). Copyright © 2009 by Oxford University Press.

may turn out to have long-lasting effects. If they do, then they have the potential to make us experience more positive emotions in the future. Because the relationship with our colleague has been strengthened, each time we meet with the same colleague again, we may feel better and the atmosphere between us may be more relaxed. The innovation that we introduced in the production area may continue to operate, and we may therefore continue to feel good about this. These good feelings from enhanced work relationships and better production may broaden our thoughts about possible future courses of action we could take. This example is based in the workplace. The same sort of process occurs when positive emotions occur in our families, with our friends or doing leisure activities. The experience of positive emotions opens up a wide range of thoughts about many possible courses of action. When we act on these, there is the possibility of doing things that will change the direction of our lives in ways that will last into the future and create opportunities for having more positive emotional experiences.

Scientific evidence from studies conducted in communities, clinics and laboratories has supported the Broaden and Build theory of positive emotions. Positive mood states broaden thought-action repertoires. Positive mood states also help people build enduring personal resources. There are now over 200 cross-sectional, longitudinal and experimental studies which show that positive emotions lead to better adjustment in the broad domains of work, relationships and health, and also to greater positive perceptions of self and others, sociability, likability, co-operation, altruism, coping, conflict resolution, creativity and problem-solving.[14]

In Broaden and Build theory it is assumed that evolution played a key role in shaping our emotional systems so that negative emotions narrow our thought-action repertoires and positive emotions expand them.[15] Evolution is about survival of the fittest; survival of those who adapt well to the challenges and threats the environment poses. It proved adaptive for our ancestors to have strong emotions in response to threats that led to a narrow range of possible responses; for example, the fight / flight / or freeze response to threat. Those who had these strong negative emotions and narrow thought-action repertoires when faced with predators survived, and those who didn't perished. However, it also proved adaptive to have positive emotions that broadened awareness and made it possible to develop resources to adapt to the environment in new and creative ways. During these creative moments new tools, dwellings, group alliances, skills and plans for dealing with threats to survival were developed. Those who used the broadened awareness associated with positive emotions to create these resources were more likely to survive than those who didn't.

A critical question is how much positive emotion is enough to facilitate positive life changes. There has been an important dialogue in the scientific literature on whether or not there is a tipping point in the ratio of positive to negative emotions that leads to flourishing.[16] A widely publicised view put forward by Barbara Fredrickson, as part of the Broaden and Build theory, is that the critical tipping point positivity ratio is 3:1. That is, in order to experience a high level of well-being, the ratio of positive to negative emotions must be greater than 3:1. The great thing about science is that it's a self-correcting enterprise. In response to dialogue with other scientists, errors in the way this conclusion was reached have been identified. Within the field of positive psychology it is now accepted that there probably isn't a tipping point in the ratio of positive to negative emotions that leads to flourishing. As more studies are done, and better ways of analysing the data from these studies become available, it will become clearer how particular positivity ratios in particular contexts contribute to well-being. In the meantime, all we can say for certain is that up to some undefined point, higher positivity ratios are usually associated with better well-being. Extremely high positivity ratios are usually problematic. For example, people in manic states who have bipolar disorder (or manic depression, as it used to be called) tend to experience intense positive emotions, but this is accompanied by severe difficulties in day-to-day functioning.

### Positive to negative emotion ratio exercise

You can use the results of this research on the ratio of positive to negative emotions to start to improve your well-being. Here is an exercise you can do right now. You can complete the scale of positive and negative experiences in Box 1.2. Then calculate your positivity ratio following the instructions at the top of the scale. For most of us, in most situations, higher positivity ratios are associated with greater well-being. In later chapters on this book there will be detailed guidance on specific positive psychology exercises you can do to increase the number of positive emotional experiences and reduce the number of negative emotions you have each day. However, at this point, maybe it's enough to acknowledge that this is an important goal in your journey towards greater well-being.

---

**Box 1.2   Scale of positive and negative experiences for assessing your positivity ratio**

Think about what you have been doing and experiencing during the past four weeks.

Then indicate how much you experienced each of the feelings in the left-hand column by circling the number from 1–5 opposite it.

To calculate your positivity ratio, divide the sum of your scores for items 1–6 by the sum of your scores for items 7–12.

Higher positivity ratios are associated with greater well-being.

The exercises in this book will help you increase your positivity ratio.

| | | | | | | |
|---|---|---|---|---|---|---|
| 1 | **Positive** | Never or very rarely 1 | Rarely 2 | Sometimes 3 | Often 4 | Always or very often 5 |
| 2 | **Good** | Never or very rarely 1 | Rarely 2 | Sometimes 3 | Often 4 | Always or very often 5 |
| 3 | **Pleasant** | Never or very rarely 1 | Rarely 2 | Sometimes 3 | Often 4 | Always or very often 5 |
| 4 | **Happy** | Never or very rarely 1 | Rarely 2 | Sometimes 3 | Often 4 | Always or very often 5 |
| 5 | **Joyful** | Never or very rarely 1 | Rarely 2 | Sometimes 3 | Often 4 | Always or very often 5 |
| 6 | **Contented** | Never or very rarely 1 | Rarely 2 | Sometimes 3 | Often 4 | Always or very often 5 |
| 7 | **Negative** | Never or very rarely 1 | Rarely 2 | Sometimes 3 | Often 4 | Always or very often 5 |

| | | Never or very rarely | Rarely | Sometimes | Often | Always or very often |
|----|------------|----------------------|--------|-----------|-------|----------------------|
| 8  | **Bad**        | Never or very rarely 1 | Rarely 2 | Sometimes 3 | Often 4 | Always or very often 5 |
| 9  | **Unpleasant** | Never or very rarely 1 | Rarely 2 | Sometimes 3 | Often 4 | Always or very often 5 |
| 10 | **Sad**        | Never or very rarely 1 | Rarely 2 | Sometimes 3 | Often 4 | Always or very often 5 |
| 11 | **Afraid**     | Never or very rarely 1 | Rarely 2 | Sometimes 3 | Often 4 | Always or very often 5 |
| 12 | **Angry**      | Never or very rarely 1 | Rarely 2 | Sometimes 3 | Often 4 | Always or very often 5 |

**Note:** Adapted with permission from the scale on pages 153–154 in Diener, E., Wirtz, D., Tov, W., Kim-Prieto, C., Choi, D., Oishi, S., & Biswas-Diener, R. (2010). New well-being measures: Short scales to assess flourishing and positive and negative feelings. *Social Indicators Research, 97*(2), 143–156. Copyright © 2009 by Ed Diener.

## Causes of happiness and well-being

Professor Sonja Lyubomirsky at the University of California has argued that three classes of factors determine our level of happiness: (1) genetic factors, (2) circumstances and (3) intentional activities.[17] This theory of sustainable happiness, which is shown in Figure 1.3, is based

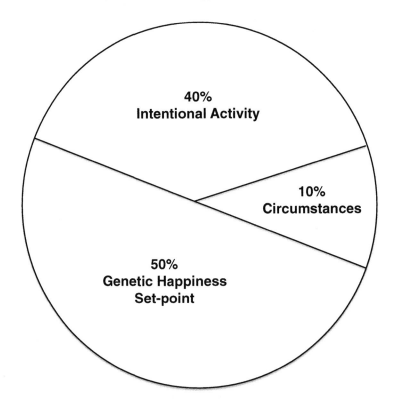

*Figure 1.3* Sonja Lyubomirsky's theory of sustainable happiness.

on scientific studies which show that about 50% of individual differences in happiness are due to genetic factors; about 10% may be accounted for by environmental circumstances; and the remaining 40% of individual differences in happiness are due to intentional activities. (These numbers are rough estimates. They refer to percentages in a whole population, not to how the three factors operate for a specific individual.) Sonja Lyubomirsky's theory is supported by a lot of evidence outlined in the next section. This is good news. It shows that we all have considerable latitude to enhance our well-being if 40% of individual differences in happiness are under our control. The positive psychology practices described in this book are intentional activities which have been scientifically proven to increase well-being.

### Genetic factors, personality traits and happiness

Many studies show that the levels of positive emotions found in identical twins are greater than those for fraternal twins.[18] This supports the view that genetic factors partly determine our level of well-being. Genetic factors set an upper limit on how much happiness we usually experience. This level is often referred to as the happiness set-point. (We will discuss the happiness set-point later, when considering adaptation of positive and negative life events.)

   Genetic factors influence happiness via their effects on major personality traits which are about 50% heritable.[19] In modern personality theory, there are five main personality traits: extraversion, neuroticism (or emotional stability), conscientiousness, agreeableness and open-mindedness. Of these five traits, extraversion is most strongly associated with positive emotions.[20] Extraverted people are generally happier than introverted people. While neuroticism (or emotional stability), conscientiousness and agreeableness have a weaker link with happiness than extraversion, these traits also affect well-being. People who are more emotionally stable, conscientious and agreeable tend to be happier than those who are not. This may be because of the impact of these traits on how people conduct their lives. A large body of research shows that extraversion, emotional stability, conscientiousness and agreeableness are associated with more satisfying relationships, better work performance and job satisfaction, healthier lifestyles, and more adaptive coping with stress and adversity.[21]

### Environmental circumstances and happiness

A range of personal and environmental circumstances influence happiness and well-being. In order of importance, people are happier when the following factors are present:

- Supportive family relationships and friendships
- Sufficient financial resources to meet basic needs
- The absence of severe illnesses
- Personal freedom
- A pleasant living environment
- Being female, under 30 or over 50.[22]

Let us look at each of these factors in a bit more detail.

### Relationships

We are happier when we have good relationships with family members and friends.[23] These relationships give us a sense of belonging, or being valued, attached, supported and loved.

However, we do adapt to major positive and negative changes in relationships, like getting married or having a divorce.[24] These major changes can make us feel very happy or very distressed for a while. Eventually, these extreme positive and negative emotional states pass. This process of adaptation is discussed in more detail below.

## Financial resources, employment and education

Increased wealth leads to long-lasting increased happiness up to the point where our basic material needs are met. After that, even large increases in wealth do not lead to large and long-lasting increases in happiness.[25] Where people have limited education or are unemployed, these factors may limit their access to sufficient money to meet basic material needs.[26] This in turn may reduce their happiness. However, for most people who are educated and employed with enough money to meet their basic needs, there are diminishing returns from trying to get more financial resources. The counterintuitive finding that increased wealth is not always associated with commensurate increases in happiness has been referred to as the Easterlin Paradox, after a seminal paper published by the economist Professor Richard Easterlin at the University of California.[27] Materialist values and the process of materialistic striving are associated with lower well-being, while freedom has a greater positive impact on well-being than wealth.[28]

## Severe illness

Severe, painful, debilitating or life-limiting illness may have a long-lasting effect on well-being. However, the relationship between ill-health and happiness is complex. People have an extraordinary capacity to adapt, in the long-term, to ill-health and disability.[29] A high degree of adaptation occurs in most cases. Adaptation is less likely to occur where illness or disability is extremely painful, life-limiting or debilitating.

## Freedom

Individuals are happier in societies that support personal freedom.[30] People report greater well-being in affluent stable democracies devoid of political oppression, social inequality and military conflict. In welfare states in which public institutions and bureaucracies run efficiently, people report greater life satisfaction. People report greater happiness in individualist (western) rather than in collectivist cultures.

## Pleasant living environment

People are happier in pleasant physical environments where they have adequate housing, close to amenities and workplaces, and far from air and sound pollution. People also report greater happiness where they are close to vegetation, water and panoramic views.[31] The effects of climate on well-being are complex. People can cope with harsh winters and summers and climatic changes if they have the economic resources to deal with these demands.[32] However, if they lack sufficient wealth or other resource to deal with harsh climates, then climate may have a negative effect on their well-being.

*Gender and age*

Well-being is higher among women, and among the old (over 50) and the young (under 30).[33] Across the lifecycle, happiness follows a U-shaped trajectory. A typical individual's happiness reaches its minimum level in middle age, between the late 30s and early 50s.

The personal and circumstantial factors listed above only account for about 10% of the long-lasting happiness people experience. This is partly explained by the fact that we all adapt or habituate to the effects that positive and negative life events have upon us.

## Adapting to positive and negative life events

Positive and negative life events have short-term effects on happiness, but in most cases these are not enduring. Professor Philip Brickman at Northwestern University and his colleague Donald Campbell coined the term 'hedonic treadmill' to describe this process of rapid adaptation.[34] People react strongly to both positive and negative recent life events, with sharp increases or decreases in happiness. However, in most instances they rapidly return to their happiness set-point in a matter of weeks or months. Brickman and Campbell proposed that each of us has a happiness set-point. This set-point is partly genetically determined.[35] It operates like a thermostat. Our happiness level may temporarily increase if we have good fortune or decrease if something terrible happens to us. After a while our happiness set-point returns us to the level of happiness at which it is set. This happens in the same way that a thermostat in a room regulates the air temperature. The thermostat keeps the average room temperature at a constant level determined by the temperature at which the thermostat is set.

This idea that we rapidly adapt to positive and negative life events is not new. It can be traced back to Stoic and Epicurean philosophers in ancient Greece. However, scientific research on its validity is new. In a series of studies Brickman showed that lottery winners or paralysed survivors of accidents eventually adapted to these major life events.[36] After about two years they returned to the level of happiness they experienced before these events happened. Subsequent research has shown that people can adapt to significant negative life events, including imprisonment and disability, and positive life events such as marriage or increases in income. However, some people do not fully adapt to extreme events such as severe disability, death of a spouse, divorce or unemployment.[37]

Another important scientific finding is that we react less strongly and adapt more rapidly to positive events than negative ones. A vast body of research on this issue was synthesised by Professor Roy Baumeister from Case Western Reserve University in a seminal paper entitled *Bad Is Stronger Than Good*.[38] Positive feelings are weaker and more fleeting than negative emotions which tend to linger and be stronger. Neuroscientist Rick Hanson expressed a similar point by saying that our minds are Velcro for negative information and Teflon for positive.[39] From an evolutionary perspective, it may be argued that those humans in our early evolutionary history who did not rapidly habituate to positive events, and who did not experience significant discomfort when exposed to negative events, were not motivated to do the things necessary to survive. They were too happy to be bothered to do the hard work required to protect themselves and their families from threats posed by predators, hunger, thirst and environmental dangers. Our ancestors who did survive responded quickly to negative events to ease their strong negative feelings. For example, they ran from large predators or fought them; removed themselves from painful situations or made them less painful; and so forth. Our ancestors who did survive also rapidly adapted to positive events, and so were motivated to continually do a wide range of things to make themselves feel happy. They engaged in activities like eating, drinking, making relationships, having sex, refining various skills, admiring nature and so forth, all of which brought them further brief spells of happiness.

The fact that positive feelings are usually less intense and briefer than bad feelings poses a significant challenge for developing positive psychology interventions that lead to sustained increases in well-being. Positive psychology interventions are based on the idea that changing our circumstances will only lead to short-term increases in happiness. Long-term increases in happiness involve changing our intentional actions. About 40% of individual differences in happiness are due to these intentional actions, according to Lyubomirsky's theory of sustainable happiness which we have seen in Figure 1.3.

There are two overarching principles that we can follow when doing things to maximise the effects of positive circumstances and intentional actions of the amount of happiness we feel. These are the principles of variety and appreciation.[40] We can make sure that we increase the *variety* of positive circumstances and positive intentional actions we engage in. If we do the same good things every day, this will not have as big an effect as if we do a variety of different good things each day. There is good scientific evidence that variety is the spice of life. The second thing we can do is consciously increase the extent to which we *appreciate* the good things in our lives. This involves taking time to pay attention to good things; appreciate just how good they are; and value them highly. Using the principles of variety and appreciation slows down the process of adapting or habituating to circumstances and activities that make us feel positive emotions.

Despite our best efforts to increase positive feelings, our happiness set-point limits the extent to which we can experience more positive emotions. We can all probably increase our average ongoing experience of positive emotions or happiness by no more than one to two points on a 10-point scale. However, well-being is not totally dependent on positive emotions. PERMA theory holds that happiness is only one of five elements in overall well-being. While our level of happiness is, to some extent, limited by our happiness set-point, the happiness set-point does not limit the levels of engagement, positive relationships, meaningful activities and accomplishments we experience. We can alter these other four elements of well-being through intentional actions. We can choose to change the way we live our lives. In doing so we can enhance our well-being.

## Predicting happiness

One of the reasons positive psychology scientifically investigates strategies for increasing well-being is because most people are not skilled at predicting what will bring them sustained happiness. In a series of experiments Professor Daniel Gilbert at Harvard University has shown that people are remarkably bad at affective or emotional forcasting.[41] At some time in our lives many of us think that more money, living in a better place, more sunshine, better health and so forth will make us happy. It's true that these things will increase our happiness for a little while. However, in the long-term, changing our circumstances will not lead to sustained increases in happiness. Gilbert's research on emotional forecasting shows that we are all bad at anticipating what will bring us lasting happiness because of the way our imaginations work. Our imaginations selectively focus on the good things and leave out the bad things. For example, we imagine that a promotion at work will give us more money and that will make us happy. However, our imaginations neglect to let us know that promotion will involve many more hassles, increased responsibilities and limited power or resources to carry these out. These negative features of promotion may erode the positive features and so reduce our happiness level.

Another thing our imaginations do is tell us that in the future we will feel like we do at present. On a cold winter's day we may imagine that a month-long sunshine holiday would make us ecstatic because it would take away the misery of being in a wintry climate. On the third week of this summer vacation we may find that the heat is oppressive, the sunburn is painful and we miss our friends. Because during the holiday we no longer feel as we did on the cold winter's day when we booked it, the joy of being in the sunshine is to some degree lessened by these negative aspects of being on vacation. However, our imaginations leave these details out when, in the depths of a cold winter, we are predicting what would make us lastingly happy. This problem that we all have with emotional forecasting partly explains why many people try unsuccessfully to improve their well-being by improving their circumstances. It also explains why there are so many myths about what will make us happy. These myths include the ideas that material wealth, beauty, health or finding the perfect partner will bring sustained happiness.[42] Our imaginations whisper to us about the greener grass on the other side of the hill. To improve our well-being, we have to develop a scepticism about these things our imagination tells us. We may also place confidence in the results of scientific studies that have measured the effects of certain interventions on well-being.[43]

## Effective positive psychology interventions

There is now a large body of scientific evidence which shows that a wide range of positive psychology interventions improve well-being.[44] Here is a list of strategies which have been found in this research to be effective:

- Setting highly valued goals
- Identifying and using personal strengths
- Mindfulness meditation
- Savouring pleasures
- Finding flow
- Being grateful
- Developing an optimistic outlook
- Relationship building
- Developing grit
- Being courageous
- Learning to live with trauma
- Practising forgiveness.

There is also evidence for the effectiveness of interventions from other areas of psychology that are closely related to positive psychology. These include:

- Getting regular physical exercise[45]
- Progressive muscle relaxation[46]
- Problem-solving[47] and solution-finding[48]
- Strengthening couple relationships[49]
- Strengthening parent–child relationships[50]
- Courageously managing anxiety[51]
- Assertively managing anger.[52]

In the rest of this book these strategies will be described in detail, so you can use them to improve your well-being. Research on these strategies shows that they have a positive effect on well-being in people with and without mental health problems.

A second important finding is that when people practise positive psychology strategies using a lot of effort for a long time, this has a bigger effect on their well-being. This occurs because the strategies turn into automatic habits.

A third critical finding is that using lots of strategies works best. When people learn and use a lot of positive psychology strategies, this works better than using just a single strategy. This is because different strategies are appropriate for different situations. If you are on your own, you can use a strategy like finding flow by engaging an absorbing task like writing or playing music. If you are with other people, you can use a strategy like kindness or expressing appreciation. Using different strategies is also more effective than using the same strategy all the time because variety prevents adaptation. Remember the hedonic treadmill? Well, you can prevent yourself from adapting to strategies that enhance your well-being by not using any one strategy too often, and changing your strategies frequently. It's a scientific fact that variety is the spice of life.

A fourth finding involves appreciating how strategies you have used have improved your well-being and being grateful for these improvements. This means not taking them for granted. Remember the principle of appreciation.

A final important finding is that you are more likely to be successful in introducing these strategies into your life if you team up with a friend, a group of friends or your family and all try to improve your well-being together. The support you get from your friends or family when you do this will make it more likely that you will keep putting in the effort. If you keep putting in effort and practising the strategies, they become habits and part of your life.

## Summary

- **PERMA theory of well-being.** Well-being involves positive emotion, engagement, relationships, meaning and accomplishment.
- **Benefits of well-being and happiness.** Happiness leads to better health and longevity.
- **Broaden and Build theory.** Positive emotions broaden thought-action repertoires and help us build enduring resources to promote well-being. This is more likely to happen if we have a higher ratio of positive to negative emotions in our lives.
- **Causes of happiness and well-being.** Forty per cent of individual differences in happiness are due to intentional activities that we can control; 10% are due to circumstances; and 50% to genetic factors.

- **Environmental circumstances and happiness.** In order of importance, people are happier when the following factors are present:

  o   Supportive family relationships and friendships
  o   Sufficient financial resources to meet basic needs
  o   The absence of severe illnesses
  o   Personal freedom
  o   A pleasant living environment
  o   Being female, under 30 or over 50.

- **Adapting to positive and negative life events.** Most people respond less strongly and adapt more quickly to positive events than to negative events. After two years, most people adapt to most positive and negative major life events.
- **Predicting happiness.** Most people are very poor at judging what will make them happy, because they are poor at imagining what the future will be like.
- **Effectiveness of positive psychology interventions.** Scientific studies have shown that a range of positive psychology interventions improve well-being.

## Where are you now?

If you wish, you may write down the most important things you learned about positive psychology from reading this chapter. This may help you to remember these important key points. Now that you have an understanding of some of the main ideas in positive psychology, you are in a good place to start practising specific positive psychology exercises. In the next chapter, you will read about setting highly valued goals. Below are some web resources and books that are relevant to topics you have read about in this chapter.

## Web resources

Martin Seligman talking about PERMA video (23:05): www.youtube.com/watch?v=iK6K_N2qe9Y
Martin Seligman talking about flourishing video (30:07): www.youtube.com/watch?v=eOLbwEVnfJA
Barbara Fredrickson talking about Broaden and Build theory video (8:37): www.youtube.com/watch?v=Z7dFDHzV36g
Barbara Fredrickson talking about how to experience positive emotions video (2:05): www.youtube.com/watch?v=5_BFsWfMkJ4
Sonja Lyubomirsky talking about the determinants of happiness video (4:34): www.youtube.com/watch?v=_URP3-V1sY4
Professor Daniel Gilbert talking about stumbling on happiness video (47:26): www.youtube.com/watch?v=6dArDQYFjC4
Positive Psychology Centre: https://ppc.sas.upenn.edu
57 positive psychology websites: https://positivepsychologyprogram.com/positive-psychology-websites-overview-topics-themes-tests

## Books

Lyubomirsky, S. (2007). *The how of happiness*. New York, NY: Penguin.
Lyubomirsky, S. (2013). *The myths of happiness*. New York, NY: Penguin.
Seligman, M. E. P. (2002). *Authentic happiness*. New York, NY: Free Press.
Seligman, M. E. P. (2011). *Flourish*. New York, NY: Free Press.
Seligman, M. E. P. (2018). *The hope circuit*. Boston, MA: Nicholas Brealey.

# 2 Highly valued goals

One of the first steps you can take to improve well-being is to create a vision for the sort of life you want to lead. We all have aspirations for the future. Because you are reading this book, one of your hopes may be to live a more fulfilling life. You can clarify these aspirations into a clear vision – a set of highly valued goals that are of vital importance to you – by reading this chapter and doing the exercises in it.

In this chapter, you will read about:

- Goals and well-being
- Goals in domains of health, relationships, work and leisure
- Characteristics of highly valued goals
- Setting and clarifying highly valued goals
- Increasing progress towards long-term highly valued goals
- Setting SMART and CLEAR short-term goals to help you achieve long-term highly valued goals.

You will also have invitations to do exercises to help you set and clarify your highly valued goals, and monitor progress towards them.

## Goals and well-being

Why is clarifying a vision for the future, and a set of highly valued goals to work towards, important? The first thing it does is gives our lives meaning and direction.[1] Highly valued goals motivate us to increase our effort. They prevent us from giving up. They inspire us to find out the best strategies for goal attainment. Without a vision for the future and highly valued goals to work towards, we risk becoming aimless, unmotivated and disorganised and wasting time doing things we don't really value. You know the old saying, 'put your money where your mouth is'. Well, when it comes to highly valued goals, the equivalent statement is 'put your time where your values are'. For example, if you really value your relationships with your family, but find yourself spending 16 hours a day at work, there is a mismatch between your values and your use of time.

When we have highly valued goals to work towards, we organise ourselves to move towards them. This process may involve making to-do lists, discovering new information, mastering skills, using strategies, monitoring progress, being careful in how we use our time, meeting deadlines and interacting with other people.

All of these activities associated with moving towards valued goals enhance our well-being.[2] In terms of PERMA theory (described in Chapter 1), pursuing highly valued goals may increase positive emotions, engagement in skilled activities, development of relationships, a sense of meaning and purpose in life and a sense of accomplishment.

## Examples of highly valued goals

Here are examples of highly valued goals in the lives of Anne, Brian and Charles.

### Anne's goal: teaching disadvantaged children

One of Anne's most highly valued goals was to be a nursery school teacher for disadvantaged children. She wanted to do this to give these children a good start in life, and break the cycle of disadvantage. To pursue this highly valued goal she completed an education degree, got a job in nursery school and did continuing professional education to improve her teaching skills. On a day-to-day basis, she planned and taught classes and developed good relationships with her pupils, their parents and her colleagues. She gave her work 110%. She did home visits to all her new pupils' houses. She thought up new themes for her lessons every few weeks: rockets and space travel, super heroes, dinosaurs and volcanoes. She made all her lessons exciting.

Despite being socially disadvantaged, Anne's pupils progressed well under her instruction. She developed a strong sense of purpose in life and sense of accomplishment from the progress her pupils made. She also found learning new skills and teaching engaging. Anne developed very supportive relationships in college during her training, and later with her colleagues at the school where she worked. Teaching is a hard job. While some days were very stressful and left her exhausted, others brought Anne positive emotions such as joy, and pride in her pupil's achievements. Overall Anne's commitment to her highly valued personal goal of being a nursery school teacher enhanced her well-being.

### Brian's goal: entertaining others

Brian worked in middle management in an insurance company. His job was well paid, and he did it efficiently. However, his most highly valued goal was to entertain people and make them laugh. He wanted to be involved in drama, especially comedy. He founded a drama club at the insurance company where he worked. Each year he took a lead role in writing, producing, directing and acting in a Christmas pantomime. His scripts and songs were full of 'in-jokes' that only colleagues in the insurance company would understand. However, he also included lots of material to make children laugh, and some political satire so the show would be appealing to friends and family members of those who worked at the insurance company.

Brian worked evenings and weekends with his club members in preparation for these shows. The pantomimes were a great success. They had a huge impact on Brian's well-being. He developed strong relationships with colleagues who were involved in the shows. The writing process gave him a strong experience of engagement. He became totally immersed in the writing process and lost all sense of time and experienced flow. (You will read more about flow in Chapter 7.) Producing Christmas pantomimes was demanding, but also engendered positive emotions, especially excitement and joy. Most importantly, Brian found the shows gave his life a sense of meaning, purpose and accomplishment (which he could not get from doing his day job). In his heart he was an entertainer. This was his most highly valued goal.

### Charles' goal: creating a supportive family

Charles was married to Wendy. They had two children: Zoe, aged 9, and Roger, aged 11. Charles' most highly valued goal was to create a really supportive and happy family life where everyone felt connected. One of the things he did to achieve this was to arrange for Wendy, Zoe, Roger and himself to have at least three evening meals together each week. He also arranged for Wendy's and his extended family to visit for dinner about once a month. During these family meals, Charles created a warm atmosphere by encouraging everyone to talk to each other about what was happening in their lives. They showed interest in each other's projects. They were generous with praise. They avoided unnecessary criticism, and unhelpful put-downs. When conflict happened, there was an acceptance that both sides would get a fair hearing, and that finding a workable compromise, or apologising for being aggressive, was a sign of strength, not weakness. During family meals, TVs, computers, tablets and phones were all turned off. The main focus was on engaging in conversation.

In his day-to-day life Charles kept in regular contact with all of his family by phone, text, email and social networking. Charles also took the lead in organising the annual family holiday. Usually most members of the extended family rented adjacent holiday homes in the west of Ireland. They went horse-riding and sailing together. Pursuing the highly valued goal of creating a supportive and happy family life enhanced Charles well-being. It involved the positive emotions of loving and being loved, contentment, joy and excitement. It strengthened his family relationships. It gave him a sense of being connected to a wide extended family who valued the same things that he did. There were other positive spin-offs. Charles was a skilled chef, and the process of cooking for his family gave him a sense of engagement and mastery.

## Goals in domains of health, relationships, work and leisure

These three examples illustrate how highly valued goals promote well-being by fostering the five elements of well-being proposed by PERMA theory: positive emotions, engagement, relationships, meaning or purpose in life and accomplishment. Anne's goal was aligned with her career as a teacher. Brian's goal was pursued through his leisure activity of amateur drama. Charles' goal was centred in family life. Of course, Anne, Brian and Charles had highly valued goals in other areas of their lives. However, I have told you about their goals of teaching, entertainment and creating supportive family relationships to illustrate how highly valued goals may be pursued in different life domains.

In clarifying your own highly valued goals it may be helpful to think about four different areas of your life: health, relationships, work and leisure.[3] In the domain of health, you may have goals related to your physical and mental health, fitness and personal growth. In the domain of relationships, you may have goals concerning your family, friends and romantic partners. In the domain of work, your goals may be about running your household, your job, your education or your involvement in volunteering. Finally, in the leisure domain you may have goals to do with sports, arts, gardening or hobbies.

## Characteristics of highly valued goals

There is a large body of research on goals. It shows that certain conditions make it more likely that we will reach our goals and that these goals will increase our well-being.[4]

### Intrinsically rewarding goals

We are more likely to achieve highly valued goals and experience increased well-being if we freely choose these goals ourselves.[5] This is because we will own them. We will be intrinsically motivated to pursue them. Pursuing intrinsically rewarding goals fulfils one or more of the most basic human needs (apart from food and sex). These include the need for feeling in control, feeling good at what we do and having good relationships.

For example, I am varnishing my 50-year-old clinker-built boat this week. I like varnishing. I also want my boat to look beautiful when I launch her at the start of the next sailing season. For me, varnishing is intrinsically rewarding. I also am doing a pile of administrative paperwork for the university this week. This is not my favourite thing in the world to do. It's fairly tedious. However, for me it is extrinsically rewarding. It gives me the cash I need to buy (among other things) the varnish for my boat. Many of us pursue goals in our jobs (like getting through tedious paperwork) that bring us money and recognition, so that we can have enough funds to take time out from work to do the things we really want to do (like varnishing our boats). Therefore, when you are setting your own highly valued goals, make sure that some of these are intrinsically rewarding, but acknowledge that extrinsically rewarding goals may also be necessary.

### Doing activities, not acquiring possessions

Goals that involve doing activities rather than acquiring possessions, or that involve creating new experiences rather than changing circumstances, are more likely to lead to sustained increases in happiness and well-being.[6] Spending quality time with our families and friends will probably increase our well-being more than buying some new stuff. This is because, as we saw in Chapter 1, we adapt to changes in circumstances more than to changes in intentional activities. Also, beyond the point where our basic needs are met, vast increases in material possessions do not lead to a commensurate increase in happiness and well-being.

### Approach-goals, not avoidance-goals

Goals that involve approaching a valued outcome (for example, making a new friend) usually lead to greater well-being than goals that involve avoiding an undesirable outcome (for example, avoiding arguments with people).[7] People who have approach-goals also have greater goal attainment than those who have avoidance-goals. This is probably because it's less complex to approach a single well-defined goal, like making a new friend, than to avoid multiple obstacles, such as having arguments with other people.

### Commitment to goals

We are more likely to achieve our goals if we are highly committed to achieving them. Therefore, when you are creating your own highly valued goals, create goals that you really want to attain and are willing to work hard to achieve. Also, we work harder at goal attainment if our goals are moderately difficult. If goals are too difficult, we may become demoralised and give up. If they are too easy, we may find it difficult to generate commitment and put in a high level of effort. If goals are moderately hard, then this makes it easier to commit to working hard to achieve them.

### Goals that fit together and don't conflict

If all of our highly valued goals fit with each other and form a coherent overall vision, then we are more likely to achieve them. We are less likely to achieve them if they conflict with each other. For example, wanting to balance the quality time you spend with your partner with the time you spend studying and playing sports is a coherent set of goals. The goals of spending most of your time with your partner and getting As on all your courses are conflicting goals, unless your partner is willing to study with you. When you are setting highly valued goals, reflect on how they fit or conflict with each other.

If your highly valued goals appear to be in conflict, look for creative solutions to resolving this conflict. For example, after they graduated from college in Ireland, Dermot and Eileen wanted to continue their relationship and pursue their careers. Unfortunately, because of the 2008 economic crisis, Eileen had to emigrate to Australia to pursue her career in architecture. Dermot, who was a very talented writer, was appointed to his dream journalism job in Ireland. For Eileen and Dermot, their relationship and careers, which were their highly valued goals, conflicted. They dealt with this in a number of ways. They skyped regularly and met during vacations. Dermot researched journalism assignments that involved travelling to Australia and arranged to be released by the paper he worked for to do these. When the economic situation in Ireland improved, Eileen arranged to be seconded periodically to work with an Irish architecture practice. While not ideal, these creative solutions allowed Eileen and Dermot to continue to pursue their conflicting highly valued goals of maintaining their relationship and pursuing their careers.

### Visualisable goals

We are more likely to achieve goals that are specific and visualisable. When we set out to achieve a vague goal like 'doing our best', we accomplish less than when we pursue a specific goal that we can visualise. For example, when Brian was clarifying his vision of being an entertainer, he imagined in his mind's eye what the Christmas pantomime would look like. He saw himself and members of his drama club on stage in costumes doing a song and dance routine, in a show based on Peter Pan. He also visualised the hall in which the show would happen. He saw the audience which included everyone from his firm who was not in the show to their families and friends. This visualisation process made his highly valued goal very concrete. It showed him that he had to form a club, write a show, support members of the club to be in the show and arrange a hall large enough for the show, as well as arranging props, costumes, music, tickets and so forth. In a later section of this chapter there are exercises that will help you visualise the things you value doing most in your life.

### Measurable and monitored goals

We are more likely to achieve our goals if they are measurable and if we regularly give our-selves feedback by measuring goal attainment. In the first example earlier in the chapter, Anne's goal of becoming a nursery school teacher to help disadvantaged children was meas-urable. She saw each exam that she passed in her education degree as step on the road to becoming a teacher. When she got her first job, each time one of her disadvantaged pupils succeeded at a task she viewed this as a measurable sign that she was achieving her highly valued goal. She kept a record of how each of her pupils was progressing. This gave her reg-ular feedback on the extent to which she was moving towards her goal.

### Appropriate goals

The pursuit of highly valued goals is more likely to enhance well-being if these goals take account of our cultural circumstances, life-stage, profile of personal characteristics, abilities, resources and strengths.[7] These factors create opportunities and pose obstacles for complet-ing a range of tasks, which most of us value, at various stages of the lifecycle: for example, completing education, being involved in sports or the arts, separating from parents, getting a job, getting married or remaining single, having children or not, retiring and dealing with the challenges of later life. We are more likely to derive increased well-being from pursuing our highly valued goals if these goals are appropriate to our life circumstances.

Let's sum up the characteristics of good highly valued goals.

- They are appropriate to our life circumstances
- They are intrinsically rewarding (not extrinsically rewarding)
- They involve doing activities (rather than acquiring possessions)
- They involve approaching a valued outcome (not avoiding an unpleasant outcome)
- They involve a high level of commitment (not a low level of commitment)
- They fit together (don't conflict with each other)
- They are visualisable (not fuzzy)
- They are measurable and can be monitored regularly (not vague).

## Setting highly valued goals

Here are two exercises to help you crystallise your vision of how you would like your life to be. One is called 'your best possible self'. The other is called the 'eulogy or legacy letter'. You may do whichever one you like, or both if you wish. Doing these exercises will help you cre-ate a vision of the sort of life you want to lead. This is the first step in clarifying your highly valued goals.

### 'Best possible self' exercise

This exercise will help you clarify your overall vision of the direction you want your life to take. It may have the added benefit of improving your feeling of well-being as you do it. The exercise involves imagining your best possible self over the next 10 years of your life. It was developed by Professor Laura King at the University of Missouri. She found that writing about life goals by imagining the best possible future self was an effective way of improving well-being and decreasing illness.[9] It was as effective as and less distressing than writing about past trauma. It also had the added benefit of clarifying highly valued personal life goals.

You are invited to do the following exercise in a quiet place where you will not be distracted or interrupted. Do it for 20 minutes a day for at least four days. However, the benefits for your well-being will be greater if you continue to do the exercise for longer than four days. Begin by sitting quietly and thinking about yourself as you will be in the future over the next 10 years.

Visualise your 'best possible self'. Imagine that everything in your life has gone as well as it possibly could. You have worked hard. This has paid off. Imagine you have succeeded at accomplishing all of your life goals. Imagine that all your life dreams have been realised. Imagine that all your hopes have been fulfilled. Imagine that you have fulfilled your potential.

Think about your best possible physical and mental health over the next 10 years. Think about what you have accomplished in your relationships with your partner, your family and your friends. Visualise what you have achieved in your career at work or in your education. Imagine how things have worked out in your leisure activities, sports or arts. In each of these domains you are visualising the best possible way that things might turn out in your life, in order to help guide your decisions now.

In your journal, write in detail about what you have imagined. Don't be concerned about grammar or spelling. The important thing is to write fluently and in detail about what you visualise.

You may not have thought about yourself in this way before. The process will help you clarify your highly valued life goals. Research shows that doing this can also have a strong positive effect on your well-being. A summary of this exercise is in Box 2.1.

---

### Box 2.1   Best possible self

Find a quiet place where you will not be distracted or interrupted.

For 20 minutes a day for at least four days, visualise your 'best possible self' and write about this in your journal.

Write about how you visualise you will be over the next 10 years if everything in your life goes as well as it possibly could and all your hopes are fulfilled in the following areas:

- Your physical and mental health.
- Your relationships with your partner, your family and your friends.
- Your achievements in your career at work or in your education.
- Your achievements in leisure activities, sports and arts.

**Note:** Based on King, L. A. (2001). The health benefits of writing about life goals. *Personality and Social Psychology Bulletin, 27,* 798-807.

---

### *Eulogy or legacy letter exercise*

This exercise will help you to clarify your highly valued goals by imagining that your life is over, and that you have reached all of your goals. By imagining that you are looking back over your life, you will be able to identify those goals that are most important to you. This exercise can be done from the perspective of a friend writing your eulogy, or from your own perspective writing an autobiographical legacy letter to your family. The exercise was developed by Professor Martin Seligman, the founder of positive psychology, and his team. It was included as one of six exercises in an effective six-session group therapy programme for people with depression.[10]

Do the following exercise in a quiet place where you will not be distracted or interrupted. Take as much time as you need. You can do it in one sitting, or you may spread it over a few sittings.

Imagine you have passed away after living a long, fruitful and satisfying life. Imagine you have lived the life you wanted to live – the best possible life you could have lived. Imagine that you have accomplished all that you wanted to do.

Now imagine that your closest friend who knows you better than anyone is speaking at your funeral. Your friend is delivering this eulogy to those who knew and loved you.

Write this eulogy now. Write about all those things that you would want your friend to mention in describing your life: your relationships, your accomplishments and the impact of your life on others. Cover all the important areas of your life, especially the things you would want to be remembered for most.

Alternatively, you may write about your life and its legacy from your own perspective. Imagine you have lived a long, fruitful and satisfying life. Imagine you have lived the life you wanted to live – the best possible life you could have lived. Imagine that you have accomplished all that you wanted to do.

Now imagine that you know you have only a short time left to live. You want to write a letter to your partner, to your children or to your grandchildren telling them about your legacy.

Write this legacy letter now. Write about the values that were most important in your life, your relationships, your accomplishments and the impact of your life on others. Cover all the important areas of your life, especially the things you would want to be remembered for most.

Take your time writing this exercise in your journal. Read back over it when you have written a first draft. If you wish, edit it by changing some parts or adding in things that you left out. A summary of this exercise is in Box 2.2.

---

### Box 2.2  Eulogy or legacy letter

Find a quiet place where you will not be distracted or interrupted.

Imagine you have passed away after living a long, fruitful and satisfying life: the best possible life you could have lived. You have accomplished all that you wanted to do. In your journal write the eulogy you imagine your closest friend would give at your funeral. Imagine that your closest friend is speaking at your funeral to those who knew and loved you about all those things that you would want your friend to mention in describing your life: your relationships, your accomplishments, the impact of your life on others and the things you would want to be remembered for most.

OR

Imagine you are close to death having lived a long, fruitful and satisfying life: the best possible life you could have lived. You have accomplished all that you wanted to do. In your journal write a legacy letter to your partner, to your children or to your grandchildren about your life and its legacy from your own perspective. Write about the values that were most important in your life, your relationships, your accomplishments and the impact of your life on others, and the things you would want to be remembered for most.

**Note:** Based on an exercise in Seligman, M. E., Rashid, T. & Parks, A. C. (2006). Positive psychotherapy. *American Psychologist, 61*(8), 774-788.

## Clarifying and refining your highly valued goals

When you have done either the best possible self exercise or the eulogy or legacy letter exercise, read what you have written. Reflect on how what you have written tells you about your answers to these questions:

- What is really important to you?
- What are your highest priorities in life?
- What sorts of things do you value most?
- What hopes and dreams for the future inspire you – draw you into the future?
- What big overall courses of action do you want to make a commitment to?
- How do you want to conduct your life?
- If you lived the sort of life you really want to, what would you be doing?
- If your life were a project, what would it be called?

Having reflected on these questions, in your journal write down your most highly valued goals. If you wish, you may organise these goals into domains to do with health, relationships, work and leisure. However, there may be other domains you consider important, for example spirituality or religious practice. A summary of this exercise is in Box 2.3.

### Box 2.3   Clarifying highly valued goals

Find a quiet place where you will not be distracted or interrupted.

Read what you have written about your best possible self, or your eulogy, or your legacy letter.

Reflect on how what you have written tells you about your answers to these questions:

- What is really important to you?
- What are your highest priorities in life?
- What sorts of things do you value most?

- What hopes and dreams for the future inspire you – draw you into the future?
- What big overall courses of action do you want to make a commitment to?
- How do you want to conduct your life?
- If you lived the sort of life you really want to, what would you be doing?
- If your life were a project, what would it be called?

Write down your highly valued goals in each of the areas of health, relationships, achievements, leisure activities and other areas you may value such as spirituality.

Now check if your goals fit with what we know about the characteristics of highly valued goals that are most likely to enhance well-being. Check if your goals:

- are appropriate to your circumstances
- are intrinsically rewarding (not extrinsically rewarding)
- involve doing activities (rather than acquiring possessions)
- involve approaching a valued outcome (not avoiding an unpleasant outcome)
- involve a high level of commitment (not a low level of commitment)
- fit together (don't conflict with each other)
- are visualisable (not fuzzy)
- are measurable and can be monitored regularly (not vague).

If your goals don't have these characteristics, you may wish to refine them. A summary of this exercise is in Box 2.4.

## Box 2.4   Refining highly valued goals

Find a quiet place where you will not be distracted or interrupted.

Read your highly valued goals in the areas of health, relationships, achievements, leisure activities and other areas you may value such as spirituality.

Check if your goals have the characteristics of highly valued goals that are most likely to enhance well-being:

- Are intrinsically rewarding (not extrinsically rewarding)
- Involve doing activities (rather than acquiring possessions)
- Involve approaching a valued outcome (not avoiding an unpleasant outcome)
- Involve a high level of commitment (not a low level of commitment)
- Fit together (don't conflict with each other)
- Are visualisable (not fuzzy)
- Are measurable and can be monitored regularly (not vague)
- Are appropriate to your life circumstances.

Consider refining your highly valued goals if they don't have these characteristics.

## Monitoring progress towards highly valued goals

Periodically, every few weeks or months, re-read your list of highly valued goals. For each goal, you may ask yourself on a scale of 1 to 10, to what extent have I made progress towards achieving this goal? On this scale 1 means that little progress has been made towards achieving your highly valued goal and 10 means a lot of progress has been made. You may record your scores for each goal in your journal each time you review progress. Notice if your scores change over time. If your scores are getting higher, this is good news. You are moving towards your highly valued goals.

If your scores are remaining the same or dropping, then this is good news too. You have an opportunity to reflect on why this is, and make constructive changes in your life to help you move towards your highly valued goals. You may ask yourself:

- Am I spending my time prioritising these goals?
- Am I spending much of my time doing other things?

If you are spending a lot of time on other things, you may wish to think about how you can change this. You may ask yourself:

- What obstacles would I have to overcome to spend more time pursuing my highly valued goals and less time doing other things?
- What would be the first small step that I could take today to start overcoming these obstacles?

This process of self-reflection will help you begin to explore ways to make progress towards your highly valued goals. A summary of this exercise is in Box 2.5.

---

### Box 2.5   Monitoring progress towards highly valued goals

Periodically, in your journal, write down your rating of progress towards each of your highly valued goals on a 10-point scale.

On this scale 1 means you have made little progress towards achieving your highly valued goals and 10 means you have made a lot of progress.

If your scores gradually increase, keep doing whatever it is that is allowing you to gradually make progress towards your highly valued goals.

If your scores are remaining the same or dropping, then ask yourself:

- Am I spending my time prioritising my highly valued goals?
- Am I spending much of my time doing other things?
- What obstacles would I have to overcome to spend more time pursuing my highly valued goals?
- What would be the first small step that I could take today to start overcoming these obstacles?

## Increasing progress towards highly valued goals

Highly valued goals tend to be large and long-term. If we want to reach these big, long-term goals and progress is slow, it's often best to break them down into a lot of smaller medium- and short-term goals and work towards these in a systematic way.[11] In the second example, earlier in the chapter, Brian wanted to entertain people. He wanted to be an entertainer. That's a big goal. It's important to have these big, highly valued goals in our lives to give us overall direction. One of Brian's medium-term goals was to set up a drama club. One of his short-term goals related to this was to send an email to everyone in the insurance company asking if they would be interested in joining a drama club.

### *Problem-solving and solution-finding*

There are usually obstacles to be overcome when making progress towards goals. For example, in Brian's company, there was a policy that employees were not allowed to email each other about matters that were not work-related. This was an obstacle Brian had to overcome to reach his short-term goal of emailing everyone. He met with his boss and explained his idea about setting up the drama club. His boss liked the idea. He saw that it would improve morale and company loyalty. He gave Brian permission to send an internal email to all staff asking about their interest in joining the drama club.

What Brian did is a good example of problem-solving. He clarified what the problem was. He thought about a range of possible solutions. He predicted the price and pay-off of each of these. Then he selected the most likely to succeed. We will be discussing problem-solving and solution-finding in detail in Chapter 10. Problem-solving and solution-finding is what we do to overcome obstacles in our paths, when we are committed to moving towards goals.

## SMART and CLEAR short-term goals

In business psychology, a few acronyms are widely used to encapsulate the features of good short-term goals; for example, SMART goals and CLEAR goals.[12] You have probably come across these.

In case you're a little rusty, let me remind you what SMART and CLEAR short-term goals are.

SMART goals are:

**S**pecific – clear and unambiguous

**M**easurable – for example, the number of things to be done

**A**ttainable – can be achieved with the skills and resources available to you

**R**elevant – to your overall vision and highly valued goals

**T**imely – have a start and end point.

CLEAR goals are:

**C**ollaborative – involve working co-operatively with others

**L**imited – in both scope and duration

**E**motional – in that they are valued and involve a high level of commitment

**A**ppreciable – insofar as they can be subdivided into smaller goals if necessary

**R**efinable – in that they may be modified in light of changing circumstances.

You will see that these characteristics of SMART and CLEAR short-term goals have some overlap with the characteristics of highly valued long-term goals. However, they are by definition different. They are short-term and time limited. Highly valued goals are long-term and it is the process of moving towards them that enhances well-being. It's all about the journey, not the destination.

## Summary

- **Goals and well-being.** Setting highly valued goals gives our lives purpose, meaning and direction. It motivates us to increase our effort. Our well-being increases as we move towards highly valued goals.
- **Best possible self, eulogy and legacy letter exercises.** These exercises help us set highly valued goals in domains of health, relationships, work and leisure.
- **Characteristics of highly valued goals.** We can refine our highly valued goals by tweaking them so that they have the following characteristics:

  o   Are appropriate to our life circumstances
  o   Are intrinsically rewarding (not extrinsically rewarding)
  o   Involve doing activities (rather than acquiring possessions)
  o   Involve approaching a valued outcome (not avoiding an unpleasant outcome)
  o   Involve a high level of commitment (not a low level of commitment)
  o   Fit together (don't conflict with each other)
  o   Are visualisable (not fuzzy)
  o   Are measurable and can be monitored regularly (not vague).

- **Monitoring progress.** Periodically rating progress towards highly valued goals can help us take corrective action. This may involve problem-solving, solution-finding and setting short-term SMART or CLEAR goals.

## Where are you now?

If you have done the exercises in this chapter, you have clarified your vision of the way you want your life to be, and your highly valued goals. You may also have a plan to monitor progress towards them, and some insights into how you might overcome obstacles in your path. You may want to read back over the chapter and summarise in your journal the main things that you found most useful about highly valued goals and well-being. The remainder of this book will include ideas and exercises from positive psychology that may help you achieve your highly valued goals. Below are some web resources that are relevant to topics you have read about in this chapter.

## Web resources

Inspirational video for setting highly valued life goals (2:45): www.youtube.com/watch?v=oR_gnzY3UgA

Setting life goals: https://positivepsychologyprogram.com/life-worth-living-setting-life-goals

Goal setting: https://positivepsychologyprogram.com/goal-setting

Setting CLEAR and SMART goals: www.inc.com/peter-economy/forget-smart-goals-try-clear-goals-instead.html

# 3 Personal strengths

In Chapter 2 you did exercises to identify your highly valued life goals. In this chapter, you will have an opportunity to identify your signature strengths and use them to help you move towards these goals. You will read about:

- The Values in Action Inventory of Strengths (VIA-IS)
- Six virtues and 24 character strengths of the VIA-IS
- Signature strengths
- The science of character strengths
- Identifying and using your signature strengths.

## The Values in Action Inventory of Strengths

One of the major achievements of positive psychology has been the development of a system for assessing character strengths. It's called the Values in Action Inventory of Strengths or VIA-IS.[1] Psychology has a long history of developing questionnaires to measure personality traits, psychological disorders and other personal characteristics. However, the VIA-IS is different. This inventory was developed explicitly to measure strengths that help people enhance their well-being.

The VIA-IS was developed by Professor Martin Seligman and the late Professor Chris Peterson.[2] They reviewed the virtues and character strengths referred to in major religious and philosophical traditions around the world. These included the bible, the Talmud, the Koran, the Upanishads and the Bushido, which is the samurai code. They also included the works of individuals such as Confucius, Buddha, Lao-Tse, Aristotle, Plato, Aquinas, Augustine and Benjamin Franklin. In this review, Seligman and Peterson found that six virtues were common to all of these religious and philosophical traditions. These were:

- Wisdom
- Courage
- Humanity
- Justice
- Temperance
- Transcendence.

These six virtues are defined in Box 3.1. They concluded that these virtues are universal because they were described in all major religious and philosophical traditions. They are also speculated that they were partly genetically determined. A recent twin study has provided some support for this idea.[3] Seligman and Peterson also proposed that evolution had a key role in the development of the six virtues. People with these virtues survived, and those without them did not. This probably happened because the six virtues helped people manage important tasks necessary for the survival of the species.

---

## Box 3.1   Virtues and character strengths

| | |
|---|---|
| *WISDOM* | *The virtue of wisdom involves the acquisition and use of knowledge. The virtue of wisdom is achieved through the strengths of creativity, curiosity, judgement, love of learning and perspective.* |
| **Creativity** | The strength of creativity includes ingenuity, originality and adaptability. Thinking of new and productive ways to do things is a crucial part of who you are. You are never content with doing something the conventional way if a better way is possible. |
| **Curiosity** | The strength of curiosity includes interest in all things, novelty seeking, exploration and openness to experience. You are curious about everything. You are always asking questions, and you find all subjects and topics fascinating. You like exploration and discovery. |
| **Judgement** | The strength of judgement includes critical thinking, thinking things through and being open-minded. Thinking things through and examining them from all sides are important aspects of who you are. You do not jump to conclusions, and you rely only on solid evidence to make your decisions. You are able to change your mind when you come across new information or develop a new perspective on things. |
| **Love of learning** | The strength of love of learning includes the desire to master new skills, learn about new topics and systematically add to knowledge. You are passionate about learning new things, whether in a class or on your own. You have always loved school, college, reading and museums – anywhere and everywhere there is an opportunity to learn. |
| **Perspective** | The strength of perspective includes wisdom, providing wise council to others and taking the big picture. Although you may not think of yourself as wise, your friends hold this view of you. They value your perspective on matters and turn to you for advice. You have a distinctive way of looking at the world that integrates many viewpoints, is 'wide-angle', takes account of the 'big picture' and makes sense to others and to yourself. |
| *COURAGE* | *The virtue of courage is the will to accomplish goals in the face of internal or external opposition. The virtue of courage is achieved through the strengths of bravery, perseverance, honesty and zest.* |
| **Bravery** | The strength of bravery includes valour; not shrinking from threat, pain, difficulty or fear; and speaking up for what is right. You are a courageous person who does not shrink from threat, challenge, difficulty or pain. You stand your ground even when frightened by physical threats. You speak up for what is right even if this makes you unpopular and there is opposition. You act on your convictions. |

| | |
|---|---|
| **Perseverance** | The strength of perseverance includes persistence, industry and diligence. You work hard to finish what you start. No matter the project, you 'get it out the door' in timely fashion. You do not get distracted when you work, and you take satisfaction in completing tasks. |
| **Honesty** | The strength of honesty includes authenticity, integrity and genuineness. You are an honest person, not only by speaking the truth but by living your life in a genuine and authentic way. You take responsibility for your feelings and actions and are slow to blame others for what you experience. You are down to earth and without pretence. |
| **Zest** | The strength of zest includes vitality, enthusiasm, vigour, energy and feeling alive and activated. Regardless of what you do, you approach it with excitement, enthusiasm and energy. You never do anything halfway or half-heartedly. For you, life is an adventure. |
| *HUMANITY* | *The virtue of humanity involves tending and befriending others in close relationships. The virtue of humanity is achieved through the strengths of love, kindness and social intelligence.* |
| **Love** | The strength of love includes the capacity to love and be loved, and to value close relations. You value close relationships with others, in particular those in which sharing and caring are reciprocated. The people to whom you feel closest are the same people who feel most close to you. |
| **Kindness** | The strength of kindness includes generosity, compassion, altruism, empathy, nurturance and care. You are kind and generous to others, and you are never too busy to do a favour. You enjoy doing good deeds for others, even if you do not know them well. You often put the needs of others ahead of your own. |
| **Social intelligence** | The strength of social intelligence includes emotional intelligence and being aware of the motives and feelings of self and others. You are aware of the motives and feelings of other people. You know what to do to fit in to different social situations, and you know what to do to put others at ease. You know what makes other people tick. |
| *JUSTICE* | *The virtue of justice underlies strong social networks and healthy community life. The virtue of justice is achieved through the strengths of teamwork, fairness and leadership.* |
| **Teamwork** | The strength of teamwork includes citizenship, social responsibility and loyalty. You excel as a member of a group, and work well with members of a group or team. You are a loyal and dedicated teammate. You always do your share. You work hard for the success of your group, even if this is not in your own best interests. |
| **Fairness** | The strength of fairness includes equity and justice. Treating all people fairly is one of your abiding principles. You do not let your personal feelings bias your decisions about other people. You give everyone a chance. |
| **Leadership** | The strength of leadership includes organising group activities and encouraging a group to achieve its goals. You excel at the tasks of leadership. You encourage a group or team to get things done and preserve harmony within the group by making everyone feel included and valued. You do a good job organising activities and seeing that they happen. |

| TEMPERANCE | The virtue of temperance protects us against excesses. The virtue of temperance is achieved through the strengths of forgiveness, humility, prudence and self-regulation. |
|---|---|
| **Forgiveness** | The strength of forgiveness includes mercy, accepting others' shortcomings and giving people a second chance. Forgiveness protects us from hatred. You forgive those who have done you wrong. You always give people a second chance. Your guiding principle is mercy and not revenge. |
| **Humility** | The strength of humility includes modesty, and letting one's accomplishments speak for themselves. Humility protects us from arrogance. You do not seek the spotlight, preferring to let your accomplishments speak for themselves. You tend to change the subject if people pay you compliments. You do not regard yourself as special, and others recognise and value your modesty. |
| **Prudence** | The strength of prudence includes caution, discretion and avoiding taking undue risks. Prudence protects us from long-term difficulties that may result from overindulging in short-term pleasures. You are a careful person, and your choices are consistently prudent ones. You do not say or do things that you might later regret. You resist impulses to do things that would feel good now, if these might involve long-term risks. |
| **Self-regulation** | The strength of self-regulation includes self-control, self-discipline and managing one's impulses and emotions. Self-regulation protects us from acting out intense emotions in problematic ways. You self-consciously regulate what you feel and what you do. You are a disciplined person. You are in control of your appetites and your emotions, not vice versa. You don't lose your temper. You can stay on a diet. |
| TRANSCENDENCE | The virtue of transcendence connects us to the larger universe and provides meaning in life. The virtue of transcendence is achieved through the strengths of appreciation of beauty and excellence, gratitude, hope, humour and spirituality. |
| **Appreciation of beauty and excellence** | The strength of appreciation of beauty and excellence includes awe, wonder and elevation. Appreciation connects us to all that is beautiful and excellent in life. You notice and appreciate beauty, excellence and/or skilled performance in all domains of life, including nature, art, mathematics, science and everyday experience. You marvel at the beauty of the world and are quickly moved to wonder. You stop to smell the roses or look at the sunset. |
| **Gratitude** | The strength of gratitude includes being thankful for the good things that happen; expressing thanks; and feeling blessed. Gratitude connects us to the good things for which we are thankful. You appreciate the good things that happen to you and you never take them for granted. Your friends and family members know that you are a grateful person because you always take the time to express your thanks. You appreciate and are thankful for how wonderful life is. |
| **Hope** | The strength of hope includes optimism, having a positive outlook and future-mindedness. Hope connects us to our future dreams and aspirations. You expect the best in the future, and you work to achieve it. You believe that the future is something that you can control. |

| Humour | The strength of humour includes playfulness and light-heartedness. Humour connects us to the challenges and complications of life in a way that brings forth positive rather than negative emotions. You like to laugh, joke and tease. Bringing smiles to other people is important to you. You try to see the light side of all situations. |
| Spirituality | The strength of spirituality includes religiousness, sense of purpose and faith. Spirituality connects us to the non-material or transcendent dimension of life, and to the ideal, universal, divine or sacred aspect of the universe. You have strong and coherent beliefs about the higher purpose and meaning of life and the universe. You know where you fit in the larger scheme. Your beliefs shape your actions and are a source of comfort to you. |

**Note:** Based on Peterson, C., & Park, N. (2009). Classifying and measuring strengths of character. In S. Lopez & C. R. Snyder (Eds.), *Oxford handbook of positive psychology* (Second Edition, pp. 25–33). New York, NY: Oxford University Press; and Peterson, C., & Seligman, M. (2004). *Character strengths and virtues: A handbook and classification*. New York, NY: Oxford University Press.

Seligman and Peterson identified character strengths associated with each of the six virtues. These 24 character strengths are listed and defined in Box 3.1. Character strengths are ways that we can achieve the virtues associated with them. For example, we can achieve the virtue of wisdom by using the character strength of curiosity. We can achieve the virtue of justice by using the strength of fairness. When we use strengths, this involves an act of will. Strengths can be developed by using them frequently, and in different situations. Seligman and Peterson developed and refined sets of questions that most accurately assessed each of these character strengths. They then selected the best questions for each strength and included these in the VIA-IS. This is now available free on the internet at www.viacharacter. org/survey/account/register. You can complete the VIA-IS online in 10–15 minutes. You will receive an instant report on your overall profile of character strengths, and a list of your top five signature strengths.

## Signature strengths

Your signature strengths are those that help you achieve greater well-being. They have the following distinctive characteristics:

- You believe that the strength is central to your character, and to the sort of person that you are or would like to be.
- You feel excited about using the strength.
- You find that you learn new skills quickly when the strength is first used.
- You find new ways to use the strength.
- You have a feeling that you will use the strength in many situations.
- You create personal projects that revolve around the strength.
- You usually feel good when using the strength or after you have used it.

You can use all of the strengths, especially your signature strengths, in day-to-day life to enhance your well-being. Later in this chapter there is an exercise that will help you to do this.

## What do we know about the science of character strengths?

The late Professor Chris Peterson and Professor Nansook Park at the University of Michigan and their international colleagues have done a series of scientific studies to investigate VIA-IS character strengths. Most of these were done on the internet. This allowed them to conduct very large studies involving thousands of people from many countries. The fact that so many people participated in these studies means that we can place considerable confidence in their results. Here are some interesting results from these studies.

The most common character strengths are kindness, gratitude, fairness, honesty and judgement. The least common strengths are self-regulation, prudence and modesty.[4]

The character strengths most strongly associated with well-being are love, hope, gratitude and zest. These strengths are strongly associated with well-being across the lifespan in children, adolescents and adults.[5]

Physical illnesses, like heart disease and cancer, take less of a toll on well-being if you have the character strengths of kindness, bravery and humour. Psychological problems, like anxiety and depression, take less of toll on life satisfaction if you have the character strengths of appreciation of beauty and love of learning.[6]

All 24 VIA-IS character strengths are associated with posttraumatic growth after trauma such as serious accidents and assaults.[7] Posttraumatic growth means responding to trauma in a positive way by re-evaluating your highly valued life goals and the relative importance of material things and relationships in your life. Posttraumatic growth will be discussed in detail in Chapter 15.

Women score higher on most VIA-IS character strength scales.[8]

As people mature, their pattern of signature strengths may change. Hope, teamwork and zest are the most common signature strengths among adolescents. Appreciation of beauty, authenticity, leadership and open-mindedness are the most common signature strengths for adults.[9]

A series of randomised controlled trials have shown that identifying your signature strengths with the VIA-IS, and then using these strengths regularly, leads to increased well-being and decreased depression.[10] The next exercise is based on the procedures evaluated in these randomised controlled trials.

## Signature strengths exercise

There is an invitation now to complete the VIA-IS at www.viacharacter.org/survey/account/register. Identify your top five signature strengths. If you don't have access to the internet, read the definitions of each of the 24 character strengths in Box 3.1. Identify which five of these best describe you. This is not the most reliable way to identify your signature strengths. However, it will allow you to move forward and do this exercise, if you wish.

Try to think of ways to use your signature strengths to help you move towards the highly valued goals you identified by doing the exercises in Chapter 2. Some examples of ways to use signature strengths are listed in Box 3.2. You can use your signature strengths at work, at home or in leisure activities.

## Box 3.2   Using your signature strengths

| | |
|---|---|
| *WISDOM* | *Achieve the virtue of wisdom by using the strengths of creativity, curiosity, judgement, love of learning and perspective* |
| **Creativity** | • Select a routine daily task and made a conscious decision to be creative and do it completely differently, using one of your other signature strengths.<br>• Develop the habit of 'brainstorming' as many solutions as possible to any problem you face, before looking at price and payoff of each and selecting the best option.<br>• Write a very brief accurate description of the most beautiful scene you can call to mind. |
| **Curiosity** | • Select a local place you pass every day, but know little about, and find out everything about it.<br>• Come home a different way from work or college and notice everything new that you see.<br>• Select an activity that you have to do regularly but dislike; as you do it pay attention to three things about the activity that you have not previously noticed; discuss these with a friend. |
| **Judgement** | • Write down an opinion you strongly hold. Then write down five reasons why someone might doubt its validity.<br>• Next time someone says something important you disagree with, ask them why they believe it so strongly. Listen carefully to what they say and try to understand their point of view.<br>• With an open mind, watch a political TV programme which advocates a position that differs from your own. |
| **Love of learning** | • Make a point of learning a new idea each day.<br>• Select a topic that really interests you and find out as much as you can about it.<br>• When you have to learn something that is boring, consider how knowing about this topic might benefit you and others.<br>• Spend 15 minutes today reading a book or article that you would not otherwise read. |
| **Perspective** | • Next time you are with two friends who are arguing, don't take sides. Instead try to understand both sides of the argument.<br>• For one day, spend more time questioning and listening than talking. Only give an opinion or advice when asked, and then only after careful deliberation. |
| *COURAGE* | *Achieve the virtue of courage by using the strengths of bravery, perseverance, honesty and zest.* |
| **Bravery** | • Catch yourself being nervous but doing whatever it was that made you nervous, and acknowledge that you can be brave.<br>• The next time you are frightened to do or say something good, acknowledge to yourself that you are frightened and then do or say something good in that situation, and acknowledge that you have been brave.<br>• When you have to do something that scares you, remind yourself of how it will help you or other people. |

| | |
|---|---|
| **Perseverance** | • Today, plan to do one thing, assignment or task to completion and follow through on this plan. |
| | • Take an important task you have been avoiding doing for some time, and plan to do it in small stages. Then follow through on your plan. |
| | • Identify a new goal today; list some of the pain obstacles to achieving it; brainstorm ways of overcoming these obstacles. |
| **Honesty** | • For one day, only say things you genuinely believe to be true. |
| | • Contact someone with whom you have not been completely honest about a particular issue and tell them the whole truth. |
| | • Do one thing each day that you think reflects your most deeply held values. |
| **Zest** | • Do something today because you really want to, not because you think you should. |
| | • Sleep for eight hours, eat three moderate-sized healthy meals and exercise vigorously outside in nature for an hour during one 24-hour period. Notice how energetic you feel as a result. |
| | • Tell a friend or family member, in vivid detail, about positive things that have happened to you today. |
| *HUMANITY* | *Achieve the virtue of humanity by using the strengths of love, kindness and social intelligence.* |
| **Love** | • Do something with your friend or partner that they really want to do. |
| | • Tell someone about one of their strengths that you really appreciate, and give them examples of how you have seen them expressing this strength. |
| | • Accept a compliment by saying 'thanks' and no more than that. |
| | • Develop a 'loving kindness' or meditation practice (described in Box 11.1). |
| **Kindness** | • Do a favour for a friend or stranger and don't make a big deal out of it. |
| | • Visit someone who is lonely and listen to them. |
| **Social intelligence** | • When someone says or does something to annoy you, don't immediately retaliate. Try to understand their motives. |
| | • Do or say something to make another person feel at ease in a tense situation. |
| | • In complex situations when you have very mixed emotions, practise naming each of them, for example feeling guilty about being angry and frightened. |
| *JUSTICE* | *Achieve the virtue of justice by using the strengths of teamwork, fairness and leadership.* |
| **Teamwork** | • Today, turn up on time and do more than your fair share of whatever team work you are involved in. |
| | • Use 'we' much more than 'I' when talking about your team's achievements, successes, hopes and positive beliefs. |
| | • Do some voluntary work for a charitable organisation. |
| **Fairness** | • Today, when you find you have made a mistake in your dealings with others, admit it and take responsibility for it. |
| | • Listen to people with whom you disagree without interrupting them. |
| | • If you have to make decisions that affect others, involve them in the decision-making process, allowing them opportunities to express and discuss ideas that differ from yours, and explain reasons for final decisions that you reach. |
| **Leadership** | • Organise a social event for your friends or family. |
| | • Make a new person or an unpopular person in your social circle feel welcome and part of the group. |

| TEMPERANCE | *Achieve the virtue of temperance by using the strengths of forgiveness, humility, prudence and self-regulation.* |
|---|---|
| **Forgiveness** | • Write a letter of forgiveness to someone who has wronged you, but don't send it. Read it each day for a week.<br>• Once a day when you feel annoyed with someone, try to understand and empathise with the other person's reasons for being annoying, and let go of your negative feeling. |
| **Humility** | • Today, don't talk about yourself.<br>• Compliment a friend on something he or she does better than you. |
| **Prudence** | • Today, ask yourself if the health risks are worth it next time you eat junk food, drink more than two units of alcohol or drive over the speed limit.<br>• Curb one excess today. |
| **Self-regulation** | • Engage in one small act of self-control every day in one area of your life where you find self-control challenging (eating healthily, drinking alcohol, exercising, shopping, expressing anger, etc.)<br>• Count to 10 the next time you feel you are going to lose your temper.<br>• Give up gossiping and saying mean things about others for today. |
| TRANSCENDENCE | *Achieve the virtue of transcendence by using the strengths of appreciation of beauty and excellence, gratitude, hope, humour and spirituality.* |
| **Appreciation of beauty and excellence** | • Stop and notice the natural beauty all around you twice a day.<br>• Write down the most beautiful thing you see every day for a week. |
| **Gratitude** | • Tell someone whose who is rarely thanked for their good work that you appreciate what they do.<br>• At the end of the day write down three good things that you experienced and for which you are grateful.<br>• Write a gratitude letter to someone who helped you and you never thanked describing in detail how they helped you, and send them the letter. |
| **Hope** | • Write down your goals for the next month and make plans for accomplishing them.<br>• Think of a thing that disappointed you, and the positive opportunities it created for you.<br>• Watch a film that contains a hopeful message, and reflect on how this applies to your life. |
| **Humour** | • Make one person smile today.<br>• Make fun of yourself today.<br>• At the end of each day, in your journal, write down the three funniest things that happened to you that day and explain why those things happened. |
| **Spirituality** | • Meditate today for 15 minutes.<br>• Think about the purpose of your life today.<br>• Think about a spiritual role model, and consider which of their positive attributes you most want to emulate. |

**Note:** This exercise is based on that given in Peterson, C. (2006). *A primer in positive psychology.* Oxford: Oxford University Press, pp. 158-162 and on exercises in Niemec, R. (2018). *Character strengths interventions: A field guide for practitioners.* Boston, MA: Hogrefe.

If you wish, make a plan to use at least one of your signature strengths in a new way every day for a week. Decide how you will use your strengths. Decide where and when you will use them. Write this plan in your journal.

After you have used your signature strengths, write about this experience in your journal. Write down what you experienced before, during and after using your signature strength.

What were you doing before you used your signature strength? At that point, how did you feel on a 10-point well-being scale, where 0 means you experienced a very low level of well-being, 5 means your feelings were neutral and 10 means you experienced an extremely high level of well-being?

When you were engaged in the activity, what were you and other involved people doing? Was the activity was challenging or easy? When you were doing the activity did you lose your sense of time and become absorbed in the activity? What positive things did you notice about your experience? At that point, how did you feel on a 10-point well-being scale, where 0 means you experienced a very low level of well-being, 5 means your feelings were neutral and 10 means you experienced an extremely high level of well-being?

When you finished doing the activity, what did you and other involved people do? What were your reflections on doing the activity? Did you think about doing the activity again? Did you think about other similar activities you could do? Did the activity help you move one step closer to one of your highly valued goals? At that point, how did you feel on a 10-point well-being scale, where 0 means you experienced a very low level of well-being, 5 means your feelings were neutral and 10 means you experienced an extremely high level of well-being?

At the end of the week review your journal and write down what you learned from doing this exercise.

If you think this exercise was useful, then you may wish to continue to use it in your life to help you move towards your highly valued goals and to enhance your well-being. Box 3.3 contains a summary of this exercise. You may find that using your signature strengths makes them stronger.

---

**Box 3.3   Using signature strengths to move towards highly valued goals**

Do this exercise to help you use signature strengths to move towards highly valued goals.

Complete the VIA-IS at www.viacharacter.org/survey/account/register and identify your top five signature strengths, or read the definitions of the 24 character strengths in Box 3.1 and identify which five of these best describe you.

In your journal, write a plan about using at least one of your signature strengths in a new way every day for a week to help you move towards the highly valued goals you identified doing the exercises in Chapter 2.

> Each evening for a week, in your journal, write down what you were doing and how much well-being you were feeling on a 10-point scale before, during and after using one of your signature strengths in a new way.
>
> On this scale 0 means you experienced a very low level of well-being, 5 means your feelings were neutral and 10 means you experienced an extremely high level of well-being.
>
> At the end of the week review what you have written in your journal, and write down if using one of your signature strengths in a new way each day for a week helped you to move towards your highly valued goals and enhanced your well-being.

## Example of signature strengths exercise

Remember Anne who we met in Chapter 2? Anne worked in a nursery school and was devoted to her job. Her most highly valued goal was to give her disadvantaged pupils a good start in life. When she took the VIA-IS she found that her top five signature strengths were kindness, love of learning, creativity, leadership and humour. She carried out a series of tasks in which she used these skills to achieve her highly valued goal of giving her disadvantaged pupils a good start in life. To use her strength of kindness, Anne carefully selected stories that she knew her pupils would like a lot, and read these to them as a treat. Their favourite story was about a giraffe who couldn't dance at the jungle party. He was too awkward and shy. He sadly left the party and walked home. On his way home, he heard the sound of the wind in the trees under the moon, and found that this music made him want to dance. The other animals saw him, and were delighted that the giraffe had finally found music he could dance to. To use her strength of love of learning, Anne searched on the internet for continuing professional development courses relevant to nursery school teachers and took one of these.

To use her strengths of creativity and humour, Anne wrote a series of funny sing-along and do-the-actions songs for her children, and taught them how to sing them and do all the actions. The kids loved the songs and they all laughed a lot about them. Anne made a point of taking her two classroom assistants for a drink after work to build team morale, and in doing so used her strengths of leadership. Anne found that using her signature strengths increase her well-being from 6 or 7 to 8 or 9. Reading the story and performing the songs led to the biggest increase in well-being, and the effects lasted for a few hours after she did them. Anne reviewed her journal at the end of the week. She reflected on what she had learned by doing this exercise. She learned that kindness, love of learning, creativity, leadership and humour were her signature strengths. She learned that she could creatively work out ways to use these strengths to move towards her highly valued goal of giving her disadvantaged pupils a good start in life. She learned that the process of doing this was fun. She wanted to do more of it. She planned to continue doing this exercise.

## Variations on the signature strengths exercise

There are variations on the basic signature strengths exercise that you may wish to try.[11]

### Using signature strengths in your relationships

If you want to strengthen your relationship with your partner or your children, identify their signature strengths, and then tell your partner or children about their signature strengths. Give them specific examples of the strengths that you observe them to have. This will let them know that you are basing your judgement about their strengths on observable facts. Then let them know that you appreciate their signature strength. For example, you might say, 'I think kindness is one of your signature strengths. You often do kind things for other people without giving it a second thought. Yesterday, you called Monica to see how she was feeling after her exam. Today, you made a special breakfast for the kids, and remembered to record a programme you knew I wanted to see. You're a really generous person. I think kindness is one of your signature strengths. It's one of the things that I really appreciate about you'. Box 3.4 contains a summary of this exercise.

---

**Box 3.4  Using signature strengths to strengthen your relationships**

Do this exercise to strengthen your relationships.

Try to catch your partner, child or friend doing something which shows that they have a particular strength (for example, creativity, bravery, kindness, fairness, forgiveness, self-control or humour or any of the other strengths in Box 3.1).

Tell your partner, child or friend that you appreciate the particular strength that you have noticed in them, and tell them about the specific situation in which you saw the using that strength.

Reflect on how this process strengthens your feeling of being connected to your partner, child or friend.

---

In my clinical practice, I see a lot of couples and families where relationships between partners, or between parents and children, have become tense and conflictual. People in these couples and families usually feel hurt and misunderstood. Rather than expressing this to each other, they express their anger. They don't say, 'I'm hurt and I need you to care about me'. They say, 'I'm angry with you'. To create an atmosphere in which it's possible to help families resolve conflicts I sometimes invite a family member to say what it was that they most like about their partner or child or parent when things are going well in their relationship. I invite them to notice each other's strengths, and express appreciation for these. I invite parents who are in conflict with their kids to 'catch their children being good'. I invite couples that are locked in conflict to 'catch their partner being kind, generous or thoughtful'. This process of noticing other's strengths and appreciating them builds good will between people. Strengthening family relationships will be discussed in detail in Chapters 12 and 13.

### Using signature strengths to overcome challenges

We all use our strengths to overcome challenges and obstacles to well-being. If you wish, you can do this exercise to help you clarify how you have used your strengths to overcome adversity. There are three parts in the exercise. The first involves thinking about the strengths of a fictional character who you identify with. The second part involves thinking about the strengths of someone you know. In the last part, you focus on your own strengths.

In the first part of this exercise, think about a character in a film, TV show or book you identify with who faced and overcame challenges. What challenges did this character face? What did they do to overcome these? What strengths did they use? In your journal, write down your answers to these questions. Reflect on why you identify with this character, the challenges they faced and their strengths. (By the way, if you would like to use films to build your signature strengths, you may find this book interesting: *Positive Psychology at the Movies: Using Films to Build Virtues and Character Strengths* by Ryan Niemiec and Danny Wedding.[12])

When you have identified character strengths in a fictional character, move on to the second part of this exercise. Select someone in real life (not a fictional character) who has overcome the sorts of challenges you face. This may be someone in your family, a friend or someone you met. What challenges did the character face? What did they do to overcome these? What strengths did they use? Write down your answers to these questions. Reflect on the parallels between the challenges that they faced and the strengths that they used to overcome these, and your life situation.

Now think about your own life. What challenges and obstacles have you faced? What exactly did you do to overcome these? What strengths did you use? What does this say about you as a person? Are you a brave person? A person who perseveres and doesn't give up? A hopeful person? How has coping with these challenges helped to build up your strengths? How might you now be better able to handle similar challenges in future? In your journal, write down your answers to these questions. Box 3.5 contains a summary of this exercise.

---

**Box 3.5   Using signature strengths to overcome challenges**

Do this exercise to identify the strengths you have shown in the past, or may need to show now or in the future to address challenges or obstacles to your well-being.

Select a **fictional character** from a book, TV show or film who you identify with, who has successfully managed challenges or obstacles similar to those in your life. In your journal, write down the challenges the character faced, what they did to overcome these and the strengths they used. Write down the parallels between the fictional character's life and your life situation.

Select **a friend or family member** who has successfully managed challenges or obstacles similar to those in your life. In your journal, write down the challenges they faced, what they did to overcome these and the strengths they used. Write down the parallels between the life of your friend or family member and your life situation

Now write down **the challenges or obstacles to your well-being that you have or are now facing**, how specifically have your addressed these, what strengths you have shown in doing so and what this says about you as a person.

How has coping with these challenges helped to build up your strengths?

How might you now be better able to handle similar challenges in future?

## Summary

- **VIA-IS.** This is the acronym for the Values in Action Inventory of Strengths which is used to assess 24 character strengths.
- **Six virtues associated with the VIA-IS.** These are wisdom, courage, humanity, justice, temperance and transcendence.
- **Twenty-four character strengths.** The 24 character strengths assessed by the VIA-IS are classified into subgroups associated with each of the six virtues, and these groups of strengths are pathways to achieving the six virtues.
- The character strengths associated with the virtue of **wisdom** are creativity, curiosity, judgement, love of learning and perspective.
- The character strengths associated with the virtue of **courage** are bravery, perseverance, honesty and zest.
- The character strengths associated with the virtue of **humanity** are love, kindness and social intelligence.
- The character strengths associated with the virtue of **justice** are teamwork, fairness and leadership.
- The character strength associated with **temperance** are forgiveness, humility, prudence and self-regulation.
- The character strengths associated with the virtue of **transcendence** are appreciation of beauty and excellence, gratitude, hope, humour and spirituality.
- **Strengths most strongly associated with well-being.** These are love, hope, gratitude and zest.
- **Signature strengths.** These are identified by completing the VIA-IS online. They are central to a person's character. Using them enhances well-being, and helps us move towards highly valued goals. They may also be used to strengthen relationships and overcome challenges.

## Where are you now?

If you have done the exercises in this chapter, you have identified your signature strengths. You have also worked out ways that you can use these strengths to move towards your highly valued goals. You have learned whether or not this exercise improves your well-being. You can now decide if you want to keep doing this exercise.

You may also have done the exercise on appreciating your partner's or children's strengths. Did doing this exercise momentarily improve the quality of your relationships?

You may have done the exercise to explore how you used your strengths to overcome difficulties and challenges in your life. If you did, did you notice that your strengths make you resilient? Did you find that they helped you to survive difficulties and challenges in your life?

You may want to read back over the chapter and summarise in your journal the main things that you have learned about strengths and well-being.

If you are concerned that certain strengths were not identified as you signature strengths when you completed the VIA-IS, and you wish to enhance these, you may use the exercises described elsewhere in this book to do so. For example, if you would like to be more hopeful, practise the exercises in Chapter 9 on optimism. If you would like to be more loving, practise the exercise in Chapters 11, 12 and 13 on improving relationships. If you would like to be more forgiving, practise the exercises in Chapter 17 on forgiveness.

In the next chapter, we will consider how to use physical exercise to enhance well-being. Below are some web resources and books that are relevant to topics you have read about in this chapter.

## Web resources

Values in Action Inventory of Character Strengths: www.viacharacter.org/survey/account/register
Martin Seligman talking about using highest strengths video (1:55): www.youtube.com/watch?v=YC1HZ qCbZ70

## Books

Niemiec, R., & Wedding, D. (2013). *Positive psychology at the movies: Using films to build virtues and character strengths* (Second Edition). Boston, MA: Hogrefe.
Niemiec, R., & McGrath, R. (2019). *The power of character strengths: Appreciate and ignite your positive personality.* Cincinnati, OH: VIA Institute of Character.

# Part 2
# Healthy body and mind

# 4  Physical exercise

There is a strong link between regular physical activity and well-being. In this chapter, you will read about

• the benefits of physical exercise for well-being
• how to develop and maintain a pattern of regular exercise, and
• how to overcome obstacles to regular physical exercise.

Since dietary and sleep problems may interfere with regular exercise, this chapter also contains guidance on a healthy eating and sleep hygiene.

Research in sports and exercise psychology, neuroscience and medicine shows that the benefits of regular daily exercise are both short-term and long-term.[1] In the short-term exercise may lead to the release of endogenous euphoriants. These amphetamine, opiate and cannabinoid-like chemicals produced in the brain induce a sense of well-being when released. When we develop a regular physical exercise routine and follow this for about three months, each time we exercise we get an 'exercise high'. When we exercise, we may also experience flow and absorption. We may become so involved in the experience of swimming, walking, running or other physical activities that we stop thinking about everyday challenges and hassles. Physical exercise, like progressive muscle relaxation and meditation discussed in Chapters 5 and 6, offers time out from the concerns that preoccupy us in our day-to-day lives. However, physical exercise makes us feel invigorated, while relaxation and meditation, in contrast, make us feel calm.

Regular exercise has long-term benefits for physical health. It promotes fitness and leads to better cardiovascular functioning. It slows down or prevents weight gain with ageing. Regular exercise throughout adulthood reduces the risk for heart disease, cancer, stroke and diabetes and is associated with longevity. Older adults who exercise have a lower risk of falling, and of hip or vertebral fractures. People who exercise regularly often do so in the company of others. This social contact may make us feel better and increase our overall level of well-being.

There are many long-term psychological benefits associated with physical exercise. Regular exercise reduces depression and anxiety. Regular aerobic exercise is as effective as antidepressant medication for mild or moderate depression.[2] It is also an excellent extra strategy to use along with antidepressants to combat severe depression. Exercise also leads to increased happiness and life-satisfaction.[3] In terms of our self-concepts, exercise can increase our sense of control, mastery and self-esteem. We may feel good about ourselves because we are doing activities that makes us stronger, fitter, mentally sharper and healthier.

## How much exercise should I do?

According to the World Health Organization,[4] if you are between 18 and 64 years of age you should do at least 150 minutes of *moderately intense* exercise throughout the week. Moderate physical activity includes brisk walking, dancing or household chores. For example, you could do 30 minutes of moderate exercise five days a week. Or just over 20 minutes of moderate exercise every day.

Alternatively, you can do at least 75 minutes of *vigorous* exercise throughout the week. Vigorous exercise includes running, fast cycling, fast swimming or moving heavy loads. For example, you could do 15 minutes of vigorous exercise five days a week. Or just over 10 minutes of vigorous exercise every day. In order to be beneficial for cardio-respiratory health, exercise sessions must be at least 10 minutes.

The World Health Organization makes different recommendations for people under 18 and over 65 years. If you are over 65, you will get more benefits from physical exercise if you increase the amount of moderate intensity physical activity from 150 to 300 minutes per week. This works out at an hour a day, five days a week, or just under three quarters of an hour seven days a week. You should also do muscle-strengthening activities for major muscle groups, two or more days a week. If you have poor mobility you should do physical activity to enhance balance and prevent falls, three or more days per week.

If you are under 18 years you should do at least 60 minutes of moderate to vigorous-intensity physical activity every day. If you do more than an hour a day, this will be better for your health and well-being.

## Set up a schedule

If you decide to introduce exercise into your life, set up a schedule. Write in your diary or journal the dates and times when you will exercise. Some people find it useful to exercise at the same time every day. Others find that it's better to work their exercise times around other fixtures like doing the shopping, picking up the kids, starting and finishing work, and so on. Some people like to exercise first thing in the morning to wake them up. Others like to exercise after work to wind down. Some like to exercise at lunchtime to take time out from the challenges of the day. The main thing is to set up an exercise schedule that suits you, and stick to it.

## Start gradually

If you are introducing exercise into your life after a long period of not exercising, it's important to do this gradually. Start with small amounts, even just a few minutes a day, and build this up gradually. If you try to make yourself do too much too soon, this will make you feel bad, and you may give up. It's also important to do the sort of exercise that you like. For example, if you like walking, that's a good activity to start with. Take a 15-minute slow walk each day. Then gradually increase the duration and speed of your walk until you are having a brisk 45-minute walk every day. If you like swimming, start with a few gentle lengths of the pool. Then gradually build this up to a 60-minute swim five days a week. If you like cycling or jogging, start with a gentle short session, and build this up to a more challenging speed and longer duration over a few weeks until you are doing 45 minutes a day.

## Do what's convenient

Only do exercise that is convenient for you to do in your life situation. If you are minding two kids under 5, then cycling may not be convenient. However, it may be convenient to get an exercise bike and use that in the play room where you can keep an eye on the kids. If you like to jog, it may only be convenient to do this if you get a two-seater jogging buggy for the kids.

## Pacing your sessions

If you decide that you want to do vigorous exercise, then it's useful to have a routine that allows you to pace yourself. Begin with a warm-up. Stretch your muscles in the major muscle groups. Then you may wish to do some strength and endurance exercises such as push-ups or pull-ups. In the middle phase of each exercise session do aerobic exercises; that is, energetic physical activity that requires high levels of oxygen. During the cool-down phase do less vigorous exercise such as walking.

## Keeping your heart rate in the target zone

Your heart rate varies from a resting level to a maximum rate. Your resting heart rate is the number of times your heart beats per minute while it's at rest. Your maximum heart rate is about 220 minus your age. So as not to strain yourself when you are doing aerobic exercise, the American Heart Association recommends that you keep your heart rate in the target zone.[5] This is between 50 and 85% of your maximum heart rate. In Table 4.1 you can check your target heart rate zone, for the age category closet to your actual age. When you are

*Table 4.1* Target heart rates

| Age in years | Target heart rate zone 50-85% in beats per minute | Average maximum heart rate 100% in beats per minute |
| --- | --- | --- |
| 20 | 100-170 | 200 |
| 30 | 95-162 | 190 |
| 35 | 93-157 | 185 |
| 40 | 90-153 | 180 |
| 45 | 88-149 | 175 |
| 50 | 85-145 | 170 |
| 55 | 83-140 | 165 |
| 60 | 80-136 | 160 |
| 65 | 78-132 | 155 |
| 70 | 75-128 | 150 |

**Note:** Reprinted with permission: www.heart.org/HEARTORG/HealthyLiving/PhysicalActivity/FitnessBasics/T arget-Heart-Rates_UCM_434341_Article.jsp#.VuAMIce50y8, Copyright © 2015 by American Heart Association, Inc.

doing moderately intense aerobic exercise your heart rate is about 50-69% of your maximum heart rate. Your heart rate is about 70% to less than 90% of your maximum heart rate during vigorous exercise. To check your heart rate when exercising, take your pulse on the inside of your wrist, on the thumb side. Use the tips of your first two fingers to press lightly over the blood vessels on your wrist. Count your pulse for 10 seconds and multiply by 6 to find your beats per minute.

## Motivating yourself

It takes about three months for exercise to become a natural part of our daily lives, and something that we really want to do every day. It's therefore important that for the first three months that you plan to stay motivated. You will be more likely to follow through on exercise plans if you formulate clear goals, set convenient times and locations for exercising, and keep a written record of progress, or an exercise log, in your journal. You can motivate yourself to stick to your plan if you exercise with a friend, or ask your family members or friends to say encouraging things to you when you follow through on your exercise plans. You may also give yourself little treats for following through on your exercise plans. Reward yourself for exercising by getting yourself something you value like a favourite food, a favourite film or a new piece of sports clothing. You may arrange to do your exercise in an environment that you find rewarding; for example, walking or jogging on the beach, cycling in the countryside, exercising in the gym listing to music that you like or running on a treadmill watching TV programmes that interest you.

## Overcoming obstacles

We often make excuses for not exercising, like 'I haven't got time', or 'I'm too tired'. These excuses prevent us from following through on our exercise plans. It's therefore essential for you to anticipate possible obstacles to following through on your exercise plan, and brainstorm possible solutions to potential obstacles and excuses. Here are some common excuses people make for not exercising and some solutions to overcoming these obstacles.

### I haven't enough time

You can exercise while watching TV. You can walk on the spot. Do squats. Lift weights. If you can't find 40-60 minutes to do your daily exercise in one big session, do your exercise in a number of smaller 10-minute sessions.

### I have to mind the kids 24/7

Take the kids with you when you exercise. Take them for a walk. Take them cycling. Take them jogging in a jogging buggy.

### My job is too demanding, or my job involves too much travelling

Exercise on the job, during breaks at work or at lunchtime. If you travel a lot, wherever you travel, go for a walk and explore the new environment. If you prefer, bring a workout DVD and exercise using this DVD in your hotel room.

### It's too dark, dangerous, cold or rainy before and after work to exercise

Exercise at lunchtime. Exercise indoors at home on a stationary bike, a treadmill or to a work-out DVD in your living room.

### I'm too tired

Exercise when you don't feel tired; for example, in the morning or at lunchtime, rather than in the evening after work. Exercise when you feel tired with the knowledge that exercise will invigorate you, once you get into it.

### Exercise is boring

Exercise by doing an activity you really like; for example, cycling, rowing or hitting a punching bag. Exercise in an environment that you really like; for example, walking by the sea, or swimming. Exercise listening to music that you love, or watching films that interest you.

### I'm too self-conscious to go to a gym

Don't exercise in a gym. Go walking with a friend. Exercise in your living room at home on a treadmill, stationary bike or to a workout DVD.

### I'm too old to start exercising

You are never too old to start exercising. Exercising when you are over 65 is a good way to prevent injuries due to falls, which become more common as we age.

### I've tried before and always failed

You probably failed before because you set the bar too high, had too few rewards and had too little support. Set small, achievable goals so you are guaranteed success. Plan to walk for 10 minutes a day, for five out of the next seven days. Tell other people about your exercise plan, and ask them to encourage you. Give yourself treats as a reward for exercising. Exercise with a friend so you can support each other when you feel like quitting.

## Keeping an exercise log

When you decide to do your exercise, keep a record or log of all you do and the effect of this on your mood. Table 4.2 is a useful format for an exercise log. You can draw this log once a week in your journal, and fill it in every day. When you fill it in, record the time you exercised and the type of exercise you did in the first two columns. For example, between 9.00 and 9.45 I went walking on Monday. Then record the possible obstacles and excuses you anticipated before you went walking. For example, you might say 'I won't go for a walk because it might rain'. Then write in the solutions you considered before you went walking, to overcome this obstacle. For example, 'I'll bring an umbrella', or 'I'll wear waterproofs'. In the last two columns of the log write down your mood rating before and after exercising. Give your

*Table 4.2* Exercise log

| | Time | Exercise type | Anticipated obstacles and excuse | Possible solutions | Mood before exercise on a scale of 1 to 10 | Mood after exercise on a scale of 1 to 10 |
|---|---|---|---|---|---|---|
| *Example* | *9.00–9.45* | *Walking* | *It might rain* | • *Bring an umbrella*<br>• *Wear waterproofs* | *6* | *8* |
| **Monday** | | | | | | |
| **Tuesday** | | | | | | |
| **Wednesday** | | | | | | |
| **Thursday** | | | | | | |
| **Friday** | | | | | | |
| **Saturday** | | | | | | |
| **Sunday** | | | | | | |

mood rating on a 10-point scale. On this scale 1 is an exceptionally low mood indicating that you felt extremely sad. In contrast, 10 is an exceptionally high mood indicating that you felt extremely happy. Using this scale, your mood might have increased from 6 before exercising to 8 after exercising. Keeping an exercise log like this, and reviewing it regularly, will allow you to keep track of how much you are exercising, and the effect of this on your mood, which is an important aspect of well-being. Box 4.1 summarises key points on following a regular physical exercise programme.

---

**Box 4.1   Regular physical exercise programme**

**Keep an exercise log**

- Plans and goals.
- Achievements.

**Exercise regularly**

- Set up a schedule.
- Start gradually.
- Exercise in a way that's convenient to you.
- Pace your sessions.
- Keep your heart rate in the target zone (50–85% of your maximum heart rate).

**Use motivational strategies**

- Exercise at a convenient time and place.
- Exercise with a friend.

- Get family encouragement.
- Reward yourself for completing regular exercise.
- Exercise in a place you like, listening to music or watching things you enjoy.

**Overcome obstacles**

- List obstacles to regular exercise and brainstorm ways around them.

## Take medical precautions

Take sensible precautions when you exercise. Don't exercise until about an hour after a big meal, so you have time to digest it. Don't eat a large meal until about an hour after exercising. Stop exercising if you experience sudden symptoms, for example chest pain, while exercising. Ask your doctor about how to proceed.

Some medical conditions limit the amount of exercise we can safely do. Don't exercise without consulting your doctor if you answer yes to any of the following questions:

- Are you over 40 and not used to vigorous exercise?
- Have you high blood pressure?
- Have you heart trouble?
- Do you frequently get chest pain?
- Do you often feel faint or dizzy?
- Have you a bone or joint problem that might be made worse by exercise?
- Have you diabetes?
- Have you any other physical problem which might be made worse by exercise?

If you answer yes to any of these problems, ask your doctor to advise you on how best to build exercise into your weekly routine.

## Diet

Diet and sleep affect our capacity to exercise. In this section, there is some guidance on diet. Sleep hygiene is dealt with in the next section.

If our diet is very unhealthy, this affects our body weight and overall health. It's more difficult to exercise when very overweight or ill. In the industrialised world, we consume too many foods high in energy, fat, sugar and salt. We also do not eat enough fruit, vegetables and dietary fibre such as whole grains. The World Health Organization and national public health services in many countries, such as the UK National Health Service, gives expert advice on diet summarised below and in Figure 4.1.[6] This advice is based on extensive international nutritional research. However, it is not about how to lose weight. It's about how to eat healthily. For good health women need 2000 calories per day, and each day men need 2500 calories. A healthy diet includes five main elements.

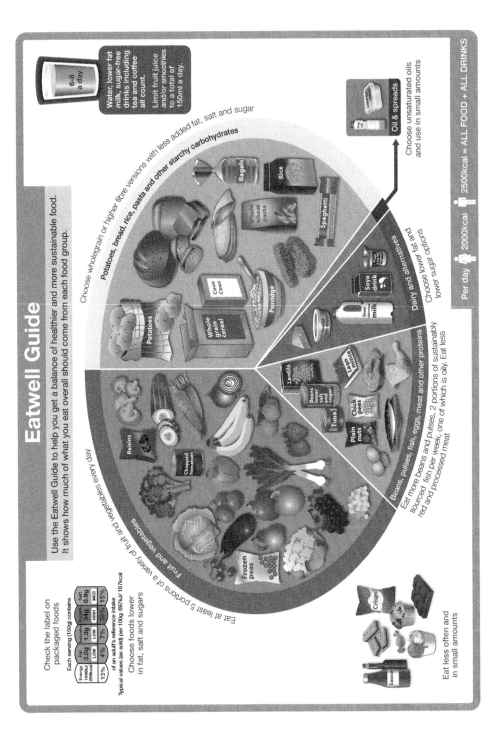

*Figure 4.1* A balanced diet.

**Note:** Reproduced with permission from *Eatwell Guide, Version 4, 2018* published by Public Health England in association with the Welsh Government, Food Standards Scotland and the Food Standards Agency in Northern Ireland © Crown copyright.

1   **Five portions (or 400g) of fruit and vegetables a day.** One portion of fruit or vegetables is about 80g or around one handful. This should make up about a third of the food you eat. Potatoes, sweet potatoes and other starchy roots are not classified as fruits or vegetables.

2   **Starchy foods and carbohydrates such as potatoes, bread, cereals, rice and pasta.** This should make up about a third of the food you eat.

3   **Milk and dairy foods such as cheese and yoghurt.** This should make up about 15% of what you eat. Mild and dairy foods are sources of protein and calcium. Protein helps our bodies to grow or repair themselves. Calcium helps to keep our bones and teeth strong. Use lower-fat milk and dairy foods.

4   **Beans, pulses, fish, eggs, poultry and meat.** This should make up about 12% of what you eat. These foods are good sources of protein, vitamins and minerals. It's better to eat beans, peas, pulses, fish and poultry than red meat. Keep your consumption of red meat to no more than 70g per day.

5   **Small amounts of fatty foods, sugar and salt.** This should make up no more than 7% of your diet. Eat a maximum of 50g (or around 12 level teaspoons) of free sugars per day. Free sugars are in fizzy drinks, cakes, sweets, honey, syrups, fruit juices and fruit juice concentrates. Eat less than 5g of salt (about a teaspoon) per day. Salt is in many fast foods and savoury snack foods.

6   **Hydration.** Drink 6–8 glasses of fluid per day. This includes water, lower-fat milk and sugar-free drinks, such as tea or coffee.

If alcohol is part of your regular diet, you may wish to follow the UK Chief Medical Officer's guideline.[7] This states that, to avoid health risks, it is safest not to drink more than 14 units of alcohol a week on a regular basis. This applies to both men and women. If you regularly drink 14 units of alcohol per week, spread your drinking evenly over three or more days. If you have one or two heavy drinking episodes a week, the risk of death from long-term illness and injuries increases. The risk of developing health problems (including cancers of the mouth, throat and breast) increases the more you regularly drink. If you want to drink less, have several drink-free days a week. If you are pregnant, to avoid putting your baby at risk, it's best not to drink any alcohol.

## Sleep

If you wake feeling refreshed, then skip the next section. However, if you often wake up feeling tired, then poor sleep hygiene may affect your capacity to engage in regular physical exercise. Fortunately, this is a solvable problem. Following an overview of some key points about the psychology of sleep, you may wish to read some guidance on sleep hygiene.

Sleep is essential for well-being.[8] In most people sleep deprivation leads to exhaustion, lack of concentration, forgetfulness, irritability, low mood, poor immune system functioning and illness. When we are asleep our bodies and brains restore themselves, and our memories are consolidated. Sleep is not a unitary process. Studies of brain activity, eye movements and muscle tension show that when sleeping we go through stages of rapid eye movement (REM) sleep and non-REM sleep on a cyclical basis. We start in non-REM sleep. We progress through three or four stages of this as our sleep becomes progressively deeper, and our level of brain activity decreases. During non-REM sleep, there are no rapid eye movements and normal muscle tension. After a period of non-REM sleep, brain activity increases and we engage in REM sleep. During this, there are frequent rapid eye movements, a high level of brain activity, low muscle tension and vivid technicolour dreams.

For most adults, a cycle of non-REM and REM sleep lasts about 90 minutes. We go through about four or five of these cycles each night. We spend about a third of our lives asleep. We spend more time asleep in childhood than in adulthood. We also spend a much higher proportion time in REM sleep as children. While sleeping, most adults spend about 20% of the time in REM sleep. Most adults need about 8 hours' sleep, although there is variation in sleep needs. Some adults need more sleep than others. The sleep-wake cycle follows a circadian rhythm, governed by a biological clock. This is controlled by a part of the brain called the hypothalamus. However, it is also affected by external environmental cues that signal to us that it's time to sleep or wake. These cues include the light–dark cycle, timing of meals, bedtime routines and knowledge of clock time.

A range of factors can disrupt the sleep-wake cycle. These include high levels of environmental stimulation (noise, light, heat etc.), extreme positive or negative mood states, alcohol or drug use, irregular sleeping hours, shift work or moving from one time zone to another. If your sleep-wake cycle is disrupted, you may wish to follow the guidance below.

### Sleep diary

For a week keep a sleep diary in your journal; that is, a written record of your sleep pattern. For each 24-hour period, write down the time you retire, the time you rise, any times at night that you remain awake and any daytime naps you take. Also record how alert you feel each morning on a scale of 1 to 10. On this scale 1 means you are extremely tired. In contrast, 10 indicates that you are extremely alert.

### Isolate the sleep problem

To awaken feeling refreshed, most adults need between 7 and 9 hours' sleep. However, there is a lot of variability from one person to the next. Review your sleep diary. Note how much sleep you got in each 24-hour period over the past week. If you awoke each day feeling tired, then you are not getting enough sleep. To find out why, ask yourself the questions listed below.

**Is my tiredness due to retiring too late?** If you awaken feeling tired it may be that you are not getting enough sleep because you are retiring too late each evening.

**Is my tiredness due to keeping very irregular retiring and rising times?** Irregular sleep routines disrupt the biological clock that regulates the sleep-wake cycle and make it difficult to go to sleep when you go to bed.

**Is my tiredness due to night waking?** Am I spending 7 or 8 hours in bed each night, but a couple of these lying awake, worrying that I can't sleep? If this is the case, your bedroom may become a place associated in your mind with worrying rather than sleeping.

**Is my tiredness due to daytime napping?** If you nap during the day because you had a bad night's sleep, then this napping may interfere with getting a good night's sleep the next night.

## Sleep hygiene

You can overcome most common sleep problems by following the sleep hygiene programme described below.[9] Box 4.2 summarises key points on sleep hygiene.

---

### Box 4.2   Sleep hygiene

- Record retiring and waking times and daytime naps in a sleep diary.
- Avoid daytime naps.
- Keep regular retiring and waking times.
- Set your biological clock using light and dark.
- Keep your bedroom quiet, dark and at a comfortable temperature.
- Don't exercise and eat large meals in the three hours before you sleep.
- Avoid stimulants and alcohol in the three hours before you sleep.
- Limit fluid intake before sleeping.
- Develop a bedtime routine.
- Use your bedroom for sleep and sex only.
- If you don't sleep after 20 minutes, leave the bedroom until tired.

---

### No naps

Avoid daytime naps.

### Regular retiring and rising times

Have a regular time for going to bed and rising. This will set your biological clock which regulates your sleep-wake cycle. You will see below that sometimes if you can't get to sleep, it's better to get up and do something relaxing until your tired. This will obviously alter your retiring time. However, keep your rising time constant, even if that means rising when feeling tired for a few mornings. Eventually your biological clock will adjust so that you feel tired at about the same time each evening. This will allow you to set a fixed bedtime.

### Use light to set your biological clock

Let light into your room as soon as you awake, and get out in the sun during the day. Natural light helps set your biological clock, and maintain a regular sleep-wake cycle.

### Exercise early

Don't exercise for at least three hours before you sleep. Making sure that there is a three-hour gap between vigorous exercise and bedtime means that you will not be 'all fired up' by exercise when you go to bed.

### Eat early

Eat your last big meal a few hours before you sleep. Avoid foods that cause indigestion, so the process of digesting foods doesn't prevent you from sleeping.

### No stimulants

Don't take caffeine, alcohol or nicotine for a few hours before you sleep. Caffeine is in coffee, tea, chocolate, cola and some medications. Caffeine is a stimulant and keeps you awake. Alcohol may put you to sleep initially, but increases the number of awakenings and decreases the quality of sleep.

### Limit fluids

In the hour before you go to bed drink enough water, warm milk or other fluids to prevent you from being thirsty at night. However, don't drink so much that you will have to awaken to go to the toilet.

### Bedtime routine

Develop a soothing bedtime routine that gets you ready to sleep. Take a bath, read a book, watch TV, practise relaxation exercises and reflect on good things that have happened to you during the day for which you are grateful. Relaxation exercises are discussed in Chapter 5 and thankfulness exercises are discussed in Chapter 8. If you do relaxation exercises to help you sleep, focus on doing the exercises well. Don't focus on trying to fall asleep, as this may make you worry and keep you awake. Avoid stimulating or stressful activities before bedtime such as doing work or arguing.

### Quiet, dark bedroom

Turn your bedroom into a sleep-inducing environment. Make your bedroom quiet, dark and heated to a level that you find comfortable. Use blackout blinds and earplugs if necessary to reduce light and noise. Make sure your bed is comfortable. If you need a clock in your room, use an electric one with a dim display. Turn off your phone, computer, TV, radio or other devices that may disrupt your sleep. If your pets keep you awake, keep them out of your bedroom. If your children keep you awake, and this is exhausting you, take turns with your partner of being 'on call' for the children.

### Sleep and sex only

Use your bedroom for sleep and sex only. Don't use it for working on your computer, watching TV or other activities associated with wakefulness. This will strengthen the mental association you make between being in bed and sleeping.

### Bed when tired

Go to bed when you are tired. If you don't fall asleep within 20 minutes, go to another room and do something relaxing, like reading or listening to gentle music until you are tired enough to sleep. If you wake during the night and don't fall asleep within 20 minutes, go to another room and do something relaxing until you feel tired enough to return to sleep. This will strengthen the mental association you make between being in bed and sleeping.

### Sleep diary

In your journal keep a sleep diary (following the guidelines given above) throughout the sleep hygiene programme. Review your sleep diary each week. Note if you are establishing a regular sleep-wake cycle. Notice if there is a gradual improvement in how alert you feel each morning.

### Medical help

If after a month this sleep hygiene programme has no effect on your sleep-wake cycle and your daytime sleepiness, consult your doctor.

## Summary

- **Exercise and well-being.** Regular daily exercise has positive short and long-term effects on physical and psychological well-being. It leads to better physical health, alleviates depression and increases self-esteem.
- **How much is enough?** For adults between 18 and 64, at least 150 minutes of moderately intense exercise throughout the week is sufficient. For adults over 65, this may be increased to 300 minutes per week.
- **Keep a log.** In your journal, write down your exercise plans, goals and achievements.
- **Exercise regularly.** Set up a schedule, start gradually, exercise in a way that's convenient to you, pace your sessions and keep your heart rate in the target zone (50-85% of your maximum heart rate).
- **Motivate yourself.** Use motivational strategies during the first three months while you are establishing a regular exercise routine. Set clear goals and record progress towards them. Exercise at a convenient time and place. Exercise with a friend. Get family encouragement. Reward yourself for completing regular exercise. Exercise in a place you like, listening to music or watching things you enjoy.
- **Overcome obstacles.** List obstacles to regular exercise and brainstorm ways around them.
- **Balanced diet.** A poor diet can interfere with keeping a regular exercise routine. A balanced diet promotes well-being. Eat a diet where 1/3 is fruit and vegetables; 1/3 is starchy foods (potatoes, bread, pasta); 15% is milk, cheese and yoghurt; 12% is meat, poultry, fish, eggs and beans; and 7% is fatty foods, sugary foods and salt. Men and women should drink no more than 14 units of alcohol per week.
- **Sleep hygiene.** Poor sleep hygiene can interfere with keeping a regular exercise routine. Sufficient regular sleep promotes well-being. Most adults need about eight hours. Children need more and older adults need less. Keeping a sleep diary can suggest factors to take into account when solving specific sleep problems. Many sleep problems may be addressed by good sleep hygiene. Avoid naps. Keep regular retiring and waking times. Set your biological clock using light and dark. Keep your bedroom quiet and dark. Don't exercise or eat large meals in the three hours before you sleep. Avoid stimulants and alcohol in the three hours before you sleep. Limit fluid intake before sleeping. Develop a bedtime routine. Use your bedroom for sleep and sex only.

## Where are you now?

If you have done the exercises in this chapter, you have introduced daily physical exercise into your weekly routine. You have found a physical activity that suits you. You have planned to do it regularly. You have gradually increased the amount of time you spent doing it. You have learned whether or not this exercise improves your well-being. You can now decide if you want to make physical exercise part of your weekly routine for the long-term.

You may also have thought about changing your diet to be more in line with international guidelines for healthy eating. If tiredness interfered with your physical exercise routines, you may have used the sleep hygiene programme to improve your sleep.

You may want to read back over the chapter and summarise in your journal the main things that you have learned about physical exercise, diet and sleep.

In the next chapter, we will consider progressive muscle relaxation. This is something that you can build into your daily routine to enhance your well-being. Below are some web resources and books that are relevant to topics you have read about in this chapter.

## Web resources

World Health Organization, ten facts on physical activity: www.who.int/features/factfiles/physical_activity/en
World Health Organization guidelines on physical activity: www.who.int/dietphysicalactivity/factsheet_
    recommendations/en
American Heart Association guidelines for healthy diet and regular exercise: www.heart.org/HEARTORG/
    HealthyLiving/PhysicalActivity/FitnessBasics/Target-Heart-Rates_UCM_434341_Article.jsp#.
    VuAMlce50y8
World Health Organization healthy diet fact sheet: www.who.int/mediacentre/factsheets/fs394/en
UK National Health Service Eatwell Plate: www.nhs.uk/Livewell/Goodfood/Pages/eatwell-plate.aspx
Video on Eatwell Plate (13:03): www.youtube.com/watch?v=Mlw6q-_DL6I
UK Chief Medical Officer's Low Risk Drinking Guidelines 2016: https://assets.publishing.service.gov.uk/
    government/uploads/system/uploads/attachment_data/file/545937/UK_CMOs__report.pdf
Colin Espie talking about the Sleepio programme video (2:52): www.youtube.com/watch?v=sepajNesSD4
Colin Espie's Sleepio programme: www.sleepio.com
A video on sleep hygiene (2:48): www.youtube.com/watch?v=TQ8uc85cEu4

## Books

Espie, C. A. (2006). *Overcoming insomnia and sleep problems: A self-help guide using cognitive behav-
    ioural techniques.* London: Constable & Robinson
Fairburn, C. (2013). *Overcoming binge eating* (Second Edition). London: Guilford.
Heather, N., & Roberson, I. (1996). *Let's drink to your health: A self-help guide to sensible drinking* (Second
    Edition). Chichester, UK: Wiley Blackwell.

# 5  Relaxation

In this chapter, you will learn how to do progressive muscle relaxation.[1] You will also learn about visualisation, auto-suggestion and applying progressive muscle relaxation skills to manage stress and anxiety in everyday life. In the next chapter, you will learn about mindfulness mediation. I mention both of these techniques now because they share some features in common. They both help us achieve a calm, peaceful state. Both can be used to reduce distress, anxiety and pain. Both are skills that can be learned through daily practice.

Progressive muscle relaxation was developed by Dr Edmund Jacobson at Harvard University. He published his first book describing it in 1929.[2] In his clinical practice, he found that a range of conditions such as headaches, ulcers and high blood pressure were due to the physiological effects of chronic muscle tension. This chronic tension arose from continually making efforts to address the demands and challenges of contemporary life. He believed that chronic muscle tension burned up the body's limited energy supply. This in turn led to a range of tension-related illnesses. Jacobson developed progressive muscle relaxation as a way of counteracting this destructive process.

You are invited now to read the set progressive muscle relaxation exercises in Box 5.1. You can see that these exercises involve focusing attention on one muscle group at a time, tensing and relaxing the muscles in that group, and then allowing the relaxation process to progress even further. Jacobson practised medicine in Chicago and New York. He used his relaxation techniques to help people with a range of psychosomatic and stress-related conditions. Jacobson and other researchers in hundreds of scientific studies have shown that progressive muscle relaxation helps people with a range of stress-related conditions. These include high blood pressure, ulcers, irritable bowel syndrome, chronic pain, headaches, arthritis, insomnia and anxiety.[3] Jacobson also wrote a book in 1959 on using progressive muscle relaxation to control pain during childbirth called *How to Relax and Have Your Baby*.[4] This was one of the first modern self-help books on natural childbirth. Subsequent scientific studies of progressive muscle relaxation have shown that during childbirth it helps control pain.[5]

---

**Box 5.1  Relaxation exercises**

- Set aside 20-30 minutes a day to do these relaxation exercises.
- Do them at the same time and in the same place every day.
- Do not do these exercises after a big meal or when intoxicated.

- Before you begin, remove all distractions (by turning off bright lights, phones, computers, TVs, radios etc.).
- Loosen any tight clothes or jewellery that may cause discomfort (like belts, ties, shoes, watchstrap etc.) and if you wear glasses, take them off.
- Lie on a bed, couch or mat, or recline in a comfortable chair.
- When you are ready, allow your eyes to close slowly.
- Before and after each exercise, breathe in deeply for three seconds and exhale slowly for six seconds, three times.
- Tense each muscle group for about five seconds, and then release tension for about ten seconds.
- You only need to tense them enough for you to able to notice the change from tension to relaxation as you release the tension. So tense them a little, not too much.
- Repeat each muscle exercise followed by three deep breaths twice.
- Before and after you do these exercises, in your journal record your level of relaxation on a scale of 1 to 10, where 1 is extremely tense and 10 is extremely relaxed.
- Each week review the relaxation ratings you have recorded in your journal.
- After a couple of weeks of daily practice, you will notice that you are becoming skilled at using these exercises to achieve a calm, peaceful relaxed state.

| Area | Exercise |
|---|---|
| **Breathing** | Settle yourself comfortably. |
| | When you are ready, allow your eyes to close gently. |
| | Focus your attention on your breathing. |
| | Take a deep breath, breathing in 1, 2, 3, and out slowly 1, 2, 3, 4, 5, 6. |
| | Take a deep breath, breathing in 1, 2, 3, and out slowly 1, 2, 3, 4, 5, 6. |
| | Take a deep breath, breathing in 1, 2, 3, and out slowly 1, 2, 3, 4, 5, 6. |
| **Right hand and forearm** | Direct your attention to your right hand. |
| | Close your **right hand into a fist**. Then allow it to open slowly. |
| | Notice the change from tension to relaxation in the muscles of your right hand and forearm. |
| | Allow this change to continue further and further still so the muscles in your right hand and forearm become more and more relaxed. |
| | Take a deep breath, breathing in 1, 2, 3, and out slowly 1, 2, 3, 4, 5, 6. |
| | Take a deep breath, breathing in 1, 2, 3, and out slowly 1, 2, 3, 4, 5, 6. |
| | Take a deep breath, breathing in 1, 2, 3, and out slowly 1, 2, 3, 4, 5, 6. |
| **Left hand and forearm** | Direct your attention to your left hand. |
| | Close your **left hand into a fist**. Then allow it to open slowly. |
| | Notice the change from tension to relaxation in the muscles of your left hand and forearm. Allow this change to continue further and further still so the muscles in your left hand and forearm become more and more relaxed |
| | Take a deep breath, breathing in 1, 2 3, and out slowly 1, 2, 3, 4, 5, 6. |
| | Take a deep breath, breathing in 1, 2 3, and out slowly 1, 2, 3, 4, 5, 6. |
| | Take a deep breath, breathing in 1, 2 3, and out slowly 1, 2, 3, 4, 5, 6. |

| | |
|---|---|
| **Right upper arm** | Focus your attention on your right arm.<br>Bend your **right arm at the elbow and touch your right shoulder** with your right hand, so that you make the muscle in your upper arm bulge up a little.<br>Then slowly return your hand to the resting position.<br>As you return your hand to the resting position, notice the change from tension to relaxation in the muscles of your upper arm.<br>Allow this change to continue further and further still so the muscles of your right arm become more and more relaxed.<br>Take a deep breath, breathing in 1, 2, 3, and out slowly 1, 2, 3, 4, 5, 6.<br>Take a deep breath, breathing in 1, 2, 3, and out slowly 1, 2, 3, 4, 5, 6.<br>Take a deep breath, breathing in 1, 2, 3, and out slowly 1, 2, 3, 4, 5, 6. |
| **Left upper arm** | Focus your attention on your left arm.<br>Bend your **left arm at the elbow and touch your left shoulder** with your left hand, so that you make the muscle in your upper arm bulge up a little.<br>Then slowly return your hand to the resting position.<br>As you return your hand to the resting position, notice the change from tension to relaxation in the muscles of your upper arm.<br>Allow this change to continue further and further still so the muscles of your left arm become more and more relaxed.<br>Take a deep breath, breathing in 1, 2, 3, and out slowly 1, 2, 3, 4, 5, 6.<br>Take a deep breath, breathing in 1, 2, 3, and out slowly 1, 2, 3, 4, 5, 6.<br>Take a deep breath, breathing in 1, 2, 3, and out slowly 1, 2, 3, 4, 5, 6. |
| **Shoulders** | Focus your attention on your shoulders.<br>**Hunch your shoulders** up to your ears.<br>Then allow them to return to the resting position.<br>Notice the change from tension to relaxation in the muscles of your shoulders.<br>Allow this change to continue further and further still so the muscles of your shoulders become more and more relaxed.<br>Take a deep breath, breathing in 1, 2, 3, and out slowly 1, 2, 3, 4, 5, 6.<br>Take a deep breath, breathing in 1, 2, 3, and out slowly 1, 2, 3, 4, 5, 6.<br>Take a deep breath, breathing in 1, 2, 3, and out slowly 1, 2, 3, 4, 5, 6.<br><br>Again, focus your attention on your shoulders.<br>**Press your shoulder blades back, trying to almost touch them together**, so that your chest is pushed forward.<br>Then allow them to return to the resting position.<br>Notice the change from tension to relaxation in the muscles of your shoulders.<br>Allow this change to continue further and further still so the muscles of your shoulders become more and more relaxed.<br>Take a deep breath, breathing in 1, 2, 3, and out slowly 1, 2, 3, 4, 5, 6.<br>Take a deep breath, breathing in 1, 2, 3, and out slowly 1, 2, 3, 4, 5, 6.<br>Take a deep breath, breathing in 1, 2, 3, and out slowly 1, 2, 3, 4, 5, 6. |
| **Back** | Focus your attention on your back.<br>**Arch your back.**<br>Then return to the resting position.<br>Notice the change from tension to relaxation in the muscles of your back.<br>Allow this change to continue further and further still so the muscles of your back become more and more relaxed. |

Take a deep breath, breathing in 1, 2, 3, and out slowly 1, 2, 3, 4, 5, 6.
Take a deep breath, breathing in 1, 2, 3, and out slowly 1, 2, 3, 4, 5, 6.
Take a deep breath, breathing in 1, 2, 3, and out slowly 1, 2, 3, 4, 5, 6.

**Right foot and lower leg**

Focus your attention on your right foot.
**Point the toes of your right foot downwards.**
Then allow your foot to return to the resting position.
Notice the change from tension to relaxation in muscles of your right foot and the front of your lower leg.
Allow this change to continue further and further still so the muscles in your right foot and the front of your lower leg become more and more relaxed.
Take a deep breath, breathing in 1, 2, 3, and out slowly 1, 2, 3, 4, 5, 6.
Take a deep breath, breathing in 1, 2, 3, and out slowly 1, 2, 3, 4, 5, 6.
Take a deep breath, breathing in 1, 2, 3, and out slowly 1, 2, 3, 4, 5, 6.

Again, focus your attention on your right foot.
**Point the toes of your right foot upwards.**
Then allow them to return to the resting position.
Notice the change from tension to relaxation in the back of your leg.
Allow this change to continue further and further still so the muscles in the back of your leg become more and more relaxed.
Take a deep breath, breathing in 1, 2, 3, and out slowly 1, 2, 3, 4, 5, 6.
Take a deep breath, breathing in 1, 2, 3, and out slowly 1, 2, 3, 4, 5, 6.
Take a deep breath, breathing in 1, 2, 3, and out slowly 1, 2, 3, 4, 5, 6.

**Right upper leg**

Focus your attention on your right thigh.
**Tighten your right thigh muscles.**
Then allow your thigh to relax.
Notice the change from tension to relaxation in your right thigh muscles.
Allow this change to continue further and further still so the muscles in your thigh become more and more relaxed.
Take a deep breath, breathing in 1, 2 3, and out slowly 1, 2, 3, 4, 5, 6.
Take a deep breath, breathing in 1, 2 3, and out slowly 1, 2, 3, 4, 5, 6.
Take a deep breath, breathing in 1, 2 3, and out slowly 1, 2, 3, 4, 5, 6.

**Left foot and lower leg**

Focus your attention on your left foot.
**Point the toes of your left foot downwards.**
Then allow your foot to return to the resting position.
Notice the change from tension to relaxation in muscles of your left foot and the front of your lower leg.
Allow this change to continue further and further still so the muscles in your left foot and the front of your lower leg become more and more relaxed.
Take a deep breath, breathing in 1, 2, 3, and out slowly 1, 2, 3, 4, 5, 6.
Take a deep breath, breathing in 1, 2, 3, and out slowly 1, 2, 3, 4, 5, 6.
Take a deep breath, breathing in 1, 2, 3, and out slowly 1, 2, 3, 4, 5, 6.

Again, focus your attention on your left foot.
**Point the toes of your left foot upwards.**
Then allow them to return to the resting position.
Notice the change from tension to relaxation in the back of your leg.
Allow this change to continue further and further still so the muscles in the back of your leg become more and more relaxed.
Take a deep breath, breathing in 1, 2, 3, and out slowly 1, 2, 3, 4, 5, 6.
Take a deep breath, breathing in 1, 2, 3, and out slowly 1, 2, 3, 4, 5, 6.
Take a deep breath, breathing in 1, 2, 3, and out slowly 1, 2, 3, 4, 5, 6.

| | |
|---|---|
| **Left upper leg** | Focus your attention on your left thigh. |
| | **Tighten your left thigh muscles.** |
| | Then allow your thigh to relax. |
| | Notice the change from tension to relaxation in your left thigh muscles. |
| | Allow this change to continue further and further still so the muscles in your left thigh become more and more relaxed. |
| | Take a deep breath, breathing in 1, 2, 3, and out slowly 1, 2, 3, 4, 5, 6. |
| | Take a deep breath, breathing in 1, 2, 3, and out slowly 1, 2, 3, 4, 5, 6. |
| | Take a deep breath, breathing in 1, 2, 3, and out slowly 1, 2, 3, 4, 5, 6. |
| **Buttocks and hips** | Focus your attention on your buttocks. |
| | **Squeeze the muscles in your buttocks.** |
| | Then allow them to relax. |
| | Notice the change from tension to relaxation in the muscles of your buttocks. |
| | Allow this change to continue further and further still so the muscles in your buttocks become more and more relaxed. |
| | Take a deep breath, breathing in 1, 2, 3, and out slowly 1, 2, 3, 4, 5, 6. |
| | Take a deep breath, breathing in 1, 2, 3, and out slowly 1, 2, 3, 4, 5, 6. |
| | Take a deep breath, breathing in 1, 2, 3, and out slowly 1, 2, 3, 4, 5, 6. |
| **Chest and stomach** | Focus your attention on your chest and stomach. |
| | **Take a deep breath and hold it for three seconds**, tensing the muscles in your stomach and chest as you do so. |
| | Then breathe out slowly, releasing the tension in the muscles of your stomach and chest. |
| | Notice the change from tension to relaxation in your stomach and chest muscles and allow this change to continue further and further still so your stomach and chest muscles become more and more relaxed. |
| | Take a deep breath, breathing in 1, 2, 3, and out slowly 1, 2, 3, 4, 5, 6. |
| | Take a deep breath, breathing in 1, 2, 3, and out slowly 1, 2, 3, 4, 5, 6. |
| | Take a deep breath, breathing in 1, 2, 3, and out slowly 1, 2, 3, 4, 5, 6. |
| **Neck** | Focus your attention on your neck muscles. |
| | **Tilt your head backwards** as far as you can without straining. |
| | Then return your head to the resting position. |
| | Notice the change from tension to relaxation in the muscles of your neck and allow this change to continue further and further still so the muscles in your neck become more and more relaxed. |
| | Take a deep breath, breathing in 1, 2, 3, and out slowly 1, 2, 3, 4, 5, 6. |
| | Take a deep breath, breathing in 1, 2, 3, and out slowly 1, 2, 3, 4, 5, 6. |
| | Take a deep breath, breathing in 1, 2, 3, and out slowly 1, 2, 3, 4, 5, 6. |
| | |
| | Focus your attention on your neck muscles once again. |
| | **Tilt your head forwards** as far as you can without straining. |
| | Then return your head to the resting position. |
| | Notice the change from tension to relaxation in the muscles of your neck and allow this change to continue further and further still so the muscles in your neck become more and more relaxed. |
| | Take a deep breath, breathing in 1, 2, 3, and out slowly 1, 2, 3, 4, 5, 6. |
| | Take a deep breath, breathing in 1, 2, 3, and out slowly 1, 2, 3, 4, 5, 6. |
| | Take a deep breath, breathing in 1, 2, 3, and out slowly 1, 2, 3, 4, 5, 6. |
| | |
| | Focus your attention on your neck muscles once again. |
| | **Tilt your head to the right side** as far as you can without straining. |
| | Then return your head to the resting position. |

Notice the change from tension to relaxation in the muscles of your neck and allow this change to continue further and further still so the muscles in your neck become more and more relaxed.

Take a deep breath, breathing in 1, 2, 3, and out slowly 1, 2, 3, 4, 5, 6.
Take a deep breath, breathing in 1, 2, 3, and out slowly 1, 2, 3, 4, 5, 6.
Take a deep breath, breathing in 1, 2, 3, and out slowly 1, 2, 3, 4, 5, 6.

**Face**    Focus your attention on the muscles in your mouth and jaw.

**Clench your teeth** tightly together. Then relax.

Notice the change from tension to relaxation in the muscles of your jaw and allow this change to continue further and further still so the muscles in your jaw become more and more relaxed.

Take a deep breath, breathing in 1, 2, 3, and out slowly 1, 2, 3, 4, 5, 6.
Take a deep breath, breathing in 1, 2, 3, and out slowly 1, 2, 3, 4, 5, 6.
Take a deep breath, breathing in 1, 2, 3, and out slowly 1, 2, 3, 4, 5, 6.

Focus your attention on the muscles around your eyes.

**Shut your eyes tightly.** Then relax.

Notice the change from tension to relaxation in the muscles around your eyes and allow this change to continue further and further still so the muscles around your eyes become more and more relaxed.

Take a deep breath, breathing in 1, 2, 3, and out slowly 1, 2, 3, 4, 5, 6.
Take a deep breath, breathing in 1, 2, 3, and out slowly 1, 2, 3, 4, 5, 6.
Take a deep breath, breathing in 1, 2, 3, and out slowly 1, 2, 3, 4, 5, 6.

Focus your attention on the muscles of your forehead.

**Furrow your forehead** as if you are worried. Then relax.

Notice the change from tension to relaxation in the muscles of your forehead and allow this change to continue further and further still so the muscles of your forehead become more and more relaxed.

Take a deep breath, breathing in 1, 2, 3, and out slowly 1, 2, 3, 4, 5, 6.
Take a deep breath, breathing in 1, 2, 3, and out slowly 1, 2, 3, 4, 5, 6.
Take a deep breath, breathing in 1, 2, 3, and out slowly 1, 2, 3, 4, 5, 6.

Focus your attention on the muscles of your forehead once again.

**Raise your eyebrows** as if you are surprised. Then relax.

Notice the change from tension to relaxation in the muscles of your forehead and allow this change to continue further and further still so the muscles of your forehead become more and more relaxed.

Take a deep breath, breathing in 1, 2, 3, and out slowly 1, 2, 3, 4, 5, 6.
Take a deep breath, breathing in 1, 2, 3, and out slowly 1, 2, 3, 4, 5, 6.
Take a deep breath, breathing in 1, 2, 3, and out slowly 1, 2, 3, 4, 5, 6.

**Body check**    Now that you've done all your muscle exercises, check that all areas of your body are as relaxed as can be.

Focus on relaxation flowing from your head down your body towards your feet.

Think of the muscles in your face and allow them to relax a little more.

Take a deep breath, breathing in 1, 2, 3, and out slowly 1, 2, 3, 4, 5, 6, and say the word 'Relax'.

Think of the muscles in your neck and shoulders and allow them to relax a little more.

Take a deep breath, breathing in 1, 2, 3, and out slowly 1, 2, 3, 4, 5, 6, and say the word 'Relax'.

Think of the muscles in your arms and hands and allow them to relax a little more.

Take a deep breath, breathing in 1, 2, 3, and out slowly 1, 2, 3, 4, 5, 6, and say the word 'Relax'.

Think of the muscles in your chest, stomach and back and allow them to relax a little more.

Take a deep breath, breathing in 1, 2, 3, and out slowly 1, 2, 3, 4, 5, 6, and say the word 'Relax'.

Think of the muscles in your buttocks, legs and feet and allow them to relax a little more.

Take a deep breath, breathing in 1, 2, 3, and out slowly 1, 2, 3, 4, 5, 6, and say the word 'Relax'.

**Breathing**    Take a deep breath, breathing in 1, 2, 3, and out slowly 1, 2, 3, 4, 5, 6.

Take a deep breath, breathing in 1, 2, 3, and out slowly 1, 2, 3, 4, 5, 6.

Take a deep breath, breathing in 1, 2, 3, and out slowly 1, 2, 3, 4, 5, 6.

**Visualising**    Imagine you are lying on a beautiful sandy beach and you feel the sun warm your body.

Make a picture in your mind of the silver sand, the calm blue sea, the clear blue sky, the sound of gentle lapping waves and the feel of the warm sun on your skin.

As the sun warms your body, you feel more and more relaxed.

As the sun warms your body, you feel more and more relaxed.

As the sun warms your body, you feel more and more relaxed.

The sky is a clear, clear blue. Above you, you can see a small white cloud drifting away into the distance.

As the white cloud drifts further and further away, it becomes smaller and smaller, and you feel more and more relaxed.

As the white cloud drifts further and further away, it becomes smaller and smaller, and you feel more and more relaxed.

As the white cloud drifts further and further away, it becomes smaller and smaller, and you feel more and more relaxed.

As the sun warms your body, you feel more and more relaxed.

As the white cloud drifts further and further away, it becomes smaller and smaller, and you feel more and more relaxed.

When you are ready, open your eyes.

You are ready to enjoy the rest of the day feeling relaxed and calm.

## Doing progressive muscle relaxation

If you would like to learn progressive relaxation skills, read the rest of the chapter. Follow the instructions as you do so to familiarise yourself with various progressive muscle relaxation exercises. Then when you have read the entire chapter, set aside an hour to follow the instructions for doing all of the exercises together. These are summarised in Box 5.2. This will allow you to experience the full set of progressive muscle relaxation exercises in a single session without the distraction of reading and thinking about the content of the chapter.

---

### Box 5.2   Summary of progressive muscle relaxation exercises

| Area | Exercise |
|---|---|
| Breathing | Take a deep breath, breathing in 1, 2, 3, and out slowly 1, 2, 3, 4, 5, 6. |
| Right hand and forearm | Close your right hand into a fist. |
| Left hand and forearm | Close your left hand into a fist. |
| Right upper arm | Bend your right arm at the elbow and touch your right shoulder with your right hand. |
| Left upper arm | Bend your left arm at the elbow and touch your left shoulder with your left hand. |
| Shoulders | Hunch your shoulders. |
| | Press your shoulder blades back, trying to almost touch them together. |
| Back | Arch your back. |
| Right foot and lower leg | Point the toes of your right foot downwards. |
| | Point the toes of your right foot upwards. |
| Right upper leg | Tighten your right thigh muscles. |
| Left foot and lower leg | Point the toes of your left foot downwards. |
| | Point the toes of your left foot upwards. |
| Left upper leg | Tighten your left thigh muscles. |
| Buttocks and hips | Squeeze the muscles in your buttocks. |
| Chest and stomach | Take a deep breath and hold it for three seconds. |
| Neck | Tilt your head backwards. |
| | Tilt your head forwards. |
| | Tilt your head to the right side. |
| | Tilt your head to the left side. |
| Face | Clench your teeth. |
| | Shut your eyes tightly. |
| | Furrow your forehead. |
| | Raise your eyebrows. |
| All-over body check | Face. |
| | Neck and shoulders. |
| | Arms and hands. |
| | Chest, stomach and back. |
| | Buttocks, legs and feet. |

| | |
|---|---|
| **Breathing** | Take a deep breath, breathing in 1, 2, 3, and out slowly 1, 2, 3, 4, 5, 6. |
| **Visualising** | Lying on a beautiful sandy beach, the sun warms your body. |
| | As the sun warms your body, you feel more and more relaxed. |
| | Small white cloud drifting away into the distance. |
| | As the white cloud drifts further and further away, it becomes smaller and smaller, and you feel more and more relaxed. |
| | You are ready to enjoy the rest of the day feeling relaxed and calm. |

When you are doing progressive muscle relaxation, do so in a quiet place where you will not be interrupted. Lie down on your back on a bed, couch or comfortable floor mat. If you prefer, sit or recline in a comfortable chair. Remove all distractions. Turn off bright lights, phones, computers, TVs and radios. Loosen any tight clothes like belts, ties or shoes. If you wear glasses, take them off. Take off your watch and any jewellery that may cause discomfort.

## Breathing

When you are ready, settle yourself comfortably. Allow your eyes to close gently. Focus your attention on your breathing. Breathe with your diaphragm. This means that when you inhale your naval is pushed out. In diaphragmatic breathing, you fill the lower and larger part of your lungs first. This is quite different from breathing with your chest where you suck in your stomach and puff out your chest. In this sort of shallow breathing you fill only the upper, smaller part of the lungs. To return to the breathing exercise, focus your attention on your breathing. Take a deep diaphragmatic breath, breathing in for three seconds. Then, breathe out slowly for six seconds. You can count the seconds in your mind: breathe in 1, 2, 3; breathe out 1, 2, 3, 4, 5, 6. Repeat this breathing exercise three times.

## Hands and forearms

For the first progressive muscle relaxation exercise, direct your attention to your right hand. Close your right hand into a fist. Not too tightly. You only need to tense your muscles enough for you to able to notice the change from tension to relaxation as you release the tension. Hold your hand closed for five seconds. Then allow it to open slowly for about 10 seconds. Notice the change from tension to relaxation in the muscles of your right hand and forearm. Allow this change to continue further and further still, so the muscles in your right hand and forearm become more and more relaxed. Take a deep breath, breathing in for three seconds. Then, breathe out slowly for six seconds. Repeat this breathing exercise three times. Now repeat the whole sequence again: closing and opening the right fist, and taking three breaths. The next exercise is the same as the first, but do it with your left hand. Repeat the left-hand exercise again, closing and opening the left fist, and taking three breaths. You have now done the exercises for the right and left hands twice. These exercises will help you to relax your right and left hands and forearms.

## Relaxation exercise rules

For all of the other exercises described below, follow these rules. Focus your attention on the specific muscle group you are aiming to relax. Tense your muscles for about five seconds and release the tension for about ten seconds. You only need to tense your muscles enough for you to able to notice the change from tension to relaxation as you release the tension. So, tense them a little, not too much. Then focus your attention on the change from tension to relaxation. This is critical. When you notice this change, allow the change to continue, so that the muscles become more deeply relaxed. When you have gone through this sequence take three deep breaths, breathing in for three seconds and out for six seconds. Then repeat the whole sequence again, tensing and relaxing the muscle group, and taking three breaths.

### Upper arms

After relaxing the hands and forearms, the next set of exercises helps you to relax the upper arms. Bend your right arm at the elbow and touch your right shoulder with your right hand, so that you make the muscle in your upper arm bulge up a little. Then slowly return your hand to the resting position. When you have done this exercise with the right arm, do it with the left arm.

### Shoulders

Having relaxed your arms, focus your attention on your shoulders. Hunch your shoulders up to your ears. Then slowly allow them to return to the resting position. Next press your shoulder blades back, trying to almost touch them together, so that your chest is pushed forward. Then slowly allow your shoulders to return to the resting position.

### Back

To relax the muscles in your back, arch your back and then return slowly to the resting position.

### Feet and lower legs

To relax your feet and lower legs, point the toes of your feet downwards, and then return them to the resting position. This relaxes the muscles in the feet and front of the legs. Then point your toes upwards and return them to the resting position. This relaxes the muscles in the backs of the legs. Do these exercises with the right foot first and then the left foot.

### Upper legs

To relax the upper legs, tighten the thigh muscles and then relax them. Do this exercise with the right leg first and then the left leg.

### Buttocks and hips

To relax the buttocks and hips, squeeze the muscles in your buttocks and then relax them.

### Chest and stomach

To relax the chest and stomach muscles, take a deep breath and hold it for three seconds, tensing the muscles in your stomach and chest as you do so. Then breathe out slowly, releasing the tension in the muscles of your stomach and chest.

### Neck

There are four exercises to help you relax your neck muscles. In these, you tilt your head backwards, forwards, to the right and to the left. In each instance, after tilting your head, return it slowly to the resting position.

### Face

There are four exercises to help you relax your face muscles. Clench your teeth together and then relax. This relaxes the muscles in the jaw. Shut your eyes tightly and then relax. This relaxes the muscles around your eyes and cheeks. Furrow your forehead and relax. Raise your eyebrows and relax. These last two exercises relax the muscles in your forehead.

### Practice makes perfect

Relaxation is a skill. To become highly skilled at relaxation, practice is essential. In the first instance, after you have read this chapter, take an hour to do all the exercises in Box 5.1 very slowly and carefully. If you wish to develop your relaxation skills so that they become automatic, set aside 20–30 minutes a day to do the exercises in Box 5.1. Ideally do them at the same time and in the same place every day. It's best to do them twice a day. Do not do these exercises after a big meal or when intoxicated. They may make you feel uncomfortable if you do so. If you use these exercises to help you sleep, do not count this as one of your daily practice sessions. This is because it's quite likely that you will nod off to sleep before you finish the full set of exercises.

Before and after you do these exercises, each day in your journal record your level of relaxation on a scale from 1 to 10, where 1 is extremely tense and 10 is extremely relaxed. Each week review the relaxation ratings you have recorded in your journal. After a couple of weeks of daily practice, you will notice that you are becoming skilled at using these exercises to achieve a calm, peaceful, relaxed state.

## Variations on a theme

Since Jacobson's early ground-breaking work, progressive muscle relaxation techniques have been refined. Jacobson's original set of exercises took weeks to learn. Modern versions of progressive muscle relaxation, like that in Box 5.1, can be practised in a single session. Visualisation and auto-suggestion have been combined with progressive muscle relaxation to aid the relaxation process. The visualisation exercise in Box 5.1 includes both visualisation and auto-suggestion. In this exercise, you imagine yourself lying on a warm beach. Then you suggest to yourself that the warmth of the sun and watching a cloud getting smaller as it drifts away relaxes you more. Very brief relaxation exercises have been developed so that you can use relaxation skills to reduce tension in distressing situations. Let's look at these variations on the theme of relaxation in a bit more detail.

## Visualisation

Progressive muscle relaxation may be combined with guided imagery or visualisation.[6] Visualisation has been found, in a series of scientific studies, to be an effective way of controlling pain associated with conditions such as arthritis and cancer.[7] When visualising, you imagine a relaxing scene in your mind's eye. Before you start a visualisation exercise, select a favourite place that you would like to visualise. Select a scene that makes you feel relaxed, safe and secure. The scene may be real or imaginary. For example, you might visualise a beautiful silver sandy beach, a peaceful green meadow, a high mountain trail lined with tall trees or a cosy kitchen with the smells of your mother's cooking and the warmth of an open fire. In your mind's eye visualise the scene in graphic detail. Call to mind all the sensations that you would experience. What would you see? What would you hear? What would you feel? What would you smell? The image of the relaxing scene will help you to sustain and deepen relaxation.

Instructions for visualising lying on a sandy beach are given in Box 5.1: 'Imagine you are lying on a beautiful sandy beach and you feel the sun warm your body. Make a picture in your mind of the silver sand, the calm blue sea, the clear blue sky, the sound of gentle lapping waves and the feel of the warm sun on your skin'. To intensify the relaxation experience, add sensory details that make the image more vivid. For example, you may imagine a vast stretch of deserted silver sand, palm trees, a grey seagull flying in the clear blue sky, a yacht with white sails in the distance on the deep blue ocean, the feel of the fine sand against your skin, the salty scent of the ocean, the sound of seashells on the sand as the waves lap the shoreline, the gentle warmth of the sun on your arms, legs, face and stomach, the distant sound of music coming from a beach house somewhere behind you, and so forth. If you prefer to visualise a different scene which makes you feel more relaxed than this warm beach scene, please do so. The important thing is that the scene helps to deepen your experience of relaxation.

## Auto-suggestion

Progressive muscle relaxation and visualisation may be combined with auto-suggestion to deepen relaxation.[8] That is, you can deepen your state of relaxation by suggesting to yourself that some aspects of the scene you are imagining are linked to your physical experience of reduced muscle tension. In the visualisation exercise in Box 5.1 you can use the feeling of warmth from the sun and the image of a white cloud drifting away and becoming smaller to deepen the feeling of relaxation by saying to yourself, 'As the sun warms your body, you feel more and more relaxed. As the white cloud drifts further and further away, it becomes smaller and smaller, and you feel more and more relaxed'. The idea here is that imagining the sun warming your body will help you deepen your experience of relaxation because usually we find it easier to relax when we are comfortably warm. The image of the cloud becoming smaller as it drifts further away may help you deepen relaxation because it acts as a visual metaphor for tension receding and being replaced by relaxation. If you prefer to use other scenes and other auto-suggestions, please do so. The key thing with auto-suggestions is that they are in some way linked to the deepening of the relaxation state.

## Applied relaxation

To do a full set of progressive muscle relaxation exercises, like those in Box 5.1, you need to be lying down or sitting in a comfortable chair and to remain there until you have completed the full routine. What if you find yourself in a distressing situation? How do you use relaxation skills to help you relax? In answer to these sorts of questions, Professor Lars-Göran Öst at Stockholm University in Sweden developed applied relaxation to help people suffering from anxiety.[9] Applied relaxation means using a very brief version of some of the relaxation exercises in Box 5.1 to induce a more relaxed state while engaging in normal daily activities.

If you find yourself in a distressing situation, to use applied relaxation, follow the guidelines in Box 5.3. First, breathe in deeply for three seconds; exhale slowly for six seconds; and say the word 'Relax'. Repeat this breathing exercise three times. Follow this with the body check exercise. With this, focus your attention on the muscles in each of the five groups listed below, one after another:

- Face.
- Neck and shoulders
- Arms and hands.
- Chest, stomach and back.
- Buttocks, legs and feet.

---

### Box 5.3  Brief applied relaxation exercise

If you find yourself in a distressing situation, do this brief applied relaxation exercise.

Breathe in deeply for three seconds, exhale slowly for six seconds and say the word 'Relax'.

Repeat this breathing exercise three times.

Focus your attention on the muscles in each of the five groups listed below one after another:

- Face.
- Neck and shoulders
- Arms and hands.
- Chest, stomach and back.
- Buttocks, legs and feet.

In each case, allow the muscle group to relax; inhale deeply for three seconds; exhale slowly for six seconds; and say the word 'Relax'.

---

In each case, allow the muscle group to relax; inhale deeply for three seconds; exhale slowly for six seconds; and say the word 'Relax'.

You may find that it is too big of a 'jump' to go from doing the full set of progressive muscle relaxation exercises in Box 5.1 at home, to doing brief applied relaxation exercises during your daily activates. That is, while you may be able to relax when you do the full set of exercises quietly at home, you may find that when you are doing daily activities the brief breathing exercise and body check don't relax you. If this is the case, there are intermediate steps you can take to train yourself to be able to do this. First, practise the progressive muscle relaxation exercises in Box 5.1 twice a day for about two weeks, doing each exercise twice at each session. The second step is, for a week, to practise the exercises in Box 5.1 twice a day, but to do each exercise only once at each session and to include only one deep breath, rather than three, between each exercise. The third step is to repeat this process with the following modification. Don't tense each muscle group; just relax it. For example, don't close your hand into a fist; simply focus your attention on your hand and allow it to relax. So, the third step involves a week of doing each exercise once without tensing, and including only one deep breath between exercises. The fourth step is to build a strong mental association between the word 'Relax' and the relaxation response that you have learned by doing the relaxation exercises. For a week do each exercise once without tensing, include only one deep breath between exercises and mentally instruct yourself with the word 'Relax' as you do each exercise. At this stage, you may be ready to start using the breathing exercise (inhaling for three seconds and exhaling slowly for six seconds, three times) and then doing the body check exercise. In the body check exercise between each muscle group, do a breathing exercise and mentally say the word 'Relax' as you exhale. Use these two exercises (the breathing exercise and the body check exercise) regularly in non-stressful situations, such as walking or shopping, to achieve a relaxed state. When you are able to do this successfully, you may be able use the brief applied relaxation exercises in Box 5.3 to relax in distressing situations.

## Dermot the IT programmer with shoulder pain

Dermot worked for an IT company as a programmer. He was excellent at his job. However, he came to see me because he had developed severe shoulder pains. This was from spending long periods of time working at his computer keyboard without taking breaks. In the past, he had managed shoulder pain by taking more frequent breaks, jogging at lunchtime and taking pain medication (Neurofen Plus, which is a combination of ibuprofen and codeine). Recently he had found that these remedies were having very little effect on the pains in his shoulders. With me he learned progressive muscle relaxation. He practised the exercises in Box 5.1 regularly each morning and evening. He also used brief applied relaxation exercises a couple of times each hour when he was working at his computer keyboard. Over a period of three months, his level of pain reduced from an average rating of 8 to 2 on a scale where 10 is extremely severe pain and 1 is no pain. His relaxation level increased from 4 to 7 over the same period on a scale where 1 indicated extreme tension and 10 indicated extreme relaxation.

## What if I can't relax? Cathy with anxiety

In my clinical practice, I occasionally meet clients who find, at first, that they can't relax. For example, Cathy, a 32-year-old mother of two young children, came to me for help with anxiety and insomnia. She felt tense much of the time. She worried a lot. She had difficulty getting off to sleep most nights of the week. Her relaxation rating on a scale of 1 to 10 was 5 before first doing progressive muscle relaxation and immediately afterwards was 3. The exercises apparently made her more tense rather than more relaxed.

When we talked about her experience of doing the exercises in Box 5.1 she said that it was the first time she could ever remember focusing so intensely on each muscle group. When she focused on each muscle group, in most instances she was distressed to notice that it was already quite tense. She became more distressed when she found that releasing the muscle group by, for example, opining her fist when doing the first exercise did not lead to a rapid reduction in muscle tension. She began to worry that she was failing to do the exercises properly. She worried that she would always be tense. These thoughts of failure and the prospect of always being tense made her feel greater muscle tension.

I suggested that to be able to relax her body, it would be important to develop a different sort of relationship with these worrying thoughts. At that point, I introduced her to mindfulness meditation which we will discuss in detail in Chapter 6. Mindfulness mediation helped Cathy come to view her worrying thoughts as transient ideas which come and go, rather than as permanent facts that define how the world is and will be. She learned to welcome in and observe these sorts of worrying thoughts as she focused on her breathing. She learned to allow the thoughts to enter her mind, linger a while and then leave without becoming attached to them or involved with them too much.

This mindfulness process freed her to be able to complete progressive muscle relaxation without interference from her worries. Over a period of months, her anxiety gradually declined and her level of relaxation improved from 5 to 7 on a 10-point scale. Cathy also used progressive muscle relaxation exercises to help her get to sleep. She found that most nights she could get off to sleep without difficulty.

## Summary

- Progressive muscle relaxation, diaphragmatic breathing, visualisation, auto-suggestion and applied relaxation enhance well-being.
- **Progressive muscle relaxation** is a series of exercises for reducing muscle tension. The exercises involve tensing and relaxing muscles groups, one at a time, in all areas of the body including the hands, arms, shoulders, back, feet, legs, buttocks, hips, stomach, chest, neck and face.
- **Diaphragmatic breathing** involves inhaling and exhaling so the lower parts of the lungs are filled with air.
- **Visualisation** involves picturing a scene in the mind's eye. To aid relaxation, the scene should be one that makes you feel relaxed, safe and secure.
- **Auto-suggestion.** Relaxation may be deepened by imagining that changes in some aspect of a visualised scene (for example, the sun warming the body) are linked to increased relaxation.
- **Applied relaxation.** A brief version of progressive muscle relaxation that may be used to reduce tension, stress and anxiety in everyday situations.

## Where are you now?

If you have done the exercises in this chapter, you have introduced progressive muscle relaxation, diaphragmatic breathing, visualisation, auto-suggestion and applied relaxation into your daily routine. These are techniques that you can use to help you achieve a relaxed, calm and peaceful state.

If you have sleep problems, you may have used progressive muscle relaxation to improve your sleep.

You may want to read back over the chapter and summarise in your journal the main things that you have learned about progressive muscle relaxation, diaphragmatic breathing, visualisation, auto-suggestion and applied relaxation.

In the next chapter, we will consider mindfulness mediation. This is another approach to achieving a relaxed, calm and peaceful state. Below are some web resources and books that are relevant to topics you have read about in this chapter.

## Web resources

Progressive muscle relaxation exercises, breathing exercises and mindfulness exercises on the Beaumont Hospital, Dublin website: www.beaumont.ie/index.jsp?p=528&n=532

Progressive muscle relaxation exercises with Colin Espie (11:05): https://soundcloud.com/mentalhealth foundation/sleep-relaxation-mp3-mental

Progressive muscle relaxation video with music (24:19): www.youtube.com/watch?v=KRUdkxQOqWM

Five-minute progressive muscle relaxation exercise video (5:32): www.youtube.com/watch?v=a123d_3SqUg

## Books

Davis, M., Eshelman, E., & McKay, M. (2008). *The relaxation and stress reduction workbook* (Sixth Edition). Oakland, CA: New Harbinger.

Madders, J. (1997). *The stress and relaxation handbook: A practical guide to self-help techniques.* London, UK: Vermillion.

# 6 Meditation

There is now a vast body of evidence showing that mindfulness and other forms of meditation have many positive effects.[1] For healthy people without a diagnosis of psychological problems, meditation leads to increases in well-being and specifically to increases or improvements in:

- positive emotions such as happiness
- mindfulness
- emotion regulation
- self-esteem
- empathy
- relationships
- thinking, attention, learning and memory.

Meditation also leads to decreases in:

- negative emotions such as depression, anxiety and anger
- stress
- negative personality traits (such as neuroticism or emotional instability).

Mindfulness not only affects psychological functioning. It also has a measurable impact on the functioning and structure of the brain.[2] You can see some of the brain regions affected by mindfulness meditation in Figure 6.1. Functional brain imaging studies have shown that mindfulness meditation affects brain regions involved in attention control (the anterior cingulate cortex and the striatum), emotion regulation (multiple prefrontal regions and limbic regions, especially the amygdala and the striatum), self-awareness and empathy (the insula, medial prefrontal cortex and posterior cingulate cortex, and praecuneus). Structural brain imaging studies have shown that long-term meditation sculpts the shape of the brain. The single most important finding is that mindfulness leads to a thickening of the cortex.[3] Changes in the structure of the brain occur at multiple sites following long-term meditation, including some sites activated in studies of brain functioning during meditation, for example the anterior cingulate (which subserves attention control) the praecuneus (which subserves self-awareness) and the insula (which subserves empathy for pain in others[4]).

Richard Davidson, a neuroscientist and friend of the Dali Lama, has shown that in happier people the left frontal lobe of the brain is more active than the right, and that regular meditation

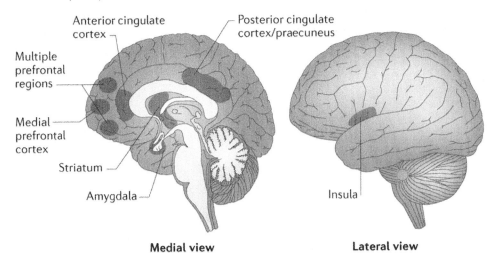

**Nature Reviews** | Neuroscience

*Figure 6.1* Brain regions involved in mindfulness meditation. Schematic view of some of the brain regions activated during mindfulness including those involved in attention control (the anterior cingulate cortex and the striatum), emotion regulation (multiple prefrontal regions, limbic regions including the amygdala and the striatum), self-awareness and empathy (the medial prefrontal cortex, the posterior cingulate cortex, the praecuneus and the insula).

practice can help people develop a more active left frontal lobe.[5] This finding of greater activation of the left side of the brain has been frequently replicated. It also improves the functioning of the immune system.

## MBSR and MBCT

Mindfulness meditation is the central component of two treatment programmes which have been shown in many studies to be particularly effective in the treatment of chronic pain and depression. These programmes are Mindfulness-Based Stress Reduction (MBSR)[6] and Mindfulness-Based Cognitive Therapy (MBCT).[7] MBSR was developed by Professor Jon Kabat-Zinn at the University of Massachusetts Medical School. MBCT was developed by Professor Zindel Segal at the University of Toronto, Professor Mark Williams at Oxford University and Professor John Teasdale at Cambridge University.

Both MBSR and MBCT programmes span eight weekly sessions, and despite their brevity, are exceptionally effective.[8] MBSR combines mindfulness meditation with yoga. It was designed to help people suffering from chronic pain associated with a variety of medical conditions and diseases. MBSR greatly enhances the quality of life of people suffering from chronic pain. MBCT combines cognitive therapy with mindfulness meditation. It was designed to prevent relapse in people suffering from chronic depression. MBCT prevents relapse in people who have recurrent episodes of depression, especially those who have experienced childhood trauma. How do MBSR and MBCT work? Research shows that these programmes reduce rumination, worry and emotional reactivity to distressing thoughts, and increase mindfulness and self-compassion in daily life.[9]

Mark Williams has developed a version of the eight-week MBCT programme specifically for people without clinical depression, but who wish to use mindfulness to increase their well-being.[10] The exercises and approach described later in this chapter are based on that programme.

## Mind-wandering and reactions to negative mood states

When we are not engaged in purposeful activity our minds tend to wander. They wander away from our present experiences to ruminating about past difficulties and worrying about future challenges. Mind-wandering is associated with a particular brain state called the default mode of brain function.[11] From an evolutionary perspective, the default mode of brain function probably developed primarily to help our ancestors automatically scan the environment for predators and other threats to safety without exerting conscious effort. This allowed our cave-dwelling ancestors to safely focus on enjoying eating, mating, working or playing without putting themselves at risk of being killed by predators. In modern industrialised society, scanning the outer environment for predators is rarely necessary. However, the default mode of brain function vigilance system still makes us scan the environment for threats to our safety.

For us, living in an industrialised world, most threats are internal. For example, we yearn for people, things, status, admiration and approval that we have lost. We fear problems that may happen in the future. Ruminating about past difficulties may make us feel a little sad. Worrying about the future may make us feel a little anxious.

Another difference between ourselves and our cave-dwelling ancestors is that our lives are far more complex. Most of us do not just have one or two past losses or one or two future challenges. We have dozens of things in the recent past that we wish had gone differently. A few may be large losses, but most are small sources of embarrassment or sadness, like losing a game or saying the wrong thing in a social situation. We also have many ongoing unfinished projects at home and work, and we worry about how these may turn out. The modern mind is like a computer with too many open files. This slows its efficiency. It also makes it more likely that we will spontaneously think of things that make us a little sad or anxious when we are not focused on a specific task.

When we become a little sad or a little anxious, it not these normal fluctuations in mood that make us distressed, but the way we react to them. Ruminating about why we are unhappy may make us feel worse. Unsuccessful efforts to free ourselves from episodes of distress may increase our distress. Judgements we pass on ourselves for being distressed can often make things worse.

When we experience a negative mood, we try to solve this problem by finding a solution. To find a solution we automatically trawl our memories for other similar episodes that occurred in the past, to see how we solved these. If we are currently uncertain about the future, we automatically remember past episodes of being worried about future threats. If we are currently sad about the loss of friendship or status, we remember other similar loss experiences. This automatic tendency to remember other similar episodes and the sorts of solutions we used in the past is a basic survival skill that has developed through millions of years of evolution. When a problem needs solving, our minds immediately and automatically look for past episodes where we successfully dealt with similar problems. For things like catching fish, gathering fruit, hunting or mending a leaky roof, this automatic tendency to look at past episodes was very adaptive for our cave-dwelling ancestors. For brief fluctuations in mood due to the sorts of concerns we have in the modern world, recalling past similar episodes creates more problems than it solves. Recalling past episodes of sadness or anxiety further lowers our mood. It also activates our 'inner critic'. This is the tendency to judge ourselves harshly and without compassion. The inner critic says things like: 'look at all those mistakes you made and couldn't put right. What is wrong with you! And now you're doing it all again! Your life is a mess!' These harsh self-judgements further lower our mood. This all happens so quickly and automatically that it may leave us wondering. 'How did I get into this really bad mood?' This may lead to a downward spiral of more self-criticism, low mood, negative memories and so forth.

There is one other problem with mind-wandering that lowers our mood. When we notice that we are having negative thoughts, being self-critical and that our mood is dropping, we may try to avoid the distress associated with this process by pushing the negative memories, self-critical thoughts and low mood out of our minds. This has the ironic or paradoxical effect of making these negative memories, thoughts and mood states all the more vivid. If you want to test this now, try not to think of a white bear for the next 30 seconds. You will find that all you can think of is – you've guessed right – a white bear![12]

You can't stop normal fluctuations in mood. You can't stop these fluctuations triggering memories of other similar episodes. However, you can stop the downward spiral. Mindfulness meditation allows us to recognise that our recollections of and ruminations about past episodes of distress are just thoughts. Our worries about the future are just thoughts. They are not facts. They are not reality. They are just thoughts.

## Mindfulness

What is mindfulness? Mindfulness involves paying attention, on purpose, in the present moment, without judgement to our immediate sensory experience with an attitude of curiosity and compassion. In mindfulness, we experience the world as it is now. Not as it was. Not as we expect, or want, or fear it may become.

Mindfulness has five facets. When we are mindful:

- We observe the world as it is now.
- We can describe these immediate experiences in words.
- We focus on what is happening in the present moment.
- We do not make judgements about whether our immediate experience is good or bad.
- We are less reactive to negative thoughts.

You can assess your current level of mindfulness by filling in the short form of the five-facet mindfulness questionnaire in Box 6.1. Alternatively, you can complete a longer online version at http://awakemind.org/quiz.php. It takes about five minutes to complete and there is no cost. The exercises described in this chapter will help you to become more mindful.

# Box 6.1 Five facets of mindfulness questionnaire

For each item circle the response that best applies to you in the past week.

To get your score on each facet, sum item scores and divide by the number of items in the facet.

To get your overall score, sum item scores and divide by 24.

Scores range from 1 to 5. Higher scores indicate greater mindfulness.

---

*Observing*

| | | | | | |
|---|---|---|---|---|---|
| 1 | I pay attention to physical experiences, such as the wind in my hair or sun on my face | Very rarely true<br>1 | Not often true<br>2 | Sometimes true<br>3 | Often true<br>4 | Very often true<br>5 |
| 2 | Generally, I pay attention to sounds, such as clocks ticking, birds chirping or cars passing | Very rarely true<br>1 | Not often true<br>2 | Sometimes true<br>3 | Often true<br>4 | Very often true<br>5 |
| 3 | I notice the smells and aromas of things | Very rarely true<br>1 | Not often true<br>2 | Sometimes true<br>3 | Often true<br>4 | Very often true<br>5 |
| 4 | I notice visual elements in art or nature, such as colours, shapes, textures, or patterns of light and shadow | Very rarely true<br>1 | Not often true<br>2 | Sometimes true<br>3 | Often true<br>4 | Very often true<br>5 |

---

*Describing*

| | | | | | |
|---|---|---|---|---|---|
| 5 | I'm good at finding the words to describe my feelings | Very rarely true<br>1 | Not often true<br>2 | Sometimes true<br>3 | Often true<br>4 | Very often true<br>5 |
| 6 | I can easily put my beliefs, opinions and expectations into words | Very rarely true<br>1 | Not often true<br>2 | Sometimes true<br>3 | Often true<br>4 | Very often true<br>5 |
| 7 | Even when I'm feeling terribly upset, I can find a way to put it into words | Very rarely true<br>1 | Not often true<br>2 | Sometimes true<br>3 | Often true<br>4 | Very often true<br>5 |
| 8 | It's hard for me to find the words to describe what I'm thinking | Very rarely true<br>5 | Not often true<br>4 | Sometimes true<br>3 | Often true<br>2 | Very often true<br>1 |
| 9 | When I feel something in my body, it's hard for me to find the right words to describe it | Very rarely true<br>5 | Not often true<br>4 | Sometimes true<br>3 | Often true<br>2 | Very often true<br>1 |

---

*Acting with awareness*

| | | | | | |
|---|---|---|---|---|---|
| 10 | I find it difficult to stay focused on what's happening in the present moment | Very rarely true<br>5 | Not often true<br>4 | Sometimes true<br>3 | Often true<br>2 | Very often true<br>1 |
| 11 | It seems I am 'running on automatic' without much awareness of what I'm doing | Very rarely true<br>5 | Not often true<br>4 | Sometimes true<br>3 | Often true<br>2 | Very often true<br>1 |

| | *Acting with awareness* | | | | | |
|---|---|---|---|---|---|---|
| 12 | I rush through activities without being really attentive to them | Very rarely true 5 | Not often true 4 | Sometimes true 3 | Often true 2 | Very often true 1 |
| 13 | I do jobs or tasks automatically without being aware of what I'm doing | Very rarely true 5 | Not often true 4 | Sometimes true 3 | Often true 2 | Very often true 1 |
| 14 | I find myself doing things without paying attention | Very rarely true 5 | Not often true 4 | Sometimes true 3 | Often true 2 | Very often true 1 |
| | *Non-judging of inner experience* | | | | | |
| 15 | I tell myself that I shouldn't be feeling the way I'm feeling | Very rarely true 5 | Not often true 4 | Sometimes true 3 | Often true 2 | Very often true 1 |
| 16 | I make judgements about whether my thoughts are good or bad | Very rarely true 5 | Not often true 4 | Sometimes true 3 | Often true 2 | Very often true 1 |
| 17 | I tell myself I shouldn't be thinking the way I'm thinking | Very rarely true 5 | Not often true 4 | Sometimes true 3 | Often true 2 | Very often true 1 |
| 18 | I think some of my emotions are bad or inappropriate and I shouldn't feel them | Very rarely true 5 | Not often true 4 | Sometimes true 3 | Often true 2 | Very often true 1 |
| 19 | I disapprove of myself when I have illogical ideas | Very rarely true 5 | Not often true 4 | Sometimes true 3 | Often true 2 | Very often true 1 |
| | *Non-reactivity to inner experience* | | | | | |
| 20 | I watch my feelings without getting carried away by them | Very rarely true 1 | Not often true 2 | Sometimes true 3 | Often true 4 | Very often true 5 |
| 21 | When I have distressing thoughts or images, I don't let myself be carried away by them | Very rarely true 1 | Not often true 2 | Sometimes true 3 | Often true 4 | Very often true 5 |
| 22 | When I have distressing thoughts or images, I feel calm soon after | Very rarely true 1 | Not often true 2 | Sometimes true 3 | Often true 4 | Very often true 5 |
| 23 | Usually when I have distressing thoughts or images I can just notice them without reacting | Very rarely true 1 | Not often true 2 | Sometimes true 3 | Often true 4 | Very often true 5 |
| 24 | When I have distressing thoughts or images, I just notice them and let them go | Very rarely true 1 | Not often true 2 | Sometimes true 3 | Often true 4 | Very often true 5 |

**Note:** Adapted with permission of SAGE publications from: Bohlmeijer, E., ten Klooster, P., Fledderus, M., Veehof, M., & Baer., R. (2011). Psychometric properties of the five-facet mindfulness questionnaire in depressed adults and development of a short form. *Assessment, 18*(3), 308–320. Copyright © 2011 by American Psychological Association.

If you would like to experience greater mindfulness now, you may wish to try doing the raisin meditation in Box 6.2. In this 10-minute exercise, you eat three raisins mindfully. You focus all of your attention on holding, seeing, touching, smelling, tasting, chewing and swallowing the raisin. Then you write down in your journal how the experience of mindful eating differs from your normal experience of eating.

---

### Box 6.2  Raisin meditation

For this exercise, you will need a few raisins, your journal and a pen. Do this exercise in a quiet place where you will not be interrupted for 10 minutes. Switch off your phone, computer, radio, TV and other potential distractions. Sit comfortably. Read through all the instructions first, so you have an overview of the process. Then do the raisin meditation. The task is to eat three raisins in a mindful way. For each raisin, spend about 30 seconds on each stage.

'First we bring our attention to seeing one of the raisins, observing it carefully as if we had never seen one before.

We feel its texture between our fingers and notice its colours and surfaces.

We are also aware of any thoughts we might have about raisins or food in general. We note any thoughts and feelings of liking or disliking raisins if they come up while we are looking at it.

We then smell it for a while, and finally, with awareness, we bring it to our lips, being aware of the arm moving the hand to position it correctly, and salivating as the mind and body anticipate eating.

The process continues as we take it into our mouth and chew it slowly, experiencing the actual taste of one raisin.

And when we feel ready to swallow, we watch the impulse to swallow as it comes up, so that even that is experienced consciously.

We even imagine, or "sense", that now our bodies are one raisin heavier.

Then we do it again with another raisin. And then with a the third.'

Write down how paying so much conscious attention to eating three raisins affected what you saw, felt, smelled, tasted and experienced. How was the experience of eating mindfully different from your usual experience of eating?

---

When you have done the exercise, you will be aware that mindful eating is different from normal eating. In normal eating, we often don't fully notice how our food looks or feels or smells or tastes. We are distracted by doing other things. We are distracted by thinking about the past or the future. We are distracted by daydreaming. In contrast, in mindful eating, all of our immediate sensations are amplified. We fully experience the food we are eating. We notice how it feels, smells and tastes.

The raisin meditation highlights an important truth. When you don't act mindfully, you miss out on experiencing many positive sensations. Much of your life passes by unnoticed because you are distracted by thoughts of the past or the future. When you act mindfully, you pay full attention to your sensations in the present moment. You experience your life as it is unfolding moment by moment. Over the next week you may wish to take one activity like brushing your teeth, drinking a cup of coffee, taking out the rubbish or loading the washing machine and do it mindfully. You don't have to do it slowly, like the raisin meditation. The invitation is to simply be mindful of your sensory experiences as you do it. If you decide to do this, in your journal write down what your experiences are of doing one thing each day mindfully.

### Mindfulness meditation

To get into the habit of attending to our immediate experience of the present moment in our daily lives, we have to break old habits. We have to break the habit of always letting our attention wander to thinking about the past, analysing the present and planning the future. Regular practice of mindfulness meditation is a good way to do this. It trains us to bring full attention to everyday activities so that we can experience our lives as they are unfolding now in the present moment.

In developing a mindfulness meditation practice, we set aside one or two periods of about 15 minutes each day to focus attention on our immediate sensory experiences in the present moment. Most people find it best to meditate in the morning and the evening. To find out what this is like, you may wish to do the mindfulness of breath and body meditation in Box 6.3. In this exercise, and in all other meditation exercises in this chapter, select a quiet place where you will not be interrupted. Turn off your phone, computer, radio, TV and other distractions. In all sitting meditations, you may use a straight-back chair, or a meditation mat, cushion or bench. In the mindfulness of body and breath meditation, first focus attention on sensations in the body for a couple of minutes. Then shift attention to the abdominal wall as it rises and falls, as you breathe in and out. Breathing, which occurs automatically, is the anchor for attention in this meditation. When your mind wanders – as it will many, many times – you acknowledge where it has wandered and gently bring your attention back to the breath. By doing this meditation twice a day you are training your attention to focus on the breath in the present moment.

---

### Box 6.3   Mindfulness of the breath and body

When we practise the mindfulness of breath and body meditation we intentionally expand our attention from the breath to the whole body. Sit in a chair with feet flat on the floor, the spine straight and not resting against the chair back, and the eyes gently closed. Adopt an erect, dignified and comfortable posture.

1   Bring awareness to sensations in the lower abdominal wall as the breath moves in and out of the body. Follow with your awareness the changing physical sensations in the abdomen as the breath enters your body as you inhale, the slight pause

that may occur before you exhale, the sensations that occur as you exhale and the slight pause that may occur before you inhale again. There is no need to control your breathing. Just allow it to occur.

2    When you feel you have settled to some degree into feeling the breath moving in and out of your body, at the belly or at the nostrils, intentionally allow the field of awareness to expand around the breath to include a sense of the various sensations throughout the body, whatever they are, and a sense of the body as a whole sitting and breathing. You may even find you get a sense of the breath moving throughout the body.

3    If you choose, include together with this wider sense of the body as a whole, and of the breath moving in and out of the body, awareness of the more local particular patterns of physical sensations that arise where the body makes contact with the chair - the sensations of touch pressure, or contact of the feet with the floor, the buttocks with whatever is supporting them, the hands where they rest on the thighs or together in the lap. As best you can, hold all these sensations, together with the sense of the breath and of the body as a whole, in a wide and spacious awareness.

4    Of course, in all likelihood, you will find the mind wandering repeatedly away from the breath and body sensations. Keep in mind that this is a natural tendency of the mind and is in no way a mistake or a sign of a failure or 'not doing it right'. As we noted before, whenever you notice that your attention has drifted away from sensations in the body, you might want to let it register that to be aware of the fact, which means that you are already back and awake to what is going on in the mind. In that very moment it can be useful to gently note what was on your mind ('thinking', 'planning', 'remembering') and then to re-establish your attention on the breath sensations and your sense of the body as a whole.

5    As best you can, rest in a gentle attending to the actuality of the field of sensations throughout the body from moment to moment, being aware of any feelings of pleasantness, unpleasantness or neutrality as they arise.

6    The longer the session continues, the more you may experience sensations arising that are particularly intense in one region of your body or another, perhaps in the back of the knees or in the shoulders. With greater intensity of sensations, especially if they feel unpleasant and uncomfortable, you may find that your attention is repeatedly drawn to them and away from your intended focus on the breath or the body as a whole. In such moments rather than shifting your posture (although you are always free to do that, of course), you might experiment even briefly with intentionally bringing the focus of attention right into the region of greatest intensity, as best you can, exploring with gentle and wise attention the detailed pattern of sensations you discover there - what, precisely, are the qualities of these sensations; where, exactly are they located; do they vary over time or shift around in the body from one place to another? This exploration is undertaken in the realm of sensing and feeling, rather than through thinking. Again, as best you

can, be open to feeling whatever is already here to be felt, allowing yourself to know what you are feeling via directly experiencing it. As in the body scan, you may play with using the breath as a vehicle to carry awareness into these regions of intensity, by 'breathing in' to them, and out of them.

7    Whenever you find yourself 'carried away' by the intensity of physical sensations, or in any other way, reconnect with the here and now by refocusing attention on the movements of the breath or on a sense of the body as a whole sitting in a balanced and dignified posture, even in the midst of the intensity of sensation, grounded in the present moment. Notice how much we create 'pain' out of discomfort through the thoughts we have about it and especially our thoughts about how long it is going to last.

**Note:** Points 2-7 are republished with permission of Guilford Publications from *The mindful way through depression* (pp. 130-131) by Williams M., Teasdale, J., Segal, Z. & Kabat-Zinn, J., copyright © 2007 by Guilford, permission conveyed through Copyright Clearance Centre, Inc.

In mindfulness meditation we accept that negative, positive and neutral thoughts will enter our minds and distract our attention away from our focus on immediate sensory experiences, from the breath or the body. Each time this happens we gently bring our attention back to our immediate sensory experience. We learn to acknowledge that the thoughts that distract us from our immediate sensory experience will stay briefly and then dissolve. We learn to avoid becoming embroiled in trying to change them, judge them or stop them. We simply acknowledge that they are occurring. We suspend attempts to look to the past for guidance on how to solve problems in the present and plan for the future. When we do this, an extraordinary thing may happen. We experience a sense of peace and well-being.

## The being mode and the doing mode

When we practise mindfulness, we move out of the doing mode, into the being mode.[13] In the being mode, we focus on being aware of our immediate sensory experiences. In the doing mode we are concerned primarily with doing things including analytical thinking, judging, trawling the past and planning the future in search of solutions. When we are in the doing mode we over-think, over-analyse, over-judge. When we are practising mindfulness, we don't use language as an intermediary between ourselves and the world. Rather, we experience the world directly through our senses. We feel the wind blowing through our hair. We hear the sound of waves breaking on the shore. We see seagulls circling in the clear blue sky. We smell the salt sea air. In mindfulness meditation, we experience the world directly, by attending to our sensory experiences. The passage of the breath as we inhale and exhale. The feelings in our bodies. These experiences also include observing thoughts entering our minds, staying for a while and then dissolving.

When we practise mindfulness, we do not completely give up the doing mode. We do not give up solving problems and finding solutions. Rather we suspend the impulse to do this as the first and only course of action when we experience difficult feelings. We take time and create space to be in in the world, to be aware, to be compassionate towards ourselves (rather than self-critical), to tolerate some distress and in time to find the best solution.

It's not the case that the doing mode is all bad, and the being mode or mindfulness is all good. The doing mode is very adaptive for solving many of life's problems. It helps us to bring the lessons of past experience to bear on present problems. It also helps us to develop automatic skills and routines. These free up spare mental capacity so we can do more complex and creative things. The doing mode is useful for solving *external* problems, from boiling an egg, to putting a man on the moon. However, the doing mode becomes maladaptive when we try to use it to solve *internal* problems, such as having distressing emotions. When we use the doing mode to try to solve problems like feeling a bit sad, we end up going over and over the problem of how to improve our mood in our minds. This rumination makes us feel worse. At these times, we need to shift gear from the doing to the being mode. The following are seven of the main characteristics of the doing and being modes.

## Conscious choice vs. automatic pilot

If we live predominantly in the doing mode, we end up spending much of our lives running on automatic pilot. We are goal-focused, continually trying to close the gap between where we are now and where we want to be. We do things without consciously choosing to do them and without being aware that we are doing them. There is a risk that we may miss much of our lives, if we live enslaved by the doing mode. In the being mode, we become mindful of what we are doing, and so our actions become based on choices we make rather than automatic habits. This prevents us from spending too much time striving for big goals that it might be wiser to let go of for a time. This gives us a sense of liberation and freedom. We may feel like we are seeing everything for the first time, with a sense of wonder.

## Waking up to the world vs. living in the head

In the doing mode, we focus on *ideas* about the world, rather than our immediate *sensations* of being in the world. In the doing mode we think about goals. We think about how to achieve them by analysing current situations, recalling similar past events and planning future strategies. This forces us to 'live inside our heads' instead of experiencing the world directly. In the being mode we are mindful not of *ideas*, but of immediate *sensations*. We 'wake up'. We see, hear, touch, smell and taste things as if for the first time. This experience of living in the world of sensations rather than in a world of ideas has an immediate effect on our well-being. (We will come back to the idea of savouring pleasurable sensations in Chapter 7.)

## Acceptance vs. striving for perfection

In the doing mode we continually make judgements. We compare the world as it is with the world as we would like it to be. Attention becomes narrowed to the gap between these two states. There is a continual perfectionistic striving to narrow this gap. In contrast, in the being mode, there is a temporary suspension of judgement. There is an acceptance of the world as it is now, in this moment. This position of mindful radical acceptance allows us to compassionately observe and experience rather than judge our current situation. It helps us to suspend knee-jerk 'emergency' emotional reactions. It prevents or slows downward spirals of negative self-judgements and negative emotions. This in turn creates space for choosing the best way to deal with distressing feelings and situations.

### Thoughts as mental events vs. thoughts as facts

In the doing mode, thoughts are seen as facts or reflections of reality. This is useful for solving some sorts of problems; for example, getting groceries. You make a list, get your credit card and head off to the supermarket. You do not question the reality of items on the list, the credit available to you on your card or the location of the supermarket. You operate as if these ideas were all facts. However, if you're stressed, seeing thoughts as facts can make you even more stressed. If when you're stressed you say to yourself 'I can't cope', your mood will drop. You may then make very harsh self-critical judgements like 'I'm weak. I'm no good. No one will ever like me. I'll be lonely forever'. If you assume that these thoughts are facts, rather than transient mental events, then they will force your mood to drop even further. In the being mode, we mindfully observe these sorts of thoughts, watching them arise, linger and dissolve in the mind. We see that they are mental events and not facts. They are not reality. They are not a true reflection of who we are in our entirety. They are simply a commentary or 'one take' on how the self and the world looks from one perspective at this moment in the changing river of life.

### Approach vs. avoidance

In the doing mode, we solve problems by pursuing goals, and actively avoid going in directions contrary to goals. This is helpful when solving *external* problems; for example, when travelling from Dublin to Moscow we head east, and avoid heading west towards New York or south towards Madrid. The doing mode has the paradoxical effect of making us more distressed if we use it to try to solve *internal* problems like stress or low mood. The doing mode makes us actively avoid negative emotions. For example, we may tell ourselves to cheer up, and stop feeling so down. Unfortunately suppressing negative emotions inevitably leads to a rebound effect. (Remember the white bear effect mentioned earlier.[12]) So, we experience more negative emotions, despite efforts to cheer ourselves up. This may lead us to make negative self-judgements like 'I shouldn't be feeling this. I'm so weak. My efforts are hopeless'. These self-critical judgements in turn make us experience more negative emotions. In contrast, in the being mode we turn towards and approach distressing emotions. We are curious about them. We acknowledge them mindfully and compassionately. This gradually weakens them, and gives us hope that things can improve.

### Living in the present vs. mental time travel

In the doing mode, we use our memory of how we solved problems in the past, and our planning or forecasting ability to anticipate how things will unfold in the future. This helps us solve a lot of life's *external* problems, like what to do when our car breaks down. We know a useful solution is to contact the Automobile Association. They will send a mechanic to help within an hour, because that's what happened the last time. With *internal* problems like stress and negative emotions, the doing mode is less useful. This is because our past memories and future forecasts are biased by our moods. If we are stressed, we only remember our failures and have difficulty recalling our successes. If we think of the future, when stressed, we tend to be pessimistic. We anticipate disaster. There is a further problem with using the doing mode to solve internal problems. Because we view our thoughts as permanent facts rather than transient mental events, we re-live our recollections of past failures and re-experience the distress that goes with this. We also pre-live anticipated catastrophes and the distress that these will cause us. That is, the doing mode condemns us to mental time travel! Mindfulness meditation trains us to live in the present moment, in the being mode where we don't engage in mental time travel. We see our memories and forecasts as transient mental events constructed by the mind, not permanent solid facts. This means that we do not have to experience the extra distress that comes from re-living past failures and pre-living antici-pated disasters.

### Nourishing vs. depleting activities

We can become trapped in the doing mode by efforts to achieve important career goals, and life goals, such as child care or looking after elderly relatives. These goals are important. They can also be very demanding. Because of this, we may spend much of our time pursuing them. This may leave little time for activities that nourish us, such as pastimes, hobbies and spending time with friends. Eventually, this can lead to exhaustion and burnout. Mindfulness and the being mode can help us restore balance to our lives. It can help us acknowledge activ-ities that nourish us and those that deplete us. It can help us acknowledge when we need to take time to nourish ourselves. It can also help us have the courage to do so.

In summary, the being and doing modes differ along these seven dimensions:

- Conscious choice vs. automatic pilot
- Waking up to the world vs. living in the head
- Acceptance vs. striving for perfection
- Thoughts as mental events vs. thoughts as facts
- Approach vs. avoidance
- Living in the present vs. mental time travel
- Nourishing vs. depleting activities

When you regularly practise mindfulness meditation exercises, like those described in this chapter, and then become more mindful in your daily activities, your life will change. You will gradually find that you can distinguish between whether you are in the doing or the being mode. You will become aware that while the doing mode is useful for solving problems in the external world, the being mode is the most helpful way to address internal problems like experiencing distress. You will begin to shift away from total immersion in the doing mode, and move towards more frequent engagement in the being mode. Regular mindful practice allows you to experience the world in your daily life directly and calmly. It helps you make conscious choices based on an awareness of what you are experiencing rather than running on auto-pilot most of the time. You will find that you are more aware of the world, and live less in your head. Mindfulness allows you to see your thoughts, memories and plans, not as permanent solid facts, but as ephemeral mental events. This means that you are less likely to react with strong negative emotions to unpleasant memories or forecasts as if they were real events. Mindfulness makes you less enslaved by striving to achieve things based on judgemental comparisons between yourself as you are, and as you imagine you should be. This gives you greater freedom to choose to balance the amount of time you spend doing nourishing activities and the amount of time you spend doing activities that deplete you. Accepting your immediate experience is liberating. However, it does not mean accepting unacceptable situations or being lazy. Mindfulness allows you to accept and tolerate your own difficult and unpleasant emotions with compassion. This, in turn, helps you to have greater empathy and compassion for others.

## Introducing mindfulness into your life

There is an invitation now for you to introduce mindfulness into your life. If you wish to do this, set aside two periods of 15–20 minutes a day for eight weeks to do this programme. The programme is based on that developed by Mark Williams[10] which in turn is based on MBSR[6] and MBCT[7] mentioned earlier. Arrange a quiet place where you will not be interrupted by phones, computers or well-meaning people. Make sure your meditation space is warm enough, but not so warm that it makes you drowsy. You will also need a mat to lie on, a straight-back chair, a cushion or bench for sitting meditations, and your journal. For each of the exercises, read the instructions through carefully before doing the exercise. Then follow the instructions from memory without referring to them during the exercise if possible. Of course, if you have to refer to them, that is OK. Alternatively, you can listen to some of the exercises online. There are online links for some exercises at the end of the chapter. Eventually you will be able to do all the exercises from memory. Although the instructions are detailed, the most important thing is to follow the 'spirit' rather than the detailed 'letter' of the instructions.

Introducing mindfulness into your life involves making a commitment. Often, we are only prepared to make a commitment if we can be clear on the benefits of doing so. In the opening sections of this chapter, you have read about research findings on the benefits of meditation. However, the most important benefits of mindfulness meditation are experiential and difficult to express in words. So, you will not know the benefits until you have practised for a while. Making a commitment to practise meditation twice a day may be challenging because you live a busy life, where there is little time for new commitments, or because it will involve disrupting your daily routines. You may wish to think about how you could make space for regular mindfulness practice in your life. You may wish to rise a little earlier in the morning, and go to bed a little earlier in the evening.

When you have made a commitment to mindfulness practice, from time to time you may become critical of the difficulty you have in focusing on your immediate sensations – the breath and the body – and the tendency of your mind to wander. When the mind wanders again and again, this is perfectly normal. It's in the nature of minds to wander. Each time the mind wanders and you gently and firmly bring your attention back to the breath, or the sensations in the body, you are learning something very important. You are learning that the thoughts of the mind are like waves on the sea, or the clouds in the sky. They come again and again without end. It is not a question of trying to stop them, so the mind goes blank. Rather, it is a question of observing them arising, lingering and dissolving in the vast open space of awareness. This wider space of awareness is calmer, wiser and more compassionate than thinking or analysing, judging or comparing, ruminating or worrying, daydreaming or planning. So, when the mind wanders, this is not a cause for self-criticism. It is an opportunity to learn about the mind. It is an opportunity to learn how to gently and firmly guide attention back to the breath or the body. It is an opportunity to observe thoughts passing across the vast space of awareness, without becoming caught up in the story these thoughts are telling.

### Week 1

In your busy life, you may find that much of the time you run on automatic pilot. For example, you may find that while you are walking or driving or eating, you are also planning one or two things, and going over a few things that recently happened. The way you run on auto-pilot when driving, eating, planning supermarket shopping and so forth reflects habits you have developed over the years. If the mind were a computer, running on auto-pilot is a bit like having a lot of programmes running all at once. Just as running many programmes at the same time causes a computer to slow down and eventually crash, so running on auto-pilot reduces the efficiency of the mind and causes us to experience stress. Mindfulness meditation is a way of going back to basics. Close down all programmes except one – focusing on the present moment. Paradoxically you don't do this by trying to screen out or suppress all the chatter of the mind. Rather, you open your awareness to it. When you do this, you become free to make choices, rather than to be driven by automatic habits. The only way to truly know this is to practise mindfulness.

In the first week of this programme the mindfulness of breath body meditation in Box 6.3 is practised twice each day for 15 minutes. In this meditation, you focus your attention initially on the body and then on the breath. You also learn how to respond to mind-wandering by bringing attention back, again and again, to focus on the breath entering and leaving the body.

The breath is an excellent target to anchor attention in the present moment. Evolution has ensured that breathing occurs automatically, because it is essential for survival. The breath is always entering and leaving the body. You cannot forget to breathe if the mind wanders. However, if the mind wanders you can bring it back to the unchanging constant rhythm of the breath. Also, the breath is a useful indicator for feelings. You can tell a lot about the way you are feeling by paying attention to the way you are breathing.

As well as practising mindfulness of body and breath twice each day for 15 minutes, in the first week of the programme there are two things you may do to bring mindfulness into your day-to-day life. This will help you to break habits that tie you into auto-pilot. If you wish, select a routine activity like brushing your teeth, showering, drinking coffee, taking out the rubbish, loading the dryer or walking from one room to another. Do the activity each day mindfully. That is, slow the activity down and focus fully on the sensations you experience moment by moment as you do it. To break the automatic habit, during the first week of the programme you may make a conscious choice to sit in a different chair or in a different way in the same chair you usually sit in at home, or work, or in a café. Notice how your perspective can change by changing chairs.

### Week 2

In the second week of the programme the body scan meditation in Box 6.3 is practised twice a day for 15 minutes. When engaged in this meditation we focus attention on one region of the body at a time, holding it in awareness for a while before progressing to the next region. In the body scan, we welcome into awareness all bodily sensations – whether they are pleasant, unpleasant or neutral. We do this in a spirit of non-judgemental friendly curiosity.

The body scan meditation takes account of the fact that our bodies and minds are intimately connected. What we think and the emotions we feel affect our bodies. For extreme emotions, the relationship between the body and the mind is very obvious to us. If we are very frightened or angry, we feel our bodies tensing up. If we are extremely sad, we cry and feel a weight on our shoulders. If we are happy, we feel light. However, most of us are unaware of the subtle connection between the mild emotional fluctuations that continually occur in our minds and how these are registered in the body. For example, Barry frequently found that when he finished work after a long stressful day his shoulders were sore. However, he did not notice the gradual process through which the tension accumulated – moment by moment - in his shoulder muscles over the course of the day. He only became aware of it at the end of the day, when the muscle tension had become painful. Linda often found that on mornings when her children were at home and she tried to do housework, by lunchtime she had a pounding headache. Like Barry, she only noticed the tension in her body when her head began to hurt quite badly. Most of us, like Barry and Linda, spend a lot of time ignoring bodily sensations, until they become quite extreme. In the doing mode, discussed earlier, we avoid or suppress mild unpleasant bodily sensations. This is unfortunate because it cuts us off from experiences that can potentially improve our well-being. The body is a very sensitive barometer for detecting subtle changes in our emotional state. In fact, often signs of sadness, anxiety and stress register in the body before we are fully aware of them. The body scan meditation helps us to tune in to these early warning sensations, and become mindful of them. One effect of this is that it makes unpleasant bodily sensations become more tolerable. Another is that it helps you become more mindful of your bodily sensations, moment by moment, in your day-to-day life. This will help you appreciate the difference between thinking about sensations and actually experiencing sensations.

As with all meditation exercise, you will find that during the body scan your mind will wander, thinking about the past, planning the future or daydreaming. You may become bored, restless or drowsy. You may judge yourself harshly for not being able to mediate properly, become frustrated and notice tension in your body. You may find yourself avoiding focusing on a part of the body that you do not particularly like, or ruminating about how much you don't like it. You may find it difficult to tune in to any sensations at all in some regions of your body. All of these experiences are normal. Training your attention is like training a muscle you have not used much. It requires daily practice. When you are doing the body scan meditation, mind-wandering, judgement, boredom, frustration and body tension are all opportunities to train your attention to focus awareness non-judgementally and with compassion on body regions.

The main exercise in the second week of the programme is practising the body scan exercise in Box 6.4 twice a day for 15 minutes. As with the first week of this programme, if you wish, select another routine activity and do it each day mindfully. That is, slow the activity down and focus fully on the sensations you experience moment by moment as you do it. During the second week of the programme you may take a mindful 15-minute walk, not rushing from one place to another, but walking so as to be mindful of what you see, hear, feel and smell, as if for the first time. Once a day, you may count on your fingers 10 things you are grateful for. When these things recur in your life, pause for a moment and mindfully notice your bodily sensations, your emotions and your thoughts. (Gratitude is discussed in detail in Chapter 8.)

---

### Box 6.4   Body scan meditation

'1   Lie down on your back on a mat in a comfortable place, such as on a foam mat or pad on the floor or on your bed. Keep in mind from the very beginning that in this lying down practice, the intention is to "fall awake" rather than to fall asleep. Make sure that you will be warm enough. You might want to cover yourself with a blanket or do it in a sleeping bag if the room is cold.

2   Allow your eyes to gently close. But if and when you find any drowsiness creeping it, feel free to open your eyes and continue with them open.

3   Gently let your attention settle on your abdomen, feeling the rising and falling of your belly with each inbreath and each outbreath; in other words "riding the waves" of your own breathing with full awareness for the full duration of each inbreath and the full duration of each outbreath.

4   Take a few moments to feel your body as a whole, from head to toe; the "envelope" of your skin; the sensations associated with touch in the places you are in contact with - the floor or the bed.

5   Bring your attention to the toes of the left foot. As you direct your attention to them, see if you can direct or channel your breathing to them as well, so that it feels as if you are breathing in *to* your toes and out *from* your toes. It may take a while to get the hang of this so that it doesn't feel effortful or contrived. It may help to imagine your breath travelling down the body from the nose into the lungs and continuing through the torso and down the left leg all the way to the toes, and then back again and out through the nose. Actually, the breath does take this and every other route in the body through the blood stream.

6   Allow yourself to *feel* any and all sensations from your toes, perhaps distinguishing between them and watching the flux of sensations in this region. If you don't feel anything at the moment, that is fine too. Just allow yourself to feel "not feeling anything".

7   When you are ready to leave the toes and move on, take a deeper, more intentional breath in all the way down to the toes and, on an outbreath, allow them to "dissolve" in your mind's eye. Stay with your breathing for a few breaths at least, and then move on in turn to the sole of the foot, the heel, the top of the foot and then the ankle, continuing to breathe in *to* and out *from* each region as you observe the sensations that you are experiencing, and then letting go of that region and moving on.

8  Bring your mind back to the breath and to the region you are focusing on each time you notice your attention has wandered off, after first taking note of what has carried you away in the first place or what is on your mind when you realise it has wandered away from the focus on the body.

9  In this way, continue moving slowly up your left leg and through the rest of your body as you maintain the focus on the breath and on the sensations within the individual regions as you come to them, breathe with them and let go of them.'

Continue to bring awareness to the physical sensations in each part of your body in turn – to your left toes, foot, ankle, calf, shin, knee, thigh; your pelvic area, groin, genitals, buttocks and hips; your lower back and abdomen; and your upper back, chest and shoulders. From the shoulders, move to the hands, doing them both at the same time. Start from the tips of the fingers and thumbs and move to the palms, backs of the hands, wrists, forearms, elbows, upper arms and shoulders again. Then move in to the neck; the face (jaw, mouth, lips, nose, cheeks, ears, eyes, forehead); and then the whole head.

10  Practise the body scan at least once a day. Again, it helps to use online guidance (www.youtube.com/watch?v=15q-N-_kkrU) in the beginning stages of your practice so that the pace is slow enough, and to help you remember the instructions and their tonal quality accurately.

**Note:** The section in quotation marks is republished with permission of Bantam Books, an imprint of Random House, a division of Penguin Random House LLC, and of Little, Brown/Piatkus from *Full catastrophe living (Revised edition)* (pp. 95–97) by Jon Kabat-Zinn, copyright © 2013 by Jon Kabat-Zinn. All rights reserved.

### Week 3

In the third week of the programme the mindfulness of movement meditation in Box 6.5 followed by the mindfulness of breath and body mediation in Box 6.3 are practised twice a day for 15 to 20 minutes. The mindfulness of movement meditation involves doing a series of simple stretching exercises in a slow mindful way to re-align muscles and joints and release stress that may build up during daily life. It is important not to push beyond the body's limits so as to cause discomfort or pain when doing these exercises. On the other hand, it is important not to be too cautious and not stretch muscles to a comfortable limit. If back problems or other medical conditions make you doubtful about the safety of these exercises, consult your physician. As you engage in these exercises, focus attention on the sensations you experience in your body. Explore these sensations so that you may discover where you carry tension in your body and the limits of your body's ability to stretch comfortably. Notice that it's possible to do these stretches without striving to exceed your limits.

### Box 6.5   Mindfulness of movement

1  First stand in bare feet or socks with your feet about hips' width apart, with the knees unlocked so that the legs can bend slightly and with the feet parallel (it's actually unusual to stand with the feet like this, and this, itself, can generate some novel body sensations).

2   Next remind yourself of the intention of this practice: to become aware, as best you can, of physical sensations and feelings throughout the body as you engage in a series of gentle stretches, honouring and investigating the limitations of your body in any and every movement as best you can, letting go of any tendency to push beyond your limits or compete with either yourself or others.

3   Then, on an inbreath, slowly and mindfully raise your arms out to the sides, parallel to the floor, and then, after breathing out, continue on the next inbreath raising them, slowly and mindfully, until the hands meet above your head, all the while perhaps feeling the tension in the muscles as they work to lift the arms and then maintain them in the stretch.

4   Then let the breath move in and out freely at its own pace, continue to stretch upward, the fingertips gently pushing towards the sky, feet firmly grounded on the floor, as you feel the stretch in the muscles and joints of the body all the way from the feet and legs up through the back, shoulders, into the arms, and hands and fingers.

5   Maintain this stretch for a time, breathing freely in and out, noticing any changes in the sensations and feelings in the body with the breath as you continue to hold the stretch. Of course, this might include a sense of increasing tension or discomfort, and if so, be open to that as well.

6   At a certain point, when you are ready, slowly, very slowly, on an outbreath, allow the arms to come back down. Lower them slowly, with the wrists bent so that the fingers point upward and the palms are pushing outward (again an unusual position) until the arms come back to rest along the sides, hanging from the shoulders.

7   Allow the eyes to close gently and focus attention on the movements of the breath and the sensations and feelings throughout the body as you stand there, perhaps noticing the contrast in the physical sense of release (and often relief) associated with returning to a neutral stance.

8   Continue now by mindfully stretching up each arm and hand in turn, as if picking from a tree fruit that is just out of reach, with full awareness of the sensations throughout the body, and of the breath; see what happens to the extension of the hand and to the breath if you lift the opposite heel off the floor while stretching up.

9   After this sequence, slowly and mindfully raise both arms up high, keeping them parallel to each other, then allow the body to bend over as a whole to the left, forming a big curve that extends sideways from the feet right though the torso, the arms, and the hands and fingers. Then come back up to standing on an inbreath, and then on an outbreath, slowly bend over, forming a curve in the opposite direction.

10  Once you have returned to standing in a neutral position with arms alongside the body, you can play with rolling the shoulders while letting the arms dangle passively, first raising the shoulders upward towards the ears as far as they will go, then backward, as if you were attempting to draw your shoulder blades together, then letting them drop down completely, then squeezing the shoulders

together in front of the body as far as they will go, as if trying to touch them together with the arms passive and dangling all the while, first in one direction, and then in the opposite direction, in a forward and backward 'rowing' motion.

11    Then, once you have rested in a neutral standing posture again, play with slowly and mindfully rolling the head around, to whatever degree you feel comfortable, and very gently as if drawing a circle with the nose in midair, allow the circling to move gently in one direction and then the other.

12    And finally, at the end of this sequence of movements, remain still for a while in a standing posture, and tune in to the sensations from the body.

**Note:** Adapted and republished with permission of Guilford Publications from *Mindfulness-based cognitive therapy for depression* (second edition, pp. 201-202), by Segal, Z., Williams M., & Teasdale, J., copyright © 2013 by Guilford, permission conveyed through Copyright Clearance Centre, Inc.

In the mindfulness of breath and body meditation, which is conducted after the mindfulness of movement meditation, initially attention is focused on breathing, and then attention is expanded to hold sensations from the whole body in the spotlight of awareness.

One of the challenges of living mindfully is to transport the skills learned in the quiet of the meditation space into the hurly-burly of day-to-day living. The three-minute breathing space in Box 6.6 provides a bridge between the meditation exercises you practise each morning and evening, and being mindful in everyday life. This very brief exercise allows you to be mindful when you are under pressure, distressed, angry, anxious or sad. During the third week of this programme, if you wish, practise the three-minute breathing space meditation twice a day.

## Box 6.6    Three-minute breathing space

**Step 1. Become aware**

Begin by deliberately adopting an erect and dignified posture, whether you are sitting or standing. If possible, close your eyes. Then, bringing your awareness to your inner experience, ask: what is my experience right now?

- What *thoughts* are going through the mind? As best you can, acknowledge thoughts as mental events, perhaps putting them into words.
- What *feelings* are here? Turn towards any sense of emotional discomfort or unpleasant feelings, acknowledging their presence.
- What *body sensations* are here? Perhaps quickly scan the body to pick up any sensations of tightness or bracing.

**Step 2. Gathering**

Then redirect your attention to focus on the physical sensations of the breath breathing itself.

Move in close to the sense of the breath in the belly . . . feeling the sensations of the belly wall expanding as the breath comes in . . . and falling back as the breath goes out.

Follow the breath all the way in and all the way out, using the breathing to anchor yourself into the present.

**Step 3. Expanding**

Now expand the field of your awareness around your breathing, so that, in addition to the sensations of the breath, it includes a sense of the body as a whole, your posture and your facial expression.

If you become aware of any sensations of discomfort, tension or resistance, zero in on them by breathing into them on each inbreath and breathing out of them on each outbreath, as you soften and open.

If you want you might say to yourself on the outbreath,

*'It's okay, whatever it is, it's already here: let me feel it.'*

As best you can, bring this expanded awareness into the next moments of your day.

**Note:** Adapted and republished with permission of Guilford Publications from *The mindful way through depression* (pp. 183–184) by Williams M., Teasdale, J., Segal, Z. & Kabat-Zinn, J., copyright © 2007 by Guilford, permission conveyed through Copyright Clearance Centre, Inc.

To break the habit of automatically watching television, one programme after another, you may do this exercise if you wish. On one day during week three, carefully select a couple of programmes that really interest you and watch these in a focused way. Pay attention to them in detail. As soon as each of these programmes is over, turn off the TV and don't watch any other programmes. When not watching TV, do something else. Read a book. Go for a walk. Phone a friend. Practise one of the meditation exercises. If you wish, write down in your journal positive things that you noticed were different about only watching the programmes that you consciously chose to watch. How did this process make you feel?

## Week 4

In week 4 a central idea is that it is not events in the world that make us feel distress, but the thoughts we have about these events. We mistake these thoughts for facts, and react to them as if they were true.

For example, on a busy Saturday morning, Sue saw her friend Anne walking down Grafton Street in Dublin on the opposite side to her. Sue waved and called out 'hello', but Anne did not respond. Sue felt sad. If we asked Sue why she was sad, she would have said, 'Because my good friend Anne just ignored me'.

Let's do an ABC analysis of this situation. That is, let's look at the

- **A**ntecedent events,
- **B**eliefs or thoughts about these events and
- **C**onsequences for mood, bodily sensations and behaviour.

The A or antecedent event was Anne not responding to Sue waving and saying 'hello'. The B or beliefs and thoughts about the situation that flitted through Sue's mind, and of which she was barely aware, were: 'Anne didn't respond to me because she was purposely ignoring me. She probably doesn't like me. This always happens to me. People don't like me'. The C or consequence of these beliefs and thoughts was that Sue felt sad, tearful and experienced a drop in her energy, so walked with a defeated posture. (ABC analysis is discussed in more detail in Chapter 9 on optimism. It was developed within cognitive behaviour therapy. Martin Seligman incorporated it into positive psychology in his book, *Learned Optimism*.[14])

Let us continue with Anne's journey. As she approached the bottom of Grafton Street, near Trinity College, Cathy also saw Anne and waved to her. Once again, Anne did not respond. Cathy felt concerned. If we asked Cathy why she felt concerned, she would have said 'Because my good friend Anne was so pre-occupied'.

Let's do another ABC analysis. The A or antecedent event was Anne not responding to Cathy waving. The B in this ABC analysis – Cathy's beliefs and thoughts about the situation – were: 'Anne didn't respond to me because she was pre-occupied. I hope she's not in trouble. I want to be there for her'. The C or consequence of these beliefs and thoughts in this ABC analysis was that Cathy felt anxious and an urge to phone Anne to ask if she was OK.

The situations that Cathy and Sue found themselves in were almost identical. Their reactions, however, were very different. Sue felt sad. Cathy felt anxious. It was not the antecedent situations (A) that led to their reactions (C), but their beliefs and thoughts (B) about these situations.

Furthermore, Sue and Cathy believed it was Anne's behaviour (A) that caused them to feel sad and concerned. They were not aware that it was their beliefs and thoughts about the situation (B) that actually led to these emotions. They mistook their *beliefs and thoughts* about Anne's behaviour for *facts*. They were not aware that they were making this mistake.

Most of us make this mistake, especially when we are stressed. We take the view that our thoughts about the world (B) are facts (A), when actually they are no more than a commentary on the world. This is partly because our beliefs and thoughts about the world race through our minds so quickly, and often with such force when we are stressed, that it's difficult to notice that they are just *thoughts* about situations, and not *facts*.

Here are some common thoughts that people have when stressed, and to which they respond as if they were facts: 'I have to keep at it or something terrible will happen. I can't fail. I must get it perfect. I can't ask for help. I'm no good. No one likes me. They are doing this to make my life difficult. I could punch them, they make me so angry. If I don't escape, I'll go crazy'. Some of these may be familiar to you. We all have these sorts of thoughts when we are stressed, and respond to them as if they were facts.

Let's conclude the story about Anne. On that particular Saturday, she was engrossed in her favourite current affairs radio programme as she walked down Grafton Street. She was listening to the programme through small, unobtrusive earphones. Neither Sue nor Cathy noticed the earphones. Anne did not notice her friends calling out and waving to her. These are the facts of the situation. Sue and Cathy did not respond to the facts. They responded to their thoughts about the situation as if they were facts.

Usually we experience distress when we respond to our thoughts as if they were facts. Mindfulness meditation helps us to recognise that our thoughts are just transient commentaries on reality that pass through the mind. In week 4 of this mindfulness programme we learn that sounds are to the ear as thoughts are to the mind. We learn this by doing the mindfulness of sounds and thoughts exercise in Box 6.7 for about 10 minutes each day for a week. In this meditation, we focus for the first few minutes on the sounds we hear as we sit and meditate. We focus on the continual soundscape of the world around us. Then after a time, we shift the spotlight of attention to the stream of thoughts that pass through the mind. We notice that sounds arise, we hear them with the ears, and then they pass. In a similar way, thoughts arise, we become aware of them in the mind and then they pass. The soundscape in the world around us is similar to the thought stream passing through the mind.

---

## Box 6.7  Mindfulness of sounds and thoughts

1   When we practise the mindfulness of sounds and thoughts, we learn that sounds arise in the air, we hear them for as long as they last and then they and dissipate. In a similar manner, thoughts arise in the mind, remain briefly and then dissolve. Sit in a chair with feet flat on the floor, the spine straight and not resting against the chair back, and the eyes gently closed. Adopt an erect, dignified and comfortable posture. Bring awareness to sensations in the lower abdominal wall as the breath moves in and out of the body, until you feel settled. Then expand your attention to take in the entire body as if the whole body were breathing. This will help you to be aware of all the sensations in the interior landscape of the body. Spend a few minutes practising mindfulness of the breath and body in this way. Remember that in the practice that follows you can always return to the breath and body to anchor yourself if your mind becomes distracted or overwhelmed.

2   Allow the focus of your awareness to shift from sensations in the body to hearing. Bring your attention to the ears and then allow awareness to open and expand, so that there is a receptiveness to sounds as they arise, wherever they arise.

3   There is no need to go searching for sounds, or listening for particular sounds. Instead, as best you can, simply open your awareness so that it is receptive to sounds from all directions as they arise - sounds that are close, sounds that are far away, sounds that are in front, behind, to the side, above or below. Open to a whole space of sound around you. Be aware of obvious sounds and of more subtle sounds, aware of the space between sounds, aware of silence.

4   As best you can, be aware of sounds simply as raw sensations. When you find that you are thinking *about* the sounds, reconnect, as best you can, with direct awareness of their sensory qualities (patterns of pitch, timbre, loudness and duration) rather than their meanings or implications.

5   Whenever you notice that your awareness is no longer focused on sounds in the moment, gently acknowledge where the mind has moved to, and then return the awareness back to sounds as they arise and pass away, from one moment to the next.

6   Mindfulness of sound can be a very valuable practice on its own, as a way of expanding awareness and giving it a more open, spacious, quality, whether or not the practice is preceded by awareness of body sensations, or followed, as here, by awareness of thoughts.

7   When you are ready, let go of awareness of sounds and refocus your attention, so that your objects of awareness are now thoughts as events in the mind. Just

as with sounds, you focused awareness on whatever sounds arose, noticing them arise, develop and pass away, so now, as best you can, bring awareness to thoughts that arise in the mind in just the same way – noticing when they arise, focusing awareness on them as they pass through the space of the mind and eventually disappear. There is no need to try to make thoughts come and go. Just let them arise naturally, in the same way that you related to sounds arising and passing away.

8   Some people find it helpful to bring awareness to thoughts in the mind in the same way they might if the thoughts were projected on the screen at the cinema. You sit, watching the screen, waiting for a thought or image to arise. When it does, you pay attention to it so long as it is there 'on the screen', and then you let it go as it passes away. Alternatively, you might find it helpful to see thoughts as clouds moving across a vast, spacious sky, or as leaves moving on a stream, carried by the current.

9   If any thoughts bring with them intense feelings or emotions, pleasant or unpleasant, as best you can, note their 'emotional charge' and intensity, and let them be as they already are.

10   If at any time you feel that your mind has become unfocused and scattered, or if it keeps getting repeatedly drawn into the drama of your thinking and imaginings, you may like to notice where this is affecting your body. Often, when we don't like what is happening, we feel a sense of contraction or tightness in the face, shoulders or torso, and a sense of wanting to 'push away' our thoughts and feelings. See if you notice any of this going on for you when some intense feelings arise. Then, once you have noticed this, see if it is possible to come back to the breath and a sense of the body as a whole, sitting and breathing, and use this focus to anchor and stabilise your awareness.

11   At a certain point, you might like to explore the possibility of letting go of any particular object of attention, like the breath, or class of objects of attention, like sounds or thoughts, and let the field of awareness be open to whatever arises in the landscape of the mind and the body and the world. See if it is possible to simply rest in awareness itself, effortlessly knowing what arises from moment to moment. That might include the breath, sensations from the body, sounds, thoughts or feelings. As best you can, just sit, completely awake, not holding onto anything, not looking for anything, having no agenda whatsoever other than embodied wakefulness.

12   And when you are ready, bring the sitting to a close, perhaps returning for a few minutes to the simple practice of mindful awareness of breath.

**Note:** Adapted and republished with permission of Guilford Publications from *Mindfulness-based cognitive therapy for depression* (second edition, pp. 221-222), by Segal, Z., Williams M., & Teasdale, J., copyright © 2013 by Guilford, permission conveyed through Copyright Clearance Center, Inc.

The random sounds we hear, for example the screech of car breaks, and the random thoughts that come into our minds, for example 'I forgot to phone Lily!', can draw us into a network of memories about the past, or fantasies about the future, and other stories which have the potential to evoke strong emotions in us. These stories are not the facts of the present moment. In the mindfulness of sounds and thoughts meditation, we focus attention on the raw sensations of the sounds that we hear, without getting drawn into the story of what the sounds mean. Similarly, when doing mindfulness meditation, we observe thoughts entering and leaving awareness, without getting drawn into the stories we associate with them. Recognising the similarity between hearing and thinking will help you to take a decentred position with respect to your thoughts. You will see them as mental events that come and go in the broad sky of awareness.

In week 4 of this programme each day before you do the 10-minute mindfulness of sounds and thoughts meditation in Box 6.7, you may begin with 5–10 minutes of the mindfulness of the breath and body meditation in Box 6.3. Each day of week 4, you may practise the three-minute breathing space exercise in Box 6.6 on at least two occasions and whenever needed to continue to bring mindfulness into your day-to-day life.

### Week 5

In week 5 the central idea is that turning towards difficulties is more liberating than turning away from them. That is, mindful acceptance of our experiences of stress and suffering with curiosity and compassion is more useful than trying to ignore, suppress or distract ourselves from the challenges we face in life.

We all face large and small challenges in our day-to-day lives: stress at work or unemployment; financial worries; demands in caring for our children or aging relatives; conflicts with other people; relationship problems, separation or divorce; personal illness or illness in those we care about; loneliness; fatigue; depression; or anxiety. A common response to life's difficulties is to try things that may have brought temporary relief in the past. Most of these strategies involve turning away from our difficulties, rather than turning towards them. We may deny that our problems are present. We may avoid situations that bring them to mind. We may try not to think about them. We may drink alcohol or take drugs. We may distract ourselves by doing other things, or thinking about other things. A problem with these avoidant strategies is that they lead to a rebound effect. That is, they make our thoughts about these challenges in our lives more salient, and our emotional and physical responses more intense.

In week 5 of this programme, the exploring difficulties and practising acceptance meditation in Box 6.8 is practised each day. This meditation involves selecting one small difficulty that is occurring in your life now, or that happened in the past, and turning attention towards it rather than away from it. It's important when engaging in this meditation for the first time not to select a difficulty that may overwhelm you. If you feel overwhelmed when doing this meditation, return your attention to the breath.

---

**Box 6.8   Exploring difficulty and practising acceptance**

1   When we engage in the exploring difficulty and practising acceptance meditation, we are intentionally focusing the spotlight of our attention on the sensations associated with difficult emotions and thoughts and accepting these rather than avoiding them. This disrupts unhelpful avoidance tendencies and allows us to

develop more skilful ways of being in relationship with uncomfortable thoughts and feelings. We come to see them not as 'bad and threatening things' but as transient mental events. Sit in a chair with feet flat on the floor, the spine straight and not resting against the chair back, and the eyes gently closed. Adopt an erect, dignified and comfortable posture. Bring awareness to sensations in the lower abdominal wall as the breath moves in and out of the body, until you feel settled. Then expand your attention to take in the entire body as if the whole body were breathing. Spend a few minutes practising mindfulness of the breath and body in this way. Remember that in the practice that follows you can always return to the breath and body to anchor yourself if your mind becomes distracted or overwhelmed.

2    When you are ready, see if you can bring to mind a difficulty that is going on in your life at the moment, something that you don't mind staying with for a short while. It does not have to be very important or critical, but it should be something that you are aware of as somewhat unpleasant, something unresolved. Perhaps a misunderstanding, or an argument, a situation where you feel somewhat angry, regretful or guilty over something that happened. If nothing comes to mind, perhaps you might choose something from the past, either recent or distant, that once caused unpleasantness.

3    Now, once you are focusing on some troubling thought or situation – some worry or difficult feeling – allow yourself to take some time to tune in to any physical sensations in the body that the difficulty evokes. See if you are able to note, approach and investigate inwardly what feelings are arising in your body, becoming mindful of these physical sensations, deliberately directing your focus of attention to the region of the body where the sensations are strongest in the gesture of an embrace, a welcoming. This gesture might include breathing into that part of the body on an inbreath and breathing out from that region on the outbreath, exploring the sensations, watching their intensity shift up and down from one moment to the next.

4    Once your attention has settled on the bodily sensations and they are vividly present in the field of awareness, unpleasant as they may be, you might try deepening the attitude of acceptance and openness to whatever sensations you are experiencing by saying to yourself from time to time, 'It's okay. Whatever it is, it's already here. Let me be open to it'. Then just stay with the awareness of these bodily sensations and your relationship to them, breathing with them, accepting them, letting them be, allowing them to be just as they are. It may be helpful to repeat 'it's here right now. Whatever it is, it's already here. Let me be open to it'. Soften and open to the sensations you become aware of, letting go of any tensing or bracing. Say to yourself: 'softening' or 'opening' on each outbreath. Remember that by saying 'It's already here' or 'it's okay' you are not judging the original situation or saying that everything is fine, but simply helping your awareness, right now, to remain open to the sensations in the body. If you like you can also experiment with holding in awareness both the sensations in the body and the feeling of the breath moving in and out as you breathe with the sensations moment by moment.

5    And when you notice that the bodily sensations are no longer pulling at your attention to the same degree, simply return 100% to the breath and continue with the breath as the primary object of attention.

6    If in the next few minutes no powerful bodily sensations arise, feel free to try the exercise with any bodily sensations you notice, even if they have no particular emotional charge.

**Note:** Adapted and republished with permission of Guilford Publications from *The mindful way through depression* (pp. 151-152) by Williams M., Teasdale, J., Segal, Z. & Kabat-Zinn, J., copyright © 2007 by Guilford, permission conveyed through Copyright Clearance Center, Inc.

This mediation is not about accepting difficult life situations, such as being bullied or unemployed, and not doing anything about them. Rather, it is about accepting the bodily sensations associated with thoughts about these challenges. In this meditation, focus your attention on the bodily sensations associated with having thoughts about the difficulty you face, and let these sensations be just as they are.

Thoughts about the difficulty you face may enter your mind. These may be about analysing the difficulty. They may be about judging yourself for how you have tried to deal with it in the past. Or they may be about planning how you will deal with it in the future. When these sorts of thoughts about the difficulty enter your mind, acknowledge them and return the spotlight of attention to the bodily sensations associated with the difficulty.

In the mindfulness exercise in Box 6.8, the invitation is for you to accept bodily experiences that occur as you turn towards a difficulty. Accept these in the 'being mode' (described earlier). Accept them with curiosity and compassion. This will create space and greater clarity about how to plan ways to skilfully address your difficulty when you have concluded your meditation practice. This planning will occur in the 'doing mode' (described earlier). Practising acceptance increases our range of choices. If we do not practise acceptance, we are likely to automatically go into the 'doing mode' and have a knee-jerk reaction to a difficult situation. Often this makes things worse.

In week 5 of this programme the exploring difficulties and practising acceptance meditation in Box 6.8 is done for 10 minutes each day. This new meditation is preceded each day by practising the mindfulness of breath and body meditation in Box 6.3 for eight minutes and the mindfulness of sounds and thoughts in Box 6.7 for eight minutes. Each day of week 5, you may practise the three-minute breathing space exercise in Box 6.6 on at least two occasions, and whenever needed to continue to bring mindfulness into your day-to-day life. You are also invited to modify the third step of the breathing space meditation to incorporate aspects of the exploring difficulties and practising acceptance meditation. Notice any part of the body where sensations are particularly intense. Breathe into these regions of the body as you did in the body scan meditation and as you breathe out say to yourself, 'It's OK to feel this. Whatever it is, it's already here now. Let me be open to it'. As best you can, bring this mindful awareness to the next moments of your day.

## Week 6

The central theme of week 6 is addressing personal shame with self-compassion. If you do something wrong, and feel bad about it, that's (healthy) guilt. With guilt, you can say, 'I was responsible for what I did. It was wrong. I apologise to you. I will make amends. I will atone for the things I did wrong. I will forgive myself'. Guilt is painful. However, it is often useful. It can motivate us to set things straight and move on.

Shame is different. With shame, we feel chronically guilty and we expand the story from 'I did something wrong on one occasion' to 'I am a bad person, and will always be a bad person'. With guilt, we feel bad about something we did. With shame, we feel bad about who we are, or what we have become as a result of our wrongdoing. We feel bad for not living up to our expectations. We feel ashamed for being a bad person, daughter or son, wife or husband, brother or sister, friend, employee, or boss.

Where does shame come from? Most of us are socialised into feeling shame from early childhood. We are socialised by the kind of society we live in with its standards and practices. These are expressed in families, schools, churches and the media. We are told if we are not good, obedient, dutiful, caring, hardworking, successful, strong, clever, beautiful, attractive, and feminine or masculine, we are bad and should be ashamed. Some of us, by our temperaments, are more sensitive to these socialisation messages than others. We internalise them more profoundly than others. Some of us have extremely stressful experiences that sensitise us to these socialisation messages. For example, we fail at school or work; we are neglected or abused in childhood; we are rejected in love; we become very ill; or we injure someone intentionally or by accident. These sorts of experiences may make us ashamed that we are not better people, and convince us that there is nothing we can do to change this.

With shame, we see ourselves as intrinsically and permanently bad. There seems to be no way to move on. We can't make amends or atone for being intrinsically bad. So, what happens? We continually criticise and punish ourselves. For example, we may say, 'I should be better. I shouldn't feel this way. I shouldn't think like this'. Driven by fear of not living up to our expectations, we may immerse ourselves in our work (at home or in our careers). We may numb our minds with alcohol and drugs. We don't forgive ourselves. We are not friendly or compassionate towards ourselves. We may find it hard to be compassionate towards others. We may emotionally cut ourselves off from them.

The loving kindness meditation in Box 6.9 is an opportunity for you to begin to address this shame. Initially you may focus on actively caring for yourself with all your failures and inadequacies. Then extend this self-compassion to compassion for others. Begin with those whom you love. Then gradually extend this to those towards whom you find it difficult to feel compassion. As you do this meditation, over time, you may find that if you can have empathy and compassion for yourself, then it is easier to have empathy and compassion for others.

---

### Box 6.9   Loving kindness meditation

To practise loving kindness meditation, we begin with awareness of our breathing.

Then we consciously invite feelings of love and kindness towards ourselves to arise, perhaps by remembering a moment when we felt completely seen and accepted by another human being, and invite those feelings of kindness and love received to re-emerge out of the memory and be held in awareness and felt in the body; and then perhaps say inwardly to ourselves simple phrases that you can either make up for yourself or take from others, such as:

'May I be free from inner and outer harm; may I be happy; may I be healthy; may I live with ease'.

Imagine what saying these things to yourself might do if you really, really, really inclined your heart in the direction the words are pointing – not to get anywhere or to pretend to feel anything, but just as an experiment, to see what already resides within you when you give yourself over to the process wholeheartedly, or even just a little.

After a time, we can then go on, if we care to, to invoke someone else, perhaps a particular person we are close to and care deeply about. We can visualise that person in our mind's eye or hold the feeling of the person in our heart as we wish that person well:

'May he or she be happy, may he (she) be free from pain and suffering, may he (she) experience love and joy, may he or she live with ease'.

In the same vein we may then include others we know and love: parents, children, friends.

Next we can identify a person with whom we may have a particularly difficult time for whatever reason, for whom feelings of aversion or antipathy arise. It should not be someone who has caused us harm in some major way, just someone we don't really care for and really don't like to feel kindness towards. Again, and only if you care to, we can intentionally cultivate feelings of kindness, generosity and compassion towards that person, intentionally recognising and letting go of our feelings of resentment and dislike for him or her and reminding ourselves instead to see that person as another human being, someone just as deserving of love and kindness as yourself, someone who also has feelings and hopes and fears, someone who feels pain and anxiety just as you do, someone who also suffers.

The practice can then move on to invoke a person who *has* caused us harm in some way. This is always optional. It does not mean that you are being asked to forgive the person for what he or she has done to hurt you or to cause harm to others. Not at all. You are simply recognising that he or she is also a human being, however damaged, that he or she also has aspirations, just like you; that he or she also suffers; that he or she also has the desire to be safe and to be happy. Since it is only we ourselves who suffer by carrying around feelings of hurt and anger, or even hatred, a willingness to experiment – even the tiniest bit, if and only if you feel receptive to the idea – with directing a modicum of kindness towards this person who is so difficult for us, who has hurt us, is really a way to bring our suffering to the fore and release it into the larger field of our own wholeness. The other person may not benefit from this at all. But you may benefit from it enormously. At this point there is also the option of purposely forgiving this person. This impulse may or may not develop spontaneously over time with ongoing practice of the loving kindness meditation. It is always entirely up to you to decide who to include in the practice and to what degree. And if we have harmed others, knowingly or unknowingly, we can also bring them to mind at some point and ask them to forgive us.

The loving kindness practice can be done with people whether they are alive or have already died. There can be a strong release of long-carried negative emotions as we ask for forgiveness and explore forgiving them. It is a profound process of coming to terms in your own heart and mind with the way things are at the moment, a deep letting go of past feelings of hurt. The cultivation of loving kindness in this way can be deeply liberating, if we follow our own lead, if we are careful not to force anything and if we honour our own boundaries and limits of the moment, just as we do in yoga.

The practice continues further as we expand the field of people we might be willing to include. We can direct loving kindness towards other individuals, known and unknown, perhaps to people we may see regularly but don't really know, such as the people who take our clothes at the cleaners, or the toll booth collector, or waiters and waitresses. We can extend the scope still further, radiating feelings of loving kindness to people anywhere and everywhere in the world who are suffering, who have been severely traumatised, who are oppressed, who are so deeply in need of human kindness and caring. The meditation can be carried even further if we care to, expanding the field of loving kindness out from our own heart in all directions until it includes all living creatures on the planet, not just people, and the life-giving planet itself.

Finally we return to our own body, we come back to our breathing for a time, and end by simply resting in the aftermath of the process itself, cradling and accepting whatever feelings may be present, and taking particular note of whatever feelings of warmth, generosity and love we may find flowing out of our own hearts.

In week 6, the invitation is to practise the loving kindness meditation in Box 6.9 for 15 minutes each day. Each day of week 6, you may also practise the three-minute breathing space exercise in Box 6.6 on at least two occasions, and whenever needed to continue to bring mindfulness into your day-to-day life. You are also invited to modify the third step of the breathing space meditation by seeing if you can relate differently to your thoughts. You may write some of them down in your journal. You may watch them come and go through your mind. You may view them as thoughts and not facts. You may label your thoughts as 'thinking', 'worrying' or 'ruminating'. You may ask yourself if you are thinking perfectionistically, overgeneralising, jumping to conclusions or exaggerating the significance of the situation. (These sorts of thinking traps will be discussed in more detail in Chapter 9 on optimism, Chapter 14 on grit and perfectionism, Chapter 15 on courage and fear and Chapter 16 on assertiveness and anger.)

### Week 7

In week 7 the theme is to improve the ratio of nourishing to depleting activities in your life through making very small changes. In your journal, list all the activities you did recently in a single, typical day. Opposite each item, write down N or D. N is for nourishing activities that make you feel happy, uplifted, calm, energised, fulfilled, connected to people you want to spend time with or more vitally alive. D is for depleting activities that are associated with feeling pressurised, stressed, tense, exhausted, anxious, angry, depressed and more like you are just existing rather than being vitally alive. For activities that were both nourishing and depleting, write down N or D, whichever letter you think best describes the impact of the activity on your overall state. If you can't decide whether an activity is more N than D, write down both N and D. Review your list of activities and ask yourself – have I a balance of nourishing and depleting activities in a typical day in my life? If not, then there are two main options for introducing greater balance into your life.

The first option is to reduce the amount of time spent doing depleting activities and increase the amount of time spent on nourishing activities. However, if many of the depleting activities are associated with your job which is essential for financial survival, or caring for family members who have no other carers (for example, aging relatives), then greatly reducing the time spent on depleting activities may not be realistically possible.

The second option is to change the way you do depleting activities. That is, instead of judging them, or wishing you could avoid them, do them mindfully. This involves paying attention in a non-judgemental way to your experience while engaging in these activities, moment by moment. This will allow you to experience both the positive and negative points of these activities, and open up possibilities for making mindful decisions. For example, if you find that you are frustrated by having to wait for your computer to boot up, or for someone to answer their phone, meet you or send you a document you must urgently respond to, you may make a decision about how best to use this 'waiting time'. You could use these 'waiting times' to do the three-minute breathing space meditation in Box 6.6.

In rebalancing your days, it's best to do both options. You may make a commitment to doing depleting activities mindfully. You may also make a plan to introduce five small changes into your typical day to increase the ratio of nourishing to depleting activities. In your journal list these five things. They should be small and achievable. For example, take a five-minute break every two hours and do something pleasant during this time; cycle with the children to school instead of driving; break large, difficult depleting tasks into smaller manageable tasks; pause for a minute before and after each depleting task; allow 10 minutes at the end of each work day to write a plan of priorities for the next day.

Next make a list of all the reasons you can't make the changes on your list to rebalance the ratio of nourishing to depleting activities in your typical day. For example, 'I don't have time. I can't do enjoyable things until I have done all my duties. It's wrong to put my needs ahead of those of others'. Reflect on the validity of these reasons, which from a mindfulness perspective are just thoughts, not facts.

During week 7 you may choose any two of the meditations in Box 6.3, 6.4, 6.5, 6.6, 6.8 and 6.9. Practise them for about 20-30 minutes each day. Choose one meditation because you found it particularly nourishing and the other because you found it challenging and did not fully master it the first time around. Each day of week 7, you may practise the three-minute breathing space exercise in Box 6.6 on at least two occasions, and whenever needed to continue to bring mindfulness into your day-to-day life. However, add a further step to this process. When you have completed the three-minute breathing space, pause and ask yourself – in this moment, what do I need right now, and how can I take care of myself? Consider each of these three options:

(1)   Doing something nourishing that brings pleasure, for example taking a bath or watering your plants. (Savouring pleasant experiences will be considered in Chapter 7.)
(2)   Doing something that gives a sense of control and mastery over your life, for example doing a job you have been postponing or taking some exercise.
(2)   Continuing to act mindfully.

Finally, during week 7 you may select one or two routine activities, such as preparing food, eating, washing up, driving or walking, and use these as reminders to stop and pay mindful attention to your moment-to-moment experiences.

## Week 8

In week 8 the theme is that it's important to live in the present because now is the only moment that you have, and to sustain mindfulness practice throughout your life. The doing mode described earlier in this chapter draws us into postponing living in the present. It makes us live in the past or the imagined future. By practising mindfulness, we are liberated to engage in the being mode and live more of our lives in the present moment. We may practise formally by regularly doing the meditations in Box 6.3, 6.4, 6.5, 6.6, 6.7, 6.8 and 6.9. We may also practise informally as we go through each day of the rest of our lives by following the guidance in Box 6.10.

---

### Box 6.10   Daily mindfulness

When we practise daily mindfulness, we are creating many opportunities in our busy lives to intentionally focus the spotlight of our attention on the breath and sensations in the body. The breath and sensations of the body bring us into the present moment.

**Waking.** When you wake, before you get out of bed, bring attention to your breathing and observe five mindful breaths. If you feel tired, sad or anxious, accept these experiences as transient mental events that will dissolve with time. If parts of your body ache, imagine breathing into these areas, accepting these aches as sensations in a compassionate and mindful way.

**Changing posture.** When you change posture, practise mindfulness. As you move from lying down, to standing, to sitting, to walking, be mindful of these changes in posture, bringing awareness to the changing sensations.

**Daily practice.** Each morning set aside a time and place for meditation. Continue this formal practice as best you can. This will help you maintain mindfulness in your daily life.

**Breathing space.** At set times each day, practice a three-minute breathing space to reconnect you with the current moment.

---

**Crises.** In times of crisis, if you feel overwhelmed with strong emotions, take a three-minute breathing space

**Environmental changes.** When there are noticeable changes in your environment, practise mindfulness. Whenever you hear a phone ring, a bird sing, a train pass by, laughter, a car horn, the wind, the sound of a door closing – use any sound as the bell of mindfulness. Really listen and be present and awake. Use the sound as a signal to observe five mindful breaths.

**Eating.** Whenever you eat or drink something, take a minute and breathe. Look at your food and realise that the food was connected to something that nourished its growth. Can you see the sunlight, the rain, the earth in your food? Pay attention as you eat, consciously consuming this food for your physical health. Bring awareness to seeing your food, smelling your food, tasting your food, chewing your food and swallowing your food.

**Routine daily activities.** Focus attention on your daily activities such as brushing your teeth, washing up, brushing your hair, putting on your shoes, doing your job. Bring mindfulness to each activity. When you do routine activities practise mindfulness. Notice your body while you walk or stand. Take a moment to notice your posture. Pay attention to the contact of your feet with the ground under them. Feel the air on your face, arms and legs as you walk. Are you rushing?

**Conversation.** Bring awareness to listening and talking. Can you listen without agreeing or disagreeing, liking or disliking, or planning what you will say when it is your turn? Can you notice how your mind and body feel?

**Queueing.** Whenever you wait in a line, use this time to notice standing and breathing. Feel the contact of your feet with the floor and how your body feels. Bring attention to the rise and fall of your abdomen. Are you feeling impatient?

**Letting go of tension.** Be aware of any points of tightness in your body throughout the day. See if you can breathe into them and as you exhale, let go of excess tension. Is tension stored anywhere in your body? For example, your neck, shoulders, stomach, jaw or lower back? If possible, stretch or do yoga once a day.

**Retiring.** Before you go to sleep at night, take a few minutes and bring your attention to your breathing. Observe five mindful breaths.

## Summary

- **Not living in the present decreases well-being.** Ruminating about past difficulties and worrying about future challenges reduces well-being.
- **Mindfulness meditation increases well-being.** It has a positive impact on many physical and mental health problems, notably depression and chronic pain.

- **Mindfulness** involves paying attention, on purpose, in the present moment, without judgement to our immediate sensory experience with an attitude of curiosity and compassion. In mindfulness meditation, when attention wanders to thoughts that enter the mind, we guide attention back to the breath or bodily sensations, and so avoid becoming embroiled in judging them or trying to change them.
- **Doing and being modes.** When not mindful, we operate in the doing mode, rather than the being mode. The doing mode is concerned with closing the gap between the way things are now and the way we want them to be. In the doing mode we focus on plans to achieve goals; judgements about our success in goal attainment; avoidance of things irrelevant to goal attainment; and we tend to think about all of these things, rather than experience our immediate sensations. In the doing mode, we live in our heads, treat thoughts as facts, operate on auto-pilot and unbalance our lives so as to exclude nourishing activities and become overwhelmed by depleting activities. The doing mode is good for solving external problems. It increases distress if we try to use it to solve internal problems like having difficult emotions. For these, the being mode is more useful. In this, we focus mindfully on sensory experiences in the present moment and accept these experiences as they are right now with curiosity and compassion.
- **Mindfulness-Based Cognitive Therapy** is an eight-week programme that has been shown in many scientific studies to prevent relapse in recurrent depression, and improve other mental health problems. This chapter presented a summary of a version of this programme that has been adapted for people without depression, who wish to increase their well-being. In the eight-week programme, each day specific meditations are practised and there are specific exercises to help introduce mindfulness into day-to-day life and break habits that may be barriers to becoming more mindful.
- **Mindfulness of breath and body and body scan** meditations are learned in weeks 1 and 2. Mindfulness of breath and body helps us to acknowledge the breath as the anchor for awareness in meditation. The body scan shows us the intimate connection between the mind and body.
- **Mindfulness of movement and the three-minute breathing space** are practised in week 3. Mindfulness of movement reveals where tension is carried in the body and the limits of the body's ability to stretch comfortably. The three-minute breathing space is practised for the remainder of the programme to help bring mindfulness into daily life.
- **Mindfulness of sounds and thoughts**, which is practised in week 4, shows that sounds are to the ear as thoughts are to the mind.
- **Exploring difficulties and practising acceptance meditation** is practised in week 5. This helps us discover that turning towards difficulties can enhance well-being more than turning away from them.
- **Loving kindness meditation**, practised in week 6, offers an opportunity to address shame and self-criticism.
- **Nourishing and depleting activities.** In week 7 small changes are made in the ratio of nourishing to depleting activities in daily life. Also, a meditation that is particularly nourishing and one that is particularly challenging are practised.
- **The future.** In the final week, the invitation is to extend formal and informal mindfulness practice in the future indefinitely.

## Where are you now?

If you have done the exercises in this chapter you have introduced mindfulness meditation into your life. Mindfulness may help you to live more of your life in the present moment. It may help you avoid ruminating about the past and worrying about the future.

You may wish to read back over the chapter and summarise in your journal the main things you have learned about the positive effects of meditation, the doing and being modes, and the various mindfulness exercises in the eight-week MBCT programme.

The next chapter will consider savouring and flow. Below are some web resources and books that are relevant to topics you have read about in this chapter.

## Web resources

Introduction to mindfulness: www.youtube.com/watch?v=D5Fa5Ooj45s
Raisin meditation. Clare Josa (2:59): www.youtube.com/watch?v=z2Eo56BLMjM
Mindfulness of the body and breath. Mark Williams (8:10): www.youtube.com/watch?v=fUeEnkjKyDs
Mindfulness of the body and breath. Jon Kabat-Zinn (10.38): www.youtube.com/watch?v=SkAMaCZtXUI
Body scan meditation. Mark Williams (14:47): www.youtube.com/watch?v=CyKhfUdOEgs
Body scan meditation. Jon Kabat-Zinn (29:02): www.youtube.com/watch?v=15q-N-_kkrU
Mindfulness of movement (Mindful standing yoga). Jon Kabat-Zinn (10:05): www.youtube.com/watch?v=6XGb3TX3g60
Mindfulness of the breath and body. Jon Kabat-Zinn (20:38): www.youtube.com/watch?v=NbXUAg5tAOs
Three-minute breathing space. Mark Williams (3:27): www.youtube.com/watch?v=rOne1POTKL8
Mindfulness of sounds and thoughts. Mark Williams (8:04): www.youtube.com/watch?v=OFeTTgl_wAI
Exploring difficulty and practising acceptance. Mark Williams (10:15): www.youtube.com/watch?v=nIEFKxGNPHk
Loving kindness meditation. Mark Williams (9:37): www.youtube.com/watch?v=pLt-E4YNVHU
Loving kindness meditation. Jon Kabat-Zinn (16.45): www.youtube.com/watch?v=WvQo4QJB400
Free mindfulness project website includes links to many downloadable audio recordings of mindfulness exercises, all based on MBSR or MBCT: www.freemindfulness.org/download

## Books

Teasdale, J., Williams, J. M. G., & Segal, Z. (2014). *The mindful way workbook: An 8-week program to free yourself from depression and emotional distress.* New York, NY: Guilford Press.
Williams, M., & Penman, D. D. (2011). *Mindfulness: A practical guide to finding peace in frantic world.* London, UK: Piatkus.
Williams M., Teasdale, J., Segal, Z., & Kabat-Zinn, J. (2007). *The mindful way through depression.* New York, NY: Guilford.

# Part 3
# Enjoying life

# 7  Savouring and flow

We all know that we can increase our immediate sense of well-being by staying in a beautiful place, doing things that we enjoy, reminiscing about these things and anticipating more good things in the future. Psychological research shows that, for most people, being in natural rather than urban environments,[1] actively doing enjoyable leisure activities,[2] listening to music,[3] singing,[4] dancing,[5] reminiscing[6] and optimistically anticipating more such things in the future[7] all enhance well-being (at least in the short-term).

I have said that these things make most, but not all, people happier, because personal vulnerabilities or particular circumstances can prevent these things from having a beneficial effect. For example, if you have hay fever, it's unlikely that walking in a meadow where there is a lot of pollen about will make you happy. If you are tone deaf, or if Beatles music is not to your taste, listening to Sergeant Pepper may not boost your happiness. If you are not too confident about your abilities, then singing and dancing when others are watching you may do little to increase your well-being. It's also unlikely that you will benefit much from beautiful environments or leisure activities if you have a lot of other concerns on your mind.

I also mentioned in the opening sentence of this chapter that we can *temporarily* increase our immediate sense of well-being by being in a beautiful place or doing things that we enjoy. In Chapter 1 it was noted that the 'hedonic treadmill'[8] – a process of rapid adaptation to pleasant events – is a major obstacle to obtaining long-term increases in well-being from engaging in pleasurable activities. People react strongly to both pleasurable and distressing experiences, with sharp increases or decreases in immediate levels of happiness. However, in most instances they rapidly return to their happiness set-point in a matter of weeks or months. This set-point is partly genetically determined and operates like a thermostat.[9]

An important question for positive psychology has been: under what conditions can we increase our well-being by having positive sensory experiences (like being in a beautiful natural environment) or engaging in pleasant leisure activities? This has led to research on savouring and flow. Savouring refers to processes that enhance positive experiences arising from pleasant sensations, or things that feel good. For example, you can savour the taste of ice cream or the smell of honeysuckle in early summer. In contrast, flow refers to positive experiences that occur during skilled activities in challenging situations, or things that you believe you are really good at. For example, you can experience flow when playing sports or a musical instrument. In this chapter, you will be invited to engage in activities that enhance your capacity for savouring and flow.

## Savouring

Professor Fred Bryant at Loyola University Chicago is the founder of savouring research, and author of the ground-breaking book: *Savouring: A new model of positive experience.*[10] When you stop and smell the roses instead of walking past without noticing them, you are savouring. Many pleasures can be savoured. They include love, sex, activities with friends and family, food, drink, nature, music, singing, dancing, entertainment, humour, art, reading, exercise, sport, games, gardening, memories and spiritual and religious practices. Savouring involves deliberately paying attention to, appreciating, enhancing and prolonging positive experiences and the positive emotions that accompany them. These positive emotions include pleasure, joy, awe, gratitude and pride. When we engage in savouring, we try to strengthen and lengthen positive emotional experiences. We try to prevent the rapid adaptation to positive experiences associated with the hedonic treadmill.

### Savouring processes

Different savouring processes regulate differing positive emotions. Luxuriating regulates pleasure. For example, we may luxuriate in the afterglow of sex or the warmth of a hot bath. Thanksgiving regulates gratitude. For example, we may give thanks for friendship or love that we have experienced. Basking regulates pride. For example, we may bask after passing an exam or winning at sports. Marvelling regulates awe. For example, we may marvel at the beauty of the dawn chorus.

### Savouring the past, present and future

We can savour by focusing on the present, past or future. When savouring the present moment, we try to lengthen and strengthen positive experiences arising from activities we are engaged in right now. We may do this by focusing on our immediate situation and sensory experiences, while blocking out all distractions. For example, we may focus on the beauty of a winter star-filled sky, and ignore the fact that it's cold. When savouring the past, we recall detailed positive memories and reminisce about these. Photographs, films, diaries and mementoes may be used to facilitate reminiscence. When savouring the future, we anticipate in detail forthcoming positive events. Invitations, photos of people who may be attending the event and other cues may be used to facilitate anticipation. (Savouring the future involves thinking optimistically, which is discussed in Chapter 9.) Most people find that they can savour best through reminiscence, moderately well through savouring the present and least well through anticipation.

### Savouring and long-term well-being

Research on savouring shows that savouring momentary positive experiences can have long-term effects on well-being.[11] This finding is consistent with the Broaden and Build theory[12] described in Chapter 1. This theory proposes that the experience of brief episodes of positive emotions broadens the range of thoughts we have about possible courses of action that may be taken. When we act on these, we may change the direction of our lives in ways that will last into the future. This may create opportunities for having more positive emotional experiences.

### Savouring exercise

To familiarise yourself with the experience of savouring, select a piece of music that really moves you; or a photograph of an occasion that made you feel good; or think of some positive event that you are looking forward to. Find a place where you will not be interrupted and take 10 minutes to listen to the music; or look at the photograph and recall the positive event; or anticipate the event you are looking forward to. Strengthen and lengthen the positive emotions you feel by using some of the following strategies. Focus on your immediate experience. Block out other irrelevant distractions. Notice and label the specific details of the situation that make you feel good. Take a mental photograph of the situation. Before and after this exercise, rate the strength of your positive emotions in your journal on a scale from 1 to 10. Note the extent to which the exercise increased the strength of your positive emotions and any aspects of the exercise that you think specifically contributed to this. This exercise is summarised in Box 7.1.

---

## Box 7.1   Savouring exercise

- **Prepare.** Find a place where you will not be interrupted by others or distracted by phones, computers, the TV, radio or other devices for about 10 minutes.
- **Choose a positive experience to savour**. For example:

  - Listen with complete concentration to a piece of music that really moves you emotionally.
  - Look at a photograph of an occasion that made you feel good, and recall the positive event.
  - Anticipate, in detail, a positive event that you are looking forward to.

- **Use some of the following strategies to strengthen and lengthen your positive emotions.**

  - Focus on your immediate experience.
  - Block out other irrelevant distractions.
  - Notice and label the specific details of the situation that make you feel good.
  - Take a mental photograph of the situation.

- **Assess effects on positive emotions.**

  - Before and after this exercise, rate the strength of your positive emotions in your journal on a scale from 1 to 10.
  - On this scale 10 means that you are experiencing extremely strong positive emotions, 1 means you are experiencing extremely strong negative emotions and 5 means you are feeling fairly neutral emotionally.
  - Note the extent to which the exercise increased the strength of your positive emotions.
  - Note any aspects of the exercise that you think specifically contributed to this.

### Strategies that facilitate savouring

Certain strategies facilitate savouring.[13] These are listed below as if they were quite separate. However, in practice, most people combine a number of strategies when savouring.

#### Sharpening your perceptions

We can facilitate savouring by sharpening our perceptions. This involves being highly attentive to positive aspects of the situation and our positive experiences within the situation, while blocking out distractions. When savouring in the present moment, this process of focusing attention involves paying attention to particular sensations in the here and now; for example, noticing the warmth of a campfire and the beauty of its flames in the darkness. When savouring past positive experiences, we may sharpen perceptions by focusing attention on mementoes, photos and films that help us to recall past positive events; for example, looking at a photo or video of a particularly happy Christmas party. When savouring anticipated future positive experiences, we may sharpen our perceptions by focusing on prompts that help us bring to mind future positive events; for example, looking at an invitation to a forthcoming wedding of our best friend, or a photo of a place we intend to visit for a vacation.

#### Absorption

Another savouring strategy is becoming absorbed in the savouring process by relaxing and focusing on the present moment; for example, noticing how good it feels to lie in a warm bath after vigorous exercise.

#### Building memories

A third strategy is actively building memories of the positive event by taking mental photographs and labelling each aspect of the situation associated with positive emotions; for example, taking a mental photograph of tropical fish when snorkelling in clear blue seas, and naming the colours and shapes of the fish. These visual and verbal process will help you to build vivid memories that can be recalled later, so that the positive experience can be vividly recollected and re-lived in the future.

#### Comparing

A fourth strategy is comparing the positive event to other less positive situations in the past or the future, or to the experiences of others who may not be experiencing such positive emotions. This highlights how positive the event is compared to other events, and sets it apart as particularly special; for example, comparing an early morning walk on a magnificent deserted beach in Donegal to the experience of walking to work through crowded city streets.

#### Awareness of transience

A fifth strategy is acknowledging that the positive event is transient, and therefore it is important to make the most of this brief and precious experience by savouring every moment; for example, noting that when you first hold your child in your arms after its birth, this is an exceptionally special and transient moment.

## Self-congratulation

Self-congratulation is a sixth strategy. This is appropriate where we are savouring success. It involves taking pride in our achievements and acknowledging that these are impressive; for example, taking time to celebrate winning a race, passing an exam or successfully completing a work project.

## Counting blessings

Being thankful that the positive event occurred is a seventh savouring strategy (gratitude is discussed in detail in Chapter 8); for example, being grateful for the smile on your partner's face when you come home after a hard day's work.

## Emotional expression

An eighth strategy is expressing positive emotions. We can do this in various ways, for example by jumping up and down, laughing or shouting with excitement or more quietly by smiling or saying things like 'mmmmm, aahh or oh yes' to ourselves.

## Sharing

A final savouring strategy is sharing good news about positive events with friends and family members. This involves giving them a blow-by-blow account of the positive experience, describing both what happened and its emotional impact on you.

You can assess the profile of savouring strategies you typically use by completing the questionnaire in Box 7.2. The items in the questionnaire illustrate the savouring strategies described above.

---

### Box 7.2  Assess your savouring and dampening strategies

This questionnaire will help assess strategies you use to savour or dampen positive emotions arising from positive experiences.

Think back to a recent positive event.

Select an event that made you feel good and that you responded to in the way that you would usually respond to positive events.

With this event in mind, for each of the following 52 items, circle the response number from 1 to 5 that best applied to you when the event happened.

1 means the item definitely didn't apply to you.

5 means the item definitely applied to you.

3 means that the item applied somewhat to you.

This is how you score the questionnaire. For each of the nine savouring scales and four dampening scales, sum the four responses you have circled to give the scale total.

Inspect the profile of total scale scores. Those with the highest scores are the strategies you use most.

Sharpening perceptions, absorption, memory building, comparing, awareness of transience, self-congratulation, counting blessings, emotional expression and sharing with others are all strategies for savouring positive experiences and enhancing positive emptions.

In contrast, distraction, suppression, kill-joy thinking and negative mental time travel are strategies that dampen positive emotions.

---

*SAVOURING STRATEGIES*

---

**Sharpening perceptions**

| | | | | | | |
|---|---|---|---|---|---|---|
| 1 | I tried to become more alert by opening my eyes wide and taking a deep breath | 1 | 2 | 3 | 4 | 5 |
| 2 | I tried to focus on certain sensory properties in particular, and perhaps block out others | 1 | 2 | 3 | 4 | 5 |
| 3 | I concentrated and blocked out distractions, and I intensified one sense by blocking another | 1 | 2 | 3 | 4 | 5 |
| 4 | I tried to slow down and move more slowly so as to stop or slow down time | 1 | 2 | 3 | 4 | 5 |
| | Total | | | | | |

**Absorption**

| | | | | | | |
|---|---|---|---|---|---|---|
| 5 | I thought only about the present and got absorbed in the moment | 1 | 2 | 3 | 4 | 5 |
| 6 | I made myself relax so that I could become more absorbed in the event | 1 | 2 | 3 | 4 | 5 |
| 7 | I closed my eyes, relaxed and took in the moment | 1 | 2 | 3 | 4 | 5 |
| 8 | I went through the event one moment at a time and tried not to look too far ahead | 1 | 2 | 3 | 4 | 5 |
| | Total | | | | | |

**Memory building**

| | | | | | | |
|---|---|---|---|---|---|---|
| 9 | I tried to memorise my surroundings | 1 | 2 | 3 | 4 | 5 |
| 10 | I took mental photographs | 1 | 2 | 3 | 4 | 5 |
| 11 | I labelled specific details of the situation explicitly – tried to find out what it was that I was enjoying and noted each aspect explicitly | 1 | 2 | 3 | 4 | 5 |
| 12 | I thought about how I'd reminisce to myself about this event later | 1 | 2 | 3 | 4 | 5 |
| | Total | | | | | |

**Comparing**

| | | | | | | |
|---|---|---|---|---|---|---|
| 13 | I thought back to events that led up to it and to a time when I didn't have it and wanted it | 1 | 2 | 3 | 4 | 5 |
| 14 | I thought about how things could never be this good again | 1 | 2 | 3 | 4 | 5 |
| 15 | I thought about ways in which the event could have turned out worse | 1 | 2 | 3 | 4 | 5 |
| 16 | I compared myself to others and asked myself – am I enjoying this as much as they are? | 1 | 2 | 3 | 4 | 5 |
| | Total | | | | | |

**Awareness of transience**

| | | | | | | | |
|---|---|---|---|---|---|---|---|
| 17 | I thought about how I wished this moment could last and reminded myself that I must enjoy it now because it would soon be over | 1 | 2 | 3 | 4 | 5 |
| 18 | I reminded myself that nothing lasts forever so I must enjoy this now | 1 | 2 | 3 | 4 | 5 |
| 19 | I reminded myself how transient this moment was and thought about it ending | 1 | 2 | 3 | 4 | 5 |
| 20 | I reminded myself that it would be over before I know it | 1 | 2 | 3 | 4 | 5 |
| | Total | | | | | |

**Self-congratulation**

| | | | | | | |
|---|---|---|---|---|---|---|
| 21 | I told myself how proud I was | 1 | 2 | 3 | 4 | 5 |
| 22 | I told myself how impressed others would be | 1 | 2 | 3 | 4 | 5 |
| 23 | I thought about what a triumph it was | 1 | 2 | 3 | 4 | 5 |
| 24 | I reminded myself how long I had waited for this to happen | 1 | 2 | 3 | 4 | 5 |
| | Total | | | | | |

**Counting blessings**

| | | | | | | |
|---|---|---|---|---|---|---|
| 25 | I reminded myself how lucky I was to have this good thing happen to me | 1 | 2 | 3 | 4 | 5 |
| 26 | I thought about what a lucky person I am that so many good things happen to me | 1 | 2 | 3 | 4 | 5 |
| 27 | I said a prayer of thanks for my good fortune | 1 | 2 | 3 | 4 | 5 |
| 28 | I was thankful and appreciative for having experienced this good thing | 1 | 2 | 3 | 4 | 5 |
| | Total | | | | | |

**Emotional expression**

| | | | | | | |
|---|---|---|---|---|---|---|
| 29 | I jumped up and down, ran around or showed other physical expressions of energy | 1 | 2 | 3 | 4 | 5 |
| 30 | I screamed or made other verbal expressions of excitement | 1 | 2 | 3 | 4 | 5 |
| 31 | I laughed or giggled | 1 | 2 | 3 | 4 | 5 |
| 32 | I sighed or made other sounds of appreciation to help myself savour the moment (e.g. saying mmm, aahh, humming or whistling | 1 | 2 | 3 | 4 | 5 |
| | Total | | | | | |

**Sharing**

| | | | | | | |
|---|---|---|---|---|---|---|
| 33 | I thought about sharing the memory of this later with other people | 1 | 2 | 3 | 4 | 5 |
| 34 | I looked for other people to share it with | 1 | 2 | 3 | 4 | 5 |
| 35 | I talked to another person about how good I felt | 1 | 2 | 3 | 4 | 5 |
| 36 | I physically expressed my feelings to others (hugging, touching) | 1 | 2 | 3 | 4 | 5 |
| | Total | | | | | |

**DAMPENING STRATEGIES**

**Distraction**

| | | | | | | |
|---|---|---|---|---|---|---|
| 37 | I distracted myself from the positive situation and thought about something else | 1 | 2 | 3 | 4 | 5 |
| 38 | I was distracted by things that worried me | 1 | 2 | 3 | 4 | 5 |
| 39 | I had other things on my mind and didn't notice the good things that were happening | 1 | 2 | 3 | 4 | 5 |

| | | | | | | |
|---|---|---|---|---|---|---|
| 40 | I was planning what to do next and didn't pay attention to what was happening | 1 | 2 | 3 | 4 | 5 |
| | Total | | | | | |
| **Suppression** | | | | | | |
| 41 | I kept my feelings inside and didn't show them | 1 | 2 | 3 | 4 | 5 |
| 42 | I didn't tell anyone what I was feeling in case it made them feel bad | 1 | 2 | 3 | 4 | 5 |
| 43 | I was too embarrassed to show how good I felt | 1 | 2 | 3 | 4 | 5 |
| 44 | I didn't think it was right to let other people know I was happy, so I said nothing | 1 | 2 | 3 | 4 | 5 |
| | Total | | | | | |
| **Kill-joy thinking** | | | | | | |
| 45 | I told myself why I didn't deserve this good thing | 1 | 2 | 3 | 4 | 5 |
| 46 | I thought about things that made me feel guilty | 1 | 2 | 3 | 4 | 5 |
| 47 | I told myself how it wasn't as good as I'd hoped for | 1 | 2 | 3 | 4 | 5 |
| 48 | I thought about ways in which it could have been better | 1 | 2 | 3 | 4 | 5 |
| | Total | | | | | |
| **Negative mental time travel** | | | | | | |
| 49 | I was reminded of difficult things that happened in the past that made me feel bad | 1 | 2 | 3 | 4 | 5 |
| 50 | I thought it was too good to be true and began to worry about future problems | 1 | 2 | 3 | 4 | 5 |
| 51 | I remembered mistakes I had made or times that things didn't go well for me | 1 | 2 | 3 | 4 | 5 |
| 52 | I thought about things in the future that could go wrong | 1 | 2 | 3 | 4 | 5 |
| | Total | | | | | |

**Note:** Items 1-27 and 29-36 and 45-48 are reproduced by permission of Taylor & Francis Group, LLC, a division of Informa plc, from the Ways of Savouring Scale in Table 2.3 on page 49-50 of *Savouring: A new model of positive experience* by Bryant, F., & Veroff, J. Copyright © 2007 by Taylor & Francis. Items for the distraction, suppression and mental time travel scales are based on dampening strategies in Quoidbach, J., Berry, E. V., Hansenne, M., & Mikolajczak, M. (2010). Positive emotion regulation and well-being: Comparing the impact of eight savouring and dampening strategies. *Personality and Individual Differences, 49*, 368-373.

## Dampening

The questionnaire in Box 7.2 also assessed dampening strategies. Dampening strategies shorten and diminish (rather than lengthen and strengthen) positive emotions.[14] These strategies include distracting yourself from positive emotions or suppressing expression of them. Kill-joy thinking is another way of dampening positive emotions. It involves looking for the cloud when presented with a silver lining; for example, noticing that the situation could be better, or that you don't deserve this good thing or feel guilty for having this good thing happen to you. Finally, negative mental time travel is another dampening strategy. It involves remembering past failures or negative experiences and anticipating future difficulties and problems. When you complete the questionnaire in Box 7.2, notice the extent to which you use dampening strategies, as well as savouring strategies. You can increase your use of savouring strategies and reduce your use of dampening strategies by doing the savouring exercises described in this chapter.

## Background factors that affect savouring and dampening

Certain background demographic, cultural factors, situational factors (especially unmet needs) and personality characteristics (notably self-esteem) affect savouring.[15] Women are better at savouring than men, and this sex difference emerges in childhood. Savouring is more consistent with western than with eastern cultures, where positive emotions are not as highly valued, and so may be less effective for people from eastern cultures.

Unmet needs associated with poverty, loneliness or not living up to our own or society's expectations can prevent savouring. It's difficult to savour when we feel destitute, unloved or a failure. Savouring may be prevented by social pressure to perform well at work, or to meet family responsibilities of caring for children or older relatives. It's difficult to savour when we are preoccupied with getting promoted, looking after the kids or caring for aging parents or in-laws. It is easier to savour simple pleasures when we take time out to temporarily suspend social pressures to achieve and perform well at work, or to care for others. It's also easier to engage in savouring when we do not feel negatively judged or threatened by others, and if we do not judge ourselves negatively. That is, if we do not have low self-esteem.

People with low self-esteem tend to dampen rather than savour positive experiences. That is, they use a range of strategies to shorten and diminish (rather than lengthen and strengthen) positive emotions. People with low self-esteem may be motivated to dampen positive emotions to maintain a consistent view of themselves as unhappy people to whom good things do not happen.[16]

## Coping and savouring

It is useful to think about the parallels between coping and savouring. Coping refers to strategies that we use to reduce the extent to which negative events lead us to experience negative emotions such as distress, sadness or anxiety. In contrast, things that we do to increase the extent to which positive events lead us to experience positive emotions such as joy, happiness or pride are referred to as savouring. Just as coping is distinct from negative emotions, so savouring is distinct from the positive emotions it enhances.

## Savouring, mindfulness and flow

Savouring may be distinguished from both flow and mindfulness. (Flow is discussed later in this chapter and mindfulness was discussed in Chapter 6.) When savouring we actively focus on a past, present or future positive experience. We are acutely aware that we are experiencing pleasurable emotions. We focus fully on the experience of these emotions. We attempt to prolong and enhance this pleasant sensory experience. We also block out distractions. In contrast, during flow our focus is on the skilled activity we are doing right now. We lose all awareness of the self and the emotions we are experiencing. With mindfulness, we focus our attention on a specific stimulus in the present moment - for example, the breath - and observe other sensations, thoughts about the past or future, and feelings arise and dissolve in awareness. However, there is no attempt to prolong experiences of pleasant sensations, or to focus on past or future positive experiences, or to block out distractions or negative emotions.

### *More savouring exercises*

Here are some more savouring exercises. You may wish to try doing them to increase your well-being.

#### Using more savouring strategies

In this exercise, there is an opportunity to review the way you use savouring and dampening strategies at the moment, and decide if you wish to change your current pattern. Review your profile of savouring and dampening scores from the questionnaire you completed in Box 7.2. In your journal make a list of your nine savouring strategies in rank order from those with the highest to those with the lowest total scores. Then make another list of your four dampening strategies, rank ordering them from those with the highest scores to those with the lowest. In your journal, write down the answers to these questions and reflect on them: Did I get higher scores for using savouring or dampening strategies? For which savouring strategies did I get the highest scores?

There is an opportunity now to make a commitment to use savouring strategies more than dampening strategies, in future, in your day-to-day life. You may practise using the full range of savouring strategies including those you scored high on as well as those on which you obtained lower scores. These is also an opportunity to decide to reduce or eliminate the use of dampening strategies in future. Box 7.3 contains a summary of this exercise.

---

### Box 7.3    Use more savouring strategies

In this exercise, you may review the savouring and dampening strategies you commonly use and commit to change your current pattern.

- Complete the questionnaire on savouring and dampening strategies in Box 7.2.
- In your journal, list your nine savouring strategies from those with the highest scores to those with the lowest.
- In your journal, list your four dampening strategies from those with the highest scores to those with the lowest.
- In your journal, write down the answers to these questions and reflect on them.

  o   Did I get higher scores for using savouring or dampening strategies?
  o   For which savouring strategies did I get the highest scores?

- Make a commitment to use the full range savouring strategies in future and to reduce or eliminate the use of dampening strategies.

---

#### Daily vacation[17]

The frequency and intensity of positive emotions affect well-being. Most people take annual vacations so that they can boost their well-being by having a single period in which they experience frequent, intense positive emotions. In this exercise, there is an opportunity to take a small vacation every day, so as to increase the frequency of positive emotions in your life. For one week, set aside 20 minutes each day for a daily vacation. Make sure you will not be interrupted or distracted while doing this exercise. Before you start, set aside your worries, concerns and responsibilities for the duration of your vacation. During your daily vacation, do something enjoyable. Vary what you do each time you engage in this exercise, so you are not doing the same activity every day. This will prevent adaptation occurring. Your daily vacation might involve going for a walk, reading a novel, taking a bath, listening to music, eating a favourite fruit, looking at a painting or doing some other activity that you find intrinsically enjoyable. During your daily vacation, try to see things as if for the first time, in a non-judgemental way. Notice, acknowledge to yourself and savour each sensation or action that you find pleasurable. Savour each positive feeling so that you strengthen and lengthen and it. Label each positive feeling that you experience, so it will be easy to recall. Actively construct positive memories of this daily vacation by taking mental photographs of the situation and your positive experiences within the situation. This will make it easy to recall and bring you pleasure when you reminisce about it at some future time. Outwardly express your positive emotions in some way that feels right to you. At the end of your daily vacation, plan your next daily vacation and anticipate it with pleasure. At the end of each day reminisce about your daily vacation, recalling and reliving the positive feelings you savoured. In your journal write down a brief account of your daily vacation and a rating on a 10-point scale of how positive you felt during your vacation. At the end of the week, take time to review your journal and reminisce about all seven daily vacations, recalling and reliving the positive experiences you savoured. In your journal write down your reflections on doing this exercise. Box 7.4 contains a summary of this exercise.

---

### Box 7.4   Daily vacation

- **Prepare.** Take a brief vacation each day for a week. Have your daily vacation in a place where you will not be interrupted by others or distracted by phones, computers, the TV, radio or other devices for about 20 minutes.
- **Set aside your worries**, concerns and responsibilities for the duration of your vacation each day.
- **Enjoyment.** Do something that you find intrinsically enjoyable like going for a walk, reading a novel, taking a bath, listening to music, eating a favourite fruit or looking at a painting.
- **Variety.** Vary what you do each time, to prevent adaptation occurring.
- **Use many savouring strategies** to strengthen and lengthen positive feelings.

  - See things as if for the first time.
  - Notice and savour each sensation or action that you find pleasurable.
  - Label each positive feeling that you experience, so it will be easy to recall.
  - Take mental photographs so that you construct vivid positive memories.
  - Outwardly express your positive emotions in some way that feels right to you.
  - At the end of your daily vacation, plan your next daily vacation and anticipate it with pleasure.

o   At the end of each day, reminisce about your daily vacation, recalling and reliving the positive feelings you savoured.

- **Assess effects on positive emotions.**

o   Each day, in your journal, write down a brief account of your daily vacation.

o   Each day, before and after your vacation, rate the strength of your positive emotions in your journal on a scale from 1 to 10, noticing the extent to which daily vacations increase your positive emotions.

o   On this scale 10 means that you are experiencing extremely strong positive emotions, 1 means you are experiencing extremely strong negative emotions and 5 means you are feeling neutral emotionally.

o   At the end of the week, review your journal and reminisce about all seven daily vacations, recalling and reliving the positive experiences you savoured.

o   In your journal write down your reflections on doing this exercise.

**Note:** This exercise is based on the daily vacation exercise on page 211 in Bryant, F. B., & Veroff, J. (2007). *Savouring: A new model of positive experience.* Mahwah, NJ: Lawrence Erlbaum.

## Relishing ordinary activities

Our lives are filled with positive experiences that we fail to notice because we are rushing to do the next thing on our endless to-do lists. This exercise is an opportunity to savour some of these things that usually go unnoticed. Each day select one pleasant activity that you normally do without thinking. For example, drinking coffee, walking to work, having lunch, looking at sunlight coming in through your window, sitting down to relax in the evening, taking a bath or shower, lying quietly in bed in the evening. Do this activity paying attention to all minute details of the activity and all of the positive experiences you have while doing so. Luxuriate in these positive experiences. Consciously try to lengthen and strengthen the positive feelings you experience. Linger over your coffee, noticing the taste and aroma. Bask in the feeling of achievement when you complete a tedious task. Marvel at the pattern sunlight makes passing through the window. Luxuriate in front of an open fire after a long day's work. In your journal, write down the ways in which savouring this activity differed from doing it without thinking. Write down the ways in which it made you feel different than usual. In one study this savouring exercise was found to reduce depression and increase well-being.[18] Box 7.5 contains a summary of this exercise.

## Box 7.5   Relishing ordinary activities

- Each day, for a week, select one pleasant activity that you normally do without thinking.
- Here are some examples: drinking coffee, walking to work, having lunch, looking at sunlight coming in through your window, sitting down to relax in the evening, taking a bath or shower, lying quietly in bed in the evening.

- Pay attention to all minute details of the activity and all of the positive experiences you have while doing it.
- Consciously try to lengthen and strengthen the positive feelings you experience by using any savouring strategies you find useful.
- Each day, in your journal, write down the ways in which savouring an ordinary activity differed from doing it without thinking.

*Reminiscence*

Our memories are vast treasure troves of past positive experiences. We rarely exploit our storehouse of positive memories to the full to enhance how happy we feel. In this exercise, there is an opportunity to use your cherished memories to enhance your well-being. Select a time and place where there are no distractions and when you will not be interrupted. You may reminisce either alone or with a family member or friend. Reminiscence has a greater impact if you do it with someone who shares your memories about the happy event you are recalling. If you reminisce on your own, you may choose to do it for a brief period, for example 20 minutes, and repeat the process each day for a week. If you reminisce with another person, you may decide to meet for an evening or to take a trip to the place you are reminiscing about for a whole day. Select a positive experience, for example a particular Christmas or birthday, a time you first met, a wedding, the birth of a child, a child achieving their first milestones, a special party, a holiday, a sporting event, a graduation, a work achievement, an adventure or a memorable happy day. Use photographs, films or mementoes of the event, or a visit to the place where the event happened to intensify recollections of it.

These sorts of reminders make reminiscence more vivid, and the positive emotions it evokes more intense and emotionally moving. While reminiscing, visualise the events as if they were happening right now. If you are reminiscing with a friend or family member, describe the events that happened in detail. When you experience positive emotions, notice these and label them. Try to lengthen and strengthen these good feelings by visualising or talking in more detail about the occasion you are remembering. Repeat and elaborate your recollections. If you decide to savour recollections each day for a week to notice their effects on your overall well-being, then select a different positive event to recollect each day to prevent adaptation occurring. Reminiscence has been shown in many studies to be especially effective in alleviating depression and increasing well-being in older adults.[19] Box 7.6 contains a summary of this exercise.

## Box 7.6   Reminiscence

### Alone or with another

- You may reminisce either alone or with a family member or friend.
- Select a positive experience, for example a particular Christmas or birthday, a time you first met, a wedding, the birth of a child, a child achieving their first

milestones, a special party, a holiday, a sporting event, a graduation, a work achievement, an adventure or a memorable happy day.

- Use photographs, films or mementoes of the event, or a visit to the place where the event happened to intensify recollections of it.
- While reminiscing, visualise the events in as much detail as possible, and as if they are happening right now.
- When you experience positive emotions, notice these and label them.

**Alone**

- If you reminisce on your own, select a time and place where there are no distractions and when you will not be interrupted.
- Reminisce for 20 minutes each day for a week.
- Select a different positive event to recollect each day to prevent adaptation.

**With another**

- Meet for an evening, or take a trip to the place you are reminiscing about for a whole day.
- Describe the events that happened in detail.
- Repeat and elaborate your recollections.

**Assess effects on positive emotions**

- Before and after this exercise, rate the strength of your positive emotions in your journal on a scale from 1 to 10.
- On this scale 10 means that you are experiencing extremely strong positive emotions, 1 means you are experiencing extremely strong negative emotions and 5 means you are feeling fairly neutral emotionally.
- Note the extent to which the exercise increased the strength of your positive emotions.
- Note any aspects of the exercise that you think specifically contributed to this.

*Make a savouring reminiscence album*[20]

This exercise allows you to use savouring cherished memories as a way of increasing positive emotions in your day-to-day life. Make an album of photos that remind you of particularly happy moments in your life, people in your life who make you feel good or places that you associate with happiness. For example, you may include pictures of special events such as graduations, weddings or parties; your children at different ages; yourself and your partner at different stages of your relationship; or places where you lived previously or were on vacation that bring happy memories to mind. You may make this album in hardcopy or on your phone, tablet or computer. From time to time, review pictures in this album and reminisce about the positive experiences prompted by the photographs. In your journal write down your reflections on doing this exercise. Box 7.7 contains a summary of this exercise.

---

## Box 7.7 Make a savouring reminiscence album

- Make an album of photos that remind you of particularly happy moments in your life, people in your life who make you feel good or places that you associate with happiness.
- You may include pictures of special events such as graduations, weddings or parties; your children at different ages; yourself and your partner at different stages of your relationship; or places where you lived previously or were on vacation that bring happy memories to mind.
- You may make this album in hardcopy or on your phone, tablet or computer.
- From time to time, review pictures in this album and reminisce about the positive experiences prompted by the photographs.
- In your journal write down your reflections on doing this exercise.

**Note:** The savouring reminiscence album exercise is based on the savouring album exercise on page 200 in Lyubomirsky, S. (2007). *The how of happiness.* New York, NY: Penguin.

---

### Optimistically anticipating

We are naturally drawn to worry about things in the future that may not go well. This disposition has served our species well by protecting us from predators and other dangers. However, we use this capacity far less frequently to vividly imagine positive things that may happen in future to make ourselves feel happy. This exercise is an opportunity for you to vividly and optimistically anticipate a positive future event. It will help you to experience some of the positive emotions associated with this special occasion. Select a time and place where there are no distractions and when you will not be interrupted. You may optimistically anticipate either alone or with a family member or friend. The process will have a greater impact if you do it with someone who will be present at the happy event you are anticipating. Select the positive experience you are optimistically anticipating, for example a party, a birthday, a wedding, the birth of a child, a holiday, a sporting event, a graduation, a work achievement or an adventure. If possible, use photographs of the place where the event will happen or of the people who will be there to intensify anticipated images of the positive event.

These sorts of reminders make anticipation more vivid, and the positive emotions it evokes more intense and moving. While optimistically anticipating, visualise the events as if they are happening right now. If you are doing this exercise with a friend or family member, describe the events as you expect them to happen in detail. When you experience positive emotions, pay attention to how you feel. Try to lengthen and strengthen these positive emotions by visualising or talking in more detail about the occasion you are anticipating. Repeat or elaborate your descriptions of what you expect will happen. When you experience positive emotions, pay attention to how you feel. In your journal write down your reflections on doing this exercise. Adopting an optimistic perspective on the future has been shown in many studies to increase well-being.[21] Box 7.8 contains a summary of this exercise.

## Box 7.8   Optimistically anticipating

- Select a time and place where there are no distractions and when you will not be interrupted.
- You may optimistically anticipate either alone or with a family member or friend.
- Select the positive experience you are optimistically anticipating, for example a party, a birthday, a wedding, the birth of a child, a holiday, a sporting event, a graduation, a work achievement or an adventure.
- Lengthen and strengthen positive emotions arising from optimistically anticipating by using these strategies:
- Use photographs of the place where the event will happen or of the people who will be there to intensify anticipated images of the positive event.
- Visualise the events as if they are happening right now.
- If you are doing this exercise with a friend or family member, describe the events as you expect them to happen in a lot of detail, repeating and elaborating your descriptions.
- When you experience positive emotions, pay attention to how you feel.
- In your journal write down your reflections on doing this exercise.

## Flow

Have you ever been so absorbed in what you were doing that you didn't notice time passing, forgot about yourself and afterwards felt really good? If you did, you were probably experiencing flow. Professor Mihaly Csikszentmihalyi at Claremont Graduate School California is the founder of the psychology of flow. He has shown through extensive research that when we engage in challenging but controllable highly skilled tasks that are intrinsically motivating, we experience a unique psychological state, referred to as flow.[22] Flow has been shown to occur in many sports,[23] when playing music,[24] when viewing beautiful art,[25] when involved in creative writing[26] or scholarship[27] and when involved in computer-based activities including video games.[28] Flow experiences are also associated with better performance and satisfaction in educational[29] and work[30] environments. After you have completed a challenging, skilled activity you can assess the intensity of your flow experience with the short flow scale in Box 7.9. You can increase the intensity of flow experiences by doing the exercises on enhancing flow described later in this chapter.

## Box 7.9   The short flow scale

After you have completed a challenging, skilled activity you can assess the intensity of your flow experience with this scale.

Rate each item on a scale of 1 to 7 where

1 means not at all

4 means partly and

7 means very much.

Sum the 10 item scores to give an overall score between 10 and 70.

Higher overall scores indicate that you experienced a higher level of flow.

| | | | | | | | | |
|---|---|---|---|---|---|---|---|---|
| 1 | I feel just the right amount of challenge | 1 | 2 | 3 | 4 | 5 | 6 | 7 |
| 2 | My thoughts/activities run fluidly and smoothly | 1 | 2 | 3 | 4 | 5 | 6 | 7 |
| 3 | I don't notice time passing | 1 | 2 | 3 | 4 | 5 | 6 | 7 |
| 4 | I have no difficulty concentrating | 1 | 2 | 3 | 4 | 5 | 6 | 7 |
| 5 | My mind is completely clear | 1 | 2 | 3 | 4 | 5 | 6 | 7 |
| 6 | I am totally absorbed in what I am doing | 1 | 2 | 3 | 4 | 5 | 6 | 7 |
| 7 | The right thoughts or movements occur of their own accord | 1 | 2 | 3 | 4 | 5 | 6 | 7 |
| 8 | I know what I have to do each step of the way | 1 | 2 | 3 | 4 | 5 | 6 | 7 |
| 9 | I feel that I have everything under control | 1 | 2 | 3 | 4 | 5 | 6 | 7 |
| 10 | I am completely lost in thought | 1 | 2 | 3 | 4 | 5 | 6 | 7 |
| | Total | | | | | | | |

**Note:** Items 1–10 are reprinted by permission from Springer Nature Customer Service Centre GmbH: Springer Nature, *Motivation and Emotion*, 32(3), 158–172, Flow, performance and moderators of challenge–skill balance by Engeser, S., & Rheinberg, F. Copyright © 2008 by Springer Nature.

Flow experiences have many benefits. They help us to feel involved and absorbed in our lives. They help us to enjoy skilled activities that we find intrinsically interesting. They allow us to experience a strong sense of control over what we are doing. They also strengthen our sense of identity by allowing us to say things like 'I am the sort of person who does XYZ well, and who likes to do this'. Collectively these benefits give our lives a sense of meaning and increase our well-being.

The defining feature of flow is total experiential absorption in an activity and temporary loss of awareness of other aspects of the self and one's life situation. For flow experiences to occur we must have a good chance of completing tasks which are intrinsically enjoyable. Tasks must be sufficiently challenging to tax our skills to the limit. There must be a balance between the challenges posed by the task and available skills. Tasks must not be so difficult that we become anxious, or not so easy that we become bored. During flow experiences, we use skills that are sufficiently well developed to be automatic. Tasks are carried out to achieve clear goals and immediate unambiguous feedback is available to indicate progress towards these goals. With flow experiences, tasks require total concentration, so we become deeply and effortlessly involved in them, so much so that we no longer think of the worries and frustrations of everyday life. During flow experiences, there is a heightened sense of control over our actions. With this sense of control there is a lack of anxiety about losing control, even though the actions may be risky; for example, when skydiving, surfing or rock-climbing. During flow experiences our sense of self disappears. Paradoxically, the sense of self emerges as strengthened after the task is completed. Time perception is altered during flow experiences, so that it appears to speed up or slow down. In summary, flow experiences have nine key attributes: (1) intrinsic enjoyment in doing the task, (2) challenge–skill balance, (3) automaticity of actions, (4) goal clarity, (5) feedback, (6) concentration on task, (7) sense of control, (8) loss of self-consciousness and (9) time transformation.

### Challenge-skill balance

The tasks which lead to flow experiences must demand that we use our skills almost to their limits. It is also important that the task be completable; for example, finishing reading or writing a piece of prose, completing a piece of music or finishing a game. In flow experiences the ratio of the challenge entailed by an activity to the skill required for the activity is close to 1:1. When in flow, we are operating at an above-average level of challenge and skill.

### Goals and feedback

Tasks that lead to flow experiences have clear, not vague, goals. Feedback about movement towards these goals is immediate, not delayed. Sports like competitive sailing or tennis involve extremely clear goals such as rounding marks before other boats or scoring points. In all sports feedback is immediate. The competitor knows on a moment-to-moment basis if they are winning or losing. This feedback is used to take corrective action by using well-developed automatic skills.

### Concentration and lack of self-awareness

Because tasks that lead to flow experiences involve working towards clear goals and receiving immediate feedback about movement towards these goals, a deep level of concentration on the task is essential. This results in a loss of awareness of the self. We stop being aware of ourselves as separate from the tasks in which we are involved. The dancer becomes the dance. The singer becomes the song. The sailor becomes one with the boat. Lapses in concentration or diversion into self-criticism can erase the flow experience and the quality of skilled task performance. So, during flow experiences we do not ask ourselves 'Should I be doing this?', or 'Is there a better alternative?', because to do so would disrupt the flow experience. One outcome of this temporary loss of self-awareness is that after flow experiences our sense of self is strengthened. This is because during flow experiences, we do not devote mental energy to thinking 'How am I doing?' or 'What do others think of me?' However, after a flow experience, we may reflect on what we have achieved and think 'Wow! I did that. I am the sort of person that can do this stuff!'

### Transformation of time

When we are involved in flow experiences our perception of time is distorted. With repetitive tasks, hours can pass in what seem to be minutes. In contrast, with tasks that require rapid complex skills, time may appear to slow down. For example, if we are fully engrossed in reading a good book, hours may fly by in what seems like minutes. The experience of elapsed time in such instances is condensed. In other flow experiences the experience of elapsed time is extended. For example, executing rapid skilled manoeuvres in competitive sailing in windy conditions may take no more than seconds, but during flow experiences these manoeuvres seem to occur almost in slow motion.

### Autotelic tasks and the autotelic personality

The defining characteristic of activities that lead to flow experiences is that they become an end in themselves or autotelic. Autotelic comes from the Greek words for self (auto) and goal (telos). Autotelic experiences are those that arise from activities which are not done primarily for some anticipated future benefit but mainly because the activity is intrinsically and immediately rewarding in itself. While these tasks may initially be done for other reasons, ultimately they are done because they are intrinsically rewarding. Writers often say that they write not for financial or occupational advancement but because it is so enjoyable. Sailors may spend a lot of money and time getting their boats into good condition, not because they want to win sailing competitions or maintain contact with other sailors, but because, for them, nothing compares with the flow experience of competitive sailing. While most people experience flow, there is considerable variability in the frequency with which people report flow and the intensity of these flow experiences. This observation led to the idea of the autotelic personality, characterised by the tendency to place greater emphasis on doing tasks for their own sake, rather than for the outcome of such tasks.[31] People with autotelic personalities have meta-skills that enable them to enter and maintain flow states with relative ease. These meta-skills include curiosity, persistence and low self-centeredness.

### Flow in families

Certain types of families promote the experience of flow.[32] Children from families characterised by optimal levels of clarity, centring, choice, commitment and challenge have more frequent flow experiences. In families with optimal levels of clarity, goals and feedback are unambiguous. Children know clearly what is expected of them. In families with optimal levels of centring, children know that their parents are interested in what they are doing and experiencing now in the present. They know that their parents are not always preoccupied with whether they will get a good job, or a place in a good college after they finished school. In families with optimal levels of choice, children believe that they have a degree of choice over how they behave. They are aware that different choices, including breaking parental rules, are associated with different consequences. In families with optimal levels of commitment, children feel that the family is sufficiently safe for them to unselfconsciously become involved in activities and sports that really interest them without fear of being judged negatively, criticised or humiliated. For children to be fully committed to activities in which they have flow experiences, they have to feel a high level of trust in their parents. In families where there is an optimal level of challenge, parents are dedicated to providing children with increasingly complex opportunities for exercising their unique and developing skills as they became older and more skilful.

There are specific things that we can do to help our children have more flow experiences. We can provide them with clear goals and feedback. We can respect what interests them now, rather than exclusively focusing on what might be good for them in the distant future. We can give them opportunities to make choices about what they do, and be mindful of the consequences of these choices. We can encourage them to unselfconsciously try their best at activities they choose. We can offer them opportunities to face bigger challenges as they get older. Box 7.10 contains a summary of these guidelines.

---

**Box 7.10   Parenting so children develop flow**

- Support children doing what interests them now, rather than exclusively focusing on what might be good for them in the distant future.
- Encourage them to unselfconsciously try their best at these activities that interest them.

- Provide them with clear goals and immediate feedback.
- Give them opportunities to make choices about what they do, and let them know the consequences of these choices.
- Offer them opportunities to face bigger challenges as they get older.

### Culture and flow

Certain cultures are conducive to flow experiences.[33] All cultures evolve goals to which citizens aspire and social norms, roles, rules and rituals which specify the ways in which these goals may legitimately be achieved. Cultures in which the goals, norms, roles, rules and rituals closely match the skills of the population afford citizens more opportunities for flow experiences. The frequency with which flow experiences occur in different cultures may vary depending upon prevailing practices in a variety of areas associated with flow experiences including work, religion and sport. Work-based flow experiences are more common in cultures that permit people to have work roles that are neither monotonously boring, nor overly challenging and stressful, but where role demands meet workers' skills levels. Flow experiences are more common in cultures where religious rituals involving dance, singing or meditation, which promote flow experiences, are widely practised. Flow experiences are more common in cultures where skilled games against well-matched competitors are widely practised.

Within our own western culture, we can increase the frequency of flow experiences by taking steps to develop work roles in which the demands of our jobs challenge us to use our skills to the limits of our abilities. We can increase our ritualistic-based flow experiences by developing skills for dance, music, rhythmic exercise or meditation and practising these skills regularly. We can increase our sports-based flow experiences by involving ourselves in one or more sports, becoming skilled in these and then practising them regularly so that our skills are moderately challenged. We can increase the frequency of flow experience associated with intellectual activities by having a commitment to lifelong learning and to maintaining an inquiring mind.

### How to create flow in physical activities

To develop the capacity to experience flow in carrying out physical activities like running or swimming, there are some straightforward guidelines to follow.[34] First, set an overall goal and break this down into a number of subgoals. Second, decide on a way of measuring progress towards the goals that you have chosen. Third, concentrate on doing the activity as well as you can when you are doing it and noting how well you are achieving your subgoals. Fourth, gradually increase the difficulty or complexity of the subgoals you are aiming for, so that the challenge you face matches your level of growing skill. Box 7.11 contains a summary of these guidelines.

### Box 7.11   Creating flow in physical activities

- Select a time and place where there are no distractions and when you will not be interrupted.
- Set an overall goal and break this down into a number of subgoals.

- Select a way of measuring progress towards the goals.
- Concentrate on doing the activity as well as you can when you are doing it and noting how well you are achieving your subgoals.
- Gradually increase the difficulty or complexity of the subgoals you are aiming for, so that the challenge you face matches your level of growing skill.

**Note:** Based on Jackson, S., & Kimiecik, J. (2008). The flow perspective of optimal experience in sport and physical activity. In T. Horn (Ed.), *Advances in sport psychology* (Third Edition, pp. 377-399, 474-477). Champaign, IL: Human Kinetics.

### Finding out what makes you flow

There is no single activity that creates flow experiences for all people. If you want to increase the amount of time you spend in flow, it would be useful find out in what activities you currently experience flow. To do this you may wish to monitor the extent to which you experience flow over a period of a few days, for example two typical weekdays (like Tuesdays and Thursday) and two weekend days. On these days, approximately once each waking hour write down in your journal the activity you were doing and what your flow rating was for the past hour. You can remind yourself to do this by setting the alarm on your smartphone. You can rate your flow experience on each occasion using the 10-item short flow scale in Box 7.9. If you circle responses to each of the items in pencil each time you complete the scale, you may then erase these marks after you calculate your total, so the scale can be re-used repeatedly. When you have monitored your flow experiences over four days, you will have a good idea about the activities in which you experience the greatest intensity of flow. You may find that spending long periods watching TV is not associated with flow, whereas working hard at something interesting is. Box 7.12 contains a summary of these guidelines.

## Box 7.12   Increasing flow in your life

**Identify activities associated with flow**

- Select two typical weekdays and two weekend days.
- Once an hour, on each of these days, in your journal write down the activity you were doing and your flow rating for the past hour.
- Rate your flow experience on each occasion using the short flow scale in Box 7.9.
- Review your flow ratings after four days, and note the activities in which you experience the greatest intensity of flow.
- Decide if you wish to spend more time doing activities associated with flow.

**Create flow in activities not normally associated with flow**

- Concentrate on tasks not normally associated with flow.
- Do them as skilfully as possible.

- Set goals and notice the extent to which you are achieving these.
- Notice the things that you could do to improve your performance the next time.
- Explore ways to match the challenge posed by the task to your skill level.
- Do complex tasks more slowly and simple tasks more quickly and carefully.
- For tedious tasks, find ways to make the task more complex and challenging.
- Divide overwhelmingly complex tasks into smaller more manageable subtasks; become skilful at completing each subtask; then combine the subtasks together.
- In your journal write down a rating of your flow experience on each occasion using the short flow scale in Box 7.9.
- Review your flow ratings after a week, and note any increases in the level of flow you are experiencing in activities not normally associated with flow.
- Decide if you wish to continue to do activities not normally associated with flow, in ways that increase your experience of flow.

### Increasing flow in your life

If you want to increase flow experiences in your life, make a commitment to doing so for a brief period, perhaps a week initially to see if this suits you. During this period, try to spend more time doing activities associated with flow that you identified by monitoring your flow experiences over four days, as described in the previous section. However, that is only one half of the plan. The other half is to learn how to create flow in activities that do not normally give you flow experiences.

In all of the activities that you do that do not normally lead to flow experiences, however tedious or overwhelming they may initially seem, look for ways of creating flow while doing them. You can do this by concentrating on the task. Consider all of its elements. Explore ways to match the challenge posed by the task to your current level of skill. This may involve doing complex tasks (like balancing your budget) more slowly and simple tasks (like vacuuming or emptying the dishwasher) more quickly and carefully. For overwhelmingly complex tasks (like assembling flatpack furniture or doing your tax return), break them down into smaller more manageable subtasks, become skilful at completing each subtask, and then gradually combine the subtasks together. For very tedious tasks, look for ways to make the task more complex and challenging. For example, you might decide to focus mindfully on a task like doing the ironing or mowing the lawn, noticing all of the sensations that occur as you do these tasks. Or you might combine these with singing or listening to a current affairs radio programme. These processes will allow you to match the complexity of the task to your skill level. When you are engaged in these tasks, try to do them as skilfully as possible. Notice the extent to which you are achieving your goals. Notice the things that you could do to improve your performance the next time. After completing activities in which you would not normally experience flow, in a new and creative way, write down a rating of your flow experience in your journal using the short flow scale in Box 7.9. Review your flow ratings after a week, and note any increases in the level of flow you are experiencing in activities not normally associated with flow. Decide if you wish to continue to do activities not normally associated with flow, in new and creative ways that increase your experience of flow.

# Summary

- **Savouring** refers to processes that enhance positive experiences arising from pleasant sensations. We can savour current experiences, past memories or anticipated future events. Savouring involves deliberately paying attention to, appreciating, enhancing and prolonging positive experiences and the positive emotions that accompany them, and preventing the rapid adaptation to positive experiences associated with the hedonic treadmill. Savouring momentary positive experiences can have long-term effects on well-being.
- **Different savouring processes regulate differing positive emotions**. Luxuriating regulates pleasure. Thanksgiving regulates gratitude. Basking regulates pride. Marvelling regulates awe.
- **Savouring strategies** include being highly attentive to positive aspects of the situation and our positive experiences within the situation, becoming absorbed and focusing on the present moment, building memories by taking mental snapshots and labelling positive experiences, comparing positive experience to less positive ones, acknowledging that positive events are transient, congratulating ourselves after success, being thankful for positive events, expressing positive emotions and sharing good news with others.
- **Dampening strategies** that diminish positive emotions include distracting ourselves from positive emotions, suppressing expression of them, kill-joy thinking and negative mental time travel.
- **Savouring differs from mindfulness** where there is no attempt to prolong experiences of pleasant sensations, or to focus on past or future positive experiences, or to block out distractions or negative emotions.
- **Savouring exercises** include taking a daily vacation, relishing ordinary activities, reminiscence, making a savouring reminiscence album and optimistically anticipating future positive events.
- **Flow** is total experiential absorption in an activity requiring a high level of control and concentration, and temporary loss of awareness of other aspects of the self and one's life situation. Paradoxically, the sense of self emerges as strengthened after flow experiences. In tasks which lead to flow experiences, skills are used almost to their limits to achieve clearly defined goals for which there is immediate feedback. Perception of time is distorted. Long periods of time may seem like minutes, or very brief episodes of skilled action may feel like they are occurring in slow motion.
- **Increasing flow.** We can improve our well-being by increasing the frequency and intensity of flow experiences in our lives. This involves doing activities in which we experience flow more frequently, and finding ways to experience flow in tedious or overwhelming activities that do not normally lead to flow experiences.
- **Flow and parenting.** Children from families characterised by optimal levels of clarity, centring, choice, commitment and challenge have more frequent flow experiences.

# Where are you now?

If you have done the exercises in this chapter, you have found out how savouring and flow can affect your well-being. Savouring involves making the most of good things in life by strengthening and lengthening pleasurable experiences. Flow experiences arise when we become absorbed in skilled activity in challenging situations.

You may want to read back over the chapter and summarise in your journal the main things that you have learned about savouring and flow. You can now decide if you want to make savouring and flow part of your day-to-day routine for the long-term.

In the next chapter, we will consider gratitude, and the benefits of being grateful for good things that happen in our lives. Below are some web resources and a book that are relevant to topics you have read about in this chapter.

## Web resources

Podcast interview with Fred Bryant talking about savouring (26:26): www.michellemcquaid.com/podcast/fred-bryant

Mihaly Csikszentmihalyi defining flow video (2:40): www.youtube.com/watch?v=GZbUDzmKvus

Tedtalk by Mihaly Csikszentmihalyi talking about flow video (18:55): www.youtube.com/watch?v=fXIeFJCqsPs

## Book

Csikszentmihalyi, M. (1997). *Finding flow: The psychology of engagement with everyday life.* New York, NY: Basic Books.

# 8  Gratitude

When we experience gratitude, it's because we have experienced good things that had definite benefits for us. Let's call these good things 'gifts'. Gratitude involves recalling these gifts, appreciating their benefits, experiencing positive emotions and expressing this appreciation by showing that we are thankful and generously giving gifts to others.[1]

There are many gifts that evoke gratitude. We can be grateful for personal strengths such as health, pregnancy, intelligence, athleticism, beauty or longevity. We can be grateful for things in our environment and wonders of the world; for example, food, housing, utilities, amenities, physical comfort, good weather, beautiful scenery and art. We can also be grateful for things that others do for us like offering employment, financial assistance, presents, celebrations, entertainment, camaraderie, practical help, emotional support, attachment and love.

## State and trait gratitude

When psychologists study gratitude they distinguish between gratitude as a transient state and gratitude as an enduring trait.[2] We may experience a state of gratitude in certain situations, for example when someone helps us. There is an immediate recognition that a gift has been received and an associated positive emotion.

Trait gratitude refers to the general disposition to be grateful, or the attitude of gratitude. The attitude of gratitude is the tendency to see all of life as a gift for which we are thankful, and to make a conscious choice to be appreciative. We acknowledge that there are good things in life and recognise that the source of these is outside ourselves. The source may be other people, nature, God or some other spiritual force. When we are grateful we don't take the good things in life for granted. We don't feel automatically entitled to certain privileges. Nor do we feel that we deserve them. We see the benevolence of others, and feel generosity, kindness and compassion towards them. However, gratitude is distinct from feeling indebted to others. With indebtedness, we are happy that someone has done something to please us. In return, we feel obliged to do something to please them.

### Profiles of grateful people

Research shows that the characteristics of people who are consistently grateful – that is, people with high levels of trait gratitude – have distinctive personal profiles.[2] They tend to be happier and healthier than those who have low levels of trait gratitude. Grateful people tend to have higher levels of positive emotions such as joy, happiness, enthusiasm and love. They also have lower levels of negative emotions such as anxiety and depression. Grateful people tend to be emotionally stable, self-confident and agreeable. They tend not to be narcissistic or self-centred. Grateful people tend to hold spiritual rather than materialistic values. You can assess your level of trait gratitude by completing the gratitude questionnaire in Box 8.1. You can increase your level of trait gratitude by doing the exercises described later in this chapter.

---

## Box 8.1   Gratitude questionnaire

You may complete this questionnaire to assess how strong your current disposition to be grateful is.

For each item circle the response that applies to you right now; add and sum the scores for all six items.

Scores between 38 and 42 are in the average range.

25% of people get scores lower than this range and 25% of people get scores higher than this range.

| | | | | | | | | |
|---|---|---|---|---|---|---|---|---|
| 1 | I have so much in life to be thankful for. | Strongly disagree | Disagree | Slightly disagree | Neutral | Slightly agree | Agree | Strongly agree |
| | | 1 | 2 | 3 | 4 | 5 | 6 | 7 |
| 2 | If I had to list everything that I felt grateful for, it would be a very long list. | Strongly disagree | Disagree | Slightly disagree | Neutral | Slightly agree | Agree | Strongly agree |
| | | 1 | 2 | 3 | 4 | 5 | 6 | 7 |
| 3 | When I look at the world, I don't see much to be grateful for. | Strongly agree | Agree | Slightly agree | Neutral | Slightly disagree | Disagree | Strongly disagree |
| | | 7 | 6 | 5 | 4 | 3 | 2 | 1 |
| 4 | I am grateful to a wide variety of people. | Strongly disagree | Disagree | Slightly disagree | Neutral | Slightly agree | Agree | Strongly agree |
| | | 1 | 2 | 3 | 4 | 5 | 6 | 7 |
| 5 | As I get older, I find myself more able to appreciate the people, events and situations that have been part of my life history. | Strongly disagree | Disagree | Slightly disagree | Neutral | Slightly agree | Agree | Strongly agree |
| | | 1 | 2 | 3 | 4 | 5 | 6 | 7 |
| 6 | Long periods of time can go by before I feel grateful to something or someone. | Strongly agree | Agree | Slightly agree | Neutral | Slightly disagree | Disagree | Strongly disagree |
| | | 7 | 6 | 5 | 4 | 3 | 2 | 1 |

**Note:** Adapted with permission from McCullough, M. E., Emmons, R. A., & Tsang, J. (2002). The grateful disposition: A conceptual and empirical topography. *Journal of Personality and Social Psychology, 82*, 112–127. Copyright © 2002 by American Psychological Association.

### Gratitude journaling, letters and visits

Professor Robert Emmons at the University of California, Davis has pioneered research on the effects of gratitude interventions on well-being. His seminal study showed that people who kept a gratitude journal in which they recorded up to five good things that they were grateful for each day showed increased positive mood compared to people who wrote about hassles they had encountered.[3] There is an example of an entry from a gratitude journal in Box 8.2. Professor Martin Seligman found that writing a gratitude letter, visiting the person to whom it was written and reading it to them had a positive effect on well-being.[4] In these gratitude letters people described how they had been helped, the effect of this on them and how thankful they were. There is an example of a gratitude letter in Box 8.3. Many other studies have confirmed Robert Emmons and Martin Seligman's findings and shown that well-being can be increased by gratitude journaling, letters and visits.[5] These positive psychology interventions help people cultivate an attitude of gratitude and enhance their well-being.

---

### Box 8.2   A page from a gratitude journal

I am thankful for four things that happened today: the alarm clock going off at 8; the robin; being with Kerry; and the hour before sundown.

**The alarm.** This morning my alarm went off at 8.00. I awoke with a start. I thought 'Oh no! I'll be late for work. I should have got up at 7.00'. Then as I jumped out of bed, I realised that it was bank holiday Monday! I was so relieved. I felt fantastic. I wasn't going to be late for work and I had a whole day to help Kerry with her garden. Brilliant!!

**The robin.** Doing the garden with Kerry was great – but the robin thing made it really special. We were planting a whole new set of shrubs in the border, when a robin came and perched on the new arch we had put in yesterday. He sat there, with his little redbreast all puffed out, turning his head right and left, keeping an eye on things. I whispered to Kerry to look. We love birds. I was amazed at the way he just perched there. Keeping an eye on everything. Like a little prince of all he surveyed. I was grateful to see this little prince. Wow!

**Kerry.** Late in the afternoon the phone rang. Kerry went in to answer it. She was gone for about 20 minutes. It was June calling her to tell her about some arrangements for next week. I was left in the garden on my own, cutting the hedge. The sun went in behind a cloud. Something about the way the light was in the garden and Kerry not being there made me think for moment what it would be like if she wasn't in my life. I mean, what would my life be like if I had never met her. Never married her. Never had kids with her. I felt cold and empty for a moment. Then I saw her standing in the doorway holding the phone to her ear. She smiled and waved to me. I'm sure to anyone else, she looked like an ordinary middle-aged woman in gardening clothes. In that moment, I thought she was the most radiant person I had ever seen. I felt a huge welling up of emotion inside me. I thought, 'I'm so glad you are in my life. If I had never met you, my life would never have been so wonderful. I'm so grateful to have met you'.

**The hour before sundown.** I noticed in the evening that the sun would soon sink below the level of the big trees at the end of the garden. Then the garden would feel gloomy. It would be time to call it a day and go inside. I like being outside in the sun. I didn't let myself sink into that sad after-sundown feeling that I sometimes get. Instead I thought, 'Let's enjoy the last hour of sunlight'. I made us both a sundowner. We sat on the porch sipping them slowly. Enjoying the last hour of sunlight. I felt really grateful for that last hour of sunlight in the garden, with Kerry, in the sunshine, sipping a sundowner. How lucky can you get?

---

## Box 8.3  A gratitude letter from James to Gerry

Dear Gerry,

I am writing to thank you for the all the help and support you gave me when I nearly dropped out of college about 10 years ago. Time has passed. I feel like I never really thanked you properly. So, this letter is my attempt to make up for that and let you know just how much you helped me and how exceptionally grateful I am for your kindness and generosity.

It was in the winter of 2003. I got the results of my first round of university exams. I didn't pass all of them. I was devastated. I thought my folks would disown me. I couldn't face my classmates. They all passed their exams. I was the only one in the class to fail. I thought my older brother would pity me. I can't stand being pitied. I'd never failed an exam before. I was always top of my class in secondary school.

The pharmacy degree programme I started in September 2002 was very competitive. When I moved for secondary school to college I was a little fish in a big pond. Halfway through my first semester my relationship with Claire ended. It broke my heart. I couldn't sleep properly or eat or concentrate for weeks. I couldn't follow the coursework at college. I couldn't study. I was a complete mess. Looking back, I can see now that it's not surprising I failed an exam. In fact, it's a miracle I passed any of them.

A couple of days after New Year's 2003 my folks had a big family get-together at our house. You found me sitting in the den playing Grand Theft Auto on the computer and said it wasn't like me to be a recluse. That's all you said at first. You just sat there for a while. Whatever way you said that, or the way you just sat there not judging me or anything, made me feel safe. You always made me feel safe. Anyway, I told you the whole story. Well, most of it.

You said you could see I was having the toughest time of my life. You asked me if I could come over the next day and help you fix up the fence at the end of your garden. For the next week, I went over to your place every day and we worked on the fence. Then we fixed up some shelves in the garage. Then we painted your spare room. Through all of this, you never asked me to pull myself together, or get a grip, or brighten up or any of that stuff. You didn't tell me that I would pass my repeats. You didn't tell me that time would heal my broken heart. You were just there. You took me as I was. You listened when I told you about how much I missed Claire. How I should have treated her better. How guilty I felt. You understood how hard failure hit me. How I thought I was no good because I had failed.

The way you were back then made it possible for me to go on. I was, I am, I will always be completely grateful to you for the way you were there for me that time. I never said thank you properly. So, I am saying it now.

I went back to college a few days after we finished fixing up your place. When I got back home in May, you had moved away. Dad said you had got a new job and that's why you moved. I guess my life had got busy. So had yours. So, I never really caught up with you again. You live in Tokyo. I live in Dublin.

I hope life is being good to you.

You probably know that I got my pharmacy degree, then went on to do graduate research. I have an academic job now. It's great. I love it. I'm doing research and teaching. My students are great. One of them failed an exam this semester, and I guessed there was some backstory in his life that explained why he failed. That made me think of you and how you helped me. So, I wrote you this letter.

Thanks Gerry. You're the best uncle a guy could have. I hope life brings you all the good things you deserve.

With much love.

James.

## *How gratitude increases well-being*

Gratitude increases well-being for a number of reasons.[6] First, when we are grateful and express gratitude, we experience positive emotions. It's difficult to feel negative emotions like fear and anxiety, sadness and depression, anger and bitterness, or greed and disgust when you are grateful for your lot in life. The positive emotions that come from gratitude, such as joy, happiness, enthusiasm and love, may momentarily broaden our perspective and allow us to create new possibilities in our lives, according to the Broaden and Build theory discussed in Chapter 1.[7] Cultivating an attitude of gratitude may also shift the ratio of positive to negative feelings discussed in Chapter 1.[8]

Second, the overall attitude of gratitude prevents us from taking enjoyable things for granted. We pay attention to the small pleasures in life, savour them and are grateful for them.[9] (Savouring was discussed in Chapter 7.) This, in turn, slows down the rate at which we adapt to pleasant experiences. (In Chapter 1 it was noted that eventually we adapt to most things that make us happy, a process referred to as the hedonic treadmill.[10])

Third, when we are grateful for the small pleasures in life, this reduces materialistic strivings which, as we saw in Chapter 1, have a negative effect on well-being.[11] Gratitude is one of the character strengths discussed in Chapter 3, associated with the virtue of transcendence, which involves a more spiritual set of values than materialism.[12]

Fourth, gratitude shifts our focus away from the negative towards the positive.[13] This has a wide range of benefits. We are more aware of our own good qualities than our deficits, and so gratitude increases self-esteem. Gratitude strengthens our relationships because we focus on the helpful things others do for us, rather than on the ways they annoy or distress us.[14] This makes us more likely to spend time with them, and be kinder to them. Thus, gratitude helps us to have more loving marriages and families and build social support networks.

Fifth, gratitude also makes us respond more positively to adversity, by being grateful that worse things did not occur. For example, we may be grateful that we were not more seriously injured in a car accident; that the prognosis for a serious illness was not worse; or that we are still healthy despite having major financial problems.

Finally, an attitude of gratitude makes it less likely that we will make negative comparisons between our situation and that of others. We are grateful for what we have got, and are less likely to be disappointed, envious or resentful that we are not keeping up with the Joneses.

### Obstacles to gratitude

There are a number of obstacles to adopting an attitude of gratitude and being grateful for the good things in life.[15] Some of these obstacles are ingrained personal habits or personality traits that are not easy to change.

It's difficult to adopt an attitude of gratitude if we firmly believe that we have few short-comings, and are more important than others, and so are entitled to many privileges. Moving from this way of looking at the world to humbly seeing others as kind and generous, and all people as being equally deserving of good things, is a difficult transition to make.

Strong materialistic values also inhibit gratitude. If we consistently engage in materialistic striving to have more and more material things, or experience envy and resentment when we see that others have more than we do, then it's difficult to develop a thankful appreciation for the good things in life and the kindness of others.

If we view ourselves as helpless victims who others take advantage of, it's difficult to be grateful. It is a challenging process to make the transition from this position, to seeing our-selves as survivors who are grateful to be alive and appreciative of the small kindnesses and good things that come our way each day.

The tendency to focus more on negative things than positive things is another obstacle to gratitude. If we regularly think of bad things that we were unable to avoid or good things that we were unable to acquire, then it will be difficult to feel grateful. Unfortunately, through nat-ural selection we are all designed to pay more attention to negative things that threaten our well-being than to positive things.[16] (This was discussed in Chapter 1.) This 'negativity bias' helped our ancestors avoid threats to our survival. However, some of us, especially those who suffer from depression, have a particularly strong negativity bias, which makes adopting an attitude of gratitude very challenging. To overcome this bias, we must exert considerable willpower to focus more on positive than negative things.

For those of us who have been socialised into thinking that expressing tender feelings is a bad thing, it may be difficult to express gratitude. It's not uncommon in some families for boys to be taught that it's a sign of weakness to express thanks, and so for them being grateful is challenging. Carefully and repeatedly reflecting on the pros and cons of expressing tender feelings including gratitude is necessary to overcome this obstacle.

When we receive a gift or a good turn from someone who has also hurt us and who we have not forgiven, the hurt and/or anger that we feel towards them may make it difficult to be grateful. Family members (parents, partners and children) may all do wonderfully gener-ous things, for which we may wish to be grateful. However, if they have let us down or hurt us in some way, and we have been unable to forgive them, then being grateful may be very difficult. Taking steps towards forgiveness is essential to overcome this obstacle. Forgiveness is discussed in Chapter 17.

When we receive gifts that are obviously given with the intention of controlling us, by making us feel indebted to the person who gave the gift, this prevents us feeling gratitude. For example, it is difficult to feel gratitude when we receive very lavish gifts that are given with a clear message that some favour is expected in return.

The expectation that others will be grateful when we show kindness and compassion towards them is an obstacle to developing an attitude of gratitude. This is because much of the time other people will not say thank you to us. They may be too busy, not notice or be too embarrassed to say thanks.

A final obstacle to gratitude is the overvaluing of self-sufficiency and devaluing of inter-dependence. Modern western culture prizes self-sufficiency, autonomy and independence. These values inhibit the cultivation of gratitude.

When we adopt an attitude of gratitude, we accept that we are interdependent. That is, we accept that we depend on each other for survival and well-being. Without our families, friends, work colleagues, communities and society, surviving would be very challenging, and life would be grim. Therefore, we are grateful for the good things we receive within these relationships.

## Gratitude journal

Gratitude journaling is a way of cultivating an attitude of gratitude. In a gratitude journal, we regularly write down things that we are grateful for. Keeping a gratitude journal increases well-being and health. Professor Robert Emmons has developed a three-week gratitude programme which is informed by important research findings on gratitude journaling.[17] The seven exercises in this programme are summarised in Boxes 8.4 to 8.10. They are:

- Box 8.4. Being thankful for three good things.
- Box 8.5. Giving thanks to whom and for what.
- Box 8.6. Giving thanks for three gifts, and paying it forward.
- Box 8.7. Being thankful for the ending of a chapter in your life.
- Box 8.8. Being thankful for a gift by imagining its absence.
- Box 8.9. Gratitude letter and visit.
- Box 8.10. Being thankful for good things that come from bad experiences.

---

### Box 8.4   Being thankful for three good things

Set aside 10 minutes for gratitude journaling.

List three good things that happened today.

These should be things for which you can give other people, God or nature some credit.

Examples include someone giving you a compliment; a friend contacting you; someone helping you at home, at work or in the community; noticing the beauty of the world; noticing your health or other personal characteristics that you have been blessed with.

For each of the three things on your list, spend some time visualising the good thing happening and then write down:

- What exactly happened.
- Why you think it happened.
- What it means to you.
- All the reasons you can think of that explain why you think it want well.
- Whether or not you told someone that it happened.
- What you can do to make it happen again, and remember next time to tell someone about it.

Before and after the exercise write down a well-being rating for how you feel at that exact moment on a 10-point scale from 1 which means you are extremely sad to 10 which means you are extremely happy.

Look at the difference between your ratings before and after the exercise and decide if this exercise improved your well-being.

**Note:** Based on an exercise in Emmons, R. (2013). *Gratitude works: A 21-day programme for creating emotional prosperity.* San Francisco, CA: Jossey-Bass.

## Box 8.5   Giving thanks to whom and for what

Set aside 10 minutes for gratitude journaling.

List five 'gifts' (benefits or good things) that you received today and the specific people from whom you received these.

In this context, a 'gift' may be a smile, a conversation, a kind word, sympathy, help, a present, an invitation to meet or any other valued thing.

For each of the five 'gifts' write down a sentence that takes the form:

I am grateful to_____ for_____

For each of the five things on your list spend some time visualising receiving the 'gift' benefit or good thing and then write down:

- Why you think you received the 'gift', benefit or good thing.
- What it means to you.

Before and after the exercise write down a well-being rating for how you feel at that exact moment on a 10-point scale from 1 which means you are extremely sad to 10 which means you are extremely happy.

Look at the difference between your ratings before and after the exercise and decide if this exercise improved your well-being.

**Note:** Based on an exercise in Emmons, R. (2013). *Gratitude works: A 21-day programme for creating emotional prosperity.* San Francisco, CA: Jossey-Bass.

## Box 8.6   Giving thanks for three gifts, and paying it forward

Set aside 10 minutes for gratitude journaling.

List three 'gifts' you have received in your life.

In this context, a 'gift' may be personal talents or characteristics (e.g. intelligence, health), people (e.g. your parents, partner, children or friends), activities (e.g. work, pastimes or sports), moments of natural beauty or gestures of kindness from others.

Think about each of the three 'gifts' that you have listed, one at a time.

- Visualise the 'gift'.
- Savour your image of the 'gift' and the feeling of gratitude that it gives rise to.
- As you do so, say the words 'I have been gifted'.
- Ask yourself: 'How might I give back to others, as a response for the gratitude I feel? How can I "pay it forward"?'

Be creative when you think about how to 'pay it forward'. You could do a random act of kindness for someone. Give change to someone to put in the parking meter. Let someone go ahead of you in the supermarket queue. Give directions to someone who is lost. Help an ageing neighbour with their shopping.

Before and after the exercise write down a well-being rating for how you feel at that exact moment on a 10-point scale from 1 which means you are extremely sad to 10 which means you are extremely happy.

Look at the difference between your ratings before and after the exercise and decide if this exercise improved your well-being.

**Note:** Based on an exercise in Emmons, R. (2013). *Gratitude works: A 21-day programme for creating emotional prosperity.* San Francisco, CA: Jossey-Bass.

## Box 8.7   Being thankful for the ending of a chapter in your life

Set aside 10 minutes for gratitude journaling.

Select a chapter of your life that will be ending soon – in the next 4–12 weeks.

This may be a job you are doing, a course you are attending, a team you are on, a place you are living or a friend who may be moving.

Visualise all the good things that have happened during this chapter of your life that will be ending soon.

Think about how much you value the time that remains in this chapter of your life that will be ending soon.

Write down all the reasons why you are grateful for this chapter of your life.

Before and after the exercise write down a well-being rating for how you feel at that exact moment on a 10-point scale from 1 which means you are extremely sad to 10 which means you are extremely happy.

Look at the difference between your ratings before and after the exercise and decide if this exercise improved your well-being.

**Note:** Based on an exercise in Emmons, R. (2013). *Gratitude works: A 21-day programme for creating emotional prosperity.* San Francisco, CA: Jossey-Bass.

---

## Box 8.8   Being thankful for a gift by imagining its absence

Set aside 10 minutes for gratitude journaling.

Select a 'gift' in your life for which you are very grateful.

This may be a person (e.g. your partner, friend or child), place (e.g. your house, workplace, school or sports club) or an activity (e.g. sports, music or work).

Visualise and write down how your life would be, what would have happened and how you would feel if this 'gift' was not in your life.

That is, visualise and write down how your life would be, what would have happened and how you would feel if, for example, you had never met your partner or friend; had your child; lived in your house; worked in your workplace; attended your school; joined your sports club; engaged in your sport; played your music; or had your job.

When you have written about life without your 'gift', write down how grateful you feel for having this 'gift' in your life.

Before and after the exercise write down a well-being rating for how you feel at that exact moment on a 10-point scale from 1 which means you are extremely sad to 10 which means you are extremely happy.

Look at the difference between your ratings before and after the exercise and decide if this exercise improved your well-being.

**Note:** Based on an exercise in Emmons, R. (2013). *Gratitude works: A 21-day programme for creating emotional prosperity.* San Francisco, CA: Jossey-Bass.

---

## Box 8.9   Gratitude letter and visit

Set aside 10 minutes to write a gratitude letter.

Remember a time in your life when you were grateful to someone for something they did for you that had a positive effect on your life, but you never properly thanked them.

It may be a teacher, mentor, sports coach, friend, family member or anyone else.

Write a letter of about 250–500 words to that person.

As you are writing, visualise the person you are writing to.

In the letter write down:

- What specifically the person did to help you.
- How the good thing they did affected your life, and changed the course of your life for the better.

- How often you reflect on how they helped you.
- How their help has made you feel in the past and how it makes you feel now.
- How grateful you are for the good thing that they did for you, for their kindness and generosity.

You can write the letter longhand or on a computer. If you prefer, you may dictate it and audio or video record it.

Read or listen to the letter when you have finished.

Imagine how it would affect the person it is intended for. Imagine what it would make them feel.

If you wish, send the letter.

If you prefer, phone them. Say you would like to visit them to catch up, or talk to them on Skype if visiting is inconvenient. Keep the letter a secret until you see them. Then read the letter to them.

Take your time reading the gratitude letter. If the person interrupts you, invite them to wait until you are finished.

After you have read the letter discuss how this process has affected each of you.

Notice how your expression of gratitude has affected the person.

Before and after the exercise write down a well-being rating for how you feel at that exact moment on a 10-point scale from 1 which means you are extremely sad to 10 which means you are extremely happy.

Look at the difference between your ratings before and after the exercise and decide if this exercise improved your well-being.

**Note:** The gratitude letter is based on an exercise in Emmons, R. (2013). *Gratitude works: A 21-day programme for creating emotional prosperity.* San Francisco, CA: Jossey-Bass. The gratitude visit is described in Seligman, M. E. P., Steen, T. A., Park, N., & Peterson, C. (2005). Positive psychology progress: Empirical validation of interventions. *American Psychologist, 60*(5), 410–421.

---

## Box 8.10   Being thankful for good things that come from bad experiences

Set aside 10 minutes for gratitude journaling.

Select a 'bad' experience that was initially unpleasant and unwanted, difficult or painful, and personally challenging for you, but which later had positive consequences for which you are now grateful.

This 'bad' experience may be a personal or family physical or mental health problem; an accident or injury; victimisation, assault or bullying; a bereavement; the end of a relationship; financial difficulties; moving to a new house and leaving an area you love; or some other life challenge.

Visualise this experience and then write a detailed description of what happened and how it felt.

Write answers to the following questions:

- How has this bad experience benefited you?
- What personal strengths did this bad experience help you discover or grow?
- What important relationships did this bad experience strengthen?
- How has this bad experience made you better able to face future challenges in your life?
- How did this bad experience help you put your life in perspective, and recognise what you value most?
- How has this experience made you more appreciative of the most important things in your life?
- What good things that have come from this bad experience are you most grateful for?

Before and after the exercise write down a well-being rating for how you feel at that exact moment on a 10-point scale from 1 which means you are extremely sad to 10 which means you are extremely happy.

Look at the difference between your ratings before and after the exercise and decide if this exercise improved your well-being.

**Note:** Based on an exercise in Emmons, R. (2013). *Gratitude works: A 21-day programme for creating emotional prosperity.* San Francisco, CA: Jossey-Bass.

With these seven exercises, there is a different exercise for each day of the week. For example, you may do the exercise in Box 8.4 on Sundays, that in Box 8.5 on Mondays, that in Box 8.6 on Tuesdays, that in Box 8.7 on Wednesdays, that in Box 8.8 on Thursdays, that in Box 8.9 on Fridays and that in Box 8.10 on Saturdays. For each week of the three-week programme, it's important to vary the experiences you write about in your journal, and avoid writing about the same experiences repeatedly. Using a variety of different gratitude exercises and varying the experiences you write about reduces 'gratitude fatigue' or adaptation. Adaptation involves experiencing less intense positive emotions after each gratitude exercise. This occurs because of the effect of the hedonic treadmill discussed in Chapter 1.

In all of the gratitude exercises, vividly visualising each thing that you are grateful for while writing about it will increase your experience of gratitude. Visualisation helps us to re-live experiences we are writing about. Visualisation helps us to feel the positive emotions they evoke more intensely. In your journal, write in great detail about what you see and feel when you visualise. Go for depth, not breadth. That is, write in depth and detail about the specific thing that you are grateful for, rather than making a long list of different things, with little mention of specific details.

In your gratitude journal write about ordinary things that you normally take for granted, but were grateful for because you paid special attention to savouring them and noticed that they were a 'gift'. For example, the fact that your car started when you turned on the ignition; the taste of your orange juice at breakfast; or the way your friend smiled when you met.

In your gratitude journal write about the unexpected gifts in your life. The challenges or crises that you thought might happen, but didn't; the chance meeting with someone you like; or the generosity of someone who normally is less thoughtful.

In your gratitude journal write about 'gifts' that have come to those you love, as well as about those that you have personally received. For example, you may be grateful for the way the teacher treated your child; the way the sales assistant helped your friend; or the way a carer helped your grandparent.

In all of the gratitude exercises, it's useful to assess the impact of doing the exercise on your mood. You can do this by writing down a mood rating for how you feel before and after each exercise. Make these mood ratings on a 10-point scale. On this scale, a rating of 1 means that you were extremely sad, and a rating of 10 means you were extremely happy. Each of the exercises takes about 10 minutes to complete, with the exception of the gratitude letter. This may take additional time if you decide to visit the person and read the gratitude letter to them.

### Being thankful for three good things

In this exercise, you are invited to list three good things that happened today. These should be things for which you can give other people, God or nature some credit. Examples of good things include someone giving you a compliment; a friend contacting you; someone helping you at home, at work or in the community; noticing the beauty of the world; noticing your health; or recognising some personal characteristics that you have been blessed with. For each of the three things on your list, spend some time visualising the good thing happening. Then write down what exactly happened and why you think it happened. Write down what it means to you. Write down all the reasons you can think of, that explain why you think it went well. Note whether or not you told someone that it happened. Finally, write down what you can do to make it happen again, and to remind yourself to tell someone about it next time. Telling other people that we are grateful enhances good feelings associated with gratitude.

### Giving thanks to whom and for what

In this exercise, you are invited to list five 'gifts', benefits or good things that you received today and the specific people from whom you received these. In this context, a 'gift' may be a smile, a conversation, a kind word, sympathy, help, a present, an invitation to meet or any other valued thing. For each of the five 'gifts' write down a sentence that takes the form:

I am grateful to _____ for _____. For each of the five things on your list spend some time visualising receiving the 'gift'. Then write down why you think you received the 'gift' and what it means to you.

### Giving thanks for three gifts, and paying it forward

In this exercise, you are invited to list three 'gifts' you have received in your life. In this context, a 'gift' may be personal talents or characteristics (e.g. intelligence or health), people (e.g. your parents, partner, children or friends), activities (e.g. work, pastimes or sports), moments of natural beauty or gestures of kindness from others. Think about each of the three 'gifts' that you have listed, one at a time, and visualise them. Savour your image of the 'gift' and the feeling of gratitude that it gives rise to. As you do so, say the words 'I have been gifted'. Ask yourself: 'How might I give back to others, as a response for the gratitude I feel? How can

I "pay it forward"?' Be creative when you think about how to 'pay it forward'. You could do a random act of kindness for someone. You could give change to someone to put in the parking meter. You could let someone go ahead of you in the supermarket queue. You could give directions to someone who is lost. You could help an ageing neighbour with their shopping.

### Being thankful for the ending of a chapter in your life

When a pleasant experience is coming to an end, you can enhance your feelings of gratitude by savouring it, rather than worrying that it will soon be over.[18] For example, your sense of gratitude for the last day of your vacation will be increased if you savour the pleasures of that day, and write about these rather than worrying about returning to work tomorrow.

In this exercise, you are invited to select a chapter of your life that will be ending in the next 4-12 weeks. This may be a job you are doing, a course you are attending, a team you are on, a place you are living or a friend who may be moving. Visualise all the good things that have happened during this chapter of your life that will be ending soon. Think about how much you value the time that remains in this chapter of your life that will be ending soon. Write down all the reasons why you are grateful for this chapter of your life.

### Being thankful for a gift by imagining its absence

Writing about what your life would be like if certain good things had not happened to you will make you feel more gratitude than thinking about their presence.[19] For example, you will probably appreciate your partner or lover more if you write about how your life would be if you had never met him or her.

In this exercise, you are invited to select a 'gift' in your life for which you are very grateful. This may be a person (e.g. your partner, friend or child), place (e.g. your house, workplace, school or sports club) or an activity (e.g. sports, music or work). Visualise and write down how your life would be, what would have happened and how you would feel if this 'gift' was not in your life. That is, visualise and write down how your life would be, what would have happened and how you would feel if, for example, you had never met your partner or friend; had your child; lived in your house; worked in your workplace; attended your school; joined your sports club; engaged in your sport; played your music; or had your job. When you have written about life without your 'gift', write down how grateful you feel for having this 'gift' in your life.

### Gratitude letter and visit

In this exercise, you are invited to remember a time in your life when you were grateful to someone for something they did for you that had a positive effect on your life, but you never properly thanked them. It may be a teacher, mentor, sports coach, friend, family member or anyone else. Write a letter of about 250-500 words to that person. As you are writing, visualise the person you are writing to. In the letter describe what specifically the person did to help you. Describe how the good thing that they did affected your life, and changed the course of your life for the better. State how often you reflect on how they helped you. Describe how their help has made you feel in the past and how it makes you feel now. State how grateful you are for the good thing that they did for you, for their kindness and for their generosity.

You can write this gratitude letter longhand or on a computer. If you prefer, dictate it and audio or video record it. Read or listen to the letter when you have finished. Imagine how it would affect the person it is intended for. Imagine what it would make them feel.

If you wish, send the letter. If you prefer, phone the person you have written to. Say you would like to visit them to catch up, or talk to them on Skype if visiting is inconvenient. Keep the letter a secret until you see them. Then read the letter to them. Take your time reading the gratitude letter. If the person interrupts you, invite them to wait until you are finished. After you have read the letter discuss how this process has affected each of you. Notice how your expression of gratitude has affected the other person.

### Being thankful for good things that come from bad experiences

Writing about being grateful for overcoming difficulties and misfortune as well as successes is more beneficial than only writing about successes.[20] When you think about an awful situation you seemed to be trapped in, and then recall how you found a way out of it, this gives rise to a profound feeling of gratitude.

In this exercise, you are invited to select a 'bad' experience that was initially unpleasant and unwanted, difficult or painful, and personally challenging for you, but which later had positive consequences for which you are now grateful. This 'bad' experience may be a personal or family physical or mental health problem; an accident or injury; victimisation, assault or bullying; a bereavement; the end of a relationship; financial difficulties; moving to a new house and leaving an area you love; or some other life challenge. Visualise this experience and then write a detailed description of what happened and how it felt. Write answers to the following questions: How has this 'bad' experience benefited you? What personal strengths did this 'bad' experience help you discover or grow? What important relationships did this bad experience strengthen? How has this bad experience made you better able to face future challenges in your life? How did this bad experience help you put your life in perspective, and recognise what you value most? How has this experience made you more appreciative of the most important things in your life? What good things that have come from this bad experience are you most grateful for?

### Reflections on the three-week gratitude programme

If you completed part or all of the three-week gratitude programme, you may wish to reflect on your experiences and write down you answers to these questions in your journal. How many days of the programme did your do? Which exercises did you do? How often did you do them? Which exercises did you find most useful? Which were least useful or most difficult to do? What obstacles did you encounter in doing the programme? How did you try to overcome these? How successful were you? Does gratitude journaling suit you? Would you like to continue doing it?

If you would like to assess the effect of the programme on your overall level of gratitude, you may wish to complete the gratitude questionnaire in Box 8.1 again and compare your score with the score you got at the start of the programme.

## Other gratitude exercises

Here are some other gratitude exercises that you may wish to try.[21] These are not scientifically validated, but they are consistent with research on the positive psychology of gratitude, and so may be helpful to you in increasing you attitude of gratitude and your well-being.

### Visual reminders

Put signs in prominent places to remind you to be grateful. For example, put a gratitude magnet on your fridge door and the dashboard of your car. Put a gratitude reminder or ringtone on your smartphone. Put a sign on the desktop of your computer, or over your desk, or somewhere else in your workplace to remind you to be grateful.

### Gratitude jar

We have all heard of a swear jar, where we put in a coin each time we swear. With a gratitude jar, your put in a coin each time you are grateful. When the jar is full, donate the contents to a charity of your choice.

### Use gratitude language

Consciously choose to use the language of gratitude in your day-to-day speech. This language includes the words thank you, thanks, grateful, gratitude, grace, gift, appreciate and blessed.

### Mindfulness of breath and gratitude

Occasionally when you are practising the three-minute breathing space mindfulness exercise described in Box 6.6 in Chapter 6, on the outbreath say the word thanks for the gift of breath and being alive.

### Gratitude chains

Occasionally when you are grateful for something good, think carefully about the chain of people who contributed to this and be grateful to each of them for their contribution to the good thing you are experiencing. For example, if you are drinking orange juice for breakfast, think about how the orange juice arrived in the carton in your fridge; the people in the factory that made the carton and the juice; the people who grew and picked the oranges; the sun and fertile soil that supported the growth of the oranges; the people who transported the oranges to the factory and the cartons to the supermarket; and so forth. In your mind or aloud, express thanks to all of them for their contribution to the orange juice you are drinking for breakfast.

### Internal gratitude monologue

When we are not engaged in purposeful activity our minds tend to wander away from our present experiences to ruminating about past difficulties and worrying about future challenges.

(Mind-wandering was discussed in Chapter 6.) You may wish to replace this tendency to have an internal monologue about what is wrong with your life with one that focuses on what is right with your life. In this internal monologue count your blessings, not your burdens. Be thankful that the half-empty glass is also half full. Be grateful for the silver lining that came with the cloud.

### Gratitude exercise for couples

If you want to strengthen your relationship with your partner, you may jointly do this exercise each evening for a week to see how it affects your well-being and the quality of your relationship. Meet by agreement with your partner at a mutually acceptable time each evening for about 20 minutes. Each of you may take a turn telling each other about good things that happened during the day in which the other partner played an important role. Describe the event in sufficient detail for you both to be able to visualise it. Explain why you appreciate this good thing. Each of you may express appreciation and thanks to your partner for their role in making these good things happen. If you wish, you may each reflect on the good things that happened before meeting, write a letter to your partner about good things that happened within your relationship during the day and thank your partner for their role in making these good things happen. Then read these letters to each other when you meet. Each day when you have done this exercise, in your journals write down how recalling these events and giving and receiving thanks makes you feel on a 10-point well-being scale, and how it affects the quality of your relationship on a 10-point scale. At the end of the week jointly review your journals and discuss what you have both learned from doing the exercise.

## Summary

- **Gratitude** involves recalling gifts and kindnesses that we have received, appreciating their benefits, experiencing positive emotions and expressing this appreciation by showing that we are thankful and generously giving gifts to others. We can be grateful for things in our environment and for things that others do for us.
- **Reasons why gratitude increase well-being.** Gratitude leads to immediate positive emotions. It makes us pay attention to and savour small pleasures. It shifts attention from the negative to the positive things in life. It makes us respond more positively to adversity, and less likely to make negative comparisons between our situation and that of others. It reduces materialistic strivings which have a negative effect on well-being.
- **Obstacles to gratitude** include lack of humility and forgiveness, overvaluing self-sufficiency, materialistic values, focusing more on negative than positive things, seeing ourselves as victims, believing that expressing tender feelings is a bad thing, expecting gratitude in return for kindness and receiving gifts that are given with the condition that we will do something in return.
- **Gratitude exercises**, most of which involve gratitude journaling, include being thankful for three good things, giving thanks to whom and for what, giving thanks for three gifts and paying it forward, being thankful for the ending of a chapter in your life, being thankful for a gift by imagining its absence, writing a gratitude letter and making a gratitude visit and being thankful for good things that come from bad experiences. Other gratitude

exercises are using visual reminders to prompt us to express thanks, having a gratitude jar, using gratitude language, doing the mindfulness of breath and gratitude meditation, thinking of gratitude chains, conducting internal gratitude monologues and expressing appreciation to your partner in the gratitude exercise for couples.

## Where are you now?

If you have done the exercises in this chapter, you have introduced gratitude journaling into your daily routine. This will help you cultivate an attitude of gratitude. In the long run gratitude enhances well-being.

You may want to read back over the chapter and summarise in your journal the main things that you have learned about gratitude.

In the next chapter, we will consider optimism and well-being. Below are some web resources and a book that are relevant to topics you have read about in this chapter.

## Web resources

Robert Emmons talking about the benefits of gratitude video (10:35): www.youtube.com/watch?v=RRrnfGf5aWE

Robert Emmons talking about cultivating gratitude video (5:42): www.youtube.com/watch?v=8964envYh58

John Templeton Foundation video summarising research on gratitude video (1:30): www.youtube.com/watch?v=sCV-mEsASLA

Summary of research on gratitude video (2:07): www.youtube.com/watch?v=JMd1CcGZYwU

## Book

Emmons, R. (2007). *Thanks: How practicing gratitude can make you happier.* Boston, MA: Houghton Mifflin.

# Part 4
# Constructive thought and action

# 9 Optimism

How you think affects how you feel.[1] Reading this chapter will help you find out how to develop a thinking style that supports well-being and helps you to feel better. In particular there will be a focus on taking an optimistic perspective on the future.

Just as Charles was leaving the office, he got an email from his boss to say that there were two major jobs that he needed to do by noon tomorrow. His mood dropped. Just as Gordon was getting ready to go home he got a very similar email. It said that by lunchtime tomorrow, he had to do two major jobs. His mood lifted. How was it that Charles' mood dropped and Gordon's mood lifted? The answer is that they each thought about the emails they received in different ways. The stories they told themselves in their minds about these very similar situations could not have been more different.

Charles thought, 'I've got so much on at the moment, I'll never get these things done by tomorrow at noon. Then my boss will be disappointed with me. He won't give me a bonus at the end of the year. We won't be able to go on the holiday we've been planning. Jeannie will be disappointed in me again. I'm such a failure. I always screw things up. I know I won't get any sleep tonight worrying about this. I will have no energy to do these two big jobs tomorrow. Why does shit always happen to me?'

Gordon thought, 'It's good to get advance warning of these two big jobs tomorrow. That gives me time to think up a plan about how best to proceed. Also, I can get an early night tonight so I will be rested in the morning. I'll come in early tomorrow and get started on them in good time to finish up by about noon. My boss will be really pleased when I meet the lunchtime deadline. Maybe I'll get a bonus for sorting this out. This is a great opportunity. Sally will joke with me about this when I get home. She says I can always find the silver lining in any cloud. As usual, I'll say, "What cloud?"'

These stories about Charles and Gordon illustrate an exceptionally important fact about the determinants of well-being. The way we think about situations, not the situations themselves, is the main thing that affects our mood. If, like Charles, we think mainly about the downside, our mood drops. If, like Gordon, we think mainly about the positives, then our mood lifts. (We came across this idea previously in Chapter 6 on meditation.)

## ABC analysis

Let's do an ABC analysis of these scenarios.[2] That is, let's look at the

- **A**ntecedent events or **A**dversity,
- **B**eliefs or thoughts about these events and
- **C**onsequences for mood, bodily sensations and behaviour.

In each scenario, the **A**ntecedent event or **A**dversity was receiving an email containing a request to do extra jobs by lunchtime the next day. The **B**eliefs or thoughts about these events were the stories Charles and Gordon told themselves when they received these emails. Charles interpreted the situation in a negative way and had pessimistic thoughts. Gordon interpreted the situation positively and had optimistic thoughts about it. The **C**onsequences for Charles were that his mood dropped, his energy decreased, he found it difficult to sleep and he had difficulties working well the next day. In contrast, the **C**onsequences for Gordon were that his mood lifted, his energy increased, he slept well and worked well the next day. Although both Charles and Gordon received very similar emails, the consequences for their mood, bodily sensations, behaviour and overall well-being were very different. This difference was largely due to their beliefs and the thinking styles these reflected. Gordon used an optimistic thinking style, whereas Charles' thinking style was pessimistic.

## Optimistic and pessimistic thinking styles

In his book *Learned Optimism*,[2] Professor Martin Seligman, the founder of positive psychology (who was first mentioned in Chapter 1), showed that the explanations people with optimistic and pessimistic thinking styles give for their successes and failures differ along three dimensions: permanence (transient vs. permanent), pervasiveness (limited to one area of life vs. pervasive to many life areas) and personalisation (mainly due to personal factors vs. mainly due to the situation or other people).

People with an optimistic thinking style explain their success in terms of permanent, pervasive, personal factors. For example, Trevor, an optimist, said that 'The reason I passed the maths exam is because I've always had a real aptitude for numbers and a knack for doing all sorts of exams'. People with an optimistic thinking style explain their failures in terms of transient factors, limited to one area of their lives, and due to situational factors (including lack of certain personal skills) or other people. For example, Trevor, said, 'The reason my art project wasn't a success is because I was tired last week when I did it; my art skills need more work; and I had other duties at home that took priority'.

People with a pessimistic thinking style explain their success in terms of transient factors, limited to one area of their lives, and due to situational factors or other people. For example, Richard, a pessimist, said, 'The reason I passed the maths exam is because I got lucky on that particular day in that specific subject'. People with a pessimistic thinking style explain their failures in terms of permanent, pervasive, personal factors. For example, Richard said, 'The reason my art project wasn't a success is because I've always been bad at art and all sorts of project work'. A pessimistic thinking style is particularly problematic. If you believe that the bad events that occur in your life are caused by permanent aspects of your character, then you probably also believe that there is nothing you can do to change this. This may lead you to not make the changes required to improve your well-being.

People with a pessimistic thinking style often fall foul of the thinking traps listed in Box 9.1.

## Box 9.1   Thinking traps that prevent optimism

**Emotional reasoning.** Thinking that feelings are facts. For example, 'I feel really sad, so the future is hopeless' or, 'I feel nervous so this situation must be really dangerous'.

**Black-and-white thinking.** Thinking about things as all good or all bad, with no shades of grey in between. For example, 'Either I'm a success or a failure'.

**Focusing on the negatives and discounting the positives.** Only paying attention to bad things, while ignoring good things or saying that they don't matter. For example, 'I made a mistake earlier today so everything I did today was wrong. The good stuff I did yesterday doesn't really count because it was just easy routine stuff'.

**Overgeneralising.** Making sweeping judgements based on one experience. For example, 'Because the meal I cooked last night wasn't perfect, this means I am a failure'.

**Labelling.** Labelling yourself in a negative way, based on a single experience. For example, 'I didn't just make a mistake, I proved that I'm a complete fool'.

**Jumping to conclusions.** Reaching a conclusion very quickly without considering alternatives and important evidence. For example, concluding that my partner is being unfaithful because he was late home from work and not considering that this is a busy time of year in his workplace.

**Making mountains out of molehills.** Ruminating for hours about disappointing things that happened in the past, so that little disappointments become blown up to be huge heart-breaking disappointments. For example, thinking over and over again about the fact that she said she couldn't meet me this weekend, so that must mean she hates me, never wants to see me again, thinks I'm a terrible person and so on.

**Disaster forecasting.** Anticipating that the future will be very distressing on the basis of limited evidence, and dwelling on this idea for a long time. For example, thinking 'My heart is racing. I must be going to have a heart attack; I'm going to die; I'm not ready for this; I can't stand it; I can't stop these thoughts; I'm losing my mind. Or no-one at the party will talk to me; it will be terrible, I'll be sad and lonely' and so on.

**Mind-reading.** Assuming that others are thinking negative things about you without having evidence for this or checking it out. For example, 'His silence means that he doesn't like me. Or I know he says he likes me, but he is thinking that he hates me'.

**Personalisation.** Attributing negative feelings of others to the self. For example, 'He looked really angry when he walked into the room, so I must have done something wrong to annoy him'.

**Blaming.** Thinking that something is all your fault or all someone's else's fault without looking at all of the evidence. For example, thinking 'It's all my fault when other people look sad'. Or thinking 'It's always all your friend's fault when you are not having a good time together'.

**Double standards.** Having one standard for yourself, and another standard for all other people. For example, thinking 'It's OK for others to make an occasional mistake, but not me. I'm a failure for making that one mistake. Everything I do must be perfect'.

**Should and must, always and never statements.** Making absolute statements about how you or others ought to be always or never. For example, 'I should always be perfect and he should never be unkind. Other people should always be fair'.

**Note:** These thinking traps are also called cognitive biases or cognitive distortions. Based on Beck, A. (1976). *Cognitive therapy and the emotional disorders.* New York, NY: International Universities Press. Burns, D. (1999). *Feeling good: The new mood therapy.* Revised and updated. New York, NY: Avon.

## When is an optimistic thinking style most useful?

People with a predominantly optimistic thinking style tend to attribute their successes to themselves and their failures or difficulties in their lives to situational factors, to skills they have not yet mastered or to other people. Clearly, in the short-term this thinking style may enhance our mood. However, if we always blame others or circumstances for our own failures, this makes it difficult to learn from mistakes. Always blaming other people or circumstances for bad events can amount to not taking responsibility for things we have done wrong, or could have done better. Recognising when we have made mistakes or could have prevented a failure from occurring is an important skill. So, knowing when to do this – knowing when a pessimistic thinking style is appropriate – is important for well-being. When it comes to optimistic and pessimistic thinking styles, well-being is enhanced by striking a balance, and knowing when optimistic and pessimistic thinking styles are most useful.

An optimistic thinking style is particularly useful if you are recovering from depression. It's also useful if you are vulnerable to depression because of a family history of depression, or because of a personal history of trauma. An optimistic thinking style is useful if you are trying to increase your morale in the face of many obstacles, for example when unemployed. It's also useful when dealing with long-term adversity, for example chronic illness. An optimistic thinking style is particularly useful if you have a strong work ethic, and are trying to achieve highly valued goals at college, work or in sports. If you don't have a strong work ethic, and blame your failures on others or circumstances, this may make you feel better in the short-term, but it will not help you achieve your valued goals. In the long-term this will reduce your well-being. Finally, an optimistic thinking style is useful when you want to inspire or lead others.

A pessimistic thinking style is appropriate in high-risk situations, where the cost of failure is very high. For example, when making risky business decisions where there are many uncertainties; when planning the family budget if you have very limited funds; or when deciding what speed to drive at in difficult weather conditions. In all of these high-risk situations, the cost of failure is very high. Your business could go bust, your family could suffer due to lack of funds or you could crash your car and be injured. In these situations, it's prudent to plan for the worst (like a pessimist). However, you can also hope for the best (like an optimist).

## Why are most people optimistic?

Most people are optimistic, unless they are suffering from depression, anxiety or other mental health problems.[3] The capacity to think in an optimistic way may be a naturally selected characteristic of our species which evolved when we developed the capacity to reflect on the future.[4] Members of our species who were pessimistic about their future and who were preoccupied with the inevitability of danger, illness and death were not motivated to do the things necessary for survival. Their optimistic counterparts, in contrast, were motivated to struggle for survival because they believed things would work out well for them.

## Long-term effects of optimism

Optimism has a profound long-term effect on well-being.[5] Compared with pessimism, an optimistic thinking style is associated with better academic achievement, sport performance, occupational adjustment, family adjustment, physical and mental health, and resilience when faced with stressful challenges.

In a study of bereavement, the late Professor Susan Nolen-Hoeksema found that optimism had an important impact on the way people dealt with loss.[6] Optimists construed bereavement as a 'wake-up call' to reprioritise their lives. They became aware of the fragility of life and lived more in the present than the past or the future. They focused more on important relationships and less on work and casual relationships. They resolved family conflicts that had been unresolved for years. They made important life changes that they had been putting off for years, such as changing jobs or pursuing retraining. They become more tolerant of others. They became aware of strengths that they did not know they had. They also became less afraid of their own death.

## Exercises for developing optimism

In his book *Learned Optimism*, Martin Seligman described how to develop an optimistic thinking style using procedures that had been tested in series of research studies with adults and children and found to be very effective.[7] He based his approach on the cognitive behaviour therapy (CBT) models of Aaron T. Beck and Albert Ellis.[8] CBT has been shown in many research studies to be particularly effective in alleviating depression, anxiety and other common psychological problems.[9] Recognising and challenging the thinking traps listed in Box 9.1 is one important part of CBT. (These thinking traps are sometimes called cognitive distortions or cognitive biases.) What follows is some guidance on how you can use these procedures to develop an optimistic thinking style.

### Monitoring optimistic and pessimistic thinking

If you wish to understand the extent to which you typically engage in optimistic and pessimistic thinking, there is an invitation now for you to keep an optimism journal for week. In your journal write an account of situations in which you faced adversity, stress or difficulty.

Write about enough situations so that you can get a sense of how you usually respond to adversity. For each of these situations do an ABC analysis, noting the:

- **A**ntecedent events or **A**dversity you faced
- **B**eliefs or thoughts that you had about these events (or the story you told yourself in your mind) and
- **C**onsequences for your mood (on a 10-point scale), your bodily sensations and your behaviour.

Earlier you read ABC analyses of Charles and Gordon's situations where they got emails at work giving them deadlines for extra jobs to be done by lunchtime the next day. Here is another example of an ABC analysis of a situation where Felicity felt sad when her boyfriend, Harry, didn't call her as promised.

> **A**dversity: Harry didn't call Felicity.
>
> **B**eliefs: Felicity thought, 'He's not interested in our friendship anymore because I'm always so boring to be with. This proves that I'm not a loveable person. No-one will ever love me. I better get used to being lonely'.
>
> **C**onsequences: Felicity changed from feeling OK to feeling fairly sad (from 7 to 3 on a 10-point scale, where 1 stands for feeling very sad and 10 stands for feeling very happy). She also felt a drop in energy, and an urge to stay home and eat a lot of chocolate or drink a lot of wine.

Not all of Felicity's responses to adversity were pessimistic. Here is an example of a situation where she had an optimistic response, and felt good about facing a challenge in her job as a teacher.

> **A**dversity: A school inspector arrived unannounced to observe Felicity teaching her class on Monday morning.
>
> **B**eliefs: Felicity thought, 'This is a bit scary. I'll focus on doing my job. My kids like me. They learn well. I'm a good teacher. I'm sure it will work out OK. I can do this'.
>
> **C**onsequences: Felicity changed from feeling good (7 on a 10-point scale, where 1 stands for feeling very scared and 10 stands for feeling very relaxed) to a bit scared (4 on the 10-point scale), and then to feeling really good (8 on the 10-point scale). She also felt an increase in energy, and found that she performed well under a bit of pressure.

These two examples give you an idea of how to write ABC analyses of challenging or stressful situations in your journal. When you have written down ABC analyses of a sufficient number of adverse situations, identify the sorts of things you tell yourself when you are using positive optimistic and negative pessimistic thinking styles. Notice that your pessimistic thinking style leads to a drop in mood. In contrast, your optimistic thinking style probably leads to your mood improving. Box 9.2 gives a summary of how to do this exercise to find out if you mainly use an optimistic thinking style.

### Box 9.2  ABC analysis: finding out if you mainly use an optimistic thinking style

- To get a sense of how you usually respond to adversity, for a week, write down in your journal an ABC analysis of difficult, stressful or challenging situations in which you faced adversity.
- In an ABC analysis, here is what A, B and C stand for.

  o **A** stands for the **Adversity** or **Antecedent event** that you found difficult.
  o **B** stands for your **Beliefs** about the situation. This is your interpretation or explanation of the situation or the story you told yourself about it.
  o **C** stands for the **Consequences** for your mood (on a 10-point scale), bodily sensations and behaviour.

- After a week review the ABC analyses in your journal and notice how often you had optimistic and pessimistic beliefs about adverse situations.
- If you had optimistic beliefs and used an optimistic thinking style, you attributed failures or difficulties to transient, situational factors, skills that you need to learn or other people. You saw the future positively because you believed you could make things better in future by changing these things that caused adversity or didn't prevent it.
- If you had pessimistic beliefs and used a pessimistic thinking style, you attributed failures or difficulties to permanent, pervasive personal shortcomings. You saw the future negatively because you believed you could not make things better in future by changing the things that caused adversity or failed to prevent it.
- Notice if you only used a pessimistic thinking style in high-risk situations where the cost of failure was very high. Where there is high risk it's often useful to take total responsibility for adversity by attributing the cause of the adversity or failure to prevent it to yourself rather than other people or circumstances, so you can prevent high-risk adversity in future.
- If you used pessimistic beliefs in some situations that were not high risk, then there is scope to increase your use of an optimistic thinking style.

**Note:** Based on Seligman, M. E. P. (2006). *Learned optimism* (Vintage Edition). New York, NY: Random House.

## Reducing pessimism and increasing optimism

There are three sets of skills you can use to increase optimistic thinking, and to prevent pessimistic thinking from dominating your mood. These are distraction, distancing and disputation.

### *Distraction*

Distraction involves doing something to change the focus of attention and stop the preoccupation with pessimistic thoughts about adversity. Simple distraction techniques include saying 'stop' loudly and hitting the table, snapping your wrist with an elastic band or looking at a flash card with STOP written on it in large letters. These simple techniques will tempo-rarily distract you, and interrupt a pessimistic train of thought. Two other useful distraction techniques are writing down the pessimistic explanation for the adversity as soon as it occurs, or postponing pessimistic rumination until later that day. For example, you might say to yourself, 'I will do all my pessimistic thinking between 7.00 and 7.20 today, and allow myself space to be as pessimistic as I can be then. Right now, I'm going to stop having pessimistic thoughts'. Distraction techniques give temporary respite from a pessimistic train of thought. However, the techniques of distancing and disputation will help you to develop a more opti-mistic thinking style.

## Distancing

Distancing involves reminding ourselves that a pessimistic explanation of a difficult situa-tion is only one possible interpretation of that situation. It is not necessarily the truth. It is not necessarily a statement of fact. While distraction is a strategy for temporarily 'turning off' pessimistic thoughts, distancing is a strategy for 'turning down' their impact on mood by recognising that beliefs are not facts, they are just one 'spin' on the situation. Distancing sets the stage for disputation. (The idea that thoughts are not facts was previously men-tioned in Chapter 6 on meditation. A key mindfulness skill is observing thoughts arising, lingering and dissolving in the mind and reminding ourselves that thoughts are mental events, not facts.)

## Disputation

With disputation, we engage in an internal dialogue. The goal of this dialogue is to show that as well as a pessimistic interpretation of a situation, there is usually an equally valid optimis-tic way of interpreting it. When disputing pessimistic explanations, we ask four questions that centre on evidence, alternatives, implications and usefulness:

- What is the evidence for the pessimistic beliefs about the situation and does this evi-dence show that these pessimistic beliefs are not 100% true?
- Are there alternative optimistic beliefs we could hold about the adversity?
- If we cannot justify optimistic beliefs about the adversity, are the implications of our pessimistic beliefs catastrophic with major long-term negative consequences or just a bit of a temporary nuisance?
- If we cannot decide whether there is more evidence for an optimistic or pessimistic interpretation of the adversity, which set of beliefs is most useful for us in terms of hav-ing a positive mood and achieving our goals?

Armed with ABC analysis skills and distraction, distancing and disputation skills, the next step is to put them together in ABCDE practice. ABCDE stands for Adversity, Beliefs, and Consequent mood changes, Disputation and Energisation or evaluation. In each adverse situ-ation, in addition to noting the adversity, beliefs and mood change consequences, also write down in your journal how you disputed your pessimistic beliefs and the impact of this on your mood state; that is, how the alternative optimistic beliefs energised you.

Let's return to Felicity who felt sad when her boyfriend, Harry, didn't call as promised, and look at a full ABCDE analysis of this situation.

**A**dversity: Harry didn't call Felicity.

**B**eliefs: Felicity thought, 'He's not interested in our friendship anymore because I'm always so boring to be with. This proves that I'm not a loveable person. No-one will ever love me. I better get used to being lonely'.

**C**onsequences: Felicity changed from feeling OK to feeling fairly sad (from 7 to 3 on a 10-point scale, where 1 stands for feeling very sad and 10 stands for feeling very happy). She also felt a drop in energy, and an urge to stay home and eat a lot of chocolate or get drunk.

**D**isputation: Felicity asked herself first about the evidence for her pessimistic beliefs. 'What is the evidence that Harry's not interested in our friendship anymore, because I'm always so boring to be with? Or that I'm not a loveable person? Or that no-one will ever love me? Or that I will be forever lonely?' She wrote the following about the evidence: 'There is evidence that he is interested in our relationship. We have seen each other two or three times a week for the past year. This means that at least some of the time I'm loveable. Therefore, it's unlikely I will be forever lonely'.

Felicity asked herself then about alternative optimistic explanations for Harry's behaviour. She wrote down: 'He may have other things on his mind? He may be dealing with a crisis?'

Felicity then asked herself if the implications of her pessimistic beliefs were catastrophic. Specifically, she asked herself: 'If Harry is losing interest in me, does that mean that I am not a loveable person; that no-one will ever love me, and that I better get used to being lonely?' In answer to this question she replied, 'Even if Harry is losing interest, it is not a catastrophe. I am loveable, and will not be lonely because I have other friends'.

Finally, Felicity asked herself which set of beliefs was more useful, the pessimistic or the optimistic. She concluded that 'It's more useful to think that he didn't call because of some temporary thing, like a crisis, not because I'm boring or some negative personal characteristic of mine'.

**E**nergisation or evaluation. Felicity then reflected on how this disputation process affected her mood. She found that she felt more upbeat and much happier (6 on a 10-point happiness scale).

To increase the frequency with which you use an optimistic thinking style and reduce the frequency with which you use a pessimistic thinking style, for a week you may wish to write down in your journal an ABCDE analysis of at least one situation each day in which you challenged your pessimistic thinking style. Box 9.3 gives a summary of this exercise for developing a more optimistic thinking style.

## Box 9.3 ABCDE strategy for developing an optimistic thinking style

- To increase your use of an optimistic thinking style, for the next week, each day do an ABCDE analysis of at least one adverse situation that you found stressful or difficult, and use this strategy to increase your well-being
- When you do an ABCDE analysis, here is what A, B, C, D and E stand for.

  o **A** stands for the **Adversity** or **A**ntecedent event that you found difficult.
  o **B** stands for your **Beliefs** about the situation. This is your interpretation or explanation of the situation or the story you told yourself about it.
  o **C** stands for the **Consequences** for your mood (on a 10-point scale), bodily sensations and behaviour.
  o **D** stands for **Distraction, Distancing or Disputation**. These strategies are described below. They will help you to move towards an optimistic thinking style and away from a pessimistic thinking style.
  o **E** stands for **Energisation** or the extent to which using distraction, distancing or disputation increased your mood.

- **Distract** yourself from pessimistic rumination about adversity by saying STOP and hitting the table, by snapping yourself with an elastic band or by looking at a flashcard with STOP written on it; or write down your pessimistic ruminations immediately; or postpone pessimistic rumination until a specific time later in the day, when you may pessimistically ruminate for a full 20 minutes.
- **Distance** yourself from pessimistic rumination by telling yourself that a pessimistic interpretation of the situation is just one set of beliefs, and not the true facts. There are always other more optimistic explanations, and some of these may be equally valid.
- **Dispute** your pessimistic beliefs by examining the evidence, alternatives, implications and usefulness related to these beliefs.

  o What is the **evidence** for the pessimistic beliefs about the situation and does this evidence show that these beliefs are not 100% true?
  o Is there an **alternative** optimistic interpretation of the situation?
  o If you cannot justify an optimistic interpretation of the situation, are the **implications** of your pessimistic beliefs catastrophic with major long-term negative consequences or just a bit of a temporary nuisance?
  o If you cannot decide whether there is more evidence for an optimistic or pessimistic interpretation of the adversity, which set of beliefs is **most useful** for you in terms of improving your mood and achieving your valued goals?

- **Energisation.** Re-rate your mood on a 10-point scale to find out the effects on your mood of having used distraction, distancing or disputation to increase your use of an optimistic thinking style and reduce your use of a pessimistic thinking style.

**Note:** Based on Seligman, M. E. P. (2006). *Learned optimism* (Vintage Edition). New York, NY: Random House.

You may also do this exercise with a close friend. This will help you both to develop your disputation skills. Select descriptions of adverse situations you have encountered and have your friend present the pessimistic interpretations of these to you. Your job is to dispute these and examine the evidence for the negative beliefs, generate optimistic alternatives, examine the real rather than catastrophic implications if the pessimistic viewpoint seems valid, and evaluate the usefulness of optimistic and pessimistic beliefs. You and your friend can then swap roles, and work on descriptions of adverse situations your friend has recently experienced.

## Questioning the evidence

Let's take a closer look at ways of questioning the evidence when you dispute pessimistic beliefs in an ABCDE analysis.[10] The two strategies are often referred to as Socratic questioning and behavioural experiments.

### Socratic questioning

Socratic questioning is a technique named after the Greek philosopher Socrates who used carefully selected questions to help people find the truth within themselves. You may use Socratic questioning when disputing pessimistic beliefs. Here are some Socratic questions you could ask yourself to try to find evidence that does not support pessimistic beliefs like 'It's all my fault. I really screwed it up because I'm so stupid. I just haven't got what it takes to do this. I'm not the sort of person people like. I'm just not attractive. Nobody likes me':

- Have I had any experiences that show that this pessimistic belief is not 100% true?
- Have I any personal strengths or positive qualities that show that this pessimistic belief is not 100% true?
- Are there any facts about the situation (however small) that I am discounting or over-looking that contradict my pessimistic beliefs and show that they are not 100% true?
- If my closest friend heard me expressing my pessimistic beliefs about myself, what would they say to me to me? What evidence would they point out to me to show that my belief was not 100% true?
- If my closest friend expressed a pessimistic belief similar to mine about themselves, what would I say to them? Could I now say what I imagine I would say to them to myself?
- When I was in this sort of situation in the past, what did I think or do to make me feel better?
- In a year's time, if I look back on this situation, will I still be convinced my pessimistic beliefs are 100% true?
- If I was not feeling stressed, low or anxious, how would I think about this situation differently?
- Am I impulsively jumping to pessimistic conclusions?
- Am I blaming myself for things that I couldn't control?
- Are my pessimistic beliefs due to black-and-white thinking?
- Are my pessimistic beliefs due to focusing on the negatives, and ignoring the positives in this situation?

- Are my pessimistic beliefs due to making a mountain out of a molehill and catastrophising about the future?
- Are my pessimistic thoughts due to mind-reading – that is, assuming I can tell what other people are thinking without asking them?
- Am I using any of the other thinking traps in Box 9.1?

If you ask yourself these questions, the answers you give may provide evidence that does not support your pessimistic belief. This provides an opportunity for you to consider optimistic alternatives.

## Behavioural experiments

Another way you can question the evidence is by carrying out behavioural experiments to test if the pessimistic beliefs you hold are true. For example, if one of your pessimistic beliefs is that you didn't succeed at a particular task because you are 'stupid and no good at anything', then a behavioural experiment may be to set yourself a moderately challenging task and notice that you can complete it competently. If another of your pessimistic beliefs is that you became involved in conflict with someone or had relationship difficulties because you are 'not the sort of person people like, or are unattractive', then a behavioural experiment may be to phone a close friend at a time you know they will be free to talk, and tell them about a recent good experience you had. These examples of behavioural experiments may provide evidence that you can do things competently and that friends are happy to hear from you. This evidence may contradict pessimistic beliefs about being stupid or unattractive, and create opportunities for considering optimistic alternatives.

### Helping children develop optimism

Research has shown that optimism flourishes in families with distinctive profiles.[11] Parents of optimists are good role models for using an optimistic thinking style. Where children come from families that have experienced major traumas (such as unemployment and poverty), they develop optimism if their families cope and recover from adversity. Parents of optimistic young people encourage their children to deal with setbacks in an optimistic way. They praise their children for using an optimistic thinking style and for persisting when the going gets tough. Optimism is related to the ability to delay gratification and to forgo short-term gains in order to achieve long-term goals, probably because optimistic people can have faith that long-term goals are achievable. Box 9.4 gives a summary of things you can do to help your children develop optimism.

---

**Box 9.4   Parenting so children develop optimism**

- Be a good role model for thinking optimistically.
- Encourage your children to deal with setbacks in an optimistic way.
- Praise your children for thinking optimistically, and persisting when faced with challenges.

# Summary

- **ABC analysis.** In an ABC analysis of a situation we identify the **A**ntecedent events or **A**dversity that preceded a change in mood; the optimistic or pessimistic **B**eliefs we had about the antecedent event or adversity; and the **C**onsequences of these beliefs for how we felt and what we did. ABC analysis shows us that how we think affects how we feel. If we have optimistic beliefs and think optimistically, we usually feel better than if we think pessimistically.

- **Optimistic thinking style.** Optimists explain their successes in terms of positive permanent, pervasive, personal characteristics. They explain failures in terms of transient characteristics, limited to one area of their lives, and due to situational factors.

- **Pessimistic thinking style.** Pessimists explain their failures in terms of negative permanent, pervasive, personal characteristics. They explain their successes in terms of transient characteristics, limited to one area of their lives, and due to situational factors.

- **Thinking traps** are automatic ways of pessimistically interpreting situations, for example black-and-white thinking.

- **Balancing the use of optimistic and pessimistic thinking styles.** Well-being is enhanced by using an optimistic thinking style most of the time, and reserving the use of a pessimistic thinking style for high-risk situations.

- **Optimism and well-being.** Using an optimistic thinking style most of the time is associated with better academic achievement, sport performance, occupational adjustment, family adjustment, physical and mental health, and resilience when faced with stressful challenges.

- **ABCDE strategy for increasing optimism.** With this strategy, we identify the **A**ntecedent events or **A**dversity associated with a drop in mood; the pessimistic **B**eliefs we had about these antecedent adversities; and the **C**onsequences of these beliefs for how our mood deteriorated and what we did. We then use **D**istraction, **D**istancing or **D**isputation to move towards an optimistic thinking style, and a happier mood state. Finally, in **E**nergisation we notice the extent to which using distraction, distancing or disputation improved our mood.

- **Distraction** involves doing something to change the focus of attention and stop the preoccupation with pessimistic thoughts about adversity.

- **Distancing** involves reminding ourselves that a pessimistic explanation of a difficult situation is only one possible interpretation of that situation.

- **Disputing** pessimistic beliefs involves examining the evidence, alternatives, implications and usefulness related to these beliefs. You may use Socratic questioning when disputing pessimistic beliefs, or conduct behavioural experiments to find evidence that contradicts pessimistic beliefs.

## Where are you now?

If you have done the exercises in this chapter, you have found out if you have a predominantly optimistic or pessimistic thinking style. You have also found out how to develop an optimistic thinking style, if you do not think this way already.

You may want to read back over the chapter and summarise in your journal the main things that you have learned about optimism. You can now decide if you want to use the exercises in this chapter for a longer period to help you consolidate a more optimistic thinking style.

In the next chapter, we will consider how to use problem-solving and solution-building skills to address challenges. Below is a web resource and book that are relevant to topics you have read about in this chapter.

## Web resource

Martin Seligman talking about optimistic explanatory style video (1:59): www.youtube.com/watch?v=8-rMuJW-UKg

## Book

Seligman, M. E. P. (2006). *Learned optimism* (Vintage Edition). New York, NY: Random House.

# 10 Solution-finding and problem-solving

Most of the time, most of us do a good job of finding solutions to problems that crop up in our lives. However, sometimes we don't. We may act impulsively without thinking things through and make things worse. We may avoid facing challenges. We may find ourselves trying the same unsuccessful solution over and over. We may get stumped and don't know what to do. We may become exhausted and give up. We may overeat or drink too much to try to make ourselves feel better. If any of these things happen to you, then this chapter may be interest. There is an invitation in this chapter for you to improve your well-being by taking a more systematic approach to problem-solving and solution-finding.

## Problem-solving and well-being

Psychological research has consistently shown that people who are good at problem-solving tend to have better well-being and better psychological adjustment.[1] People with good problem-solving skills are less likely to become depressed, hopeless and suicidal when faced with life stresses and challenges.

People who are good at problem-solving tend to have a positive solution-oriented attitude to problems. They see negative emotions as important signals that they are facing problems that need to be solved. They view problems as challenges, rather than major threats. They are optimistic, and believe that most problems are solvable. They believe that they have the ability to handle difficult problems. They believe that they will have to put in time and effort to reach a successful solution.

However, sometimes problems get the better of us. We may view problems as major threats to our well-being which we do not have the ability to resolve. We may become overwhelmed by negative emotions. We may feel the urge to respond to problems impulsively or find ourselves avoiding facing the problem. Fortunately, these tendencies are not set in stone. We can all develop a positive, optimistic solution-focused attitude to problem-solving. We can all learn or refine the skills for systematically finding successful solutions to the challenges that we meet in our lives.

### Problems

Life continually presents us with many challenges. There are daily hassles like money problems, relationship problems, family difficulties and conflict with co-workers. There are also major stressful life events like bereavement, divorce, redundancy, illness, victimisation and bullying. Some problems are single time-limited events, like missing the bus or getting a puncture. Others are repetitive events like regular conflict at work, family arguments, over-eating or drinking too much. There may also be other problems which are continuous like chronic pain or loneliness.

## Problems and barriers to goals

A useful way to think about problems is that they are life situations that prevent us from achieving goals that would improve our well-being. Problems place barriers or obstacles between us and our goals. These barriers may be physical, for example getting caught in a snow storm, or they may be to do with relationships, for example facing unfair criticism at work. The barriers that problems place between us and our goals may occur for a number of reasons. The situation may be new and unfamiliar, for example starting a new job. The situation may be unpredictable, for example an unexpected increase in workload. The situation may be confusing or ambiguous, for example not understanding exactly what your partner wants from you. The situation may involve conflicting goals, for example wanting to spend time with your family, and also wanting to do well in your job or at college. The situation may need a response that, in the first instance, seems to be beyond our capabilities; for example, having to do something at home, at work or in college for which you do not currently have the skills. The situation may need resources that you do not have, for example money or time. To summarise, problems may occur in situations that are new, confusing or unpredictable, or in situations where we face conflicting goals, or lack the skills and resources to achieve our goals.[1]

## Solutions

If we think of problems as situations that place barriers or obstacles between us and our goals, then we can think of solutions as ways of overcoming barriers or obstacles and achieving our goals. The kinds of goals we set depend on how controllable the situation is. Where situations are controllable, we can aim to change the situation. For example, if the problem is dealing with heavy morning traffic or parking difficulties, then the solution may be to take the train to work. Where situations are uncontrollable, then a useful goal is to change the amount of distress the situation causes us. For example, if the problem is bereavement, then the solution may be spending time with close friends or family members reminiscing about the person who has died and sharing the grieving process within the context of these supportive relationships. To be good at problem-solving and solution-finding, it's important to make the distinction between controllable and uncontrollable problems. This will allow you to decide if your goal should be changing the situation, or changing your distressing reaction to the situation.

## Automatic fight / flight / or freeze responses

We sometimes resort to impulsive solutions when faced with problems. Often these impulsive solutions make things worse. For example, we may get inappropriately angry or we may avoid facing the problem, even when we know that these solutions will only make the problem worse. Why do we do this again and again? The answer goes back to our prehistoric ances-tors, from whom we have evolved. Only our fittest ancestors survived. We have inherited the characteristics that made these ancestors the best survivors. Our tendency to automatically react to some problems in particular ways is partly inherited.

Evolution has designed us to automatically react to many problematic situations as if they were threats to our physical well-being.[2] These automatic reactions are the fight / flight / or freeze responses. During these automatic responses, adrenaline pumps into our blood stream. There are increases in heart rate, respiration and muscle strength. Our bodies become prepared to attack the thing that threatens us, to run from it or to freeze and become 'invisible' so a predator will not attack us. These responses were adaptive for our prehistoric ancestors who mainly faced physical threats. These simple automatic responses helped them to survive.

In the modern world, most problems are social rather than physical. That is, they prevent us from achieving social goals like getting along well with friends, family members and colleagues. Relatively few problems in our day-to-day lives prevent us from achieving physical goals such as avoiding serious physical injury. Because most of the problems we face are social rather than physical, they require complex planned social responses rather than simple, automatic, physical reactions.

In our daily lives, dealing with problems rarely involves fighting, fleeing or freezing. It usually involves calming down our automatic fight or flight reactions, breaking out of our 'freeze' reactions, thinking carefully about the situation and talking calmly with people involved about how best to proceed.

## Too much of a good thing

Some of our problems come from having too much of a good thing, like food, sex and resources, or indulging in these things as a solution to feeling distressed. By resources, I mean things that make us feel good and give us power – like money, alcohol, drugs and leisure activities. By power, I mean the capacity to keep ourselves and those we care about healthy, safe and secure. Eating food, having sex and acquiring or using resources make us feel good in the short-term. In the long-term, too much of these things may create problems such as overeating, sexual infidelity with multiple partners, gambling, gaming, being a 'workaholic', problem-drinking and drug addiction.

Why are we drawn to want too much of a good thing? Just like the fight / flight / or freeze reaction described in the previous section, the answer goes back to our prehistoric ancestors, from whom we have evolved.[2] We have inherited the tendency to crave good things, because this tendency helped our ancestors survive as individuals and as a species. People who didn't have a very strong desire for food, sex and resources didn't survive. Those who did survived, and we inherited their tendency to want more of these things.

In our daily lives, taking too much of a good thing, especially as a solution to distress, can create long-term problems. The alternatives are problem-solving and solution-finding which we will look at in the remainder of this chapter.

## Problem-solving therapy and solution-focused therapy

Problem-solving therapy and solution-focused therapy are two psychological treatments specifically designed to improve skills for overcoming obstacles that stand between us and our goals.

In problem-solving therapy, we learn to define our problems in a specific rather than a vague way, brainstorm a wide range of possible solutions, consider the payoff and price of each of these, pick the one which we think will be most successful, try this out and see if it works.

In contrast, in solution-focused therapy we clarify what the smallest noticeable change in the situation would be to indicate that the problem was being solved, identify exceptional circumstances when movement towards this goal happened in the past and consciously amplify these exceptional moments in the future to create more exceptions.

Building on the pioneering work of Professor Thomas D'Zurilla at the State University of New York, Professor Arthur Nezu and Professor Chrisine Maguth Nezu at Drexel University, Philadelphia have developed problem-solving therapy within the cognitive behaviour therapy tradition.[3] Problem-solving therapy has been shown to be effective in improving well-being for adults with a range of clinical problems, especially depression.[4]

Solution-focused therapy, in contrast, was originally developed by Steve deShazer and Insoo Kim Berg at the Milwaukee Brief Family Therapy Centre within the systemic therapy tradition.[5] Solution-focused therapy has been shown to be effective for improving the well-being of young people and adults with a range of mental health and relationship problems.[6]

In both problem-solving and solution-focused therapy, people are invited to set very specific goals and regularly track their progress towards these goals. Problem-solving therapy helps people develop skills for clarifying problems, generating solutions, doing a cost-benefit analysis of these and selecting one, then using it and seeing if its effective. In contrast, solution-focused therapy helps people identify exceptional circumstances in which the problem was expected to occur but didn't because the person spontaneously found an effective solution. They are then helped to recreate and amplify these exceptions in a deliberate planned way. Of course, there are other processes involved in problem-solving and solution-focused therapies, like building a strong therapist–client relationship and dealing with setbacks. However, the strategies outlined above are the central features of these two deceptively simple, but effective, approaches to psychotherapy.

In the remainder of this chapter you will read about how to apply the core skills learned in problem-solving therapy and solution-focused therapy to address problems in your life.

## Problem-solving

When we are faced with a problem, there are five steps we can follow to cope with the challenge. The first letter of each of the key words in these steps makes up the acronym COPER.

1   Be **C**alm and **C**larify what the problem is.
2   List **O**ptions.
3   **P**redict the **P**ayoff and **P**rice of each option; **P**ick and **P**lan the best option.
4   **E**valuate the outcome.
5   **R**eward yourself.

### 1. Be Calm and Clarify what the problem is

Successful problem-solving is easier when we are calm. Unfortunately, many challenging problems automatically cause the fight / flight / or freeze response which makes us feel keyed up. When we are keyed up our brains work less efficiently, so we are less likely to find successful solutions. It's useful, therefore, as a first step, to calm ourselves before problem-solving. Calm yourself by saying STOP in your mind. Breathe in for three and out for six, and say the word RELAX as you exhale. If you are very keyed up, you may wish to do the brief applied relaxation exercise in Box 5.3, or the three-minute breathing space meditation in Box 6.6.

Once you have become calm, clarify what the challenge is that you have to cope with by identifying the specific barriers you have to overcome to achieve a particular goal. For example, if the goal is having a more satisfying relationship with your partner, the barriers you have to overcome may be reducing the number of arguments you have. It's important that problem-solving goals are realistic and that we monitor our progress towards them as we engage in the problem-solving process. Aiming to have a more satisfying relationship is more realistic than aiming to have an idyllic relationship. A very specific problem is easier to solve than a vague problem. For example, it's harder to solve a vague problem like 'generally arguing less' than a specific problem like 'not arguing with my partner on weekday evenings when we are both tired'. It's also better to frame problems positively rather than negatively. So 'constructively dealing with conflict with my partner on weekday evenings when we are both tired' is a better and more positive statement of the problem than 'not arguing with my partner on weekday evenings when we are both tired'.

If you are facing a very big challenge, break it down into a few smaller problems and solve them one at a time. For example, a big apparently unsolvable problem such as falling behind with everything at work may be broken down into a few more solvable problems. For example,

Problem 1: Contacting 20 suppliers by Friday

Problem 2: Drafting a report by the end of the month

Problem 3: Meeting the accounts manager for 30 minutes each Thursday for the next three weeks to check progress.

## 2. List Options

Once you are calm and have clarified the specific problem you want to solve, the next step is to brainstorm at least three possible solution or options. At this stage, there is no need to judge them as good or bad. Judging prevents us from coming up with creative solutions. So, at this point in the problem-solving process, just list the options. For example, if the problem is constructively dealing with conflict with my partner on weekday evenings when we are both tired, three possible solutions are:

Solution 1. On a Saturday afternoon when we are both rested suggest that if there are issues we need to discuss in the evenings during the week, we postpone these discussions until an agreed time when are both rested, and more likely to be constructive.

Solution 2. When I feel the urge to argue with my partner on weekday evening, I will tell her that I am tired and so prone to arguing over silly things, and that probably I probably would not argue about if I was rested and feeling more tolerant.

Solution 3. Get more sleep during the week so I am not tired on weekday evenings, and more likely to have the energy to resolve conflicts constructively.

If the problem is contacting 20 suppliers by Friday, three possible solutions are:

> Solution 1. Make a plan to phone four suppliers per day between 9.00 and 10.00am each morning of the week.

> Solution 2. Put all other tasks on hold and contact all 20 suppliers on Monday, working overtime if necessary.

> Solution 3. Ask a colleague to help so that we each contact 10 suppliers.

In these examples, for simplicity and brevity, I have kept the number of solutions to three. Three is the minimum. However, when it comes to generating options, more is better. Think of as many solutions as you can. Variety is better homogeneity. Be creative and think of as many different types of solutions as you can. Being playful is better than being too serious. When we adopt a playful approach to thinking up new solutions, and try to feel good and have fun doing it, we are more likely to generate creative options. In Chapter 1, we came across the Broaden and Build theory. This predicts that when we experience positive emotions our thought-action repertoires broaden. This is why we are more likely to generate more creative solutions when we adopt a playful attitude.

### 3. Predict the Payoff and Price of each option; Pick and Plan the best option

When you have listed at least three possible solutions, conduct a cost-benefit analysis by predicting the short- and long-term payoff and price for each of these. Box 10.1 contains a cost-benefit analysis of solutions to the problem of constructively dealing with conflict with my partner on weekday evenings when we are both tired. Box 10.2 contains a cost-benefit analysis of solutions to the problem of contacting 20 suppliers by Friday.

---

**Box 10.1   Payoffs and prices of solutions to the problem of constructively dealing with conflict with my partner on weekday evenings when we are both tired**

| Solution | Payoff | Price |
|---|---|---|
| Solution 1. On a Saturday afternoon when we are both rested suggest that if there are issues we need to discuss in the evenings during the week, we postpone these discussions until an agreed time when we are both rested and more likely to be constructive. | The short-term payoff is that arguments will be avoided. It will probably reduce the number of arguments that occur during the week. | The long-term price is that there may be a build-up of tension over the week, as there is an accumulation of unresolved issues. The accumulation of unresolved issues may make it difficult to have a constructive conversation on Saturdays. |

| | | |
|---|---|---|
| Solution 2. When I feel the urge to argue with my partner on weekday evenings, I will tell her that I am tired and so prone to arguing over silly things, and that I probably would not argue about if I were rested and feeling more tolerant. | Making this statement may clear the air when potential conflicts arise during the week. Over the long-term it may reduce tension within the relationship. | The short-term price may be that the statement may sometimes lead to an argument. |
| Solution 3. Get more sleep during the week so I am not tired on weekday evenings, and more likely to have the energy to resolve conflicts constructively. | I will feel more rested and better able to deal with potential conflicts constructively. | I will have to plan to go to bed early and possibly miss some good TV programmes. |

## Box 10.2 Payoffs and prices of solutions to the problem of contacting 20 suppliers by Friday

| Solution | Payoff | Price |
|---|---|---|
| Solution 1. Make a plan to phone four suppliers per day between 9.00 and 10.00am each morning of the week. | All suppliers will be contacted by Friday. | Some suppliers will not be contacted until Friday. This may mean that they do not have enough time to send supplies by the time they are needed in the next week, if there are unforeseen supply problems. |
| Solution 2. Put all other tasks on hold and contact all 20 suppliers on Monday, working overtime if necessary. | All suppliers will be contacted sooner rather than later. Their supplies will arrive in good time. This will prevent problems associated with late arrival of essential supplies in the following week. | In the short-term, this will involve very hard work and long hours on Monday, and a build-up of other work to do on Tuesday. |
| Solution 3. Ask a colleague to help so that we each contact 10 suppliers. | In the short-term this will reduce my workload for this job. | In the long-term I may have to 'pay back' my colleague for helping me out and this may create an increased workload at a later date. |

Looking at both short- and long-term effects is important. This is because some very good long-term solutions have a short-term downside or price. In the example of having to contact 20 suppliers, the second solution involved putting all other tasks on hold and contacting all

20 suppliers on Monday, working overtime if necessary. This solution has a high short-term price. It involves very hard work and long hours on Monday, and creating a build-up of other work to do on Tuesday. However, it has a very good long-term payoff, because all suppliers will be contacted sooner rather than later. The supplies will arrive in good time. This will prevent problems associated with late arrival of essential supplies in the following week.

Looking at both short- and long-term effects is also important because some very good short-term solutions have a high long-term price. For example, avoiding problems, procrastinating, doing things which distract us from the problem, becoming intoxicated or inappropriately expressing rage may all create a strong short-term sense of well-being. In the long-term, however, these solutions may have a high price and create further problems. When we come up with solutions that have a big short-term payoff, it's useful to ask ourselves questions like this:

- Am I acting impulsively – being driven by the fight / flight / freeze reaction?
- Does my solution involve indulging in 'too much of a good thing'?
- Will this short-term solution lead to long-term problems?

When you have predicted the payoff and price of each option, pick the best option. Then develop a plan about how to actually do it. For example, if I decided that getting more sleep was the best solution to the problem of constructively dealing with conflict with my partner on weekday evenings when we are both tired, then the plan might involve organising my day so that I could go to bed by 10.30pm.

### 4. Evaluate the outcome

When you have put your plan into action, the next step is to evaluate what effect this has on the problem. Does it help you achieve your goal or not? If it does, then proceed to step 5, which is to reward yourself for solving the problem successfully. If you don't achieve your goal, then go back to step 3, and choose the next best option. For example, if the option of getting more sleep was not an effective solution to the problem of constructively dealing with conflict with my partner on weekday evenings when we are both tired, then I would choose the next best option. This might be telling my partner, when I feel the urge to argue, that I am tired and prone to arguing over silly things, and that probably I probably would not argue about if I was rested and feeling more tolerant. I would then develop a plan for implementing this solution, and evaluate how successful it was. When we are trying to solve complex problems, we may have to try a few solutions before we find one that works. 'If at first you don't succeed, try and try again' is bad advice. For successful problem-solving the key is: if at first you don't succeed, try the next best option.

### 5. Reward yourself

When you successfully solve a problem, mark the occasion by rewarding yourself. In your mind say 'Well Done!' or whatever is your equivalent of this sentiment. Acknowledge that it was a difficult challenge. Acknowledge that you successfully coped with it by using problem-solving skills to find an effective way to reach your goal. Then reward yourself by doing something you enjoy. For example, you may take a short walk in the sunshine, listen to a favourite song or have your favourite snack. Savour your reward by focusing on the sensations you experience as you engage in your rewarding activity.

Box 10.3 contains a summary of the key steps in successful problem-solving. Angela's story, below, illustrates what problem-solving looks like in practice.

---

### Box 10.3   Problem-solving: coping with challenges

1   **Be Calm and Clarify what the problem is**

- Calm yourself by saying STOP in your mind – breathe in for three and out for six – say the word RELAX.
- Clarify what the challenge is that you have to cope with by stating, in a positive way, the specific barriers you have to overcome to achieve a specific goal.
- If it's a very big challenge, break it down into a few smaller problems and solve them one at a time.

2   **List Options**

- Brainstorm at least three options to cope with the challenge and overcome the barriers to achieve your specific goal.
- Don't judge them as good or bad at this point; just list them.

3   **Predict the Payoff and Price of each option; Pick and Plan the best option**

- Predict what the short-term and long-term payoff and price of each option will be.
- Pick the best option and develop a plan to do it.

4   **Evaluate the outcome**

- Evaluate what happens when you do the option with the best payoff and lowest price.
- If it solves the problem and helps you achieve your goal, go to step 5.
- If it doesn't, select the next best option.
- Keep going till you find an option that works.

5   **Reward yourself**

- In your mind say 'Well Done!'
- Give yourself a little treat.

---

### Angela's story

Angela usually meets her partner Hector outside his office at 5.30 and drives him home. This arrangement developed because there are convenient parking arrangements at Angela's workplace, but not at Hector's. Therefore, Angela usually drives Hector to work, and then parks her car at her office where there is free parking. After work, she usually collects him on her way home. The problem for Angela is that she often has to wait for up to 20 minutes in her parked car, because Hector is frequently late. She finds waiting distressing, especially since a police officer asked her on one occasion to move on from the place where she was waiting, otherwise she would get a fine for illegal parking on a double yellow line outside Hector's office.

When Hector is late and she is waiting, Angela often anticipates getting a parking ticket or getting into a distressing argument with Hector about his lateness. While doing this, she notices that she becomes keyed up. She has a fight / flight reaction and feels scared and angry. Sometimes when Hector shows up, to prevent an argument, Angela avoids mentioning how waiting has affected her. She ends up feeling bad for not expressing herself. On other occasions, Angela impulsively criticises Hector for his thoughtless tardiness. This often results in an argument which leads her to feel distressed.

Angela's situation is confusing and involves conflicting goals. She wants to support Hector by driving him home in a relaxing atmosphere after work. She also wants him to be more punctual, so she doesn't get a ticket for illegally parking outside his office, but fears if she mentions this, they will get into an argument.

One day Angela decides to solve this problem. She calms herself and clarifies what the problem is. Her problem is finding a way to collect Hector that leaves her feeling OK. Her goal is to be able to collect Hector and drive him home without feeling distress. The barriers to this are her worry about getting a parking ticket while waiting, and her worry that she and Hector will argue on the way home, if she says she was distressed by him keeping her waiting.

Angela brainstorms the following four solutions:

Solution 1. She could tell Hector that if he does not arrive punctually, she will call or text him and let him know that she has driven to a nearby car park where she will wait until he arrives.

Solution 2. She could ask Hector to phone or text her at about 4.30pm and let her know if he will finish work by 5.30pm, and if not, what time would be convenient for her to meet him.

Solution 3. She could tell Hector that if he does not turn up at 5.30, she will drive home without him, and he can travel home by bus, train or taxi.

Solution 4. She could ask Hector to help her find a solution that will take account of her wish not to be distressed when she collects him, and his need for a flexible collection time.

Angela then lists the payoffs and prices associated with each of these solutions, taking account of their short- and long-term effects. These are in Box 10.4. She picks solution 2. She asks Hector to phone or text her at about 4.30pm and let her know if he will finish work by 5.30pm, and if not, what time would be convenient for her to meet him. She puts this solution into practice for three weeks. Hector calls or texts her every day at 4.30. True to his word, he is always standing outside his office when she arrives at the time he says he will be finished work. Angela does not have to wait and worry about parking tickets. However, after three weeks, she decides that the solution is not working. Hector postpones their going home time each day so it becomes progressively later. During the third week of trying this solution Hector texts Angela to ask if she will collect him at 7.00. She agrees to do this. On the way home, they have an argument. Angela says she feels controlled by Hector, and that 7.00 is too late. Hector says that he was co-operating with her plan of texting or calling about going home time at 4.30, and that she should support him when he is under so much work pressure.

---

### Box 10.4   Payoffs and prices of solutions to Angela's problem: collecting Hector

| Solution | Payoff | Price |
|---|---|---|
| Solution 1. Angela could tell Hector that if he does not arrive punctually, she will call or text him and let him know that she has driven to a nearby car park where she will wait until he arrives. | Angela will not worry about getting a parking ticket. Hector will get some exercise and fresh air. | Angela may feel guilty for making Hector walk to the car park after he has done a hard day's work. Hector may get caught in the rain walking to the car park and this may lead to an argument. |
| Solution 2. Angela could ask Hector to phone or text her at about 4.30pm and let her know if he will finish work by 5.30pm, and if not, what time would be convenient for her to meet him. | In the short-term Angela will feel less distress because she will not have to wait when parked illegally outside his office, as Hector will be on time. | In the long-term if Hector often postpones their going home time, Angela will feel controlled by Hector for frequently deciding on their going home time, become angry and pick a fight with him. |
| Solution 3. Angela could tell Hector that if he does not turn up at 5.30, she will drive home without him, and he can travel home by bus, train or taxi. | Angela will not have to park illegally outside Hector's office for long periods of time, and worry about getting a parking ticket. The couple will not fight on the way home when Hector is late, as they will be travelling separately. In the long-term, Hector will be on time more days than not, because he prefers travelling by car than the alternatives, so will gradually be motivated to finish work on time. | In the short-term Hector will get angry and they will argue when Angela proposes the solution and when she puts it into effect, and does not drive Hector home from work. |
| Solution 4. Angela could ask Hector to help her find a solution that will take account of her wish not to be distressed when she collects him, and his need for a flexible collection time. | The couple may find a joint solution that meets both their needs. | Hector and Angela may spend a lot of time looking for a solution, and not find one that they both agree with. The constructive search for a solution they can both agree to may turn into a big argument. |

When they calm down after the argument, Angela says that solution 2 is not working for her. She suggests they change to solution 1 where she tells Hector that if he does not arrive punctually at 5.30, she will call or text him and let him know that she has driven to a nearby car park where she will wait until he arrives. This solution works well for a few months. Angela thinks it's a success, and gives herself a treat for solving the problem. Most days Hector is on time. When he is not, she rarely has to wait longer than 10 minutes for him at the nearby car park, where she does not worry about getting a parking ticket. However, when winter arrives, Hector catches a bad cold after getting caught in a torrential downpour while walking to the car park to meet Angela. She feels very guilty about this. She abandons solution 1.

She decides to try solution 4 where she asks Hector to help her find a solution that will take account of her wish not to be distressed when she collects him, and his need for a flexible collection time. After a lot of discussion, they find a new solution that suits both of them. Hector offers to do the driving, and both drop off and pick up Angela from work. This solution is partly facilitated by Hector's employer making basement car parking available to him. This solution is a lasting success. Hector picks up Angela most days between 5.30 and 5.45. Angela doesn't have to worry about parking tickets and the couple usually enjoy each other's company on the journey home. After a month Angela rewards herself for this successful outcome by arranging a special date night for herself and Hector.

## Solution-finding

When we engage in problem-solving, we focus on the details of our problems and then plan new solutions. In contrast, with solution-finding, we focus our attention on exceptional times when we expected our problems to occur but they didn't. Or if they did, they were less noticeable, less intense, more bearable or we coped better with them. That is, we remember episodes that contain the seeds of solutions to our current problems. Then we plan to build solutions to our current problems from these things that we have already done. These are things which we know have had a positive effect on our problems in the past. There are six steps in solution-finding.

1   Set small measurable goals.
2   Identify exceptions.
3   Spot the difference between problem and exception episodes.
4   Create more exceptions.
5   Track progress towards your goals.
6   Reflect on who you are becoming.

### *1. Set small measurable goals*

A central part of solution-finding is identifying the smallest goal that will make the biggest difference to you. One way to do that is to ask yourself this miracle question: Imagine while you are sleeping tonight, without you knowing, there is a miracle and the problem that concerns you now is solved. When you wake up tomorrow, what would be the smallest change you would notice that would make you say – My problem is gone! How would you be acting differently? How would you be thinking differently? How would you be feeling differently? The answers to these questions tell you what your goals are in terms of finding a solution to your problem. These are the smallest changes that would make the biggest difference to you.

Katie's problem was that she drank too much at weekends and so felt hungover on Saturdays, Sundays and Mondays. The smallest changes that would make the biggest difference to her were that she be able to pause after having three alcoholic drinks and ask herself: Do I want to drink iced water now and wake feeling refreshed tomorrow, or do I want to drink more alcohol and risk a hangover?

Simon's problem was that he suffered from chronic pain following a road traffic accident. The smallest changes that would make the biggest difference to him were that once a day he able to do a physical activity that made him feel good, and that distracted him from his pain.

When solution-finding, it's best to state our goals positively. That is, state what we will be doing rather than what we will not be doing. For Katie her goal was being able to pause after having three alcoholic drinks and ask: Do I want to drink iced water now and wake feeling refreshed tomorrow, or do I want to drink more alcohol and risk a hangover? A negative statement of her goal might be – I want to stop drinking alcohol after three drinks. For Simon, his goal was once a day to do a physical activity that made him feel good, and which distracted him from his pain. A negative statement of his goal might be – I want to not be in pain once a day. Stating goals as positive rather than negative actions, thoughts and feelings is a better strategy to use.

It's useful to think of goals as involving changes in the way we act; the way we think; and the way we feel. Katie had goals in the domains of action, thinking and feeling.

The action goal was: I will pause after having three alcoholic drinks.

The thinking goal was: I will ask myself: Do I want to drink iced water now and wake feeling refreshed tomorrow, or do I want to drink more alcohol and risk a hangover?

The feeling goal was: The next day I will feel refreshed.

It's important to state our goals in ways that can be easily measured so that we will be able to judge how much progress we are making towards them. For action and thinking goals, we can state measurable goals as the number of times we will be acting or thinking in a particular way. For feeling goals, we can state measurable goals as a rating of how we will feel on a scale of 1 to 10. Katie's measurable goals may be stated as follows:

Action goal: On at least one occasion in a weekend, I will pause after having three alcoholic drinks.

Thinking goal: On at least one occasion in a weekend I will ask myself: Do I want to drink iced water now and wake feeling refreshed tomorrow, or do I want to drink more alcohol and risk a hangover?

Feeling goal: I will rate my mood on Saturday, Sunday or Monday morning as 6 or greater on a scale of 1 to 10 where 1 is bad or very hungover and 10 is good or very refreshed.

For Simon the smallest measurable goals that would make the biggest difference to him are listed below.

Action goal: I will do at least one enjoyable physical activity a day.

Thinking goal: I will think positively about the physical activity I am doing once a day (rather than think about back pain).

Feeling goal: At least once a day, I will rate my mood as 6 or greater on a scale of 1 to 10 where 1 is bad or in severe pain and 10 is good or not in pain at all.

## 2. Identify exceptions

The second step in solution-finding is to identify exceptions. We think about recent situations where we expected the problem to occur but it didn't occur at all, or was less noticeable, less intense, more bearable or where we coped better with it. For Katie whose problem was that she drank too much alcohol at weekends and so felt hungover on Saturdays, Sundays and Mondays, there may have been occasions when she drank more moderately or not at all and awoke feeling less hungover or more refreshed. These occasions might have involved being alone or socialising with particular friends, colleagues or family members. These exceptions might have occurred in situations where she drank alcohol with a meal rather than without food, or situations where she drank wine or beer rather than spirits. These exceptions might have occurred in situations where she was involved in activities on Friday, Saturday and Sunday nights that were incompatible with drinking alcohol, for example sports or work. Exceptions might also have occurred in situations where she had enjoyable activities planned for Saturday and Sunday for which she wanted to feel refreshed, or where she had work responsibilities on Monday for which she did not want to be hungover, and so refrained from drinking alcohol. These were just some of the possibilities that she could have considered.

For Simon whose problem was chronic pain, there might have been exceptional circumstances where he noticed that it was less intense, more bearable or where he coped better with it; for example, when he was with certain people whose company he enjoyed; when he was involved in distracting physical activities; or when he was absorbed in interesting non-physical activity involving a high level of attention.

## 3. Spot the difference between problem and exception episodes

The third step in solution-finding is to identify differences between situations where the problem occurs and exceptional situations where it is expected to occur but doesn't. In order to spot these differences there is a series of questions you may ask yourself.

- What are the main differences between episodes where the problem did occur and exceptional episodes where the problem was expected to occur or get worse but didn't, or was less noticeable, intense or bearable, or where you coped better?
- What is it that I did differently to create these exceptional episodes?
- What is it that other people in my life did differently to create these exceptional episodes?

- What is the difference between episodes where the problem did occur and these exceptional episodes were the problem didn't happen or get worse, or was less noticeable, intense or bearable, or where I coped better?
- How would a close friend or member of my family explain the difference between episodes where the problem did occur and these exceptional episodes?

For Katie whose problem was that she drank too much alcohol at weekends and so felt hungover on Saturdays, Sundays and Mondays, these questions helped her to realise that there were three main differences between episodes where the problem occurred and exceptional episodes where it didn't. Exceptional episodes occurred when she was with people who were not heavy drinkers and did not put social pressure on her to drink a lot; where she was playing tennis on weekend nights; and when she had something important to do at work on Monday for which she wanted to feel refreshed. The main things that she did differently to set up these exceptional episodes were to make plans to see people who were not heavy drinkers and who did not put social pressure on her to drink excessively; to make arrangements to play tennis on weekend evenings; or where she or her work colleagues scheduled important meetings on Monday mornings. In these exceptional episodes, Katie believed that she drank less because she was not under social pressure to drink excessively, or she was playing tennis (an activity which left no opportunity for drinking), or she was motivated to perform well at work on Monday and so didn't drink excessively.

For Simon whose problem was chronic pain, questions about differences between episodes where the problem occurred and exceptional episodes where it didn't helped him to realise that there were a number of differences between episodes where he felt intense pain and exceptional episodes in which the pain was less noticeable, more bearable or where he coped better. Exceptional episodes occurred when he was with his girlfriend, walking by the sea or swimming; reading an absorbing novel or writing an absorbing document; or meditating. The main things that he did differently to arrange these exceptional episodes was to make plans to be with his girlfriend; to walk or swim rather than stay late at work or watch TV; and to take time to read or write or meditate and prioritise these activities. In exceptional episodes, Simon believed that he experienced less pain because he focused his attention on things that were more highly valued, important, compelling and enjoyable than pain.

### 4. Create more exceptions

The fourth step in solution-finding is to plan to create more exceptional episodes, over a period of a week or two, where the problem doesn't happen or get worse, or is less noticeable, intense or bearable or where you cope better. This involves doing things that we already have done in previous exceptional episodes.

Katie, whose problem was that she drank too much alcohol at weekends and so felt hungover on Saturdays, Sundays and Mondays, made plans to see people at the weekend who were not heavy drinkers and who did not put social pressure on her to drink excessively. She also made arrangements to play tennis on some weekend evenings. Where there were important meetings to be held at work, she scheduled these for Monday mornings whenever possible. She hoped that these solutions that had worked in the past would help her to drink alcohol moderately in future.

Simon, whose problem was chronic pain, arranged to go for a walk or have a swim with his girlfriend a few times a week and to prioritise reading novels or doing creative writing, or meditating. He hoped that these solutions that had worked in the past would help him to control his pain in future.

## 5. Track progress towards your goals

The fifth step in solution-finding is to notice the extent to which we are achieving our goals over a period of a week or two. That is, to notice how much more frequently we are acting and thinking the way we aimed to when we started this process, and to rate on a scale of 1 to 10 how much better we are feeling. If our problem is not improving, we may consider what we are doing to prevent it from getting worse. Then we may continue to create exceptional episodes and track changes towards our goals.

Katie, whose problem was that she drank too much alcohol at weekends and so felt hungover, found that after two weeks, on four occasions she had paused after having three alcoholic drinks and asked herself: Do I want to drink iced water now and wake feeling refreshed tomorrow, or do I want to drink more alcohol and risk a hangover? On five occasions, she rated her mood on Saturday, Sunday or Monday morning as 6 or greater, and her most frequent weekend morning mood-rating was 7.

Simon, whose problem was chronic pain, found that he achieved his goals over the first week. He did one enjoyable physical activity a day and thought positively about it. On five of the seven days he did three or four pleasant activities. He rated his mood as 7 or 8 on five of seven days, and 6 on the other two days.

Both Simon and Katie continued to track progress by keeping daily notes of the extent to which they were achieving their goals in their journals. They both found that over a period of 4–6 months they continued to maintain the gains they made in their first few seeks, although they had occasional setbacks. For example, one Friday evening after work Katie met a group of old college friends, and awoke the next day with a bad hangover. She had succumbed to social pressure to drink to excess. Simon had a week where his well-being ratings were all below 6. This was because he had the flu and so didn't engage in physical activities or absorbing pastimes or meet with his girlfriend during this week.

## 6. Reflect on who you are becoming

The final step in solution-finding is to reflect on the following questions as we create more exceptions in our lives and move towards our goals:

- How did I decide that now was the time to solve this problem?
- What insights from my life was I able to use to find a solution and move towards my goals?
- How am I different now that I have made these positive changes in my life?
- How will I maintain the gains that I have made?
- What does it say about me as a person that I have made these positive changes in my life?

In the sections that follow, Katie and Simon's stories illustrate how reflecting on these questions after engaging in the solution-finding process can change our views of ourselves.

Box 10.5 contains a summary of steps in the solution-finding process.

---

## Box 10.5  Solution-finding

1  **Set small measurable goals**

- Imagine while you are sleeping tonight, without you knowing, there is a miracle and the problem that concerns you now is solved. When you wake up tomorrow, what would be the smallest change you would notice that would make you say – My problem is gone!.
- How would you be ACTING differently?
- How would you be THINKING differently?
- How would you be FEELING differently?
- The answers to these questions tell you what your goals are in terms of finding a solution to your problem.
- Your goals are the smallest changes that would make the biggest difference to you.
- State your goals positively (what you will be doing rather than what you will not be doing).
- State your goals in a way that can be measured (the number of times you will be acting or thinking in a particular way, or the way you will rate how you feel on a scale of 1 to 10 where 1 is feeling really low or anxious or bad and 10 is feeling really happy, relaxed or good).

2  **Identify exceptions**

- Think about recent situations where you expected the problem to occur but it didn't occur at all, was less noticeable, less intense, more bearable or where you coped better with it.

3  **Spot the difference between problem and exception episodes**

- What are the main differences between episodes where the problem did occur and these exceptional episodes were the problem was expected to occur but didn't happen or get worse, or was less noticeable, intense or bearable, or where you coped better?
- What is it that you did differently to create these exceptional episodes?
- What is it that other people in your life did differently to create these exceptional episodes?
- How do you explain the difference between episodes where the problem did occur and these exceptional episodes where the problem didn't happen or get worse, or was less noticeable, intense or bearable, or where you coped better?
- How would a close friend or member of your family explain the difference between episodes where the problem did occur and these exceptional episodes?

4   **Create more exceptions**

- Plan to create more exceptional episodes where the problem doesn't happen or get worse, or is less noticeable, intense or bearable or where you cope better.
- This will involve doing things that you already have done in previous exceptional episodes.
- Create a number of exceptional episodes over a period of a week or two.

5   **Track progress towards your goal**

- Over a period of a week or two, notice the extent to which you are achieving your goals.
- How much more frequently are you acting and thinking the way you aimed to when you started this process?
- On a scale of 1 to 10 how much better are you feeling?
- If your problem is not improving, consider what you are doing to prevent it from getting worse.
- Continue to create exceptional episodes and track changes towards your goals.

6   **Reflect on who you are becoming**

- As you create more exceptions in your life and move towards your goals, reflect on the following questions:
- How did you decide that now was the time to solve this problem?
- What insights from your life were you able to use to find a solution and move towards your goals?
- How are you different now that you have made these positive changes in your life?
- How will you maintain the gains that you have made?
- What does it say about you as a person that you have made these positive changes in your life?

## Katie's story

When Katie reflected on the questions listed above, she wrote the following in her journal.

I decided to sort out my weekend binges when I had to cancel two tennis matches in a row because I was too hungover to play. I let myself down and I let my friends down. I knew it was time to do something about it. I found that when I looked back on my life there were definitely situations where I drank less. These were situations where I went out with friends who knew how to have a good time without becoming legless, blotto drunk. I also noticed that when I played evening tennis, rather than going drinking, I felt better the next day. Big things at work on Mondays also made me watch how much I drank on Sunday nights. I used all these insights to help me move towards a more moderate drinking pattern.

I feel much better about myself now. I feel like I am in control of my life. I feel like weekends are a time for doing more things and feeling good. They are not times for getting drunk, not being able to remember what happened and feeling hungover all the time. I know how to keep this going. I just have to go out with people who are not complete piss-heads, but who enjoy a drink and can have a good time without getting blotto. I have to pause after three drinks and ask myself, do I want to feel good tomorrow? I have to make sure to play some evening tennis on some weekends. I have to make sure some of the time to have important stuff to do at work on Mondays so as to motivate myself to stick to my moderate drinking plan. This experience of finding my own solution has shown me that I am in charge of my own life. I'm in charge of how I run it. I control how I think. I am in control of what I decide to do and ultimately how good I feel. That's what this change in my life says about me as a person. It's my life and it's down to me to take charge of the direction it moves in. I can do this now.

## Simon's story

Simon reflected on the questions listed above. Here is what he wrote in his journal.

Chronic pain is very difficult to live with. It never goes away. It can eat into every corner of your life and suck the good out of it. I let it do this to me. I had got to the point where I didn't want to do anything because I hurt too much. I was feeling really sorry for myself. I felt hopeless. My girlfriend, Maeve, told me that I was bigger than the pain. She said she believed that I could do something about it. I think I was scared that if I didn't, she would leave me. So, I started this process. When I looked back on my life, I saw that the pain was not constant. It went up and down. Or there were sometimes when I noticed it more than others. That was a really important insight. Through detective work I found out when I felt better or coped better or noticed the pain less. It was really clear to me after a bit of detective work and reflection that when I was with Maeve, especially if we were walking on the beach or swimming, I hardly noticed the pain at all. Walking or swimming without Maeve – I felt OK doing that too, but not as good.

The other thing I found out was that if I was really deeply absorbed in reading a good book or doing my creative writing, I forgot about the pain. I learned to meditate. That helped too. That made me change the sort of relationship I had with my pain. I can let it in when I meditate and not lock it out. In a funny sort of way that makes it more bearable. All of these things helped me put together a survival plan. Now most days I make sure to go for a walk or swim with Maeve. I read or write. I meditate. I'm not cured. The pain probably is with me for life. The difference is that now I no longer feel helpless or hopeless. I know I can do this. I know the pain and how good I feel fluctuate. These things are not constant. I can influence the way they fluctuate and how I react to that. I think of myself now as much stronger. When you accept that pain is part of your life, from now till your dying day, it makes you strong. The other side of the coin is that you find yourself accepting the good things in life too. There are so many wonderful, beautiful things in the world: people I love; stories I read; new stories I create; the extraordinary beauty of the world when the sun is setting, the clouds are turning crimson and I walk along the deserted beach with Maeve and listen to seagulls crying before a storm. When I accept that pain is part of my life, I have to accept that all these good things are part of my life too. That makes me strong. I know I will keep on keeping on.

### *Problem-solving and solution-finding exercise*

There is an invitation for you to select a problem in your life that concerns you right now. Read through the problem-solving guidelines in Box 10.3 and the solution-finding guidelines in Box 10.5. Decide which approach suits you best at the moment. Solve your problem or find your solution using the approach that suits you. In your journal, write about your progress as you move though each step in the process. Before and after this exercise, rate your well-being in your journal on a scale of 1 to 10. Note the extent to which the exercise increased your well-being and any aspects of the exercise that you think specifically contributed to this.

Then, possibly a week or two later, select another problem. Try the approach that you have not previously tried – problem-solving or solution-finding. Once again, in your journal, write about your progress as you move through each step in the process. Before and after this exercise, rate your well-being in your journal on a scale of 1 to 10. Note the extent to which the exercise increased your well-being and any aspects of the exercise that you think specifically contributed to this.

Compare and contrast the two approaches – problem-solving or solution-finding – and reflect on the extent to which each of these approaches are useful for you. Write your reflections on this in your journal.

## Summary

- **Problems are barriers to goals.** Problems are life situations that prevent us from achieving goals that would improve our well-being.
- **Hassles, life events and chronic conditions.** Problems include daily hassles, major stressful live events (like bereavement) and chronic ongoing problems (like chronic illness).
- **Problem-solving and well-being.** People with good problem-solving skills have better well-being, and become less distressed and depressed when faced with life challenges.
- **Controllable and uncontrollable problems.** For controllable problems, the goal is changing the situation. For uncontrollable problems, the goal is changing our distressing reactions to the situation.
- **Fight / flight / or freeze reactions**. When faced with problems that threaten our well-being, we automatically have a fight / flight / or freeze reaction. Adrenaline is released into the blood stream and increases in heart rate, muscle tension and strength occur. This is a reaction which we have inherited from our ancestors and is good for dealing with physically threatening problems. It's not good for dealing with problems that threaten us socially. This automatic reaction may lead us to deal with problems in impulsive ways that may make the situation worse.
- **Too much of a good thing.** We have evolved to be highly motivated to want things that make us feel good and give us power. We may use in acquiring these things as a solution to our problems. Unfortunately, too much food, sex, alcohol, drugs, work or leisure activities can create more problems than they solve. Problem-solving and solution-finding are usually better alternatives.
- **Problem-solving.** Remember the five steps for problem-solving with the acronym COPER. Be **C**alm and **C**larify what the problem is. List **O**ptions for solving the problem.

**P**redict the **P**ayoff and **P**rice of each option; **P**ick and **P**lan the best option. **E**valuate the outcome. **R**eward yourself.

* **Solution-finding.** There are six steps in solution-finding. (1) Set small measurable goals. (2) Identify exceptions. (3) Spot the difference between problem and exception episodes. (4) Create more exceptions. (5) Track progress towards your goals. (6) Reflect on who you are becoming.

## Where are you now?

If you have done the exercise at the end of this chapter using the skills in Boxes 10.3 and 10.5, you have found out how problem-solving or solution-finding can affect your well-being. Problem-solving involves focusing on the details of our problems and then planning new creative solutions. In contrast, solution-finding involves remembering exceptional times when we expected our problems to occur but they didn't, and developing solutions from these things that previously worked for us.

You may want to read back over the chapter and summarise in your journal the main things that you have learned about problem-solving and solution-finding. You can now decide if you want to make problem-solving and solution-finding part of the way you address challenges in your life.

In the next part, we will consider relationships and well-being. Below is a web resource and books that are relevant to topics you have read about in this chapter.

## Web resource

Animated video on systematic problem-solving (4.28): www.youtube.com/watch?v=Bt7i0UyLjmg

## Books

Duncan, B. (2005). *What's right with you? Debunking dysfunction and changing your life.* Deerfield Beach, FL: Health Communications Inc.

Nezu, A., Nezu, M., & D'Zurilla, T. (2007). *Solving life's problems: A 5-step guide to enhance well-being.* New York, NY: Springer.

# Part 5
# Strengthening relationships

# 11 Compassionate relationships

A vast body of psychological research shows that relationships are central to our well-being.[1] Our well-being is enhanced by good relationships, with our families, friends, work colleagues and people in the wider community. When we have good relationships, we are happier. We experience more positive emotions. When we have good relationships, we find it easier to co-operate with each other. We accomplish more when we have co-operative relationships at home, at work, in sports and in other activities.

Supportive close relationships also make us more resilient. Numerous research studies have shown that people with supportive relationship show better recovery and quality of life following major illnesses like cancer, heart attacks and stroke; better self-management of chronic conditions like diabetes; and better adjustment following childbirth.[2]

How is it that most of us are able to form close relationships? The main reason is that we have evolved over millions of years to be the sort of species that can do this.[3] From an evolutionary perspective, the capacity to make and maintain close relationships was adaptive for our prehistoric ancestors. People who could do this survived. They formed relationships to hunt and gather food; to create safe dwelling places; to mate; to bear and bring up children; and to protect their group from larger and stronger predators. None of these tasks could have been done alone. People who couldn't form close relationships to do these tasks didn't survive.

Why are close relationships so good for us? Psychological research points to four key processes that link good relationships to well-being. They help us to co-operate. They provide us with a context within which to celebrate and capitalise upon our successes. They give our lives meaning. Most importantly, relationships provide us with support.

## Co-operation

Our teamwork is better when we have good relationships with our team-mates.[4] We co-operate better with each other. The goodwill that comes from co-operation allows us to work together more efficiently. Co-operation improves the efficiency of all sorts of teams: parenting teams, sports team, work teams. Children of parents who co-operate well with each other are better adjusted. They are happier, have fewer problems and do better at school. In work situations, colleagues who co-operate well together do a better job and return better profits. In sports, teams who co-operate well together are more likely to win.

### Capitalisation

In close relationships, we not only benefit from telling others about out difficulties, and getting their support, as discussed below. We also benefit from telling them about our successes. This process of sharing good news with our nearest and dearest is referred to as capitalisation. By telling others about our good fortune, we are making the most of, or capitalising on, our positive experiences. When our partners, family members and close friends respond to our good news with enthusiasm, this increases our well-being.[5] In a series of studies Professor Shelly Gable at the University of California, Santa Barbara has found that sharing good news with others makes people feel more positive emotions, increases their self-esteem and reduces their loneliness. She also found that these sorts of positive benefits were greatest when others responded to their good news with enthusiasm.

### Meaning

Relationships with our families, friends and colleagues may give us a sense of belonging, identity, purpose and meaning.[6] They allow us to say things like 'I am a member of this family and in this family, we have strong values that mean a lot to me'; or 'I play on this team, and our team does its best'; or 'I work for this organisation; the work we do and the way we do it is important to me'.

### Social support

Perhaps one of the most important reasons why close relationships are so good for us is that they provide us with support. In close relationships we feel supported, understood, valued and loved, especially when under stress. Psychologists refer to these experiences as social support. Social support counteracts the negative effects of stress on the way we think and feel, and on our neuro-endocrine systems.[7] When we talk with someone who 'is there for us' and who empathises with our situation, this allows us to get things off our chest. We feel understood. This soothes us. We become less revved up. Our physiological stress responses calm down. Our heart rate, blood pressure and cortisol levels all gradually return to normal. This, in turn, has a positive effect on our immune systems and so healing processes work more efficiently. People with high levels of social support when under stress experience less distress, and fewer physical health problems.

Remember Professor Barbara Fredrickson's Broaden and Build theory which we came across in Chapter 1.[8] This theory says that when we feel positive emotions, our thought-action repertoires broaden. It becomes possible to see situations in far more flexible ways and generate new and creative solutions, which in turn helps us to build resources for repeating this process. There is little doubt that this occurs in socially supportive relationships, when we tell our nearest and dearest our troubles. As we calm down and experience the good feeling that goes with getting things off our chest, our thinking becomes less rigid and more flexible. It becomes possible to see complex and challenging situations in a new light. Talking with someone who understands us may also help us to view our situation in a more optimistic way. We may begin to see the wood and not just the trees. We may see the glass is half full, not half empty. It may also become possible with this new perspective to be more creative about finding useful solutions.

## Love 2.0

One of Barbara Fredrickson's remarkable discoveries is that positive Broaden and Build experiences occur not only in close long-term relationships, but also in momentary interactions with acquaintances. These moments of connection between ourselves and others – whether family, close friends or acquaintances – have a more profound effect on well-being than other positive emotions. This has led to her expanding the Broaden and Build theory, to take account of the very special case of positive emotions shared with others in momentary interactions. She refers to these episodes of emotional connection as 'love' in her book *Love 2.0*.[9] Her scientific definition of love is so distinctive that I will refer to it here as Love 2.0 (in keeping with the name of her book). Love 2.0 does not refer to the sort of love we associate with long-term close emotional bonds between romantic partners, between parents and children, or between best friends. When Fredrickson talks about Love 2.0, she is referring to those fleeting moments of connection that feel good, and that occur between any two people. For example, you meet a colleague in the corridor at work, smile at each other and briefly joke about an email that was circulated to all staff that morning about not wasting time talking in corridors. You ask the shopkeeper in the convenience store how business is, and he tells you an amusing anecdote about the rush on his new sandwiches, which leads you both to laugh. You arrive home from work at exactly the same time as your partner, look at each other and smile, while simultaneously collapsing into your favourite chairs in the living room and saying, 'you'll never guess what happened to me today?', and then burst out laughing because (once again) you have both said the same thing at the same time.

During these moments of connection, three events occur: (1) a positive emotion is shared, (2) mutual care is expressed and (3) for those involved, a synchrony occurs between their behaviour and between certain biological processes particularly in the brain and nervous system. In these fleeting moments of shared emotions, mutual care and biobehavioural synchrony, a process of positivity resonance occurs, where you each amplify the experiences of the other person. You both experience and amplify the positive emotion. You both experience and amplify each other's impulse to express care. You also mirror each other's gestures and mirror certain processes within the brain, nervous system and some other biological systems. This positivity resonance doesn't happen with any other positive emotion.

Certain conditions are essential for moments of Love 2.0 or positivity resonance to occur. We must feel safe. We must be present in the same physical place at the same moment in time. This sort of connection does not easily occur when we interact electronically by phone or Skype. Eye contact is the most potent trigger, but touch, voice and mirrored gestures (especially smiles or laughter) may also help us to create this type of connection.

When we experience moments of interpersonal connection characterised by positivity resonance, neural coupling occurs in that moment when we 'get' each other.[10] There is a very significant overlap between the areas of my brain and your brain that become particularly active in these moments of connection. Our oxytocin waves also synchronise.[11] Oxytocin is the hormone that regulates the calm-and-connect response. It calms fears that might make us avoid strangers, and sharpens our skills for connecting with others.

This extension of the Broaden and Build theory proposes that thought-action repertoires are broadened in these moments of social connection – of Love 2.0. We both see the world in a broader and less narrowly focused way. We both experience a broader range of possibilities about what we could do next. We are both enriched by these experiences and so can build on them in the future. Fredrickson proposes that we can enhance well-being by actively organising our lives to create more micro-moments of Love 2.0.[9] We can prepare ourselves to make the most of such opportunities by regularly engaging in meditation practices in which we focus on compassion and loving kindness.[12]

## Positive psychology techniques focusing on relationships

A range of scientifically based positive psychology techniques focus on relationships. These include:

- Compassion and loving kindness meditation
- Acts of kindness
- Volunteering
- Celebrating success
- Understanding attachment styles

### *Compassion and loving kindness meditation*

Compassion and loving kindness meditation may be found in a number of spiritual traditions. However, positive psychology has drawn on Buddhism as the primary source for this meditation. The aim of compassion and loving kindness meditation is to cultivate a strong positive disposition towards the self and others. In loving kindness meditation, we wish to develop unconditional kindness for the self and all people. With compassion meditation, we want to generate a deep, genuine sympathy for ourselves and those experiencing misfortune, along with an earnest wish to ease this suffering. These two meditations have been combined in two of the most widely researched mindfulness-based psychological intervention programmes: Mindfulness-Based Stress Reduction (MBSR)[13] and Mindfulness-Based Cognitive Therapy (MBCT).[14] These were described in Chapter 6.

In compassion and loving kindness meditations, positive feelings are directed towards the self, then towards loved ones, then towards strangers, then towards someone with whom we experience conflict or difficulty, and finally towards all people. This continuum from the self to all people represents a progression from a relatively easy task to a more difficult one. It's relatively easy to feel compassion for loved ones and relatively difficult to feel it for people whom we do not know.

Compassion and loving kindness-based meditations usually involve the repetition of the same phrases for each object of compassion. For example:

> May I (or he / she / they) be free from suffering (or harm or pain or distress).
>
> May I (or he / she / they) be healthy (or have well-being).
>
> May I (or he / she / they) be happy (or have joy in my life).
>
> May I (or he / she / they) live with ease (or live in peace, or be safe).

This may be combined with visualisation to generate a feeling of compassion and loving kindness towards the object of the meditation. For example, in our mind's eye we may create as vivid an image of the other person as possible and visualise light flowing from ourselves to the other person. Between each phrase we pause and are open to any thoughts that come into our awareness. As with all mindfulness meditations, we observe and accept these thoughts, without judgement, and let them pass. We mindfully note the urge to be swept into the stream of thought by judging, ruminating, worrying, planning and so forth. However, we simply notice these thoughts and urges, and let them pass.

There is a loving kindness meditation in Box 11.1. If you practise the meditation regularly, then it will increase your compassion for other people and may enhance your relationships.

---

## Box 11.1   A loving kindness meditation

The loving kindness meditation is an opportunity to experience compassion towards the self and others.

### Settling

Sit in a chair with feet flat on the floor, the spine straight and not resting against the chair back, and the eyes gently closed. Adopt an erect, dignified and comfortable posture.

Bring awareness to sensations in the lower abdominal wall as the breath moves in and out of the body. Then expand attention to your whole body.

When your mind wanders, as it inevitably will, acknowledge where it went. Then bring your attention back to the breath or the body, whichever you were focusing on when the mind wandered.

### Self-compassion

When you are ready, allow some of these phrases to come to mind:

May I be free from suffering / harm / pain / distress / illness
May I be healthy / have well-being
May I be happy / have joy in my life
May I live with ease / live in peace / be safe

Select three or four phrases that feel right for you, for example:

May I be free from pain
May I be healthy
May I have joy in my life
May I be safe

Allow these phrases to become a doorway through which you can experience a deep sense of compassion, kindness or friendship towards yourself.

Taking your time, imagine that each phrase is a small stone dropped into a deep well. As you drop each one in turn, pause, breathe and listen attentively for any responses that may come in thoughts, feelings, urges to act or images. Accept whatever arises, without judgement.

If you find it difficult to feel friendship towards yourself, visualise a person or a pet who has loved you. When you have a clear image in your mind of them showing their love for you, see if you can offer this love to yourself by saying the phrases that suit you, for example:

May I be free from pain

May I be healthy

May I have joy in my life

May I be safe

Remain with this step as long as you wish before moving on to the next step.

### Compassion for someone you love

Now visualise someone you love. Wish them well in the same way. Acknowledging that they, like you, have challenges in their lives and want to be happy. Once again, choose phrases that suit you from the selection below, or others if you prefer:

May they be free from suffering / harm / pain / distress / illness

May they be healthy / have well-being

May they be happy / have joy in their lives

May they live with ease / live in peace / be safe

Once again, imagine that each phrase is a small stone dropped into a deep well. As you drop each one in turn, pause, breathe and listen attentively for any responses that may come in thoughts, feelings, urges to act or images. Accept whatever arises, without judgement.

### Compassion for a stranger

When you are ready to move on, visualise a stranger. This may be someone you see regularly when shopping or travelling to work. Although you recognise them, you do not know them well, and have no strong feelings about them, either positive or negative. Although you do not know them, acknowledge that they, like you, have challenges in their lives and want to be happy. Once again, choose phrases that suit you from the selection below, or others if you prefer:

May they be free from suffering / harm / pain / distress / illness

May they be healthy / have well-being

May they be happy / have joy in their lives

May they live with ease / live in peace / be safe

Once again, imagine that each phrase is a small stone dropped into a deep well. As you drop each one in turn, pause, breathe and listen attentively for any responses that may come in thoughts, feelings, urges to act or images. Accept whatever arises, without judgement.

### Compassion for someone whom you find difficult

When you are ready to move on, visualise someone whom you find difficult form you, someone who you find it hard to experience kindness towards, but not the most difficult person you know.

Although you find them difficult and would rather avoid them, acknowledge that they, like you, have challenges in their lives, hopes and dreams, and want to be happy. Once again, choose phrases that suit you from the selection below, or others if you prefer.

May they be free from suffering / harm / pain / distress / illness

May they be healthy / have well-being

May they be happy / have joy in their lives

May they live with ease / live in peace / be safe

Once again, imagine that each phrase is a small stone dropped into a deep well. As you drop each one in turn, pause, breathe and listen attentively for any responses that may come in thoughts, feelings, urges to act or images. Accept whatever arises, without judgement.

### Feeling overwhelmed

If, at any time, you feel overwhelmed by intense feelings or thoughts, direct your attention to the breath to anchor yourself in the present moment, treating yourself with kindness and compassion.

### Compassion for all

Finally, extend loving kindness to all beings including people you love, strangers, those whom you find difficult and yourself. All people, like you, have challenges in their lives; they suffer; they have hopes and dreams; they wish for peace, love and joy in their lives. Once again, choose phrases that suit you from the selection below, or others if you prefer, directing your compassion to all people.

May they be free from suffering / harm / pain / distress / illness

May they be healthy / have well-being

May they be happy / have joy in their lives

May they live with ease / live in peace / be safe

Once again, imagine that each phrase is a small stone dropped into a deep well. As you drop each one in turn, pause, breathe and listen attentively for any responses that may come in thoughts, feelings, urges to act or images. Accept whatever arises, without judgement.

### Mind wandering

From time to time, the mind will wander away from the focus of compassion. You may find thoughts, images, plans or daydreams coming up. This is what the mind naturally does. When this happens acknowledge it, noticing where the mind has wandered. For example, you may note 'that's planning', 'that's thinking', 'that's worrying', 'that's judging', 'that's surprise', 'that's boredom', 'that's sadness' etc. Just label these thoughts and feelings. There is no need to judge them. Then gently return your attention to the focus of your compassion.

---

**Concluding**

At the end of this meditation direct your attention to the breath in the body, resting in clear awareness of the present moment; accepting whatever feelings may be present without judgement; and taking particular note of whatever feelings of warmth, generosity and love you may find in your heart.

---

It's easy to feel compassion for people you love. However, there may be obstacles to feeling compassion towards other people or yourself.[15] It's more difficult to feel compassion for strangers, for people who you find difficult, for all people or possibly for yourself if you are ashamed of some things that you have done. You may fear being compassionate to others because you have thoughts that they may take advantage of you, become dependent on you or that you may be overwhelmed by their distress. You may fear being compassionate towards yourself because you may believe that it's a sign of being selfish or weak. Other thoughts that may make it difficult for us to be compassionate towards ourselves are that we may not believe we deserve compassion, or we may fear being overcome by sadness and grief about the suffering we have experienced in our lives. If you have any of these fears, no doubt you have had challenging experiences that have given rise to them.

While you are practising the loving kindness meditation, welcome fears or negative thoughts about the self and others into your mind if they arise. There is no need to judge them. Acknowledge them as 'just thoughts' and let them go. There is no need to condone the undesirable things that you, or others have done. However, there is the opportunity to experience compassion for yourself and other people. You and they are all trying to make your way through life as best you can. This is the great equaliser. We all experience the suffering and challenges of life. We are all trying to do the best we can to make our way despite this suffering and these challenges. To those who care about us, we are deserving of compassion. So, if you are having difficulty feeling compassion towards someone you find difficult, imagine how their best friend or partner sees them. Then notice if you can feel an increase in the level of compassion you feel towards them.

Despite fear you may have about this exercise, cultivating compassion by practising the loving kindness meditation will not make your life situation worse. It will probably make it better. With the increasing popularity of mindfulness meditation, extensive research has been done on the effects of compassion and loving kindness meditation. Results from available studies show that when practised regularly over periods of 3–12 weeks, this type of meditation increases the experience of compassion towards the self and others, as well as positive emotions such as happiness.[16]

## Compassion-focused therapy

Professor Paul Gilbert at the University of Derby in the UK developed compassion-focused therapy.[17] Compassion involves a sensitivity to suffering in self and others along with a commitment to use skills try to alleviate it. While compassion-focused therapy helps us develop compassion for others, and feel compassion coming to us from others, a central part of it is developing self-compassion. That is, compassion-focused therapy helps us to develop a better relationship with ourselves. For those of us who are self-critical, and experience guilt or shame, developing self-compassion – a better relationship with ourselves – is an important way to achieve well-being. Research shows that self-compassion is correlated with well-being,[18] and compassion-focused therapy increases self-compassion.[19] Meditation involving compassion and loving kindness is an important element of compassion-focused therapy.

Compassion-focused therapy is based on a large body of scientific evidence about the evolution and neurobiology of human emotions;[20] and also on effective psychotherapy interventions for problems like anxiety, depression and aggression.[21] Paul Gilbert proposed that there are three main systems for regulating emotions. To make it easy to remember, he has referred them as the red, blue and green systems.

- **The red, threat and self-protection system** operates when we are threatened. It underpins fight, flight or freeze reactions. It is associated with the emotions of anger, fear, anxiety, disgust and also with defeat, depression and despair. It activates us to defend or protect ourselves by being aggressive or escaping from threatening situations; by avoiding things that disgust us; or by 'shutting down' and becoming less noticeable to predators.
- **The blue, resource-seeking system** energises us to pursue goals. It is linked to feelings of pleasure, excitement, desire and wanting to achieve things that are important to us. It activates us to go after things that we want, and to solve solvable problems that are important to us.
- **The green, soothing and contentment system** motivates us to be content in the moment and express kindness. It is linked to feeling safe, and being soothed. It is activated when we feel secure, cared for or connected to other people.

All three emotion regulation systems have evolved over millions of years to help our species survive. The red system evolved to help us protect ourselves from predators or other humans who threatened us. The blue system evolved to help us get the things we needed to survive, like food, shelter and sexual partners. The green system evolved to help us rest and digest between episodes of dealing with threats and pursuing goals. It also evolved to help us develop close co-operative relationships with other people in our families and tribe.

About 2 million years ago, our species evolved the ability to imagine the future, and make plans about what to do in the future. This was long after the three emotion regulation systems, mentioned above, were in place. Having the ability to imagine the future and plan for it helped our species to be better able to defend ourselves from threats, and pursue goals. There was, however, a downside to these new abilities. They led us to keep thinking about threats that had passed; to imagine awful future threats; and to continually ruminate about how to achieve goals, long after sunset. These new abilities allowed us to become worriers, ruminators and pessimists.

In compassion-focused therapy, Paul Gilbert invites us, any time we feel threatened, to recognise that we are in the red threat-focused system. Then we may ask ourselves, if we moved to the blue resource-seeking system, what kind of resources could we look for, so we would no longer feel threatened? Alternatively, we could ask ourselves, if we moved to the green soothing and contentment system, what sorts of things could we do to calm ourselves so that we would feel content in the moment, safe and secure? This would include activities that help soothe us and experience self-compassion, including compassion-focused or loving kindness meditation, as well as thinking in more compassionate ways, and behaving with greater compassion towards ourselves and others.

## Acts of kindness

Being kind to other people is a central value in many ethical, spiritual and religious traditions around the world. Valuing altruism is not new. The idea that it is desirable to do good things for other people has been around for thousands of years. One of the first interventions to be developed and evaluated in modern positive psychology was carrying out random acts of kindness for other people. This research has shown that acts of kindness not only make the recipients feel better, they also enhance the well-being of the person who carries out the acts of kindness.[22] Acts of kindness enhance the quality of our relationships with others. They create better communities by inspiring others to carry our acts of kindness. This is sometimes called the 'pay it forward effect'. If a person does you a good turn, you feel inspired to respond by 'paying it forward' and doing a good turn for someone else. For example, in the USA when people saw the kindness and heroism of fire fighters in response to the 9/11 disaster in New York, they donated blood at two to five times the normal rate.[23]

Acts of kindness may be large or small; for example, helping a disabled person to cross the street, or helping a neighbour whose house has been flooded. They may be one-off acts, like giving someone change for a parking meter, or they may be ongoing, for example regularly helping an elderly neighbour with their shopping. They may be carried out to help people we know and care about, or strangers. The recipients of our acts of kindness may or may not know that we have done something to help them. The main thing is that we do something to improve the quality of another person's life without expectation of a payback.

Professor Sonja Lyubomirsky at the University of California has shown in her research that for acts of kindness to make a difference to well-being the number of acts, the size of the acts, the variety of acts and the time frame for doing these acts are important to take into account.[24] The number of acts of kindness must be sufficiently high within a short time frame to make an impact on our perception of ourselves as being kind. For example, Sonja Luybomirsky found that carrying out five relatively small acts of kindness in a day had a bigger impact on well-being than carrying out five acts of kindness spaced out over a week. This was probably because the day stood out in people's minds as one on which they were noticeably kinder than on other days. She also found that in the long-term carrying out a wider variety of different types of acts of kindness led to greater well-being than repeating the same act again and again. This is probably because if we repeat the same act, we may feel that we are getting stuck in a rut. Larger acts of kindness (for example, regularly helping a disadvantaged child learn to read), up to a point, may boost our well-being more than smaller acts (for example, lending someone your bicycle). Box 11.2 contains guidance on carrying out acts of kindness and recording the effects of this in your journal.

## Box 11.2   Acts of kindness

In this exercise, there is an invitation for you to plan to carry out acts of kindness for others.

Here are some examples:

- helping a friend carry their shopping to the car
- visiting an older person who may be lonely
- helping a colleague at work who is overloaded with tasks and up against a deadline
- helping someone with their homework
- giving money to charity
- lending a friend some money
- minding a neighbour's child during an emergency
- getting a coffee for a colleague at work
- helping someone with their computer problems.

During this week, select a day. On that day do five small acts of kindness, or one or two large acts of kindness.

The important thing is that you are aware that you are *being much kinder on this day* than you normally would be on other days. That is, the day must stand out in your mind as one on which you were very kind.

It's also important that you *do a variety of different acts of kindness,* so that you do not feel like you are mechanically repeating the same act again and again. This is particularly important if you decide to repeat this exercise regularly.

*Do not bite off more than you can chew,* and do so much that you feel overwhelmed. This is particularly important if you decide to repeat this exercise regularly.

You do not have to do all the acts of kindness for the same person.

The acts of kindness do not need to be the ones listed above – these are just examples.

The person or people who you help does not have to know that you have helped them. You may find that it gives your well-being an extra lift when you do an act of kindness for a person who never knows that you helped them.

Before and after you do this task, in your journal write down your well-being rating on a scale of 1 to 10 where 1 is a very low level of well-being and 10 is a very high level of well-being. Notice the effect of this acts of kindness task on your level of well-being. Also write down the acts of kindness that you carried out and reflect on what they say about you as a person that you did these acts.

**Note:** Based on an exercise in Lyubomirsky, S. (2008). *The how of happiness: A scientific approach to getting the life you want.* New York, NY: Penguin.

## Volunteering

Volunteering is a special case of carrying out acts of kindness. Usually it involves making a commitment over a period of time to engaging in sustained acts of kindness. Research consistently shows that membership of voluntary organisations improves well-being.[25] Therefore, you can enhance your well-being by volunteering in an organisation that helps others. There are many organisations that accept volunteers, and a very wide range possible volunteering activities, for example:

- Working for local charities
- Coaching or helping out at all types of children's sports
- Visiting older people in their homes
- Helping at homeless shelters
- Working with sea or mountain search and rescue teams
- Helping with community development projects in local disadvantaged areas or developing countries
- Helping with disaster relief.

If volunteering is something that you wish to do, select an organisation that has a good fit with you in terms of your availability; skills, experiences and resources required; and team work. You may wish to ask yourself these questions. Can I make myself available at the required times and in the necessary locations to volunteer? Have I the skills, experiences and resources required to do this sort of voluntary work? Would I be prepared to do training necessary for specialist volunteer work? Could I develop good team working relationships with other volunteers in the organisation? If you decide to volunteer, before and after each meeting or event, in your journal write down your well-being rating on a scale of 1 to 10 where 1 is a very low level of well-being and 10 is a very high level of well-being. Notice the effect of volunteering on your level of well-being. Also write down the volunteering activities that you carried out and reflect on what they say about you as a person that you volunteered to do these activities.

### *Why does helping help?*

There are a number of reasons why helping others by doing acts of kindness or volunteering improves our well-being. It may lead us to view others more positively and deserving of help. It may make us appreciate our own good fortune, and the fact that we have the opportunity, skills and resources to help others. It may relieve guilt we feel over others' misfortune. It may enhance our view of ourselves as compassionate and altruistic. The gratitude that people express when we help them may make us feel good. Volunteering may create opportunities for learning new skills and forming new supportive relationships. Volunteering to work in an organisation that helps others involves a special type of relationship. With volunteering the work is done without payment, with others who are also volunteering, and for a good cause. These features of being a member of a voluntary organisation create a very particular ethos. This ethos involves the belief that we are all in this together, working towards a common goal for the good of others. This ethos, central to volunteering, gives meaning and direction to our lives and contributes to the positive effects of volunteering on well-being.

While acts of kindness and volunteering have many benefits, there may also a potential cost if the demands of helping others are too great. It's important not to bite off more than you can chew. If you do too much, you may feel overwhelmed and develop burnout or compassion fatigue.[26]

## Celebrating successes

Earlier in this chapter you read about Professor Shelly Gable's research on capitalisation. She found that how we respond to others when they tell us good news has a profound impact on personal well-being and the quality of our relationships.[5] Our partners, family members and close friends often tell us about minor successes in their lives. We have a choice about how we respond. For example, there are many ways you can respond if your partner says, 'A good thing happened at work today. I finished that project I've been working on for the past few weeks. My boss was pleased with how I did it'. Professor Gable has classified responses to this sort of good news into four categories, based on whether they are passive or active, and destructive or constructive.

- With an active and constructive response, we react in a positive, enthusiastic way to good news; for example, by saying 'That's brilliant. I'm proud of you. Tell me the whole story. How did you complete the project? What were the trickiest things in getting it finished? When did you talk to your boss about it? What did he say? How did you feel? Let's celebrate!'
- A passive and constructive response would involve expressing some support, with little enthusiasm; for example, saying 'That's good' with little emotional expression.
- A passive and destructive response would involve paying little attention to the good news; for example, by saying 'I had a bad day at work today, what's for dinner?' while having little eye contact.
- With an active and destructive response, the downside or problems associated with the good event are pointed out; for example, saying 'Don't be getting too cocky. Don't be surprised if next week he's criticising you for not doing the next project as well as you did the last one'.

Shelly Gable's research has shown that active and constructive responses have a marked positive impact on well-being and strengthen close relationships. In contrast, passive or destructive responses have a negative impact on the quality of our relationships.

You can use active and constructive responding to strengthen relationships with your partner, people in your family and your close friends. The first thing is to be on the lookout for any mention of good things that happen to them. These may be positive experiences, like a chance meeting with an old friend; achievements, like finishing a project; success, like passing an exam; or triumphs, like winning a race. We often let these things slide, so it's important to make the effort to spot these successes. Once you detect a success, respond actively and constructively. When you're responding actively, respond with a lot of enthusiasm and positive emotion in the way you talk and act. When you're responding constructively, ask the person to re-construct the good thing or positive experience with you. You may ask them to talk to you about the success or good thing that happened in detail, so that they can relive it and re-experience the positive emotions that go with it. Try to extend the time you spend talking about the event so that they experience the positive emotions associated with the good thing or success for an extended period of time. Pay attention to how they respond to you. Note on a 10-point scale how this process makes you feel.

If you find that active constructive responding does not come easily to you, then you can use the following exercise to rehearse your responses. Set aside side some time each day or each week and write the following things in your journal. First write down the names of the people to whom you want to respond actively and constructively. Call them to mind one at a time. Visualise them. Imagine meeting them. Imagine the sorts of good things they are likely to mention. Write down all of these possible successes. Then, for each of these possible successes, write down the active constructive responses you would like to give when they mention these good things or successes. When you have done this rehearsal, be on the lookout for opportunities to put this rehearsal into action by responding actively and constructively to your partner, family and friends.

There are a couple of caveats to this exercise, summarised in Box 11.3. Active constructive responding doesn't work if you fake it. It's important that you are congruent. That is, what you say and display on the outside must match what you think and feel emotionally on the inside. Therefore, it is vital that you really allow yourself to experience positive emotions such as enthusiasm, joy or pride about the other person's success or good fortune.

---

### Box 11.3   Active and constructive responding

- Visualise meeting the people to whom you want to respond actively and constructively.
- Imagine the sorts of good things or successes that they are likely to mention to you when you meet and write these in your journal.
- For each of these possible successes, write down the active and constructive responses you would like to give when they mention these good things or successes to you.

  o Plan to ask them to describe their successes in great detail, so that their account is lengthened.
  o Plan to elaborate on their account.
  o Plan to celebrate their success.
  o Be on the lookout for opportunities to put this rehearsal into action by responding actively and constructively.
  o When you give an active and constructive response, allow yourself to experience positive emotions such as enthusiasm, joy or pride about the other person success or good fortune. Don't fake it.

---

A second issue has to do with the norms for responding to success and displaying emotions within your culture. It's important that you fine tune your active constructive response so that it fits with, and is not completely out of step with, the norms of your culture. I have lived in Ireland, the UK and North America. There are very different cultural norms in these countries about responding to success and displaying emotions. For example, in Ireland and the UK, people mention their success a lot less than in North America. This is because it's against the cultural norm in Ireland and the UK to tell people how proud you are of your achievements. In keeping with this, when someone mentions personal success, there is a tendency for people in Ireland and the UK to give passive constructive responses at best, and active destructive responses at worst. Some would say that in Ireland we are a nation of begrudgers! For example, remarkable rock stars turned philanthropists, like Bono and Bob Geldof, are sometimes the target for active destructive responding in public and on social media. In contrast, in North America it's the norm for people to openly talk about their successes. I remember the first few months I spent in Queen's University, Kingston, Ontario, wondering why everyone I met seemed to be boasting all the time! Eventually I twigged that there was a different cultural norm for talking about success across the Atlantic from Ireland. When you are responding actively and constructively to your family and friends telling you about their successes, it will be important for you to do so with an awareness of cultural norms. Otherwise, it will not have a positive effect on others and yourself.

## Understanding attachment styles

John Bowlby in the UK developed attachment theory to explain how children exposed to different parenting experiences developed distinctive styles for interacting with their parents.[27] Children whose parents regularly met their needs in a predictable way developed secure attachments. Those whose parents failed to do this developed insecure attachments. Subsequent research has shown that the kinds of close romantic attachments we develop as adults, to some degree, mirror the kinds of attachments we learned to have with our parents when we were children.[28] Each of us as adults has a particular adult attachment style that influences the way we engage in close romantic relationships. What follows is a description of these attachment styles.

### *Secure attachment*

As infants and children, we had many needs that we relied on our parents to meet. These included the need for food, warmth, protection from harm, safety and security. They also included the need for company when we wanted someone to talk to or play with. If our parents were sensitive to our needs, and responded to them in a timely way, then we gradually learned that our parents were a 'secure-base' from which to explore the world. We gradually learned that we could depend on them to be there for us. If we had these sorts of experiences as children, then we probably developed a secure adult attachment style. With this attachment style, we assume that our partners will be there for us. We are comfortable with our partners depending on us, and we are comfortable depending on our partners.

### *Insecure attachment*

If our parents were not very sensitive to our needs, and did not respond to them in a timely way, then we gradually learned that our parents were not a 'secure-base'. We learned that we couldn't depend on them to be there for us. If we had these sorts of early experiences, we may have developed one of two insecure attachment styles for coping with our parents' unavailability. We may have become either sulky or clingy. We may have taken the position 'If you don't want to be there for me, then I don't want to be there for you'. Alternatively, we may have taken the position 'I am frightened that you will abandon me, so I will not let you out of my sight'. These positions reflect avoidant and anxious insecure attachment styles.

These two parent–child attachment styles lay the foundations for developing similar adult attachment styles in romantic relationships.

## Avoidant attachment

In adult romantic relationships, people with an avoidant attachment style assume that their partners will not be there for them, just as their parents weren't. They want to trust their partners, but find it difficult to do so because they fear their partners will hurt them by leaving them. They deal with this fear by avoiding psychological intimacy or closeness. They find that their partners often want more closeness than they feel comfortable with. Paradoxically, their attempts to create more distance in their relationships often make their partners seek more closeness. This can lead to conflict within romantic relationships.

## Anxious attachment

In adult romantic relationships, people with an anxious attachment style assume that their partners will not be there for them, just as their parents weren't. They worry that their partners will abandon them. They therefore pressurise their partners into having frequent contact with them, and letting them know what they are doing when they are elsewhere. Paradoxically, they sometimes find that their attempts to get their partners to be so close to them make their partners become more distant. Conflict within romantic relationships may occur because of this.

You can find your current predominant adult attachment style by completing the questionnaire in Box 11.4. Not surprisingly, research has shown people with secure adult attachment styles have more satisfying romantic relationships than those with insecure attachment styles.[29]

---

## Box 11.4   Adult attachment scale

Read each of the following statements and circle the answer opposite it that shows the extent to which it describes your feelings about romantic relationships. Think about all your relationships (past and present) and respond in terms of how you generally feel in these relationships.

Add up your scores for the secure, avoidant and anxious attachment scales. On each scale, scores range from 6 to 30. If you get a high score (over 24) on one scale, and low scores (under 12) on the other two scales, then the scale you score high on is your main attachment style. If you do not score high on one scale and low on the other two, then you do not have one main attachment style as assessed by this scale.

*Secure*

| | | 1 | 2 | 3 | 4 | 5 |
|---|---|---|---|---|---|---|
| 1 | I am comfortable depending on others | Not at all like me | Not really like me | In between | Somewhat like me | Very like me |
| 2 | I know that others will be there when I need them | Not at all like me | Not really like me | In between | Somewhat like me | Very like me |

| 3 | I do not often worry about being abandoned | 1 Not at all like me | 2 Not really like me | 3 In between | 4 Somewhat like me | 5 Very like me |
|---|---|---|---|---|---|---|
| 4 | I find it relatively easy to get close to others | 1 Not at all like me | 2 Not really like me | 3 In between | 4 Somewhat like me | 5 Very like me |
| 5 | I do not often worry about someone getting close to me | 1 Not at all like me | 2 Not really like me | 3 In between | 4 Somewhat like me | 5 Very like me |
| 6 | I am comfortable having others depend on me | 1 Not at all like me | 2 Not really like me | 3 In between | 4 Somewhat like me | 5 Very like me |

**Avoidant**

| 7 | I find it difficult to allow myself to depend on others | 1 Not at all like me | 2 Not really like me | 3 In between | 4 Somewhat like me | 5 Very like me |
|---|---|---|---|---|---|---|
| 8 | People are never there when you need them | 1 Not at all like me | 2 Not really like me | 3 In between | 4 Somewhat like me | 5 Very like me |
| 9 | I find it difficult to trust others completely | 1 Not at all like me | 2 Not really like me | 3 In between | 4 Somewhat like me | 5 Very like me |
| 10 | I am somewhat uncomfortable being close to others | 1 Not at all like me | 2 Not really like me | 3 In between | 4 Somewhat like me | 5 Very like me |
| 11 | I am nervous when anyone gets too close | 1 Not at all like me | 2 Not really like me | 3 In between | 4 Somewhat like me | 5 Very like me |
| 12 | Often, love partners want me to be more intimate than I feel comfortable being | 1 Not at all like me | 2 Not really like me | 3 In between | 4 Somewhat like me | 5 Very like me |

**Anxious**

| 13 | I am not sure that I can always depend on others to be there when I need them | 1 Not at all like me | 2 Not really like me | 3 In between | 4 Somewhat like me | 5 Very like me |
|---|---|---|---|---|---|---|
| 14 | I often worry that my partner does not really love me | 1 Not at all like me | 2 Not really like me | 3 In between | 4 Somewhat like me | 5 Very like me |
| 15 | I find others are reluctant to get as close as I would like | 1 Not at all like me | 2 Not really like me | 3 In between | 4 Somewhat like me | 5 Very like me |

| | *Secure* | | | | | |
|---|---|---|---|---|---|---|
| 16 | I often worry my partner will not want to stay with me | 1<br>Not at all like me | 2<br>Not really like me | 3<br>In between | 4<br>Somewhat like me | 5<br>Very like me |
| 17 | I want to merge completely with another person | 1<br>Not at all like me | 2<br>Not really like me | 3<br>In between | 4<br>Somewhat like me | 5<br>Very like me |
| 18 | My desire to merge sometimes scares people away | 1<br>Not at all like me | 2<br>Not really like me | 3<br>In between | 4<br>Somewhat like me | 5<br>Very like me |

**Note:** Adapted with permission from Table 2, page 647 of Collins, N. L., & Read, S. J. (1990). Adult attachment, working models, and relationship quality in dating couples. *Journal of Personality and Social Psychology, 58*(4), 644–663. Copyright © 1990 by American Psychological Association.

## Moving towards secure attachment

If you have read the previous sections on attachment styles, completed the questionnaire in Box 11.4 and concluded that you have an insecure, avoidant or anxious adult attachment style, you have an opportunity now to start changing this by doing the exercises described below. Attachment styles are not set in stone. They reflect 'internal working models' that we have for relationships. They are 'relationship maps' that we hold in our minds to guide us when we form close relationships with others. Maps and models are malleable. They can be changed. If you have an insecure anxious or avoidant adult attachment style, then there is an invitation for you to move towards developing a more secure adult attachment style. With this new secure attachment style your relationship map will be 'I will be there for my partner, and I will work on the assumption that may partner will be there for me'.

## Choose a partner with secure attachment

Regardless of the type of insecure adult attachment style that you have, one way to move towards a secure attachment style is to select a partner who has a secure attachment style. By living with someone who believes that you will be there for them, this will help you come to believe that they will be there for you.

## Write a coherent life narrative

A second thing that you can do is write your life story from the earliest years to the present time. In your journal, write this narrative with the aim of trying to make sense of the way your parents treated you, and led you to believe that other people can't be trusted to be there for you. What were all the things that they did in your childhood that led you to believe that they were not a 'secure-base' and consequently your current romantic partner(s) cannot be your 'secure-base' in adulthood? Write about the relationship habits you have developed as a result of assuming that in adulthood your romantic partner(s) cannot be trusted to be a 'secure-base' for you. Write also about exceptional events in your development, where your parents were there for you, met your needs in a timely way and gave you hope that secure attachment might be a possibility in your life.

### Explore alternatives to an avoidant adult attachment style

If you have an avoidant adult attachment style, write answers to these questions: How do I avoid closeness and commitment in romantic relationships? Do I select partners who live a long distance away; contact them infrequently; spend less time with them than they would like; have angry arguments when they ask for greater closeness? What effect does this have on my romantic partner(s) and me in these relationships? What do I fear will happen if I develop closer relationships with romantic partners? If I decided to form closer relationships with romantic partners, what sorts of things would I do? What would be the costs and benefits for me in doing this? If you have an avoidant attachment style, and you decide to move towards having a secure attachment style, the challenge for you will be to accept that to reap the benefits of being closer to your partner, you must tolerate the uncomfortable risk of them hurting you, by leaving you. However, eventually this discomfort will pass and you will enjoy greater closeness and intimacy. Once this begins to happen, and this may take months or even years, you may find that your partner puts less (uncomfortable) pressure on you for closeness.

### Explore alternatives to an anxious adult attachment style

If you have an anxious attachment style, write answers to these questions: How do I pressurise romantic partners into contacting me more often or spending more time with me than they would like? How do I pressurise romantic partners into limiting their contact with others or asking them to account for time they do not spend with me and becoming angry if they don't do this? What effect does this have on my romantic partners and me in these relationships? What do I fear will happen if I allow my partner(s) greater distance? If I decided to have relationships with romantic partners that allowed them a greater say in the frequency of our contact with each other and less pressure to account for their activities when they are not with me, what sorts of things would I do? What would be the costs and benefits for me in doing this? If you have an anxious attachment style, and you decide to move towards having a secure attachment style, the challenge for you will be to accept that to reap the benefits of having more distance between you and your partner, you must tolerate the uncomfortable risk of them hurting you by leaving you. You will have to learn to tolerate the discomfort that comes with allowing more space to develop between you and your partner, and trusting that they will come to you when you need their support. However, eventually this discomfort will pass and you will enjoy greater intimacy. Once this begins to happen, and this may take months or even years, you may find that your partner puts less (uncomfortable) pressure on you for distance.

Of course, you can explore moving from an insecure to a secure attachment style with a psychotherapist, and use psychotherapy as a place to work out a coherent life narrative.

## Summary

- **Relationships and well-being.** Good relationships enhance well-being. They improve our mood, health and resilience.
- **Relationships and evolution.** Our species has evolved to be able to form good relationships because these were essential for survival.
- **Co-operation, capitalisation, meaning and support** are four processes through which relationships affect well-being. They help us to co-operate. They provide us with a context within which to capitalise upon our successes. They give our lives meaning. They provide us with support.
- **Love 2.0** is Barbara Fredrickson's term for brief moments of positive social connection that enhance well-being, by broadening thought-action repertoires and creating opportunities for building lasting resources. This is an extension of her Broaden and Build theory discussed in Chapter 1.
- **Compassion and loving kindness meditation.** In this meditation, positive feelings are mindfully directed towards the self, then towards loved ones, then towards strangers, then towards someone with whom we experience conflict or difficulty and finally towards all people. Practising this meditation regularly enhances well-being.
- **Altruistic acts of kindness** enhance well-being. Larger, more frequent and more varied acts of kindness have a stronger effect on well-being.
- **Volunteering**, which involves making a commitment over a period of time to engaging in sustained acts of kindness, increases well-being.
- **Compassion fatigue** occurs when too great a commitment is made to helping others. Individuals 'bite off more than they can chew' and experience burnout.
- **Capitalising** involves reacting to another person's good news or success stories in a positive, enthusiastic, constructive way. We invite them to talk in detail about their good news and to celebrate their successes in ways that generate positive emotions.
- **Adult attachment styles** are dispositions to develop particular types of romantic relationships.
- With a **secure adult attachment style**, we assume that our partners will be there for us. We are comfortable with our partners depending on us, and we are comfortable depending on our partners. Secure adult attachment styles lead to greater well-being.
- With an **insecure adult attachment style**, we assume that our partners will not be there for us. This leads us to have either an avoidant or anxious insecure adult attachment style. If we have an avoidant insecure adult attachment style, we avoid intimacy, so as to avoid being hurt by our partner not being there for us. If we have an insecure anxious adult attachment style, we worry that our partners will not remain with us, and do not want the kind of closeness that we need. Insecure adult attachment styles tend to result in lower levels of relationship satisfaction.
- **Strategies for developing a secure adult attachment style** include choosing a partner with a secure adult attachment style, developing a coherent life narrative, exploring alternatives to being avoidant or anxious in close relationships and engaging in psychotherapy.

## Where are you now?

If you have done the exercises in this chapter you may have found that the loving kindness meditation, the acts of kindness task, volunteering, active and constructive responding to good news, and understanding attachment styles affect your well-being.

You may want to read back over the chapter and summarise in your journal the main things that you have learned from this chapter about improving relationships. You can now decide if you want to include the practices described in this chapter in your life.

In the next two chapters, you will have an opportunity to read more about relationships. The next two chapters will be specifically about family relationships. Chapter 12 is about relationship with long-term partners. Chapter 13 is about parent–child relationships. Below are some web resources and books that are relevant to topics you have read about in this chapter.

## Web resources

Barbara Fredrickson talking about love video: www.youtube.com/watch?v=fHoEWUTYnSo
The befriending or loving kindness meditation. Mark Williams (9:37): www.youtube.com/watch?v=pLt-E4YNVHU
The loving kindness meditation. Jon Kabat-Zinn (9:37): www.youtube.com/watch?v=WvQo4QJB4O0
Shelly Gable talking about active constructive responding video (1:11): www.youtube.com/watch?v=OF9kfJmS_Ok
Adult attachment styles video (8:36): www.youtube.com/watch?v=U-GPID1cy2o
Adult attachment styles podcast (15:58): www.youtube.com/watch?v=GLNaKCk_Pjo

## Books

Fredrickson, B. (2014). *Love 2.0: Creating happiness and health in moments of connection.* New York, NY: Penguin.
Gilbert, P. (2009). *The compassionate mind: A new approach to the challenges of life.* London, UK: Constable & Robinson.

# 12 Couple relationships

Having a spouse, romantic partner or soul mate has a profound impact on health and well-being. A vast research literature shows that married people and their children are happier and healthier than those who are unmarried.[1]

This is not surprising. We have evolved to find long-term relationships very satisfying.[2] Our prehistoric ancestors who sustained long-term relationships helped their children survive into adulthood. This was a major achievement. The prehistoric environment in which they lived was very dangerous. There were many predators. Food and shelter were scarce. Committed couples provided their children with food, shelter and protection from predators and other hazards until they were mature enough to fend for themselves. By being members of a group of other similar couples, they also gave their children a community in which to learn survival skills for hunting, gathering, building shelters, defending against predators, mating and rearing children.

In the modern world, marriage (and other long-term committed relationships) still gives us many good things.[1] Married people have better health and well-being than those who are single. There are benefits similar to those appreciated by our prehistoric ancestors: a context for safely rearing children where the costs of meeting the family's needs are shared, and a community of other similar families. However, there are also profound psychological benefits to long-term committed relationships. Our partners meet our needs for companionship and intimacy. Intimacy includes both sexual and psychological intimacy. What is psychological intimacy? It is the closeness and trust we experience when our partners communicate that they care deeply for us and understand us. It is the closeness and trust we experience when our partners communicate that they share our values, support us in pursuing our dreams and are emotionally committed to being with us for the long haul in good times and bad.

## Positivity and repairing conflicts

At the University of Washington, Professor John Gottman conducted a series of ground-breaking research studies on the stability of couple relationships.[3] In these, he interviewed couples at various stages in their relationships. He also observed them doing normal daily activities and discussing disagreements. For example, in his first study he met with couples who were newly married and then six and nine years later when some were still married and others had divorced. He then identified things that they said, ways that they interacted with each other and patterns of physiological arousal (for example, heart rate and blood pressure) that predicted which couples divorced and which couples stayed together.

He found that all couples had disagreements and ongoing unresolved 'perpetual' relationship conflicts. However, certain factors distinguished those who divorced from those who didn't. Chief among these were positivity and repairing conflicts. Those who stayed together engaged in five times more positive exchanges than negative exchanges, both when discussing disagreements and at other times. They also actively worked to repair relationship conflicts when they arose.

### Repairing relationships

Couples with stable relationships didn't let disagreements escalate so they became intense, emotionally negative exchanges in which they both became extremely angry and distressed. Nor did they become very cold and emotionally distant. Rather, they began discussions of disagreements with a 'gentle start-up' in which they expressed a very low level of negative emotions. During disagreements, as well as mild negative emotions, they also expressed positive emotions, humour and affection for their partners. They prevented themselves from expressing negative emotions by calming themselves down when they noticed they were becoming distressed or angry. They also didn't take it personally when their partners did or said things that affected them negatively. They reminded themselves of how much they both valued their relationship. They reminded themselves that above all else, they were best friends! They tried to understand, respect and accept their partner's point of view as valid, and take it into account when reaching compromises or making decisions. They accepted that some conflicts or differences were unresolvable, and these were fuelled by partners' commitment to underlying highly valued goals. Partners in stable relationships responded positively towards attempts their partners made to increase emotional connection during conflicts. They also shared power, and allowed their partners to influence their decisions.

### Positivity - 5:1 ratio

When not actively discussing a conflict, couples who stayed together built positivity into their relationships, so the ratio of positive to negative exchanges was about 5:1. They expressed admiration and fondness for each other. They responded to each other's 'bids' for emotional connection far more frequently than those who separated. They usually saw each other in a positive light and gave their partners the benefit of the doubt if they let them down by, for example, not following through on something they said they would do. They took time to understand their partners' way of looking at the world and their life goals, hopes and dreams. They also talked about things that they both valued and gave meaning to their relationships. These ongoing positive exchanges built a sense of trust and commitment, strengthening couples' relationships.

In contrast, couples who eventually divorced had difficulty discussing conflicts calmly. They usually escalated conflict until they became gridlocked in angry, disrespectful, unproductive exchanges. Between episodes of conflict, couples in unstable marriages were critical of each other, commenting on the bad rather than the good. They were also defensive, blaming their partners for all of their problems, and not taking responsibility for their half of the difficulties they faced in their relationships. They expressed contempt by taking a morally superior position or putting their partner down. They engaged in stonewalling, by emotionally or physically withdrawing. Gottman referred to these processes – criticism, defensiveness, contempt and stonewalling – as the four horsemen of the apocalypse since it was these four processes that predicted divorce. Of the four, contempt was the strongest predictor of divorce. This is not surprising, because contempt involves expressing a lack of respect and a lack of fondness. It's difficult to maintain any friendship without mutual fondness and respect.

## Sound Relationship House Theory

Arising from this research, Gottman proposed his Sound Relationship House Theory,[4] which is in Figure 12.1. In this theory, he proposed a hierarchy of seven positive strategies that couples may use to strengthen trust and commitment within their relationships:

- Build love maps
- Share fondness and admiration
- Turn towards your partner
- Take a positive perspective
- Manage conflict
- Make life dreams come true
- Create shared meaning

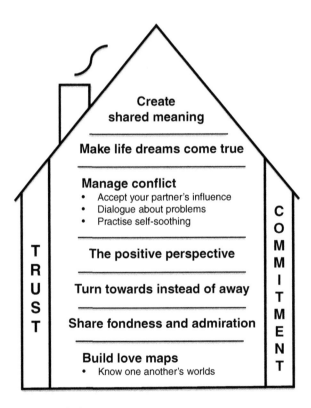

*Figure 12.1* Sound relationship house.

**Note:** Reproduced with permission from the Gottman Institute Inc. Copyright © 2019, the Gottman Institute Inc.

Gottman has shown in a series of research studies that when couples are trained to use these strategies, they enrich their relationships.[5] The rest of this chapter offers guidance on how you can use these positive strategies to enhance your relationship.

### Build love maps

In any relationship, each person has their own 'take' on the world. Their own unique perspective. When we build love maps, our aim is to create and regularly update our understanding of how we each see the world. Love maps cover the past, present and future. They include our personal life stories; our current concerns, challenges and successes; and our future hopes, dreams and highly valued goals. Love maps also cover important people and projects in our lives. They include our 'take' on other family members, friends and colleagues. They include our views of our roles at work or education, in our families and in our leisure pursuits.

We make love maps by communicating with our partners. In the early stages of a relationship we may tell each other our life stories and our dreams for the future. When our relationships are established, we may ask each other how our day or week has been, and listen to each other's stories about challenges and successes as they arise. However, as life becomes busy with multiple demands on our time, we may find that we spend less and less time updating our love maps. We may spend less and less time really listening to our partner's take on the world. We may lose touch with what their priorities are, the things that are most important to them and the things they most value.

The exercise in Box 12.1 is a way of updating your love maps. It has a number of important features. First, you are invited to spend uninterrupted time together without distractions. This means turning off phones, computers, TVs and radios. It also means selecting a time when you will not be interrupted by children, other family members, friends or work colleagues. Second, you are invited to take turns at being the speaker or the listener. If you are taking a turn as the speaker, the invitation is to talk about things that matter to you in a way that lets your listening partner know what you think and how you feel about the issue. If you are taking a turn as the listener, the invitation is to listen without interrupting; summarise what you have heard; and check with your partner that you have heard correctly *before* responding. When you respond, let your partner know you appreciate them letting you know their 'take' on the issue they have been talking about.

---

### Box 12.1   Create love maps: get to know your partner better

**Aim**

The aim of this exercise is to get to know your partner better.

**Setting up the exercise**

- Invite your partner to spend 30–60 minutes with you doing this exercise.
- Select a private place and time that suits you both when you will not be interrupted or distracted.

- Turn off phones, computers, tablets, TVs, radios and other potential distractions.
- Take turns of being the speaker and listener.

### Listening

- When you are the listener, select a few of the open questions on the list below, and ask them one at a time.
- When your partner answers these questions, listen without interrupting.
- Listen so carefully that you will be able to remember all that your partner has said.
- If your partner pauses, leave space for them to collect their thoughts and continue.
- When your partner finishes their answer, summarise the key points they made.
- Check with them that you have understood them accurately *before* replying.
- Reply by letting your partner know how you appreciate them helping you to understand how they view the aspect of their life they have been talking about.

### Speaking

- When you are answering a question your partner has asked, reflect on the main themes or key points you want to communicate.
- If you are describing a situation, say what the situation was, what you thought about the situation, how you felt emotionally about the situation and what you did.
- Frame what you have to say as honestly, positively and constructively as possible.
- *Avoid* blaming, criticising and attributing negative intentions to your partner.
- Check that you have been understood.
- Allow space for your partner to reply and listen to this following the guidelines for listening listed above.

### Questions about the past

- What are your most treasured memories about growing up in your family?
- What strengths did you get from your mother / father / grandparents / siblings?
- How did people in the family you grew up in express love or affection / gratitude / hope / pride in one another/ happiness or joy / forgiveness / spirituality?
- When they did it well, how did people in the family you grew up in express and deal with danger, fear and courage / hurt, anger and forgiveness / loss, sadness, grief and mourning?
- When they did it well, how did people in the family you grew up in deal with conflict or differences of opinion?
- What positive things did you learn from the family you grew up in about relationships between partners / relationships between parents and children / relationships between the nuclear family and the extended family?
- In what positive ways did the family you grew up in influence your approach to education / work / career choice / ambition / money / teamwork / leadership / creativity / curiosity / honesty / fairness?

- Describe the most important friendships or romantic relationships you had as a child / teenager / young adult.
- Describe the best things that happened to you when you were a child / teenager / young adult / in the recent past.
- Describe how you successfully managed difficult challenges that you faced when you were a child / teenager / young adult / in the recent past.
- How have the ways you have successfully managed challenges in your life prepared you to deal with future challenges you and your current family may face?

**Questions about your current relationship**

- What most attracted you to your partner when you first met?
- What other positive qualities have you noticed in your partner since you first met?
- What is the story of your relationship from your perspective?
- How is this story different from the story you think your partner might tell?
- What are the main areas where you and your partner hold similar views, beliefs, preferences, values and goals? (Think of daily routines, food, hygiene, sleep-wake cycle, housework, child care, career, education, religion, TV programmes, entertainment, leisure activities, holidays, sex, money management, contact with extended family, approach to communicating and solving problems, etc.)
- What are the main areas where you and your partner hold different views, beliefs, preferences, values and goals? (Think of daily routines, food, hygiene, sleep-wake cycle, housework, child care, career, education, religion, TV programmes, entertainment, leisure activities, holidays, sex, money management, contact with extended family, approach to communicating and solving problems etc.)

**Questions about the present**

- Who are the most important people – family, friends and work colleagues – in your life right now?
- What are the most important projects in your life right now?
- Today / this week / this month what specific situations have brought you greatest happiness or joy / hope for the future?
- Describe how you successfully managed difficult challenges that you faced recently.
- What do you value most about your current family relationships?
- When you do it well, how do you, your partner and your children express and deal with danger, fear and courage / hurt, anger and forgiveness / loss, sadness, grief and mourning?
- When you do it well, how do you, your partner and your children deal with conflict or differences of opinion?
- In what positive ways do your partner and children influence your approach to education / work / career choice / ambition / money / teamwork / leadership / creativity / curiosity / honesty / fairness?

**Questions about the future**

- What are your most highly valued goals in family life / at work / in your leisure activities?
- To what extent have you achieved these and to what extent are there things that you still wish to achieve in family life / at work / in your leisure activities?
- If you could have a different career, what would it be?
- If you could have lived in a different time in history, when would that be?
- If you could change one thing about the sort of person you are, what would that be?
- Describe in detail how you would like the future to turn out for you and your current family.
- What do you need from your partner / children / parents / friends / colleagues to help you achieve your highly valued goals?
- To what extent do you believe that your partner and children share your highly valued goals?
- What do you think your partner and children need from you to help them achieve their highly valued goals?

If you are taking a turn as the speaker and the issue you are talking about is an area of conflict between you and your partner, it will strengthen your relationship if you talk about this in as positive and constructive a way as possible. Avoid blaming, criticising and attributing negative intentions to your partner. For example, Eve's following statement to Adam isn't constructive. 'You don't care how it makes me feel when you come home late. You do it to annoy me. It's your fault I was so upset last night'. A more constructive approach would be for Eve to explain to Adam how the situation affected her; what she thought and how she felt. For example, 'When you came home late, I was worried about what might have happened to you. I was imagining you being in a car crash or mugged or something. I was really scared. Then I flipped into being angry, because I was so scared. I really care about you, Adam. I would hate it if something bad happened to you'.

If you are taking a turn as a listener, there may be a temptation to rehearse your response or defence while your partner is speaking, rather than actively listening to them. There may also be a temptation to immediately respond to what your partner has said before summarising and checking that what you heard was what your partner intended. Try to avoid these two temptations. Actively listening, summarising and checking are very important because they allow your partner to know that you have empathy for their situation. They allow your partner to know that you know what it's like to stand in their shoes. For example, Adam saying, 'I was late because I got stuck in a meeting and the traffic was bad' does not let Eve know that he understands her thoughts and feelings about the situation. However, the following statement does let Eve know that Adam understood exactly how his lateness affected her: 'When I came home late, you worried that I was in a car crash or mugged. You got angry because you were so scared. This was because you care about me'. When communicating about things that matter, empathy is very important. So, actively listen, summarise and check that you have understood your partner's take on the situation before responding.

Building love maps, deepening our understanding of each other, is a first step towards strengthening relationships. The next step is using this knowledge to express fondness and admiration.

### Share fondness and admiration

Sharing fondness and admiration is about letting your partner know that you care deeply about them and respect them. Early in a relationship most of us spontaneously express fondness and admiration very frequently, and express criticism very infrequently. As time passes, there is a risk that we assume our partners know that we are fond of them and admire them, and so express these feelings less often. As relationships evolve, we also become less tolerant of each other's idiosyncrasies and so are more likely to express criticism about these more frequently. These two tendencies have the effect of reducing the ratio of positive to negative exchanges below the optimum level of 5:1, which Gottman found to be one of the hallmarks of satisfying long-term relationships, mentioned above. Fortunately, you can change this if it has happened in your relationship. You can both decide to regularly catch each other 'doing things right' and express appreciation and gratitude (rather than catching each other 'doing things wrong' and expressing criticism) by doing the exercise in Box 12.2. If you do this, you will build a culture of appreciation and respect, where the ratio of positive to negative exchanges is above the 5:1 ratio.

---

**Box 12.2   Express fondness and appreciation**

**Aim**

The aim of this exercise is to maintain the ratio of positive to negative exchanges within your relationship above 5:1.

**Practice**

Every day, on a moment-to-moment basis, notice when your partner is 'doing things right' or being the kind of person you admire.

Tell your partner that you admire, appreciate or are grateful for the positive things they do and that you admire their positive personal characteristics.

If you regularly let your partner know that you admire and appreciate their positive attributes and the things they do, this will maintain the ratio of positive to negative exchanges above 5:1 and enhance the quality of your relationship.

Here are some things you may notice:

- Being kind / gentle / funny / strong / sexy / brave / thoughtful / loyal / generous / beautiful / dependable / calm / hardworking / fair / energetic / forgiving / flexible / honest / tolerant / wise
- Showing affection, kissing, having sex

- Reminding you about something that you might forget, making breakfast with you, getting the kids ready, organising laundry or dry cleaning, organising transport to school or work
- Contacting you during the day, organising or doing house/garden maintenance, getting groceries, collecting the kids, taking the kids to activities / appointments / playdates, taking care of grandparents
- Making dinner, cleaning up after dinner, helping kids with homework
- Being patient with kids / in-laws / ex-partners / friends / neighbours who irritate you
- Playing music or movies that you like, listening to how your day went, understanding you
- Planning stuff to do with the house, planning holidays, paying bills, doing tax returns, doing house finances and administration
- Supporting your involvement in leisure activities / sports / arts
- Supporting you during big transitions and life challenges: births, deaths, moving house, changing jobs, illnesses, injuries.

### Turn towards your partner

On a moment-to-moment basis in our relationships we make 'bids' to each other for emotional connection. These are usually not dramatic displays of passion. They are hum-drum bids for attention, and bids to give or receive support: for example, saying 'Do we need more pickle?' when doing the shopping; saying 'Hey, look at that' when watching the news together; asking for help with doing a job; or accepting help when it's offered. In long-lasting, satisfying relationships partners tend to regularly make bids to each other for emotional connection, and to respond to most of these bids. Turning towards your partner involves responding to their bids for attention and support. You can strengthen your relationship by being on the lookout for your partner's bids for moments of emotional connection with you. These may be comments or questions about things that interest you both, requests for help or open invitations to provide emotional connection and support. Tune in to these, and respond. This is what turning towards your partner means. Also, give your partner opportunities to turn towards you. Let them know when you need their support. Appreciate their support when they provide it.

There are many obstacles to tuning in to our partner's bids. Distractions such as phones, computers, tablets, TVs and radios may prevent us from noticing them. Another obstacle to recognising partner's bids is that sometimes they come wrapped in criticism or anger. For example, Eve wanted Adam's support with clearing up after dinner. She said in a frustrated way, 'Are you just going to sit there and watch TV?' Adam unwrapped the anger from around this bid and said with a smile, 'How about I give you a hand with that'. Adam recognised that the request for help was wrapped up in anger. He saw Eve was exhausted and frustrated with him relaxing while she continued to work after a long day. She was asking for help. This turning towards Eve that Adam did strengthened their emotional connection in that moment. Also, it prevented the potential escalation of a negative exchange, which might have happened if Adam had said defensively, 'You've no right to criticise me for watching TV. I've done a 10-hour day at work and put the kids to bed. It's your turn to do the dishes'.

Bids often occur during joint activities. If you plan some joint activities in your daily, weekly, monthly and annual schedules, you will create opportunities for turning towards each other. For example, you may wish to plan to spend some time together most days talking about how your days went; watching a TV programme or listening to music you both enjoy; taking the dog for a walk; or having breakfast or dinner together. You may wish to plan joint weekly or monthly outings, leisure activities, dinner dates, entertainment dates, periods of housework, gardening or other activities together. On an annual basis, you may wish to plan joint holidays, volunteering or long-term projects. During all of these joint activities be on the lookout for your partner's bids for moments of emotional connection with you.

One daily activity that creates an opportunity for you and your partner to turn towards each other is to spend uninterrupted time listening to how each other's day has been, as described in Box 12.3. Like the exercise in Box 12.1, this exercise involves setting aside inter-rupted time to have a conversation in which partners take turns at being the speaker and the listener. The aim of the exercise is for partners to offer each other emotional support. The aim is not for the listener to give the speaker unsolicited advice. This makes it different from normal conversations. For example, in a normal conversation if Eve said, 'My car ran out of petrol today. I was so stressed. I ended up being late picking up the kids', Adam might give a problem-solving reply like this: 'You should fill up your tank on Sundays at the station by the football field, when you drop Kane off for soccer' or this: 'Don't worry. I'll make sure your tank is full, from now on'. These responses offer Eve a solution to the petrol problem, but little emotional support. If the couple were doing the exercise in Box 12.3 and Adam were consciously aiming to give emotional support his response might be: 'That sounds really stressful. Running out of petrol on such a busy day. Tell me more about how you felt'.

---

### Box 12.3  Turn towards your partner: how was your day?

**Aim**

The aim of this exercise is for you and your partner to offer each other emotional support.

**Setting up the exercise**

- Invite your partner to spend 30 minutes with you doing this exercise on most days.
- Select a private place and time that suits you both, when you will not be inter-rupted or distracted.
- Turn off phones, computers, tablets, TVs, radios and other potential distractions.
- Take turns of being the speaker and listener.

**Speaking**

- Invite your partner to listen to how your day went.
- Reflect on the main themes or key points you want to talk about.
- Organise them logically in your mind.

- If you are describing a situation, say what the situation was; what you thought about the situation; how you felt emotionally about the situation; and what you did.
- If you felt happy, joyful, excited, proud, grateful, inspired or other positive emotions, express these.
- If you felt sad and want to cry, express this.
- If you felt hurt or frightened, express this.
- If you felt angry towards someone other than your partner, express this.
- If you felt anger towards your partner, you probably also felt hurt that they let you down in some way. Express this sense of hurt, and of needing your partner to be there for you. *Avoid* blaming, criticising and attributing negative intentions to your partner.
- Check that you have been understood.

**Listening**

- Listen without interrupting.
- Listen so carefully that you will be able to remember all that your partner has said.
- Occasionally, let your partner know that you understand the emotions they felt and support them by saying things like, 'I see' / 'That sounds very difficult / wonderful / scary / sad / frustrating', 'I understand', 'I would have felt the same way' etc.
- If your partner expresses positive emotions, respond in a positive, enthusiastic way.
- If your partner expresses negative emotions like sadness, hurt, fear or anger towards others (rather than you), listen carefully with the goal of *understanding* their reaction, not solving their problem.
- If your partner expresses anger towards you, and you find yourself becoming keyed up, soothe yourself by taking a brief period of time out. If you wish, do the brief relaxation or meditation exercises in Boxes 5.3 or 6.6.
- If your partner pauses, leave space for them to collect their thoughts and continue, or invite them to do so by repeating the last thought they expressed, for example, 'You said you were really sacred and wanted to run away'. Or by asking open questions like:

  o   What was the hardest thing about that situation?
  o   Can you say more about that?'
  o   Can you help me understand the situation from your point of view?

- Avoid asking questions that may sound like criticism, for example, 'Why did you do that?' or 'What is that supposed to mean?'
- Don't offer unsolicited advice on what your partner can or could have done.
- If your partner is sad, don't try to cheer them up; acknowledge that they are sad.
- If your partner is angry, don't tell them to calm down; acknowledge that they are angry.
- If your partner is frightened or worried, don't tell them that they shouldn't be worried; acknowledge that they are scared.

- If you have difficulty tolerating your partner's expression of strong negative emotions (like sadness, fear or anger), let your partner know this, and take a couple of minutes to soothe yourself using the exercises in Boxes 5.3 or 6.7 before proceeding.
- When your partner finishes telling you about their day, summarise what they have said.
- Check with them that you have understood them accurately.

If you are the speaker in the exercise in Box 12.3, you are invited to describe situations that occurred during the day, saying what you thought about the situation, how you felt emotionally about it and what you did. You also have the opportunity to fully express your positive emotions (like happiness, gratitude and pride), and negative emotions (like sadness, fear and anger). However, there is one exception to this. If you felt anger towards your partner, it is highly likely that this was because you felt hurt because they let you down in some way. Express this sense of hurt, and of needing your partner to be there for you. Your partner will find it easier to offer you emotional support if they understand the hurt behind your anger. Expressing the hurt behind the anger also allows you to avoid blaming, criticising and attributing negative intentions to your partner, all of which would diminish rather than enhance the quality of your relationship.[6]

If you are the listener in the exercise in Box 12.3, you are invited to listen so carefully that you will be able to remember all that your partner has said. Occasionally, let your partner know that you that you understand the emotions that they felt by saying things like, 'I see' / 'That sounds very difficult / wonderful / scary / sad / frustrating', 'I understand', 'I would have felt the same way' etc. If your partner expresses positive emotions, respond in a positive, enthusiastic way using the active, constructive responding described in Chapter 11. If your partner expresses negative emotions like sadness, hurt, fear or anger towards others (rather than you), listen carefully with the goal of *understanding* their reaction, not solving their problem. If your partner expresses anger towards you, and you find yourself becoming keyed up, soothe yourself by taking a brief period of time out. If you wish, do the brief relaxation or meditation exercises in Boxes 5.3 or 6.7. When pauses occur, leave space for your partner to collect their thoughts and continue, or invite them to do so by saying things like, 'What was the hardest / best thing about that situation?', 'Can you say more about that?', 'Help me understand the situation from your point of view', or by simply repeating the last thought they expressed, for example, 'You said you were really sacred and wanted to run away'. Avoid asking questions that may sound like criticism, for example, 'Why did you do that?', or 'What is that supposed to mean?' Your role is to allow your partner space to fully express what they are feeling, not to actively try to change their emotional state. If your partner is sad, don't try to cheer them up; acknowledge that they are sad. If you partner is angry, don't tell them to calm down; acknowledge that they are angry. If you partner is frightened or worried, don't tell them that they have nothing to be frightened of; acknowledge that they are scared and feel unsafe.

This is not always easy to do. Many of us find it hard to tolerate people we love expressing distress. If you have difficulty tolerating your partner's expression of strong negative emotions (like sadness, fear or anger), let your partner know this, and take a couple of minutes to soothe yourself using the exercises in Boxes 5.3 or 6.7 before proceeding with the exercise in Box 12.3. When your partner finishes telling you about their day, summarise what they have said. Check with them that you have understood them accurately. The process of providing emotional support, or turning towards your partner, may help them capitalise upon the benefits of positive emotions and bear the burden of negative emotions.

### Take a positive perspective

Taking a positive perspective means believing that fundamentally your partner has your best interests at heart, and highly values your relationship. A positive perspective arises from practising the three strategies mentioned above: (1) building love maps, so you know each other well, (2) regularly expressing fondness and admiration, so you have a ratio of at least five positive exchanges to every one negative exchange and (3) regularly turning towards your partner and responding to their bids for emotional connection. Having a positive perspective allows you to give your partner the benefit of the doubt when they do things that annoy or irritate you, and when they hold views that are different than yours.

If your partner does things that irritate you, assume that they love you and are not aware that whatever it is they are doing is annoying you. Don't jump to conclusions, or engage in mind-reading and assume that they are doing these things purposely to annoy you. Let your partner know that you would prefer if they did not do those things that irritate you. If you and your partner have differences that are difficult to resolve, listen to them and understand them. Often issues that couples disagree on are linked to highly valued personal long-term goals. For example, Adam and Eve disagreed about how late Adam should work in the evenings, and how much should be spent on holidays. Adam worked late many evenings because his personal long-term goal was to be successful in his career. Eve spent a lot of money on family holidays because one of her highly valued goals was for her children to have wonderful memories of their childhood.

Discuss how your beliefs differ. Discuss the highly valued personal goals that underpin these. Jointly accept that in any relationship, it is inevitable that people will agree on some things, but disagree on others. Agree to differ with good grace, and allow this agreement to bring you closer together.

### Manage conflict

Accept that conflict is a normal healthy part of all relationships. In any relationship, there are two distinct kind of conflicts. (1) There are short-term conflicts that can be resolved by skilled negotiation and compromise. These are solvable problems. For example, deciding what to eat for dinner, or what to do on Saturday night. (2) There are long-term differences that can't be quickly resolved. These include disagreements about major issues like what country to live in, how many children to have or the extent to which you want to spend time with certain friends or members of the extended family. They also include differences in personal style for dealing with core needs for safety and security, physical and psychological intimacy, and power and resources (money, property, earning capacity etc.). These long-term differences often involve important dreams, hopes or highly valued goals. They are rarely resolved by rapid negotiation and compromise. They are managed by ongoing dialogue and understanding. In his research Gottman found that in long-term relationship, more than four out of five arguments are about long-term differences that we need to learn to manage, understand and accept, rather than resolve.

### Solvable problems

Box 12.4 contains an exercise for helping you to resolve solvable problems. For solvable problems, when you decide to talk to your partner about it, open the conversation with a soft rather than a harsh initial statement or question. The most useful initial statements never contain criticism or contempt. They take the form (1) There is a difficulty. (2) Both of us are involved in it. (3) This is how I feel about it. (4) This is what I need or would prefer. Here is an example of a soft initial statement where Eve asks Adam about dropping the kids to school: 'Wednesday mornings are difficult for us because we both have to get to work extra early and the kids need to be dropped to school. I have done the drop-off for the past month. I know it was my choice to do it. Anyway, it's made me late for important meetings. I'm now dreading Wednesdays. I'd like for us to agree on sharing the drop-offs. What do you think?' This is better than a harsh start-up where Eve says, 'You've made me late for work every Wednesday of the last month. You never do the drop-offs. You can do the drop-off tomorrow!'.

---

### Box 12.4 Resolving solvable relationship problems

**Aim**

The aim of this exercise is for you and your partner to resolve a solvable problem.

**Setting up the exercise**

- Invite your partner to spend 30 minutes with you doing this exercise.
- Select a private place and time that suits you both when you will not be interrupted or distracted.
- Turn off phones, computers, tablets, TVs, radios and other potential distractions.
- Take turns of being the speaker and listener.

**Start-up**

Begin with a soft 'start-up' that takes the form:

- There is a difficulty.
- Both of us are involved in it.
- This is how I feel about it.
- This is what I need or would prefer.

**Problem-solving**

- Break big problems into a number of smaller problems and then deal with these one at a time.
- For each small problem, brainstorm solutions.
- Look at the price and payoff of each solution, for each of you.
- Settle on the solution that suits you both best.
- Agree to try out the solution, and then afterwards to review how well it worked.

**Negotiating a compromise**

- Accept that finding a solution that suits you both will involve a degree of compromise.
- Let each other know the needs you can compromise on, and the core needs on which you can't compromise.
- When reaching a compromise, allow your partner to influence you.

**Self-soothing**

- If you become keyed up while negotiating a compromise, take a couple of minutes to soothe yourself using the exercises in Box 5.3 or 6.7 before proceeding.

**Repair connection**

- If you become involved in negative emotional exchanges, repair the connection in your relationship.
- Remind yourself how much you and your partner care about each other and value your relationship.
- Remind yourself that it's important to keep the ratio of positive to negative exchanges above 5:1.
- Express positive emotions, show affection or make a humorous comment about the situation.
- Be tolerant of your partner's idiosyncrasies and imperfections and remind yourself that these are not intended to make your life difficult. They are unfortunate incompatibilities.

After the soft initial statement, explore solutions that ideally would suit you both. Break big problems into a number of smaller problems and then deal with these one at a time. This may involve using problem-solving skills we came across in Box 10.3. For each small problem, brainstorm solutions. Look at the price and payoff of each solution, for each of you. Settle on the solution that suits you both best. Agree to try out the solution, and then afterwards to review how well it worked. In the example above about dropping the kids to school, there were a range of solutions including Eve getting up earlier and continuing to do the drop-off; Adam doing the drop-off; Adam and Eve doing the drop-off on alternate weeks; arranging for a neighbour or grandparent to do the drop-off, etc. The couple discussed the price and payoff for all of these solutions, with a lot of good humour, and settled on each getting up a bit earlier and doing the drop-off on alternate weeks.

Accept that often finding a solution that suits you both will involve a degree of compromise. An important issue is how much you should compromise in a relationship. You may find it helpful to distinguish between core needs on which you cannot compromise, and other needs where you are more flexible. Core needs include, for example, the need for safety, security, feeling loved, having a degree of influence in your relationship, maintaining your career, protecting the children from harm etc. Examples of other needs include the need for tidiness, punctuality, having sex in the morning, eating particular sorts of food etc. When you are negotiating a compromise, let each other know the needs you can compromise on, and the core needs on which you can't compromise.

When reaching a compromise avoid being rigid, and allow your partner to influence you during this compromise process. This tends to be easier for women to do than men. This is because traditionally men have been socialised into believing that accepting the influence of their partner is a sign of weakness, and a bad thing. In fact, allowing our partners to influence us is vital to enhancing the quality and stability of long-term relationships.

If the conversation begins to escalate into a heated argument where you or your partner experience strong negative emotions, attempt to soothe yourselves and repair this negative emotional exchange before it gets too heated. Tune in to your own physiological state of arousal. If you become keyed up and your heart rate increases, use the brief relaxation or meditation exercises in Boxes 5.3 or 6.7 to soothe yourself. If you wish, you can do these exercises together as a couple listening to a recording of them; or saying the instructions out loud; or one of you may guide the other through these exercises. While there are great benefits to these joint soothing processes, they may be difficult to do in the heat of a conflict. If one or both of you become very keyed up and your heart rate exceeds 100 beats per minute, take time out for a few minutes until your heart rate returns to normal, before resuming.

When you become keyed up and involved in negative emotional exchanges, repair the connection in your relationship. During repair attempts, remind yourself how much you and your partner care about each other. Remind yourself how much you both value your relationship. Remind yourself that it's important to keep the ratio of positive to negative exchanges above 5:1. Express positive emotions. Show affection. Make a humorous comment about the situation. Be tolerant of your partner's idiosyncrasies and imperfections and remind yourself that when these affect you negatively, this is not an attempt by your partner to make your life difficult. It is an unfortunate incompatibility.

For example, in a heated exchange about driving on the way to a dinner party, Eve shouted at Adam that he should not drive so quickly. Adam responded by shouting that if Eve had been ready on time, he would not have to speed. Then Eve shouted, 'You're so selfish. All you think about is what you want. You don't care about how scared I get when you speed'. Adam noticed that in response to the heated exchange and this criticism, his heart rate increased. He took a few moments to relax. He thought about how much he and Eve cared about each other. Then he slowed down a bit and said in a quieter, playful, humorous way, 'Now you're just trying to soft-soap me, you old scallywag!' Eve laughed and thanked Adam for slowing down. Both Adam and Eve felt like the emotional connection between them had been repaired.

### *Processing emotional injuries*

Conflicts that involve heated exchanges of negative emotions and in which criticism, defensiveness, contempt and/or stonewalling occur may lead to emotional injuries. These are not visible, like physical injuries. However, they are just as significant. Just as physical injuries leave scars on our bodies, emotional injuries may leave emotional scars on our relationships. The good news is that these can be prevented if we process emotional injuries. The aim is for you each to listen to and understand your partner's perspective on the argument or conflict; to acknowledge your contribution to it; to apologise for the emotional injury it caused; and to plan to manage differences more constructively in future.

Box 12.5 contains an exercise for processing emotional injuries. As with previous exercises in this chapter, agree a time and place where you will not be interrupted. Take turns at being a speaker or a listener. When you are the speaker, start by describing the complex set of difficult feelings that you had during the episode. Include the soft emotions, like feeling hurt, sad, scared, worried, unsafe, unloved, unappreciated, abandoned, lonely, hopeless, powerless, foolish. Also include the hard emotions like feeling frustrated, angry, enraged, defensive, morally justified, righteously indignant etc. In as objective a way as you can, without attacking, blaming or criticising your partner, try to accurately describe the experiences you had that led to these feelings, and what you needed. As far as possible use statements that begin with 'I' rather than 'you'. Statements that begin with 'I' will make your partner less defensive and more able to listen than statements that begin with 'you'. Identify the trigger that set off the strong negative emotions. If you can see a connection between the trigger and something from your childhood or a past relationship, mention this. If you expressed unjustified anger, criticism or contempt towards your partner, apologise for this. If you can think of a way to avoid engaging in this sort of negative exchange again, let your partner know what you intend to do and what you would like them to do. For example, Adam said to Eve, 'On Saturday morning, I felt unloved, and angry. I needed you to hold me just for a couple of minutes to feel OK. Then you seemed not to hear me and got up. That was the trigger for me. I exploded with rage. I felt like you didn't care about me. I know that's my Achilles heel. In my family, I was never sure my folks would be there when I needed them. So, any sign of that in our relationship is like kryptonite to me. I'm sorry I blew a gasket and shouted at you. Next time something like this happens, I want to be able to let you know what's going on inside me, and for you to say you understand'.

---

### Box 12.5   Processing emotional injuries

**Aim**

The aim of this exercise is for you and your partner to process an emotional injury after a hurtful exchange.

**Setting up the exercise**

- Invite your partner to spend 30 minutes with you doing this exercise.

- Use a soft 'start-up' that takes the form:

  - There is a difficulty.
  - Both of us are involved in it.
  - I want to talk about it.

- Select a private place and time that suits you both when you will not be interrupted or distracted.
- Turn off phones, computers, tablets, TVs, radios and other potential distractions.
- Take turns of being the speaker and listener.

## Speaking

- Describe the complex set of difficult feelings that you had during the episode.

  - Include the soft (or primary emotions), like feeling hurt, sad, scared, worried, unsafe, unloved, unappreciated, abandoned, lonely, hopeless, powerless, foolish, etc.
  - Include the hard (or secondary) emotions like feeling frustrated, angry, enraged, defensive, morally justified, righteously indignant etc.

- As objectively as possible without attacking, blaming or criticising your partner, accurately describe the experiences you had that led to these feelings, and what you would have needed to avoid these.
- Use 'I' statements rather than 'you' statements.
- Identify the trigger that set off the strong negative emotions.
- Point out connections you see between the trigger and past experiences in your childhood or difficult past relationships.
- Apologise for expressions of unjustified anger, criticism or contempt.
- To avoid similar emotional injuries in future, let your partner know what you intend to do, and what you would like them to do.

## Listening

- Listen without interrupting.
- Listen so carefully that you will be able to remember all that your partner has said.
- If your partner pauses, leave space for them to collect their thoughts and continue or invite them to do so by repeating the last thought they expressed; for example, 'You said you felt unloved'. Or ask open questions like:

  - What was the hardest thing about that situation?
  - Can you say more about that?
  - Can you help me understand the situation from your point of view?

- Avoid asking questions that may sound like criticism; for example, 'Why did you do that?' or 'What is that supposed to mean?'
- When your partner has finished, summarise what they have said.
- Check with them that you have understood them accurately.
- Swap roles.

If you are having a turn as the listener, listen so carefully that you will be able to remember all that your partner has said. If your partner pauses, leave space for them to collect their thoughts and continue or invite them to do so by saying things like, 'What was the hardest thing about that situation?', 'Can you say more about that?', 'Help me understand the situation from your point of view' or by simply repeating the last thought they expressed; for example, 'You said you felt unloved'. Avoid asking questions that may sound like criticism; for example, 'Why did you do that?' or 'What is that supposed to mean?' When your partner finishes telling you about the 'take' on the episode, summarise what they have said. Check with them that you have understood them accurately. Then swap roles.

### Overcoming gridlock and managing ongoing differences and incompatibilities

When you enter into a long-term relationship, like marriage, along with all the good things, you take on board a set of long-term incompatibilities. You will recognise these issues because they have four defining characteristics. (1) You have the same argument, following the same pattern, again and again without resolution. (2) Often these arguments are devoid of empathy, affection or good humour. (3) You and your partner become more polarised each time the argument occurs. (4) You both feel unable to compromise because it would be like giving up some important part of yourself and not being true to your core beliefs, values and highly valued goals. If we become gridlocked over these inevitable incompatibilities, they can make us miserable. It's therefore essential for a satisfying long-term relationship to find a way to live with these incompatibilities.

Gridlock occurs when we don't fully acknowledge, understand and accept each other's primary needs, deeply held beliefs, highly valued goals, hopes for the future and visions of the sorts of people we want to become. For short, let's call these dreams. These dreams usually have their roots in our childhood. We may want to recreate powerful positive experiences we had as children or avoid particularly distressing childhood experiences. For example, Adam may want to always have a big family dinner on Sundays, because these sorts of events were such happy occasions in his childhood. Eve may never want to have such meals because in her childhood, drunken family rows usually happened at these sorts of events. To overcome gridlock, we must understand the dream behind the conflict. We must become aware of our own and our partner's dreams – deeply held beliefs, highly valued goals, hopes for the future and vision of our identities. Then we have an opportunity to empathise with, accept and respect each other's dreams, and explore creative ways to help each other move towards them if possible.

These dreams may include living in a particular place, having a particular type of home, having a specific number of children, having certain types of relationships within the nuclear family and the extended family, organising routines within the home in a particular way, arranging children's education in a particular way, engaging in particular religious practices, organising holidays and celebrations in a particular way, organising rituals around life transitions (births, deaths, marriages, illnesses) in a particular way, engaging in or achieving success in particular sports, arts or leisure activities, achieving a certain qualification, having or avoiding a specific job or career, attaining a specific level of career or financial success, maintaining particular friendships, and having a particular role in the community. Our dreams may also include some more hidden and hard-to-get-at aspirations, for example achieving a certain degree of intimacy (physical and psychological) and power-sharing within our long-term relationships, resolving things that have hurt us in the past, expressing talents that have no outlet in our job, leisure activities or family, exploring the world, exploring ourselves and finding a satisfying way to grow old.

A problem with dreams that lead to gridlock is that they often remain unspoken or secret. When this is the case, it may be because we feel that they are impractical or childish, or that we are not entitled to them. For example, Adam and Eve's repeated arguments about whether to save or spend money reflected an underlying conflict about Adam's deeply felt need for security and Eve's wish for equitable power-sharing within the relationship. Adam felt that his need for security and his terror of becoming destitute, like his father, was childish. Eve thought that she was not entitled to talk about her feeling of being powerless within her relationship with Adam, like her mother had been in her marriage, because in most areas, except spending disposable income, Adam was extremely reasonable.

Box 12.6 contains an exercise for addressing conflicts that have become gridlocked. As with previous exercises in this chapter, agree a time and place where you will not be interrupted. Take turns at being the speaker or listener. Give each other 15 minutes in each role. Agree to discuss a particular conflict that is gridlocked. Agree that the aim of the discussion is to understand the primary needs, deeply held beliefs, highly valued goals, hopes for the future and visions of the sorts of people you both want to become that lie beneath the conflict. The aim is not to resolve the conflict. It is to find a way to live more peacefully with it as an unresolved conflict that you both accept is part of your relationship.

---

### Box 12.6   Overcoming gridlock

**Aim**

The aim of this exercise is for you and your partner to understand the primary needs, deeply held beliefs, highly valued goals, hopes for the future and visions of the sorts of people you both want to become that lie beneath a conflict that has become gridlocked. The aim is not to resolve the conflict. It is to find a way to live more peacefully with it as an unresolved conflict that you both accept as part of your relationship.

**Setting up the exercise**

- Invite your partner to spend 30 minutes with you doing this exercise so you can both better understand your positions on an issue over which you have become gridlocked.
- Use a soft 'start-up' that takes the form:

  o   There is a difficulty.
  o   Both of us are involved in it.
  o   I want to talk about it.

- Select a private place and time that suits you both when you will not be interrupted or distracted.

- Turn off phones, computers, tablets, TVs, radios and other potential distractions.
- Take turns of being the speaker and listener.

**Speaking**

- Explain your primary needs, or deeply held beliefs, or your highly valued goals, or your hopes for the future, or your vision of the sort of person you want to become that lies beneath your position in the conflict.
- Don't censor your expression of these 'dreams' because they seem impractical or childish, or because you don't feel entitled to them due to the negative effect they would have on your relationship.
- Say how much these 'dreams' mean to you and how big a loss it would be if you let go of them.
- Make 'I' statements, expressing your needs and feelings, and avoid making critical 'you' statements.

**Listening**

- Listen without interrupting.
- Listen so carefully that you will be able to remember all that your partner has said.
- Don't use this listening time to think of responses to what your partner is saying. Use it to deepen your understanding of their position.
- If your partner pauses, leave space for them to collect their thoughts and continue or invite them to elaborate on their dreams by saying:

  o Can you say more about that?
  o What do you strongly believe about this issue?
  o What do you really want or need?
  o What do you long for?
  o What kind of person do you want to become?
  o If there was a miracle and you got exactly what you wanted, what would your life look like?
  o If you didn't get what you want / need / long for, how would that affect you?

- If your partner's description of their 'dream' makes you feel keyed up, soothe yourself by taking a brief period of time out or doing the brief relaxation or meditation exercises in Boxes 5.3 or 6.6.
- When your partner has finished, summarise what they have said.
- Check with them that you have understood them accurately.
- Swap roles.

**Acceptance**

Conclude the exercise by each of you taking a turn of saying that you:

- Understand how important your conflicting 'dreams' are to each other
- Accept that these 'dreams' are not childish
- Accept that you are both entitled to your 'dreams'
- Accept that living with these incompatible 'dreams' will continue to be part of your relationship indefinitely
- Realise that this acceptance will help you avoid repeating pointless distressing patterns of conflict associated with your incompatible 'dreams'.

**Appreciation**

Select three specific things that your partner did or said during the discussion of a gridlocked conflict that you appreciated and thank them for these.

**Temporary or partial compromise**

From time to time, revisit the discussion of this incompatibility:

- Tentatively explore temporary or partial compromises.
- When compromising, let each other know the needs you can compromise on, and the core or primary needs on which you can't compromise.

When you are the speaker, explain your primary needs, or deeply held beliefs, or your highly valued goals, or your hopes for the future, or your vision of the sort of person you want to become that lies beneath the conflict. Don't censor your expression of these dreams because they seem impractical or childish, or because you don't feel entitled to them due to the negative effect they would have on your relationship. It may help if you imagine you are explaining your dreams to a good friend, and not your partner. Explain them fully. Say how much they mean to you. Say how much it would hurt you, or how big a loss it would be if you let go of these dreams. Whenever possible make 'I' statements, expressing your needs and feelings. For example, 'I want to feel free' or 'I need adventure'. Avoid making critical 'you' statements. For example, 'You always say it's not practical' or 'You never imagine how it affects me'. When you are finished, check that your partner has understood what you have said.

If you are taking the listener role, listen so carefully that you will be able to summarise what your partner has said when they have finished. Don't use this listening time to think of responses to what your partner is saying. Use it to deepen your understanding of their position. If your partner pauses, leave space for them to collect their thoughts and continue or invite them to elaborate on their dreams by saying: Can you say more about that?, What do you strongly believe about this issue?, What do you really want or need?, What do you long for?, What kind of person do you want to become?, If there was a miracle and you got exactly what you wanted, what would your life look like? If you didn't get what you want / need / long for, how would that affect you? If your partner's description of their dream makes you feel distressed, and you find yourself becoming keyed up, soothe yourself by taking a brief period of time out. If you wish, do the brief relaxation or meditation exercises in Boxes 5.3 or 6.7. When your partner finishes explaining their dream to you, summarise what they have said. Check that you have understood them accurately.

Understanding each other's dreams that underpin repeated conflicts opens up possibilities for enhancing our relationships. We can tell our partners that we understand how important their dreams are to them. We can say that we understand where their deeply held beliefs, needs or wishes for themselves come from. We can say that we do not see having these dreams as childish. We can say that our partners are entitled to have these dreams. We can decide with our partners not to regularly repeat pointless distressing patterns of conflict associated with these dreams. When we notice ourselves beginning to engage in one of these patterns, we can say to each other, 'Uh-oh – we're about to have another of these pointless arguments. Let's stop now. We both know this argument and the pattern it follows. You need X and I need Y. This is one of our incompatibilities. We both want the best for each other and our relationship, so let's not do that fight – that pattern – again and upset each other'. We can say that we are open to supporting our partners in exploring ways that these dreams that may seem impractical now, but may be achieved in the future at some point. In some cases, a temporary compromise may be possible. As with forming compromises about solvable problems, you may find it helpful to distinguish between core or primary needs on which you cannot compromise, and other needs where you are more flexible. When you are negotiating a compromise, let each other know the needs you can compromise on, and the core or primary needs on which you can't compromise.

For example, Adam and Eve did the exercise in Box 12.6 to release themselves from gridlock about how to deal with disposable income. Eve let Adam know that she understood he was frightened that he would end up destitute like his father, and this led him to want to save all of their disposable income. Adam was able to tell Eve that he understood her wish to have a say over how their disposable income was spent, and met her need to feel like she had equal power within the relationship. She needed this because she feared becoming powerless like her mother, who was very unhappy in her marriage to a dictatorial husband. This mutual understanding and empathy softened Adam and Eve's feelings towards each other around how to deal with disposable income. They agreed to be on the lookout for their habitual pattern of arguing about money, and nip it in the bud if it happened again. They also agreed to a temporary compromise, where each month they would save some of their disposable income and Eve would decide how to spend the remainder.

Adam and Eve also had frequent arguments about physical and psychological intimacy. Adam wanted to have sex more often than Eve. Compared with Adam, Eve wanted to spend more time talking with him about things that mattered to both of them. Both of these issues led to angry arguments. In these arguments, Adam and Eve criticised each other, were defensive and sometimes lapsed into expressing contempt. Afterwards, Adam sometimes stonewalled Eve for a couple of days, while Eve used every available opportunity to try to engage Adam in constructive and conciliatory conversations. All four horsemen of the apocalypse, mentioned at the start of this chapter, were associated with this pattern: criticism, defensiveness, contempt and stonewalling. Adam and Eve did the exercise in Box 12.6 to release themselves from gridlock about how to deal with their differing needs for physical and psychological intimacy. In these conversations, Adam came to understand that Eve had begun to doubt that Adam loved her, and would always be there for her, because of the hurtful things he had said to her in their arguments. He understood that she really needed him, loved him and was scared he would leave her. She needed him to regularly tell her what he was thinking about her, and how much he cared about her. These conversations also led Eve to understand Adam's position better. She understood that Adam had begun to doubt that Eve loved him, and would always be there for him because of her frequent and unpredictable refusal to have sex, and her criticism of him. She understood that he really needed her, loved her and was scared she would leave him. He needed her to express this by making love with him regularly, and for their way of communicating about how to arrange this to be clearer and more predictable for both of them. This mutual understanding and empathy softened Adam and Eve's feelings towards each other around how to deal with their need for psychological and physical intimacy. They agreed to be on the lookout for their habitual pattern of arguing about sex and communication, and nip it in the bud if it happened again. They also agreed to an arrangement where they set aside particular times each week, to talk and have sex, and a way of communicating to each other outside of these times if they were open to additional episodes of physical or psychological intimacy.

When concluding the exercise in Box 12.6, there is an invitation to end on a positive note because these conversations can be very stressful. Select three specific things that your partner did or said during the conversation and thank them for these.

Having conversations about gridlocked conflicts has the positive spin-off of creating an atmosphere that encourages us to talk honestly about our primary needs, deeply held beliefs, highly valued goals, hopes for the future and visions of the sorts of people we want to become. This is the starting point for supporting each other to make our life dreams come true, which is the sixth strategy in Figure 12.1.

## Create shared meaning

There is more to our long-term relationships than dividing up the chores, caring for the kids and grandparents, managing finances, dealing with conflict, having fun and making love. The over-arching factor that brings extraordinary satisfaction to long-term relationships is a sense of shared meaning and purpose in life. We develop this by (1) having formal and informal rituals for emotional connection, (2) supporting each other's life roles, (3) working towards shared goals and (4) developing shared values and symbols.

## Establishing formal and informal rituals for emotional connection

In our long-term relationships and marriages, we bring two separate family traditions together and create a new family, with its own culture and rituals. Rituals are structured routines we create to strengthen our emotional connection to each other. Rituals are agreed, planned and predictable. They have a strong meaning for us that makes us feel closer together. There are daily, weekly, annual and lifetime rituals.

Daily rituals include those for parting and returning, for connecting by phone, text or email during the day, for talking intimately together without distractions, and for initiating and refusing physical affection and sex. Weekly rituals include those for managing leisure, meeting friends, doing things at weekends and caring for each other when ill. Annual rituals include those associated with Christmas, Easter, annual holidays, birthdays and anniversaries.

Lifetime rituals for managing major life transitions include those for graduation, changing jobs, moving house, births, deaths and weddings. Some of these rituals may involve keeping photos, videos and other records as a family legacy. Box 12.7 contains an exercise to help you make your rituals for connection more explicit, or develop such rituals for connection if you do not have them already.

---

## Box 12.7   Creating rituals of connection

### Aim

The aim of this exercise is for you and your partner to make your rituals for connection more explicit, or develop such rituals for connection if you do not have them already.

### Setting up the exercise

- Invite your partner to spend 30 minutes with you doing this exercise.
- Select a private place and time that suits you both when you will not be interrupted or distracted.
- Turn off phones, computers, tablets, TVs, radios and other potential distractions.
- Take turns of being the speaker and listener.

### Speaking

- Select a ritual from the lists below that you would like to make more explicit or develop.

| | | | |
|---|---|---|---|
| • Breakfast | • Date night | • Birthdays | • Graduation |
| • Dinner | • Meeting friends | • Anniversaries | • Changing jobs |
| • Parting in the morning | • Hosting parties | • Christmas | • Moving house |
| • Returning in the evening | • Weekend outings | • Easter | • Births |
| • Connecting by phone, text or email during the day | • Sporting activities | • Vacations | • Deaths |
| • Talking intimately together without distractions | • Artistic activities | • Annual holidays | • Other losses |
| • Initiating physical affection and sex | • Leisure activities | | • Weddings |
| • Gently refusing physical affection and sex | • Caring for each other when ill | | |
| • Getting ready for bed | | | |
| • Going to sleep | | | |

- Say why the ritual is important to you.
- Describe how you have experienced this ritual within your relationship with your partner, and if relevant, within your birth family when you were growing up.
- If you would like to develop this ritual, say how you would prefer this ritual to unfold between you in future, giving details of the specific things you and your partner would do.
- Check with your partner that they have understood what you have said.

**Listening**

- Listen without interrupting.
- Listen so carefully that you will be able to remember all that your partner has said.
- When your partner has finished, summarise what they have said.
- Check with them that you have understood them accurately.
- Let your partner know if you agree or disagree with the way they would like to develop the ritual.

### *Supporting each other's life roles*

We each fulfil many roles in our lives. We are spouses or parents within our nuclear families. We are sons or daughters, and brothers or sisters within our birth families. We are friends, neighbours, team mates or competitors within our leisure activities and communities. Within our work lives and careers we also have distinct roles. Roles are important to us because they help us define who we are, and our place in the world. Our well-being is affected by our evaluation of how well we are being the sort of partner we want to be, the sort of parent we want to be, the sort of son or daughter we want to be, the sort of friend we want to be and the sort of worker we want to be. When our partners support us in fulfilling our roles in the ways we think we should, this increases our well-being and strengthens our relationship. This is more likely to happen when our partners and ourselves have shared values.

In traditional marriages, the husband's role is to provide financial support and the wife's role is to provide emotional support. In egalitarian marriages, the role for both partners is to support each other financially and emotionally. If both partners share traditional marriage values, or if both partners share egalitarian marriage values, they will be able to support each other in their roles as spouses. Tension will occur in relationships where partners don't share the same values. For example, if Adam holds traditional marriage values, and Eve holds egalitarian marriage values, then their expectations of each other will not fit well together. It will be difficult for them to support each other. If partners hold similar values about how best to care for and discipline children, they will be able to support each other in their roles as parents. If they hold differing values on childrearing, then it will be more difficult for them to support each other. If partners fully support each other in their careers, this enhances their relationship. If partners have the same views on how much contact they should have with their own parents, then it will be easier for them to support each other than if they have very different views on this. If partners have different views on balancing the demands of work and responsibilities of family life, then this may create tension within the relationship. Box 12.8 contains an exercise to help you and your partner communicate about your life roles and increase mutual support in this area.

---

### Box 12.8   Supporting each other's life roles

**Aim**

The aim of this exercise is for you and your partner to let each other know your deeply held views about your life roles, how you support each other in these roles and how you could support each other more.

**Setting up the exercise**

- Invite your partner to spend 30 minutes with you doing this exercise.
- Select a private place and time that suits you both when you will not be interrupted or distracted.
- Turn off phones, computers, tablets, TVs, radios and other potential distractions.
- Take turns of being the speaker and listener.

**Speaking**

- Each time you do this exercise, select one or two of the roles listed below:

  - My role as a partner, husband or wife in this relationship
  - My role as a mother or father to my children
  - My role as a son or daughter to my parents
  - My role as a worker or student in my job, occupation or education
  - My role as a friend to people I know well
  - My role as a member of my community

- Tell your partner your answers to these questions about the roles you have selected:

  - What do you think and feel about the way you fulfil this role?
  - What did your mother or father think and feel about how they fulfilled this role?
  - How are your views and those of your parents about fulfilling this role similar or different?
  - How would you like to develop the way you fulfil this role?
  - How would you like to balance the way you fulfil this role and the way you fulfil other roles in your life?
  - How does your partner currently support you in fulfilling this role?
  - How would you like your partner to support you more in fulfilling this role?

**Listening**

- Listen without interrupting.
- Listen so carefully that you will be able to remember all that your partner has said.
- When your partner has finished, summarise what they have said.
- Check with them that you have understood them accurately.
- Let your partner know how you would like to support them more in fulfilling their life roles.

### Working towards shared life goals

We can strengthen our long-term relationships by talking with our partners about our highly valued life goals, and helping them understand why these goals mean so much to us. The 'best possible self' and 'obituary' strategies for clarifying life goals described in Chapter 2 may be useful in this contex.[7] Some of your goals will be specific to you, and some will be shared by your partner. Your relationship and well-being will be strengthened if you support each other to achieve your individual goals, and work together towards shared life goals. For example, Adam and Eve supported each other to achieve success in their respective careers. They also worked together towards the shared goals of rearing their children to be good people, making their home-life happy and strengthening their community by volunteering together. Box 12.9 contains an exercise to help you and your partner communicate about your highly valued life goals and increase mutual support in this area.

## Box 12.9    Discussing highly valued life goals

**Aim**

The aim of this exercise is for you and your partner to let each other know your highly valued life goals, so you can support each other in achieving these, and so you can identify shared goals.

**Setting up the exercise**

- Invite your partner to spend 30 minutes with you doing this exercise.
- Select a private place and time that suits you both when you will not be interrupted or distracted.
- Turn off phones, computers, tablets, TVs, radios and other potential distractions.
- Take turns of being the speaker and listener.

**Speaking**

- Tell your partner about your most highly valued goals: the main things you want to achieve in your life. It may help you to do this if you tell your partner:

o   What you think the 'mission statement' is for your life, or

o   About how you visualise your 'best possible self' (mentioned in Chapter 2), or

o   About what you imagine a close friend would say in your eulogy (mentioned in Chapter 2).

- Cover the following areas and other areas that may be important to you:

   o   Your relationships with your partner, family and friends

   o   Your career

   o   Your involvement in the community, sports, arts or leisure activities

   o   Your physical health and well-being.

- Tell your partner how they support you in achieving these highly valued goals.
- Ask your partner which of your goals they share.

**Listening**

- Listen without interrupting.
- Listen so carefully that you will be able to remember all that your partner has said.
- When your partner has finished, summarise what they have said.
- Check with them that you have understood them accurately.
- Let your partner know which of their life goals you share.
- Let your partner know how you would like to support them more in achieving their life goals.

### Developing shared values and symbols

Your well-being will be strengthened if you and your partner agree on what things in life are most important. That is, if you share similar values. For example, you may both hold similar views on the importance of some of the following: love, respect, trust, commitment, freedom, independence, interdependence, religious beliefs, education, excellence, diligence, fun, caring for the environment, physical fitness, owning possessions and financial security. Box 12.10 contains an exercise to help you and your partner identify your shared values.

---

### Box 12.10   Discussing shared values

**Aim**

The aim of this exercise is for you and your partner to let each other know your values, so you can identify shared values.

**Setting up the exercise**

- Invite your partner to spend 30 minutes with you doing this exercise.

- Select a private place and time that suits you both when you will not be interrupted or distracted.
- Turn off phones, computers, tablets, TVs, radios and other potential distractions.
- Take turns of being the speaker and listener.

**Speaking**

- Tell your partner about the top three to five values you hold to be most important in life, and give examples to show how these are important to you.
- Consider the following values in identifying yours: love, respect, trust, commitment, freedom, independence, interdependence, courage, hope, honesty, fairness, education, diligence, excellence, creativity, fun, spirituality, caring for the environment, physical fitness, owning possessions and financial security.
- Tell your partner how they support you in living by these values.
- Ask your partner which of these values they share.

**Listening**

- Listen without interrupting.
- Listen so carefully that you will be able to remember all that your partner has said.
- When your partner has finished, summarise what they have said.
- Check with them that you have understood them accurately.
- Let your partner know which of their main values you share.

## Summary

- **Couple relationships and well-being.** Satisfying couple relationships enhance well-being and health.
- **Couple relationship and evolution.** Our species has evolved to find long-term couple relationships satisfying because these sorts of relationships ensured survival and propagation of the species.
- **Couples in stable long-term relationships** engage in five times more positive exchanges than negative exchanges, and repair relationship conflicts. They begin disagreements with a gentle start-up; express positive emotions, humour and affection during conflicts; try to understand their partner's point of view; accept that some conflicts are unresolvable, and these are fuelled by partners' commitment to underlying highly valued goals; respond positively towards partners' bids emotional connection; and allow their partners to influence them when negotiating.
- **Couples in unstable long-term relationships** engage in criticism, defensiveness, contempt and stonewalling.
- **Sound Relationship House Theory** was developed by John Gottman based on research on couples in stable long-term relationships and couples who divorced. The theory involves a hierarchy of seven positive strategies that couples may use to strengthen trust and commitment within their relationships. These are: build love

maps to get to know each other; share fondness and admiration; turn towards your partner; take a positive perspective; manage conflict; make life dreams come true; and create shared meaning.

- A **positive perspective** arises from practising the three first strategies in the Sound Relationship House Theory: (1) build love maps, so you know each other well, (2) regularly express fondness and admiration, so you have a ratio of at least five positive exchanges to every one negative exchange and (3) regularly turn towards your partner and respond to their bids for emotional connection.
- **Conflict.** Conflict is a normal, healthy part of all relationships. All couples have short-term conflicts that can be resolved by skilled negotiation, and long-term differences which often involve important dreams, hopes or highly valued goals. These are managed by ongoing dialogue. Gottman found that four out of five arguments are about long-term differences that the couple learn to manage, understand and accept, rather than resolve.
- **Shared meaning and purpose** makes long-term relationships satisfying. We develop this by having formal and informal rituals for emotional connection, supporting each other's life roles, working towards shared goals and developing shared values and symbols.

## Where are you now?

If you and your partner have done the exercises in this chapter, you may have found that they improved the quality of your relationship and your personal well-being.

You may want to read back over the chapter and summarise in your journal the main things that you have learned from this chapter about improving your relationship. You can now decide if you want to include the practices described in this chapter in your relationship in future.

You may also wish to think about how you could deepen your relationship with your partner and enhance your well-being by jointly engaging in conversations, activities, arts, sports, entertainments or other things that you both enjoy that involve you using your strengths (discussed in Chapter 3), exercising (discussed in Chapter 4), being mindful (discussed in Chapter 6) and engaging in savouring and flow (discussed in Chapter 7).

In the next chapter, you will have an opportunity to read about enhancing relationships with your children. Below are some web resources and books that are relevant to topics you have read about in this chapter.

## Web resources

John Gottman talking about seven things that make relationships work video (0:57): www.youtube.com/watch?v=AEF3OdvNNzk

John Gottman talking about improving marriage in 30 seconds video (1:31): www.youtube.com/watch?v=G_Vz_Cbsu3o

John Gottman talking about building trust video (4:42): www.youtube.com/watch?v=rgWnadSi91s

John Gottman talking about repairing relationships video (3:24): www.youtube.com/watch?v=SqPvgDYmJnY

John Gottman talking about making relationships work video (47:03): www.youtube.com/watch?v=
    AKTyPgwfPgg
Sue Johnson talking about close relationships video (2:47): www.youtube.com/watch?v=Su9GmkL9T1M

## Books

Gottman, J. M., & Silver, N. (2015). *The seven principles for making marriage work (Second edition)*. New
    York, NY: Harmony Books.
Johnson, S. M. (2008). *Hold me tight: Seven conversations for a lifetime of love*. New York, NY: Little,
    Brown.

# 13 Positive parent-child relationships

We all want the best for our children. We want them to grow up to be strong and healthy. We want them to be happy and popular. We want them to be successful at school and work. We want them to do well at sports, arts or other activities that interest them. This is not surprising. Evolution has designed us to want nothing but the best for our offspring so our species will survive.[1] If we want the best for our kids, how is it that our children do not always make us ecstatic? How is it that some of the time, most us find parenting challenging?

This is because rearing children is both demanding and rewarding. It requires a vast amount of time for many years to care for children and meet all of their needs. We have to meet their need to be loved, fed, housed, to go to school, to develop friendships, to be involved in sports, arts, clubs and activities, to go to college, to develop independence, to leave home and possibly to start their own family. Rearing children may lead to many sleepless nights when they are infants, but also when they are adolescents. When we have children, there is less time for us to focus on our romantic relationships. Rearing children may give rise to arguments about how couples jointly manage issues such as housework, childcare, work outside the home, relationships with the couple's parents and how to manage the financial demands of rearing children. If our children have illnesses, disabilities or special educational needs, this may lead us to experience profound grief, and demand a high level of skill to care for them properly.

On the other hand, rearing children is also very rewarding. Having children meets a basic human need to procreate, and care for someone who is our own flesh and blood. Supporting children as they grow, develop and achieve their potential is an extraordinarily positive experience. Having children creates opportunities to be connected to our wider families and communities. The process of loving our children and being in lifelong relationships with them may give our lives meaning and direction.

Psychological research shows that parents' well-being depends on the balance of the demands of childrearing, and their available coping resources.[2] When we have the time, energy, skill, social support and money to meet the demands of rearing children, and our children fulfil our needs to be parents and to be connected to our wider families and communities, and give our lives meaning and direction, then children enhance our well-being. However, where the demands our children place upon us outstrip our capacity to cope, then our well-being is diminished. We are more likely to have positive relationships with our children when we have the resources to cope with the demands they place upon us. If our children have positive relationships with us, then they are more likely to experience greater well-being while growing up, and also as adults than those who are less fortunate.[3]

Because the demands that children place upon us tend to be greatest during infancy, childhood and adolescence, it is not surprising that it is during these times that parents report greatest stress and lower levels of well-being. As our children mature into adulthood, our own well-being increases.[4]

Professor Diana Baumrind at the University of California, Berkeley in her ground-breaking work identified three distinct parenting styles.[5] Authoritarian parents were strict or demanding, and emotionally aloof or unresponsive to their children's emotional needs. Permissive parents were not at all strict or very undemanding, and highly responsive to their children's emotional needs. Authoritative parents in contrast to these two non-optimal parenting styles combined high levels of both demandingness and responsiveness. They expected their children to comply with their expectations, and combined this with a high level of warmth and responsiveness to their children's emotional needs. Baumrind's original study in 1967, and over five decades of subsequent research, has shown that authoritative parenting is the optimal parenting style in western industrialised cultures.[6] Children whose parents expect their children to follow direction, and who are also warm and responsive to their children's emotional needs, show high levels of well-being, prosocial behaviour, achievement motivation, self-reliance, self-control and confidence.

A vast body of research shows that the following discrete parenting skills, which constitute an authoritative parenting style, lead to better parent–child relationships and greater well-being in children.[7]

- Make and maintain a good relationship
- Accommodate to your child's temperament
- Nurture and reward prosocial behaviour
- Reduce opportunities for problem behaviour, and discourage it
- Use problem-solving and negotiation skills
- Be a good, consistent role model

In the rest of this chapter, guidance on how you can use these parenting skills will be given.

## Make and maintain a good relationship

The most important thing we can do to enhance our children's well-being is to make and maintain a good relationship with them across the lifespan. At any stage of the lifespan we can deepen our relationship with our children and enhance their well-being by jointly engaging in conversations, activities, arts, sports, entertainments or other things that we both enjoy. In particular we can do things that involve our children and ourselves using our strengths (discussed in Chapter 3), exercising (discussed in Chapter 4), being mindful (discussed in Chapter 6) and engaging in activities that promote savouring and flow (discussed in Chapter 7).

At particular stages of the lifespan, psychological research points to very specific parenting skills that we can use to enhance our children's well-being. When they are infants we can be responsive to our children's needs so that they develop a secure attachment to us. When they become older and attend school we can spend special time with them so that our children know we are interested in things that interest them. As they move into adolescence and adulthood we can develop a deep understanding of how our teenagers see the world by actively listening to them. We will now look at these skills in more detail.

## Attachment

John Bowlby, in the UK, developed attachment theory (which was mentioned at the end of Chapter 13). The theory was published in four volumes between 1969 and 1988.[8] This theory lets us know how to develop good relationships with our infants. Bowlby developed attachment theory to explain why some infants and children tend to have very secure relationships with their parents, and others don't. Attachment theory proposes that children are more likely to develop secure attachments to their parents and derive feelings of safety and security from being close to them, if parents are attuned to children's needs, and respond to them in timely and predictable ways. When children have regular experiences of their parents meeting their needs for food comfort and other essentials, they develop expectations that this will continue to happen in the future. When this doesn't occur, they develop expectations that their parents will not be there for them, when they need them. This leads them to become very clingy or very sulky in their relationships with their parents. These clingy and sulky relationships reflect anxious and avoidant insecure attachment styles.

Children experience greater well-being when they develop secure attachments to their parents. This is because when they have a secure attachment they experience their parents as a 'secure-base' from which to explore the world. For secure attachments to develop between our children and ourselves, we must be responsive to our children's needs, especially when they are infants.[9] When we are responsive we 'tune in' to their wavelength. We accurately interpret the messages they are sending us when they cry, express distress or express happiness. We respond to these messages in a timely way by meeting their needs to be cuddled, fed, changed, warmed up, cooled down, put to sleep, treated for illness or played with. When we regularly and predictably respond to their messages by meeting their needs, they gradually learn that we (and others) are trustworthy, and that they can rely on us to be there for them when they need us. You can strengthen your infant's attachment to you, and enhance their well-being, by using the responsive parenting guidelines in Box 13.1.

---

### Box 13.1   Guidelines for responsive parenting

- When you are with your infant or child, tune in to their wavelength.
- Listen to the messages they are sending you when they vocalise, make gestures or cry.
- Guess what they are asking for.
- Do they need to be cuddled, fed, changed, warmed up, cooled down, put to sleep, treated for illness or injury or played with?
- Give them what they need in a timely way.
- If their response tells you they still need something else, guess what that is, and give it to them in a timely way.
- If their response tells you that their need has been fulfilled, you have enhanced their well-being, and strengthened the security of their attachment to you.

## *Special time*

As they develop into toddlers and then into school-age children, we can enhance the quality of our relationships with our children by making a point of spending one-to-one 'special time' with them. Special time is a central part of many parent training programmes that have been developed by psychologists and scientifically evaluated.[10] During special time, we let our children take the lead in deciding what activities to do, what games to play and what things to talk about. We follow their lead. We show interest in things that interest them. We empathise with their way of looking at the world. We avoid directing them, correcting them, criticising them or teaching them. Our focus is on showing full interest in things that our children choose to do, in the same way that we would show interest in the views of a close friend telling us about something that is important to them. However, with young children we show this interest by 'running a commentary' on the whatever they are playing. This lets our children know that we are genuinely interested in their 'take' on the world. This makes them feel strong positive emotions. Special time can occur at any time, and can be incorporated into routines such as returning home after school or going to bed at night. For example, Claire was spending special time with Josh after school. He was playing with his toy cars. She asked him who was in each car and what they were doing. She 'ran a commentary' on the play session by saying things like, 'The van man is driving to the supermarket with lots of stuff to go on the shelves for all the customers. The bin man is collecting all the bins and then will drive to the dump. Oh! There's been an accident. Here comes the ambulance. The ambulance is speeding along to the crash . . .' etc. You can strengthen your relationship with your child and enhance their well-being by practising the special time exercise in Box 13.2.

---

### Box 13.2   Special time

**Aim**

The aim of the exercise is to strengthen your relationship with your child by letting your child know that you are interested in the things that interest them, and their way of making sense of the world.

**Setting up the exercise**

- Invite your child to spend 20–30 minutes with you doing this exercise on most days.
- Select a private place and time that suits you both, when you will not be interrupted or distracted.
- Turn off phones, computers, tablets, TVs, radios and other potential distractions.

**Practice**

- Ask your child to select something to play with.
- The exercise may work better if the play is make-believe and not digital, although if digital/electronic games are the consuming interest of your child then agree to this.

- During special time, let your child take the lead.
- Participate in the activity wholeheartedly.
- Run a commentary on what your child is doing or saying, to show your child that you understand in detail what they are doing.
- Make congruent *I like it when you* ... statements, to show your child you feel good about being there.
- Praise your child repeatedly.
- Laugh and make physical contact through hugs or rough and tumble.
- Avoid using commands, instructions, teaching or other 'parent-directed' activity. You are aiming to engage in a 'child-directed' activity.
- Try to foresee rule-breaking, and prevent it from happening, or ignore it.
- Notice how much you enjoy being with your child.
- Finish the episode by summarising what you did together, and how much you enjoyed it.

### Active listening

With the transition to adolescence, having regular one-to-one conversations with our teenagers is an important way of enhancing the quality of our relationships with them. We may find that our teenagers talk most feely with us when we are in the car together, working together on household chores or around sports, arts, camping or other recreational activities. During these times, we can enhance our relationship with our teenagers by using active listening skills. Family therapy programmes that facilitate active listening between parents and adolescents (among other skills) have been shown scientifically to help families of troubled teenagers.[11] These programmes that facilitate active listening are effective partly because in such families, communication between parents and teenagers has broken down. With active listening, we listen to what our teenagers have to say without interrupting, with the primary aim of understanding how they see the world. When we do this, it is important that we avoid criticising or correcting them, or giving unsolicited advice. When they have finished speaking, we let them know that we have understood them by summarising what they have said, and check with them that our summary is accurate. We then say whether we agree with them or take a different view. This use of active listening skills helps us to avoid getting into heated arguments, when our teenagers want to tell us about ideas that they have, which may differ in important ways from our own views. When we use these active listening skills in talking to our teenagers it lets them know that we want to hear and understand their position, even though we may disagree with it. For example, Martin, aged 17, was telling his mother, Amy, about his interest in the rock band, Pink Floyd. He said, 'I really think Roger Waters was the driving force behind their best work. He had the vision. He wrote their best lyrics and did the most creative arrangements, especially on *Dark of Side of the Moon* and *The Wall*. Dave Gilmore is gifted with a beautiful voice and is a brilliant guitarist. But I feel like ... Roger was the soul of the band. I love his new album *Is This the Life You Really Want?* It's like he says things that I think, or might think if I took the time to think about it'. Amy said in response, 'I know where you're coming from, Martin. You really identify with Roger Waters. Even if he's not as musically talented in some ways as Dave, Roger was the soul of Floyd. You feel like he does about injustice'. You can strengthen your relationship with your teenager and enhance their well-being by practising the active listening exercise in Box 13.3.

---

### Box 13.3   Active listening

#### Aim

The aim of the exercise is to strengthen your relationship with your teenager by letting them know that you are interested in their views on the world.

#### Setting up the exercise

- Select a private place and time that suits you both when you will not be inter-rupted or distracted to do this exercise.
- Turn off phones, computers, tablets, TVs, radios and other potential distractions.

#### Practice

- Make an opening for your teenager to speak freely to you by using a strategy that suits them.

  o Ask open questions like: How are things? What do you think of . . .? How do you make sense of . . .?
  o Make statements that invite an answer like: You've been really busy recently? I suppose that has an effect on you? Everybody has their own view of the situation?
  o Follow your teenager's lead when they talk spontaneously.

- Once your teenager gets 'on a roll' and starts talking, listen without interrupting, or expressing your opinion.
- Listen so carefully that you will be able to remember all that your teenager has said when they have finished.
- Occasionally, let your teenager know that you understand what they think and emotions that they feel by saying things like 'I see', 'I understand', 'That sounds very difficult / wonderful / scary / sad / frustrating', 'I would have felt the same way' etc.
- If your teenager expresses positive emotions, respond in a positive, enthusiastic way.
- If your teenager expresses negative emotions like sadness, hurt, fear or anger towards others (rather than you), listen carefully with the goal of *understanding* their reaction, not solving their problem.
- If your teenager expresses anger towards you, and you find yourself becoming keyed up, soothe yourself by doing brief relaxation or meditation exercises in Boxes 5.3 or 6.7.
- If your teenager pauses, leave space for them to collect their thoughts and con-tinue or invite them to do so by repeating the last thought they expressed, for

example, 'You said you found it hard to make sense of that' or by asking open
questions like:

- o   What was the most puzzling thing about that situation?
- o   Can you say more about that?
- o   How did that look from your point of view?

- Avoid asking questions that may sound like criticism, for example, 'Why did you do
  that?' or 'What is that supposed to mean?'
- Don't offer unsolicited advice on what your teenager should do.
- If your teenager is sad, don't try to cheer them up; acknowledge that they are sad.
- If you teenager is angry, don't tell them to calm down; acknowledge that they are angry.
- If your teenager is frightened or worried, don't tell them that they shouldn't be
  worried; acknowledge that they are scared.
- When your teenager finishes, summarise what they have said.
- Check with them that you have understood them accurately.

### Accommodate to your child's temperament

Professors Alexander Thomas and Stella Chess in their New York Longitudinal study, which
began in the 1950s, showed that children are born with different temperaments.[12] Some have
easy temperaments and some have difficult temperaments. Children with different temperaments have different outcomes as adults, but their outcomes partly depend on how parents
respond to their temperaments. The quality of our relationships with our children, and their
well-being over the lifecycle, is enhanced when there is a 'goodness of fit' between their temperaments and our approach to caring for them.[13] That is, when we understand that all infants
are born with different temperaments, and accommodate our parenting style to match our
children's unique temperament, then our relationships with our children are better, and children experience greater well-being. It's a lot less challenging to care for children with easy
temperaments than to care for those with difficult temperaments. Children with easy temperaments are born with the sorts of nervous systems that made it easy for them to learn
regular routines for feeding, toileting, sleeping, waking and experiencing positive emotions
when they enter unfamiliar situations. In contrast, children with difficult temperaments are
born with the sorts of nervous systems that made it very difficult for them to learn regular
routines for feeding, toileting, sleeping and waking. They need us to be very patient with them
as we help them develop routines. They need us to understand that learning routines is hard
for them. They need us not to express our impatience, frustration or exhaustion in ways that
distress them, when they are having difficulty learning routines. If they typically respond to
unfamiliar stimulating situations by crying, and find it hard to calm down, they need us to
anticipate and pre-empt this whenever possible. For example, when visiting with family and
friends, they need us to sit calmly and quietly with them, soothing them before stimulating
them by passing them to other family members or friends to hold or interact with.

   As they develop into toddlers, they need us to be patient in helping them soothe the negative
emotions they experience during their daily transitions between home and preschool or school.

As they develop into school-age children, and adolescents, they need us to help them develop self-soothing skills so they can regulate intense negative emotions that may be triggered during transitional or other stressful times. You can strengthen your relationship with your child and enhance their well-being by using the exercise in Box 13.4 to reflect on how you could improve the goodness of fit between your child's temperament and the way you interact with them.

## Box 13.4   Finding a good fit with your child's temperament

**Aim**

The aim of this exercise is for you to plan fit in with your child's temperament.

**Practice**

- For each of the nine temperament factors below read the questions and then circle the number that best describes where your child is on that factor.
- The factors on which you have given your child higher scores are those where your child places greater demands on you, and makes it more difficult for you to have a good fit with their temperament.
- Reflect on how the ratings you have given your child on each of the nine temperament factors differ from how you expected your child to be or how you would prefer your child to be.
- Think about strategies you could use to fit in better with those temperamental characteristics of your child that you find challenging.
- Reflect on specific temperamental characteristic of your child that will require you to be more understanding, patient and accepting.
- Plan to take one or two steps towards improving the goodness of it between your child's temperament and your way of interacting with them.

| 1 | Activity level | How much does your child wiggle and move around when being read to, sitting at a table or playing alone? | 1<br>Not very<br>active | | 2  3  4 | 5<br>Highly<br>Active |
|---|---|---|---|---|---|---|
| 2 | Distractibility | Is your child easily distracted, or do they ignore distractions? | 1<br>Not<br>distractible | | 2  3  4 | 5<br>Very<br>distractible |
| 3 | Intensity of reactions | How strong or violent are your child's emotional reactions? Does your child laugh and cry energetically, or do they just smile and express distress mildly? | 1<br>Not intense | 1 | 3  4 | 5<br>Very intense |
| 4 | Regularity | Is your child regular about eating times, sleeping times, amount of sleep needed and bowel movements? | 1<br>Regular | | 2  3  4 | 5<br>Irregular |

| 5 | Sensitivity | How aware is your child of slight noises, slight changes in temperature, differences in taste and the feel of different sorts of clothing? | 1<br>Not<br>  sensitive | 2 | 3 | 4 | 5<br>Very sensitive |
|---|---|---|---|---|---|---|---|
| 6 | Approach / Withdrawal | How does your child usually react the first time to new people, new foods, new toys and new activities? | 1<br>Approaches | 2 | 3 | 4 | 5<br>Withdraws |
| 7 | Adaptability | How quickly does your child adapt to changes in their schedule or routine?<br>How quickly does your child adapt to new foods and transitions from one place to another? | 1<br>Adapts<br>  quickly | 2 | 3 | 4 | 5<br>Slow to adapt |
| 8 | Persistence | How long does your child continue with one activity?<br>Does your child usually continue if it is difficult? | 1<br>Long<br>  attention<br>  span | 2 | 3 | 4 | 5<br>Short<br>  attention<br>  span |
| 9 | Mood | How much of the time does your child show pleasant, joyful behaviour compared with unpleasant crying and distressed behaviour? | 1<br>Positive<br>  mood | 2 | 3 | 4 | 5<br>Negative mod |

**Note:** The nine dimensions of temperament are from Chess, S., & Thomas, A. (1995). *Temperament in clinical practice*. New York, NY: Guilford.

### Nurture and reward prosocial behaviour

Our children will have better relationships with us and experience greater well-being if we focus on catching them being good and rewarding them for this, more than catching them misbehaving and punishing them. This overall strategy is a central part of many parent training programmes that have been developed by psychologists and scientifically evaluated.[10] From infancy, through to the end of adolescence, it will improve our children's well-being if we develop the habit of actively looking for opportunities to let our children know that they are doing something good. These good things may be simple prosocial behaviours like saying please or thank you, sharing toys with siblings or friends or doing chores. For example, Mary asked her 15-year-old son Colin to take a break from mowing the lawn. When he came into the kitchen, she gave him a glass of juice and said how much she appreciated him doing the grass. We can also reward our children's sophisticated prosocial behaviours like controlling their temper, and not hitting a child who breaks their toys, or waiting their turn when queuing. For example, when Anthony saw that his six-year-old son Keith was going to hit Gary who had broken his truck, he said, 'Anthony, I know you're annoyed at Gary and sad your truck is broken. We'll try and fix it in a minute. Right now, you are being very grown up, by keeping calm.

I like when you are grown up and calm'. If we catch our children putting in effort to achieve a goal, it may enhance their perseverance in future if we praise them for their effort to achieve their goal, rather than praise them for achieving the goal, or having a particular ability. For example, when James saw his eight-year-old daughter Jacintha doing her homework in her bedroom, he simply said, 'Jacintha, I like to see you working hard at your homework. You will do well if you work hard'. We will see in Chapter 14 that research on achievement indicates that rewarding effort is more effective than rewarding task completion or ability.[14] We can help our children develop strengths listed in Chapter 3[15] by rewarding them for using these strengths in their day-to-day lives.

### Reduce opportunities for problem behaviour, and discourage it

Our children will have better relationships with us and experience greater well-being if we reduce opportunities for problem behaviour, and discourage it. This overall strategy, and procedures for implementing it, is a central part of many parent training[10] and family therapy[11] programmes that have been developed by psychologists and scientifically shown to be effective.

#### Clear communication

To reduce problem behaviour, we let our children know what we expect of them in a clear direct way. With young children, this involves giving very clear direct commands. For example, 'Timmy, it's tea time. Come and sit up at the table'. 'Margie and Val, take turns with the scooter. Margie, you have a go around the garden first. Then Val, you have your turn'. With older children and adolescents, we make expectations or rules, the reasons for them and the consequence for rule-breaking very clear. For example, 'Homework is to be done before watching TV, so you are not too tired. There will be no TV until homework is done'. When it comes to rules about problem behaviours, the fewer and the clearer these are, the better.

#### Supervision

To reduce opportunities for problem behaviour, it's essential that we know where our children are. It's also essential that we know what opportunities for problem behaviour and prosocial behaviour are available to them. We then encourage them to move towards situations where there are opportunities for prosocial behaviour, and away from situations where there are opportunities for problem behaviour.

How we do this varies depending on our children's age. With pre-schoolers, we keep them in sight all or most of the time. We may have only one or two rules. We may pre-empt problem behaviour by anticipating it, and offering immediate alternatives. With teenagers, we may have half a dozen rules. We may ask our children where they are going, who they will be with and what time they will be home. We may explore prosocial activities that they would like to do, if they become involved in problem behaviour.

Here are two examples. Henry made sure to keep his two-year-old Tina in sight at all times when he was cooking dinner. He explained to Tina that the main rule was not to touch the stove because it would burn her. When he saw she was in danger of touching the stove, Henry encouraged her to move away from it by saying, 'Tina, come and sit up here at the table and help daddy to put all these carrot slices in the big pot'.

The second example concerns Ellen and Mike's 14-year-old son, Joe, who took longer than he should coming home from school on a few occasions. Mike saw him, on one occasion, outside the supermarket with a group of older boys who had a bad reputation in their neighbourhood. That evening, he asked Joe about the friends he was seeing after school, and what he found exciting about being with them. Joe said he liked being with the older boys because it made him feel more like an adult. Mike said he understood this, but was concerned that Joe might get into trouble if he hung around with the older boys, because they had a reputation for vandalism. Mike asked Joe if there were any activities, other than hanging around with these older boys, that he would really like to do, that would make him feel more grown up. After talking about a range of options, Mike agreed for Joe to join a rock climbing and mountaineering club and Joe agreed not to hang around with the older boys with the bad reputation after school.

### Separate the person from the problem

So far, we have been talking in this section about guiding our children away from opportunities for problem behaviour, and towards opportunities for prosocial behaviour. The next set of parenting skills is about discouraging problem behaviour when it actually occurs. If our children engage in problem behaviour that's not too serious, we may ignore it. However, if it's dangerous or harmful, we may let them know we disapprove. The important thing is to convey that we disapprove of their behaviour, not of them. That is, we view our child as a good person, who did something bad, not a bad child. If it happens repeatedly, we view them a good person with a bad habit, not as a bad person.

### Time out from reinforcement

We can back up our disapproval of problem behaviour by giving our young children time out from reinforcement. Time out from reinforcement is always brief. We withdraw our child from situations that are rewarding until they control their negative emotions. Often, children intensify angry outbursts when they enter time out. This is normal. As soon as they control their negative emotions, we praise and reward them for exercising self-control. Effective time out always ends with our children having a positive experience of having controlled their negative emotions, impulses and problem behaviours, and being rewarded for doing so. Time out is not a punishment. It is a learning opportunity that concludes with the child experiencing mastery, success and positive emotions.

Effective time out happens in a place where there are no enjoyable activities or toys. If a child is sent to their room for time out, and there are many enjoyable activities and toys there, then it's not time out from reinforcement, since many enjoyable reinforcers are present. Effective time out is brief. If a child spends a long time in time out, during which they are no longer having a tantrum, then an important opportunity has been missed for praising the child as soon as they have controlled their temper or problem behaviour.

## Contracts

Our relationships with our teenagers will be strengthened by the way we manage their problem behaviour if the consequences of rule-breaking are very clear, and if the consequences are proportionate to the degree to which the rule was broken. For example, Ian knew that if he was home after midnight, he would not be allowed out on Sunday after supper. His parents, May and Seth, had made this very clear to him. In a sense, this was a contract that Ian had agreed with May and Seth. To maintain a positive relationship with teenagers when we have withdrawn privileges, following rule-breaking we can couple this with offering to help them avail of opportunities for prosocial behaviour in future. This may involve planning activities that they value, where there are many opportunities for prosocial behaviour, to substitute for situations or activities where problem behaviour occurred, as discussed earlier.

## Consistency

Our children will find it easier to learn how to avoid engaging in problem behaviour if we and our partners are consistent with rules about what sorts of behaviour are unacceptable, and the consequences for rule-breaking and problem behaviour.[16] This means that each parent should be consistent over time, so our children know that the rules are the same from one day to the next. It also means that both parents should be consistent with each other, for the main rules and consequences. This is often quite challenging, but particularly important when parents are separated. However, it's far less confusing for children of separated parents if there are similar expectations, rules and consequences in both their mother's and their father's homes.

You can strengthen your relationship with your child and enhance their well-being by following the guidelines for promoting positive child behaviour and discouraging problem behaviour in Box 13.5.

---

**Box 13.5   Guidelines for promoting positive child behaviour and discouraging problem behaviour**

**Catch your child being good**

- Focus on catching your child being good and rewarding them for this, more than catching them misbehaving and punishing them.
- Catch them being good and praise or reward them for:

    o   Simple prosocial behaviours, like saying 'please' and 'thank you'
    o   Sophisticated prosocial behaviours, like controlling their temper
    o   Putting in a lot of effort to achieve a goal.

- Use giving your attention, praise and approval as the main reward for prosocial behaviour.

- If you want to help your child overcome behaviour problems, use symbolic systems (star charts, sticker charts, token systems or point systems) for rewarding prosocial behaviour. With symbolic systems, stars, stickers, tokens or points can by accumulated and exchanged for tangible rewards or privileges that your child values.

**Communicate rules clearly**

- Tell your children clearly and directly what you expect of them.
- Give very clear direct commands to young children.
- With older children and adolescents, clearly state rules, reasons for them and consequences for rule-breaking.
- Consequences should be fair, and based on 'care' more than 'control'.
- Consequences should reflect how much you care about your child: your wish to help you child learn how to be safe, secure and considerate.
- Consequences should not reflect your anger at your child for upsetting you, or your wish to impose unfair control on your child as a punishment.

**Supervise your child**

- Know where your children are. Keep young children in sight. Ask older children and adolescents about where they are going, with whom and when they will return.
- Encourage children to move towards opportunities for prosocial behaviour, and away from opportunities for problem behaviour.

**Separate the person from the problem**

- If your child engages in problem behaviour, view them as a good person with a bad habit, not as a bad person.

**Give time out from reinforcement**

- If your young child misbehaves, give three warnings, and suggest alternatives to engaging in problem behaviour.
- If they continue to misbehave, withdraw them from situations that are rewarding, for a brief period, until they control their negative emotions and problem behaviour.
- As soon as they do so, praise them for exercising self-control.

**Make contracts for rule-breaking**

- With older children and teenagers make the consequences of rule-breaking very clear and proportionate to the degree to which the rule was broken – this is an informal contract.
- If adolescents engage in problem behaviour and have privileges withdrawn as a consequence, help them identify opportunities for prosocial behaviour which they can substitute, in future, for situations where problem behaviour occurred.

**Be consistent**

- Be consistent with rules and consequences.
- Each parent should be consistent from one day to the next, and both parents should be consistent with each other.

## Use problem-solving and negotiation skills

We and our adolescents have different needs and preferences. Because of this, conflict in parent–adolescent relationships is inevitable. We can resolve these conflicts and strengthen our relationships with our adolescents by using problem-solving and negotiation skills. This will also enhance the well-being of our teenagers and ourselves. Problem-solving and negotiation skills are an integral part of parent training[10] and family therapy[11] programmes that have been developed by psychologists and scientifically shown to be effective in resolving a range of clinical problems involving parent–child conflict. Problem-solving skills are discussed in Chapter 11. Combining problem-solving and negotiation skills in managing conflict in long-term couple relationships was discussed in Chapter 12. Here we will discuss how to use these skills to constructively manage parent–adolescent conflict.

With problem-solving, we break big problems into a number of smaller problems. For each small problem, we brainstorm solutions. We look at the price and payoff of each solution, for ourselves and our children. We settle on the solution that suits us both best. Agree to try out the solution, and then afterwards to review how well it worked. These are the problem-solving skills we came across in Box 10.3. For example, Simon and his 18-year-old son, Kevin, were considering how best for Kevin to get home from a music gig on Friday night. The main options were by bus and taxi. They agreed that the bus was cheap, but might be full and stopped a mile from the house, leaving Kevin with a long walk home on a lonely and potentially dangerous road. The taxi would leave Kevin at the door, and was more likely to be available, but would be more expensive than the bus. On balance, they both opted for the taxi as the best solution. Simon lent Kevin some extra money towards the taxi fare. Kevin agreed to do some chores to pay off this debt. Both Simon and Kevin felt good after this brief episode of problem-solving. It also strengthened their relationship.

Often finding a solution that suits ourselves and our youngsters involves compromise. This is increasingly the case as our children mature into adolescents and young adults. During this period in the family lifecycle, our youngsters and ourselves have conflicting drives. Our youngsters have a strong drive to achieve greater independence, freedom and privacy. They have a desire to become identifiably distinct from us – their parents – and eventually to leave home and create their own lives separate from ours. In contrast, we are motivated to keep them safe, prevent them from harm, and help them become the sorts of people we want them to be. An important issue is how much you should compromise when negotiating with your adolescent or young adult offspring when resolving a conflict through negotiation.

You may find it helpful to distinguish between core issues on which you cannot compromise, and other issues on which you are more flexible. Core issues include, for example, protecting yourself and your children from serious harm. Examples of other issues include tidiness, punctuality or for your children to do particular chores, participate in certain family events, study particular courses, work at particular jobs, engage in particular sports, dress in particular ways, eat particular sorts of food, etc. When you are negotiating a compromise with your youngster, let each other know the issues on which you can compromise, and the core issues on which you can't compromise.

When reaching a compromise avoid being rigid, and allow your youngster to influence you during this compromise process. If the conversation begins to escalate into a heated argument where you or your youngster experience strong negative emotions, use the brief relaxation or meditation exercises in Boxes 5.3 or 6.7 to soothe yourself. If you become very keyed up and your heart rate exceeds 100 beats per minute, take time out for a few minutes until your heart rate return to normal, before resuming.

When you become keyed up and involved in negative emotional exchanges, repair the connection in your relationship. During repair attempts, remind yourself how much you and your youngster care about each other. Remind yourself how much you both value your relationship. Express positive emotions. Make a humorous comment about the situation. Be tolerant of your youngster's idiosyncrasies and remind yourself that when these affect you negatively, this is not an attempt by your youngster to make your life difficult. It is an inevitable consequence of living in a family where you and others will inevitably have different needs and preferences. Chief among these are your need for your youngster's safety and security, and their need for autonomy and independence.

For example, Alice, aged 20, wanted to drop out of college and work with a digital company her older boyfriend, Steve, and his colleagues were developing. Alice was still living with her parents Sally and Nick, who were paying her college fees, and who disapproved of Alice's wish to drop out. Alice saw her career plan as a way of doing something new and exciting; of spending more time with Steve; of earning money so she could move out of her parents' house; and of becoming independent. She felt trapped in her parents' house, and in her degree programme which would take two more years to complete. Sally and Nick were concerned that if Alice's relationship with Steve ended, she could end up either in a very uncomfortable work situation or unemployed, and with poor employment prospects because she had dropped out of college. A core issue for Alice was moving out of her parents' house. A core issue for Nick and Sally was that Alice complete her degree programme. They reached a compromise in which it was agreed that Alice would take a year's leave of absence from university, move out of her parents' house and work with Steve's company. After that year, Alice would return to college on a part-time basis, continue working with Steve's company on a part-time basis and remain living independently from her parents. During heated moments in this negotiation, Alice and her mother Sally took time out to calm down. When they had done so, Sally made this repair attempt. She said, 'Alice, you know I love you and only want the best for you. It's not that I want to take away your independence now. I worry about you, and want you to be qualified so you will have a bright future'.

You can strengthen your relationship with your child and enhance their well-being by following the guidelines for problem-solving and negotiation in Box 13.6.

## Box 13.6   Guidelines for problem-solving and negotiation

**Setting up**

- Select a private place and time that suits you both when you will not be interrupted or distracted.
- Turn off phones, computers, tablets, TVs, radios and other potential distractions.
- Take turns of being the speaker and listener.

**Problem-solving**

- Break big problems into a number of smaller problems and then deal with these one at a time.
- For each small problem, brainstorm solutions.
- Look at the price and payoff of each solution, for each of you.
- Settle on the solution that suits you both best.
- Agree to try out the solution, and then afterwards to review how well it worked.

**Negotiating a compromise**

- Accept that finding a solution that suits you both will involve a degree of compromise.
- Let each other know the issues you can compromise on, and the core issues on which you can't compromise.
- When reaching a compromise, allow your youngster to influence you.

**Self-soothing**

- If you become keyed up while negotiating a compromise, take a couple of minutes to soothe yourself using exercise 5.3 or 6.7 before proceeding.

**Repair connection**

- If you become involved in negative emotional exchanges, repair the connection in your relationship.
- Remind yourself how much you and your youngster care about each other and value your relationship.
- Express positive emotions, show affection or make a humorous comment about the situation.
- Be tolerant of your youngster's idiosyncrasies and remind yourself that these are not intended to make your life difficult. They are inevitable conflicts that arise partly because you want your youngster to be safe and secure, and partly because they yearn for independence.

## Be a good consistent role model

Our children are programmed through millions of years of evolution to imitate us.[1] One of the best ways we can help our children enhance their well-being is to be good role models, for skills and practices that improve well-being. In being good role models we can do some or all of the following things mentioned in this book:

- understand well-being (discussed in Chapter 1)
- set and pursue important life goals (discussed in Chapter 2)
- identify and use signature strengths (discussed in Chapter 3)
- exercise regularly (discussed in Chapter 4)
- incorporate relaxation and mindfulness meditation exercises into our lives (discussed in Chapters 5 and 6)
- engage in activities that promote savouring and flow (discussed in Chapter 7)
- show gratitude and appreciation (discussed in Chapter 8)
- adopt an optimistic perspective (discussed in Chapter 9)
- use systematic approaches to solving problems and finding solutions (discussed in Chapter 10)
- practise kindness and compassion (discussed in Chapter 11)
- enhance our relationships with our partners and our children's other parent (discussed in Chapter 12)
- enhance our relationship with our children (discussed in this chapter)
- cultivate perseverance and grit (discussed in Chapter 14)
- be courageous and re-evaluate our lives positively when we encounter trauma and loss (discussed in Chapter 15)
- practice assertiveness rather than aggression when threatened (discussed in Chapter 16)
- practise forgiveness when wronged (discussed in Chapter 17).

We transmit our values to our children through our actions. They look at what we do. They infer what it is that we value. Then they adopt those values.

## Summary

- **Evolution and parenting.** Evolution has designed us to want nothing but the best for our children so our species will survive.
- **Parenting and well-being.** Parents' well-being depends on the balance of the demands of childrearing, and their available coping resources. When parents have the time, energy, skill, social support and money to meet the demands of rearing children, and children fulfil their needs to be parents and to be connected to their extended family and community, and give their lives meaning and direction, then children enhance parental well-being.
- **Well-being and the family lifecycle.** In western industrialised countries, couples report lower well-being when their children are in infancy, childhood and adolescence. They report higher well-being before the birth of children, and when their children mature into adults. This pattern reflects the fact that, for many families, the demands of childrearing exceed parental resources.

- **Authoritative parenting** involves expecting children to follow direction, and also being warm and responsive to children's emotional needs. Children whose parents adopt this parenting style show high levels of well-being, prosocial behaviour, achievement, motivation, self-reliance, self-control and confidence.
- **Authoritative parenting skills** include making and maintaining a good parent–child relationship, accommodating to your child's temperament, nurturing and rewarding prosocial behaviour, reducing opportunities for problem behaviour and discouraging it, using problem-solving and negotiation skills with adolescents and being a good, consistent role model.
- **Making and maintaining a good parent–child relationship** involves being responsive to infants' needs to help them develop secure attachment, spending 'special time' with children doing activities they enjoy and letting them direct these activities, and actively listening to teenagers to understand their views.
- **Accommodating to your child's temperament** involves developing a good fit between their temperaments and the way you help them develop routines, emotional self-control and skills. Children with difficult temperaments need you to be more patient and thoughtful.
- **Nurturing and rewarding prosocial behaviour** involves catching your children for being good and praising them for this. This should be prioritised over catching your children misbehaving and reprimanding them.
- **Reducing opportunities for problem behaviour** involves clearly communicating expectations and rules, the reasons for them and the consequence for rule-breaking. Consequences for rule-breaking should be fair, and based more on care than control. Know where your children are most of the time, and encourage them to move towards opportunities for prosocial behaviour and away from opportunities for problem behaviour.
- **Negotiation with adolescents.** With young children, it's reasonable to set rules without negotiation. With adolescents, rule setting often involves negotiation.
- **Discouraging problem behaviour.** Ignore problem behaviours that are not too serious. Divert children towards prosocial activities and praise them for doing these. For serious problem behaviour, let your child know that they are good but that their behaviour is not good. With young children who do not respond to requests to follow directives, use time out from reinforcement that concludes with them being praised for showing self-control. With older children, establish contracts for rule-breaking that include opportunities for being rewarded for prosocial behaviour in future.
- **Consistency.** Your children are more likely to follow rules if you and others involved in parenting are consistent with each other about rules, and if rules are consistent from one day to the next.
- **Being a good role model.** Your children are more likely to develop well-being if you are a good role model for the sorts of values and behaviour you expect of them.

## Where are you now?

If you have done the exercises and followed the guidelines in this chapter, you may have found that they have improved the quality of your relationship with your children.

You may wish to read back over the chapter and summarise in your journal the main things that you have learned from this chapter about improving your relationship with your children. You can now decide if you want to include the practices in your relationship with your children in future.

In the next chapter, you will have an opportunity to read about cultivating perseverance and grit. Below are some web resources and books that are relevant to topics you have read about in this chapter.

## Web resources

Authoritative parenting - nine tips video (10:33): www.youtube.com/watch?v=tZ62NAoGnE4
Authoritative parenting video (2:49): www.youtube.com/watch?v=7MOa7YR7H3U
Four parenting styles - three less good styles compared with authoritative parenting video (3:27): www.youtube.com/watch?v=P3gOkKD4txo
Four parenting styles - three less good styles compared with authoritative parenting video (4:15): www.youtube.com/watch?v=nUYOq1__C2Y
Creating secure attachment video (22:09): www.youtube.com/watch?v=w3lB1cSMMFU
Explanation of secure attachment video (4:13): www.youtube.com/watch?v=n2ypDPqs9AO
Child temperament and goodness of fit video (15:20): www.youtube.com/watch?v=-TH_3h_6bgk
Child temperament and goodness of fit video (18:27): www.youtube.com/watch?v=gp3LmoAcfPA
Active listening comedy video (2:58): www.youtube.com/watch?v=4VOubVB4CTU
Active listening with parents and children video (2:23): www.youtube.com/watch?v=kCgZ-6Jrwll
How to change bad to good behaviour video (7:71): www.youtube.com/watch?v=xkao9LETulQ
Good parenting by role modelling video (2:05): www.youtube.com/watch?v=CuNUnnf3OdY
Teens on talking with parents video (2:28): www.youtube.com/watch?v=uPT6-ASRhzo
Parent-teen negotiation video (5:17): www.youtube.com/watch?v=nTXj-zWVzhc
Importance of repairing your mistakes video (7:10): www.youtube.com/watch?v=uBPtp-tFOq8

## Books

Sharry, J. (2010). *Positive parenting: Bringing up responsible, well-behaved and happy children.* Dublin, Ireland: Veritas.
Sharry, J. (2013). *Parenting teenagers: A guide to solving problems, building relationships, and creating harmony in the family.* Dublin, Ireland: Veritas.
Sharry, J. (2016). *Bringing up happy, confident children. A practical guide to nurturing resilience, self-esteem and emotional well-being.* Dublin, Ireland: www.eprint.ie.
Sharry, J., Hampson, G., & Fanning, M. (2005) *Parenting preschoolers and young children.* Dublin, Ireland: Veritas.

# Part 6
# Overcoming challenges

# 14 Grit and perfectionism

Accomplishment is one of the key elements of well-being. That is, our well-being depends on achieving highly valued goals. In Chapter 1, we saw that PERMA theory proposes that well-being involves accomplishment in addition to positive emotion, engagement, relationships and meaning.[1] In this chapter, you will have an opportunity to read about grit which is a character trait that leads to accomplishment, and has been studied extensively in positive psychology. You will also have an opportunity to read about how to overcome problematic perfectionism and social comparisons, which can be obstacles to accomplishment.

## Grit

There is no doubt that achieving highly valued goals depends to some extent on inborn talent. However, talent alone is not enough. Persistent hard work is vital. Accomplishment does not depend on ability or IQ alone; it also depends on effort or character. Professor Angela Duckworth at the University of Pennsylvania has named this aspect of character grit.[2] Grit is the tendency to work towards very long-term goals with a high level of interest and effort. Grit involves focusing on the big picture, and selecting a highly valued, specific long-term goal and pursuing it with passion and persistence. It is critical that the goal is highly valued and of great long-term interest. This sustained interest motivates gritty people to maintain a high level of effort for years and years, pursuing the same goal without changing their target when progress is slow. Gritty people view their work as a marathon, not a sprint. They pace themselves and cultivate stamina. While disappointment, fatigue or episodes of boredom may lead others to change goals, gritty people see these experiences as signals to persist towards their original long-term goals, no matter how many years it takes.

Interest, practice, purpose and hope are the key characteristics of gritty people. Gritty people are passionately interested in their work, and so are intrinsically motivated to persevere at it for a long time. They engage in daily practice to improve their skills so that they become better and better at pursuing their overall goal. They see their work as having a purpose, as making a difference for themselves and others, and hold a strong conviction that their work matters. Finally, they are hopeful and optimistic that no matter how many setbacks they encounter, they will overcome them and achieve their long-term goal. (Optimism was discussed in Chapter 9.)

Angela Duckworth's research has shown that people who score high on the grit scale have very high levels of achievement in school and work.[3] You can complete the grit scale online at http://angeladuckworth.com/grit-scale in less than five minutes and there is no cost. On the grit scale you are invited to rate yourself from 1 to 5 on items such as 'I'm a hard worker', 'I finish whatever I begin' or 'setbacks don't discourage me'. In longitudinal studies that followed people up over a number of years she found that grit predicted surviving the arduous first summer of military training for the US army, retention in the US Special Forces, retention and performance among novice teachers, graduation from Chicago public high schools and reaching the final rounds of the US National Spelling Bee competition. Grit predicted these accomplishments, beyond the level of prediction made by measures of relevant talents such as IQ, standardised achievement test scores and physical fitness. Duckworth found that grit correlated with lifetime educational attainment, and that people who had high grit scores made fewer lifetime career changes and fewer people with high grit scores divorced.

### Cultivating grit

You can cultivate grit by engaging in a number of steps and strategies.[4] These are listed in Box 14.1. Carefully select a main long-term goal that you value very highly. It's useful to distinguish between career goals, goals to do with family life and goals to do with leisure activities. In each domain you may have a single overarching goal; for example, raising your children in the best possible way, achieving something of benefit to the world in your career or making a contribution to you community. Here we are talking mainly about accomplishment-related goals in the work or career domain. (Goals setting was discussed in Chapter 2.)

---

**Box 14.1   Cultivating grit**

- Carefully select a single highly valued long-term goal that is connected to some greater good beyond yourself.
- Expect to work hard towards this goal for years.
- Set or select short- and medium-term goals, to help you achieve your main long-term, highly valued goal.
- Say 'no' to goals, projects and activities that distract you from pursuing your long-term goal.
- Develop a work routine that suits you.
- Work at the limits of your competence, so the challenges you face are at or just beyond the level of your skill.
- Expect mistakes and setbacks.
- Think of mistakes, setbacks, slow progress, frustration and confusion as signals that you are gaining expertise and so are likely to succeed in the long-term.
- Distinguish between setbacks that can be overcome by trying harder and doing 'more of the same', and those that that can be overcome by changing course and 'doing something different'.
- Each day notice how intrinsically rewarding it is for you to put in the *effort* to work for your highly valued goal.
- Each day reward your *efforts* for doing tasks that are not intrinsically rewarding by giving yourself a treat.

---

- Grow a network of family, friends, colleagues, mentors and coaches who understand your passionate pursuit of your goals, believe that your efforts will be successful and support you in your work.
- Regularly take stock of all the steps you have taken towards your highly valued long-term goal; reflect on how much you enjoy this work; check that that you are still on course; and reflect on the additional steps you have to take in future to keep your support network going, and to achieve your overall goal.

The main accomplishment-related goal that you work towards should be connected to some greater good, beyond you and your own self-interest; for example, producing energy in a cost-effective way without using fossil fuels; creating a work environment that is collaborative and supportive; providing a service that makes customers feel valued; alleviating suffering; or promoting learning.

If you have many goals and they are conflicting, you are unlikely to make progress. You will need to identify and prioritise your main goal if you want to be successful in reaching it. One way to do this is to list all the work-related goals that you think are important in your life at the moment. Review these and divide them into long-term, highly valued goals and short- or medium-term goals. Circle the single main long-term goal that you value most highly. Circle about three short- or medium-term goals that that you think will be most helpful in moving you towards your long-term goal. Your long-term goal is like a compass that guides all your work. Your short- and medium-term goals are the things you must do to get there.

Now for the hard part. Decide not to pursue any of the other goals on your list. Decide to say 'no' to them. If you continue to pursue all short- and medium-term goals, projects and activities that come your way, you will be too thinly stretched. Your time will be used up doing lots of little things that are only marginally related to your long-term goal. Progress towards your long-term goal will become very slow. So, only spend time pursuing a relatively small number of short- and medium-term goals that help you make progress towards your long-term goal. Don't be distracted by other activities.

Expect to work hard towards this long-term goal for years. Research on expert performance in sports, chess and other areas suggests that it may take as long as 10,000 hours, or 10 years of daily deliberate practice, to achieve expert performance in any specific area (although there is controversy about the exact number of hours[5]). Because your long-term goal is highly valued, the process of working towards it will be of great interest to you, and this high level of interest will help you to remain motivated for the long-term.

When you work towards your goals, develop a work routine that suits you. This routine may involve plans for what you do each day, week, month or year. Your work routine will also depend on family responsibilities and leisure activities.

When you work towards your goal, try to work at the limits of your competence. You can do this by setting short-term micro-goals that you can just about achieve. Research on developing expertise shows that greatest gains are made when we work at challenging tasks that are at the limit of our competence.[6]

Expect setbacks as you work hard towards achieving your long-term goals. Treat mistakes, setbacks, slow progress, frustration and confusion as signals – not that you should quit – but as signs that you are gaining expertise and so are likely to succeed in the long-term. This way of thinking about setbacks makes them easier to overcome. Mistakes, setbacks and periods where progress proceeds slowly are the rule rather than the exception in the lives of people who accomplish a great deal.[7]

A crucial strategy is distinguishing between setbacks that can be overcome by trying harder and doing 'more of the same', and those that that can be overcome by changing course and 'doing something different'. When setbacks last a long time, gritty people look at all the evidence and ask themselves, 'Will I achieve my goal by continuing in this direction, or by pulling out of this cul-de-sac and changing direction?'

Each day when you are working towards your long-term goal notice how intrinsically rewarding it is for you to *put in the effort*. For aspects of your work that are not intrinsically rewarding, each day reward your efforts by giving yourself a treat. This may be as small as taking a break, phoning friend or having a snack. These strategies of noticing how intrinsically rewarding some aspects of your work is, and of rewarding yourself with treats for aspects of the work which are not intrinsically rewarding, are based on results from two lines of research. Research on intrinsic and extrinsic motivation suggests that often it is more effective not to use external rewards as motivators where tasks are intrinsically rewarding, and to use external rewards (like a snack or a break) for tasks that are not (yet) intrinsically rewarding.[8] Research on achievement indicates that rewarding effort is more effective than rewarding task completion or ability.[9]

We all need support when working for years towards long-term goals. Therefore it's vital to grow a network of family members, friends, colleagues, mentors and coaches who support you in your work. It is important they understand and sympathise with your passionate pursuit of your long-term goal. It is also important that they convey to you that they believe that your efforts will lead to success.

Finally, regularly take stock of what you have achieved and how you are progressing towards your long-term goal. Notice all the steps you have taken towards your highly valued long-term goal. Reflect on how much you enjoy the process of working towards that goal. Check that you are still on course. Think about the additional steps you have to take in future to achieve your overall goal. (Monitoring progress towards goals was discussed in detail in Chapter 2.)

## Perfectionism

Grit involves striving to do our best to successfully achieve long-term goals. Gritty people have high standards. High standards and persistence help us to perform well. When we perform well, this increases our confidence, self-esteem and well-being. There is, therefore, an adaptive form of perfectionism that involves aiming to do your best or to do a 'good enough' job.[10] However, you can get too much of a good thing. The relentless pursuit of high standards, regardless of the cost, and the belief that self-worth is completely dependent on consistently achieving high standards can lead to suffering. These are the hallmarks of problematic perfectionism.[11] Problematic perfectionism may affect one life domain (for example, work), or many domains (for example, work, hygiene, appearance, relationships, house cleanliness etc.). If you have very high standards, you can assess whether your perfectionism is adaptive or problematic with the questionnaire in Box 14.2. If your perfectionism is problematic, there is an opportunity for you to change this by doing the exercises in the remainder of the chapter.

# Box 14.2 Perfectionism questionnaire

You can complete this questionnaire to assess if your perfectionism is adaptive or problematic.

For each item circle the response that applies to you right now.

Sum scores for items 1 to 4 to get your High Standards score.

Sum the scores items 5 to 8 to get your Self-Criticism score.

If you get a High Standards score of 27 or more and a Self-Criticism below 19, then your perfectionism is adaptive.

If you get a High Standards score of 27 or more and a Self-Criticism above 27, then your perfectionism is problematic.

| | | Strongly disagree | Disagree | Slightly disagree | Neutral | Slightly agree | Agree | Strongly agree |
|---|---|---|---|---|---|---|---|---|
| 1 | I have high expectations of myself. | 1 | 2 | 3 | 4 | 5 | 6 | 7 |
| 2 | I set very high standards for myself. | 1 | 2 | 3 | 4 | 5 | 6 | 7 |
| 3 | I expect the best from myself. | 1 | 2 | 3 | 4 | 5 | 6 | 7 |
| 4 | I have a strong need to strive for excellence. | 1 | 2 | 3 | 4 | 5 | 6 | 7 |
| | **High Standards score** | | | | | | | |
| 5 | Doing my best never seems to be enough. | 1 | 2 | 3 | 4 | 5 | 6 | 7 |
| 6 | My performance rarely measures up to my standards. | 1 | 2 | 3 | 4 | 5 | 6 | 7 |
| 7 | I am hardly ever satisfied with my performance. | 1 | 2 | 3 | 4 | 5 | 6 | 7 |
| 8 | I often feel disappointed after completing a task because I know I could have done better. | 1 | 2 | 3 | 4 | 5 | 6 | 7 |
| | **Self-Criticism score** | | | | | | | |

**Note:** Adapted with permission of Taylor & Francis, http://www.tandfonline.com, from: Rice, K. G., Richardson, C. M. E., & Tueller, S. (2014). The short form of the revised almost perfect scale. *Journal of Personality Assessment, 96*(3), 368-379. Copyright © 2014 by Taylor & Francis.

### Brigid, the perfectionist

Brigid suffered from problematic perfectionism. She was married to Sean, and had a teenage daughter, Susan. She also ran her own clothing shop. She demanded the highest standards from herself as a mother, wife, homemaker and shop owner. She tried to spend time with her daughter each day helping her with her homework, because she wanted Susan to do well at school. She expected Susan to do her homework perfectly. These expectations often led to conflict between mother and daughter.

Brigid prided herself on producing different evening meals each day, cooked perfectly from natural ingredients. She did this to please Sean who liked good home cooking. She would cook all the meals for the week on Sundays, put them in the deep freeze, and then serve them each evening to her family.

She kept her home like a show house. She had done the interior design herself, and kept the house exceptionally neat and clean. A number of housemaids whom she had employed to clean her home had left because of the way that Brigid criticised the standards of their cleaning.

Brigid's shop was exceptionally well laid out and her business procedures were all conducted to a high standard. Brigid worked long hours, starting each day at 5.30 or 6.00am so she could get all of her office work (ordering, book keeping etc.) done perfectly before the shop opened at 9.00. Brigid found that, despite her best efforts, she often came home from work later than she wished; did not serve the evening meal until later than planned; spent too much time cleaning up after dinner; got to bed too late; was exhausted when she awoke in the morning; and spent too much time double checking her paperwork at her shop in the morning. This problem with missing deadlines distressed her and reduced her well-being.

In all areas of her life, tasks took far longer than Brigid planned because she double checked everything to make sure it was perfect. She continually worried that her performance as a mother, wife, homemaker and shop owner was not perfect, and criticised herself for this. She was sad much of the time because she thought she was a failure. She believed that she was consistently failing to achieve her standards in all of the important areas of her life. She believed that this meant she was a bad person. She also criticised herself for rarely meeting her deadlines and for the conflict she had with her daughter and housemaids. The conflict with her daughter was about homework. The conflict with her housemaids was about the standards of their cleaning.

Some of the time she felt that her personal style alienated her husband. This also depressed her mood. Brigid longed to have a circle of close friends. Over the years she had lost touch with friends from school and college because she never had time meet with them.

### Problematic perfectionism

People with problematic perfectionism, like Brigid, have exceptionally high standards in most or all important areas or their lives. They believe that if they do not meet these standards, they are worthless. They say things to themselves like, 'I'm no good unless I do tasks perfectly'.

In any episode of problematic perfectionism, this belief that self-worth depends on perfect performance can lead to one of three main scenarios which are diagrammed in

Figure 14.1. In the first of these, perfectionists finish tasks perfectly and on time. If this happens, they feel good briefly because they tell themselves that they have done a perfect job, and they believe that their self-worth depends on perfect performance. However, this increased well-being is transient. Fairly soon, they question their standards. They think things like, 'My standards were not high enough. Anyone could have done what I did'. This self-critical way of thinking inevitably leads them to feel sad. They try to make themselves feel happier by striving for perfection in the next task that they do. And so the vicious cycle of perfectionistic striving and self-criticism continues.

In the second scenario diagrammed in Figure 14.1 perfectionists fail to do tasks perfectly, as judged by their own high standards. In response, they criticise themselves for doing a bad job. They feel sad for failing. They try to overcome the failure and sad feeling by doing tasks more slowly and carefully. They may repeat tasks over and over again, each time trying to do them a little better. They may check and re-check their work to make sure it's perfect. They may compare their performance to that of others, and usually this comparison is with other people who they believe are performing better than them. They may ask other people for reassurance that they are performing well. Inevitably these strategies lead to tasks taking a long time to complete. Deadlines are missed. Perfectionists criticise themselves for missing

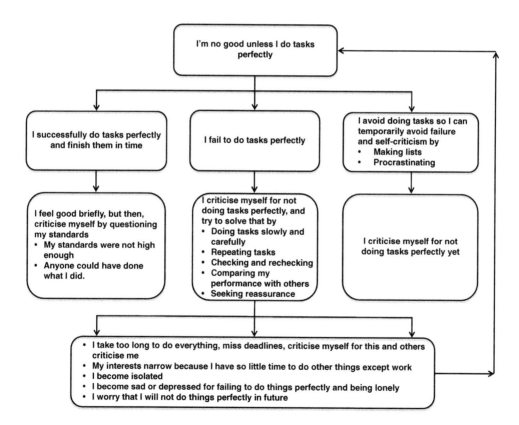

*Figure 14.1* A map of problematic perfectionism.

deadlines. Others may criticise them for this too. They spend more and more time at work, and less and less time with family and friends to compensate for their slowness in completing tasks. Their interests narrow. They become isolated and lonely. They continue to worry that they will not do things perfectly in future and miss more deadlines. They try to make themselves feel happier by striving for perfection in the next task that they do. And so the vicious cycle of perfectionistic striving and self-criticism continues.

In the third scenario diagrammed in Figure 14.1 perfectionists avoid doing tasks so that they can temporarily avoid failing to perform perfectly, and the self-criticism and low mood that goes with this failure. This avoidance may involve postponing doing tasks, or making long to-do lists so that they will not forget things that would prevent them from doing tasks perfectly. This avoidance leads to missed deadlines. Perfectionists may then criticise themselves for not doing tasks on time, or perfectly. Others may also criticise them for missing deadlines. As with the previous scenario, this may lead to a narrowing of interests, isolation, loneliness and worry that they will miss more deadlines in the future. They try to make themselves feel happier by striving for perfection in the next task that they do. And so the vicious cycle of perfectionistic striving and self-criticism continues.

All three scenarios diagrammed in Figure 14.1 lead to reduced well-being and reinforce perfectionistic striving. Some perfectionists extend their high expectations to others. They may be extremely critical of family members, friends and colleagues who do not strive to meet their high standards. This personal style may alienate others and contribute to the social isolation that many perfectionists experience.

### *Perfectionistic thinking traps*

People who engage in problematic perfectionism often fall into thinking traps that make their perfectionism worse. Thinking traps specifically associated with problematic perfectionism are listed in Box 14.3. (Thinking traps were also mentioned in Chapter 9 on optimism, and a longer list of thinking traps associated with pessimism is given in Box 9.1.) With black-and-white thinking, there is a tendency to think in extreme categorical terms. For example, 'if I don't do it perfectly, then I am a complete failure'. In focusing on the negatives and discounting the positives, there is a selective focus on the negative aspects of a situation. For example, 'I made a mistake earlier today so everything I did today was wrong'. Or, 'I got an A on that exam, but it doesn't really count because the exam was too easy'. With overgeneralisation, there is generalisation from one instance to all possible instances. For example, 'because the meal I cooked last night wasn't perfect, this means I am a failure'. With should and must, always and never statements, absolute statements are made about yourself or others. For example, 'I should always be perfect and they should never be unkind'. With double standards, there is one standard for yourself, and another standard for all other people. For example, 'it's OK for others to make an occasional mistake, but not me. I'm a failure for making that one mistake'. These sorts of thinking traps are usually woven into the story that people with problematic perfectionism continually tell themselves. The main theme of this story is that to be a good person, you have to do things perfectly.

## Box 14.3 Thinking traps associated with problematic perfectionism

**Black-and-white thinking.** Thinking in extreme categorical terms. For example, 'If I don't do it perfectly, then I am a complete failure'.

**Focusing on the negatives and discounting the positives.** Selectively focusing on the negative aspects of a situation, filtering out positive aspects of the situation and basing conclusions on this unequal consideration of negative and positive aspects of the situation. For example, 'I made a mistake earlier today so everything I did today was wrong'. Or, 'I got an A on that exam, but it doesn't really count because the exam was too easy'.

**Overgeneralisation.** Generalising from one instance to all possible instances. For example, 'Because the meal I cooked last night wasn't perfect, this means I am a failure'.

**Should and must, always and never statements.** Making absolute statements about how the self or others ought to be always or never. For example, 'I should always be perfect and he should never be unkind'.

**Double standards.** Having one standard for yourself, and another standard for all other people. For example, 'It's OK for others to make an occasional mistake, but not me. I'm a failure for making that one mistake'.

**Note:** These thinking traps are also called cognitive biases or cognitive distortions. Based on Shafran, R., Egan, S., & Wade, T. (2010). *Overcoming perfectionism: A self-help guide using cognitive behavioural techniques.* London: Robinson, and Egan, S., Wade, T., Sharfan, R., & Antony, M. (2014). *Cognitive behavioural treatment of perfectionism.* New York, NY: Guilford.

### The effect of problematic perfectionism on well-being

Problematic perfectionism has a negative impact on well-being. It may lead to a range of mental and physical health problems including anxiety, obsessive compulsive disorder, depression, eating disorders (bulimia and anorexia), chronic fatigue, insomnia, burnout and exacerbation of physical health problems.[12]

### Overcoming problematic perfectionism

There is good evidence from a number of clinical studies that cognitive behavioural treatment programmes can help reduce problematic perfectionism.[13] These programmes focus predominantly on helping people to change their perfectionistic habits and time management skills. They also help challenge the conviction that self-worth is completely dependent on perfect performance.

### Do you want to overcome problematic perfectionism?

If you got high scores on both the high standards and self-criticism scales of the perfectionism questionnaire in Box 14.2, then you may wish to consider reducing your problematic perfectionism. If you wish to do this, look at Figure 14.1 and see if any of the three scenarios in it apply to you. Perhaps they all do at different times. If these scenarios (or approximations to them) describe the way you strive for high standards and criticise yourself for not always reaching them, then there is now an invitation for you to consider the downside of holding onto problematic perfectionism and the advantages of giving it up.

The approach to addressing problematic perfectionism described in the remainder of this chapter has been developed and evaluated by a group of psychologists and found to be exceptionally effective.[14] The group includes Dr Sarah Egan from Curtin University, Australia; Professor Tracy Wade from Flinders University, Australia; Professor Roz Shafran from University College London in the UK; and Professor Martin Antony from Ryerson University, Canada. Their approach is described in a number of books including *Overcoming Perfectionism* and *When Perfect Isn't Good Enough*.

The idea is not to give up your high standards. Rather, it is to uncouple your sense of self-worth from how perfectly you perform tasks or how well you stick to your rules about what constitutes a good job. The idea is to move from a position where you think, 'I am only good if my performance at work is always absolutely perfect and reaches the highest standards' to a position where you think, 'I believe I am good and have a lot to offer others in many areas of my life. I will do a "good enough" job and work towards high standards in a balanced way across all areas of my life'.

### Motivating yourself

To motivate yourself to overcome problematic perfectionism, it's important to convince yourself that it's in your best interests to change. If you wish to motivate yourself, start off by making two lists in your journal.

> List 1: The advantages of holding onto problematic perfectionism and disadvantages of giving up problematic perfectionism.
>
> List 2: The advantages of giving up problematic perfectionism and the disadvantages of not giving up problematic perfectionism.

When you are writing these lists consider various areas of your life, for example:

- Work (including home-making and education)
- Relationships with family, friends and colleagues
- Physical, mental and spiritual health
- Your body shape and appearance
- Sports and leisure activities

Think about the extent to which holding onto or giving up problematic perfectionism will help you achieve highly valued life goals in a balanced way across all areas of your life over the next 12 months. Read through these lists, and ask yourself if you really want to give up problematic perfectionism. If you want to make this change, then read on.

## *ABC analysis of perfectionism*

To get a clearer idea of how often you have episodes of problematic perfectionism, and how these affect your well-being, for a week keep a diary of episodes of problematic perfectionism in your journal. Each time you have an episode of problematic perfectionism write down the time and date when it occurred and an ABC analysis. (ABC analysis is also discussed in Chapters 6 and 9). In these analyses A stands for the **A**ntecedent situation. B stands for the perfectionistic **B**eliefs you had in this situation. Usually these will be about being bad for not achieving very high standards, and will involve some of the thinking traps in Box 14.3. C stands for the **C**onsequences of well-being and behaviour and of having these beliefs. Usually the behavioural consequences of perfectionistic beliefs will be some of those listed in Figure 14.1. These include doing tasks slowly, repeating tasks, checking, comparing, reassurance seeking, making lists or procrastinating. You can record the consequences of your perfectionistic beliefs for well-being by giving a rating on a 10-point scale where 1 stands for low well-being (feeling extremely anxious or sad) and 10 stands for high well-being (for example, feeling very happy and not at all anxious or sad).

Here is an example from Brigid's journal of how to write in your journal about an ABC analysis of a perfectionistic episode.

**Antecedent situation**: I had to write an email to order supplies.

**Beliefs**: I must write the email so it's really clear and friendly or I will be a complete failure.

**Consequences**: I spent 50 minutes writing it, which was far too long for a brief email. My main perfectionistic behaviours were rewriting the email 9 or 10 times, checking and rechecking it was OK and comparing my performance to emails I have seen produced by other people. While I was writing the email and after I sent it, I was worried it wasn't perfect. On a 10-point well-being scale, where 1 is low and 10 is high, I felt about 3 when I had sent the email.

Here is another example from Brigid's diary.

**Antecedent situation**: I had to cook all the evening meals for the week and freeze them on Sunday.

**Beliefs**: If I don't cook a variety of meals perfectly before 10 pm tonight, I will be a complete failure as a wife and mother.

**Consequences**: I spent 3 hours writing menus and cooking to-do lists. I knew this was my way of avoiding starting to actually cook. It gave me some relief from the anxiety I knew I would feel once I started cooking. Once I finally got down to cooking, I got really anxious about not cooking nice enough meals and finished well after 10 pm on Sunday night. I worried that I would be exhausted and possibly make mistakes at work on Monday. I had to get up by about 5 on Monday morning. On a 10-point well-being scale I felt about 2 when I had finished the task. I felt really awful.

By reviewing your diary at the end of the week, you will have an idea of how many episodes of problematic perfectionism you experience in a week. You will be able to see the sorts of **A**ntecedent situations that trigger episodes of problematic perfectionism. You will also be able to identify some of your perfectionistic **B**eliefs. Finally, you will be able to see the sorts of negative **C**onsequences that these beliefs lead to. That is, you will be able to see the perfectionistic behaviour that you engage in and the deterioration in your sense of well-being that arises from these perfectionistic beliefs. You may use this insight into the way your problematic perfectionism reduces your well-being to begin to modify it.

## Surveys

One way to begin to modify problematic perfectionism is to compare your own standards beliefs, behaviour and emotions to those of others. Surveys are a useful strategy for finding out about other people's standards, beliefs, behaviour and emotions. In this context, a useful survey asks a small number of highly specific questions. Usually surveys should contain between three and eight questions. The questions should be designed to test specific beliefs. For example, Brigid conducted an email survey with 10 other shopkeepers to test the belief that to be successful people should work 12 hours a day, with about 4 spent on paperwork. Here are the questions she asked:

- What time do you start and complete work each day?
- How long do you spend on paperwork each day (book keeping, ordering and correspondence)?
- To be successful in retail, how much time do you think people should spend at work and on paperwork each day?

Some examples of survey questions to test out specific beliefs are given in Box 14.4. You may give surveys electronically (for example, by email), by phone or face-to-face. Give your surveys to small numbers of relevant people. For example, Brigid gave her survey to 10 other retailers in her district. The survey results from small numbers of relevant people will be manageable and relevant to you. Surveys will let you know if other people agree with you, or hold different standards and beliefs. Surveys usually show that there is a range of different viewpoints, and not one right answer to each question. Surveys may also prompt you to test your beliefs out with behavioural experiments.

---

### Box 14.4   Example of surveys to test out perfectionistic beliefs

| Belief | Survey questions |
|---|---|
| To be successful you should work 14 hours a day | How many hours a day do you work? |
| | How many hours a day do you think people need to work to be successful? |
| To be successful you should be available by phone or email 24/7, 365 days a year | How often do you answer your phone and emails outside office hours? |
| | How much time do you spend on work-related phone-calls or emails when you are on vacation? |
| | Do you think that you need to be available 24/7, 365 days a year by phone and email to be successful? |
| To be successful you should not have outside interests, and devote all your time to work | How much time do you spend each weekday with your family, friends or doing leisure activities? |
| | At weekends how much time do you spend working? |
| | How much time do you think people can spend with family, friends and on outside interests and be successful? |

| To be successful you should never make mistakes at work | In the past month how many mistakes have you made at work?<br>What sort of mistakes have you made?<br>What do you think of people who make mistakes? |
|---|---|
| To be a good home maker you should keep your home like a show house and clean it thoroughly every day | How often do you clean, vacuum and dust your house, top to bottom?<br>What do you think of people who don't clean their house top to bottom every day? |
| To be a good home maker you should cook really good meals every day | How often do you cook really good meals for your family?<br>What do you think of people that don't cook really good meals for their family every day? |

## Behavioural experiments

Behavioural experiments are a way of testing out whether or not the beliefs you have that motivate your perfectionistic behaviour are 100% true. Brigid did this behavioural experiment to test the belief that repeatedly rechecking her book keeping figures reduces worry.

First, she converted this belief into this prediction: 'If I check my daily book keeping totals 10 times, I will worry less than if I check them twice'.

Second, she did this experiment. On one day she checked her daily book keeping totals 10 times. On the following day she checked them only twice. On both days immediately after checking her book keeping totals, and then one hour later, she wrote down in her journal how worried she was on a scale of 1 to 10, where 1 is not worried and 10 is very worried.

Third, she reviewed the worry ratings she made on both days which were as follows:

| | Worry rating on 10-point scale<br>1 = not worried<br>10 = very worried | Worry rating on 10-point scale<br>1 = not worried<br>10 = very worried |
|---|---|---|
| Day 1. Checked totals 10 times | 8 | 7 |
| Day 2. Checked totals twice | 6 | 4 |

Finally, she drew these conclusions: 'Before the experiment I was 100% convinced that repeatedly rechecking book keeping figures always reduces worry. Now I am only 75% certain that this is true. I am beginning to believe that checking book keeping figures only twice may be less worrying than doing it repeatedly'.

You can use behavioural experiments to test out any perfectionistic beliefs by following the steps in Box 14.5.

## Box 14.5   Behavioural experiments

- Write down the perfectionistic belief.
- Convert the belief into a specific prediction: 'If I do X, then Y will happen'.

- Design and conduct a behavioural experiment to test if the prediction is some-times false. In the experiment make sure to measure the outcome on a scale of 1 to 10.
- Record and review the results.
- Draw a conclusion about how strongly you hold the belief now compared to the start of the experiment, and the revised belief that you are starting to consider: For example, at the start I held the belief 100%, but now only hold it 65%. I am beginning to consider an alternative belief.

Below are some beliefs that people with problematic perfectionism may hold about work and success. Suggestions are given for behavioural experiments that may be conducted to test out the validity of these erroneous beliefs or myths. If you believe any of these myths, there is an opportunity now to test it out by conducting a behavioural experiment.

**The harder you work, the better you will do, and the closer to perfection you will get.** A prediction based on this belief is that if you work really hard on one task and less hard on another similar task, then the task you worked harder on will have a better outcome. To test this prediction, select two work-related emails of about equal importance. Revise and edit one email 20 times and the other one three times. Ask a colleague to rate how clearly they each communicate the intended message on a scale of 1 to 10. You may find there is little dif-ference between them. The belief 'The harder you work, the better you will do, and the closer to perfection you will get' is not always true. Very low effort and very high effort both lead to poorer performance than the optimal level of effort.

**To be successful you have to give up outside interests and work hard.** A prediction based on this belief is that if you devote time to activities other than work, then you will be less successful. You can test this out by comparing your performance at work over two months. In the first month work hard and devote little or no time to family, friends or leisure activities. In the second month, work hard but also plan to spend some time on family, friends or leisure activities. At the end of each of these months, write down what you have achieved at work and in terms of your overall well-being. Rate your overall success for each month. Notice if the month in which you worked hard, to the exclusion of all else, led to better work performance and overall well-being. The belief 'To be successful you have to give up outside interests and work hard' is not always true. Many very successful people, for example Richard Branson, have multiple interests and a balanced lifestyle.

**Mistakes are always bad.** A prediction based on this belief is if you make mistakes, then nothing of value can come from them. You can test this out by writing down all the mis-takes you make over the next week or month, and then recording all the important things you learned from each of these mistakes. You can rate the importance of these things you learned on a scale from 1 to 10. The belief that 'mistakes are always bad' is not true. Mistakes are essential for learning.

**All people notice every little thing that you do wrong and are always critical of you for these.** A prediction based on this belief is that if you make some minor mistakes, then they will be noticed and you will be judged harshly for these errors. To test this out, make a few minor mistakes at work, for example mis-spell a few words in an email or don't vacuum as well as you usually do. Note what percentage of people notice your errors (from 0–100%). Ask those that do notice the errors to rate them on a scale of 1 to 10. The belief that 'all people notice every little thing that you do wrong and are always critical of you for these' is a myth. Most people miss many errors, and when they do notice errors, many are forgiving.

**If you avoid or postpone a problem, it always sorts itself out and you will worry less.** A prediction based on this belief is that if you review the last month or year, then all problems that you ignored or postponed sorted themselves out and you did not worry about them. To test this out, think back over the past year. List all the problems you avoided or postponed addressing that didn't sort themselves out. Write down the negative consequences for you of avoiding or postponing these problems. Rate how much you worried about them on a scale of 1 to 10. Some problems sort themselves out if you don't solve them. However, others get worse, and many cause significant worry.

### Time management for delaying starting and finishing

Delaying starting things (or procrastination) and delaying finishing things are common problems associated with problematic perfectionism. For example, Brigid often delayed starting her cooking on Sunday by spending a lot of time on menus and to-do lists. She did this because she believed that if her cooking wasn't perfect, she would be a failure. The more she procrastinated, the more likely it was that she would have to rush to finish her cooking, and possibly spoil it. Or if she didn't rush to finish it, and delayed finishing it so it was perfect, she would get to bed late and make errors in her work the next day because of exhaustion. This in turn would reinforce her determination to strive harder the next day to do her work perfectly and avoid 'being a failure'. From this you can see that procrastination and delaying finishing are part of a vicious cycle of perfectionistic striving and self-criticism that keep problematic perfectionism going.

There are a few strategies that are helpful in managing delaying starting and finishing. Break big tasks down into smaller tasks. Make a timetable for doing each of the smaller tasks. Allow yourself a reasonable amount of time to do each of the smaller tasks. Aim to do them within the allotted time, and to do a 'good enough' job, rather than a perfect job. Allow a brief break between each of the smaller tasks. Each time you complete one of the small elements of the big task on time, reward yourself with a small treat during the break.

If you wish, set this time management task up as a behavioural experiment. Your prediction may be that if you use this time management system you will feel very distressed because the work you produce will be 'good enough' and not perfect. You may try using this system for one job and your usual work practices for another similar job. Make well-being ratings on a scale of 1 to 10 after using each system and compare these. Notice the effect of this time management system on your well-being immediately after and one hour after doing these two jobs. You may find that this time management system leads to greater efficiency and well-being.

### Developing flexible beliefs: ABCDE analysis

You may use an ABCDE analysis of episodes of problematic perfectionism to challenge perfectionistic beliefs and begin to develop more flexible beliefs. (ABCDE analysis was discussed in Chapter 9 on optimism.) When you do an ABCDE analysis, here is what A, B, C, D and E stand for.

> **A** stands for the **Antecedent event** that triggered problematic perfectionism.
>
> **B** stands for your perfectionistic **Beliefs** about the situation.
>
> **C** stands for the **Consequences** for your well-being (on a 10-point scale), and perfectionistic behaviour.
>
> **D** stands for **Disputation**.
>
> **E** stands for **Evaluation** in terms of improved well-being and reduced perfectionistic behaviour.

With disputation you examine the evidence for your perfectionistic beliefs. You ask yourself: What is the evidence for the perfectionistic beliefs about the situation and does this evidence show that these beliefs are 100% true?

You consider if this evidence suggests that alternative, more flexible beliefs may be true. That is, you ask yourself: Is there an alternative, more flexible way of viewing the situation? What would a friend say to me about this?

If you cannot decide whether there is more evidence for a perfectionistic or flexible belief, decide which belief is most useful for you in terms of improving your well-being and achieving your valued goals.

Let us return to the example of Brigid's episode of perfectionistic behaviour mentioned earlier, and do an ABCDE analysis of this episode.

> **Antecedent situation**: Brigid had to write an email to order supplies.
>
> **Beliefs**: Brigid believed that she must write the email so it was really clear and friendly or she would be a complete failure.
>
> **Consequences**: Her main perfectionistic behaviours were rewriting the email 9 or 10 times, checking and rechecking it was OK, and comparing her performance to emails she had seen produced by other people, all of which took her 50 minutes. On a 10-point well-being scale she felt about 3 when she had sent the email.
>
> **Disputation**: Brigid asked herself: What is the evidence that she would be a complete failure if she didn't write the email really clearly and in a friendly tone? What would a friend say to her? She thought that a friend would tell her that her shop had been making a good profit for the past year. Many customers had become regulars, and commented on how much they liked doing their shopping there. Most suppliers responded to her emails in a polite, friendly way. She concluded that this evidence showed that even if she wrote a bad email, she was not a complete failure.

**Evaluation**: Brigid found that after this exercise her well-being increased from 3 to 6 and she thought that next time around she would spend less time revising her emails to suppliers.

### Disputing and thought traps

When you are disputing perfectionistic beliefs, watch out for the thought traps listed in Box 14.3.

**Black-and-white thinking.** If your beliefs involve black-and-white thinking, remember that in most areas of life things come in shades of grey. Look for evidence that you fall somewhere on a continuum between being a success and being a failure. For example, if the belief is that you are either a success or a failure, then look for evidence that you are usually partially successful, or very successful sometimes.

**Focusing on the negatives and discounting the positives.** If your perfectionistic beliefs involve focusing on the negatives and discounting the positives, then broaden your attention and look for positives. For example, if you believe, 'My work was a complete disaster today, therefore I'm a total disgrace!' try to recall some things that you did well today.

**Overgeneralisation.** If you overgeneralise from one instance to all possible instances, remember that one swallow doesn't make a summer. If you believe that 'I messed up today, so I will always mess up', remember all the days when you didn't mess up, and think about how this does not support the conclusion that you will always mess up in future.

**Should and must, always and never.** If you find yourself making absolute statements that involve should and must, or always and never, make them less absolute. For example, instead of believing 'I should always be perfect and he should never be unkind', try thinking 'I would like to be very good some of the time, and for him to be nice some of the time'. There is rarely any evidence that we or others should or must always be one way and not another. It is usually a matter of preference. Saying statements that begin with 'I would like if sometimes . . .' or 'I would prefer if usually . . .' makes us feel less stressed than making absolute statements that include words like must or should, always and never. For this reason they are more useful. It's therefore better for our well-being to replace beliefs that involve absolute statements with beliefs stated as preferences.

**Double standards.** If your perfectionistic beliefs involve having one standard for yourself, and another standard for all other people, try applying the same standard to yourself and others. For example, instead of thinking 'It's OK for others to make an occasional mistake, but not me' try changing to 'It's OK for everybody to make mistakes sometimes, including me'. There is rarely any evidence that it's fair or justified to apply one exceptionally high standard to ourselves, and a much lower standard to all other people. Having double standards is stressful, unfair and decreases well-being. For this reason, its preferable to have a single set of standards for ourselves and others.

In the exercise in Box 14.6 you are invited first to find out how perfectionism affects your well-being by doing an ABC analysis of all problematic perfectionistic episodes for a week. Then, to begin to develop a more flexible thinking style, for the next week, each day do an ABCDE analysis of at least one situation that triggered problematic perfectionism.

## Box 14.6   Developing a flexible (non-perfectionistic) thinking style

To get a sense of how perfectionism affects your well-being, write down in your journal an ABC analysis of all problematic perfectionistic episodes for a week.

In an ABC analysis, here is what A, B and C stand for.

**A** stands for the **Antecedent event** that triggered problematic perfectionism.

**B** stands for your perfectionistic **Beliefs** about the situation. This is the story you told yourself about being bad for not achieving high standards and may involve thinking traps listed in Box 14.4 (black-and-white thinking, selective attention, overgeneralisation, should and must statements, and double standards).

**C** stands for the **Consequences** for your well-being (on a 10-point scale), and perfectionistic behaviour (doing tasks slowly, repeating tasks, checking, comparing, reassurance seeking, making lists or procrastinating).

After a week, review the ABC analyses in your journal and note

- How often you had problematic perfectionistic episodes
- The sorts of situations that trigger these
- Your main perfectionistic beliefs
- The effects of these in terms of perfectionistic behaviour and reduced well-being.

To develop a more flexible thinking style, for the next week each day do an ABCDE analysis of at least one situation that triggered problematic perfectionism

When you do an ABCDE analysis, here is what A, B, C, D and E stand for.

**A** stands for the **Antecedent event** that triggered problematic perfectionism.

**B** stands for your perfectionistic **Beliefs** about the situation.

**C** stands for the **Consequences** for your well-being (on a 10-point scale), and perfectionistic behaviour.

**D** stands for **Disputation.**

Dispute your pessimistic beliefs by examining the evidence, alternatives and usefulness related to these beliefs.

- What is the **evidence** for the perfectionistic beliefs about the situation and does this evidence show that these beliefs are 100% true?
- Is there an **alternative**, more flexible way of viewing the situation? What would a friend say?

- If you cannot decide whether there is more evidence for a perfectionistic or flex-ible belief, decide which belief is **most useful** for you in terms of improving your well-being and achieving your valued goals.

  **E** stands for **Evaluation**. Evaluate the extent to which using disputation improved your well-being and reduced your perfectionistic behaviour.

**Note:** Based on Shafran, R., Egan, S., & Wade, T. (2010). *Overcoming perfectionism: A self-help guide using cognitive behavioural techniques.* London: Robinson, and Egan, S., Wade, T., Sharfan, R., & Antony, M. (2014). *Cognitive behavioural treatment of perfectionism.* New York: Guilford.

## Basing self-worth on your whole life (not just work)

For people who engage in problematic perfectionism mainly at work, most of their sense of self-worth comes to depend on how much they accomplish in their career. They put all their eggs in one basket. This can have a negative effect on well-being. If things do not go well at work, they judge themselves to have failed and feel bad, even though things may be going well in other areas of their lives. If this sounds familiar, you may wish to do the following exercise.

In this exercise, the idea is to find out how judgements about self-worth are made now, and if there is a more balanced way to make them that you would prefer to work towards. Let's illustrate this with the case of Kevin. Kevin reflected on the relative importance of dif-ferent areas of his life in contributing to his self-criticism, or judgements he made about his self-worth. He believed his overall self-worth as a person depended mainly on his work performance; a bit on family relationships; and a little on relationships with friends. He gave these percentage weights to these three areas:

- Work: 70%
- Family: 20%
- Friends: 10%

Notice that the percentages sum to 100%. (This sort of list can also be drawn as a pie chart with three slices: a 70% slice for work; a 20% slice for family; and a 10% slice for friends.)

After some reflection Kevin decided that he would prefer if judgements about his self-worth were spread more evenly across more areas. Here is a list of areas that he considered.

- Work
- Home-making
- Education
- Relationships with family
- Relationships with friends
- Relationships with colleagues
- Physical health
- Mental health

- Spiritual health
- Body shape and appearance
- Sports
- Leisure activities
- Community involvement
- Travel

After reflecting on his preferences, Kevin drew up the following more balanced list of areas and percentage weights on which he wished to make judgements about his self-worth in future:

- Work: 40%
- Family: 20%
- Friends: 20%
- Sports: 10%
- Community involvement: 10%

When he found himself not reaching his high standards at work and telling himself that he was a complete failure, he disputed this by considering the successes he was having in other areas of his life with family and friends, at sports and with community involvement.

If you would like to do this exercise, reflect on the relative importance of different areas of your life in contributing to your self-criticism, or judgements you make about your self-worth. Give a percentage weighting to each area. Now draw up a preferred list of areas and percentage weights, so that your judgements about self-worth are spread more evenly across more areas. If you find that you do not reach your standards at work and view yourself as a complete failure, disputed this belief by considering the successes you have in other areas of your life.

### Self-compassion and self-criticism

Self-criticism is central to problematic perfectionism. Unfortunately, self-criticism makes us feel bad, reduces our confidence and makes it harder to learn useful lessons from our mistakes. An important challenge in addressing problematic perfectionism is developing self-compassion and reducing self-criticism.

Throughout our development we internalise the compassionate and critical voices of our parents, carers, teachers, coaches and others. Unfortunately for people with problematic perfectionism, the internalised critical voices speak louder than the compassionate voices. What follows are some exercises to help strengthen your internalised self-compassionate voice, and reduce the impact of your internalised self-critical voice.

**Identify the self-critical voice.** Review the diary you kept in your journal for a week in which you recorded ABC analyses of episodes of problematic perfectionism. For each episode, look at the beliefs you wrote down. That is, the stories you told yourself about having to be perfect. These are examples of your internalised self-critical voice. If you wish, in your journal keep an ABC diary of episodes of problematic perfectionism for a further week and try to identify more of your self-critical beliefs. For Brigid, some of the things her internalised self-critical voice said were:

- I made a mistake at work, so I'm no good.
- I didn't do the book keeping perfectly, so I'm a complete failure.
- I didn't finish work on time and will be late home, I'm a failure as a mother.
- My cooking is not perfect, so I am a terrible wife.
- I never get to see my friends at the club anymore, I'm a useless friend.
- I look so old and frumpy. I'm an awful person.

**Origin of the self-critical voice.** Write down in your journal where you think your self-critical voice came from. Can you remember situations in which your parents, carers, teachers, coaches or others said these critical things to you when you were growing up? The strength of our self-critical voice depends upon the emotional intensity of the critical messages we received as children and how significant the people who gave us these messages were in our lives. For example, if your parents were very angry or cold when you didn't do well at school or in sports, then this may have a bigger impact on you than if a classmate criticised you. The strength of our self-critical voice also depends on how sensitive we were to picking up and internalising these messages. So if you were a sensitive child, then that influenced how strongly you internalised critical messages from others.

**Identify your self-compassionate voice.** Reflect on the values that are important to you in strong friendships. That is, think about how would you like to treat your friends. Would you like to treat them with acceptance, compassion, forgiveness, generosity, hope, kindness, support and respect? To develop your self-compassionate voice, make a commitment to apply the values that are important in friendship to the way you treat yourself. That is, treat yourself with acceptance, compassion, forgiveness, generosity, hope, kindness, support and respect. In practice this would involve making the following commitments to yourself.

- Acceptance: I accept myself as a good person, no matter what I achieve.
- Compassion: I care for myself when I am feeling bad. I don't criticise myself.
- Forgiveness: When I make mistakes, I forgive myself.
- Generosity: I give myself the benefit of the doubt.
- Hope: I believe in myself, even when I fail.
- Kindness: I am kind to myself, and gentle with myself when I feel bad.
- Support: When the going is tough, I support myself and don't criticise myself.
- Respect: Whether I succeed or fail at a task, I respect myself.

**Practice self-compassion.** Over the next week when you experience episodes of problematic perfectionism, write down an ABC analysis of the episode. Then respond to the episode by writing down a self-compassionate statement. Finally, rate your well-being on a 10-point scale to see the effect of practising self-compassion on your well-being.

To illustrate practising self-compassion let us return to Brigid's ABC analysis of an episode of problematic perfectionism mentioned earlier.

**Antecedent situation:** I had to cook all the evening meals for the week and freeze them on Sunday.

**Beliefs:** If I don't cook a variety of meals perfectly before 10 pm tonight, I will be a complete failure as a wife and mother.

**Consequences:** I spent 3 hours writing menus and cooking to-do lists. I knew this was my way of avoiding starting to actually cook, and gave me some relief from the anxiety I knew I would feel once I started cooking. Once I finally got down to cooking, I got really anxious about not cooking nice meals and finished well after 10 pm on Sunday night. I worried that I would be exhausted and possibly make mistakes at work on Monday, because I had to get up by about 5 on Monday morning. On a 10-point well-being scale I felt about 2 when I had finished the task. I felt really awful.

**Self-compassionate statement:** I care deeply for my family, and have put in a lot of effort to make sure they will have good evening meals all next week. That was a kind thing to do. I forgive myself for taking too long to do this, and will take it a little easier tomorrow at work if I am tired.

**Effects of self-compassionate statement:** On a 10-point well-being scale I felt about 5 when I had been compassionate to myself. I felt a bit better.

Another option for dealing with self-critical thoughts is to mindfully observe them and not react to them. Mindfulness is discussed in Chapter 6.

### *Caveat*

If your problematic perfectionism and related difficulties do not improve when you use the techniques described in this book, then it is a good idea to seek treatment from a mental health professional skilled in treating the sorts of challenges you face. Your GP may be able to arrange a referral to a clinical psychologist or psychotherapist who can help you.

### Social comparison

While perfectionism involves comparing our performance to very high internal standards, upward social comparison involves comparing our performance to people who are performing better than ourselves.[15] Upward social comparison can occur in all areas of life. We can compare our bodies and our attractiveness to others who are fitter, slimmer and more attractive. We can compare our work performance or achievements in sports to that of others who are performing at a higher level than we are.

Upward social comparison can be inspiring or demoralising. It is inspiring if we think, 'I could be like that some day!'. It can be demoralising if we think, 'I'll never be as good as that!'. Idealising successful sports stars and aspiring to be like them is an example of inspirational upward social comparison. Trying to keep up with the Joneses is an example of demoralising upward social comparison, especially if your earning potential is not as high as the neighbours who you compare ourselves to. Demoralising upward social comparisons inevitably lead us to conclude that we are not as good as some other people, and this conclusion lowers our mood and decreases our well-being.

Research shows that making upward social comparisons that involve contrasting the self to others who have a more favourable position has a negative effect on well-being in a range of areas including school, work, family life, appearance, aging and adjustment to chronic illness.[16] People with problematic perfectionism typically engage in this sort of demoralising upward social comparison.

Demoralising upward social comparisons are based on *contrasting* ourselves to others. Inspiring upward social comparisons are based on *identifying* ourselves with people who we aspire to be like. These processes of contrast and identification also operate when we make downward social comparisons. When we contrast ourselves with people who have not accomplished as much as we have, this can lift our mood because we focus on how much more we have accomplished than them. However, when we identify with people who have not accomplished as much as we have, this can depress our mood because we realise that we could become like them by losing some or all of what we have achieved.

If you wish to use social comparison to enhance your well-being, use an identification strategy for upward social comparisons and a contrast strategy for downward social comparisons.[17]

When making upward social comparisons, only make them with people who you can identify with and who you aspire to be like. Compare yourself to your heroes. Don't make upward social comparisons where you contrast your lesser accomplishments with the greater accomplishments of others, because this will lower your mood. Don't compare yourself to the Joneses, or you will be disappointed that you can't keep up with them.

When you make downward social comparisons, focus on how much more you have accomplished than others. Notice how much more successful you are in your family life, at work and in your health, attractiveness and well-being. Don't dwell on the possibility that you could lose your accomplishments and become like them.

## Summary

- **Grit** is the tendency to work towards very long-term goals with a high level of interest and effort. Grit leads to accomplishment, which is a key element of well-being in Seligman's PERMA theory.
- To **cultivate grit**, work at the limits of your competence towards a single highly valued long-term goal that is connected to some greater good. Develop short- and medium-term goals, a work routine that suits you, a support network, a positive way of thinking about setbacks and a system for regularly reviewing progress. Value intrinsically rewarding aspects of your work and reward your efforts for doing tasks that are not intrinsically rewarding.
- **Adaptive and problematic perfectionism.** Perfectionism involves holding high standards. Perfectionism is problematic when high standards are coupled with excessive self-criticism.
- **Negative consequences of problematic perfectionism** include a vicious cycle of perfectionistic striving and self-criticism, doing task extremely slowly and carefully, and avoiding tasks. These may lead to missed deadlines, a narrowing of interests, isolation, low mood and worry.
- **Perfectionistic thinking traps** include black-and-white thinking, focusing on the negatives and discounting the positives, overgeneralisation, making absolute statements and holding double standards.

- **Perfectionistic beliefs.** The following are some beliefs associated with problematic perfectionism: The harder you work, the better you will do, and the closer to perfection you will get. To be successful you have to give up outside interests and work hard. Mistakes are always bad. All people notice every little thing that you do wrong and are always critical of you for these. If you avoid or postpone a problem, it always sorts itself out and you will worry less.
- **Surveys.** You may survey people by email in situations similar to yours with six to eight questions to test the validity of your perfectionistic beliefs.
- **Behavioural experiments.** You may check if perfectionistic beliefs are 100% true by conducting behavioural experiments to test predictions which are based on perfectionistic beliefs.
- You may use **ABCDE analysis** to test out the effects of challenging perfectionistic beliefs. In ABCDE analysis A stands for the **A**ntecedent event that triggered an episode of problematic perfectionism. B stands for your perfectionistic **B**eliefs about the situation. C stands for the **C**onsequences for your well-being (on a 10-point scale), and perfectionistic behaviour. D stands for **D**isputation where you examine the evidence for your perfectionistic beliefs. E stands for **E**valuation in terms of improved well-being and reduced perfectionistic behaviour.
- **Base self-worth on more than one life area.** If all your self-worth is based on one life area, consider the extent to which you would like to base self-worth on a range of areas such as home-making, education, relationships, health, leisure activities, community involvement or travel.
- **Self-compassion.** When you experience self-criticism, counter this with self-compassion and treat yourself with acceptance, compassion, forgiveness, generosity, hope, kindness, support and respect.
- **Social comparison.** Inspiring upward social comparisons are based on *identifying* ourselves with people who we aspire to be like who have achieved exceptionally well. Demoralising upward social comparisons are based on *contrasting* ourselves to others who have achieved more than we have. To enhance well-being use identification for upward social comparisons and a contrast for downward social comparisons.

## Where are you now?

If you have done the exercises in the first part of this chapter you have begun to develop grit. In the long run grit enhances your accomplishments and well-being.

Having high standards is important for achieving success at work. However, when judgements of self-worth are completely based on achieving these high standards, this leads to problematic perfectionism. If you found that problematic perfectionism is part of your personal style and read the second half of the chapter, then you have discovered that there are a series of exercises that you can do to address this problem.

You may want to read back over the chapter and summarise in your journal the main things that you have learned about grit, problematic perfectionism and social comparison.

In the next chapter we will consider courage, fear and posttraumatic growth. Below are some web resources and books that are relevant to topics you have read about in this chapter.

## Web resources

Angela Lee Duckworth talking about grit: the power of passion and perseverance video (5:12): www.youtube.com/watch?v=H14bBuluwB8
Grit animated video (6:11): www.youtube.com/watch?v=sWctLEdIgi4
Martin Antony talking about perfectionism video (18:50): www.youtube.com/watch?v=TTbnBmwKuCI

## Books

Antony, M., & Swinson, R. (2009). *When perfect isn't good enough* (Second Edition). Oakland, CA: New Harbinger.
Duckworth, A. (2016). *Grit: The power of passion and perseverance.* New York, NY: Scribner.
Dweck, C. (2006). *Mindset: The new psychology of success.* New York, NY: Ballantine books.
Shafran, R., Egan, S., & Wade, T. (2010). *Overcoming perfectionism: A self-help guide using cognitive behavioural techniques.* London, UK: Robinson.

# 15 Courage, fear and posttraumatic growth

In this chapter, you will read about three related themes: courage, fear and posttraumatic growth. You will read about how to be courageous. You will read about how to courageously overcome anxiety and fear. You will also read about how to benefit from life crises and trauma.

Courage is the capacity to move towards valued goals in the face of threat. Diving into a stormy sea to rescue a floundering swimmer is courageous. The valued goal is saving a life, and the threat is drowning. Saying something unpopular, which we strongly believe in, is also courageous. The valued goal is standing up for what we believe in, and the threat is being ostracised. Facing threats to our safety and security is risky. In these two examples the risks are that we might drown or be ostracised. Usually we take the risk of acting courageously to reduce threat. In the two examples the threats we are trying to reduce are loss of life and violation of strongly held beliefs.

When we are faced with a threat to our safety or security most of us feel scared or angry. Automatically our bodies get ready for us to run away, to fight or to become less noticeable to potential predators by making us stay very still. This automatic physiological process is called the fight / flight / or freeze response.[1] (This was mentioned in Chapter 10 on problem-solving and solution-finding.) The response begins in a primitive area of the brain – the amygdala – and through a complex chain reaction triggers the release of adrenaline and cortisol into the blood stream. There is an associated cascade of physiological responses that will be familiar to you. These include increased heart rate, increased muscle tension and increased strength as well as many other transient physiological changes. This automatic fight / flight / or freeze response has developed over millions of years of evolution. Our ancestors whose bodies automatically turned on the fight / flight / or freeze response when faced with threats survived. If this response didn't automatically kick in, when faced with a threatening predator, then those early humans didn't survive. Threating predators, natural disasters and other dangers ended their lives.

In the short-term, and for many types of physical threats, the fight / flight / or freeze response motivates and energises us to take very adaptive courses of actions. For example, if we accidentally step from the path onto a busy street and a car toots its horn at us, then the fight / flight / or freeze response may energise us to step back onto the path very quickly, preventing us from being knocked down. However, in the long-term, often a response to threat other than running away, fighting or freezing is necessary for us to achieve our valued goals. This is where courage comes into play. Courage is required to intentionally move towards valued goals, even though this places us at risk of harm because the threat is still present. It is still making us feel scared and is still making our bodies 'rev up'.

Courage involves (1) intentionally taking a course of action (2) that puts us at risk of harm (3) because of the presence of a threat, (4) despite feeling extremely frightened, anxious and/or angry, (5) to achieve valued goals, usually by reducing threat.[2] Distinctions are made between different types of courage. Physical courage is required to face threats where there is risk of injury or death, for example involvement in firefighting, law enforcement, bomb-disposal or military combat. Moral courage is necessary to take courses of action such as civil disobedience or whistle blowing that may lead to social condemnation. Psychological courage is essential for being assertive in awkward social situations, confronting workplace bullying, leaving abusive relationships and facing fears associated with mental or physical health problems like anxiety or chronic pain, or addiction.

## Engaging in courageous action

The process of engaging in courageous action involves some or all of the elements in the sequence in Box 15.1. Studies of courage in military situations show that we can strengthen our courage by having leaders who are good role models for coping with threatening situations, having the support of a small cohesive group, having prior training in facing specific risks and receiving recognition from respected people for acting bravely.[3] These external supports facilitate the development of skills for carrying out tasks necessary to reduce risk, confidence in using these skills when under threat, mental toughness, persistence and resilience in the face of adversity, and values such as duty, honour and loyalty which motivate courageous behaviour.[4]

---

### Box 15.1   Engaging in courageous action

**Prepare**

- Work with leaders who are courageous role models.
- Build a team who will support you when facing threats.
- Train in skills needed to manage specific threats.

**Plan**

- Use problem-solving skills to plan the most useful way to reduce the specific threat you are about to face.
- Break a big problem into a number of smaller ones.
- Brainstorm possible solutions to each of these.
- Consider the payoff and price or risks associated with each potential solution.
- Select the one that will be most useful in reducing the threat.
- Avoid the extremes of cowardice or reckless risk-taking.

**Take courageous action**

- Follow your plan.
- Modify your plan if it is ineffective, or the situation demands it.
- Use coping strategies to encourage yourself and manage fear in the face of threat.
  - ○ Do brief relaxation (in Box 5.3) or mindfulness exercises (in Box 6.6).
  - ○ Remind yourself of past successes when you have been courageous.
  - ○ Think of the good you will do, or the people you will protect by reducing the threat.
  - ○ Think of how your courageous action will help you achieve your valued goals.
  - ○ Think of how your team support you, and the fact that you do not want to let them down.
  - ○ Think of brave role models.

**Debrief**

- Evaluate how effective your courageous action has been in reducing threat.
- Reflect on what your courageous action says about you as a person with specific valued goals.
- Accept recognition from respected people for acting bravely.

In addition to these broad factors which prepare us for courageous action, in any given situation requiring courage, planning is a critical first step. Before engaging in a courageous action, we use problem-solving skills to plan the most useful way to reduce threat. (Problem-solving was discussed in Chapter 10.) We break big problems into smaller ones. We brainstorm possible solutions. We consider the payoff and price or risks associated with each potential solution. We then select the one that will be most useful in achieving our valued goal or reducing risk. We aim to avoid the extremes of cowardice or reckless risk-taking.

For example, Benny heard a little girl screaming from the upstairs window of an isolated two-storey farm house while he was cycling home on a sparsely populated country road. There was smoke coming from the window, and clearly the house had caught fire. Benny broke the big problem – a girl trapped in a house fire – into two smaller problems: (1) putting out the fire, and (2) rescuing the child.

To deal with the fire there were two main options: (1) call the fire brigade, or (2) try to put out the fire himself. The payoff for calling the fire brigade was that it would be effective. The price for calling the fire brigade was that a lot of damage would be done to the house because it would take some time for the fire brigade to arrive. The payoff for trying to put the fire out himself was that he could act quickly and prevent damage to the house. The price for trying to put the fire out himself was that he might not be effective, and it would delay him rescuing the child. On balance, he decided to call the fire brigade and focus most of his energy on rescuing the girl. When he called the fire brigade on his mobile phone, he was informed that they would arrive within 30 minutes.

For the second problem, Benny considered two options: (1) taking the girl down the stairs, (2) taking the girl down from the window using an outside ladder. The payoff of taking the girl down the stairs was that it would be quick. The price of this option was that he might have to break down the front door if it was locked, and he and the girl might get burned or suffocate if the fire in the house was widespread. The payoff of using an outside ladder was that there was little risk of being burned or choking. The price of this option was that it might take a lot of time to find a ladder; there might not be one in the outhouse; and they might fall off the ladder and be injured. On balance, he decided to use the stairs.

As we embark on courageous action, ideally, we follow our plan. However, if it is ineffective or if the situation changes and our plan does not fit the demands of the situation, we will need to modify it. In the example involving Benny and the little girl, his plan was to use the stairs. He quickly and effectively kicked in the front door, and following his plan went upstairs. However, as he arrived on the upstairs landing, he found that the fire prevented him from reaching the room where the girl was trapped. He had to modify his plan. He ran downstairs and over to the outhouse, where he found a ladder and used this to climb to the window and rescue the little girl.

When we engage in courageous action, we may use a range of coping strategies to encourage ourselves and manage the anxiety and fear we experience in the face of threat. We may remind ourselves of our past successes when we have been courageous. We may think of the good we will do, or the people we are protecting by being brave. If we are acting as part of a team, we may think of how they support us and the fact that we do not want to let them down. We may think of people who have been valued role models of bravery for us. We may think of how the course of action we are taking will reduce risk, help us achieve our valued goals, be true to our values and help us become the sort of individual we aspire to be.

Afterwards we evaluate how effective we have been. We reflect on what it says about us as a person that we engaged in courageous action. This is how we reward ourselves for being courageous and strengthen our belief in ourselves as a courageous individual. If we are offered recognition from people we respect for acting bravely, accepting this recognition will strengthen our courage in future.

When faced with a threat, the fight / flight / or freeze response may catapult us into anxiety or impulsive anger or rage. To be courageous we must tolerate these feelings of fear and anger and prevent ourselves from impulsively avoiding the situation or flying into an uncontrolled rage. Courage involves channelling our fight / flight / or freeze energy into appropriate constructive action. In awkward social situations, giving an assertive response may be the most courageous way to proceed. When there are injustices or unethical practices within organisations, whistle blowing may be the most appropriate courageous response. We may channel our anger into civil disobedience where social injustice demands a courageous response. In law enforcement and military combat, anxiety and anger control are essential for thoughtful courageous action which effectively reduces threat.

Anxiety and anger prevent us from engaging in these sorts of flexible responses. In the next section of this chapter we will consider how best to manage anxiety and fear. In the next chapter, we will consider anger management, along with the related theme of assertiveness.

## Fear and anxiety

Fear and anxiety are complex phenomena.[5] When we experience fear or anxiety there are distinct changes in

- Feeling
- Physiological sensations
- Thinking and
- Behaviour.

### Feeling

Fear and anxiety involve feelings that may range from mild apprehension to extreme terror.

### Physiological sensations

Fear and anxiety involve all the physiological sensations associated with the fight / flight / or freeze reaction. These include increased heart and respiration rates, muscle tension, sweating, difficulty concentrating and so forth.

### Thinking

Anxiety and fear also affect thought processes. We become hypervigilant for signs of danger. People with anxiety disorders have a distinctive thinking style. (Anxiety disorders will be described in the next section.) People with anxiety disorders are prone to see danger where it may not in fact be present. They are hypersensitive to threats to safety and security. They are prone to the thinking traps listed in Box 15.2, especially disaster forecasting. This is where the future is assumed to hold many dangers, based on limited evidence. For example, thinking 'My heart is racing. I must be going to have a heart attack. I'm going to die. I can't stand it. I can't stop these thoughts. I'm losing my mind'.

---

**Box 15.2   Thinking traps that fuel anxiety**

**Disaster forecasting.** Assuming that the worst possible outcome is inevitable, on the basis of limited evidence. For example, a person with panic disorder thinking 'This tightness is my chest is a heart attack'; or a person with generalised anxiety disorder thinking 'I may be fired for making a mistake'.

   **Jumping to conclusions.** Quickly reaching a conclusion that some dreaded outcome will occur without considering alternatives and contradictory evidence. For example, a person with exam anxiety thinking 'I'm unsure about this exam question, so I'll definitely fail the exam'; or a person with health anxiety thinking 'This pain in my back is definitely a spinal tumour, so I haven't long to live'.

   **Tunnel vision.** Hypervigilance for potential threats, while ignoring signs of safety. For example, a person with obsessive compulsive disorder thinking 'That one spot of

---

urine on the public toilet floor means the whole bathroom is covered with germs, so I will definitely be contaminated'.

**Near-sightedness.** Assuming that a threat is about to happen in the very near future. For example, a person with generalised anxiety disorder thinking 'I will definitely be fired today'.

**Emotional reasoning.** Assuming that the more intense the subjective feeling of anxiety, the greater the objective danger. For example, a person with panic disorder thinking 'Everything looks unreal, so I'm definitely going insane'.

**Black-and-white thinking.** Threat and safety are viewed as present or absent, with no shades of grey in between. For example, a person with posttraumatic stress disorder thinking 'Because I had a trauma in the past, I must avoid absolutely everything that might remind me of that or I'll have flashbacks and will not be able to handle them'; or a person with social phobia thinking 'If I ever speak up at meetings, I will be incompetent'.

**Note:** These thinking traps are also called cognitive biases or cognitive distortions. Based on Clark, D., & Beck, A. (2010). *Cognitive therapy of anxiety disorders: Science and practice* (p. 169). New York: Guilford.

## Behaviour

Both fear and anxiety are associated with avoidance of situations or memories of things that frighten us. Avoidance is the behavioural hallmark of anxiety and fear.

## Difference between fear and anxiety

A distinction is made between fear and anxiety. Fear is the experience we have when faced with a clearly identifiable, realistic threat to our safety or security; for example, finding that your brakes don't work when driving at high speed on a motorway, or receiving a diagnosis of cancer. In contrast, anxiety is a term often used for the fear we experience in situations that are not objectively threatening, but which we interpret as placing us in danger; for example, a fear of heights, travelling by plane or being contaminated by germs in relatively clean situations. Normal fear is adaptive. It helps us avoid realistic threats. Anxiety, in contrast, is not adaptive. It makes us avoid things that are not really that dangerous. In doing so, it may prevent us from leading full and enjoyable lives. The next part of this chapter is mainly about anxiety and how to courageously manage it.

## Anxiety and mental health

In the mental health field, distinctions are made between a number of different conditions that involve anxiety.[5] These include phobias, separation anxiety disorder, panic disorder, generalised anxiety disorder, health anxiety, obsessive compulsive disorder and posttraumatic stress disorder. While this is a book on positive psychology with a primary emphasis on strengths, if you are reading this chapter and suffer from anxiety, it may be helpful to have a description of the main anxiety disorders. What follows is thumbnail sketch of each of these conditions.

## Phobias

Phobias involve anxiety about relatively circumscribed situations, for example fear of blood, spiders, snakes, heights, enclosed spaces, public speaking, meeting new people and flying. People with phobias develop strategies for avoiding the situations that frightened them. For example, a person with a fear of enclosed spaces may take the stairs instead of the lift. People with phobias may also develop routines for helping them to feel safe if forced into situations that make them anxious. For example, a person with a fear of meeting new people may spend time helping in the kitchen at a party to avoid being introduced to new people in the living room. The process of approaching feared situations and then leaving them before anxiety subsides makes the situations seem more frightening the next time around.

## Separation anxiety

Separation anxiety is the fear that bad things will happen to family members if separated from them. Children with separation anxiety may refuse to go to school because they are frightened that something dangerous will happen to their parents. Adults with separation anxiety may have difficulty letting their partners travel abroad, fearing that they may be involved in a plane crash.

## Panic disorder

In panic disorder people are frightened of the sensations of fear such as increased heart rate, chest pain, difficulty breathing or swallowing, sweating, gastric discomfort, trembling, feeling numbness or tingling, strange sensations that the self or the world look unreal and feeling faint. This 'fear of fear' brings on panic attacks. During panic attacks, fear sensations are experienced extremely intensely for a few minutes. The intensity of the symptoms leads some people to believe that they are having a heart attack or going crazy. Situations where panic attacks occurred may come to be feared and avoided, and people with panic disorder may eventually become housebound. This is referred to a panic disorder with agoraphobia.

## Generalised anxiety disorder

People with generalised anxiety disorder worry about the same things that all of us worry about; for example, the health, safety and security now and in the future of ourselves and the people we care about. However, in generalised anxiety disorder this worry is excessive, intrusive and disruptive. It fills every waking minute, and makes it difficult to focus on normal activities. Attempts to suppress worries are successful in the short-term. However, in the long-run, suppression causes worrying to intensify. This leads to a fear that the worrying process has gone out of control.

## Health anxiety

With health anxiety, there is an overwhelming fear that every minor ailment may turn out to be a life-threatening illness. This leads to frequent visits to the doctor. However, the relief that follows receiving reassurance from doctors is short-lived. Therefore, people with health anxiety feel compelled to visit their doctors very frequently. This may lead to tensions in doctor-patient relationships. These tensions, in turn, make health anxiety worse.

## Obsessive compulsive disorder

With obsessive compulsive disorder, a wide range of cues can cause obsessional thoughts that lead to anxiety. This anxiety is temporarily reduced by carrying out a compulsive action. For example, contact with objects believed to be dirty may lead to obsessive thoughts about contamination. This causes anxiety which is temporarily reduced by handwashing. However, this relief soon passes, so the compulsive handwashing is repeated.

## Posttraumatic stress disorder

Posttraumatic stress disorder occurs after a life-threatening event, such as an earthquake, or a serious car crash. Memories of the trauma or reminders of the trauma cause flashbacks (during wakefulness) or nightmares (during sleep). During these flashbacks or nightmares, the trauma is re-experienced. This re-experiencing is terrifying. Attempts are made to suppress memories of the trauma and avoid reminders of it, to prevent re-experiencing the terror of the traumatic event. These strategies temporarily reduce anxiety. However, in the long-term they make flashbacks and nightmares happen more frequently.

## Avoidance

Avoidance feeds fear and anxiety. Every time a person with a phobia, separation anxiety or panic disorder avoids the situation they are frightened of, their anxiety about being in that situation gets stronger. Every time a person with obsessive compulsive disorder carries out a ritual like handwashing to avoid anxiety, their anxiety about a particular cue, like contamination, is strengthened. Health anxiety escalates every time a person with this condition seeks medical reassurance to avoid the idea that they have a fatal illness. Every time a person with generalised anxiety suppresses their worries because they fear their worrying is out of control, their worries and generalised anxiety are strengthened. Every time reminders of trauma are avoided or traumatic memories are suppressed, they become stronger triggers for posttraumatic anxiety.

## Courage and facing fears

Research on the psychological treatment of anxiety disorders converges on one main conclusion. To overcome anxiety, we must be courageous and face our fears. We must purposely expose ourselves to those situations and memories that we are frightened of until our fear subsides.[6]

Fear and anxiety follow a very predictable course when we courageously face our fears. First, we become very scared. Then our fear reaches a peak. Eventually, our fear gradually subsides. Figure 15.1 is a graph of this courage curve. For exposure to feared situations or memories to lead to a lasting improvement, we must be courageous and tolerate the distress we experience as our anxiety rises, peaks and subsides. If we expose ourselves to our fears for a little while, and when we become very scared, withdraw from the situation or push the memories or ideas we are frightened of out of our minds, this actually makes our anxiety stronger. This is because the next time we are exposed to the situation or memory we are frightened of, we will remember that the last time we faced our fear it was very distressing, and when we withdrew it brought us relief.

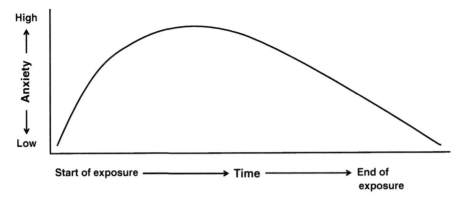

*Figure 15.1* The courage curve.

## Courageous steps to overcoming anxiety

Research conducted mainly within the cognitive behaviour therapy tradition points to certain things that we can do to overcome anxiety.[7] These are summarised in Box 15.3. They include the following:

- Prepare for exposure
- Monitor your anxiety level
- Make a courage ladder
- Do exposure exercises to items on your courage ladder in real life, imagination, by writing or through virtual reality
- Don't withdraw from exposure until you're no longer frightened
- Use effective coping strategies during exposure exercises (social support, relaxation, meditation, optimism)
- Don't use safety routines during exposure
- Reward yourself for being courageous.

---

### Box 15.3   Courageously facing fears

**Prepare for exposure**

- Find and brief a support partner.
- Find a role model who has courageously faced fears like yours.
- Practise coping skills.

    o   Relaxation exercises in Boxes 5.1, 5.2 and 5.3.
    o   Mindfulness exercises in Boxes 6.3 and 6.7.
    o   Optimistic thinking skills (detailed below) to challenge thinking traps in Box 15.2.

---

**Monitor your anxiety level**

- Use a 10-point scale where 1 indicates you are not anxious at all, and 10 means that you are extremely anxious.

**Make a courage ladder**

- Write down a courage ladder with about five or six rungs.
- The highest rung on this ladder is for situations or memories that would lead to an anxiety level of 10 and require extreme courage to face.
- The lowest rung on this ladder is for situations or memories that would lead to an anxiety level of about 4 or 5 and require a moderate level of courage to face.
- Put a few situations that give rise to the same amount of anxiety on each rung of the ladder.

**Do exposure exercises**

- Do exposure exercises to items on the courage ladder, starting at the least anxiety-provoking and working upwards to the most anxiety-provoking.
- Whenever possible, do exposure exercises in real life.
- Do exposure exercises in imagination, through writing or in virtual reality when doing exposure exercises in real life is not possible or appropriate, or as a lower rung on the courage ladder.
- Do exposure through expressive writing for posttraumatic stress, flashbacks and nightmares.
- Do exposure through planned worrying and writing out multiple fears, if you are scared your worrying has gone out of control.

**Don't withdraw from exposure until you're no longer frightened**

- During exposure exercises your anxiety will follow the courage curve in Figure 15.1, increasing, peaking and gradually subsiding.
- Don't stop the exposure exercise until your anxiety level is half as high as your peak level. If your peak is 10, don't stop until you reach 5.

**Use effective coping strategies during exposure exercises**

- Invite your partner, a friend or other trusted person to support you during exposure.
- Do the relaxation exercises in Boxes 5.1, 5.2 and 5.3 to reduce muscle tension.
- Do the mindfulness exercises in Boxes 6.3 and 6.7 to remind yourself that your fears are just thoughts that arise in consciousness, linger a while and then pass.

- Use optimistic thinking skills to challenge thinking traps (in Box 15.3). Ask yourself these questions:

  o   What is the **evidence** for the pessimistic beliefs about the situation and does this evidence show that these beliefs are not 100% true?
  o   Is there an **alternative** optimistic interpretation of the situation?
  o   If you cannot justify an optimistic interpretation of the situation, are the **implications** of your pessimistic beliefs catastrophic with major long-term negative consequences or just a bit of a temporary nuisance?
  o   If you cannot decide whether there is more evidence for an optimistic or pessimistic interpretation of the adversity, which set of beliefs is **most useful** for you in terms of improving your mood and achieving your valued goals?

**Don't use safety routines during exposure**

- During exposure don't use any routines that help you avoid, escape from or minimise exposure to a situation or memory that you are frightened of.

**Reward yourself for being courageous**

- Reward yourself each time you expose yourself to a feared situation on your courage ladder, and tolerate the anxiety it causes you until your fear subsides to half its peak level.

### Prepare for exposure

If you suffer from anxiety and have courageously decided to overcome it, then preparing yourself for the ordeal of facing your fears is a good place to start. Find someone to support you during your ordeal. Explain to them that you want to overcome your fear and invite them to support you during this process. This could be a member of your family. It could be a support group for people with anxiety problems. Or it could be a mental health professional. You may also wish to find a role model. This is someone you can look up to, who has courageously and successfully taken on the challenge that you are preparing to face. You may wish to look on the internet for some well-known person whose anxiety disorder was similar to yours.

To be able to courageously endure anxiety during exposure, select coping skills that suit you and practise these until you are proficient in them.

You may use relaxation skills described in Chapter 5 and summarised in Boxes 5.1, 5.2 and 5.3 to reduce the tension in your body that anxiety causes. You may use meditation skills, especially the exercises in Boxes 6.3 and 6.7, to focus your attention on the breath, and recognise that your anxious thoughts are not facts about how the world actually is, but just thoughts that arise in the mind, linger for a while and then pass.

If you prefer, you may wish to use skills for optimistic thinking described in Chapter 9 to challenge your pessimistic, threat-oriented 'dangerous' thinking style. When you have dangerous thoughts like 'something terrible will happen if I enter this situation or remember these traumatic events', ask yourself the following questions, to challenge these sorts of thoughts:

- What is the **evidence** for the pessimistic beliefs about the situation and does this evidence show that these beliefs are not 100% true?
- Is there an **alternative** optimistic interpretation of the situation?
- If you cannot justify an optimistic interpretation of the situation, are the **implications** of your pessimistic beliefs catastrophic with major long-term negative consequences or just a bit of a temporary nuisance?
- If you cannot decide whether there is more evidence for an optimistic or pessimistic interpretation of the adversity, which set of beliefs is **most useful** for you in terms of improving your mood and achieving your valued goals?

### Monitor your fear or anxiety level

During exposure exercises, when you are courageously facing your fears, keep track of your anxiety level on a 10-point scale where 1 indicates you are not anxious at all, and 10 means that you are extremely anxious. By regularly monitoring your anxiety level on a 10-point scale during exposure exercises, you will be able to judge where you are on the courage curve in Figure 15.1. You will be able to tell if your anxiety is still increasing; if it has peaked; or if it is declining. This is vital, because it is essential that you do not end an exposure exercise until your anxiety has dropped to at least half its peak value. For example, if doing an exposure exercise to face a fear of heights, as you stood looking down from a 30-storey window your anxiety peaked at 8, then it would be essential to remain there until your anxiety level dropped to 4.

### Work your way up courage ladders

When courageously facing your fears, start by exposing yourself to situations or memories that give rise to moderate levels of anxiety, for example 4 or 5 on your 10-point anxiety scale. As you master these, progress to more challenging exercises that give rise to higher levels of anxiety. To plan for this, write down a courage ladder with about five or six rungs. The highest rung on this ladder is a situation or memory that would lead to an anxiety level of 10. In contrast, the lowest rung on this ladder is a situation that would lead to an anxiety level of about 4 or 5. In between these two extremes, write down situations that you imagine would lead to anxiety levels of 6, 7, 8 and 9.

For example, Rory made the fear ladder in Figure 15.2 for his fear of heights. The lowest rung on this ladder is standing on the balcony on the second storey of his house about 5 metres off the ground. Rory gave this an anxiety rating of 5. In contrast, the highest rung on this ladder is standing on One Man's Path at Slieve League in Donegal which is 601 metres above sea level. Rory gave this an anxiety rating of 10. The other rungs on Rory's courage ladder fall between these extremes. I have only written one situation on each rung of Rory's ladder in Figure 15.2. However, Rory actually put a few situations, each with the same anxiety rating, at each rung of his courage ladder. This is a good idea, which I invite you to do. It gives you an opportunity to practise a few times being courageous with challenges of about the same magnitude.

| | | |
|---|---|---|
| **Rung 1** | Standing on the balcony on the second storey of our house about 5 metres off the ground (anxiety rating of 5) |  |
| **Rung 2** | Standing on Howth Cliffs about 50 metres from sea level (anxiety rating of 6) |  |
| **Rung 3** | Standing at a window on the 16th floor of Liberty Hall in Dublin which is about 59 metres from the ground (anxiety rating of 8) |  |
| **Rung 4** | Standing at the top of Skellig Michael in Kerry which is 218 metres high |  |
| **Rung 5** | Standing on One Man's Path, Slieve League in Donegal which is 601 metres high |  |

*Figure 15.2* Rory's courage ladder.

Una suffered from posttraumatic nightmares about a near-fatal car crash. She was also frightened of things that reminded her of the car crash. The lowest rung of Una's ladder was standing 100 yards from the corner where the accident happened, or seeing cars that were the same model and colour as the one she was driving when she crashed (a blue BMW 320). At the highest rung of her ladder there were vivid descriptions of two recurring nightmares. In the first she re-experienced the car going into a spin on black ice, leaving the road and rolling over, before smashing into a wall. In the second she was paralysed in a crashed car upside down, and was scared it was going to burst into flames at any moment.

### Real life, imagination, virtual reality or by writing

When we face our fears, we can do it in real-life situations, in imagination or in virtual reality. For example, if like Rory we are afraid of heights and want to overcome this fear, we may face our fears by going to the various locations in Figure 15.2 (the balcony, Howth Cliffs, Liberty Hall,

Skellig Michael and One Man's Path) and remain there until our fear subsides. That is doing courageous exposure in real life. We could also do exposure in imagination. For this, we adopt a relaxed posture, lying down or sitting with the eyes closed. In our mind's eye, we imagine as vividly as possible being exposed to the things we are frightened of. With Rory, he did exposure to each of the situations in his courage ladder in imagination before exposing himself to them in real life. Like most people who do this, he found that exposure in imagination made him feel less anxiety than exposure in real life, but it was a good rehearsal for the real thing.

In recent years exposure has been conducted with virtual reality technology.[8] This is useful for some phobias, for example fear of flying, or fear of memoires of armed combat. However, whenever possible, exposure in imagination or virtual reality should be followed by real-life exposure, for maximum effectiveness.

Writing about the things that make us anxious is another type of exposure.[9] For example, Una, who we mentioned earlier, wrote in detail about recurring nightmares of her car skidding on black ice, rolling over and crashing into a wall, and of being paralysed in her overturned car, terrified that it was about to burst into flames. If you decide to write out your fears, write in an uncensored way describing vividly how you see your memories in your mind's eye, moment by moment. Write in detail about what you see, hear, feel and think. If you still feel a high level of anxiety when you have written a complete description, repeat the writing exercise over and over again until your fear peaks and subsides to, at most, half the level at which it peaked.

Writing down fears is a particularly useful type of exposure for posttraumatic stress and generalised anxiety disorder, where the main fear is that worrying has gone out of control. If you suffer from generalised anxiety disorder and write out all your fears in detail, again and again, you will come to recognise two important things. First, the list of things that you are frightened of is limited. Second, you are in control of the worrying process. When you write down your worries again and again at a time and place of your choosing, you are actually doing planned worrying. Many people find that doing planned worrying and recognising these two things reduces their anxiety.

For example, Bernadette worried about everything: her health, her family's health, the family's finances, the security of her job and that of her husband, the safety of the house, the safety of her children, parents, in-laws and pets, terrorism, natural disasters, and extreme weather. All of these worries made her feel an anxiety level of about 5 or 6. Her greatest worry was her fear that she could no longer control her worry. This made her feel an anxiety level of 10. She did planned worrying for 50 minutes a day at her kitchen table. She wrote down a vivid account of all the worries that were in her mind at that time. In each session, her anxiety level dropped to between 2 and 3. She found that over two months her fear that her worrying was out of control decreased from 10 to about 4 or 5.

### Don't withdraw from exposure until you're no longer frightened

During each exposure exercise, be courageous and stay in the anxiety-provoking situation until your fear subsides. Expect your anxiety to follow the courage curve in Figure 15.1, increasing, peaking and then gradually subsiding. Don't stop the exposure exercise until your anxiety level is, at most, half as high as your peak level. If your peak is 10, don't conclude until you reach 5.

### Use effective coping strategies during exposure

For most anxiety problems relaxation, meditation, challenging thinking traps and getting social support from partners or parents are helpful coping strategies to use during exposure.

#### Relaxation

Doing relaxation exercises like those described in Chapter 5 and summarised in Boxes 5.1, 5.2 and 5.3 is a very useful way of managing anxiety.[10] This is because it helps to reduce physiological arousal. The only anxiety condition where this is not helpful is panic disorder. For panic disorder, the main thing that is feared is signs of physiological arousal, so part of the challenge in overcoming panic disorder is getting used to high levels of physiological arousal and seeing that they do not lead to catastrophes like having a heart attack.

#### Meditation

You can also manage anxiety by practising meditation exercises like those described in Chapter 6, especially the exercises in Boxes 6.3 and 6.7.[11] Meditation helps us manage anxiety by focusing attention on the breath and the body. It helps us recognise that our anxious thoughts are not facts, but just thoughts that arise in consciousness and which eventually dissipate.

#### Challenging thinking traps and being optimistic

Challenging thinking traps that fuel anxiety, like those in Box 15.2, is good way of coping with anxiety during exposure to feared situations. When we challenge thinking traps, such as disaster forecasting, we ask ourselves the following sorts of questions: Is any evidence that contradicts the story we are telling ourselves about the threat we perceive? Is there an alternative optimistic interpretation or the situation? Will the outcome be a catastrophe or just a nuisance? Is an optimistic interpretation more useful than a pessimistic interpretation?[12] For example, after her car crash Una often got snared by the black-and-white thinking trap. She would think 'I must avoid absolutely everything that reminds me of the crash or I'll have flashbacks and will not be able to handle them'. She challenged this by asking herself: Are there times when I have had the courage to manage flashbacks? When I did have a flashback, how well did I cope with it? Am I exaggerating my vulnerability? Optimistically, what is likely to happen?

#### Social support

In Chapter 11 you read about the extraordinarily positive effects that close supportive relationships can have on well-being. It is therefore not surprising that research on couple and family therapy has shown that we can use social support to help manage anxiety during exposure to feared situations.[13] It may be helpful to invite your partner or a trusted friend to help support you when you are doing exposure exercises. The only situation where this may be counterproductive is where you are frightened of social situations. If you always bring along a supportive companion to new or unfamiliar social situations, then this may prevent you from facing your fear of meeting new people on your own.

### Don't use safety routines during exposure

During exposure, it's helpful to use relaxation or meditation to help you tolerate distress and courageously face your fear. It's also helpful to accept support from a friend or family member who helps you be courageous and face your fear. Relaxation, meditation, challenging thinking traps and social support are useful coping strategies because they help you be courageous.

In contrast, safety routines are problematic.[14] These are any routines that help you avoid, escape from or minimise exposure to a situation or memory that you are frightened of. Here are some examples: using stairs instead of lifts when claustrophobic, repeatedly washing hands when frightened of contamination, avoiding eye contact and speaking quietly when frightened of social situations, repeatedly seeking reassurance from a doctor when frightened that health problems may be fatal, and suppressing frightening memories. In the short-term, safety routines give relief. In the long-term, they prevent us from overcoming anxiety. This is because they interfere with the vital process of entering and remaining in anxiety-provoking situations until anxiety has peaked and subsided, following the courage curve in Figure 15.1. If you don't do this, you will not learn that those situations that make you feel anxiety are in fact quite safe.

### Reward yourself for being courageous

Reward yourself with a treat after each exposure exercise. Only reward yourself if you achieved your goal of showing courage. By that I mean staying exposed to the anxiety-provoking situation or memory until your anxiety level falls to, at most, half that of your peak anxiety level for that exercise.

## Posttraumatic growth

All of us have experienced or in the future will experience events that seriously threaten our lives or those we care for. These crises include losing a loved one, facing our own mortality, suffering a serious injury, receiving a diagnosis of life-limiting illness like cancer, being mugged or burgled, having a near-fatal accident, experiencing a natural disaster such as an earthquake or becoming involved in armed conflict or war. These sorts of events may lead to suffering, grief or in some cases posttraumatic stress disorder (which was described earlier in this chapter). However, personal growth is the silver lining in the dark cloud of trauma and loss. From antiquity, it has been acknowledged within religious, spiritual, philosophical and literary traditions that trauma and suffering may lead to positive changes in our lives.

Within the field of positive psychology, Professors Lawrence Calhoun and Richard Tedeschi at the University of North Carolina Charlotte have pioneered the scientific study of posttraumatic growth.[15] They have found that positive changes which follow trauma fall into five distinct categories: recognition of personal strength, improved relationships with other people, a greater appreciation of life, spiritual and existential transformation and an increased openness to new possibilities.

### Recognition of personal strength

When we successfully cope with trauma and suffering, we may discover that while we are vulnerable in a dangerous world filled with hazards, we are also stronger and more resilient than we ever imagined. This may lead to increased confidence in our ability to handle future challenges, and a greater sense of self-reliance. Sorcha found that following successful treatment of breast cancer, she was aware that she would always be vulnerable to further tumours. However, she was also aware that she would have the strength to cope with this and any other challenges that occurred in her life.

### Improved relationships with other people

When we turn to others to support us through hard times, because we cannot make it alone, this affects our relationships. It makes us accept that we need others. It makes us express our needs and emotions to others in more open and direct ways. It makes us appreciate others and value our relationships more, because we realise that we can count on others when we need them. It may also show us who our real friends are: those who support us and do not abandon us when we most need them. It makes us feel closer to other people and have more compassion for the suffering of others. Reggie, aged 23, broke both legs in a skiing accident. He spent a few months in a wheelchair and then on crutches. His relationships with his close friends at college deepened during his recovery. This was partly because of the generosity they showed in helping him with his mobility problems during recovery. He also found that he felt greater sympathy and compassion towards people he didn't know; for example, an older woman using a Zimmer frame to help her walk, and a child who fell at the bus-stop and hurt his knee.

### Greater appreciation of life

Surviving a bereavement or a brush with death may increase our awareness of how valuable life is, and what things in our lives are most valuable to us. After a heart attack, Rex cut his working week from 70 to 30 hours and spent more time with his family. He realised that these close relationships were more important than the growth of his very successful business.

### Spiritual and existential transformation

Facing our own mortality or that of someone close to us can clarify our beliefs about the meaning of life and the significance of death. For those who are religious like Mary, a devout Christian, her survival following a terrorist bombing in London deepened her religious faith. In contrast, Neville, her agnostic partner, found that the same experience made him feel more connected to other people, to nature and the universe.

### Increased openness to new possibilities

Facing a life crisis may change our view of how best to spend the rest of our lives. It may help us to discover new opportunities, interests and directions. It may energise us to try to change things in our lives or in the world which previously we would not have attempted. Harry joined Friends of the Earth and became a renewable energy and climate change activist after his son was killed in an accident on an oil rig.

### Factors that promote posttraumatic growth

Research in positive psychology has shown that posttraumatic growth occurs for some but not all people following bereavement, diagnosis with diseases such as cancer or HIV/AIDS and violent victimisation, as well as a range of other life crises.[16] People who experience posttraumatic growth tend cope with adversity using particular coping strategies that may facilitate it.[17] They turn to their friends and family for social support. They accept the reality of the crisis they have been through, and the situation in which they now find themselves. That is, they do not dwell on what should or could have happened, but rather accept that what happened has occurred and cannot be changed. However, they are reflective and optimistic, not fatalistic. They actively reflect on the crisis they have been through. They look for the positives in the adversity they have endured. They also draw on their spiritual or religious beliefs to help them to make sense of their situation. These coping strategies help them to develop a new story or narrative about their lives that accounts for their experiences before, during and after the crisis.

Posttraumatic growth has been found to occur following psychotherapeutic approaches that enhance social support (for example, couple therapy), that foster acceptance and self-regulation of fear and anger (for example, mindfulness-based therapies), that facilitate deliberate exposure to traumatic memories (for example, cognitive behaviour therapy) and that help survivors develop a coherent narrative about their crisis (for example, expressive writing or speaking about trauma).[18]

### Engaging in posttraumatic growth

When we face a crisis that shatters our beliefs about the world, our lives, our relationships and the future, we have an opportunity to engage in posttraumatic growth. The research on posttraumatic growth summarised above points to very specific things we can do to facilitate this process. These are summarised in Box 15.4.

---

## Box 15.4   Facilitating posttraumatic growth

**Find support**

- Find a trusted companion to listen to your story about the crisis.
- This may be someone from your family, a friend, a support group or a professional therapist or counsellor.
- Ask for understanding, not advice, or to be cheered up.
- Meet regularly and tell the story of the crisis, again and again.

**Write the story of the crisis**

- Describe the crisis in as much detail as possible.
- Write it again and again.
- Write in an uncensored way.

---

**Create a coherent narrative**

- Through talking to a trusted companion or writing, create a coherent narrative.
- Link your story of the crisis to your life before it happened and your life since the crisis.

**Look for posttraumatic growth themes in your story**

- Each time you write this story, notice if any of the themes of posttraumatic growth are emerging in your account of your life by considering these questions:
    - How has the crisis helped you recognise your personal strengths and resilience?
    - How has the crisis improved your relationships with other people?
    - In what ways has the crisis given you a greater appreciation of life?
    - In what ways has the crisis changed your relationship with God (if you have religious beliefs) or with the natural world (if you do not have religious beliefs)?
    - How has the crisis changed how you see your future and what your future priorities will be?

**Practice mindfulness**

- Use mindfulness exercises to help you accept the suffering you have experienced.
- Use mindfulness exercises to help you manage painful feelings like sadness, fear and anger.

**Draw on spiritual, religious and existential beliefs**

- Draw on your spiritual, religious or existential beliefs to help you make sense of the crisis.

**Note:** Based on: Calhoun, L. G., & Tedeschi, R. G. (2013). *Posttraumatic growth in clinical practice*. New York, NY: Routledge.

Getting social support is the first priority. This involves finding someone we can trust and talk to regularly about the crisis. It may be a close friend, family member, support group of people who have faced crises like yours or a professional counsellor or therapist. In conversations with people supporting us, it's useful to make it clear that we are asking the other person to listen and understand, not to advise us on what to do or try to cheer us up. A second useful practice is to regularly write about the traumatic event or crisis.

Whether we are talking or writing about the crisis, the main aim is to gradually work towards a coherent narrative about how the story of the crisis fits into our understanding of ourselves and our lives. We may start off by simply recounting, in as much detail as possible, the facts of the crisis as we remember it or currently understand it. We may find it necessary to do this many, many times. This is like repeated exposure to anxiety-provoking situations or memories discussed in the previous section of this chapter. This repeated telling and retelling, or writing and rewriting, gradually makes painful feelings and emotions related to the crisis less difficult to tolerate.

As we become better able to tolerate the painful feelings associated with the crisis, there is the opportunity to begin to link the story of the crisis to life before it happened and life since the crisis. Crises or trauma, by definition, have the potential to shatter our beliefs about the world and our place in it. Before Karen, aged 24, was mugged in Grafton Street, she experienced Dublin as a safe city, and herself as relatively invulnerable. After the mugging, she was terrified to go out alone at night, viewed Dublin as a dangerous place, had regular nightmares and flashbacks and experienced herself as extremely vulnerable. In the telling and retelling of her story, she struggled to fit these two different views of herself and her home-city together in a way that had some sort of continuity that made sense to her.

Each time we retell or rewrite the story of the crisis and its links to our lives before and after it, there is an opportunity to notice if any of the themes of posttraumatic growth are emerging in our account of our lives. We may ask ourselves these sorts of questions: How has the crisis helped me to recognise my personal strengths and resilience? How has the crisis improved my relationships with other people? In what ways has the crisis given me a greater appreciation of life? In what ways has the crisis changed my relationship with God (if you have religious beliefs) or with the natural world (if you do not have religious beliefs)? How has the crisis changed how I see my future and what my future priorities will be?

Karen came to see her experience of being mugged as an event that helped her to mature out of a child-like view of Dublin as a very safe place, to a more realistic view of it as a city in which there are places that are never safe, and others that are safe some of the time. She also came to view herself as somewhat vulnerable rather than invulnerable, but also as having considerable personal resilience. This was because she overcame all of the posttraumatic anxieties, nightmares and flashbacks that she initially experienced in the aftermath of being mugged. Her relationship with her partner, Freddie, deepened because he was so understanding and supportive as she recovered from the crisis. She also became more tolerant of what she previously had thought of as her mother's overprotectiveness. Her crisis had no major effect on her appreciation of life, her view of the future or her spirituality.

In contrast, Doreen, whose best friend since childhood died in a tragic car crash, found that this experience radically altered her appreciation of the little things in life, and helped her consolidate her decision to prioritise having children sooner rather than later. Previously she had been delaying pregnancy, because she had been prioritising her career.

In addition to getting support, and developing a coherent narrative that incorporates posttraumatic growth themes, it may be useful to practise mindfulness skills, described in Chapter 6. These help us to accept the fact that suffering in life is inevitable, and also to manage extreme emotions especially sadness, fear and anger that usually follow a major life crisis. It is also important to draw on spiritual, religious or existential beliefs to help make sense of the crisis.

## Summary

- **Courage** involves intentionally taking a course of action that puts us at risk of harm, because of the presence of a threat, despite feeling extremely frightened, anxious and/or angry, to achieve valued goals, usually by reducing threat.
- **Fight / flight / or freeze reactions.** Courage often involves overriding the automatic fight / flight / or freeze reaction. During this reaction adrenaline is released into the blood stream and increases in heart rate, muscle tension and strength occur. This prepares our bodies to run away, to fight or to become less noticeable to potential predators by making us stay very still. This reaction which we have inherited from our ancestors is good for dealing with some physically threatening problems, but the impulse to run, fight or freeze may not be useful for complex threats that require thoughtful responses.
- **Preparation for courageous action** involves working with leaders who are courageous role models, building a supportive team, relevant skills training for managing specific threats, planning using problem-solving skills and avoiding the extremes of cowardice or reckless risk-taking.
- **Coping strategies.** Thinking of past successful courageous actions, the benefits of courageous actions, team support and brave role models are coping strategies that may support courageous action. Relaxation (in Box 5.3) and mindfulness (in Box 6.6) exercises are other useful coping strategies.
- **To debrief after courageous action**, evaluate its effectiveness, reflect on what it says about you as a person and accept recognition from respected people for bravery.
- **Fear and anxiety are multidimensional.** They involve feelings of apprehension; physiological sensations such as increased heart and respiration rates; changes in thinking especially hypervigilance for threat and a tendency to fall into thinking traps; and avoidance of threat.
- **Thinking traps that fuel anxiety** include disaster forecasting, jumping to conclusions, tunnel vision, near-sightedness, emotional reasoning and black-and-white thinking.
- **Fear** is the experience we have when faced with a clearly identifiable, realistic threat to our safety or security. It is adaptive.
- **Anxiety** occurs in situations that are not objectively threatening, but which are interpreted as placing us in danger. It is not adaptive.
- **Mental health problems where anxiety is a central feature** include phobias, separation anxiety disorder, panic disorder, generalised anxiety disorder, health anxiety, obsessive compulsive disorder and posttraumatic stress disorder.
- **Avoidance** of feared situations and memories makes anxiety disorders worse.
- **Courageously facing fears** is the most effective way to overcome anxiety disorders. This involves preparing for exposure to feared situations, monitoring anxiety levels, making a courage ladder, doing exposure exercises to items on the courage ladder, not withdrawing from exposure until you're no longer frightened, using effective coping strategies during exposure exercises (social support, relaxation, meditation, optimism), not using safety routines during exposure and rewarding yourself for being courageous as you complete each step of the process.

- **Posttraumatic growth** following a trauma or crisis may involve recognition of personal strength, improved relationships with other people, a greater appreciation of life, spiritual and existential transformation and an increased openness to new possibilities.
- **Facilitating posttraumatic growth** involves finding support, writing or talking in detail about the story of the crisis, linking the story of the crisis to life before and after the crisis, looking for posttraumatic growth themes in the story, practising mindfulness and drawing on spiritual, religious and existential beliefs.

## Where are you now?

If you have done the exercises and followed some of the guidelines in this chapter, you may have found that they have helped you feel more courageous when facing things that threaten you or make you feel scared or anxious. If you have experienced a life crisis or trauma, you may find that some of the exercises have helped you experience posttraumatic growth.

You may want to read back over the chapter and summarise in your journal the main things that you have learned from this chapter about being courageous in situations that you find threatening, and experience growth and transformation following a life crisis. You can now decide if you want to use the strategies for managing anxiety to help you be courageous in situations that you find particularly threatening.

In the next chapter, you will have an opportunity to read about managing anger when threatened and responding assertively. Below are some web resources and books that are relevant to topics you have read about in this chapter.

## Web resources

Face your fear video (5:13): www.youtube.com/watch?v=MTJaPozjeF8
Exposure therapy for anxiety video (4:57): www.youtube.com/watch?v=JCXitNs_JEc
Exposure treatment for anxiety video (33:49): www.youtube.com/watch?v=QHDTXT7OwSM
Posttraumatic growth 'science of people' video (4:14): www.youtube.com/watch?v=u2tkEk6MgWA
ReSolve: A guide to posttraumatic growth documentary video (1.21:03): www.youtube.com/watch?v=n4bgOspacmw

## Books

Antony, M. M., & Swinson, R. P. (2017). *The shyness and social anxiety workbook: Proven techniques for overcoming your fears* (Third Edition). Oakland, CA: New Harbinger.
Bourne, E. (2015). *The anxiety and phobia workbook* (Sixth Edition). Oakland, CA: New Harbinger.
Butler, G. (2016). *Overcoming social anxiety and shyness: A self-help guide to using cognitive behavioural techniques* (Second Edition). London, UK: Robinson.
Tedeschi, R. G., & Moore, B. A. (2016). *The posttraumatic growth workbook: Coming through trauma wiser, stronger, and more resilient*. Oakland, CA: New Harbinger.

# 16 Assertiveness and anger

In this chapter, you will read about how to respond assertively, rather than aggressively, when threatened. When we are faced with a threat to our safety or security most of us feel angry or scared.[1] In Chapters 10 and 15, it was explained how, when threatened, our bodies prepare for battle, retreat or become less noticeable to potential predators by making us stay very still. This automatic physiological process is called the fight / flight / or freeze response.

From an evolutionary perspective, the automatic fight / flight / or freeze response helped our ancestors deal effectively with many threats.[2] It helped them fight predators or competitors who they knew they could physically overpower. It helped them to run away from predators who were large but slow, or groups of people who could overpower them. It also helped them to hide from predators who were strong and quick. Our ancestors who fought aggressively, ran away quickly or became unnoticeable by staying very still survived. Because of this, we have all inherited the fight / flight / or freeze reaction.

In modern life, most threats we face are social. Much of the time, annoying things that other people do make our lives difficult. It's rare that the solution to these situations involves fighting, fleeing or freezing. Many of these social threats that we face require us to be assertive.[3] They require us to say clearly what we would like another person to do, in a way that is neither too submissive nor too aggressive. For example, if our neighbours are playing very loud music at four in the morning, then the assertive thing to do is to ask them to lower the volume so we can sleep. The automatic fight / flight / or freeze reaction may make it difficult to be assertive. In the example of the noisy neighbours, we may find ourselves either flying into an aggressive rage, or timidly backing down. In Chapter 15, we discussed how to manage fear courageously. In this chapter, we will consider how to express anger assertively rather than aggressively when feeling threatened.

## Assertiveness

Anger is a very useful emotion. Anger, like all emotions, gives us information important for our well-being. Anger tells us that we must protect ourselves so that our needs will be met, and our rights will be protected. The uncontrolled, impulsive, aggressive expression of anger is problematic. It may violate the rights of others, and lead to an escalating angry conflict. This, in turn, may reduce our well-being. If you wish, complete the exercise in Box 16.1. In this exercise, you indicate whether you are more likely to respond aggressively or assertively when you come into conflict with others. The challenge in expressing anger assertively is to control angry feelings using the skills described later in this chapter, and then to tell the right person, at the right time, in the right place, in the right way, specifically what we are angry about, and how we would prefer them to behave in future. Box 16.2 contains a summary of key assertiveness skills. These will be expanded below, in light of the following example.

---

### Box 16.1   Do you usually respond to conflict with assertiveness or aggression?

Below there is an aggressive and assertive response given to five situations. For each of these situations circle the response that reflects how you would typically respond. Review your responses and decide if, overall, you are more likely to respond aggressively or assertively to these sorts of situations.

| | Situation | Aggressive response | Assertive response |
|---|---|---|---|
| 1 | When someone close to me unjustly criticises my behaviour | I react angrily and tell the person that people in glass houses shouldn't throw stones. | I openly discuss the criticism with the person. |
| 2 | When someone I don't know well borrows something from me and forgets to return it | I demand it back. | I ask if they are finished using it and ask for it back. |
| 3 | When I have to return an item to a shop without the original receipt | I take it to the shop and demand a refund. | I stand my ground if the sales person gives me a hard time. |
| 4 | If a neighbour I know well returns something of mine in poor shape | I get angry and demand that it be replaced. | I request that my neighbour replace or fix it. |
| 5 | If the new newspaper deliverer does not deliver the newspaper a couple of days | I shout at the newspaper deliverer the next time I see them. | I mention the oversight next time I see them. |

**Note:** Items are based on Thompson, R. J., & Berenbaum, H. (2011). Adaptive and aggressive assertiveness scales (AAA-S). *Journal of Psychopathology and Behavioral Assessment, 33*(3), 323-334.

---

### Box 16.2   Assertive communication

- **Right person.** Tell the person directly. Don't just complain to others.
- **Right time.** Talk sooner rather than later.
- **Right place.** Talk in a place without distractions or an unnecessary audience.
- **Right way.** Speak in a respectful, calm, co-operative, solution-focused way.

  o **Positive opening.** Start positively.
  o **Clear goal.** State the aim of the conversation.

- o  **Specific issue.** Pinpoint one specific issue. Don't mention many vague issues. Don't criticise the personality of the other person.
- o  **I statements, not you statements.** Say in this situation, I felt X because of Y, not 'You made me feel X'.
- o  **Preferred plan.** Say how you would like things to be in future.
- o  **Avoid aggression and passivity.** Don't be a tyrant or a doormat.
- o  **Avoid thinking traps.** These are listed in Box 16.3.

Audrey was angry with Fay because on two occasions she had not turned up for a meeting that was important for their business. This occurred in a context where Fay had been late for two previous meetings. Audrey approached Fay in the corridor and asked if now was a good time to talk. Fay agreed. They went to Fay's office and Audrey said, 'Thank you for making time to talk to me now. I want to sort this out because it's important to me that we work well together. Here is the issue I would like resolved. We had scheduled a meeting for nine this morning, and you didn't turn up. I feel angry about that. I would prefer, in future, if you came to meetings we have set up or let me know in advance if you can't make it'. Let's look at this example in terms of the person, time, place and way of communicating.

### *Right person*

Audrey spoke to the right person. Audrey was angry with Fay, so she spoke directly to Fay about this issue. She didn't complain to other people in her office about Fay.

### *Right time*

Audrey also spoke at the right time. She didn't wait for days to pass, during which she would have felt ongoing anger. She spoke to Fay as soon as possible, and at a time that was convenient for her.

### *Right place*

Audrey spoke to Fay in the right place. She didn't speak to hear in the corridor where others would overhear this private conversation and possibly embarrass Fay. She spoke to her in her office, where there was privacy.

### *Right way*

Audrey spoke to Fay in the right way. She used a positive opening, set a clear goal for the meeting, focused on a specific issue and used 'I statements' and not 'you statements' to describe the situation and the anger she felt in it. The difference between 'I statements' and 'you statements' will be explained below. (These were discussed in Chapter 12 and mentioned in exercises in Boxes 12.5 and 12.6.) Audrey concluded by stating her preferred plan for the future. Let's look at each of these elements of Audrey's assertive speaking style in more detail.

### Positive opening

She opened by expressing appreciation. She said, 'Thank you for making time to talk to me now'. This set a positive tone for the meeting.

### Clear goal

She made the goal of the meeting – sorting out a specific issue – very clear, and she also mentioned the broader goal of working together well. This was a goal that they both valued. She said: 'I want to sort this out because it's important to me that we work well together'.

### Specific issue

Audrey described the issue she wanted resolved. She said: 'Here is the issue I would like resolved. We had scheduled a meeting for nine this morning, and you didn't turn up. I feel angry about that'. She didn't bring in other related issues by, for example mentioning that Fay had been late for two previous meetings. She focused on one specific issue. She also didn't attack Fay's personality by, for example, saying, 'You're self-absorbed. You never think about how you affect others. You're so selfish!'

### I statements

Audrey described the situation in which she felt angry, and used an 'I statement' to let Fay know that she owned her anger. She said: 'We had scheduled a meeting for nine this morning, and you didn't turn up. I feel angry about that'. Audrey avoided making a 'you statement' like 'You made me angry when you didn't turn up this morning'. Usually 'you statements' make others feel criticised and so they become more defensive than when responding to 'I statements'.

### Preferred plan

Audrey let Fay know her preferred plan for the future. She said: 'I would prefer, in future, if you came to meetings we have set up or let me know in advance if you can't make it'. Audrey's plan was clear and suggested a goal that both Fay and Audrey could realistically achieve. She didn't say something vague or unachievable like, 'Fay, would you not just cop yourself on. Just get a proper work attitude!' In some situations, the main outcome we want is for the other person to acknowledge that they have not respected our rights and to apologise. In other situations, we may wish that they apologise and agree that in future they will treat us differently. It's important to be clear about our preferred outcome.

### Avoid aggression and passivity

The conversational style that Audrey used helped her to avoid being either too aggressive, or too passive. She avoided being aggressive by not shouting at her, or ignoring her in the corridor. Audrey also avoided passivity. She didn't behave as if Fay missing the meeting didn't matter to her. Assertiveness involves avoiding being aggressive or passive when someone's actions unfairly affect our rights. It is about avoiding being a tyrant or a doormat. This sort of assertiveness balances our needs and rights with those of others.

## Thinking traps

Another thing about the way that Audrey spoke to Fay that made her conversational style assertive rather than aggressive was her avoidance of thinking traps. Thinking traps commonly associated with anger are listed in Box 16.3. Audrey didn't fall into any of these when she was speaking to Fay. For example, Audrey didn't use name-calling ('Fay, you're such a loser!'), mind-reading ('Sometimes I think you do this just to annoy me!') or black-and-white thinking ('You're always late, you're never on time!'). We will discuss thinking traps associated with anger in more detail below, when considering the complex nature of anger. (Thinking traps were discussed in three previous chapters. Thinking traps that prevent optimism were considered in Chapter 9 and Box 9.1; those associated with perfectionism were considered in Chapter 14 and Box 14.4; and those that fuel anxiety were considered in Chapter 15 and Box 15.2.)

---

**Box 16.3   Thinking traps associated with anger**

- **Thresholding.** Setting an arbitrary limit, standard or threshold, which when crossed justifies your anger. For example, 'That's the last straw. I've given him three chances, and he blew it. I'm going to let him know how angry I am'.
- **Blaming.** Thinking that something is all someone's else's fault without looking at all of the evidence. For example, 'It's all the other person's fault, not mine, so I am angry'.
- **Name-calling.** Labelling others in a negative way based on a single experience. For example, 'He said he was not satisfied with my work last week, therefore he is a jerk/prat/SOB for criticising me'.
- **Mind-reading.** Assuming that others are intentionally trying to hurt or annoy you without having evidence for this or checking it out. For example, 'He's just doing that to annoy me, so I am angry at him'.
- **Jumping to conclusions.** Reaching a conclusion very quickly without considering alternatives and important evidence. For example, 'She forgot to bring back the book she borrowed, and this means she is taking advantage of my generosity, so I am angry at her'.
- **Black-and-white thinking.** Thinking about things as all good or all bad, with no shades of grey in between. For example, 'It's all your fault. It's nothing to do with me, so I'm angry'.
- **Focusing on the negatives and discounting the positives.** Only paying attention to bad things, while ignoring good things or saying that they don't matter. For example, 'He didn't do his fair share of the work. He was supposed to do 10

---

things but he left one out. But that one thing is really important, so I am angry at him'.

- **Overgeneralising.** Making sweeping judgements based on one experience. For example, 'Because he said one critical thing about me, that means he will always be critical, so I am angry at him'.
- **Making mountains out of molehills.** Ruminating for hours about threatening things that happened in the past, so that little challenges become blown up to be huge anger-fuelling threats. For example, 'She disrespected me once, but that was just the tip of the iceberg. She will probably do it again and again. I hate her and am angry at her'.
- **Disaster forecasting.** Anticipating that the future will be very distressing on the basis of limited evidence, and dwelling on this idea for a long time. For example, 'He is going to criticise or humiliate me, therefore I am angry'.
- **A rule containing should or must, and always or never.** Making absolute statements about how things ought to be always or never.
- **A rule about lack of control.** 'I can never control my anger or aggression (because I inherited my temper, or was traumatised)'.
- **A rule about overcontrol.** 'I should always be in control of my feelings and never get angry'.
- **A rule about letting off steam.** 'I must always express my anger aggressively to let off steam and get rid of it'.
- **A rule about sharing.** 'It's always a good thing to share anger and let off steam with other victims like me to help me control my anger about being victimised'.
- **A rule about getting respect.** 'I must always express my anger aggressively to make others respect me and my rights'.
- **A rule about getting even.** 'I must always take revenge and get even, to make me feel better when someone hurts or threatens me'.
- **A rule about avoiding fear and sadness.** 'It's always better to feel and express anger, rather than to feel and express fear or sadness'.
- **A rule about entitlement.** 'I am always entitled to be treated as special, and if I'm not treated as special I will be uncontrollably angry'.

**Note:** These thinking traps are also called cognitive biases, cognitive distortions, beliefs or assumptions. Based on Beck, A. (1999). *Prisoners of hate: The cognitive basis of anger hostility and violence.* New York, NY: Harper/Collins. Burns, D. (1999). *Feeling good: The new mood therapy.* Revised and updated. New York, NY: Avon.

## Active listening and problem-solving

Sometimes assertive communication leads to conversations that require active listening, and problem-solving. Key elements of these skills are listed in Box 16.4. (Active listening was discussed in Chapter 12 on couple relationships and Chapter 13 on parent-child relationships. Problem-solving was discussed in Chapter 10.)

**Box 16.4   Active listening and problem-solving**

**Active listening.**

- Listen without interruption.
- Summarise.
- Check you have heard correctly.
- Reply.

**Problem-solving.**

- Clarify the problem calmly and break a big problem into smaller problems.
- Brainstorm options.
- Predict the price and payoff of each.
- Negotiate the one that suits both of you best.
- Agree to review progress.

### Active listening

When we have told the right person, at the right time, in the right place, in the right way, specifically what we are angry about, and how we would prefer them to behave in future, the next step is to listen to their response and understand their perspective. In some situations, this may be sufficient to resolve the situation. The other person may acknowledge how their behaviour has affected us, apologise and offer to behave differently in future. The main skill that is required here is active listening.[4] That is, listening without interrupting, and in such a way that when the person finishes speaking we will be able to summarise what they have said accurately. This is relatively easy to do if the other person apologises and agrees with our point of view. However, it is difficult to do if they disagree with us. Our natural tendency is to stop actively listening to them. Instead, in our minds we rehearse ways to refute their arguments and support our preferred position. With active listening, the challenge is to avoid the temptation to do this. Rather, we listen, summarise and check that we have accurately understood the other person accurately, before telling the other person how our view differs from theirs. For example, when Audrey said, 'I would prefer, in future, if you came to meetings we have set up or let me know in advance if you can't make it', Fay replied, 'I've been snowed under recently. I've so much on, and so many different projects at critical points, I've been letting things slip though the net. Don't take it personally that I missed our meeting. I'm at breaking point. In fact, I was going to call in sick today!' Audrey listened to this actively. She then summarised by saying: 'Fay, I can see you have a lot on, and it's taking its toll on you. It's making it hard to remember everything, like our meeting this morning?' Fay let Audrey know that she had understood correctly. This is a good example of active listening.

### *Problem-solving*

In situations where we have assertively let another person know about our anger at a particular situation, and our preferred plan for the future, the other person may believe that they were justified in doing whatever made us angry. The assertive response is to actively listen to their position, understand it and use this understanding as the starting point for joint problem-solving about how best to proceed.[5] Break big problems into a number of smaller problems and then deal with these one at a time. This may involve using the problem-solving skills we came across in Box 10.3. For each small problem, brainstorm solutions. Look at the price and payoff of each solution, for each of you. Settle on the solution that suits you both best. Agree to try out the solution, and then afterwards to review how well it worked. Accept that often finding a solution that suits you both will involve a degree of compromise.

Assertive communication in tense conflictual situations is hard work. It takes time and effort. Each of us has a limited supply of time and energy. Therefore, it is better for our well-being to pick our battles carefully. One of the reasons assertive communication is demanding is because it involves preventing angry feelings from escalating into aggressive behaviour. In the remainder of this chapter the focus will be on anger control, and preventing aggression.

## Anger and aggression

Anger and aggression are complex phenomena.[6] There are things that trigger anger, for example being insulted. There are also risk factors that make triggers more likely to lead to impulsive aggression, for example being tired and hungry. Situations that trigger anger automatically lead to physiological sensations associated with the fight / flight / or freeze response; for example, increased heart and respiration rates. The stories we tell ourselves about trigger situations have a big impact on how angry we end up feeling. Often these stories contain thinking traps associated with anger mentioned earlier and listed in Box 16.3. For example, if we tell ourselves the story that our noisy neighbours play loud music late at night to intentionally annoy us, this story contains the 'mind-reading' thinking trap. In the mind-reading thinking trap we assume we know what others are thinking, in this case that our neighbours were intentionally trying to annoy us. If we tell ourselves stories that contain thinking traps, this has the potential to increase how angry we feel. This, in turn, may affect how aggressively we behave towards others. Ultimately this affects our relationships and our well-being. It's useful to make these distinctions between risk factors, triggers, sensations, stories we tell ourselves that contain thinking traps and aggressive behaviour. A diagram of them is given in Figure 16.1.

These distinctions point to ways to prevent anger from escalating to aggression. For example, we can learn what our triggers and risk factors are. We can try to minimise risk factors. We can be careful to avoid lethal cocktails of multiple risk factors (for example, noise, heat, hunger) and triggers to which we are particularly sensitive (for example, harsh criticism). We can challenge the stories we tell ourselves and the thinking traps they contain that intensify our anger. We can learn to recognise and reduce physiological sensations associated with anger. All of these things can free us behave assertively rather than aggressively and increase our well-being.

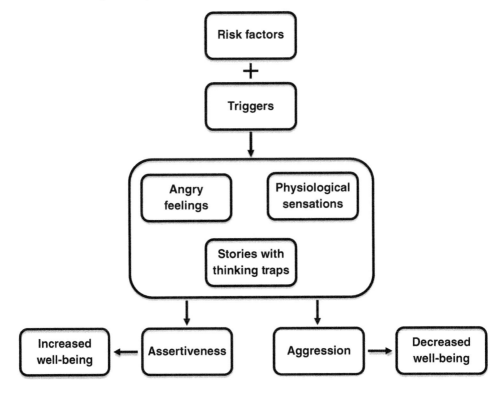

*Figure 16.1*  Assertiveness and anger.

### Triggers

Anger is typically triggered by situations that we find threatening. We all have our own anger triggers – things that push our anger buttons and make us likely to flip into the automatic fight / flight / or freeze reaction. Most of us will become angry if we are assaulted, threatened, insulted, humiliated, shouted at or harshly criticised. These are fairly universal anger triggers. Other possible anger triggers are being treated unfairly, disagreed with, exploited, told what to do or asked to do too much. Making mistakes, fail- ure, financial problems or jealousy may be triggers for anger. Some people's anger button involves being told what they think or feel or do, or what they should think or feel or do. For example, Margie saw red when her friend Kate said, 'You shouldn't be upset. You think she should have been on time. We all know she never is. So just get over it'. For other people, anger is sparked by waiting in a queue, or being ignored, taken for granted, disre- spected or interrupted. For example, Tom became furious with his team leader when he repeatedly interrupted his presentation, and later ignored his suggestions for improving teamwork. For people who have been traumatised, being reminded of trauma can trigger anger. For example, Gregory became angry anytime he thought of the borstal where he was abused as a teenager. Being forced to face something that we are frightened of can make us angry. This is particularly relevant for people with anxiety problems. For example,

Carl, who was terrified of flying, found that he became very angry anytime he had to get on a plane. Box 16.5 contains a list of situations that are often triggers for anger. Are there any situations on this list to which you are particularly sensitive and make it very likely that you will become aggressive?

---

## Box 16.5   Trigger situations for aggression

Are there any situations on this list to which you are particularly sensitive and make it very likely that you will become impulsively aggressive?

- Failing
- Waiting in a queue
- Financial problems
- Jealousy
- Being taken for granted
- Being told what you think or feel or do
- Being told what you should think or feel or do
- Being reminded of trauma
- Being spoken to aggressively
- Being interrupted
- Being disrespected
- Being sworn at
- Being called names
- Being insulted
- Being humiliated
- Being blamed
- Being criticised
- Making mistakes
- Being disagreed with
- Being treated unfairly
- Being exploited
- Being asked to do too much
- Being shouted at
- Being threatened
- Being ignored
- The transgressor stomps out of the room
- Being pushed
- Being hit
- Being assaulted
- Being injured
- Being forced to do something against your will

---

- Being betrayed
- Having your property harmed
- Having your projects sabotaged
- Having people you care about harmed
- Having others turned against you
- Having negative rumours spread about you
- Others driving aggressively

### Risk factors

There may be risk factors that make triggers far more likely to spark off an episode of impulsive aggression. People are more susceptible to their anger triggers in environments that they find too noisy, too hot, too cold or too crowded. Being stuck in traffic is a special case of being too crowded, associated with 'road rage'. Other risk factors that make us more susceptible to anger triggers include being drunk or 'high', in pain or ill, tired or hungry, frustrated or frightened, and sad or excited. Box 16.6 contains a list of situations that are often risk factors for anger. Are there any things on this list that make you more likely to become aggressive in trigger situations?

---

### Box 16.6 Risk factors for aggression

Are there any things on this list that make you more likely to become aggressive in trigger situations?

- Being too hot
- Being too cold
- Noise
- Crowding
- Traffic
- Being drunk
- Being high
- Being tired
- Being hungry
- Being in pain
- Being ill
- Being under pressure
- Being frustrated
- Being frightened
- Being sad
- Being excited

### Anger and the body

When an episode of impulsive anger is triggered by a particular situation, anger affects how our bodies work. It makes us physiologically aroused or revved up. Our hearts race. We may breathe faster. Our muscles become tense. We may perspire. We may become 'hot and bothered'. We may become restless. Our stomachs may churn. We may get headaches. We may find it difficult to concentrate. We may also feel the impulse to behave aggressively. Box 16.7 lists some of the physiological sensations associated with anger. Which of these sensations do you notice are most prominent when you become angry? Are there any that are particularly associated with becoming more aggressive than you would like to be? Would you consider any to be early warning signs that you may lose your temper?

---

### Box 16.7 Physiological sensations associated with aggression

Which of these sensations do you notice when you are angry and at risk of becoming impulsively aggressive?

- High heart rate
- Rapid breathing
- Muscle tension
- Feeling hot
- Restlessness
- Stomach churning
- Headaches
- Difficulty concentrating

---

### Thinking traps

Our thinking becomes rigid when we are angry and physiologically revved up. When our thinking becomes rigid, we are more likely to fall into thinking traps. Thinking traps make us tell ourselves stories about the triggering situation in which we find ourselves that makes us angrier. We may use these stories we tell ourselves to justify becoming aggressive. For example, when Paul's manager asked him to take on a new project, he became revved up, and angry. The story he told himself made him even angrier. He said to himself, 'I have too much on to do a new project. I should be treated fairly. I'm entitled to it. My boss is a jerk. He's just doing this to make my life difficult. He always does this. Next week he'll be criticising me for not having made enough progress'. Box 16.3 contains a list of thinking traps particularly associated with anger. Look at the list in Box 16.3 and see if you can spot the thinking traps in the story Paul told himself.

The thinking traps associated with anger fall into two broad categories. The first mainly affects our *style* of thinking. The second mainly affects the *content* of our thoughts. In Box 16.3 the thinking traps that influence our thinking style are listed first and those that affect the content of our thoughts are listed second.

The following thinking traps mainly influence our style of thinking: thresholding, blaming, name-calling, mind-reading, jumping to conclusions, black-and-white thinking, focusing on the negatives and discounting the positives, overgeneralising, making mountains out of molehills, and disaster forecasting. All of these thinking traps make our thinking style rigid and inflexible.

The remaining thinking traps in Box 16.3 may be thought of as rules that we believe we should always follow. Our conviction in these rules tends to become stronger the more revved up and angry we become. These thinking traps all contain words like 'should' or 'must', and 'always' or 'never'. This set of thinking traps includes rules about lack of control over aggression, overcontrol of anger, the necessity to let off steam when angry, the value of sharing angry feelings with other victims of injustice, using aggression to get respect, resolving hurt through revenge, using aggression to avoid fear and sadness, and a belief that entitlement justifies aggression. In fact, all of these rules are myths. There is very little evidence to support them. Re-evaluating these myths and challenging thinking traps are very effective ways of controlling anger and aggression. These will be discussed later in the chapter.

### Anger and aggressive behaviour

When we are angry, physiologically keyed up and thinking in a rigid way, we are at risk of behaving aggressively. We may say things that we later regret. We may insult or disrespect others. We may shout, storm off, hit out or react in other unplanned, hurtful ways. Box 16.8 contains a list of aggressive behaviours that may occur when angry. Can you spot the things that you do when you are very angry that you wish you didn't? Have your aggressive reactions been disproportionate to the incidents that triggered them? If so, you may wish to read the remainder of the chapter which is on anger management.

---

**Box 16.8   Aggressive behaviour**

When you are angry, which of these aggressive things do you find yourself doing?

- Speaking aggressively
- Interrupting
- Disrespecting
- Swearing
- Name-calling
- Insulting
- Humiliating
- Blaming
- Criticising
- Pointing out mistakes
- Disagreeing
- Treating unfairly

---

- Exploiting
- Demanding
- Shouting
- Threatening
- Ignoring
- Stomping out of the room
- Pushing
- Hitting
- Assaulting
- Injuring
- Forcing another person to do something they do not want to do
- Betraying
- Harming the transgressor's property
- Sabotaging the transgressor's projects
- Harming people the transgressor cares about
- Turning others against the transgressor
- Spreading negative rumours
- Driving aggressively

## Anger management

If you find that you can't always behave in a thoughtful and assertive way in the face of threats, then it may be worth considering learning to control anger and aggression. Extensive research evaluating cognitive-behavioural anger management programmes points to certain steps that we can take to reduce aggression and impulsive outbursts of anger.[7] There is an invitation now for you to decide if anger and aggression are preventing you from achieving important goals in your life. For example, Seamus noticed that at work he frequently became involved in heated arguments. He became very keyed up and said things that he regretted. On some occasions, he shouted, overturned furniture, walked out of meetings and slammed doors. It took a long time for him to calm down after these episodes. He found he couldn't concentrate. He got behind in his work. This was pointed out in a weekly review meeting with his line manager. He decided that he needed to find a way to control his anger, because it was interfering with his work as a design engineer which he valued highly.

Anger management involves the following:[8]

- Keeping an anger diary
- Developing strategies to prevent angry or aggressive episodes
- Developing skills for calming down when the fight / flight / or freeze response occurs
- Challenging thinking traps that fuel anger
- Replacing aggression with assertion.[3]

### Anger diary

If you have decided that you wish to develop better control over your anger and aggression, then you may find it helpful to get a snap-shot of how you manage anger over the course of a typical week in your life. Keep a diary for a week, noting each time you find yourself becoming irritated, angry or aggressive. Box 16.9. contains guidelines for keeping an anger diary. For each episode, write down (1) your rating of how intense your anger was on a scale of 1 to 10, where 1 is not angry at all and 10 is extremely angry; (2) the duration of the episode; (3) any background risk factors that made your anger worse like being drunk, tired or hungry; (4) the situation that triggered your anger (the time, place, people involved and what they said or did); (5) the physiological sensations that were most noticeable to you when you were angry; (6) the story you told yourself about the situation and any thinking traps you fell into; (7) aggressive things you did and said when angry; (8) the effect that your impulsive aggressive behaviour had on the situation. Especially note the extent to which the episode moved you towards or away from your valued goals. Box 16.10 contains a summary of all of the risk factors, trigger situations, physiological sensations associated with anger, thinking traps and aggressive behaviours we have discussed so far. It may be helpful to refer to this when writing about episodes in your anger diary. Review your anger diary after a week. Draw conclusions about what usually happens during your anger episodes. Does the way you handle these situations move you closer to or further away from your highly valued goals? This information may help you to plan to reduce the number of anger episodes you have in future, and handle trigger situations better.

---

### Box 16.9  Keep an anger diary

For a week, after each anger episode write a description of the episode using these headings:

- Anger rating on a 10-pont scale, where 1 is not angry and 10 is extremely angry
- Duration of the episode
- Risk factors that were there before you entered the trigger situation
- Trigger situation
- Physiological sensations you felt when angry
- Story you told yourself, and any thinking traps you fell into when angry
- Aggressive things you did and said when angry
- Did anger move you towards or away from valued goals?

Review your diary after a week and draw conclusions about what usually happens in your anger episodes.

## Box 16.10 Summary of risk factors, trigger situations, physiological sensations associated with anger, thinking traps and aggressive behaviour

| Risk factors | Trigger situations | Sensations | Thinking traps | Behaviour |
|---|---|---|---|---|
| • Being too hot<br>• Being too cold<br>• Noise<br>• Crowding<br>• Traffic<br>• Being drunk<br>• Being high<br>• Being tired<br>• Being hungry<br>• Being in pain<br>• Being ill<br>• Being under pressure<br>• Being frustrated<br>• Being frightened<br>• Being sad<br>• Being excited | • Failing<br>• Waiting in a queue<br>• Financial problems<br>• Jealousy<br>• Being taken for granted<br>• Being told what you think or feel or do<br>• Being told what you should think or feel or do<br>• Being reminded of trauma<br>• Being spoken to aggressively<br>• Being interrupted<br>• Being disrespected<br>• Being sworn at<br>• Being called names<br>• Being insulted<br>• Being humiliated<br>• Being blamed<br>• Being criticised<br>• Making mistakes<br>• Being disagreed with<br>• Being treated unfairly<br>• Being exploited<br>• Being asked to do too much | • High heart rate<br>• Rapid breathing<br>• Muscle tension<br>• Feeling hot<br>• Restlessness<br>• Stomach churning<br>• Headaches<br>• Difficulty concentrating | • **Thresholding.** Setting an arbitrary limit, standard or threshold, which when crossed justifies your anger. For example, 'That's the last straw. I've given him three chances, and he blew it. I'm going to let him know how angry I am'.<br>• **Blaming.** Thinking that something is all someone's else's fault without looking at all of the evidence. For example, 'It's all the other person's fault, not mine, so I am angry'.<br>• **Name-calling.** Labelling others in a negative way based on a single experience. For example, 'He said he was not satisfied with my work last week, therefore he is a jerk/prat/ SOB for criticising me'.<br>• **Mind-reading.** Assuming that others are intentionally trying to hurt or annoy you without having evidence for this or checking it out. For example, 'He's just doing that to annoy me, so I am angry at him'.<br>• **Jumping to conclusions.** Reaching a conclusion very quickly without considering alternatives and important evidence. For example, 'She forgot to bring back the book she borrowed, and this means she is taking advantage of my generosity, so I am angry at her'. | • Speaking aggressively<br>• Interrupting<br>• Disrespecting<br>• Swearing<br>• Name-calling<br>• Insulting<br>• Humiliating<br>• Blaming<br>• Criticising<br>• Pointing out mistakes<br>• Disagreeing with<br>• Treating unfairly<br>• Exploiting<br>• Demanding<br>• Shouting<br>• Threatening<br>• Ignoring<br>• Stomping out of the room<br>• Pushing<br>• Hitting<br>• Assaulting<br>• Injuring<br>• Forcing the transgressor to do something they do not want to do |

| Risk factors | Trigger situations | Sensations | Thinking traps | Behaviour |
|---|---|---|---|---|
| | • Being shouted at<br>• Being threatened<br>• Being ignored<br>• The transgressor stomps out of the room<br>• Being pushed<br>• Being hit<br>• Being assaulted<br>• Being injured<br>• Being forced to do something against your will<br>• Being betrayed<br>• Having your property harmed<br>• Having your projects sabotaged<br>• Having people you care about harmed<br>• Having others turned against you<br>• Having negative rumours spread about you<br>• Others driving aggressively | | • **Black-and-white thinking.** Thinking about things as all good or all bad, with no shades of grey in between. For example, 'It's all your fault. It's nothing to do with me, so I'm angry'.<br>• **Focusing on the negatives and discounting the positives.** Only paying attention to bad things, while ignoring good things or saying that they don't matter. For example, 'He didn't do his fair share of the work. He was supposed to do 10 things but he left one out. But that one thing is really important, so I am angry at him'.<br>• **Overgeneralising.** Making sweeping judgements based on one experience. For example, 'Because he said one critical thing about me, that means he will always be critical, so I am angry at him'.<br>• **Making mountains out of molehills.** Ruminating for hours about threatening things that happened in the past, so that little challenges become blown up to be huge anger-fuelling threats. For example, 'She disrespected me once, but that was just the tip of the iceberg. She will probably do it again and again. I hate her and am angry at her'.<br>• **Disaster forecasting.** Anticipating that the future will be very distressing on the basis of limited evidence, and dwelling on this idea for a long time. For example, 'He is going to criticise or humiliate me, therefore I am angry'. | • Betraying<br>• Harming the transgressor's property<br>• Sabotaging the transgressor's projects<br>• Harming people the transgressor cares about<br>• Turning others against the transgressor<br>• Spreading negative rumours<br>• Driving aggressively |

- **A rule containing should or must, and always or never.** Making absolute statements about how I or others ought to be always or never.

- **A rule about lack of control.** I can never control my anger (because I inherited my temper, or was traumatised).

- **A rule about overcontrol.** I should always be in control of my feelings and never get angry.

- **A rule about letting off steam.** I must always express my anger aggressively to let off steam and get rid of it.

- **A rule about sharing.** It's always a good thing to share anger and let off steam with other victims like me to help me control my anger about being victimised.

- **A rule about getting respect.** I must always express my anger aggressively to make others respect me and my rights.

- **A rule about getting even.** I must always take revenge and get even, to make me feel better when someone hurts or threatens me.

- **A rule about avoiding fear and sadness.** It's always better to feel and express anger, rather than to feel and express fear or sadness.

- **A rule about entitlement.** I am always entitled to be treated as special, and if I'm not treated as special, I will be uncontrollably angry.

For example, when Seamus reviewed his anger diary he noticed that in one week he had seven episodes at work and none at home. Most episodes occurred when he was tired or hungry. They were triggered by his colleagues suggesting courses of action with which he disagreed. In these situations, he would tell himself that they were intentionally disagreeing with him to annoy or disrespect him. These thoughts led him to become very keyed up. He noticed that his heart raced, and he couldn't think clearly. In all situations, he raised his voice. On one occasion, he insulted a colleague. His anger intensity ratings ranged from 7 to 9. The episodes lasted from 5 to 15 minutes. However, on all occasions he was relatively unproductive for a couple of hours after an anger episode. He found that he rehearsed arguments with his colleagues over and over in his mind. This prevented him from focusing on his work. He used this information to reduce his number of anger episodes as follows. He decided not to start conversations with colleagues that might trigger his anger when he was tired or hungry. He also planned to learn and use anger control skills to calm himself down, if he got into disagreements with his colleagues. He decided, in future, to challenge the stories he told himself when he got angry. His colleagues, he thought on reflection, were probably not trying to annoy him. They probably wanted their work team to be productive, just like he did. Finally, he planned to find some alternative, more respectful and assertive ways to talk to his colleagues when they disagreed with him.

### Preventing aggression

You can prevent unnecessary episodes of anger and aggression by using the strategies listed in Box 16.11.

- Learn your risk factors, triggers and early warning physiological signs
- Change your routines so there are fewer risk factors
- Avoid anger triggers when there are many unavoidable risk factors
- Re-evaluate unhelpful beliefs about anger.

---

**Box 16.11   Prevent unnecessary angry episodes**

- Learn your:

  o   Risk factors
  o   Triggers
  o   Physiological sensations

- Change your routines so there are fewer risk factors
- Avoid triggers when there are many unavoidable risk factors (like noise, tiredness, traffic, hunger)
- Re-evaluate the extent to which you hold unhelpful beliefs about anger:

  o   A rule about lack of control. 'I can never control my anger (because I inherited my temper, or was traumatised)'.

- o   A rule about overcontrol. 'I should always be in control of my feelings and never get angry'.
- o   A rule about letting off steam. 'I must always express my anger aggressively to let off steam and get rid of it'.
- o   A rule about sharing. 'It's always a good thing to share anger and let off steam with other victims like me to help me control my anger about being victimised'.
- o   A rule about getting respect. 'I must always express my anger aggressively to make others respect me and my rights'.
- o   A rule about getting even. 'I must always take revenge and get even, to make me feel better when someone hurts or threatens me'.
- o   A rule about avoiding fear and sadness. 'It's always better to feel and express anger, rather than to feel and express fear or sadness'.
- o   A rule about entitlement. 'I am always entitled to be treated as special, and if I'm not treated as special, I will be uncontrollably angry'.

## Learn your pattern

When we keep an anger diary for a week and review it, it helps us to become aware of our risk factors and triggers for anger episodes as they occur in day-to-day life. You will have learned from your anger diary the sorts of risk factors that make it likely that you will become angry, and the threatening situations that are likely to trigger aggressive or disrespectful behaviour. These situations are the ones that push your anger buttons. Be on the lookout for them. However, even if you are very vigilant, you may not notice them all. Because of this, it's important also to be on the lookout for early warning signs that your automatic fight / flight / or freeze reaction has started. Keep an eye out for increased heart rate, breathing more rapidly, feeling hot or sweating. For example, in the week following keeping an anger diary, Seamus was aware of four situations that could have triggered angry episodes. These all occurred when he was very tired and was criticised by work colleagues. There were two situations where he did not anticipate feeling threatened. He only noticed these when he had to take his jacket off because he was too warm. In these situations, he was tired and hungry, having returned home from work. Both his wife and children were talking loudly at the same time, and asking for his help with different things. Instead of shouting at them, as he usually would, he took some time out to calm down. He changed out of his work suit into his casual clothes, while listening to some calming music. Then he returned to the living room and offered to help his family.

## Change your routines

You may wish to review your anger diary and reflect on the factors that put you at risk of becoming angry. These risk factors may include heat, cold, noise, crowding or traffic, or where you are drunk, high, tired, hungry, in pain, ill, under pressure, frustrated, frightened, sad or excited. Any time there are a lot of these risk factors present, you are at high risk of anger episodes if you end up in a trigger situation. Think about how you could re-organise your average weekday or weekend so that there are fewer of these factors present that put you at risk of becoming angry, acting aggressively and moving away from, rather than towards, your highly valued goals when you encounter anger triggers. This process of reorganisation may involve getting more sleep, eating regular meals, commuting earlier or later in the day to avoid traffic, regulating use of alcohol or drugs, exercising regularly, practising relaxation or meditation, and balancing the demands of work and family life in a different way. Some of these issues are addressed in Chapters 4–6.

### Avoid anger triggers when there are many unavoidable risk factors

It's rarely possible for us to re-organise our routines so that they contain no risk factors for anger. There will always be some anger risk factors in our lives. When there are many risk factors like heat, cold, noise, crowding or traffic, or where you are drunk, high, tired, hungry, in pain, ill, under pressure, frustrated, frightened, sad or excited, avoid situations that usually trigger anger for you. That is, avoid trigger situations where you may be threatened, insulted, humiliated, shouted at, harshly criticised, treated unfairly, disagreed with, exploited, told what to do, asked to do too much, or where you may make mistakes, fail, have financial problems, be jealous, have to wait in a queue, be ignored, be taken for granted, be disrespected, be interrupted, be told what you think or feel or do, be told what you should think or feel or do, be reminded of trauma, or be forced to face something you are frightened of. For example, Seamus knew that when he had drunk alcohol, was tired and in a noisy environment, he was more likely to become angry if interrupted. On Friday, after a tiring week at work, he went for drinks with some colleagues. He knew from experience that his colleague, Rupert, would repeatedly interrupt him with tasteless jokes, after he had had a couple of drinks, if they become involved in long conversation. Seamus knew that he would react to Rupert by becoming angry. He therefore decided, as they entered the pub, not to get into a long conversation with Rupert.

### Re-evaluate anger myths

In the lower half of Box 16.3 we came across a number of thinking traps that often occur in our minds as rules associated with anger and threat. For example, 'I must always express my anger aggressively to let off steam and get rid of it'. There is little evidence to support this, or any of the other rules listed in the lower half of Box 16.3. These are myths. If we believe in any of these myths, they may stop us from controlling anger and expressing it in an assertive or respectful way. If you believe any of these myths, there is an invitation now for you to re-evaluate them. This may help you prevent unnecessary anger episodes.

#### Anger is uncontrollable

The myth that anger is uncontrollable may be tied to the idea that having a bad temper is inherited, that trauma leads to uncontrollable rage or that working in a high-pressure job makes the anger we feel uncontrollable. For example, Sean believed that he had an uncontrollable temper, just like his father. Malachy, who had been abused for many years in a child-care institution, and Howard, a war veteran, who had been traumatised by armed combat, both believed that their traumatic experiences had made them uncontrollably angry. Sue, a surgeon, believed that the anger she expressed towards junior doctors on her team for being less skilled than she would prefer was uncontrollable and justified her verbally abusing them when they were slow to follow her directives in the operating theatre. It's true that people born with a difficult temperament, trauma survivors and people in high-pressure jobs find that they are more easily provoked to anger by smaller triggers than others. However, all of us can learn to identify our triggers and risk factors, and then use anger management skills to prevent or regulate impulsive aggressive outbursts.

## You can decide never to be angry

It is a myth that we can simply decide never to be angry, because our bodies automatically respond to threats with the fight, flight or freeze reaction. It is not possible to go through life without encountering threats to our safety and security. It is, therefore, inevitable that we will experience anger at these times. However, we can decide how we deal with anger when we experience it. We can learn to avoid expressing anger in impulsive, destructive, abusive or aggressive ways. We can become skilled at recognising situations in which we are at risk of expressing anger aggressively. We can develop skills for calming ourselves down, so we don't act impulsively in the heat of the moment. We can learn to challenge the stories we tell ourselves about situations that we find anger-provoking. We can also develop skills for expressing anger in assertive rather than aggressive ways.

## Letting off steam

It is a myth is that letting off steam will get rid of our anger. By letting off steam, I mean name-calling, insulting, humiliating, shouting, kicking something, punching a pillow or hitting someone with a foam baton. In the past, some psychotherapists advocated that partners in unhappy relationships hit each other with foam batons to help them manage anger. It doesn't work. Letting off steam doesn't act like a safety valve and help us control or reduce anger. Letting off steam is effectively practising being angry and aggressive. It makes it more likely that we will say angry things or behave aggressively in future.

## Sharing

A related myth is that sharing angry feelings in an uninhibited way with others who have been on the receiving end of the same sort of oppression that we have suffered will help with anger management. Sharing anger with fellow survivors of abuse or armed combat is equivalent to a group of people collectively letting off steam together. Just like letting off steam on our own, this doesn't work. It is like practising being angry and aggressive in a group format. It makes it more likely that we will behave aggressively in future. However, sharing the expression of anger with other survivors of similar sorts of oppression may generate group support. This may mobilise group members to take collective assertive action against an oppressor. Sharing anger, in this way, is a common strategy used in civil rights movements.

## Anger makes people respect you

It's a myth that if we don't express anger in a forceful way, people will disrespect us, take advantage of us or think we're weak. If we allow ourselves to express anger in an aggressive or disrespectful way; if we lose our tempers; if we use abusive language; if we threaten others; then in the short-term people may defer to us. However, in the long-term this may lead to our colleagues, friends and family avoiding us because our anger is unpleasant, and possibly because it is not easy for others to predict what will trigger these unpleasant outbursts. If we talk to others in an assertive, respectful way, in most situations they will be more likely to treat us with respect. Bullies are rarely respected.

## Revenge

It's a myth that the best way to control anger is by taking revenge and getting even. Paying someone back for threatening or hurting us may bring temporary relief. In the long run, however, it is likely to lead to reprisals. An escalating pattern of attack and counter-attack will inevitably follow. One of the reasons civilised societies developed laws, law-enforcement systems and courts was to prevent blood feuds. Such feuds led to lengthy conflicts between families involving an escalating cycle of retaliatory killings. The costs were high. Many were killed. The benefits were few.

## It's better to feel and express anger than fear or sadness

Sometimes when we are frightened, sad or emotionally hurt, we avoid these painful feelings by becoming angry. It may feel better in the short-term to experience and express anger, rather than to allow ourselves to feel tender emotions like fear or sadness behind the anger. In close, intimate relationships this can be counterproductive. For example, when Vanessa said she couldn't help her partner, Scott, with the gardening on Saturday, he got into an angry fight with her, telling her that she was selfish and lazy. Beneath this anger, Scott felt hurt because he worried that Vanessa did not care about him enough to spend time with him. The fight led to Vanessa storming out of the house and not talking to him for 24 hours. This led Scott to feel lonely. The next day, Scott apologised and told Vanessa he was angry, because he worried that Vanessa did not care about him enough to work on the garden with him. This expression of primary emotions (worry or hurt) was far more effective than the expression of the secondary emotion (anger) in helping Scott achieve his valued goal of maintaining a close relationship with Vanessa. (Addressing anger in close relationships is discussed in detail in Chapter 12, and in particular in the exercise in Box 12.5.)

## Entitlement

The idea that there some people who are 'special' and are therefore entitled to be treated far better than others is an unhelpful idea for most of us. If we cling to this idea or rule, then every time we are treated the same as other people, we will feel short-changed and angry. It's far more useful to view all of humanity as being entitled to the same rights. Any time we are treated in a way where we get more than is our right, this will be a bonus and may increase our well-being.

### Anger control

When we find ourselves in situations where there are anger triggers, where we notice that we are becoming physiologically aroused and where we are at risk of becoming aggressive, we may use well-rehearsed skills, listed in Box 16.12, to calm ourselves down.

---

**Box 16.12 Anger control**

If you begin to become angry, calm yourself down using any of these skills:

- **Stop.** Say stop to yourself and imagine a stop sign, a red light or someone shouting stop.
- **Breath.** Take a few deep diaphragmatic breaths, breathing in for three and out for six.
- **Count.** Slowly count from 1 to 10 in your mind. If you are not calm when you get to 10, keep counting until you become calm.
- **Time out.** Take time out for a couple of minutes.
- **Walk.** Take a walk.
- **Distract.** Do something distracting that is pleasant, for example listen to music, watch a comedy clip on your computer or smartphone, visualise a pleasant scene etc.
- **Relax.** Do the brief relaxation exercise in Box 5.3. Pay special attention to particularly tense muscle groups, for example shoulders, neck and hands.
- **Meditate.** Do the brief meditation exercise in Box 6.6. Pay special attention to sensations of physiological arousal, especially rapid breathing, increased heart rate, hotness and muscle tension.

After you have used any of these skills in a real-life situation, notice how angry you feel on a scale of 1 to 10, where 1 is not angry at all and 10 is extremely angry. If you have successfully calmed yourself down, praise yourself for this.

---

**Stop.** Say 'stop' to yourself. Imagine a stop sign, a red light or someone shouting stop in your mind's eye. Use this as a signal to stop the anger you are beginning to feel from escalating into aggression.

**Breathe.** Take a few deep diaphragmatic breaths, breathing in for three and out for six.

**Count till you're calm.** Slowly and carefully count from 1 to 10 in your mind, pausing between each number. If you are not calm when you get to 10, keep counting until you become calm.

**Take time out.** Excuse yourself from the situation for a couple of minutes to calm yourself down.

**Walk.** Take a walk.

**Distract yourself.** Do something distracting that is pleasant, for example listen to music, or watch a comedy clip on your computer or smartphone.

**Relax.** Do the brief relaxation exercise in Box 5.3. Pay special attention to particularly tense muscles, for example those in your shoulders, neck and hands.

**Meditate.** Do the brief meditation exercise in Box 6.6. Pay special attention to sensations of physiological arousal such as increased heart rate, rapid breathing, hotness etc.

After you have used any of these skills in a real-life situation, notice how angry you feel on a scale of 1 to 10, where 1 is not angry at all and 10 is extremely angry. If you have successfully calmed yourself down, praise yourself for this.

### Challenge thinking traps

When we reflect on a situation in which we were angry, and ask ourselves what was most threatening about it, we often find the answer in the story we told ourselves about this situation. It is usually these stories about situations and not the situations themselves that make us feel threatened, and provoke our anger.

These stories may be threatening because they contain thinking traps. Stories that contain thinking traps are rarely true, or useful. When Seamus, in the example mentioned earlier, heard his colleagues disagree with him and he became angry, his anger was mainly fuelled by the story that he must always be right, and also by the story that his colleagues might be disagreeing with him to annoy him. The story that Seamus was telling himself contained two thinking traps listed in Box 16.3. The first thinking trap was a rule containing 'must' and 'always': 'I must always be right'. The second thinking trap was mind-reading: 'My colleagues are disagreeing with me to annoy me'.

The 'I must always be right' thinking trap fuelled Seamus' anger in the following way. When his colleagues disagreed with him, this threatened the image he had of himself as someone who must always be right. He had learned this from his father, who strongly believed in this rule. He identified with his father, and so he had come to adopt this rule in his own life. When this rule was challenged, he felt it was a personal attack and so he became very angry.

However, he came to see that this story or rule, 'I must always be right', was preventing him from achieving his valued goals of having a cohesive team at work, and a happy family at home. He decided to modify it to 'I may often, but not always, be right. I would prefer to listen to my team mates more, and to my wife and children more, because sometimes they will be right. I do not want to miss those important opportunities when I might learn something new'. Seamus still became irritated when his colleagues and family members disagreed with him. However, he did not fly into a rage, and become aggressive, because he had let go of the story that he must always be right.

The 'mind-reading' thinking trap fuelled Seamus' anger as follows. He assumed that his colleagues were intentionally trying to annoy or disrespect him. This hurt him deeply because he wanted their respect and he reacted by becoming angry. Reflecting on this story he told himself, Seamus acknowledged that he couldn't read other people's minds. It was possible that his colleagues were suggesting courses of action with which he disagreed for reasons other than trying to annoy or disrespect him. He decided to ask them about these reasons. He found that this process of challenging the stories he told himself reduced the intensity of the anger he felt.

When you reflect on a situation in which you were angry, bring to mind the story you told yourself about this situation. It is often these stories about the situation, and not the situations themselves, that makes us feel threatened and angry. These stories may be threating because they contain thinking traps. Stories that contain thinking traps are rarely true or useful.

Most of the thinking traps in Box 16.3 refer to rigid thinking styles. For example, with black-and-white thinking, we view people or situations as all good or all bad. Rigid thinking styles fuel anger and conflict. Flexible thinking styles, in contrast, help us to form good relationships and improve our well-being. With flexible thinking styles, we see the shades of grey between black and white. We see people as having both positive and negative characteristics. We see situations as having advantages and disadvantages.

Many stories we tell ourselves in situations that trigger anger involve us judging others to have broken a rule that we learned early in life. These rules contain the words should or must, and always or never. Here are some examples of these sorts of rules: I'm entitled to be able to relax when I get home from work; you should know what I feel or think without me having to explain; people should always be fair; I must always be right; no-one should ever make mistakes; everyone should always work as hard as I do; no-one should ever break a promise.

It may be that we have not explicitly stated these rules, or acknowledged that we believe them. We may have learned these rules when we were growing up in our own families, or in other relationships. We may have assumed that they were true, or right, or just, without questioning them. When these implicit rules are broken, and we become angry, it's helpful to challenge them. To challenge them, we need first to state them as simply as possible. Then, we can re-evaluate them, as discussed above.

When we are all revved up, it's difficult to clearly see the thinking traps woven into the fabric of the stories we tell ourselves. It is usually after we have used the skills in Box 16.12 to calm ourselves down that we can see the thinking traps that are embedded in stories we tell ourselves. Often these stories come to us as a 'hot thoughts'. They seem to flash into our minds unbidden, and we notice that they instantly fuel our anger. Here are some examples of 'hot thoughts': 'That's not fair!'; 'Don't tell me what to do, you stupid idiot!'; 'Stop annoying me on purpose!'; 'That's the last straw!'; 'It's all your fault, you jerk, stop getting at me!'; 'That's typical of you, here you go again, you've ruined my day!' etc. As you become more skilled at finding thinking traps in the stories you tell yourself when angry, you may find you can do this not only when you have calmed down, but also in the heat of the moment.

You may challenge these stories you tell yourself that contain thinking traps by asking yourself important questions like these:

- Does this 'hot thought' contain a thinking trap that will prevent me from achieving my highly valued goals?
- Does this 'hot thought' fit with my 'big picture'?
- Is there any evidence that this 'hot thought' or story I'm telling myself is not completely true?
- How could I modify my story to make it truer, and more useful to me in achieving my highly valued goals?

## Summary

- **Anger** is a useful emotion that motivates us to protect ourselves from threats to our safety, security or well-being. The assertive expression of anger enhances well-being. The impulsive, aggressive expression of anger may reduce well-being.
- **Fight / flight / or freeze reactions** automatically occur in response to threats to our safety, security or well-being. During these reactions adrenaline is released into the blood stream and increases in heart rate, muscle tension and strength occur. This prepares us to attack those that threaten us, or to escape or hide from them. This reaction, which we have inherited from our ancestors, is good for dealing with some physically threatening problems. However, the impulse to behave aggressively is rarely useful for complex social threats that require thoughtful, assertive responses.
- **Assertiveness.** The challenge in expressing anger assertively is to control angry feelings, and to tell the right person, at the right time, in the right place, in the right way, specifically what we are angry about, and how we would prefer them to behave in future. It involves speaking in a positive, respectful, calm, co-operative, solution-focused way, using I statements, and avoiding thinking traps.
- **Anger and aggression are multidimensional**. Risk factors, like noise or crowding, increase the risk that specific triggers, like being criticised, will be perceived as threatening, and lead to physiological sensations associated with the fight / flight / or freeze reaction, such as increased heart and respiration rates, a tendency to fall into thinking traps and aggressive behaviour.
- **Thinking traps that fuel anger**. Traps that affect thinking style include thresholding, blaming, name-calling, mind-reading, jumping to conclusions, black-and-white thinking, focusing on the negatives and discounting the positives, overgeneralising, making mountains out of molehills, and disaster forecasting. Thinking traps that affect thought content include rules about lack of control over aggression, overcontrol of anger, the necessity to let off steam when angry, the value of sharing angry feelings with other victims of injustice, using aggression to get respect, resolving hurt through revenge, using aggression to avoid fear and sadness, and a belief that entitlement justifies aggression.
- **Anger management** involves learning risk factors and triggers by keeping an anger diary, developing strategies to prevent angry or aggressive episodes, developing skills for calming down when the fight / flight / or freeze response occurs, challenging thinking traps and replacing aggression with assertion.
- **Strategies to prevent angry or aggressive episodes** include changing routines so there are fewer risk factors, avoiding anger triggers when there are many unavoidable risk factors and re-evaluating unhelpful beliefs about anger.
- **Anger control skills** include saying 'stop' to yourself, diaphragmatic breathing, counting till you're calm, taking time out, taking a walk, distraction, relaxation (the exercise in Box 5.3) and meditation (the exercise in Box 6.6).
- **Challenge thinking traps** by asking if there is any evidence to show that the story you are telling yourself is not 100% true, and whether there is a more useful story that will help you achieve your highly valued goals.

## Where are you now?

Anger control strategies liberate us to embrace assertiveness and let go of aggression.

If you have done the exercises and followed some of the guidelines in this chapter, you may have found that they have helped you respond assertively when facing things that threaten you and make you feel angry.

You may want to read back over the chapter and summarise in your journal the main things that you have learned from this chapter about being assertive and controlling anger in situations that you find threatening. You can now decide if you want to use these strategies for anger management and being assertive in situations that you find particularly threatening.

In the next chapter, you will have an opportunity to read about forgiving those who have wronged you. Below are some web resources and books that are relevant to topics you have read about in this chapter.

## Web resources

Video on being assertive (3:48): www.youtube.com/watch?v=ubSL1tFmgDc
Video on being assertive (6:50): www.youtube.com/watch?v=OpXmRjbCNOM
Video on anger control using cognitive behaviour therapy (4:00): www.youtube.com/watch?v=umeicApyjug
Video on anger control (5:14): www.youtube.com/watch?v=oByJpMHFM1g

## Books

Alberti, R., & Emmons, M. (2017). *Your perfect right: Assertiveness and equality in your life and relationships* (Tenth Edition). Atascadero, CA: Impact Publishers.

Dansiger, S. (2018). *Mindfulness for anger management: Transformative skills for overcoming anger and managing powerful emotions.* New York, NY: Althea Press.

McKay, M., & Rogers, P. (2000). *The anger control workbook.* Oakland, CA: New Harbinger.

Tafrate, R. C., & Kassinove, H. (2019). *Anger management for everyone: Ten proven strategies to help you control anger and live a happier life* (Second Edition). Atascadero, CA: Impact Publishers.

# 17 Forgiveness

In this chapter, you will read about forgiveness as a response to being hurt or harmed by another person. When we have been threatened or harmed, we initially experience the fight / flight / or freeze automatic reaction.[1] This reaction was discussed in the opening paragraphs of Chapters 15 and 16. This may be followed by an urge for revenge.[2] We may find ourselves ruminating about how we have been hurt or wronged. We may think repeatedly about the grudge we hold against the transgressor. We spend time developing revenge plans. We may engage in acts of revenge. These may be met with further acts aggression in an escalating spiral of tit-for-tat battles that get worse each time. This process of rumination, holding grudges, plotting and engaging in revenge may reactive the fight / flight / or freeze reaction. This, in turn, may reduce our well-being, leaving us feeling distressed much of the time.

For example, at work, Lillian overheard Denise telling her colleagues that she couldn't be trusted with challenging projects. Later, the manager gave Denise, and not Lillian, a challenging project to direct. If Lillian had been given this project, it could have led to her getting an end-of-year bonus. Lillian spent weeks thinking about how to 'get even' and show Denise that there was a high price to pay for ruining her reputation, and jeopardising the possibility of an end-of-year bonus. She hacked into Denise's final report on the challenging project, and edited it so that it contained errors. Denise was reprimanded by the manager for producing such shoddy work. Denise suspected that Lillian had hacked into her report and altered it. In retaliation, Denise spread further negative rumours about Lillian. The feud between them escalated. Both Denise and Lillian spent a great deal of time thinking about how to get back at each other and feeling angry, frightened, sad and guilty about these events. Eventually, they both left the company and took jobs elsewhere. This could have worked out differently. Lillian could have made a decision early in the process to forgive Denise. This would have saved her a significant amount of distress. Practising forgiveness is important because a lack of forgiveness is a hidden and highly significant factor underpinning a great deal of unhappiness.

## Benefits of forgiveness

Research in the field of positive psychology has shown that forgiveness is associated with many benefits.[3] It leads to better psychological and physical well-being. Where grudges are held for a long time, these can be experienced as an ongoing psychological weight to carry. When we forgive others, there is a sense of a burden being lifted. Forgiveness stops us ruminating. This, in turn, prevents chronic negative mood states, especially anger, anxiety and depression. Because forgiveness reduces chronic negative mood states, it also prevents health problems that occur when people hold onto grudges and do not forgive. These include problems with the immune system, the gastrointestinal system and the cardiovascular system. Forgiveness can lead to a deepening of relationships with transgressors. This may involve repentance on the part of the transgressor. Forgiveness can lead to greater marital satisfaction when the transgressor is a spouse. It can also lead to better adjustment to bereavement, where the deceased has wronged us.

## Evolution, revenge and forgiveness

We have evolved to engage in both revenge and forgiveness in response to dealing with situations where we have been threatened or harmed.[4] Revenge acts as a deterrent against further transgressions. In contrast, forgiveness maintains relationships between victims and transgressors.

For our prehistoric ancestors, taking revenge by harming transgressors acted as a deterrent. It prevented the transgressor, or others who witnessed acts of revenge, from harming the victim again. In this context, harm refers to direct physical harm to a person, or indirect harm. This includes harm to those the victim cares for, their possessions or their reputations.

For our prehistoric ancestors, there were, however, costs associated with revenge. First, in certain circumstances it led to an escalating tit-for-tat spiral of attacks and reprisals, where both the victim and the transgressor suffered severe losses. Second, in most circumstances it led to victims losing the support of transgressors, and those affiliated with them. This was problematic. Because humans are a relatively weak and vulnerable species, our prehistoric ancestors depended on the co-operation and support of other group members, especially those within their family. They depended on them to help defend themselves from predators, and manage tasks vital for survival. These included acquiring food, building dwellings, forming families and childrearing. We have therefore evolved so that, in certain circumstances, we can forgive people who have harmed us. In doing so, we prevent the loss of their support. We also prevent the risk to the survival of the group that a revenge-motivated blood-feud would cause. In many circumstances forgiveness is adaptive. It is not surprising, therefore, that forgiveness leads to greater well-being.

In modern life, betrayal, breaches of trust and acts of physical or psychological hostility occur within friendships, romantic relationships, families and at work. For example, a friend breaks a promise, one partner lies to another about an extramarital affair, a sibling lets you down or a work colleague spreads a negative rumour about you. In some instances, like the example of Denise and Lillian mentioned above, these transgressions lead to revenge. Spirals of retribution and retaliation which culminate in the destruction of relationships may follow.

Forgiveness is an important way for curbing such escalating spirals.[5] It is a way of transforming conflict into co-operation. Forgiveness is a way of reacting to being wronged that aims to make our relationship with the person who wronged us better, rather than worse. With forgiveness, we experience sentiments like this: 'I acknowledge that you made a transgression against me, but I am not looking for retribution. I forgive you. The debt you owe me for your transgression is cancelled'. When we forgive someone who has hurt us, we let go of the wish to seek revenge. We give the person who has transgressed against us the gifts of forgiveness and mercy, even though the transgressor does not deserve these gifts. We do not give these gifts out of pity, or a sense of obligation. We make a personal choice to be merciful and forgiving. Our motivation may be altruistic. By altruistic, I mean a selfless concern for others' well-being. We may want to be generous to the other person. Our motivation may also be self-serving. We may be forgiving to experience greater well-being.

## Barriers to forgiveness

There are barriers to the expression of forgiveness.[6] We may feel that our forgiveness will be interpreted as a sign of weakness and that this will lead to repeated transgressions. This is probably what motivated Lillian to hack into Denise's report and make errors in it, in the example described above. Also, when we forgive others, we give up our position as an aggrieved victim and lose the power to induce guilt and the luxury of experiencing and expressing righteous indignation. Forgiveness requires us to put pride aside and be humble. Humility involves seeing ourselves as no better or no worse than others. Forgiveness requires us to empathise with the other person and understand how the situation looks from their perspective. Setting pride aside and engaging in humility and empathy are extremely challenging processes. They render us vulnerable to attack. They are, therefore, obstacles to engaging in forgiveness.

## Factors that make it easier to forgive

It's easier to forgive some people than others.[7] We find it easier to forgive people whose transgressions were unintentional, less severe, less dangerous and led to fewer negative consequences for us. It's also easier to forgive people who we feel close to; who we think will be valuable to us in the future; who apologise; and who we judge to be unlikely to harm us again. All of these conditions reduce our bad feelings towards transgressors. This makes it easier for us to empathise with them. It makes forgiveness easier. In the example of Lillian and Denise mentioned above, Lillian found it very difficult to forgive Denise for a number of reasons. She knew that Denise had intentionally spread malicious rumours about her. She knew that these rumours would prevent her from getting assigned challenging projects and earning related bonus payments. She did not have a close relationship with Denise. She did not think that her relationship with Denise would ever be one of deep friendship or important work-related collaboration. Therefore, she did not think her relationship with Denise was valuable. She also did not judge Denise to be safe, because Denise didn't apologise. Lillian felt she was likely to be hurt her again. In contrast, Lillian had no difficulty forgiving her sister, Maura, when she accidentally spilled coffee on a dress she had borrowed. This was because the harm done was unintentional, not severe and had limited negative consequences for Lillian. Also, Lillian was close to Maura, valued her relationship with her sister and did not think that Maura would do this sort of thing again. Within romantic relationships, people find it easier to forgive their partners if they have a high level of relationship satisfaction, a high level of commitment to the relationship and a high level of psychological intimacy with their partners.

## How forgiveness differs from other non-aggressive responses

Forgiveness may be distinguished from other non-aggressive responses to transgression.[8] Forgiveness is distinct from legal pardoning, since it is a personal response to a breach in a relationship rather than the result of a legal process. Forgiveness is distinct from condoning or justifying the transgression; rationalising or excusing the transgression as arising from extenuating circumstances; denying the seriousness of the transgression; or forgetting that the transgression occurred. None of these involve acknowledging that another person was responsible for harming us. Forgiveness is also distinct from reconciliation. Reconciliation entails a willingness to form a contract to come together to live or work in an atmosphere of trust on an ongoing basis. It is possible for us to forgive another person without progressing to reconciliation. It is also possible for us to agree to reconciliation, without having forgiven another person. Reconciliation can create a context within which it becomes possible for us to forgive.

## Decisional and emotional forgiveness

Positive psychology interventions that increase forgiveness enhance psychological and physical well-being.[9] Interventions that promote forgiveness help people do two key things: (1) make a personal decision, choice or commitment to forgive the transgressor, and (2) develop emotional empathy for the person who has done them wrong. These things are linked to two different aspects of forgiveness: decisional forgiveness and emotional forgiveness. With **decisional forgiveness**, we decide that we will not look for revenge or avoid the transgressor. Instead we will try to make the relationship with the transgressor as good as it was before the transgression. **Emotional forgiveness** involves experiencing less negative and more positive feelings towards the transgressor. Decisional and emotional forgiveness may occur together. In the example, where Maura spilled coffee on Lillian's dress which she had borrowed, Lillian experienced both decisional and emotional forgiveness simultaneously. However, often it takes longer to experience emotional forgiveness than decisional experience. For example, Rob decided to forgive Ken for lying to him about why he didn't turn up for an important work meeting. However, it took him a couple of weeks to feel positively about Ken. Decisional and emotional forgiveness have different benefits.[10] Decisional forgiveness often is a stepping stone to emotional forgiveness. It improves our relationship with transgressors. We may feel better about viewing ourselves as being forgiving rather than resentful. In contrast, the main benefit of emotional forgiveness is that it improves mental and physical well-being.

## Practising forgiveness

Professor Everett Worthington, Jr at Virginia Commonwealth University, USA has pioneered a highly effective approach to facilitating forgiveness, which he calls the REACH programme.[11] REACH is an acronym which stands for **R**ecall the hurt, focusing more on its effects on you, and less on blame. **E**mpathise with the offender, by imagining what it was like to be them. Give the **A**ltruistic gift of forgiveness. Make a **C**ommitment to being forgiving by making the private experience public. This may involve, for example, writing a forgiveness letter and reading it to a trusted friend. **H**old onto forgiveness when doubts occur, by referring back to the commitment to forgive and planning to deal with triggers for unforgiving thoughts, feelings and behaviours. The five steps in the REACH programme are conceptualised as forming a forgiveness pyramid, shown in Figure 17.1. There is an invitation, now, for you to follow key elements from the REACH programme to help you bring forgiveness into your life, especially

*Figure 17.1* Forgiveness pyramid.

**Note:** Adapted with permission from Figure 3.1 on page 38 of Worthington, E. (2001). *Five steps to forgiveness: The art and science of forgiving.* New York, NY: Crown. Copyright © 2001 by Everitt Worthington.

if there is a particular incident in which you were hurt, and following which you have found it difficult to forgive. Conduct the exercises in this programme in a place where you feel safe and secure, and where you will not be interrupted.

### *Rate your level of decisional and emotional forgiveness*

Recall an event where another person hurt you emotionally or physically. Throughout the rest of this chapter we will call this the 'target event'. This may be an event for which you have tried unsuccessfully to forgive the transgressor, or for which you have only been able to reach decisional forgiveness, but not emotional forgiveness. Before and after you do this programme, in your journal write down your levels of decisional and emotional forgiveness towards the transgressor for that target event. Rate your level of decisional forgiveness on a scale from 1 to 10, where 1 means I am completely unwilling to make a decision to forgive, and 10 means I am completely willing to make a decision to forgive. Rate your level of emotional forgiveness towards the transgressor on a scale from 1 to 10 where 1 means I experience very strong negative feelings and no positive feelings towards the transgressor; 5 means I experience a mixture of mild negative feelings and mild positive feelings towards the transgressor; and 10 means I experience no negative feelings and very strong positive feelings towards the transgressor.

### Recall the hurt

The following two exercises focus on recalling the hurt you have suffered. The first is an invitation for you to connect with the hurt you have experienced as a result of the transgressor's actions by comparing a personal perspective and an objective perspective on the events that hurt you. The second is an invitation for you to make a decision to let go of the hurt which the target event caused you.

#### Compare a personal perspective and objective perspective on events that hurt you

In your journal write down two stories about the target event in which you were hurt, mentioned in the previous section. Write the first story from a distinctly personal perspective. Focus on how much the target event hurt you; how deeply you were affected emotionally; how the transgressor's actions and intentions affected your life; how negatively you saw the transgressor; and how much you wanted to take revenge. Write the second story from an 'outsider perspective', giving an objective account of the target event. Describe what a person would see if they were watching a video of the situation. Do not focus on the transgressor's 'badness', or possible negative intentions. Do not focus on the emotional impact of the event on you, or its negative consequences for your life. Read the two versions of the story and identify the differences between them. Write these differences down. These differences reflect the difference between your victim perspective, and an outsider perspective on the situation. They may help you to become aware of how much hurt you have experienced as a result of the target event.

#### Decide to let go of the hurt

Stand up and stretch your hands straight out in front of you at shoulder height with the fingers locked together. In your hands clasp an object to symbolise the hurt you have suffered and the grudge you feel towards the person who has hurt you during the target event. This symbolic object may be a small bag of sand, a stone or some other heavy object. Imagine that you are holding the hurt and the grudge you feel in your clasped hands. Imagine that you are trying to keep this hurt and this grudge against the person who has hurt you trapped and contained in your hands at arm's length from you. This grudge is heavy. It contains the hurt you have suffered; your unwillingness to forgive; and your wish for revenge. Hold this position for a minute, two minutes or maybe a little longer. Notice how your arms become tired and sore holding this hurt and this grudge. Think of all of the things you could be doing with your hands and with your life if you could let go of this hurt and this grudge and move on. Holding onto this hurt and this grudge is hurting you. It is not hurting the transgressor. Letting go may help you both. In the safe and secure place where you are doing this exercise, say, 'I am deciding to forgive you'. Let the object that you are holding, which symbolises the hurt and the grudge you feel, drop to the floor. Let your arms fall down by your sides. Notice the physical relief you feel, as you do this. Think of this as a metaphor for the mental relief you will begin to feel as you let go of the hurt and the grudge that you are holding, and begin to forgive. Forgiveness may free you. The process of forgiving will involve both decisional forgiveness and emotional forgiveness.

With decisional forgiveness, you have a choice now. You may decide to forgive, or not. If you find it difficult to decide to forgive now, you may come back to it later. With decisional forgiveness, you make a decision to let go of the wish to get even. You make a decision to treat the person as a valued, though flawed, individual. With decisional forgiveness, you may not feel any differently towards the person who hurt you. Your feelings will be more affected by the exercises that follow, which facilitate emotional forgiveness.

### Empathise with the person who hurt you

The following are five exercises that may help you develop empathy for the person who has hurt you:

- Understand the reasons for your own hurtful actions.
- Understand why the person you have decided to forgive hurt you.
- Write an imagined conversation with the person who hurt you.
- Act out an imagined conversation with the person who hurt you.
- Reflect on your empathy for the person who hurt you.

#### Understand the reasons for your own hurtful actions

In your journal, write about a time when you did something that hurt someone. Write about the thoughts that were going through your mind, what you were feeling, and what you were doing before you hurt this person, during the event itself and afterwards. When you have finished, read what you have written. Notice that when you hurt this person, you probably had a good reason for your actions. From your perspective, you did what you did for good reasons. You may even have had good intentions. However, your actions and the reasons for them were not justifiable from the other person's perspective, because your actions hurt them. Then, ask yourself, is it possible that the person who you have decided to forgive had good reasons for doing things that hurt you?

#### Understand why the person you have decided to forgive hurt you

In your journal, write about what you imagine the person who you have decided to forgive was thinking and feeling when they did things that hurt you during the target event. When you are doing this exercise, try to imagine what it was like to be them. Try to see the world from their point of view. Imagine pressures that were on them, things in their personal history that may have caused them to act as they did, their needs and wishes, and their hopes for the future.

#### Write an imagined conversation with the person who hurt you

Imagine that you are having a conversation with the person who hurt you. In your journal, write down what you would say to them about how they hurt you during the target event. Then write down what they would say in response to this. After that, write down how you would reply to this, and so on, until you have written about four conversational turns for you (the victim) and the person who hurt you (the transgressor). When you are writing conversational turns for the transgressor, try to imagine the reasons they did things to hurt you, and the associated feelings or emotions. Take account of the pressures that were on them, things in their personal history that may have caused them to act as they did, their needs and wishes, and their hopes for the future.

## Act out an imagined conversation with the person who hurt you

When you have written out this conversation, set up two chairs facing each other.[12] Sit in the first chair. (Let's call this the victim's chair.) Imagine the person who has hurt you is sitting facing you in the second chair. (Let's call this the transgressor's chair.) Read out the first conversational turn for the victim that you have written. As you do so, imagine as vividly as you can that you are speaking to the transgressor in the opposite chair. Try to feel, as fully as you can, all the emotions and feelings associated with what you are saying to the transgressor. If necessary, repeat the lines you are reading a few times so that you can fully feel the emotions associated with them. If new lines come to mind that express your thoughts and feelings more fully than those you have written, say these new lines, as if you were improvising in a drama class.

Then sit in the transgressor's chair. Imagine that you are the transgressor speaking to the victim. Read out the lines you have written for the transgressor to say in response to the victim's first conversational turn. As you do so, imagine as vividly as you can that you are the transgressor speaking to the victim. Try to feel, as fully as you can, all the emotions and feelings associated with what the transgressor is saying to the victim. If necessary, repeat the lines you are reading a few times so that you can fully feel the emotions associated with them. If new lines come to mind that express your thoughts and feelings more fully than those you have written, say these new lines, as if you were improvising in a drama class.

When you have finished this turn as the transgressor, move back to the victim's chair and read out the victim's reply to the transgressor. Continue this process of reading the conversational turns of the victim and transgressor from the victim's and transgressor's chairs, until you reach the end of the conversation. The most important thing in this exercise is to try to evoke the emotions and feelings of the victim and transgressor associated with the things that you imagine they would say.

If you find this process too emotionally challenging when working with a 'live' issue from your own life, then you may wish to learn how to do this sort of 'chair work' by practising first using the example of Denise and Lillian mentioned in the opening paragraph of chapter.

## Reflect on your empathy for the person who hurt you

When you have finished acting out this conversation, in your journal, write down the answers to these questions:

- What are the possible reasons (and associated feelings) that caused the transgressor to hurt me?
- If I was the transgressor, would I want to be forgiven for the hurt I caused?
- Having done this exercise, to what extent do I feel empathy, sympathy or compassion for the person who hurt me?

### *Give the altruistic gift of forgiveness*

Altruism occurs when we do something selfless for the good of another person. In the third part of the REACH forgiveness process we are invited to give the altruistic gift of emotional forgiveness to the person who has hurt us in the target event. The following four exercises may help you to do this:

- Write about a time when you did something altruistic.
- Write a letter of gratitude to someone you hurt and who forgave you.
- Imagine helping the person who hurt you.
- Rate your level of emotional forgiveness, after reflecting on the benefits of forgiveness.

### *Write about a time when you did something altruistic*

In your journal, write in detail about a specific occasion when you did something selfless to benefit another person. Write down exactly what you did, and how this helped the other person. Write down what you thought and how you felt when you were being altruistic. Write down how you felt after you had done this altruistic act. Notice that being altruistic may have made you feel good.

### *Write a letter of gratitude to someone you hurt and who forgave you*

In your journal, write a letter to a person who forgave you for hurting them or doing something wrong to them. (This is a letter to help you clarify your feelings about being forgiven, not a letter which you intend to send.) You may write to a person who forgave you in your childhood, your teenage years or in early or later adulthood. It may be a parent, a sibling, a teacher, a coach, a colleague, a friend, your partner or someone else. Describe what you did to hurt the other person. Describe what you thought and how you felt about doing something wrong to them. Write about the guilt, shame, fear, sadness or other negative emotions and painful feelings you felt after you hurt them. Describe how you needed them to forgive you to relieve your painful feelings. Describe how they forgave you. Write down how it made you feel when the person you hurt forgave you. Write down how grateful you were then, and are now for their forgiveness. Explain how their forgiveness freed you by lifting your burden of guilt, and other negative emotions that you felt for having hurt them. Reflect on how grateful you were to be forgiven.

### *Imagine helping the person who hurt you*

Imagine the person who hurt you was in serious trouble. (I'm referring here to the person in the target event you brought to mind at start of the REACH process earlier in this chapter.) Imagine that they were very ill, or someone close to them had died, or they had lost their job, or their home had been destroyed in flood, or they had been mugged. In your journal, write down any positive things you would be willing to say to that person or any things you would be willing to do to help that person. Reflect on the extent to which you were willing to help someone who hurt you.

*Rate your level of emotional forgiveness, after reflecting on the benefits for forgiveness*

Reflect on the important things you noticed while doing the three exercises in this section which highlighted the benefits of emotional forgiveness.

- When you were writing about a time when you did something altruistic, did you notice that being altruistic may have made you feel good?
- When you wrote a letter of gratitude to someone you hurt and who forgave you, did you notice how grateful you were to be forgiven?
- When you were imagining that the person who hurt you was in trouble, did you notice the extent you were willing to help them, even though they had hurt you?

Noticing these benefits of forgiveness may have helped you begin to replace the negative feelings you have towards the person who hurt you with positive feelings. At the start of the REACH process you rated your level of emotional forgiveness. Having now thought about the benefits of being emotionally forgiving, there is an invitation for you to rate your level of emotional forgiveness towards the transgressor again. You may make this rating on a scale from 1 to 10 where 1 means I experience very strong negative feelings and no positive feelings towards the transgressor; 5 means I experience a mixture of mild negative feelings and mild positive feelings towards the transgressor; and 10 means I experience no negative feelings and very strong positive feelings towards the transgressor. In your journal, write down your rating of emotional forgiveness, at this point. Noticed if it has changed since you started the REACH process. Notice if you have begun to give the altruistic gift of forgiveness to the transgressor for hurting you during the target event, which you brought to mind at the start of this process. Now write down in your journal the answer to this question: What percentage of emotional forgiveness do you experience towards the transgressor? If you have only mild negative feelings, strong positive feelings and little desire to get even, then you may say that you experience 85% or 90% emotional forgiveness. In contrast, if you continue to have strong negative feelings, and continue to have a strong desire to get even, then you may say that you experience only 5 or 10% emotional forgiveness.

### Make a commitment to being forgiving

The following four exercises may help you make a commitment to being forgiving. The first is writing a commitment letter. This is a letter to help you clarify your thoughts and process your feelings, not a letter to be sent to the transgressor. The second exercise is telling someone you trust about your forgiveness. The third exercise involves repeatedly washing your hands to remove a symbolic statement of the hurt written in ink. This metaphorically shows that it may be necessary to repeat REACH exercises described earlier to achieve emotional forgiveness. The fourth exercise involves processing a small number of the worst hurts inflicted by a single transgressor, as a way of forgiving them for the many times they have hurt you.

*Write a forgiveness letter*

Write a letter to the person who hurt you. In this letter explain to the transgressor how their actions during the target event hurt you. Tell them how you have tried to understand why they hurt you, and develop empathy for them. Let them know that you have decided to forgive them rather than get even. Let them know how you feel towards them right now. Describe your positive and negative feelings towards them. Describe how much you have emotionally forgiven them. You may express this as a percentage. Anticipate how you expect your feelings of emotional forgiveness towards them to develop in future. Conclude by letting the transgressor know how committed you are open to fully forgiving them in the long-term for hurting you during the target event.

*Tell someone you trust about your forgiveness*

Make your forgiveness public by telling someone you trust that you have forgiven the transgressor for the target event. For example, you may tell your partner, a family member, a close friend or a counsellor about your forgiveness. You may wish to read them the forgiveness letter you have written.

*Hand-washing*

Write a few words on your hand, in ink, that symbolise the target event. For example, 'He hurt me', 'She lied to me', 'They bullied me'. Then try to wash it off by rinsing your hands briefly under the tap. Notice that a quick rinse does not remove all the ink. You may need to wash your hands a few times with soap to get rid of all the ink. Similarly, you may need to move through the REACH forgiveness steps more than once to remove most of the negative unforgiving feelings about the target event. If you find that in your forgiveness letter, you write that you are experiencing a low level of emotional forgiveness, you may find that going back to the start of the programme and doing the exercises again may help you deepen you experience of emotional forgiveness.

*Multiple hurts*

If the transgressor has hurt you a number of times, and the target event is only one of these, you do not have to recall every single hurtful event to experience emotional forgiveness towards the transgressor. Select two or three of the most hurtful things you have experienced. Allow these to stand for all of the hurts that the transgressor has caused you. Using the steps of the REACH process described above, work through these hurtful events one at a time, until you experience emotional forgiveness about each transgression. Eventually you may find that you have forgiven enough specific transgressions to allow you to emotionally forgive the transgressor for all the hurt they have caused you.

## Hold onto forgiveness when doubts occur

Through following the REACH process, you may now have experienced some degree of emotional forgiveness. An inevitable part of reaching complete emotional forgiveness is experiencing doubts about its permanence. There are a number of exercises that may help you hold onto forgiveness, when feelings of unforgiveness give rise to doubts about your sincerity or the permanence of your forgiveness. You may identify triggers situations that make you doubt your forgiveness. Then, you may learn about switching emotional channels from those focused on hurt, fear, anger and bitterness, to those focused on compassion and forgiveness. A number of strategies may help you to switch channels. These include both short-term avoidant strategies, and longer-term strategies such as meditation, reminding yourself that you are forgiving, and becoming a more forgiving person.

### Identify triggers that make you doubt your forgiveness

There is an invitation now for you to think about situations that may trigger doubts that you have not fully forgiven your transgressor for the target event. These triggers are probably situations where you are reminded about the target event. For example, you see the transgressor; you are hurt in the same way again by the transgressor or someone else; it's the anniversary of the target event; you find yourself in the place where the target event happened; or you find yourself in a situation that that looks, sounds or smells like the place where the target event happened. These are all 'hot' reminders of hurt. You may also be reminded of the target event by worrying about it, or by ruminating.

When trigger situations remind us of times when we have been hurt and we experience negative emotions of fear and anger, this is the body preparing us to protect ourselves by getting ready to run away from the threat of harm or by preparing to fight it. This is the fight / flight / or freeze response we discussed previously in chapters on courage and fear, and assertiveness and anger. For example, Bill feels angry each time he sees Kevin. Kevin has refused to pay back money he borrowed from Bill. Bill's angry feelings are Bill's body warning him to beware of being conned by Kevin again. This is not unforgiveness. This is a warning to be self-protective.

### Switch emotional channels

Worrying and ruminating about past hurts can bring back negative unforgiving feelings. However, we have a choice about whether to ruminate or not. When you think about the transgressor and the target event in which you were hurt, you may choose to experience negative unforgiving emotions or positive forgiving emotions. Experiencing negative emotions is like watching a TV channel where the story evokes anger, fear, sadness, bitterness and a desire for revenge. If you regularly ruminate and tell yourself a story about the target event that highlights the bad intentions of the transgressor, and how much they are to blame for the hurt you experienced, then you will experience negative unforgiving emotions. In contrast, you will experience positive emotions like empathy, sympathy and compassion if you counter negative ruminations by telling yourself a story that emphasises the external pressures that may have pushed the transgressor to hurt you. You will amplify these positive emotions if you remember how good it felt when you were forgiven for wrongdoing and how you could give this altruistic gift to the transgressor. You may also enhance your positive emotions if you recall how good it has felt in the past any time you were altruistic. Whenever you find yourself ruminating, or when trigger situations make you doubt your forgiveness, you can choose to switch from a negative emotional channel to a positive emotional by changing the story you are telling yourself. Right now, you can make a commitment to change channels from negative emotions to positive emotions any time you doubt your forgiveness.

## Use strategies to switch channels when memories of hurt are triggered

You may plan to use strategies that help you to switch channels when a trigger reminds you how angry or frightened you felt when you were hurt. It's useful to distinguish between short-term avoidant strategies that may be useful in the heat of the moment, and strategies that will help you develop long-term forgiveness. These include meditation, reminding yourself that you have forgiven the transgressor and becoming a more forgiving person.

## Short-term avoidant strategies

If you become overwhelmed by feelings of anger or fear, you may wish to use strategies that help you avoid or block out memories of being hurt; for example, leaving the situation, taking few deep breaths, breathing in for three and out for six, counting from 1 to 10, practising brief relaxation exercises (like those in Box 5.3) or distracting yourself by doing something pleasant like listening to music. These strategies are described in Box 16.12 and discussed in Chapter 16. While these are useful short-term strategies for dealing with overwhelming anger or fear, the long-term exclusive use of avoidance strategies may slow down the process of experiencing emotional forgiveness. In the long-term, meditation, reminding yourself that you have forgiven the transgressor and taking steps to becoming a more forgiving person are strategies that will promote emotional forgiveness.

## Meditation

Meditation can facilitate forgivness.[13] With meditation, which is discussed in Chapter 6, begin with mindfulness of breath and body in Box 6.3. In this meditation, attention is initially focused on the body and then on the breath. As the mind wanders acknowledge it, noticing where the mind has wandered. For example, you may note 'that's remembering', 'that's planning', 'that's thinking', 'that's worrying', 'that's judging', 'that's anger', 'that's fear', 'that's sadness' etc. Just label these thoughts and feelings. If you have memories of being hurt or unforgiving thoughts about revenge and getting even, there is no need to judge them. Label them 'just thoughts' that arise in the mind, linger a while and then dissolve. If you try to suppress these sorts of memories of being hurt or unforgiving thoughts about revenge, they will 'rebound' again and again. Therefore, during meditation, accept them as 'just thoughts' that will eventually pass. Then gently return your attention to the abdominal wall again as the breath moves in and out of the body. When you are settled, move to the exercise in Box 6.8 – exploring difficulty and practising acceptance. Intentionally focus attention on the sensations associated with difficult emotions, especially anger, fear and distress, and thoughts – both forgiving and unforgiving – you are experiencing and accepting these rather than avoiding them. Finally, you may wish to practise the loving kindness meditation in Box 6.9. In this meditation, positive feelings are directed towards the self, then towards loved ones, then towards strangers, then towards someone with whom we experience conflict or difficulty and whom we may wish to forgive, and finally towards all people.

*Reminding yourself that you are forgiving*

Remind yourself that you are a forgiving person and that you have forgiven the transgressor. Recall the distinction between granting decisional forgiveness and experiencing emotional forgiveness. With decisional forgiveness, we decide that we will not look for revenge or avoid the transgressor. Instead we will try to make the relationship with the transgressor as good as it was before the transgression. Emotional forgiveness involves experiencing less negative and more positive feelings towards the transgressor. This takes more time to experience than decisional forgiveness. Look at the list of forgiveness exercises in Box 17.1. Identify those that work best for you, and revisit them. For example, you may wish to re-read the forgiveness letter you have written. Or you may wish to tell someone you trust again about your forgiveness and ask them to reassure you that you have forgiven the transgressor.

---

**Box 17.1   REACH forgiveness process exercises**

**Recall the hurt**

- Compare a personal perspective and objective perspective on events that hurt you.
- Decide to let go of the hurt.

**Empathise with the person who hurt you**

- Understand the reasons for your own hurtful actions.
- Understand why the person you have decided to forgive hurt you.
- Write an imagined conversation with the person who hurt you.
- Act out an imagined conversation with the person who hurt you.
- Reflect on your empathy for the person who hurt you.

**Give the altruistic gift of forgiveness**

- Write about a time when you did something altruistic.
- Write a letter of gratitude to someone you hurt and who forgave you.
- Imagine helping the person who hurt you.
- Rate your level of emotional forgiveness, after reflecting on the benefits for forgiveness.

**Commit publicly to forgive**

- Write a forgiveness letter.
- Tell someone you trust about your forgiveness.
- Hand-washing.
- Forgive multiple hurts.

**Hold onto forgiveness when doubts occur**

- Identify triggers that make you doubt your forgiveness.
- Switch emotional channels.
- Use strategies to switch channels when memories of hurt are triggered.

  o   Short-term avoidant strategies.
  o   Meditation.
  o   Reminding yourself that you are forgiving.
  o   Becoming a more forgiving person.

**Note:** Based on exercises in Worthington, E. L., Jr. (2016). *The path to REACH forgiveness: Less than two hours to becoming a more forgiving person self-directed learning workbook.* Virginia Commonwealth University, USA. www.evworthington-forgiveness.com/diy-workbooks.

*Becoming a more forgiving person*

In this final exercise, there is an invitation for you to write in your journal a response to each of the 12 steps towards being more forgiving in Box 17.2.

## Box 17.2   Twelve steps to being more forgiving

In your journal, write down responses to each of the 12 steps below.

Step 1. List the main **reasons** why you want to be a more forgiving person.

Step 2. Write a list of **five of the greatest hurts** you have experienced in your life. These may be:

- Disappointments by your parents
- Criticisms by teachers
- Betrayals by friends or romantic partners or
- Being criticised or let down by people at work.

Step 3. Pick one of the hurts you listed in step 2, and write a brief description for each of the elements in the REACH process.

**R: Recall** the hurt by writing a brief description of how you were hurt and its effect on you.

**E: Empathise** with the transgressor by writing a brief description of what external pressures caused them to hurt you.

**A:** Give the **Altruistic gift** of forgiveness by writing down a reason why you may want to unselfishly grant forgiveness.

**C: Commit** to forgiveness by writing down your intention to forgive the transgressor now, or at some point in the future.

**H:** Write down the strategies you will use when doubts make it difficult for you to **Hold** onto this forgiveness.

Step 4. Write down what you admire most about two **forgiveness role models** from your current life or from the past (e.g. Nelson Mandela, Jesus of Nazareth, Mahatma Gandhi, Martin Luther King, etc.).

Step 5. Write a letter to yourself **expressing your desire** to be a more forgiving person.

Step 6. Write down specific things you could do to **begin** to become a more forgiving person.

Step 7. Write down how you are going to **think and talk differently**, in future, about one of the five hurts you listed in step 2 to show that you are more forgiving.

Step 8. Write down something that you intend to **do differently** to become more forgiving.

Step 9. **Imagine** how you would talk to one of the people you listed in step 2 so that they would know you are forgiving them.

Step 10. **List the strengths** of the person towards whom you have the most negative feelings (from your list of five hurts in step 2).

Step 11. Write down the name of **a person you trust** to whom you have said you want to be more forgiving. Try to give to another person whatever it is that the person you trust gives you that makes it possible for you to say that you want to be more forgiving.

Step 12. Write a list of specific **things you could do to show warmth towards the people who have hurt you**, listed in step 2. Use this as a first step to start a campaign of feeling warmth towards your 'enemies'.

**Note:** Based on exercise H-8 in Worthington, E. L., Jr. (2016). *The path to REACH forgiveness: Less than two hours to becoming a more forgiving person self-directed learning workbook.* Virginia Commonwealth University, USA. www.evworthington-forgiveness.com/diy-workbooks.

When you have finished this exercise, reflect on Everett Worthington's metaphor of the pencil for becoming a more forgiving person. Everett Worthington, who developed the REACH programme, has used all of the exercises in it and the metaphor of the pencil to help him forgive the young man who shot his mother. He has made it his life's work to understand forgiveness from a scientific perspective, and to help others become more forgiving in his clinical practice. Here is his metaphor of the pencil.

Imagine you are like a pencil with an eraser at one end. You have a short life in the grand scheme of the universe, but you can make a significant mark. You are not like a pen, whose mistakes cannot be corrected. Because you are a pencil, your mistakes can be corrected, but it often means standing on your head to rub them out! It is not what is outside but what is inside you that is responsible for your mark. So instead of making an external display of power and revenge, you experience internal compassion and forgiveness. A pencil needs to be sharpened regularly. The hurts you feel as painful may sharpen you, so you can make your mark in this wonderful world.

## Summary

- **Forgiveness** is a way of reacting to being wronged that aims to make our relationship with the person who wronged us better, rather than worse. The victim shows mercy, does not seek revenge and cancels the debt the transgressor owes them. Forgiveness may be motivated by altruism: a wish to enhance the transgressor's well-being. It may also be self-serving: a wish to enhance the victim's well-being. Being forgiving involves both decisional and emotional forgiveness.
- With **decisional forgiveness**, there is a decision not to look for revenge or avoid the transgressor. Instead a commitment is made to restore the relationship with the transgressor to the way it was before the transgression.
- **Emotional forgiveness** involves experiencing less negative and more positive feelings towards the transgressor. This usually occurs more slowly than decisional forgiveness, and has a greater impact on well-being.
- **Forgiveness is distinct from other responses to transgressions.** It is distinct legal pardoning, since it is a personal response. It is distinct from condoning, justifying, rationalising, excusing, denying or forgetting transgressions. These responses fail to acknowledge the responsibility of the transgressor for wrongdoing. It is also distinct form reconciliation which can occur without forgiveness.
- **Evolution, revenge and forgiveness.** Our species has evolved to engage in both revenge and forgiveness. Revenge acts as a deterrent against further transgressions, which promotes survival of the individual. Forgiveness maintains relationships between victims and transgressors, which promotes survival of their social group.
- **Factors that facilitate forgiveness.** We find it easier to forgive people whose transgressions were unintentional, less severe, less dangerous and led to fewer negative consequences for us. It's also easier to forgive people who we feel close to; who we think will be valuable to us in the future; who apologise; and who we judge to be unlikely to harm us again.
- **Forgiveness and well-being.** Forgiveness leads to better health and well-being than holding grudges and seeking revenge. It also prevents escalating spirals of retribution and retaliation which erode group cohesion. That is, forgiveness prevents tit-for-tat battles that make people trust each other less.
- **REACH forgiveness programme.** This was developed by Everett Worthington. REACH is an acronym which stands for **R**ecall the hurt, focusing more on its effects on you, and less on blame. **E**mpathise with the offender, by imagining what it was like to be them. Give the **A**ltruistic gift of forgiveness. Make a **C**ommitment to being forgiving by making the private experience public. **H**old onto forgiveness when doubts occur, by referring back to the commitment to forgive and planning to deal with triggers for unforgiving thoughts, feelings and behaviours.

## Where are you now?

If you have done the exercises and followed some of the guidelines in this chapter, you may have found that they have helped you feel greater forgiveness. In your journal write down your levels of decisional and emotional forgiveness towards the transgressor for the target event you wrote down before engaging in the REACH forgiveness process. Compare your current levels of decisional and emotional forgiveness with those you wrote down at the start of the process. Rate your level of decisional forgiveness on a scale from 1 to 10, where 1 means I am completely unwilling to make a decision to forgive, and 10 means I am completely willing to make a decision to forgive. Rate your level of emotional forgiveness towards the transgressor on a scale from 1 to 10 where 1 means I experience very strong negative feelings and no positive feelings towards the transgressor; 5 means I experience a mixture of mild negative feelings and mild positive feelings towards the transgressor; and 10 means I experience no negative feelings and very strong positive feelings towards the transgressor.

You may want to read back over the chapter and summarise in your journal the main things that you have learned about forgiveness. You can now decide if you want to use these strategies for becoming a more forgiving person. Below are some web resources and books that are relevant to topics you have read about in this chapter.

## Web resources

Everett Worthington talking about forgiveness video (18:40): www.youtube.com/watch?v=5Or9OuxuYKw
Robert Enright talking about forgiveness video (17:54): www.youtube.com/watch?v=dXGIpFmFBbc

## Books

Worthington, E. L., Jr., (2001). *Five steps to forgiveness: The art and science of forgiving.* New York, NY: Crown.
Worthington, E. L., Jr. (2016). *The path to REACH forgiveness: Less than two hours to becoming a more forgiving person self-directed learning workbook.* Virginia Commonwealth University, USA. www.evworthington-forgiveness.com/diy-workbooks.

# 18 Managing your life

In this final chapter, there is an opportunity for you to reflect on what you have learned from reading this book and doing the exercises in it. There is also an opportunity for you to reflect on how you may now use what you have learned in the future.

## Part 1: creating resilience

Part 1 offered an opportunity to lay the foundations for creating resilience. It contained chapters on key ideas from positive psychology, valued goals and personal strengths.

### Positive psychology

In Chapter 1 you learned that well-being involves positive emotion, engagement, relationships, meaning and accomplishment. This is Seligman's PERMA theory. Research on well-being shows that it has major long-term effects. It makes us have fewer illnesses and increases the length of our lives. Reading about Frederickson's Broaden and Build theory, you learned that positive emotions broaden thought-action repertoires and help us build enduring resources to promote well-being. This is more likely to happen if we have a higher ratio of positive to negative emotions in our lives.

Forty per cent of individual differences in happiness are due to intentional activities, such as the positive psychology exercises that you read about in this book. The remainder are due to genetic factors (50%) and circumstances (10%). Supportive relationships increase happiness more than any other circumstantial factor including wealth and health. You can strengthen your relationships with the exercises you read about in Part 5 of this book.

There are three scientific findings that have been taken into account in designing effective positive psychology exercises. The first one is that most of us respond less strongly and adapt more quickly to positive than to negative events. The second one is that after two years, most of us adapt to most positive and negative major life events. The third one is that most of us are very poor at judging what will make us happy, because we are poor at imagining what the future will be like.

### Valued goals

In Chapter 2 you learned that setting highly valued goals gives our lives purpose, meaning and direction. Our well-being increases as we move towards highly valued goals. You may have used the best possible self, eulogy and legacy letter exercises described in Chapter 2 to set highly valued goals in domains of health, relationships, work and leisure. Periodically rating progress towards highly valued goals can help us take corrective action if we veer away from the path that leads to our highly valued goals. Corrective action may involve setting short-term SMART or CLEAR goals. SMART goals are **S**pecific, **M**easurable, **A**ttainable, **R**elevant and **T**imely. CLEAR goals are **C**ollaborative, **L**imited, **E**motional, **A**ppreciable and **R**efinable.

### Strengths

In Chapter 3 you learned about the Values in Action Inventory of Strengths (VIA-IS) which you may have used to identify your signature strengths. Your signature strengths are central to your character. Using them enhances well-being, and helps you move towards highly valued goals. You may also use them to strengthen relationships and overcome challenges.

## Part 2: healthy body and mind

Part 2 offered an opportunity to develop routines for becoming physically and mentally healthier. It had chapters on physical exercise, relaxation and mindfulness meditation.

### Physical exercise

In Chapter 4 you learned that regular daily exercise has positive short- and long-term effects on physical and psychological well-being. It leads to better physical health, alleviates depression and increases self-esteem. For adults, at least 150 minutes of moderately intense exercise throughout the week is sufficient. You may have found that it was useful to set up a schedule, start gradually and exercise in a way that was convenient to you and that motivated you to continue. A balanced diet, moderate alcohol use and good sleep hygiene make it easier to exercise and promote well-being.

### Relaxation

In Chapter 5 you had an opportunity to practise progressive muscle relaxation, diaphragmatic breathing, visualisation, auto-suggestion and applied relaxation. All of these exercises reduce stress and enhance well-being.

### Mindfulness meditation

In Chapter 6 you learned that ruminating about past difficulties and worrying about future challenges reduce well-being. Developing mindfulness skills helps us address these tendencies. When reading Chapter 6 you had an opportunity to develop mindfulness skills by doing an eight-week Mindfulness-Based Cognitive Therapy programme.

## Part 3: enjoying life

Part 3 offered an opportunity to develop skills for enjoying life to the full. It had chapters on savouring, flow and gratitude.

## *Savouring*

In Chapter 7 you learned about savouring. Savouring involves deliberately paying attention to, appreciating, enhancing and prolonging positive experiences and the positive emotions that accompany them. There was an opportunity to engage in savouring exercises including taking a daily vacation, relishing ordinary activities, reminiscence, making a savouring reminiscence album and optimistically anticipating future positive events.

## *Flow*

In Chapter 7 you also had an invitation to experience flow, by allowing yourself to become absorbed in activities requiring a high level of control and concentration. Both savouring and flow may have long-term effects on well-being.

## *Gratitude*

In Chapter 8 you learned that gratitude enhances well-being. You had an opportunity to practise gratitude exercises such as being thankful for three good things, paying it forward, being thankful for a gift by imagining its absence, writing a gratitude letter and making a gratitude visit.

## Part 4: constructive thought and action

In Part 4 there was an invitation to learn skills for engaging in constructive thought and action. It had chapters on optimism, problem-solving and solution-finding.

## *Optimism*

In Chapter 9 you learned that you could increase your well-being by using an optimistic thinking style most of the time, and reserving the use of a pessimistic thinking style for high-risk situations. An optimistic thinking style involves explaining your successes in terms of positive permanent, pervasive, personal characteristics. You may also have practised the ABCDE strategy for increasing optimism. With this strategy, we identify the **A**ntecedent events or **A**dversity associated with a drop in mood; the pessimistic **B**eliefs we had about these antecedent adversities and related thinking traps; and the **C**onsequences of these beliefs and thinking traps for how our mood deteriorated and what we did. We then use **D**istraction, **D**istancing or **D**isputation to move towards an optimistic thinking style, and a happier mood state. Finally, in **E**nergisation we notice the extent to which using distraction, distancing or disputation improved our mood.

## *Problem-solving*

In Chapter 10 you learned about problem-solving. Controllable and uncontrollable problems require different types of solutions. For controllable problems, the goal is changing the situation. For uncontrollable problems, the goal is changing our distressing reactions to the situation. The five steps for problem-solving are given in the acronym COPER. Be **C**alm and

Clarify what the problem is. List Options for solving the problem. Predict the Payoff and Price of each option; Pick and Plan the best option. Evaluate the outcome. Reward yourself.

### Solution-finding

In Chapter 10 you also learned about solution-finding. There are six steps in solution-finding. (1) Set small measurable goals. (2) Identify exceptions. (3) Spot the difference between problem and exception episodes. (4) Create more exceptions. (5) Track progress towards your goals. (6) Reflect on who you are becoming.

## Part 5: strengthening relationships

Part 5 offered an opportunity to develop skills for strengthening relationships. It had chapters on developing compassionate relationships, as well as chapters on enhancing relationships with partners and children.

### Relationships with self and others

In Chapter 11 you read that good relationships enhance well-being. They help us to co-operate. They provide us with a context within which to celebrate our successes. They give our lives meaning. They provide us with support. In Chapter 11 you were invited to revisit the loving kindness meditation described previously in Chapter 6. In this meditation, positive feelings are mindfully directed towards the self, then towards loved ones, then towards strangers, then towards someone with whom we experience conflict or difficulty, and finally towards all people. Practising this meditation regularly enhances relationships with ourselves and others.

There was also an opportunity to engage in acts of kindness and volunteering. Larger, more frequent and more varied acts of kindness have a stronger effect on well-being. You may also have practised capitalising. This involves reacting to another person's good news by inviting them to talk in detail about it and celebrate their successes in ways that generate positive emotions.

There was also an opportunity in Chapter 11 to identify your adult attachment style. If you found that you had an insecure attachment style, there was an invitation for you to reflect on ways to address this. Strategies for developing a secure adult attachment style include choosing a partner with a secure adult attachment style, developing a coherent life narrative, exploring alternatives to being avoidant or anxious in close relationships and engaging in psychotherapy.

### Relationships with partners

In Chapter 12 you read that having a satisfying relationship with your partner may enhance your well-being and health. You learned that research shows that couples in stable long-term relationships have distinctive characteristics. They engage in five times more positive exchanges than negative exchanges, and repair relationship conflicts. They begin disagreements with a gentle start-up; express positive emotions, humour and affection during conflicts; try to understand their partner's point of view; accept that some conflicts are unre-solvable, and these are fuelled by partners' commitment to underlying highly valued goals; respond positively towards partners' bids for emotional connection; and allow their partners to influence them when negotiating.

You also had an opportunity to read about Gottman's Sound Relationship House Theory which included seven positive strategies for strengthening trust and commitment within relationships. These are: build love maps to get to know each other; share fondness and admiration; turn towards your partner when they make bids for emotional connection; take a positive perspective; manage conflict; help each other achieve highly valued goals; and create shared meaning. We develop shared meaning by having rituals for emotional connec-tion, supporting each other's life roles, working towards shared goals and developing shared values and symbols. Conflict is a normal, healthy part of all relationships. All couples have short-term conflicts that can be resolved by skilled negotiation, and long-term differences which are managed by ongoing dialogue.

### Relationships with children

In Chapter 13 you had an opportunity to read about strengthening relationships with your children. You learned that in western industrialised countries, couples report lower well-being when their children are in infancy, childhood and adolescence. They report higher well-being before the birth of children, and when their children mature into adults. This pat-tern reflects the fact that, for many families, the demands of childrearing exceed parental resources. Children whose parents adopt an authoritative parenting style show high levels of well-being.

Authoritative parenting skills include creating and maintaining a good parent–child relationship, accommodating to your child's temperament, nurturing and rewarding prosocial behaviour, reducing opportunities for problem behaviour and discouraging it, using problem-solving and negotiation skills with adolescents, and being a good, consistent role model. Creating and maintaining a good parent–child relationship involves being responsive to infants' needs to help them develop secure attachment, spending 'special time' with children doing activities they enjoy and letting them direct these activities, and actively listening to teenagers to understand their views. Accommodating to your child's temperament involves developing a good fit between their temperaments and the way you help them develop routines, emotional self-control and skills.

Children with difficult temperaments need us, as parents, to be more patient and thought-ful. Nurturing and rewarding prosocial behaviour involve catching your children being good and praising them for this. Reducing opportunities for problem behaviour involves clearly communicating expectations and rules, the reasons for them and the consequences of rule-breaking. With young children, it's reasonable to set rules without negotiation. With ado-lescents, rule-setting often involves negotiation.

To discourage problem behaviour, ignore problem behaviours that are not too serious. Divert children towards prosocial activities and praise them for doing these. For serious prob-lem behaviour, let your child know that they are good but that their behaviour is not good. With young children who do not respond to requests to follow directives, use time out from reinforcement that concludes with them being praised for showing self-control. With older children, establish verbal contracts for rule-breaking that include opportunities for being rewarded for prosocial behaviour in future. Your children are more likely to follow rules if you and others involved in parenting are consistent with each other about rules, and if rules are consistent from one day to the next. Your children are more likely to develop well-being if you are a good role model for the sorts of values and behaviour you expect of them.

## Part 6: overcoming challenges

Part 6 offered an opportunity to develop skills for overcoming a number of life challenges. It had chapters on grit and perfectionism; courage, fear and posttraumatic growth; assertiveness and anger; and forgiveness.

### Grit

In Chapter 14 you learned that grit is the tendency to work towards long-term goals with a high level of interest and effort. Grit leads to accomplishment, which is a key element of well-being in Seligman's PERMA theory. You had an opportunity to begin to cultivate grit by working at the limits of your competence towards a single highly valued long-term goal that was connected to some greater good. There was an invitation to develop short- and medium-term goals, a work routine that suits you, a support network, a positive way of thinking about setbacks and a system for regularly reviewing progress. You learned that to motivate yourself you should value intrinsically rewarding aspects of your work and reward your efforts for doing tasks that are not intrinsically rewarding.

### Perfectionism

In Chapter 14 you also learned that perfectionism is adaptive when it helps us achieve our highly valued goals. However, perfectionism is problematic when high standards are coupled with excessive self-criticism. This leads to a vicious cycle of perfectionistic striving and self-criticism, avoiding completing tasks, missing deadlines and worry. You learned how to overcome problematic perfectionism. This involves challenging maladaptive perfectionistic beliefs by gathering evidence that lessens the conviction that these beliefs are true. It also involves practising self-compassion, and basing self-worth on more than one life area such as home-making, education, relationships, health, leisure activities, community involvement or travel.

### Courage in dangerous professions

In Chapter 15 there was an opportunity to strengthen courage. In dangerous professions that require courage (like firefighting, law enforcement or the military), you learned that preparation for courageous action involves working with leaders who are courageous role models, building a supportive team, engaging in relevant skills training for managing specific threats, planning using problem-solving skills and avoiding the extremes of cowardice or reckless risk-taking.

There was also an invitation to reflect on coping strategies that support courage. These include acknowledging team support and thinking of past successful courageous actions, the benefits of courageous actions and brave role models. Relaxation and mindfulness exercises are other useful coping strategies. You also learned that you can strengthen courage by debriefing after courageous action. You may reflect on how effective you were, and what this says about you as a person. You may also accept recognition from respected people for your bravery.

## Courage and anxiety

In Chapter 15 you also had an opportunity to strengthen the sort of courage that is essential for overcoming anxiety. Fear is the experience we have when faced with a realistic threat to our safety or security. Anxiety occurs in situations that are not objectively threatening, but which are interpreted as placing us in danger. Mental health problems where anxiety is a central feature include phobias, separation anxiety disorder, panic disorder, generalised anxiety disorder, health anxiety, obsessive compulsive disorder and posttraumatic stress disorder.

Avoidance of feared situations and memories makes anxiety disorders worse. Courageously facing fears is the most effective way to overcome anxiety disorders. This involves preparing for exposure to feared situations, monitoring anxiety levels, making a courage ladder, doing exposure exercises to items on the courage ladder, not withdrawing from exposure until you're no longer frightened, using effective coping strategies during exposure exercises (social support, relaxation, meditation, optimism), not using safety routines during exposure and rewarding yourself for being courageous as you complete each step of the process.

## Posttraumatic growth

In Chapter 15 you also learned that following a trauma or crisis, we may experience distress, but there is also an opportunity for posttraumatic growth. This involves recognising personal strengths, deepening relationships with other people, developing a greater appreciation of life, experiencing spiritual and existential transformation and cultivating an increased openness to new possibilities. Facilitating posttraumatic growth involves finding support, writing or talking in detail about the story of the crisis, linking the story of the crisis to life before and after the crisis, looking for posttraumatic growth themes in the story, practising mindfulness and drawing on spiritual, religious and existential beliefs.

## Assertiveness and anger

In Chapter 16 you had an opportunity to learn skills for assertively expressing anger. This way of expressing anger can enhance well-being. In contrast, the impulsive, aggressive expression of anger may reduce well-being. The challenge in expressing anger assertively is to control angry feelings, and to tell the right person, at the right time, in the right place, in the right way specifically what we are angry about, and how we would prefer them to behave in future. It involves speaking in a positive, respectful, calm, co-operative, solution-focused way, using 'I' statements and avoiding thinking traps.

### *Forgiveness*

In Chapter 17 there was an invitation to embrace forgiveness. Being forgiving involves making a decision not to look for revenge or avoid the person who has wronged you. It also involves experiencing less negative and more positive feelings towards that person. Forgiveness leads to better health and well-being than holding grudges and seeking revenge. It also prevents tit-for-tat battles that make people trust each other less. You may remember a five-step approach to forgiveness by thinking of the acronym: REACH. The steps are as follows. **R**ecall the hurt, focusing more on its effects on you, and less on blame. **E**mpathise with the offender, by imagining what it was like to be them. Give the **A**ltruistic gift of forgiveness. Make a **C**ommitment to being forgiving by making the private experience public. **H**old onto forgiveness when doubts occur, by referring back to the commitment to forgive and planning to deal with triggers for unforgiving thoughts, feelings and behaviours.

## Identify the positive psychology exercises that are most relevant to you

From this brief review of most of the exercises in this book, there is an opportunity now for you to reflect on which are most relevant to your life situation. Doing positive psychology exercises that are very relevant to your life is more likely to increase your well-being than doing those that are less relevant.[1] If you kept a journal when you were reading this book, you may wish to review what you have written to help you identify the exercises that you thought worked best for you. Not all exercises will be relevant to everybody at all times in their lives. Some of the exercises in Chapters 2-10 and Chapter 11 are probably relevant to everyone at most times in their lives. The exercises in Chapter 12 are relevant to you if you are in a long-term committed relationship and want to improve the quality of this relationship. The exercises in Chapter 12 are only relevant to you if you have children, or are involved in caring for children, and want to improve the quality of your relationships with children.

If you suffer from any mental health problem, especially depression, then all of the exercises in Chapters 2-10 and Chapter 11 on compassionate relationships may help with your recovery. However, it's important that you select those that suit you best. You don't have to do all of them; just those that suit you. Trying to do too many may make you feel overwhelmed. Just do those that work for you at this point in your life.

The exercises in the chapters in Part 6 are not relevant to everyone. These chapters deal with specific life challenges. If you want to accomplish excellence at work, but find that self-criticism is preventing you from doing so, then the exercises in Chapter 14 on grit and perfectionism may help you deal with problematic perfectionism. If your work is intrinsically dangerous, if you suffer from anxiety or if you have survived a major trauma, then the exercises in Chapter 15 on courage, anxiety and posttraumatic growth may be of particular interest to you. These exercises show how you can develop courage and enhance your well-being. If you have difficulty controlling your temper, and would like to find a way to become less aggressive, then the exercises in Chapter 16 on assertiveness and anger control may help you achieve these goals. If you find that you hold grudges and ruminate about revenge, and this reduces your quality of life, then you may find the exercises in Chapter 17 help you embrace forgiveness.

## Motivate yourself to continue to put in effort

Some positive psychology exercises involve developing routines (like taking daily physical exercise) or refining skills (like practising mindfulness meditation). We will be more success-ful in developing routines and skills if we put considerable effort into routine-building and skills-practice.[2] When we put a lot of effort into practising skills regularly they are more likely to become skilled automatic habits. You are more likely to maintain your motivation to keep putting effort into doing positive psychology exercises if you do them with your partner, a friend or a group of like-minded friends.[3]

## Create variety to avoid adaptation

Most positive psychology exercises work best if you do them regularly. However, there is a risk that the benefits you get from doing positive psychology exercises may lessen, each time you do them, because you adapt to them. (You read about adaptation and the 'hedonic treadmill' in Chapter 1.) To offset the effects of adaptation, you may vary the specific details of positive psychology exercises each time you do them.[4] If you repeatedly savour the same experience, for example a particular food, you may find that eventually it brings you less pleasure. So, if you think you are going to get used to a specific exercise, like savouring, or being grateful, then creatively vary the specific details of the exercise so you do not adapt to its beneficial effects.

## Welcome setbacks

The process of changing your routines to make room for positive psychology exercises in your everyday life will probably involve setbacks. You are invited to expect these, and to plan how you will manage them. Setbacks are to be anticipated. You may wish to write in your journal about those circumstances when you are most likely to not follow through on your plan to do positive psychology exercises. For example, you may anticipate on busy days you may not find time to take physical exercise, to meditate or to volunteer. You may anticipate that when you are tired, or intoxicated, you may be more likely to be unforgiving, and angry rather than forgiving and assertive. When you have anticipated setbacks, make a plan for how you will notice these, and then get back on track. When setbacks occur, write about these in your journal and identify the circumstances that contributed to the setback happening. Then write about how you used your plan to get back on track.

Setbacks are to be welcomed. When we notice setbacks, they are a sign that we are chang-ing our lifestyles. Setbacks tell us that we are on a journey moving towards certain goals, and that temporarily we have deviated from the path towards those goals.

If you have a mental health problem or addiction, setbacks or slips tell you that you are recovering. You are moving towards recovering your life. On this specific occasion, when you experienced a setback or slip, your movement forward stalled. However, the process of recovery always involves moving forward, stalling and then overcoming slips and setbacks.[5] Therefore setbacks or slips are to be welcomed. Every setback or slip takes you one step closer to full recovery. You can't recover without slipping.

Steps you can take to keep using positive psychology to improve your well-being are sum-marised in Box 18.1.

**Box 18.1   Bring positive psychology exercises into your everyday life**

- Use positive psychology exercises, web-based resources and self-development books that are most relevant to you at your particular stage of life, in your current life circumstances.
- Motivate yourself to continue to put effort into doing positive psychology exercises by practising with a like-minded companion.
- Vary the details of positive psychology exercises to avoid adaptation.
- Welcome setbacks. Each time you overcome a setback, you increase well-being. Each time you overcome a slip, you are one step closer to recovery.

## Final word if you are feeling good

If you are healthy and well and read this book to enhance your well-being, I wish you well in using the exercises you have read about to make your life better.

## Final word if you are feeling like it's all too much

If you feel that everything seems to be too much, then there is the risk that reading this book may have been discouraging. If you feel too overwhelmed to respond to the invitations to do the exercises in this book, that's OK. That's how your life is right now. Please consider talking to a clinical psychologist or other mental health professional about your difficulties. Maybe after you have done that, and feel less overwhelmed, you may wish to revisit this book. At that point you may find it helpful to bring some of the positive psychology exercises described in the book into your life. I wish you well in your recovery.

# References and notes

## Chapter 1. Positive psychology

1 Snyder, C. R., Lopez, S. J., Edwards, L. M., & Marques, S. C. (2016). *Oxford handbook of positive psychology* (Third Edition). New York, NY: Oxford University Press.
Diener, E., Tay, L., Heintzelman, S. J., Kushlev, K., Wirtz, D., Lutes, L. D., & Oishi, S. (2017). Findings all psychologists should know from the new science on subjective well-being. *Canadian Psychology, 58*(2), 87-104.
2 Seligman, M. E. P., & Csikszentmihalyi, M. (Eds.) (2000). Special issue on happiness, excellence and optimal human functioning. *American Psychologist, 55*(1), 1-190.
3 Seligman, M. E. P. (2002). *Authentic happiness.* New York, NY: Free Press.
Seligman, M. E. P. (2011). *Flourish.* New York, NY: Free Press.
Seligman, M. E. P. (2018). *The hope circuit.* Boston, MA: Nicholas Brealey.
4 International Positive Psychology Association: www.ippanetwork.org. Positive Psychology Centre: www.positivepsychology.org.
5 Templeton foundation: www.templeton.org.
6 The *Journal of Positive Psychology* published by Taylor and Francis is the leading positive psychology journal. The *Oxford handbook of positive psychology* (cited in note 1) is the leading academic source on modern positive psychology.
7 Seligman, M. E. P. (2011). *Flourish: A visionary new understanding of happiness and well-being.* New York, NY: Free Press.
8 Biswas-Diener, R., Kashdan, T. B., & King, L. A. (2009). Two traditions of happiness research, not two distinct types of happiness. *Journal of Positive Psychology, 4,* 208-211.
Deci, E., & Ryan, R. (2008b). Hedonia, eudaimonia, and well-being: an introduction. *Journal of Happiness Studies, 9,* 1-11.
9 Hone, L. C., Jarden, A., Schofield, G. M., & Duncan, S. (2014). Measuring flourishing: The impact of operational definitions on the prevalence of high levels of wellbeing. *International Journal of Wellbeing, 4*(1), 62-90.
10 Boehm, J. K., & Kubzansky, L. D. (2012). The heart's content: The association between positive psychological well-being and cardiovascular health. *Psychological Bulletin, 138,* 655-691.
Diener, E., & Chan, M. Y. (2011). Happy people live longer: Subjective well-being contributes to health and longevity. *Applied Psychology: Health and Well-Being, 3*(1), 1-43.
Diener, E., Tay, L., Heintzelman, S. J., Kushlev, K., Wirtz, D., Lutes, L. D., & Oishi, S. (2017). Findings all psychologists should know from the new science on subjective well-being. *Canadian Psychology, 58*(2), 87-104.
Howell, R. T., Kern, M. L., & Lyubomirsky, S. (2007). Health benefits: Meta-analytically determining the impact of well-being on objective health outcomes. *Health Psychology Review, 1*(1), 83-136.
Lamers, S. M. A., Bolier, L., Westerhof, G. J., Smit, F., & Bohlmeijer, E. T. (2012). The impact of emotional well-being on long-term recovery and survival in physical illness: A meta-analysis. *Journal of Behavioural Medicine, 35*(5), 538-547.
Miller, S. M., Sherman, A. C., & Christensen, A. J. (2010). Introduction to special series: The great debate - evaluating the health implications of positive psychology. *Annals of Behavioural Medicine: A Publication of the Society of Behavioural Medicine, 39*(1), 1-3.

Seligman, M. E. P. (2008). Positive health. *Applied Psychology: An International Review, 57,* 3-18.

Steptoe, A., Dockray, S., & Wardle, J. (2009). Positive affect and psychobiological processes relevant to health. *Journal of Personality, 77*(6), 1747-1775.

11  Chida, Y., & Steptoe, A. (2008). Positive psychological well-being and mortality: A quantitative review of prospective observational studies. *Psychosomatic Medicine, 70*(7), 741-756.

Diener, E., & Chan, M. Y. (2011). Happy people live longer: Subjective well-being contributes to health and longevity. *Applied Psychology: Health and Well-Being, 3*(1), 1-43.

12  Danner, D., Snowdon, D., & Friesen, W. (2001). Positive emotions early in life and the longevity: Findings from the nun study. *Journal of Personality and Social Psychology, 80,* 804-813.

13  Conway, A. M., Tugade, M. M., Catalino, L. I., & Fredrickson, B. L. (2013). The broaden-and-build theory of positive emotions: Form, function, and mechanisms. In S. David, I. Boniwell, & A. Conley Ayers (Eds.), *The Oxford handbook of happiness* (pp. 17-34). New York, NY: Oxford University Press.

Fredrickson, B. L. (2013). Positive emotions broaden and build. In P. Devine & A. Plant (Eds.), *Advances in experimental social psychology* (Vol. 47, pp. 1-54). San Diego, CA: Academic Press.

14  Lyubomirsky, S., King, L., & Diener, E. (2005). The benefits of frequent positive affect: Does happiness lead to success? *Psychological Bulletin, 131,* 803-855.

15  Fredrickson, B. L. (2013). Updated thinking on positivity ratios. *American Psychologist, 68*(9), 814-822.

16  There has been an important dialogue in the scientific literature on positivity ratios, tipping points, and flourishing. The seminal paper on this topic was: Fredrickson B., & Losada M. (2005). Positive affect and the complex dynamics of human flourishing. *American Psychologist, 60,* 678-686. In this paper, Fredrickson and Losada used complex mathematical modelling on daily ratings of positive and negative affect from samples of university students to show that a positive ratio of 3:1 was a tipping point for flourishing. Flourishing was assessed with a scale that measured self-acceptance, purpose in life, environmental mastery, positive relations with others, personal growth and autonomy. The positivity ratio tipping point of 3:1 was challenged in the following paper which showed that mathematical modelling had been incorrectly applied and there was no convincing evidence that a positivity ratio of 3:1 was a tipping point for flourishing: Brown N. J., Sokal A. D., & Friedman, H. L. (2013). The complex dynamics of wishful thinking: the critical positivity ratio. *American Psychologist, 68*(9), 801-813. Fredrickson, in a retraction, conceded that the mathematical modelling that underpinned her initial 2005 paper with Losada was problematic. However, in the following paper she maintained that data from a number of studies continue to show that a moderately high ratio of positive to negative affective experiences contributes to well-being: Fredrickson, B. L. (2013). Updated thinking on positivity ratios. *American Psychologist, 68*(9), 814-822. In the following two papers, there is a strong argument that there is no convincing evidence for a discontinuous positivity ratio tipping point: Brown, N. J., Sokal, A. D., & Friedman, H. L. (2014). The persistence of wishful thinking. *American Psychologist, 69*(6), 629-632. Brown, N. J., Sokal A. D., & Friedman, H. L. (2014). Positive psychology and romantic scientism. *American Psychologist, 69*(6), 636-637. Research on positivity ratios continues within positive psychology. As more data become available, it will become clearer how particular positivity ratios in particular contexts contribute to well-being. In the meantime, all we can say for certain is that up to some undefined point, higher positivity ratios are usually associated with better well-being. Extremely high positivity ratios, for example where individuals are hypomanic, are usually problematic.

17  Lyubomirsky, S. (2007). *The how of happiness.* New York, NY: Penguin.

Lyubomirsky, S., Sheldon, K. M., & Schkade, D. (2005). Pursuing happiness: The architecture of sustainable change. *Review of General Psychology, 9,* 111-131.

18  Lykken, D., & Tellegen, A. (1996). Happiness is a stochastic phenomenon. *Psychological Science, 7*(3), 186-189.

Bartels, M. (2015). Genetics of wellbeing and its components satisfaction with life, happiness, and quality of life: A review and meta-analysis of heritability studies. *Behaviour Genetics, 45,* 137-156.

19  Krueger, R. F., & Johnson, W. (2008). Behavioural genetics and personality. In L. A. Pervin., O. P. John., & R. W. Robins (Eds.), *Handbook of personality: Theory and research* (Third Edition, pp. 287-310). New York, NY: Guilford.

Steel, P., Schmidt, J., & Shultz, J. (2008). Refining the relationship between personality and subjective well-being. *Psychological Bulletin, 134,* 138-161.

Vukasović, T., & Bratko, D. (2015). Heritability of personality: A meta-analysis of behaviour genetic studies. *Psychological Bulletin, 141*(4), 769-785.

Weiss, A., Bates, T. C., & Luciano, M. (2008). Happiness is a personal(ity) thing: The genetics of personality and well-being in a representative sample. *Psychological Science, 19*(3), 205-210.

20  Steel, P., Schmidt, J., & Shultz, J. (2008). Refining the relationship between personality and subjective well-being. *Psychological Bulletin, 134*, 138-161.

21  Bogg, T., & Roberts, B. W. (2004). Conscientiousness and health-related behaviours: A meta-analysis of the leading behavioural contributors to mortality. *Psychological Bulletin, 130*, 887-919.

Connor-Smith, J., & Flachsbart, C. (2007). Relations between personality and coping: A meta-analysis. *Journal of Personality and Social Psychology, 93*, 1080-1107.

Judge, T. A., Heller, D., & Mount, M. K. (2002). Five-factor model of personality and job satisfaction: A meta-analysis. *Journal of Applied Psychology, 87*, 530-541.

Kern, M. L. & Friedman, H. S. (2008). Do conscientious individuals live longer? A quantitative review. *Health Psychology, 27*(5), 505-512.

Ozer, D., & Benet-Martínez, V. (2006). Personality and the prediction of consequential outcomes. *Annual Review of Psychology, 57*, 401-421.

Peeters, M. A. G., Van Tuijl, H. F. J. M., Rutte, C. G., & Reymen, I. M. M. J. (2006). Personality and team performance: A meta-analysis. *European Journal of Personality, 20*, 377-396.

Zhao, H., Seibert, S., & Lumpkin, G. (2010). The relationship of personality to entrepreneurial intentions and performance: A meta-analytic review. *Journal of Management, 36*, 381-404.

22  Argyle, M. (2001). *The psychology of happiness* (Second Edition). London, UK: Routledge.

Blanchflower, D. (2009). International evidence on well-being. In A. Krueger (Ed.), *Measuring the subjective wellbeing of nations* (pp. 155-226). Chicago, IL: University of Chicago Press.

Clark, A., Fleche, S., Layard, R., Powdthavee, N., & Ward, G. (2018). *The origins of happiness: The science of well-being over the life course*. Princeton, NJ: Princeton University Press.

Diener, E., Suh, E. M., Lucas, R. E., & Smith, H. L. (1999). Subjective well-being: Three decades of progress. *Psychological Bulletin, 125*(2), 276-302.

Layard, R. (2005). *Happiness*. New York, NY: Penguin.

23  Diener, M., & Diener McGavran, M. (2008). What makes people happy? A developmental approach to the literature on family relationships and well-being. In M. Eid & R. Larsen (Eds.), *The science of subjective well-being.* (pp. 347-375). New York, NY: Guilford Press.

Lucas, R., & Dyrenforth, P. S. (2006). Does the existence of social relationships matter for subjective well-being? In K. D. Vohs & E. J. Finkel (Eds.), *Self and relationships: Connecting intrapersonal and interpersonal processes* (pp. 254-273). New York, NY: Guilford Press.

Masten, A., Cutuli, J., Herbers, J., & Reed, M. (2009). Resilience and development. In S. Lopez & C. R. Snyder (Eds.), *Oxford handbook of positive psychology* (Second Edition, pp. 117-132). New York, NY: Oxford University Press.

Myers, D. (2000). The funds, friends and faith of happy people. *American Psychologist, 55*, 56-67.

24  Luhmann, M., Hofmann, W., Eid, M., & Lucas, R. E. (2012). Subjective well-being and adaptation to life events: A meta-analysis. *Journal of Personality and Social Psychology, 102*(3), 592-615.

25  Diener, E., & Biswas-Diener, R. (2009). Will money increase subjective wellbeing? A literature review and guide to needed research. In E. Diener (Ed.), *The science of wellbeing* (pp. 119-154). New York, NY: Springer.

Howell, R. T., & Howell, C. J. (2008). The relation of economic status to subjective well-being in developing countries: A meta-analysis. *Psychological Bulletin, 134*(4), 536-560.

26  Diener, E., Suh, E. Lucas, R. & Smith, H. (1999). Subjective well-being: Three decades of progress. *Psychological Bulletin, 125*, 273-302.

McKee-Ryan, F., Song, Z., Wanberg, C. R. & Kinicki, A. J. (2005). Psychological and physical well-being during unemployment: A meta-analytic study. *Journal of Applied Psychology, 90*, 53-76.

Michalos, A. (2008). Education, happiness and wellbeing. *Social Indicators Research, 87*, 347-366.

27  Easterlin, R. (1974). Does economic growth improve the human lot? In P. David and M. Reder (Eds.), *Nations and households in economic growth: Essays in honor of Moses Abramovitz* (pp. 89-125). New York, NY: Academic Press.

Stevenson, B., & Wolfers, J. (2008). Economic growth and happiness: Reassessing the Easterlin paradox. *Brookings Papers on Economic Activity*, Spring, 1-87.

28  Dittmar, H., Bond, R., Hurst, M., & Kasser, T. (2014). The relationship between materialism and personal well-being: A meta-analysis. *Journal of Personality and Social Psychology, 107*(5), 879-924.

Fischer, R., & Boer, D. (2011). What is more important for national well-being: Money or autonomy? A meta-analysis of well-being, burnout, and anxiety across 63 societies. *Journal of Personality and Social Psychology, 101*(1), 164-184.

29  Bishop, M. (2012). Quality of life and psychosocial adaptation to chronic illness and acquired disability: A conceptual and theoretical synthesis. In I. Marini & M. Stebnicki (Eds.), *The psychological and social impact of illness and disability* (Sixth Edition, pp. 179-191). New York, NY: Springer.

   Livneh, H., & Antonak, R. F. (2012). Psychological adaptation to chronic illness and disability: A primer for counsellors. In I. Marini & M. Stebnicki (Eds.), *The psychological and social impact of illness and disability* (Sixth Edition, pp. 95-107). New York, NY: Springer.

30  Diener, E. (2009). *Culture and well-being.* New York, NY: Springer.

   Diener, E., & Suh, E. (2000). *Culture and subjective well-being.* Cambridge, MA: MIT Press.

31  Brereton, F., Clinch, J., & Ferreira, S. (2008). Happiness, geography and the environment. *Ecological Economics, 65*, 386-396.

   Diener, E., Oishi, S., & Lucas, R. (2009). Well-being: The science of happiness and life satisfaction. In S. Lopez & C. R. Snyder (Eds.), *Oxford handbook of positive psychology* (Second Edition, pp. 187-194). New York, NY: Oxford University Press.

   Martens, D., & Bauer, N. (2013). Natural environments: A resource for public health and well-being? A literature review. In E. Noehammer (Ed.), *Psychology of well-being: Theory, perspectives and practice* (pp. 173-217). Hauppauge, NY: Nova Science.

   Thompson, C. W., & Aspinall, P. A. (2011). Natural environments and their impact on activity, health, and quality of life. *Applied Psychology: Health and Well-Being, 3*(3), 230-260.

32  Fischer, R., & Van, d. V. (2011). Does climate undermine subjective well-being? A 58-nation study. *Personality and Social Psychology Bulletin, 37*(8), 1031-1041.

33  Blanchflower, D. (2009). International evidence on well-being. In A. Krueger (Ed.), *Measuring the subjective wellbeing of nations* (pp. 155-226). Chicago, IL: University of Chicago Press.

   Diener, E., Suh, E. M., Lucas, R. E., & Smith, H. L. (1999). Subjective well-being: Three decades of progress. *Psychological Bulletin, 125*(2), 276-302.

   Layard, R. (2005). *Happiness.* New York, NY: Penguin.

34  Brickman, P., & Campbell, D. (1971). Hedonic relativism and planning the good society. In M. H. Apley (Ed.), *Adaptation-level theory: A symposium* (pp. 287-302). New York, NY: Academic Press.

35  Lykken, D., & Tellegen, A. (1996). Happiness is a stochastic phenomenon. *Psychological Science, 7*, 186-189.

36  Brickman, P., Coates, D., & Janoff-Bulman, R. (1978). Lottery winners and accident victims: Is happiness relative? *Journal of Personality and Social Psychology, 36*, 917-992.

37  Diener, E., Lucas, R. E., & Scollon, C. N. (2006). Beyond the hedonic treadmill: Revising the adaptation theory of well-being. *American Psychologist, 61*, 305-314.

   Luhmann, M., Hofmann, W., Eid, M., & Lucas, R. E. (2012). Subjective well-being and adaptation to life events: A meta-analysis. *Journal of Personality and Social Psychology, 102*(3), 592-615.

38  Baumeister, R. F., Bratslavsky, E., Finkenauer, C., & Vohs, K. D. (2001). Bad is stronger than good. *Review of General Psychology, 5*(4), 323-370.

39  Hanson, R. (2009). *Buddha's brain: The practical neuroscience of happiness love and wisdom.* Berkeley, CA: New Harbinger.

40  Bao, K. J., & Lyubomirsky, S. (2014). Making happiness last: Using the hedonic adaptation prevention model to extend the success of positive interventions. In A. Parks & S. Schueller (Eds.), *The Wiley Blackwell handbook of positive psychological interventions* (pp. 373-384). Chichester: Wiley.

41  Gilbert, D. (2006). *Stumbling on happiness.* New York, NY: Knopf.

   In 2016 Martin Seligman and colleagues published a book called *Homo prospectus* which argued that modern psychology should shift its focus from investigating how behaviour is influenced by past developmental and genetic factors, or present circumstantial factors. Instead it should investigate how behaviour is largely influenced by our predictions, both accurate and inaccurate, of what the future will hold. Seligman, M., Railton, P., Baumeister, R, & Sripada, C. (2016). *Homo prospectus.* New York, NY: Oxford University Press

42  Lyubomirsky, S. (2013). *The myths of happiness.* New York, NY: Penguin.

43  To test the effectiveness of positive psychology strategies or interventions in improving well-being, researchers have conducted studies or experiments referred to as randomised controlled trials. In these trials participants are assigned at random to either a treatment or control group. Their well-being is assessed before and after the trial. The patterns of improvement in the treatment and control groups are compared. The significance of the difference between the treatment and control group is evaluated with statistical tests, to check if the difference could have occurred by chance. We can place considerable confidence in the results of these sorts of trials, especially if a number of trials conducted in different centres reach the same conclusions. This is usually assessed by combining the

results of many controlled trials into a single statistical analysis, to check that the overall results of all the trials could not have happened by chance. This sort of procedure is called a meta-analysis.

Randomisation is used in controlled trials to prevent results being biased by, for example, all the people with high happiness set-points being assigned to one group and all those with low happiness set-points being assigned to another group.

In randomised controlled trials, usually participants in treatment groups receive a specific positive psychology intervention or use a positive psychology strategy, and those in the control group do not. Treatment groups may receive positive psychology interventions or learn positive psychology strategies in one-to-one meetings with a psychologist or other professional, in group training or therapy sessions or via the internet.

In randomised controlled trials, usually control groups receive no intervention or a placebo. The idea of a placebo comes from medicine. In randomised controlled trials, to test the effectiveness of a new medicine treatment groups are given pills containing the medicine and control groups are given sugar pills. Both treatment and control groups will have expectations of the pill curing their illness, but only those in the treatment group receive the medicine being tested. Therefore, if at the end of the trial the treatment group has improved more than the placebo group, it may be concluded that this was due to the active ingredient in the medicine and not just the expectation of improvement arising from taking a pill. In positive psychology trials, placebos are usually plausible, but inert, activities. For example, if those in the treatment group were invited to write down each evening three things that happened to them that day for which they were grateful, the placebo control group might be asked to write down an early childhood memory each evening.

Randomised controlled trials (and therefore meta-analyses of these trials) have some limitations. For example, people in randomised trials don't choose the sort of treatment they get, and this is quite different from normal help-seeking, where people often choose the treatments they receive or interventions they use. Therefore, the results of randomised controlled trials may not be fully generalisable to normal help-seeking behaviour, where we choose the treatments we get or the positive psychology interventions we want to do, rather than being randomised to them.

44  Bolier, L., Haverman, M., Westerhof, G. J., Riper, H., Smit, F., & Bohlmeijer, E. (2013). Positive psychology interventions: A meta-analysis of randomized controlled studies. *BMC Public Health*, *13*(1), 119.

Carr, A., Cullen, K., & Keeney, C. (2019). Positive psychology interventions: A systematic review and meta-analysis or over 400 randomized controlled trials. Unpublished manuscript.

Casellas-Grau, A., Font, A., & Vives, J. (2014). Positive psychology interventions in breast cancer. A systematic review. *Psycho-Oncology*, *23*(1), 9–19.

Davis, D. E., Choe, E., Meyers, J., Wade, N., Varjas, K., Gifford, A., . . . Worthington, E. L., Jr. (2016). Thankful for the little things: A meta-analysis of gratitude interventions. *Journal of Counselling Psychology*, *63*(1), 20–31.

Diener, E., Tay, L., Heintzelman, S. J., Kushlev, K., Wirtz, D., Lutes, L. D., & Oishi, S. (2017). Findings all psychologists should know from the new science on subjective well-being. *Canadian Psychology*, *58*(2), 87–104.

D'raven, L. L., & Pasha-Zaidi, N. (2014). Positive psychology interventions: A review for counselling practitioners. *Canadian Journal of Counselling and Psychotherapy*, *48*(4), 383–408.

Frisch, M. B. (2013). Evidence-based well-being/positive psychology assessment and intervention with quality of life therapy and coaching and the quality of life inventory (QOLI). *Social Indicators Research*, *114*(2), 193–227.

Hone, L. C., Jarden, A., & Schofield, G. M. (2015). An evaluation of positive psychology intervention effectiveness trials using the re-aim framework: A practice-friendly review. *The Journal of Positive Psychology*, *10*(4), 303-322.

Meyers, M. C., van Woerkom, M., & Bakker, A. B. (2013). The added value of the positive: A literature review of positive psychology interventions in organizations. *European Journal of Work and Organizational Psychology*, *22*(5), 618–632.

Parks, A., & Schueller, S. (2014). *The Wiley Blackwell handbook of positive psychological interventions*. Chichester: Wiley.

Parks, A. C., & Layous, K. (2016). Positive psychological interventions. In J. C. Norcross, G. R. VandenBos, D. K. Freedheim, & R. Krishnamurthy (Eds.), *APA handbook of clinical psychology: Applications and methods* (Volume 3, pp. 439–449). APA, Washington, DC: American Psychological Association.

Quoidbach, J., Mikolajczak, M., & Gross, J.J. (2015). Positive interventions: An emotion regulation perspective. *Psychological Bulletin*, *141*, 655–693.

Rashid, T. (2015). Positive psychotherapy: A strength-based approach. *The Journal of Positive Psychology,10*(1), 25-40.

Rashid, T., & Seligman, M. (2018). *Positive psychotherapy: Clinician manual.* New York, NY: Oxford University Press.

Seligman, M. E. P., Ernst, R. M., Gillham, J., Reivich, K., & Linkins, M. (2009). Positive education: Positive psychology and classroom interventions. *Oxford Review of Education, 35*(3), 293-311.

Seligman, M. E. P., Steen, T. A., Park, N., & Peterson, C. (2005). Positive psychology progress: Empirical validation of interventions. *American Psychologist, 60*(5), 410-421.

Seligman, M. E., Rashid, T., & Parks, A. C. (2006). Positive psychotherapy. *American Psychologist, 61*(8), 774-788.

Sheldon, K. M., & Lyubomirsky, S. (2012). The challenge of staying happier: Testing the hedonic adaptation prevention model. *Personality and Social Psychology Bulletin, 38*(5), 670-680.

Sin, N., & Lyubomirsky, S. (2009). Enhancing well-being and alleviating depressive symptoms with positive psychology interventions: A practice-friendly meta-analysis. *Journal of Clinical Psychology, 65,* 467-487.

Slade, M., Brownell, T., Rashid, T., & Schrank, B. (2017). *Positive psychotherapy for psychosis: A clinician's guide and manual.* Oxford, UK: Routledge.

Walsh, S., Cassidy, M., & Priebe, S. (2016). The application of positive psychotherapy in mental health care: A systematic review. *Journal of Clinical Psychology, 73*(6), 638-651.

Waters, L. (2011). A review of school-based positive psychology interventions. *The Australian Educational and Developmental Psychologist, 28*(2), 75-90.

Wood, A. M., & Johnson, J. (2016). *The Wiley handbook of positive clinical psychology.* Chichester, UK: Wiley

Wood, A. M., & Tarrier, N. (2010). Positive clinical psychology: A new vision and strategy for integrated research and practice. *Clinical Psychology Review, 30,* 819-829.

45  Bridle, C., Spanjers, K., Patel, S., Atherton, N. M., & Lamb, S. E. (2012). Effect of exercise on depression severity in older people: Systematic review and meta-analysis of randomised controlled trials. *The British Journal of Psychiatry, 201*(3), 180-185.

Brown, J. C., Huedo-Medina, T., Pescatello, L. S., Ryan, S. M., Pescatello, S. M., Moker, E., . . . Johnson, B. T. (2012). The efficacy of exercise in reducing depressive symptoms among cancer survivors: A meta-analysis. *PLoS ONE, 7*(1), doi: 10.1371/journal.pone.0030955.

Heinzel, S., Lawrence, J. B., Kallies, G., Rapp, M. A., & Heissel, A. (2015). Using exercise to fight depression in older adults: A systematic review and meta-analysis. *GeroPsych: The Journal of Gerontopsychology and Geriatric Psychiatry, 28*(4), 149-162.

Josefsson, T., Lindwall, M., & Archer, T. (2014). Physical exercise intervention in depressive disorders: Meta-analysis and systematic review. *Scandinavian Journal of Medicine & Science in Sports, 24*(2), 259-272.

Krogh, J., Nordentoft, M., Sterne, J. A. C., & Lawlor, D. A. (2011). The effect of exercise in clinically depressed adults: Systematic review and meta-analysis of randomized controlled trials. *Journal of Clinical Psychiatry, 72*(4), 529-538.

Rethorst, C., Wipfli, B., & Landers, D. (2009). The antidepressive effects of exercise: A meta-analysis of randomized trials. *Sports Medicine, 39,* 491-511.

Silveira, H., Moraes, H., Oliveira, N., Coutinho, E. S. F., Laks, J., & Deslandes, A. (2013). Physical exercise and clinically depressed patients: A systematic review and meta-analysis. *Neuropsychobiology, 67*(2), 61-68.

46  Carlson, C., & Hoyle, R. (1993). Efficacy of abbreviated progressive muscle relaxation training: A quantitative review of behavioural medicine research. *Journal of Consulting and Clinical Psychology, 61*(6), 1059-1067.

Chellew, K., Evans, P., Fornes-Vives, J., Pérez, G., & Garcia-Banda, G. (2015). The effect of progressive muscle relaxation on daily cortisol secretion. *Stress: The International Journal on the Biology of Stress, 18*(5), 538-544.

Esch, T., Fricchione, G., & Stefano, G. (2003). The therapeutic use of the relaxation response in stress-related diseases. *Medical Science Monitor, 9*(2), RA23-34.

Jacobson, E. (1978). *You must relax* (Fifth Edition). New York, NY: McGraw Hill.

Jorm, A., Morgan, A., & Hetrick, S. (2008). Relaxation for depression. *Cochrane Database of Systematic Reviews, 4,* CD007142.

Klainin-Yobas, P., Oo, W. N., Suzanne Yew, P. Y., & Lau, Y. (2015). Effects of relaxation interventions on depression and anxiety among older adults: A systematic review. *Aging & Mental Health, 19*(12), 1043-1055.

Kwekkeboom, K. L., & Gretarsdottir, E. (2006). Systematic review of relaxation interventions for pain. *Journal of Nursing Scholarship, 38*(3), 269-277.

Luebbert, K., Dahme, B., & Hasenbring, M. (2001). The effectiveness of relaxation training in reducing treatment-related symptoms and improving emotional adjustment in acute non-surgical cancer treatment: A meta-analytical review. *Psycho-Oncology, 10*(6), 490-502.

Manzoni, G. M., Pagnini, F., Castelnuovo, G., & Molinari, E. (2008). Relaxation training for anxiety: A ten-years systematic review with meta-analysis. *BMC Psychiatry, 8*, ArtID 41. doi: 10.1186/1471-244X-8-41.

Pagnini, F., Manzoni, G. M., Castelnuovo, G., & Molinari, E. (2013). A brief literature review about relaxation therapy and anxiety. *Body, Movement and Dance in Psychotherapy, 8*(2), 71-81.

47  Bell, A. C., & D'Zurilla, T. J. (2009). Problem-solving therapy for depression: A meta-analysis. *Clinical Psychology Review, 29*(4), 348-353.

Cuijpers, P., van Straten, A., & Warmerdam, L. (2007). Problem solving therapies for depression: A meta-analysis. *European Psychiatry: The Journal of the Association of European Psychiatrists, 22*(1), 9-15.

Kirkham, J. G., Choi, N., & Seitz, D. P. (2016). Meta-analysis of problem solving therapy for the treatment of major depressive disorder in older adults. *International Journal of Geriatric Psychiatry, 31*(5), 526-535.

Malouff, J. M., Thorsteinsson, E. B., & Schutte, N. S. (2007). The efficacy of problem solving therapy in reducing mental and physical health problems: A meta-analysis. *Clinical Psychology Review, 27*, 46-57.

48  Bond, C., Woods, K., Humphrey, N., Symes, W., & Green, L. (2013). Practitioner review: The effectiveness of solution focused brief therapy with children and families: A systematic and critical evaluation of the literature from 1990-2010. *Journal of Child Psychology and Psychiatry, 54*(7), 707-723.

Gingerich, W. J., & Peterson, L. T. (2013). Effectiveness of solution-focused brief therapy: A systematic qualitative review of controlled outcome studies. *Research on Social Work Practice, 23*(3), 266-283.

Kim, J. S. (2008). Examining the effectiveness of solution-focused brief therapy: A meta-analysis. *Research on Social Work Practice, 18*(2), 107-116.

Kim, J. S., Franklin, C., Zhang, Y., Liu, X., Qu, Y., & Chen, H. (2015). Solution-focused brief therapy in china: A meta-analysis. *Journal of Ethnic & Cultural Diversity in Social Work: Innovation in Theory, Research & Practice, 24*(3), 187-201.

Schmit, E. L., Schmit, M. K., & Lenz, A. S. (2016). Meta-analysis of solution-focused brief therapy for treating symptoms of internalizing disorders. *Counselling Outcome Research and Evaluation, 7*(1), 21-39.

49  Babcock, J. C., Gottman, J. M., Ryan, K. D., & Gottman, J. S. (2013). A component analysis of a brief psycho-educational couples' workshop: One-year follow-up results. *Journal of Family Therapy, 35*(3), 252-280.

Gottman, J. M., & Gottman, J. (2015). Gottman couple therapy. In A. Gurman, J. Lebow, & D Snyder (Eds.), *Clinical handbook of couple therapy* (Fourth Edition, pp. 129-157). New York, NY: Guilford.

Gottman, J. M., Gottman, J. S., & Atkins, C. L. (2011). The comprehensive soldier fitness program: Family skills component. *American Psychologist, 66*(1), 52-57.

Shapiro, A., & Gottman, J. M. (2005). Effects on marriage of a psycho-communicative-educational intervention with couples undergoing the transition to parenthood, evaluation at 1-year post intervention. *Journal of Family Communication, 5*(1), 1-24.

Navarra, R. J., Gottman, J. M., & Gottman, J. S. (2016). Sound relationship house theory and relationship and marriage education. In J. J. Ponzetti Jr. (Ed.), *Evidence-based approaches to relationship and marriage education* (pp. 93-107). New York, NY: Routledge.

50  Carr, A., Brosnan, E., & Sharry, J. (2017). Parents Plus systemic, solution-focused parent training programs: Description, review of the evidence-base, and meta-analysis. *Family Process, 56*(3), 652-668.

Forgatch, M. S., & Kjøbli, J. (2016). Parent management training – Oregon model: Adapting intervention with rigorous research. *Family Process, 55*(3), 500-513.

Henggeler, S. W., & Schaeffer, C. M. (2016). Multisystemic therapy®: Clinical overview, outcomes, and implementation research. *Family Process, 55*(3), 514-528.

Horigian, V. E., Anderson, A. R., & Szapocznik, J. (2016). Taking brief strategic family therapy from bench to trench: Evidence generation across translational phases. *Family Process, 55*(3), 529-542.

Kazdin, A. (2017). Parent management training and problem-solving skills training for child and adolescent conduct problems. In J. Weisz & A. Kazdin, (Eds.), *Evidence-based psychotherapies for children and adolescents* (Third Edition, pp. 142-158). New York, NY: Guilford.

Liddle, H. A. (2016) Multidimensional family therapy: Evidence base for transdiagnostic treatment outcomes, change mechanisms, and implementation in community settings. *Family Process, 55*(3), 558-576.

Menting, A. T. A., de Castro, B. O., & Matthys, W. (2013). Effectiveness of the incredible years parent training to modify disruptive and prosocial child behaviour: A meta-analytic review. *Clinical Psychology Review, 33*(8), 901-913.

Robbins, M. S., Alexander, J. F., Turner, C. W., & Hollimon, A. (2016). Evolution of functional family therapy as an evidence-based practice for adolescents with disruptive behaviour problems. *Family Process, 55*(3), 543-557.

Sanders, M. R., Kirby, J. N., Tellegen, C. L. and Day, J. J. (2014). The triple P-positive parenting program: A systematic review and meta-analysis of a multi-level system of parenting support. *Clinical Psychology Review, 34*(4), 337-357.

Thomas, R., Abell, B., Webb, H. J., Avdagic, E., & Zimmer-Gembeck, M. (2017). Parent–child interaction therapy: A meta-analysis. *Paediatrics, 140*(3), doi: 10.1542/peds.2017-0352.

51  Barlow. D., Conklin, L., & Bently, K. (2015). Psychological treatments for panic disorders, phobias, and social and generalized anxiety disorders. In P. E. Nathan and J. M. Gorman (Eds.), *A guide to treatments that work* (Fourth Edition, pp. 409-462). New York, NY: Oxford University Press.

Clark, D., & Beck, A. (2010). *Cognitive therapy of anxiety disorders: Science and practice.* New York, NY: Guilford.

Cooper, K., Gregory, J. D., Walker, I., Lambe, S., & Salkovskis, P. M. (2017). Cognitive behaviour therapy for health anxiety: A systematic review and meta-analysis. *Behavioural and Cognitive Psychotherapy, 45*(2), 110-123.

Cusack, K. J., Jonas, D. E., Forneris, C. A., Wines, C., Sonis, J., Middleton, J. C., . . . Gaynes, B. N. (2016). Psychological treatments for adults with posttraumatic stress disorder: A systematic review and meta-analysis. *Clinical Psychology Review, 43*, 128-141.

Dougherty, D. D., Rauch, S. L., & Jenike, M. A. (2015) Treatments for obsessive-compulsive disorder. In P. E. Nathan and J. M. Gorman (Eds.), *A guide to treatments that work* (Fourth Edition, pp. 545-570). New York, NY: Oxford University Press.

Hofmann, S. G., Wu, J. Q., & Boettcher, H. (2014). Effect of cognitive-behavioural therapy for anxiety disorders on quality of life: A meta-analysis. *Journal of Consulting and Clinical Psychology, 82*(3), 375.

Najavits, L., & Anderson, M. (2015). Psychosocial treatments for posttraumatic stress disorder. In P. E. Nathan and J. M. Gorman (Eds.), *A guide to treatments that work* (Fourth Edition, pp. 571-593). New York, NY: Oxford University Press.

Olatunji, B. O., Cisler, J. M., & Deacon, B. J. (2010). Efficacy of cognitive behavioural therapy for anxiety disorders: A review of meta-analytic findings. *Psychiatric Clinics of North America, 33*(3), 557-577.

Olatunji, B. O., Davis, M. L., Powers, M. B., & Smits, J. A. J. (2013). Cognitive-behavioural therapy for obsessive-compulsive disorder: A meta-analysis of treatment outcome and moderators. *Journal of Psychiatric Research, 47*(1), 33-41.

Pozza, A., & Dèttore, D. (2017). Drop-out and efficacy of group versus individual cognitive behavioural therapy: What works best for obsessive-compulsive disorder? A systematic review and meta-analysis of direct comparisons. *Psychiatry Research, 258*, 24-36.

52  Beck, R. & Fernandez, E. (1998). Cognitive-behavioural therapy in the treatment of anger: A meta-analysis. *Cognitive Therapy and Research, 22*, 63-74.

Del Vecchio, T., & K. D. O'Leary (2004). Effectiveness of anger treatments for specific anger problems: A meta-analytic review. *Clinical Psychology Review, 24*, 15-34.

DiGuiseppe, R., & Tafrate, R. C. (2003). Anger treatments for adults: A meta-analytic review. *Clinical Psychology: Science and Practice, 10*, 70-84.

Edmonson, C. B., & Conger, J. C. (1996). A review of treatment efficacy for individuals with anger problems: Conceptual, assessment, and methodological issues. *Clinical Psychology Review, 16*, 251-275.

Gansle, K. A. (2005). The effectiveness of school-based anger interventions and programs: A meta-analysis. *Journal of School Psychology, 43*, 321-341.

Henwood, K. S., Chou, S., & Browne, K. D. (2015). A systematic review and meta-analysis on the effectiveness of CBT informed anger management. *Aggression and Violent Behaviour, 25*, 280-292.

Ho, B. P. V., Carter, M., & Stephenson, J. (2010). Anger management using a cognitive-behavioural approach for children with special education needs: A literature review and meta-analysis. *International Journal of Disability, Development and Education, 57*, 245-265.

Saini, M. (2009). A meta-analysis of the psychological treatment of anger: Developing guidelines for evidence-based practice. *Journal of the American Academy of Psychiatry and the Law, 34*, 473-488.

Speed, B. C., Goldstein, B. L., & Goldfried, M. R. (2017). Assertiveness training: A forgotten evidence-based treatment. *Clinical Psychology: Science and Practice*, http://dx.doi.org/10.1111/cpsp.1221.

Sukhodolsky, D. G., Kassinove, H., & Gorman, B. S. (2004). Cognitive-behaviour therapy for anger in children and adolescents: A meta-analysis. *Aggression and Violent Behaviour, 9*, 247-269.

Tafrate, R. C. (1995). Evaluation of treatment strategies for adult anger disorders. In H. Kassinove (Ed.), *Anger disorders: Definition, diagnosis, and treatment* (pp. 109-129). Washington, DC: Taylor and Francis.

## Chapter 2. Highly valued goals

1  Locke, E., & Latham, G. (Eds.) (2013). *New developments in goal setting and task performance.* New York, NY: Routledge.
   Seligman, M. E. P., Railton, P., Baumeister, R. F., & Sripada, C. (2013). Navigating into the future or driven by the past. *Perspectives on Psychological Science, 8*(2), 119-141.
   Shin, J. Y., & Steger, M. F. (2014). Promoting meaning and purpose in life. In A. Parks & S. Schueller (Eds.), *The Wiley Blackwell handbook of positive psychological interventions* (pp. 90-110). Chichester, UK: Wiley.
2  Klug, H. J. P., & Maier, G. (2015). Linking goal progress and subjective well-being: A meta-analysis. *Journal of Happiness Studies, 16*(1), 37-65.
   McLeod, A. (2017). *Prospection, well-being and mental health.* Oxford, UK: Oxford University Press.
   Toli, A., Webb, T. L., & Hardy, G. E. (2016). Does forming implementation intentions help people with mental health problems to achieve goals? A meta-analysis of experimental studies with clinical and analogue samples. *British Journal of Clinical Psychology, 55*(1), 69-90.
   Seligman, M. E. P. (2018). *The hope circuit.* London, UK: Nicholas Brealey.
3  Lundgren, T., Luoma, J. B., Dahl, J., Strosahl, K., & Melin, L. (2012). The Bull's-Eye Values Survey: A psychometric evaluation. *Cognitive and Behavioural Practice, 19*, 518-526.
4  Locke, E. & Latham, G. (Ed.) (2013). *New developments in goal setting and task performance.* New York, NY: Routledge.
   Lyubomirsky, S. (2007). *The how of happiness.* New York, NY: Penguin.
5  Ryan, R. M., & Deci, E. L. (2000). Self-determination theory and the facilitation of intrinsic motivation, social development, and well-being. *American Psychologist, 55*, 68-78.
6  Sheldon, K. M., & Lyubomirsky, S. (2006). Achieving sustainable gains in happiness: Change your actions, not your circumstances. *Journal of Happiness Studies, 7*(1), 55-86.
7  Tamir, M., & Diener, E. (2008). Approach-avoidance goals and well-being. One size does not fit all. In A. Elliot (Ed.), *Handbook of approach and avoidance motivation* (pp. 415-431). New York, NY: Psychology Press.
8  Cantor, N., & Sanderson, C. (1999). Life-task participation and well-being. The importance of taking part in daily life. In D. Kahneman E. Dienenr, & N. Schwartz (Eds.), *Well-being: The foundations of hedonic psychology* (pp. 230-243). New York, NY: Russell Sage.
9  King, L. A. (2001). The health benefits of writing about life goals. *Personality and Social Psychology Bulletin, 27*, 798-807.
   Sheldon, K., & Lyubomirsky, S. (2006). How to increase and sustain positive emotion: The effects of expressing gratitude and visualizing best possible selves. *Journal of Positive Psychology, 1*(2), 73-82.
10 Seligman, M. E., Rashid, T., & Parks, A. C. (2006). Positive psychotherapy. *American Psychologist, 61*(8), 774-788.
11 Locke, E., & Latham, G. (Eds.) (2013). *New developments in goal setting and task performance.* New York, NY: Routledge.
12 Doran, G. T. (1981). There's a S.M.A.R.T. way to write management's goals and objectives. *Management Review, 70* (11), 35-36.
   Economy, P. (n.d.). Forget SMART goals - Try CLEAR goals instead. www.inc.com/peter-economy/forget-smart-goals-try-clear-goals-instead.html.

# Chapter 3. Personal strengths

1 Values in action inventory of character strengths: www.viacharacter.org/survey/account/register.

2 Peterson, C. (2006). *A primer in positive psychology.* Oxford, UK: Oxford University Press.
Peterson, C., & Park, N. (2009). Classifying and measuring strengths of character. In S. Lopez & C. R. Snyder (Eds.), *Oxford handbook of positive psychology* (Second Edition, pp. 25-33). New York, NY: Oxford University Press.
Peterson, C., & Seligman, M. (2004). *Character strengths and virtues: A handbook and classification.* New York, NY: Oxford University Press.
Park, N., Barton, M., & Pillay, J. (2017). Strengths of character and virtues: What we know and what we still want to learn. In M. Warren & S. Donaldson (Eds.), *Scientific advances is positive psychology* (pp. 73-102). Santa Barbara, CA: Praeger.

3 Steger, M. F., Hicks, B., Kashdan, T. B., Krueger, R. F., & Bouchard Jr., T. J. (2007). Genetic and environmental influences on the positive traits of the values in action classification, and biometric covariance with normal personality. *Journal of Research in Personality, 41*, 524-539.

4 Park, N., Peterson, C., & Seligman, M. E. P. (2006). Character strengths in fifty-four nations and the fifty U.S. states. *Journal of Positive Psychology, 1*, 118-129.

5 Park, N., Peterson, G., & Seligman, M. E. P. (2004). Strengths of character and well-being. *Journal of Social and Clinical Psychology, 23*, 603-619.
Park, N., & Peterson, C. (2006). Moral competence and character strengths among adolescents: The development and validation of the values in action inventory of strengths for youth. *Journal of Adolescence, 29*, 891-905.
Park, N., & Peterson, C. (2006). Character strengths and happiness among young children: Content analysis of parental descriptions. *Journal of Happiness Studies, 7*, 323-341.
Peterson, C., Ruch, W., Beermann, U., Park, N., & Seligman, M. E. P. (2007). Strengths of character, orientations to happiness, and life satisfaction. *The Journal of Positive Psychology, 2*, 149-156.
Shimai, S., Otake, K., Park, N., Peterson, C., & Seligman, M. E. P. (2006). Convergence of character strengths in American and Japanese young adults. *Journal of Happiness Studies, 7*, 311-322.

6 Peterson, C., Park, N., & Seligman, M. E. P. (2006). Greater strengths of character and recovery from illness. *Journal of Positive Psychology, 1*, 17-26.

7 Peterson, C., Park, N., Pole, N., D'Andrea, W., & Seligman, M. E. (2008). Strengths of character and posttraumatic growth. *Journal of Trauma and Stress, 21*, 214-217.

8 Linley, P., Maltby, J., Wood, A., Joseph, S., Harrington, S., & Peterson, C. (2007). Character strengths in the United Kingdom: The VIA inventory of strengths. *Personality and Individual Differences, 43*, 341-351.

9 Park, N., & Peterson, C. (2006). Moral competence and character strengths among adolescents: The development and validation of the values in action inventory of strengths for youth. *Journal of Adolescence, 29*, 891-905.

10 A summary of the research on the effects of using signature strengths is available at: www.viacharacter.org/www/Research/What-the-Research-Says-About-Character-Strengths-Signature-Strengths.
Allan, B. A., & Duffy, R. D. (2014). Examining moderators of signature strengths use and well-being: Calling and signature strengths level. *Journal of Happiness Studies, 15*(2), 323-337.
Duan, W., Ho, S. M. Y., Tang, X., Li, T., & Zhang, Y. (2014). Character strength-based intervention to promote satisfaction with life in the Chinese university context. *Journal of Happiness Studies, 15*(6), 1347-1361.
Gander, F., Proyer, R. T., Ruch, W., & Wyss, T. (2013). Strength-based positive interventions: Further evidence for their potential in enhancing well-being. *Journal of Happiness Studies, 14*(4), 1241-1259.
Louis, M. C., & Lopez, S. J. (2014). Strengths interventions: Current progress and future directions. In A. Parks & S. Schueller (Eds.), *The Wiley Blackwell handbook of positive psychological interventions* (pp. 66-89). Chichester: Wiley.
Madden, W., Green, S., & Grant, A. M. (2011). A pilot study evaluating strengths-based coaching for primary school students: Enhancing engagement and hope. International. *Coaching Psychology Review, 6*(1), 71-83.
Mitchell, J., Stanimirovic, R., Klein, B., & Vella-Brodrick, D. (2009). A randomised controlled trial of a self-guided internet intervention promoting well-being. *Computers in Human Behaviour, 25*, 749-760.

Mongrain, M., & Anselmo-Matthews, T. (2012). Do positive psychology exercises work? A replication of Seligman et al. *Journal of Clinical Psychology, 68*(4), 382-389.

Proyer, R. T., Gander, F., Wellenzohn, S., & Ruch, W. (2015). Strengths-based positive psychology interventions: A randomized placebo-controlled online trial on long-term effects for a signature strengths vs. a lesser strengths intervention. *Frontiers in Psychology, 6,* 456. doi: 10.3389/fpsyg.2015.00456.

Proyer, R. T., Gander, F., Wellenzohn, S., & Ruch, W. (2014). Positive psychology interventions in people aged 50-79 years: Long-term effects of placebo-controlled online interventions on well-being and depression. *Aging & Mental Health, 18*(8), 997-1005.

Rust, T., Diessner, R., & Reade, L. (2009). Strengths only or strengths and relative weaknesses? A preliminary study. *Journal of Psychology, 143*(5), 465-476.

Seligman, M. E. P., Steen, T. A., Park, N., & Peterson, C. (2005). Positive psychology progress: Empirical validation of interventions. *American Psychologist, 60,* 410-421.

11  Niemiec, R. (2018). *Character strengths interventions: A field guide for practitioners.* Boston, MA: Hogrefe.

12  Niemiec, R., & Danny Wedding, D. (2013) *Positive psychology at the movies: Using films to build virtues and character strengths* (Second Edition). Boston, MA: Hogrefe.

# Chapter 4. Physical exercise

1  Acevedo, E. (2012). *The Oxford handbook of exercise psychology.* New York, NY: Oxford University Press.

Eddekakis, P. (Ed.) (2013). *Routledge handbook of physical activity and mental health.* New York, NY: Routledge.

Lox, C., Ginis, K., & Petruzzello, S. (2014). *The psychology of exercise: Integrating theory and practice* (Fourth Edition). Scottsdale, AZ: Holcomb Hathaway.

World Health Organization (n.d.). Ten facts on physical activity: www.who.int/features/factfiles/physical_activity/en.

2  Bridle, C., Spanjers, K., Patel, S., Atherton, N. M., & Lamb, S. E. (2012). Effect of exercise on depression severity in older people: Systematic review and meta-analysis of randomised controlled trials. *The British Journal of Psychiatry, 201*(3), 180-185.

Brown, J. C., Huedo-Medina, T., Pescatello, L. S., Ryan, S. M., Pescatello, S. M., Moker, E., . . . Johnson, B. T. (2012). The efficacy of exercise in reducing depressive symptoms among cancer survivors: A meta-analysis. *PLoS ONE, 7*(1) doi: 10.1371/journal.pone.0030955.

Heinzel, S., Lawrence, J. B., Kallies, G., Rapp, M. A., & Heissel, A. (2015). Using exercise to fight depression in older adults: A systematic review and meta-analysis. *GeroPsych: The Journal of Gerontopsychology and Geriatric Psychiatry, 28*(4), 149-162.

Josefsson, T., Lindwall, M., & Archer, T. (2014). Physical exercise intervention in depressive disorders: Meta-analysis and systematic review. *Scandinavian Journal of Medicine & Science in Sports, 24*(2), 259-272.

Krogh, J., Nordentoft, M., Sterne, J. A. C., & Lawlor, D. A. (2011). The effect of exercise in clinically depressed adults: Systematic review and meta-analysis of randomized controlled trials. *Journal of Clinical Psychiatry, 72*(4), 529-538.

Rethorst, C., Wipfli, B. & Landers, D. (2009). The antidepressive effects of exercise: A meta-analysis of randomized trials. *Sports Medicine, 39,* 491-511.

Silveira, H., Moraes, H., Oliveira, N., Coutinho, E. S. F., Laks, J., & Deslandes, A. (2013). Physical exercise and clinically depressed patients: A systematic review and meta-analysis. *Neuropsychobiology, 67*(2), 61-68.

3  Wiese, C., Kuykendall, L., & Tay, L. (2018). Get active? A meta-analysis of leisure-time physical activity and subjective well-being. *Journal of Positive Psychology, 13*(1), 57-66.

4  WHO guidelines on physical activity: www.who.int/dietphysicalactivity/factsheet_recommendations/en.

5  American Heart Association guidelines at: www.heart.org/HEARTORG/HealthyLiving/PhysicalActivity/FitnessBasics/Target-Heart-Rates_UCM_434341_Article.jsp#.VuAMIce5Oy8.

6  World Health Organization healthy diet fact sheet: www.who.int/mediacentre/factsheets/fs394/en.

UK Public Health England Eatwell Guide Booklet: https://assets.publishing.service.gov.uk/government/uploads/system/uploads/attachment_data/file/742750/Eatwell_Guide_booklet_2018v4.pdf.

7   UK Chief Medical Officer's Low Risk Drinking Guidelines 2016: https://assets.publishing.service.gov.uk/government/uploads/system/uploads/attachment_data/file/545937/UK_CMOs__report.pdf.

8   American Academy of Sleep Medicine (2014). *International Classification of Sleep Disorders Third Edition (ICSD-3)*. Darien, IL: American Academy of Sleep Medicine.
    During, E. H., & Kawai, M. (2017). The functions of sleep and the effects of sleep deprivation. In M. Miglis (Ed.), *Sleep and neurologic disease* (pp. 55-72). New York, NY: Elsevier.
    Morin, C. M., & Espie, C. A. (2012). *The Oxford handbook of sleep and sleep disorders*. Oxford, UK: Oxford University Press.

9   Edinger, J., & Carney, C. (2015). *Overcoming insomnia: A cognitive behavioural therapy approach* (Second Edition). New York, NY: Oxford University Press.
    Espie, C. A. (2006). *Overcoming insomnia and sleep problems: A self-help guide using cognitive behavioural techniques*. London, UK: Constable & Robinson.

# Chapter 5. Relaxation

1   Bernstein, D., & Borkovec, T. (1973). *Progressive relaxation training: A manual for the helping professions*. Champaign, IL: Research Press.
    Bernstein, D., Borkovec, T., & Hazlett-Stevens, H. (2000). *New directions in progressive relaxation training: A guidebook for helping professionals*. Westport, CT: Praeger.
    Davis, M., Eshelman, E., & McKay, M. (2008). *The relaxation and stress reduction workbook* (Sixth Edition). Oakland, CA: New Harbinger.
    Madders, J. (1997). *The stress and relaxation handbook: A practical guide to self-help techniques*. London, UK: Vermillion.
    McCallie, M., Blum, C., & Hood, C. (2006). Progressive muscle relaxation. *Journal of Human Behaviour in the Social Environment*, 13(3), 51-66.

2   Jacobson, E. (1929). *Progressive relaxation*. Chicago, IL: University of Chicago Press. Reprinted in 1974.
    Jacobson, E. (1934). *You must relax*. New York, NY: Whittlesey House. The fifth edition was published in 1978.

3   Carlson, C., & Hoyle, R. (1993). Efficacy of abbreviated progressive muscle relaxation training: A quantitative review of behavioural medicine research. *Journal of Consulting and Clinical Psychology*, 61(6), 1059-1067.
    Chellew, K., Evans, P., Fornes-Vives, J., Pérez, G., & Garcia-Banda, G. (2015). The effect of progressive muscle relaxation on daily cortisol secretion. *Stress: The International Journal on the Biology of Stress*, 18(5), 538-544.
    Esch, T., Fricchione, G., & Stefano, G. (2003). The therapeutic use of the relaxation response in stress-related diseases. *Medical Science Monitor*, 9(2), RA23-34.
    Jacobson, E. (1978). *You must relax* (Fifth Edition). New York, NY: McGraw Hill.
    Jorm, A., Morgan, A., & Hetrick, S. (2008). Relaxation for depression. *Cochrane database of systematic reviews*, 4, CD007142.
    Klainin-Yobas, P., Oo, W. N., Suzanne Yew, P. Y., & Lau, Y. (2015). Effects of relaxation interventions on depression and anxiety among older adults: A systematic review. *Aging & Mental Health*, 19(12), 1043-1055.
    Kwekkeboom, K. L., & Gretarsdottir, E. (2006). Systematic review of relaxation interventions for pain. *Journal of Nursing Scholarship*, 38(3), 269-277.
    Luebbert, K., Dahme, B., & Hasenbring, M. (2001). The effectiveness of relaxation training in reducing treatment-related symptoms and improving emotional adjustment in acute non-surgical cancer treatment: A meta-analytical review. *Psycho-Oncology*, 10(6), 490-502.
    Manzoni, G. M., Pagnini, F., Castelnuovo, G., & Molinari, E. (2008). Relaxation training for anxiety: A ten-years systematic review with meta-analysis. *BMC Psychiatry*, 8, ArtID 41. doi: 10.1186/1471-244X-8-41.
    Pagnini, F., Manzoni, G. M., Castelnuovo, G., & Molinari, E. (2013). A brief literature review about relaxation therapy and anxiety. *Body, Movement and Dance in Psychotherapy*, 8(2), 71-81.

4   Jacobson, E. (1959). *How to relax and have your baby*. New York, NY: McGraw Hill.

5   Fink, N. S., Urech, C., Cavelti, M., & Alder, J. (2012). Relaxation during pregnancy: What are the benefits for mother, foetus, and the new-born? A systematic review of the literature. *The Journal of Perinatal & Neonatal Nursing*, 26(4), 296-306.

6   Utay, J., & Miller, M. (2006). Guided imagery as an effective therapeutic technique: A brief review of its history and efficacy research. *Journal of Instructional Psychology, 33*(1), 40-43.

7   Giacobbi, P. R., Jr., Stabler, M. E., Stewart, J., Jaeschke, A., Siebert, J. L., & Kelley, G. A. (2015). Guided imagery for arthritis and other rheumatic diseases: A systematic review of randomized controlled trials. *Pain Management Nursing, 16*(5), 792-803.

Gruzelier, J. H. (2002). A review of the impact of hypnosis, relaxation, guided imagery and individual differences on aspects of immunity and health. *Stress: The International Journal on the Biology of Stress, 5*(2), 147-163.

King, K. (2010). A review of the effects of guided imagery on cancer patients with pain. *Complementary Health Practice Review, 15*(2), 98-107.

Posadzki, P., & Ernst, E. (2011). Guided imagery for musculoskeletal pain: A systematic review. *The Clinical Journal of Pain, 27*(7), 648-653.

Posadzki, P., Lewandowski, W., Terry, R., Ernst, E., & Stearns, A. (2012). Guided imagery for non-musculoskeletal pain: A systematic review of randomized clinical trials. *Journal of Pain and Symptom Management, 44*(1), 95-104.

Trakhtenberg, E. (2008). The effects of guided imagery on the immune system: A critical review. *International Journal of Neuroscience, 118*(6), 838-855.

8   Sheikh, A. (2002). *Handbook of therapeutic imagery techniques.* Amityville, NY: Baywood.

Stetter, F., & Kupper, S. (2002). Autogenic training: A meta-analysis of clinical outcome studies. *Applied Psychophysiology and Biofeedback, 27*(1), 45-98.

9   Ost, L. G. (1987). Applied relaxation: Description of a coping technique and review of controlled studies. *Behaviour Research and Therapy, 25*, 397-409.

Hayes-Skelton, S., Roemer, L., Orsillo, S. M., & Borkovec, T. D. (2013). A contemporary view of applied relaxation for generalized anxiety disorder. *Cognitive Behaviour Therapy, 42*(4), 292-302.

## Chapter 6. Meditation

1   Brown, K., Creswell, J., & Ryan, R. (2015). *Handbook of mindfulness: Theory, research, and practice.* New York, NY: Guilford.

Eberth, J., & Sedlmeier, P. (2012). The effects of mindfulness meditation: A meta-analysis. *Mindfulness, 3*(3), 174-189.

Ivtzan, I., & Lomas, T. (2016). *Mindfulness in positive psychology: The science of meditation and well-being.* Oxford, UK: Routledge.

Sedlmeier, P., Eberth, J., Schwarz, M., Zimmermann, D., Haarig, F., Jaeger, S., & Kunze, S. (2012). The psychological effects of meditation: A meta-analysis. *Psychological Bulletin, 138*(6), 1139-1171.

2   Boccia, M., Piccardi, L., & Guariglia, P. (2015) The meditative mind: A comprehensive meta-analysis of MRI studies. *BioMed Research International, 419808*, doi: 10.1155/2015/419808.

Fox, K. C. R., Nijeboer, S., Dixon, M. L., Floman, J. L., Ellamil, M., Rumak, S. P., . . . Christoff, K. (2014). Is meditation associated with altered brain structure? A systematic review and meta-analysis of morphometric neuroimaging in meditation practitioners. *Neuroscience and Biobehavioural Reviews, 43*, 48-73.

Gotink, R. A., Meijboom, R., Vernooij, M. W., Smits, M., & Hunink, M. G. M. (2016). 8-week mindfulness-based stress reduction induces brain changes similar to traditional long-term meditation practice: A systematic review. *Brain and Cognition, 108*, 32-41.

Tang, Y., Hölzel, B., & Posner, M. (2015). The neuroscience of mindfulness meditation. *Nature Reviews: Neuroscience, 16*, 213-225.

3   Lazar, S. W., Kerr, C. E., Wasserman, R. H., Gray, J. R., Greve, D. N., Treadway, M. T., . . . Fischl, B. (2005). Meditation experience is associated with increased cortical thickness. *NeuroReport: For Rapid Communication of Neuroscience Research, 16*(17), 1893-1897.

4   Shamay-Tsoory, S. (2015). The neuropsychology of empathy: Evidence from lesion studies. *Revue De Neuropsychologie, Neurosciences Cognitives Et Cliniques, 7*(4), 237-243.

5   Davidson, R., Kabat-Zinn, J., Schumacher, J., Rosenkranz, M., Muller, D. et al. (2003). Alterations in brain and immune function produced by mindfulness meditation. *Psychosomatic Medicine, 65*, 564-570.

6   Kabat-Zinn, J. (2004). *Wherever you go, there you are* (Revised Edition). London, UK: Piatkus.

Kabat-Zinn, J. (2005). *Coming to our senses.* London, UK: Piatkus.

Kabat-Zinn, J. (2013). *Full catastrophe living* (Revised Edition). London, UK: Piatkus.

7   Segal, Z., Williams M., & Teasdale, J. (2013). *Mindfulness-based cognitive therapy for depression* (Second Edition). New York, NY: Guilford.
    Teasdale, J., Williams, J. M. G., & Segal, Z. (2014). *The mindful way workbook: an 8-week program to free yourself from depression and emotional distress.* New York, NY: Guilford Press.
    Williams, M., Teasdale, J., Segal, Z., & Kabat-Zinn, J. (2007). *The mindful way through depression.* New York, NY: Guilford.
    Williams, M., & Penman, D. D. (2011). *Mindfulness: A practical guide to finding peace in frantic world.* London, UK: Piatkus.
8   Galante, J., Iribarren, S. J., & Pearce, P. F. (2013). Effects of mindfulness-based cognitive therapy on mental disorders: A systematic review and meta-analysis of randomised controlled trials. *Journal of Research in Nursing, 18*(2), 133–155.
    Crowe, M., Jordan, J., Burrell, B., Jones, V. Gillon, D. et al. (2016). Mindfulness-based stress reduction for long-term physical conditions: A systematic review. *Australian and New Zealand Journal of Psychiatry, 50,* 21–32.
    Khoury, B., Sharma, M., Rush, S. E., & Fournier, C. (2015). Mindfulness-based stress reduction for healthy individuals: A meta-analysis. *Journal of Psychosomatic Research, 78*(6), 519–528.
    Gotink, R. A., Chu, P., Busschbach, J. J. V., Benson, H., Fricchione, G. L., & Hunink, M. G. M. (2015). Standardised mindfulness-based interventions in healthcare: An overview of systematic reviews and meta-analyses of RCTs. *PLoS ONE, 10*(4), doi: 10.1371/journal.pone.0124344.
9   van, d. V., Kuyken, W., Wattar, U., Crane, C., Pallesen, K. J., Dahlgaard, J., . . . Piet, J. (2015). A systematic review of mechanisms of change in mindfulness-based cognitive therapy in the treatment of recurrent major depressive disorder. *Clinical Psychology Review, 37,* 26–39.
    Gu, J., Strauss, C., Bond, R., & Cavanagh, K. (2015). How do mindfulness-based cognitive therapy and mindfulness-based stress reduction improve mental health and wellbeing? A systematic review and meta-analysis of mediation studies. *Clinical Psychology Review, 37,* 1–12.
10  Williams, J. M. G., & Penman, D. D. (2011). *Mindfulness: A practical guide to finding peace in frantic world.* London, UK: Piatkus.
11  Sood, A. (2013). On mind-wandering, attention, brain networks, and meditation. *Explore, 9,* 136.
12  Wegner, D. (1989). *White bears and other unwanted thoughts: Suppression, obsession, and the psychology of mental control.* New York, NY: Viking.
13  The distinctions between the doing and being mode described in the text are based on:
    Chapter 2 in: Teasdale, J., Williams, J. M. G., & Segal, Z. (2014). *The mindful way workbook: An 8-week program to free yourself from depression and emotional distress.* New York, NY: Guilford Press.
    Chapter 3 in: Williams, M., & Penman, D. D. (2011). *Mindfulness: A practical guide to finding peace in frantic world.* London, UK: Piatkus.
    Chapter 4 in: Segal, Z., Williams M., & Teasdale, J. (2013). *Mindfulness-based cognitive therapy for depression* (Second edition). New York, NY: Guilford.
14  Beck, A. (1976). *Cognitive therapy and the emotional disorders.* New York, NY: International Universities Press.
    Ellis, A., & Harper, R. (1975). *A new guide to rational living.* North Hollywood, CA: Wiltshire.
    Seligman, M. E. P. (2006). *Learned optimism* (Vintage Edition). New York, NY: Random House.

# Chapter 7. Savouring and flow

1   Martens, D., & Bauer, N. (2013). Natural environments: A resource for public health and well-being? A literature review. In Noehammer, E. (Ed.), *Psychology of well-being: Theory, perspectives and practice* (pp. 173–217). Hauppauge, NY: Nova Science Publishers.
2   Ekers, D., Webster, L., Van Straten, A., Cuijpers, P., Richards, D. & Gilbody, S. (2014). Behavioural activation for depression: An update of meta-analysis of effectiveness and sub-group analysis. *PLoS ONE, 9*(6), e100100. doi: 10.1371/journal.pone.0100100.
    Kuykendall, L., Tay, L., & Ng, V. (2015). Leisure engagement and subjective well-being: A meta-analysis. *Psychological Bulletin, 141*(2), 364–403.
    Mazzucchelli, T. G., Kane, R. T., & Rees, C. S. (2010). Behavioural activation interventions for well-being: A meta-analysis. *The Journal of Positive Psychology, 5*(2), 105–121.
3   MacDonald, R., Kreutz, G., & Laura Mitchell, L. (2012). *Music, health, and well-being.* New York, NY: Oxford University Press.
4   Gick, M. L. (2011). Singing, health and well-being: A health psychologist's review. *Psychomusicology: Music, Mind and Brain, 21*(1-2), 176–207.

5   Burkhardt, J., & Brennan, C. (2012). The effects of recreational dance interventions on the health and well-being of children and young people: A systematic review. *Arts & Health: An International Journal of Research, Policy and Practice, 4*(2), 148-161.

6   Pinquart, M., & Forstmeier, S. (2012). Effects of reminiscence interventions on psychosocial outcomes: A meta-analysis. *Aging & Mental Health, 16*(5), 541-558.

7   Forgeard, M. J. C., & Seligman, M. E. P. (2012). Seeing the glass half full: A review of the causes and consequences of optimism. *Pratiques Psychologiques, 18*(2), 107-120.

8   Brickman, P., & Campbell, D. (1971). Hedonic relativism and planning the good society. In M. H. Apley (Ed.), *Adaptation-level theory: A symposium* (pp. 287-302). New York, NY: Academic Press.

9   Lykken, D., & Tellegen, A. (1996) Happiness is a stochastic phenomenon. *Psychological Science, 7,* 186-189.

10  Bryant, F. B., & Veroff, J. (2007). *Savouring: A new model of positive experience.* Mahwah, NJ: Lawrence Erlbaum.

11  Quoidbach, J., Mikolajczak, M., & Gross, J. (2015). Positive interventions: An emotion regulation perspective. *Psychological Bulletin, 141*(3), 655-693.
    Hurley, D. B., & Kwon, P. (2013). Savouring helps most when you have little: Interaction between savouring the moment and uplifts on positive affect and satisfaction with life. *Journal of Happiness Studies, 14,* 1261-1271.
    Jose, P. E., Lim, B. T., & Bryant, F. B. (2012). Does savouring increase happiness? A daily diary study. *The Journal of Positive Psychology, 7*(3), 176-187.
    Quoidbach, J., Berry, E. V., Hansenne, M., & Mikolajczak, M. (2010). Positive emotion regulation and well-being: Comparing the impact of eight savouring and dampening strategies. *Personality and Individual Differences, 49,* 368-373.
    Smith, J. L., Harrison, P. R., Kurtz, J. L., & Bryant, F. B. (2014). Nurturing the capacity to savour: Interventions to enhance the enjoyment of positive experiences. In A. Parks & S. Schueller (Eds.), *The Wiley Blackwell handbook of positive psychological interventions* (pp. 42-65). Chichester: Wiley.
    Smith, J. L., & Hollinger-Smith, L. (2015). Savouring, resilience, and psychological well-being in older adults. *Aging & Mental Health, 19*(3), 192-200.
    Speer, M. E., Bhanji, J. P., & Delgado, M. R. (2014). Savouring the past: Positive memories evoke value representations in the striatum. *Neuron, 84,* 847-856.

12  Conway, A. M., Tugade, M. M., Catalino, L. I., & Fredrickson, B. L. (2013). The broaden-and-build theory of positive emotions: Form, function, and mechanisms. In S. David, I. Boniwell, & A. Conley Ayers (Eds.), *The Oxford handbook of happiness* (pp. 17-34). New York, NY: Oxford University Press.
    Fredrickson, B. L. (2013). Positive emotions broaden and build. In P. Devine & A. Plant (Eds.), *Advances in experimental social psychology* (Vol. 47, pp. 1-54). San Diego, CA: Academic Press.

13  Bryant, F. B., & Veroff, J. (2007). *Savouring: A new model of positive experience.* Mahwah, NJ: Lawrence Erlbaum.

14  Quoidbach, J., Berry, E. V., Hansenne, M., & Mikolajczak, M. (2010). Positive emotion regulation and well-being: Comparing the impact of eight savouring and dampening strategies. *Personality and Individual Differences, 49*(5), 368-373.
    Miyamoto, Y., & Ma, X. (2011). Dampening or savouring positive emotions: A dialectical cultural script guides emotion regulation. *Emotion, 11*(6), 1346-1357.
    Wood, J. V., Heimpel, S. A., & Michela, J. L. (2003). Savouring versus dampening: Self-esteem differences in regulating positive affect. *Journal of Personality and Social Psychology, 85,* 566-580.

15  Bryant, F. B., & Veroff, J. (2007). *Savouring: A new model of positive experience.* Mahwah, NJ: Lawrence Erlbaum.

16  Wood, J. V., Heimpel, S. A., & Michela, J. L. (2003). Savouring versus dampening: Self-esteem differences in regulating positive affect. *Journal of Personality and Social Psychology, 85,* 566-580.

17  This exercise is based on the daily vacation exercise on page 211 in Bryant, F. B., & Veroff, J. (2007). *Savouring: A new model of positive experience.* Mahwah, NJ: Lawrence Erlbaum.

18  Seligman, M. E., Rashid, T., & Parks, A. C. (2006). Positive psychotherapy. *American Psychologist, 61*(8), 774-788.

19  Pinquart, M., & Forstmeier, S. (2012). Effects of reminiscence interventions on psychosocial outcomes: A meta-analysis. *Aging & Mental Health, 16*(5), 541-558.

20  The savouring reminiscence album exercise is based on the savouring album exercise on page 200 in Lyubomirsky, S. (2007). *The how of happiness.* New York, NY: Penguin.

21  Forgeard, M. J. C., & Seligman, M. E. P. (2012). Seeing the glass half full: A review of the causes and consequences of optimism. *Pratiques Psychologiques, 18*(2), 107-120.

22  Csikszentmihalyi, M. (1990). *Flow: The psychology of optimal experience.* New York, NY: Harper Row.
    Csikszentmihalyi, M. (1997). *Finding flow: The psychology of engagement with everyday life.* New York, NY: Basic Books.

Csikszentmihalyi, M. (2000). *Beyond boredom and anxiety: Experiencing flow in work and play.* San Francisco, CA: Jossey-Bass. (Original work published 1975.)

Csikszentmihalyi, M. (2014). *Applications of flow in human development and education: The collected works of Mihaly Csikszentmihalyi.* New York, NY: Springer.

Csikszentmihalyi, M. (2014). *Flow and the foundations of positive psychology: The collected works of Mihaly Csikszentmihalyi.* New York, NY: Springer.

Csikszentmihalyi, M., & Csikszentmihalyi, I. (1988). *Optimal experience: Psychological studies of flow in consciousness.* Cambridge: Cambridge University Press.

Nakamura, J., & Csikszentmihalyi, M. (2009). Flow theory and research. In S. J. Lopez & C. R. Snyder (Eds.), *Oxford handbook of positive psychology* (Second Edition, pp. 195-206). New York, NY: Oxford University Press.

23  Jackson, S. (1995). Factors influencing the occurrence of flow sate in elite athletes. *Journal of Applied Sport Psychology, 7,* 138-166.

Jackson, S., & Csikszentmihalyi, M. (1999). *Flow in sports: The keys to optimal experiences and performances.* Lower Mitcham, South Australia: Human Kinetics.

Jackson, S., Eklund, R., & Martin A. (2010). *The FLOW manual.* Mind Garden Inc. www.mindgarden.com.

Jackson, S., & Kimiecik, J. (2008). The flow perspective of optimal experience in sport and physical activity. In T. Horn (Ed.), *Advances in sport psychology* (Third Edition, pp. 377-399, 474-477). Champaign, IL, US: Human Kinetics.

24  de Manzano, Ö., Theorell, T., Harmat, L., & Ullén, F. (2010). The psychophysiology of flow during piano playing. *Emotion, 10*(3), 301-311.

25  Csikszentmihalyi, M., & Robinson, R. (1990). *The art of seeing.* Malibu, CA: Getty Publications.

26  Perry, S. K. (1999). *Writing in flow.* Cincinnati, OH: Writer's Digest Books.

27  Neumann, A. (2006). Professing passion: Emotion in the scholarship of professors at research universities. *American Educational Research Journal, 43,* 381-424.

28  Finneran, C. M., & Zhang, P. (2005). Flow in computer-mediated environments: Promises and challenges. *Communications of the Association for Information Systems, 15,* 82-101.

Fang, X., Zhang, J., & Chan, S. S. (2013). Development of an instrument for studying flow in computer game play. *International Journal of Human-Computer Interaction, 29*(7), 456-470.

29  Csikszentmihalyi, M. (2014). *Applications of flow in human development and education: The collected works of Mihaly Csikszentmihalyi.* New York, NY: Springer.

30  Fullagar, C., & Kelloway, E. (2013). Work-related flow. In A. Bakker & K. Daniels (Eds.), *A day in the life of a happy worker* (pp. 41-57). New York, NY: Psychology Press.

31  Csikszentmihalyi, M. (1997). *Finding flow: The psychology of engagement with everyday life.* New York, NY: Basic Books.

32  Rathunde, K. (1988). Optimal experience and the family context. In M. Csikszentmihalyi & I. Csikszentmihalyi (Eds.), *Optimal experience: Psychological studies of flow in consciousness* (pp. 342-363). Cambridge: Cambridge University Press.

33  Csikszentmihalyi, M., & Csikszentmihalyi, I. (1988). *Optimal experience: Psychological studies of flow in consciousness.* Cambridge: Cambridge University Press.

34  Jackson, S., & Kimiecik, J. (2008). The flow perspective of optimal experience in sport and physical activity. In T. Horn (Ed.), *Advances in sport psychology* (Third Edition, pp. 377-399, 474-477). Champaign, IL: Human Kinetics.

# Chapter 8. Gratitude

1  Emmons, R. (2004). *The psychology of gratitude.* New York, NY: Oxford University Press.

Emmons, R. (2007). *Thanks: How practicing gratitude can make you happier.* Boston, MA: Houghton Mifflin.

Emmons, R. (2013). *Gratitude works: A 21-day programme for creating emotional prosperity.* San Francisco, CA: Jossey-Bass.

Rusk, R. D., Vella-Brodrick, D., & Waters, L. (2016). Gratitude or gratefulness? A conceptual review and proposal of the system of appreciative functioning. *Journal of Happiness Studies, 17*(5), 2119-2212.

Watkins, P. C. (2014). *Gratitude and the good life: Toward a psychology of appreciation.* New York, NY: Springer.

Wood, A. M., Froh, J. J., & Geraghty, A. W. A. (2010). Gratitude and well-being: A review and theoretical integration. *Clinical Psychology Review, 30*(7), 890-905.

2  Watkins, P. C. (2014). *Gratitude and the good life: Toward a psychology of appreciation*. New York, NY: Springer.

3  Emmons, R. A., & McCullough, M. E. (2003). Counting blessings versus burdens: An experimental investigation of gratitude and subjective well-being in daily life. *Journal of Personality and Social Psychology, 84*(2), 377-389.

4  Seligman, M. E. P., Steen, T. A., Park, N., & Peterson, C. (2005). Positive psychology progress: Empirical validation of interventions. *American Psychologist, 60*(5), 410-421.

5  Davis, D. E., Choe, E., Meyers, J., Wade, N., Varjas, K., Gifford, A., ... Worthington, E. L., Jr. (2016). Thankful for the little things: A meta-analysis of gratitude interventions. *Journal of Counselling Psychology, 63*(1), 20-31.

   Lomas, T., Froh, J. J., Emmons, R. A., Mishra, A., & Bono, G. (2014). Gratitude interventions: A review and future agenda. In A. Parks & S. Schueller (Eds.), *The Wiley Blackwell handbook of positive psychological interventions* (pp. 3-19). Chichester: Wiley.

6  Emmons, R., & Mishra, A. (2011). Why gratitude enhances wellbeing: What we know and what we need to know. In K. Sheldon, T. Kashdan, & M. Steger (Eds.), *Designing positive psychology: Taking stock and moving forward* (pp. 248-262). New York, NY: Oxford University Press.

   Watkins, P. C. (2014). *Gratitude and the good life: Toward a psychology of appreciation*. New York, NY: Springer.

7  Conway, A. M., Tugade, M. M., Catalino, L. I., & Fredrickson, B. L. (2013). The broaden-and-build theory of positive emotions: Form, function, and mechanisms. In S. David, I. Boniwell, & A. Conley Ayers (Eds.), *The Oxford handbook of happiness* (pp. 17-34). New York, NY: Oxford University Press.

   Fredrickson, B. L. (2013). Positive emotions broaden and build. In P. Devine & A. Plant (Eds.), *Advances in experimental social psychology* (Vol. 47, pp. 1-54). San Diego, CA: Academic Press.

8  Fredrickson, B. L. (2013). Updated thinking on positivity ratios. *American Psychologist, 68*(9), 814-822.

9  Smith, J. L., Harrison, P. R., Kurtz, J. L., & Bryant, F. B. (2014). Nurturing the capacity to savour: Interventions to enhance the enjoyment of positive experiences. In A. Parks & S. Schueller (Eds.), *The Wiley Blackwell handbook of positive psychological interventions* (pp. 42-65). Chichester: Wiley.

10  Brickman, P., & Campbell, D. (1971). Hedonic relativism and planning the good society. In M. H. Apley (Ed.), *Adaptation-level theory: A symposium* (pp. 287-302). New York, NY: Academic Press.

11  Dittmar, H., Bond, R., Hurst, M., & Kasser, T. (2014). The relationship between materialism and personal well-being: A meta-analysis. *Journal of Personality and Social Psychology, 107*(5), 879-924.

   Fischer, R., & Boer, D. (2011). What is more important for national well-being: Money or autonomy? A meta-analysis of well-being, burnout, and anxiety across 63 societies. *Journal of Personality and Social Psychology, 101*(1), 164-184.

12  Wirtz, D., Gordon, C. L., & Stalls, J. (2014). Gratitude and spirituality: A review of theory and research. In C. Kim-Prieto (Ed.), *Religion and spirituality across cultures* (pp. 287-301). New York, NY: Springer.

13  Watkins, P. C. (2014). *Gratitude and the good life: Toward a psychology of appreciation*. New York, NY: Springer.

14  Algoe, S. B. (2012). Find, remind, and bind: The functions of gratitude in everyday relationships. *Social and Personality Psychology Compass, 6*(6), 455-469.

15.  Emmons, R. (2009). Gratitude. In S. Lopez (Ed.), *The encyclopaedia of positive psychology: Volume 1* (pp. 442-447). Chichester, Wiley.

   Chapter 5 in Emmons, R. (2007). *Thanks: How practicing gratitude can make your happier.* Boston, MA: Houghton Mifflin.

16  Baumeister, R. F., Bratslavsky, E., Finkenauer, C., & Vohs, K. D. (2001). Bad is stronger than good. *Review of General Psychology, 5*(4), 323-370.

17  Emmons, R. (2013). *Gratitude works: A 21-day programme for creating emotional prosperity.* San Francisco, CA: Jossey-Bass.

18  Kurtz, J. L. (2008). Looking to the future to appreciate the present: The benefits of perceived temporal scarcity. *Psychological Science, 19*(12), 1238-1241.

19  Koo, M., Algoe, S. B., Wilson, T. D., & Gilbert, D. T. (2008). It's a wonderful life: Mentally subtracting positive events improves people's affective states, contrary to their affective forecasts. *Journal of Personality and Social Psychology, 95*(5), 1217-1224.

20  Watkins, P. C., Cruz, L., Holben, H., & Kolts, R. L. (2008). Taking care of business? Grateful processing of unpleasant memories. *The Journal of Positive Psychology, 3*(2), 87-99.

21  Emmons, R. (2007). *Thanks: How practicing gratitude can make you happier.* Boston, MA: Houghton Mifflin.

# Chapter 9. Optimism

1   The idea that thought is the primary determinant of mood is a central tenet of cognitive behaviour therapy. Hofmann, S. (2013). *The Wiley handbook of cognitive behavioural therapy* (Volumes 1-3). Chichester: Wiley.
2   Seligman, M. E. P. (2006). *Learned optimism* (Vintage Edition). New York, NY: Random House.
3   Matlin, M., & Stang, D. (1978). *The Pollyanna principle*. Cambridge, MA: Schenkman.
4   Tiger, L. (1979). *Optimism: The biology of hope*. New York, NY: Simon and Schuster.
5   Forgeard, M. J. C., & Seligman, M. E. P. (2012). Seeing the glass half full: A review of the causes and consequences of optimism. *Pratiques Psychologiques, 18*(2), 107-120.
6   Nolen-Hoeksema, S. (2000). Growth and resilience among bereaved people. In J. Gillham (Ed.), *The science of optimism and hope* (pp. 107-127). Philadelphia, PA: Templeton Foundation Press.
7   Seligman, M. E. P. (2006). *Learned optimism* (Vintage Edition). New York, NY: Random House.
8   Beck, A. (1976). *Cognitive therapy and the emotional disorders*. New York, NY: International Universities Press.
    Ellis, A., & Harper, R. (1975). *A new guide to rational living*. North Hollywood, CA: Wiltshire.
9   Hofmann, S. (2013). *The Wiley handbook of cognitive behavioural therapy* (Volumes 1-3). Chichester: Wiley.
10  In CBT pessimistic beliefs are referred to as negative automatic thoughts. Socratic questioning or guided discovery are the terms used to describe the sort of questions listed in this section. Behavioural experiments are also used in CBT to find evidence that does not support negative automatic thoughts. Hofmann, S. (2013). *The Wiley handbook of cognitive behavioural therapy* (Volumes 1-3). Chichester: Wiley.
11  Gillham, J. (2000). *The science of optimism and hope*. Philadelphia, PA: Templeton Foundation Press.
    Peterson, C., & Steen, T. (2009). Optimistic explanatory style. In S. Lopez & C. R. Snyder (Eds.), *Oxford handbook of positive psychology* (Second Edition, pp. 313-322). New York, NY: Oxford University Press.
    Seligman, M. E. P. (2006). *Learned optimism* (Vintage Edition). New York, NY: Random House.

# Chapter 10. Solution-finding and problem-solving

1   D'Zurilla, T. J., & Nezu, A. M. (2007). *Problem-solving therapy: A positive approach to clinical intervention* (Third Edition). New York, NY: Springer.
    Nezu, A., Nezu, M., & D'Zurilla, T. (2013). *Problem-solving therapy: A treatment manual*. New York, NY: Springer.
2   Buss, D. (2014). *Evolutionary psychology: The new science of the mind* (Fifth Edition). New York, NY: Routledge.
    Buss, D. (2016). *Handbook of evolutionary psychology: Volumes 1 and 2* (Second Edition). Chichester: Wiley.
3   D'Zurilla, R., & Goldfried, M. (1971). Problem solving and behaviour modification. *Journal of Abnormal Psychology, 78*, 107-126.
    D'Zurilla, T. J., & Nezu, A. M. (2007). *Problem-solving therapy: A positive approach to clinical intervention* (Third Edition). New York, NY: Springer.
    Heppner, P., & Lee, D. (2009). Problem solving appraisal and psychological adjustment. In S. Lopez & C. Snyder (Eds.), *Oxford handbook of positive psychology* (Second Edition, pp. 345-355). New York, NY: Oxford University Press.
    Nezu, A., Nezu, M., & D'Zurilla, T. (2013). *Problem-solving therapy: A treatment manual*. New York, NY: Springer.
    Nezu, A., Nezu, M., & D'Zurilla, T. (2007). *Solving life's problems: A 5-step guide to enhance wellbeing*. New York, NY: Springer.
4   Bell, A. C., & D'Zurilla, T.J. (2009). Problem-solving therapy for depression: A meta-analysis. *Clinical Psychology Review, 29*(4), 348-353.
    Cuijpers, P., van Straten, A., & Warmerdam, L. (2007). Problem solving therapies for depression: A meta-analysis. *European Psychiatry: The Journal of the Association of European Psychiatrists, 22*(1), 9-15.
    Kirkham, J. G., Choi, N., & Seitz, D. P. (2016). Meta-analysis of problem solving therapy for the treatment of major depressive disorder in older adults. *International Journal of Geriatric Psychiatry, 31*(5), 526-535.

Malouff, J. M., Thorsteinsson, E. B., & Schutte, N. S. (2007). The efficacy of problem solving therapy in reducing mental and physical health problems: A meta-analysis. *Clinical Psychology Review, 27*, 46–57.

5   Berg, I. K. (1994). *Family-based services: A solution focused approach*. New York, NY: Norton.

Berg, I. K., & Dolan, Y. (2001). *Tales of solutions: A collection of hope-inspiring stories*. New York, NY: Norton.

Berg, I. K., & Kelly, S. (2000). *Building solutions in child protective services*. New York, NY: Norton.

Berg, I. K., & Miller, S. D. (1992). *Working with the problem drinker: A solution-oriented approach*. New York, NY: Norton.

Berg, I. K., & Reuss, N. (1997). *Solutions step by step: A substance abuse treatment manual*. New York, NY: Norton.

Berg, I. K., & Shilts, L. (2004). *Classroom solutions: The WOWW approach*. Milwaukee, WI: Brief Family Therapy Centre Press.

Berg, I. K., & Steiner, T. (2003). *Children's solution work*. New York, NY: Norton.

Berg, I. K., & Szabó, P. (2005). *Brief coaching for lasting solutions*. New York, NY: Norton.

deShazer, S. (1985). *Keys to solutions in brief therapy*. New York, NY: Norton.

deShazer, S. (1988). *Clues: Investigating solutions in brief therapy*. New York, NY: Norton.

deShazer, S. (1991). *Putting difference to work*. New York, NY: Norton.

deShazer, S. (1994). *Words were originally magic*. New York, NY: Norton.

deShazer, S., & Dolan, Y. (2007). *More than miracles: The state of the art of solution-focused brief therapy*. Binghamton, NY: Haworth.

Duncan, B. (2005). *What's right with you*. Deerfield Beach, FL: Health Communications Inc.

Franklin, C., Trepper, T., Gingerich, W., & McCollum, E. (Eds.) (2012). *Solution-focused brief therapy: A handbook of evidence-based practice*. New York, NY: Oxford University Press.

6   Bond, C., Woods, K., Humphrey, N., Symes, W., & Green, L. (2013). Practitioner review: The effectiveness of solution focused brief therapy with children and families – A systematic and critical evaluation of the literature from 1990–2010. *Journal of Child Psychology and Psychiatry, 54*(7), 707–723.

Gingerich, W. J., & Peterson, L. T. (2013). Effectiveness of solution-focused brief therapy: A systematic qualitative review of controlled outcome studies. *Research on Social Work Practice, 23*(3), 266–283.

Kim, J. S. (2008). Examining the effectiveness of solution-focused brief therapy: A meta-analysis. *Research on Social Work Practice, 18*(2), 107–116.

Kim, J. S., Franklin, C., Zhang, Y., Liu, X., Qu, Y., & Chen, H. (2015). Solution-focused brief therapy in china: A meta-analysis. *Journal of Ethnic & Cultural Diversity in Social Work: Innovation in Theory, Research & Practice, 24*(3), 187–201.

Schmit, E. L., Schmit, M. K., & Lenz, A. S. (2016). Meta-analysis of solution-focused brief therapy for treating symptoms of internalizing disorders. *Counselling Outcome Research and Evaluation, 7*(1), 21–39.

## Chapter 11. Compassionate relationships

1   Demir, M., Orthel, H., & Andelin, A. K. (2013). Friendship and happiness. In S. A. David, I. Boniwell, & A. Conley Ayers (Eds.), *The Oxford handbook of happiness* (pp. 860–870). New York, NY: Oxford University Press.

Lakey, B. (2013). Perceived social support and happiness: The role of personality and relational processes. In S. A. David, I. Boniwell, & A. Conley Ayers (Eds.), *The Oxford handbook of happiness* (pp. 847–859). New York, NY: Oxford University Press.

Saphire-Bernstein, S., & Taylor, S. E. (2013). Close relationships and happiness. In S. A. David, I. Boniwell, & A. Conley Ayers (Eds.), *The Oxford handbook of happiness* (pp. 821–833). New York, NY: Oxford University Press.

2   Barth, J., Schneider, S., & Von Känel, R. (2010). Lack of social support in the aetiology and the prognosis of coronary heart disease: A systematic review and meta-analysis. *Psychosomatic Medicine, 72*(3), 229–238.

Compare, A., Zarbo, C., Manzoni, G. M., Castelnuovo, G., Baldassari, E., Bonardi, A., . . . Romagnoni, C. (2013). Social support, depression, and heart disease: A ten year literature review. *Frontiers in Psychology, 4*, doi: 10.3389/fpsyg.2013.0038.

Decker, C. L. (2007). Social support and adolescent cancer survivors: A review of the literature. *Psycho-Oncology, 16*(1), 1–11.

Graven, L. J., & Grant, J. (2013). The impact of social support on depressive symptoms in individuals with heart failure: Update and review. *Journal of Cardiovascular Nursing, 28*(5), 429-443.

Graven, L. J., & Grant, J. S. (2014). Social support and self-care behaviours in individuals with heart failure: An integrative review. *International Journal of Nursing Studies, 51*(2), 320-333.

Holt-Lunstad, J., Smith, T. B., & Layton, J. B. (2010), Social relationships and mortality risk: A meta-analytic review. *PLoS Med, 7*(7), e1000316. doi: 10.1371/journal.pmed.1000316.

Kruithof, W. J., van Mierlo, M. L., Visser-Meily, J., van Heugten, C. M., & Post, M. W. M. (2013). Associations between social support and stroke survivors' health-related quality of life: A systematic review. *Patient Education and Counselling, 93*(2), 169-176.

Luszczynska, A., Pawlowska, I., Cieslak, R., Knoll, N., & Scholz, U. (2013). Social support and quality of life among lung cancer patients: A systematic review. *Psycho-Oncology, 22*(10), 2160-2168.

Nausheen, B., Gidron, Y., Peveler, R., & Moss-Morris, R. (2009). Social support and cancer progression: A systematic review. *Journal of Psychosomatic Research, 67*(5), 403-415.

Paterson, C., Jones, M., Rattray, J., & Lauder, W. (2013). Exploring the relationship between coping, social support and health-related quality of life for prostate cancer survivors: A review of the literature. *European Journal of Oncology Nursing, 17*(6), 750-759.

Razurel, C., Kaiser, B., Sellenet, C., & Epiney, M. (2013). Relation between perceived stress, social support, and coping strategies and maternal well-being: A review of the literature. *Women & Health, 53*(1), 74-99.

Stopford, R., Winkley, K., & Ismail, K. (2013). Social support and glycaemic control in type 2 diabetes: A systematic review of observational studies. *Patient Education and Counselling, 93*(3), 549-558.

Zarbo, C., Compare, A., Baldassari, E., Bonardi, A., & Romagnoni, C. (2013). In sickness and in health: A literature review about function of social support within anxiety and heart disease association. *Clinical Practice and Epidemiology in Mental Health, 9,* 255-262.

3 Griskevicius, V., Haselton, M. G., & Ackerman, J. M. (2015). Evolution and close relationships. In M. Mikulincer, P. R. Shaver, J. A. Simpson, & J. F. Dovidio (Eds.), *APA handbook of personality and social psychology, volume 3: Interpersonal relations* (pp. 3-32). Washington, DC: American Psychological Association.

Kurzban, R., Burton-Chellew, M., & West, S. A. (2015). The evolution of altruism in humans. *Annual Review of Psychology, 66,* 575-599.

4 DeChurch, L. A., & Mesmer-Magnus, J. (2010). The cognitive underpinnings of effective teamwork: A meta-analysis. *Journal of Applied Psychology, 95*(1), 32-53.

LePine, J. A., Piccolo, R. F., Jackson, C. L., Mathieu, J. E., & Saul, J. R. (2008). A meta-analysis of teamwork processes: Tests of a multidimensional model and relationships with team effectiveness criteria. *Personnel Psychology, 61*(2), 273-307.

McEwan, D., & Beauchamp, M. R. (2014). Teamwork in sport: A theoretical and integrative review. *International Review of Sport and Exercise Psychology, 7*(1), 229-250.

Teubert, D., & Pinquart, M. (2010). The association between co-parenting and child adjustment: A meta-analysis. *Parenting: Science and Practice, 10*(4), 286-307.

5 Gable, S. L., & Gosnell, C. (2011). The positive side of close relationships. In K. Sheldon, T. Kashdan, & M. Steger (Eds.), *Designing positive psychology: Taking stock and moving forward* (pp. 265-279). New York, NY: Oxford University Press.

Donato, S., Pagani, A., Parise, M., Bertoni, A., & Iafrate, R. (2014). The capitalization process in stable couple relationships: intrapersonal and interpersonal benefits. *Procedia - Social and Behavioural Sciences, 140,* 207-211.

Gable, S. L., & Reis, H. T. (2010). Good news! Capitalizing on positive events in an interpersonal context. In M. P. Zanna (Ed.), *Advances in experimental social psychology* (Volume 42, pp. 195-257). San Diego, CA: Academic Press.

Gable, S. L., Reis, H. T., Impett, E. A., & Asher, E. R. (2004). What do you do when things go right? The intrapersonal and interpersonal benefits of sharing positive events. *Journal of Personality and Social Psychology, 87*(2), 238-245.

Woods, S., Lambert, N., Brown, P., Fincham, F., & May, R. (2015). 'I'm so excited for you!' How an enthusiastic responding intervention enhances close relationships. *Journal of Social and Personal Relationships, 32*(1), 24-40.

6 O'Donnell, M. B., Bentele, C. N., Grossman, H. B., Le, Y., Jang, H., & Steger, M. F. (2014). You, me, and meaning: An integrative review of connections between relationships and meaning in life. *Journal of Psychology in Africa, 24*(1), 44-50.

Wissing, M. P. (2014). Meaning and relational well-being: A reflection on the state of the art and a way forward. *Journal of Psychology in Africa, 24*(1), 115-121.

7   Dickerson, S., & Zoccola, P. (2009). Towards a biology of social support. In S. Lopez & C. R. Snyder (Eds.), *Oxford handbook of positive psychology* (Second Edition, pp. 519-526). New York, NY: Oxford University Press.

Eisenberger, N. I. (2013). An empirical review of the neural underpinnings of receiving and giving social support: Implications for health. *Psychosomatic Medicine, 75*(6), 545-556.

Uchino, B. N. (2006). Social support and health: A review of physiological processes potentially underlying links to disease outcomes. *Journal of Behavioural Medicine, 29*(4), 377-387.

8   Conway, A. M., Tugade, M. M., Catalino, L. I., & Fredrickson, B. L. (2013). The broaden-and-build theory of positive emotions: Form, function, and mechanisms. In S. David, I. Boniwell, & A. Conley Ayers (Eds.), *The Oxford handbook of happiness.* (pp. 17-34). New York, NY: Oxford University Press.

Fredrickson, B. L. (2013). Positive emotions broaden and build. In P. Devine & A. Plant (Eds.), *Advances in experimental social psychology* (Vol. 47, pp. 1-54). San Diego, CA: Academic Press.

9   Fredrickson, B. (2014). *Love 2.0: Creating happiness and health in moments of connection.* New York, NY: Penguin.

10  Hasson, U., Ghazanfar, A. A., Galantucci, B., Garrod, S., & Keysers, C. (2012). Brain-to-brain coupling: A mechanism for creating and sharing a social world. *Trends in Cognitive Sciences, 16*(2), 114-121.

Stephens, G. J., Silbert, L. J., & Hasson, U. (2010). Speaker–listener neural coupling underlies successful communication. *PNAS Proceedings of the National Academy of Sciences of the United States of America, 107*(32), 14425-14430.

11  De Dreu, C. K., & Carsten, K. W. (2012). Oxytocin modulates cooperation within and competition between groups: An integrative review and research agenda. *Hormones and Behaviour, 61*(3), 419-428.

IsHak, W. W., Kahloon, M., & Fakhry, H. (2011). Oxytocin role in enhancing well-being: A literature review. *Journal of Affective Disorders, 130*(1-2), 1-9.

12  Fredrickson, B. L., Boulton, A. J., Firestine, A. M., Van Cappellen, P., Algoe, S. B., Brantley, M. M., ... Salzberg, S. (2017). Positive emotion correlates of meditation practice: A comparison of mindfulness meditation and loving-kindness meditation. *Mindfulness, 8*(6), 1623-1633.

Zeng, X., Chiu, C. P. K., Wang, R., Oei, T. P. S., & Leung, F. Y. K. (2015). The effect of loving-kindness meditation on positive emotions: A meta-analytic review. *Frontiers in Psychology, 6*, 14.

13  Kabat-Zinn, J. (2013). *Full catastrophe living* (revised edition). London, UK: Piatkus.

14  Williams, M., & Penman, D. D. (2011). *Mindfulness: A practical guide to finding peace in frantic world.* London, UK: Piatkus.

15  Gilbert, P., McEwan, K., Matos, M., & Rivis, A. (2011). Fears of compassion: Development of three self-report measures. *Psychology and Psychotherapy: Theory, Research and Practice, 84*(3), 239-255.

16  Galante, J., Galante, I., Bekkers, M., & Gallacher, J. (2014). Effect of kindness-based meditation on health and well-being: A systematic review and meta-analysis. *Journal of Consulting and Clinical Psychology, 82*(6), 1101-1114.

Hofmann, S. G., Grossman, P., & Hinton, D. E. (2011). Loving-kindness and compassion meditation: Potential for psychological interventions. *Clinical Psychology Review, 31*(7), 1126-1132.

Shonin, E., Van Gordon, W., Compare, A., Zangeneh, M., & Griffiths, M. D. (2015). Buddhist-derived loving-kindness and compassion meditation for the treatment of psychopathology: A systematic review. *Mindfulness, 6*(5), 1161-1180.

Zeng, X., Chiu, C. P. K., Wang, R., Oei, T. P. S., & Leung, F. Y. K. (2015). The effect of loving-kindness meditation on positive emotions: A meta-analytic review. *Frontiers in Psychology, 6*, 14.

17  Gilbert, P. (2009). *The compassionate mind: A new approach to the challenges of life.* London, UK: Constable & Robinson.

Gilbert, P. (2010). *Compassion focused therapy: The CBT distinctive features series.* London, UK: Routledge.

Gilbert, P., & Choden. (2013). *Mindful compassion.* London, UK: Constable & Robinson.

18  Zessin, U., Dickhäuser, O., & Garbade, S. (2015). The relationship between self-compassion and well-being: A meta-analysis. *Applied Psychology. Health and Well-being, 7*(3), 340-364.

19  Kirby, J. N., Tellegen, C. L., & Steindl, S. R. (2017). A meta-analysis of compassion-based interventions: Current state of knowledge and future directions. *Behavior Therapy, 48*(6), 778-792.

20  Depue, R. A., & Morrone-Strupinsky, J. (2005). A neurobehavioral model of affiliative bonding: Implications for conceptualizing a human trait of affiliation. *Behavioural and Brain Sciences, 28*(3), 313-395.

21  Gilbert, P. (2014). The origins and nature of compassion focused therapy. *British Journal of Clinical Psychology, 53*(1), 6-41.

22  Aknin, L. B., Barrington-Leigh, C., Dunn, E. W., Helliwell, J. F., Burns, J., Biswas-Diener, R., . . . Norton, M. I. (2013). Prosocial spending and well-being: Cross-cultural evidence for a psychological universal. *Journal of Personality and Social Psychology, 104*(4), 635-652.

Alden, L. E., & Trew, J. L. (2013). If it makes you happy: Engaging in kind acts increases positive affect in socially anxious individuals. *Emotion, 13*(1), 64-75.

Layous, K., Lee, H., Choi, I., & Lyubomirsky, S. (2013). Culture matters when designing a successful happiness-increasing activity: A comparison of the United States and South Korea. *Journal of Cross-Cultural Psychology, 44*(8), 1294-1303.

Nelson, S. K., Della Porta, M. D., Bao, K. J., Lee, H. C., Choi, I., & Lyubomirsky, S. (2015). 'It's up to you': Experimentally manipulated autonomy support for prosocial behaviour improves well-being in two cultures over six weeks. *The Journal of Positive Psychology, 10*(5), 463-476.

Nelson, S. K., Layous, K., Cole, S. W., & Lyubomirsky, S. (2016). Do unto others or treat yourself? The effects of prosocial and self-focused behaviour on psychological flourishing. *Emotion, 16*(6), 850-861.

Oarga, C., Stavrova, O., & Fetchenhauer, D. (2015). When and why is helping others good for well-being? The role of belief in reciprocity and conformity to society's expectations. *European Journal of Social Psychology, 45*(2), 242-254.

Otake, K., Shimai, S., Tanaka-Matsumi, J., Otsui, K., & Fredrickson, B. L. (2006). Happy people become happier through kindness: A counting kindnesses intervention. *Journal of Happiness Studies, 7*(3), 361-375.

Pressman, S. D., Kraft, T. L., & Cross, M. P. (2015). It's good to do good and receive good: The impact of a 'pay it forward' style kindness intervention on giver and receiver well-being. *The Journal of Positive Psychology, 10*(4), 293-302.

Velasquez, K. R. (2016). *Altruistic behaviour and subjective well-being: A metaanalytic perspective* (Order No. 10116399). ProQuest Dissertations & Theses A&I: Social Sciences, and Health & Medicine.

Weinstein, N., & Ryan, R. M. (2010). When helping helps: Autonomous motivation for prosocial behaviour and its influence on well-being for the helper and recipient. *Journal of Personality and Social Psychology, 98*(2), 222-244.

23  Glynn, S., Busch, M., Schreiber, G., Murphy, E., Wright, D., Tu, Y. et al. (2003). Effect of a national disaster on blood supply and safety: The September 11 experience. *Journal of the American Medical Association, 289*(17), 2246-2253.

24  Lyubomirsky, S. (2008). *The how of happiness: A scientific approach to getting the life you want.* New York, NY: Penguin.

25  Anderson, N. D., Damianakis, T., Kröger, E., Wagner, L. M., Dawson, D. R., Binns, M. A., . . . Cook, S. L. (2014). The benefits associated with volunteering among seniors: A critical review and recommendations for future research. *Psychological Bulletin, 140*(6), 1505-1533.

Höing, M., Bogaerts, S., & Vogelvang, B. (2016). Helping sex offenders to desist offending: The gains and drains for CoSA volunteers – A review of the literature. *Sexual Abuse: Journal of Research and Treatment, 28*(5), 364-402.

Okun, M. A., Yeung, E. W., & Brown, S. (2013). Volunteering by older adults and risk of mortality: A meta-analysis. *Psychology and Aging, 28*(2), 564-577.

Piliavin, J. A., & Siegl, E. (2015). Health and well-being consequences of formal volunteering. In D. A. Schroeder, & W. G. Graziano (Eds.), *The Oxford handbook of prosocial behaviour* (pp. 494-523). New York, NY: Oxford University Press.

Wheeler, J. A., Gorey, K. M., & Greenblatt, B. (1998). The beneficial effects of volunteering for older volunteers and the people they serve: A meta-analysis. *International Journal of Aging & Human Development, 47*(1), 69-79.

26. Oakley, B., Knafo, A., Madhavan, G., & Sloan Wilson, D. (Eds.) (2012). *Pathological altruism.* New York, NY: Oxford University Press.

Thormar, S. B., Gersons, B. P. R., Juen, B., Marschang, A., Djakababa, M. N., & Olff, M. (2010). The mental health impact of volunteering in a disaster setting: A review. *Journal of Nervous and Mental Disease, 198*(8), 529-538.

27  Bowlby, J. (1988). *A secure base: Clinical implications of attachment theory.* London, UK: Routledge.

28  Cassidy, J., & Shaver, P. (2016). *Handbook of attachment: Theory, research, and clinical applications* (Third Edition). New York, NY: Guilford.

29  Feeney, J. (2016). Adult romantic attachment: Development in the study of couple relationships. In J. Cassidy & P. Shaver (Eds.), *Handbook of attachment: Theory, research, and clinical applications* (Third Edition, pp. 435-463). New York, NY: Guilford.

## Chapter 12. Couple relationships

1   Proulx, C. M., Helms, H. M., & Buehler, C. (2007). Marital quality and personal well-being: A meta-analysis. *Journal of Marriage and Family*, *69*(3), 576-593.
    Robles, T. F., Slatcher, R. B., Trombello, J. M., & McGinn, M. M. (2014). Marital quality and health: A meta-analytic review. *Psychological Bulletin*, *140*(1), 140-187.
    Saphire-Bernstein, S., & Taylor, S. E. (2013). Close relationships and happiness. In S. A. David, I. Boniwell, & A. Conley Ayers (Eds.), *The Oxford handbook of happiness* (pp. 821-833). New York, NY: Oxford University Press.
    Wilcox, W. (2011). *Why marriage matters: Thirty conclusions from the social sciences* (Third Edition). New York, NY: Institute of American Values.

2   Buss, D. M. (2007). The evolution of human mating. *Acta Psychologica Sinica*, *39*(3), 502-512.

3   Gottman, J. M., Driver, J., & Tabares, A. (2015). Repair during marital conflict in newlyweds: How couples move from attack-defend to collaboration. *Journal of Family Psychotherapy*, *26*(2), 85-108.
    Gottman, J. M., Murray, J., Swanson, C., Tyson, R., & Swanson, K. *The mathematics of marriage: Dynamic non-linear models.* Cambridge, MA: MIT Press.
    Gottman, J. M. & Gottman, J. (2015). Gottman couple therapy. In A. Gurman, J. Lebow, & D. Snyder (Eds.), *Clinical handbook of couple therapy* (Fourth Edition, pp. 129-157). New York, NY: Guilford.
    Gottman, J. M., & Gottman, J. (2018). *The science of couples and family therapy: Behind the scenes at the love lab.* New York, NY: Norton.
    Gottman, J. M., Coan, J., Carrere, S., & Swanson, C. (1998). Predicting marital happiness and stability from newlywed interactions. *Journal of Marriage and the Family*, *60*(1), 5-22.
    Gottman, J. M., & Levenson, R. W. (1992). Marital processes predictive of later dissolution: Behaviour, physiology, and health. *Journal of Personality and Social Psychology*, *63*(2), 221-233.
    Gottman, J. M., & Levenson, R. W. (2002). A two-factor model for predicting when a couple will divorce: Exploratory analyses using 14-year longitudinal data. *Family Process*, *41*(1), 83-96.
    Driver, J., Tabares, A., Shapiro, A. F., & Gottman, J. M. (2012). Couple interaction in happy and unhappy marriages: Gottman laboratory studies. In F. Walsh (Ed.), *Normal family processes: Growing diversity and complexity* (Fourth Edition, pp. 57-77). New York, NY: Guilford Press.

4   Gottman, J. M. (1994). *What predicts divorce.* Hillsdale, NJ: Erlbaum.
    Gottman, J.M. (1999). *The marriage clinic.* New York, NY: Norton.
    Gottman, J. M. (2004). *The marriage clinic casebook.* New York, NY: Norton.
    Gottman, J. M. (2011). *The science of trust: Emotional attunement for couples.* New York, NY: Norton.
    Gottman, J. M. (2015). *Principia amoris: The new science of love.* New York, NY: Routledge.
    Gottman, J. S., & Gottman, J. M. (2015). *10 principles for doing effective couples therapy.* New York, NY: Norton.
    Gottman, J. M., & DeClaire (2001). *The relationship cure.* New York, NY: Simon Schuster.
    Gottman, J. M., & Gottman, J. (2015). Gottman couple therapy. In A. Gurman, J. Lebow, & D Snyder (Eds.), *Clinical handbook of couple therapy* (Fourth Edition, pp. 129-157). New York, NY: Guilford.
    Gottman, J. M., & Silver, N. (2015). *The seven principles for making marriage work* (Second Edition). New York, NY: Harmony Books.
    Gottman, J. M., & Silver, N. (2015). *What makes love last.* New York, NY: Simon & Schuster.

5   Babcock, J. C., Gottman, J. M., Ryan, K. D., & Gottman, J. S. (2013). A component analysis of a brief psycho-educational couples' workshop: One-year follow-up results. *Journal of Family Therapy*, *35*(3), 252-280.
    Gottman, J. M., & Gottman, J. (2015). Gottman couple therapy. In A. Gurman, J. Lebow, & D Snyder (Eds.), *Clinical handbook of couple therapy* (Fourth Edition, pp. 129-157). New York, NY: Guilford.
    Gottman, J. M., Gottman, J. S., & Atkins, C. L. (2011). The comprehensive soldier fitness program: Family skills component. *American Psychologist*, *66*(1), 52-57.
    Shapiro, A., & Gottman, J.M. (2005). Effects on marriage of a psycho-communicative-educational intervention with couples undergoing the transition to parenthood, evaluation at 1-year post intervention. *Journal of Family Communication*, *5*(1), 1-24.
    Navarra, R. J., Gottman, J. M., & Gottman, J. S. (2016). Sound relationship house theory and relationship and marriage education. In J. J. Ponzetti Jr. (Ed.), *Evidence-based approaches to relationship and marriage education* (pp. 93-107). New York, NY: Routledge.

6   The practice of helping partners express primary emotions - like hurt - that lie behind secondary emotions - like anger - as a way of improving the quality of couple relationships is central to many

approaches to couple therapy, especially emotion-focused therapy (Greenberg, 2015; Greenberg, Elliott & Pos, 2008). Sue Johnson (2004), who developed emotionally focused couple therapy, has shown that when our need for a secure attachment to our partner is not met, we feel hurt, and often express this as anger. This tends to make our partners become more distant rather than closer to us, and is the root cause of much relationship distress. However, if we express the hurt behind the anger, our partners respond by meeting our need for closeness and attachment. A large body of research shows that emotionally focused couple therapy is a highly effective way of helping distressed couples improve the quality of their relationships (Wiebe & Johnson, 2016).

Greenberg, L. S. (2015). *Emotion-focused therapy* (Second Edition). Washington, DC: American Psychological Association Press.

Greenberg, L. S., Elliott, R., Pos, A. E. (2008). Emotion-focused therapy: An overview. *European Journal of Experiential Psychotherapy, 7,* 19-40.

Johnson, S. (2004). *The practice of emotionally focused couple therapy: Creating connection* (Second Edition). New York, NY: Routledge.

Wiebe, S. A., & Johnson, S. M. (2016). A review of the research in emotionally focused therapy for couples. *Family Process, 55*(3), 390-407.

7   King, L. A. (2001). The health benefits of writing about life goals. *Personality and Social Psychology Bulletin, 27,* 798-807.

Sheldon, K., & Lyubomirsky, S. (2006). How to increase and sustain positive emotion: The effects of expressing gratitude and visualizing best possible selves. *Journal of Positive Psychology, 1* (2), 73-82.

Seligman, M. E., Rashid, T., & Parks, A. C. (2006). Positive psychotherapy. *American Psychologist, 61*(8), 774-788.

## Chapter 13. Positive parent-child relationships

1   Bjorklund, D. F., Yunger, J. L., & Pellegrini, A. D. (2002). The evolution of parenting and evolutionary approaches to childrearing. In M. H. Bornstein (Ed.), *Handbook of parenting: Biology and ecology of parenting* (vol. 2, Second Edition, pp. 3-30). Mahwah, NJ: Lawrence Erlbaum.

Buss, D. (2015). *Evolutionary psychology: The new science of the mind* (Fifth Edition). New York, NY: Routledge.

2   Nelson, S. K., Kushlev, K., & Lyubomirsky, S. (2014). The pains and pleasures of parenting: When, why, and how is parenthood associated with more or less well-being? *Psychological Bulletin, 140*(3), 846-895.

3   Biglan, A., Flay, B. R., Embry, D. D., & Sandler, I. N. (2012). The critical role of nurturing environments for promoting human well-being. *American Psychologist, 67*(4), 257-271.

Bornstein, M. (2002). *Handbook of parenting* (Second Edition, volumes 1-5). Mahwah, NJ: Erlbaum.

Cassidy, J., & Shaver, P. (2016). *Handbook of attachment: Theory, research, clinical applications* (Third Edition). New York, NY: Guilford.

4   Olson, D. (1993). Circumplex model of marital and family systems: Assessing family functioning. In F. Walsh (Ed.). *Normal family processes* (Second Edition, pp. 104-1137). New York, NY: Guilford.

5   Baumrind, D. (1967). Child care practices anteceding three patterns of preschool behaviour. *Genetic Psychology Monographs, 75*(1), 43-88.

6   Larzelere, R., Morris-Sheffield, A., Harrist, A. W. (Eds.). (2013). *Authoritative parenting: Synthesizing nurturance and discipline for optimal child development.* Washington, DC. American Psychological Association.

7   Berlin, L., Zeanah, C., & Lieberman, A. (2016) Prevention and intervention programmes for supporting early attachment. In J. Cassidy and P. Shaver (Eds.), *Handbook of attachment* (Third Edition, pp. 739-758). New York, NY: Guilford.

Biglan, A., Flay, B. R., Embry, D. D., & Sandler, I. N. (2012). The critical role of nurturing environments for promoting human well-being. *American Psychologist, 67*(4), 257-271.

Carr, A. (2014). The evidence-base for family therapy and systemic interventions for child-focused problems. *Journal of Family Therapy, 36*(2), 107-157.

Kaminski, J. W., Valle, L. A., Filene, J. H., & Boyle, C. L. (2008). A meta-analytic review of components associated with parent training program effectiveness. *Journal of Abnormal Child Psychology, 36*(4), 567-589.

Johnson, B. D., Berdahl, L. D., Horne, M., Richter, E. A., & Walters, M. (2014). A parenting competency model. *Parenting: Science and Practice, 14*(2), 92–120.

Leeman, J., Crandell, J. L., Lee, A., Bai, J., Sandelowski, M., & Knafl, K. (2016). Family functioning and the well-being of children with chronic conditions: A meta-analysis. *Research in Nursing & Health, 39*(4), 229–243.

Van Ryzon, M., Kumpfer, C., Fosco, G., & Greenberg, M. (2016). *Family-based prevention programmes for children and adolescents: Theory, research, and large-scale dissemination.* New York, NY: Psychology Press.

8  Bowlby, J. (1969/1982). *Attachment and loss: Volume 1* (First and Second Editions). London, UK: Hogarth Press.

Bowlby, J. (1973). *Attachment and loss: Volume 2.* London, UK: Hogarth.

Bowlby, J. (1980). *Attachment and loss: Volume 3.* London, UK: Hogarth.

Bowlby, J. (1988). *A secure base: Clinical implications of attachment theory.* London, UK: Routledge.

9  Berlin, L., Zeanah, C., & Lieberman, A. (2016). Prevention and intervention programmes for supporting early attachment. In J. Cassidy & P. Shaver (Eds.), *Handbook of attachment* (Third Edition, pp. 739–758). New York, NY: Guilford.

10 Carr, A., Brosnan, E., & Sharry, J. (2017). Parents Plus systemic, solution-focused parent training programs: Description, review of the evidence-base, and meta-analysis. *Family Process, 56*(3), 652–668.

Forgatch, M. S., & Kjøbli, J. (2016). Parent management training – Oregon model: Adapting intervention with rigorous research. *Family Process, 55*(3), 500–513.

Kazdin, A. (2017). Parent management training and problem-solving skills training for child and adolescent conduct problems. In J. Weisz & A. Kazdin (Eds.), *Evidence-based psychotherapies for children and adolescents* (Third Edition, pp. 142–158). New York, NY: Guilford.

Menting, A. T. A., de Castro, B. O., & Matthys, W. (2013). Effectiveness of the incredible years parent training to modify disruptive and prosocial child behaviour: A meta-analytic review. *Clinical Psychology Review, 33*(8), 901–913.

Sanders, M. R., Kirby, J. N., Tellegen, C. L., & Day, J. J. (2014). The triple P-positive parenting program: A systematic review and meta-analysis of a multi-level system of parenting support. *Clinical Psychology Review, 34*(4), 337–357.

Thomas, R., Abell, B., Webb, H. J., Avdagic, E., & Zimmer-Gembeck, M. (2017). Parent–child interaction therapy: A meta-analysis. *Paediatrics, 140*(3), doi: 10.1542/peds.2017-0352.

11 Henggeler, S. W., & Schaeffer, C. M. (2016). Multisystemic therapy®: Clinical overview, outcomes, and implementation research. *Family Process, 55*(3), 514–528.

Horigian, V. E., Anderson, A. R., & Szapocznik, J. (2016). Taking brief strategic family therapy from bench to trench: Evidence generation across translational phases. *Family Process, 55*(3), 529–542.

Liddle, H. A. (2016). Multidimensional family therapy: Evidence base for transdiagnostic treatment outcomes, change mechanisms, and implementation in community settings. *Family Process, 55*(3), 558–576.

Robbins, M. S., Alexander, J. F., Turner, C. W., & Hollimon, A. (2016). Evolution of functional family therapy as an evidence-based practice for adolescents with disruptive behaviour problems. *Family Process, 55*(3), 543–557.

12 Chess, S., & Thomas, A. (1995). *Temperament in clinical practice.* New York, NY: Guilford.

Zentner, M., & Shiner, R. (2012). *Handbook of temperament.* New York, NY: Guilford.

13 Graham McClowry, S. G., Rodriguez, E. T., & Koslowitz, R. (2008). Temperament-based intervention: Re-examining goodness of fit. *European Journal of Developmental Science, 2*(1–2), 120–135.

14 Dweck, C. 2006). *Mindset: The new psychology of success.* New York, NY: Ballantine Books.

15 Peterson, C., & Park, N. (2009). Classifying and measuring strengths of character. In S. Lopez & C. R. Snyder (Eds.), *Oxford handbook of positive psychology* (Second Edition, pp. 25–33). New York, NY: Oxford University Press.

Peterson, C., & Seligman, M. (2004). *Character strengths and virtues: A handbook and classification.* New York, NY: Oxford University Press.

16 Teubert, D., & Pinquart, M. (2010). The association between co-parenting and child adjustment: A meta-analysis. *Parenting: Science and Practice, 10*(4), 286–307.

## Chapter 14. Grit and perfectionism

1  Seligman, M. E. P. (2011). *Flourish: A visionary new understanding of happiness and well-being.* New York, NY: Free Press.

2  Duckworth, A. (2016). *Grit: The power of passion and perseverance.* New York, NY: Scribner.

3 Duckworth, A. L., Peterson, C., Matthews, M. D., & Kelly, D. R. (2007). Grit: Perseverance and passion for long-term goals. *Journal of Personality and Social Psychology, 9*, 1087-1101.
Duckworth, A. L., & Quinn, P. D. (2009). Development and validation of the Short Grit Scale (Grit- S). *Journal of Personality Assessment, 91*, 166-174.
Eskreis-Winkler, L., Duckworth, A. L., Shulman, E., & Beale, S. (2014). The grit effect: Predicting retention in the military, the workplace, school and marriage. *Frontiers in Personality Science and Individual Differences, 5*(36), 1-12.
4 Duckworth, A. (2016). *Grit: The power of passion and perseverance.* New York, NY: Scribner.
5 Macnamara, B. N., Hambrick, D. Z., & Oswald, F. L. (2014). Deliberate practice and performance in music, games, sports, education, and professions: A meta-analysis. *Psychological Science, 25*(8), 1608-1618.
Ericsson, K. A. (2016). Summing up hours of any type of practice versus identifying optimal practice activities: Commentary on MacNamara, Moreau, & Hambrick (2016). *Perspectives on Psychological Science, 11*(3), 351-354.
6 Ericsson, K. A. & Charness, N., Feltovich, P., & Hoffman, R. (2006). *The Cambridge handbook of expert performance.* Cambridge: Cambridge University Press.
Ericsson, K. A. (2006). *Development of professional expertise: Toward measurement of expert performance and design of optimal learning environment.* Cambridge: Cambridge University Press.
7 Howe, M. J. A. (1999). *Genius explained.* New York, NY: Cambridge University Press.
8 Cameron, J., & Pierce. W. (2002). *Rewards and intrinsic motivation: Resolving the controversy.* Westwood, CT: Bergin & Garvey.
Deci, R., Koestner, R., & Ryan, R. (1999). A meta-analytic review of experiments examining the effects of extrinsic rewards on intrinsic motivation. *Psychological Bulletin, 125*, 627-668.
Ryan, R., & Deci, E. (2000). Self-determination theory and the facilitation of intrinsic motivation, social development and well-being. *American Psychologist, 55*, 68-78.
9 Dweck, C. (2006). *Mindset: The new psychology of success.* New York, NY: Ballantine Books.
10 Stoeber, J., & Otto, K. (2006). Positive conceptions of perfectionism: Approaches, evidence, challenges. *Personality and Social Psychology Review, 10*(4), 295-319.
Stoeber, J., Otto, K., & Dalbert, C. (2009). Perfectionism and the big five: Conscientiousness predicts longitudinal increases in self-oriented perfectionism. *Personality and Individual Differences, 47*(4), 363-368.
Lo, A., & Abbott, M. J. (2013). Review of the theoretical, empirical, and clinical status of adaptive and maladaptive perfectionism. *Behaviour Change, 30*(2), 96-116.
11 Shafran, R., Egan, S. & Wade, T. (2010). *Overcoming perfectionism. A self-help guide using cognitive behavioural techniques.* London, UK: Robinson.
Egan, S., Wade, T., Sharfan, R., & Antony, M. (2014). *Cognitive behavioural treatment of perfectionism.* New York, NY: Guilford.
12 Egan, S. J., Wade, T. D., & Shafran, R. (2011). Perfectionism as a transdiagnostic process: A clinical review. *Clinical Psychology Review, 31*(2), 203-212.
Sirois, F., & Molnar, D. (2016). *Perfectionism, health, and well-being.* Cham, Switzerland: Springer.
13 Lloyd, S., Schmidt, U., Khondoker, M., & Tchanturia, K. (2015). Can psychological interventions reduce perfectionism? A systematic review and meta-analysis. *Behavioural and Cognitive Psychotherapy, 43*(6), 705-731.
14 Antony, M., & Swinson, R. (2009). *When perfect isn't good enough* (Second Edition). Oakland, CA: New Harbinger.
Egan, S., Wade, T., Sharfan, R., & Antony, M. (2014). *Cognitive behavioural treatment of perfectionism.* New York, NY: Guilford.
Shafran, R., Egan, S., & Wade, T. (2010). *Overcoming perfectionism: A self-help guide using cognitive behavioural techniques.* London, UK: Robinson.
15 Corcoran, K., Crusius, J., & Mussweiler, T. (2011). Social comparison: Motives, standards, and mechanisms. In D. Chadee (Ed.), *Theories in social psychology* (pp. 119-139). Chichester: Wiley Blackwell.
Suls, J., & Wheeler, L. (2012). Social comparison theory. In P. Van Lange, A. Kruglanski, & E. Higgins (Eds.), *Handbook of theories of social psychology* (Volume 1, pp. 460-482). Thousand Oaks, CA: Sage.
16 Arigo, D., Suls, J. M., & Smyth, J. M. (2014). Social comparisons and chronic illness: Research synthesis and clinical implications. *Health Psychology Review, 8*(2), 154-214.
Ben-Zur, H., & Michael, K. (2009). Social comparisons and well-being following widowhood and divorce. *Death Studies, 33*(3), 220-238.

Brown, D. J., Ferris, D. L., Heller, D., & Keeping, L. M. (2007). Antecedents and consequences of the frequency of upward and downward social comparisons at work. *Organizational Behaviour and Human Decision Processes, 102*(1), 59-75.

Dijkstra, P., Kuyper, H., van, d. W., Buunk, A. P., & van, d. Z. (2008). Social comparison in the classroom: A review. *Review of Educational Research, 78*(4), 828-879.

Myers, T. A., & Crowther, J. H. (2009). Social comparison as a predictor of body dissatisfaction: A meta-analytic review. *Journal of Abnormal Psychology, 118*(4), 683-698.

Stewart, T. L., Chipperfield, J. G., Ruthig, J. C., & Heckhausen, J. (2013). Downward social comparison and subjective well-being in late life: The moderating role of perceived control. *Aging & Mental Health, 17*(3), 375-385.

17  Buunk, B. P., Collins, R. L., Taylor, S. E., Vanyperen, N. W., & Dakof, G. A. (1990). The affective consequences of social comparison: Either direction has its ups and downs. *Journal of Personality and Social Psychology, 59*, 1238-1249.

## Chapter 15. Courage, fear and posttraumatic growth

1  Blanchard, R., Blanchard, C., Griebel, G., & Nutt, D. (2008). *Handbook of anxiety and fear.* Oxford, UK: Academic Press.

LeDoux, J. E., & Pine, D. S. (2016). Using neuroscience to help understand fear and anxiety: A two-system framework. *The American Journal of Psychiatry, 173*(11), 1083-1093.

2  Pury, C., & Lopez, S. (2010). *The psychology of courage. Modern Research on an ancient virtue.* Washington, DC: American Psychological Association.

Pury, C., Starkey, C., Breeden, C., Kelley, C. Murphy, H., & Lowndes, A. (2014). Courage interventions: Future direction and cautions. In A. Parks & S. Schueller (Eds.), *The Wiley handbook of positive psychological intervention* (pp. 168-177). Chichester: Wiley.

3  McGurk, D., & Castro, C. (2010). Courage in combat. In S. Pury & S. Lopez (Eds.), *The psychology of courage: Modern research on an ancient virtue* (pp. 167-185). Washington, DC: American Psychological Association.

Rachman, S. (2010). Courage: A psychological perspective. In S. Pury & S. Lopez (Eds.), *The psychology of courage: Modern research on an ancient virtue* (pp. 91-107). Washington, DC: American Psychological Association.

4.  Hannah, S., Sweeney, P., & Lester, P. (2010). The courageous mindset: A dynamic personality system approach to courage. In S. Pury & S. Lopez (Eds.), *The psychology of courage: Modern research on an ancient virtue* (pp. 125-148). Washington, DC: American Psychological Association.

McGurk, D., & Castro, C. (2010). Courage in combat. In S. Pury & S. Lopez (Eds.), *The psychology of courage: Modern research on an ancient virtue* (pp. 167-185). Washington, DC: American Psychological Association.

5.  Emmelkamp, P., & Ehring, T. (Eds.) (2014). *Wiley handbook of anxiety disorders (Volumes 1 and II).* Chichester: Wiley Blackwell.

6  Abramowitz, J. S., Deacon, B. J., & Whiteside, S. P. (2011). *Exposure therapy for anxiety: Principles and practice.* New York, NY: Guilford Press.

Barrera, T. L., Mott, J. M., Hofstein, R. F., & Teng, E. J. (2013). A meta-analytic review of exposure in group cognitive behavioural therapy for posttraumatic stress disorder. *Clinical Psychology Review, 33*(1), 24-32.

Jayasinghe, N., Finkelstein-Fox, L., Sar-Graycar, L., Ojie, M., Bruce, M. L., & Difede, J. (2017). Systematic review of the clinical application of exposure techniques to community-dwelling older adults with anxiety. *Clinical Gerontologist: The Journal of Aging and Mental Health, 40*(3), 141-158.

Neudeck, P., & Wittchen, H. (Eds.) (2012). *Exposure therapy: Rethinking the model - refining the method.* New York, NY: Springer.

Powers, M. B., Halpern, J. M., Ferenschak, M. P., Gillihan, S. J., & Foa, E. B. (2010). A meta-analytic review of prolonged exposure for posttraumatic stress disorder. *Clinical Psychology Review, 30*(6), 635-641.

Weisman, J. S., & Rodebaugh, T. L. (2018). Exposure therapy augmentation: A review and extension of techniques informed by an inhibitory learning approach. *Clinical Psychology Review, 59*, 41-51.

Woody, S., & Ollendick, T. (2006). Technique factors in treating anxiety disorders. In L. Castonguay & L. Beutler (Eds.), *Principles of therapeutic change that work* (pp. 167-186). Oxford, UK: Oxford University Press.

7   Barlow. D., Conklin, L., & Bently, K. (2015). Psychological treatments for panic disorders, phobias, and social and generalized anxiety disorders. In P. E. Nathan and J. M. Gorman (Eds.), *A guide to treatments that work* (Fourth Edition, pp. 409-462). New York, NY: Oxford University Press.

Clark, D., & Beck, A. (2010). *Cognitive therapy of anxiety disorders: Science and practice*. New York, NY: Guilford.

Cooper, K., Gregory, J. D., Walker, I., Lambe, S., & Salkovskis, P. M. (2017). Cognitive behaviour therapy for health anxiety: A systematic review and meta-analysis. *Behavioural and Cognitive Psychotherapy, 45*(2), 110-123.

Cusack, K. J., Jonas, D. E., Forneris, C. A., Wines, C., Sonis, J., Middleton, J. C., . . . Gaynes, B. N. (2016). Psychological treatments for adults with posttraumatic stress disorder: A systematic review and meta-analysis. *Clinical Psychology Review, 43*, 128-141.

Dougherty, D. D., Rauch, S. L., & Jenike, M. A. (2015) Treatments for obsessive-compulsive disorder. In P. E. Nathan and J. M. Gorman (Eds.), *A guide to treatments that work* (Fourth Edition, pp. 545-570). New York, NY: Oxford University Press.

Hofmann, S. G., Wu, J. Q., & Boettcher, H. (2014). Effect of cognitive-behavioural therapy for anxiety disorders on quality of life: A meta-analysis. *Journal of Consulting and Clinical Psychology, 82*(3), 375.

Najavits, L., & Anderson, M. (2015). Psychosocial treatments for posttraumatic stress disorder. In P. E. Nathan & J. M. Gorman (Eds.), *A guide to treatments that work* (Fourth Edition, pp. 571-593). New York, NY: Oxford University Press.

Olatunji, B. O., Cisler, J. M., & Deacon, B. J. (2010). Efficacy of cognitive behavioural therapy for anxiety disorders: A review of meta-analytic findings. *Psychiatric Clinics of North America, 33*(3), 557-577.

Olatunji, B. O., Davis, M. L., Powers, M. B., & Smits, J. A. J. (2013). Cognitive-behavioural therapy for obsessive-compulsive disorder: A meta-analysis of treatment outcome and moderators. *Journal of Psychiatric Research, 47*(1), 33-41.

Pozza, A., & Dèttore, D. (2017). Drop-out and efficacy of group versus individual cognitive behavioural therapy: What works best for obsessive-compulsive disorder? A systematic review and meta-analysis of direct comparisons. *Psychiatry Research, 258*, 24-36.

8   Cardo , R. A. I., David, O. A., & David, D. O. (2017). Virtual reality exposure therapy in flight anxiety: A quantitative meta-analysis. *Computers in Human Behaviour, 72*, 371-380.

Powers, M. B., & Emmelkamp, P. M. G. (2008). Virtual reality exposure therapy for anxiety disorders: A meta-analysis. *Journal of Anxiety Disorders, 22*(3), 561-569.

9   Frattaroli, J. (2006). Experimental disclosure and its moderators: A meta-analysis. *Psychological Bulletin, 132*(6), 823-865.

Pennebaker, J. W., & Smyth, J. M. (2016). *Opening up by writing it down: How expressive writing improves health and eases emotional pain* (Third Edition). New York, NY: Guilford.

Pennebaker, J. W., & Chung, C. K. (2011). Expressive writing: Connections to physical and mental health. In H. S. Friedman (Ed.), *The Oxford handbook of health psychology* (pp. 417-437). New York, NY: Oxford University Press.

10  Kim, H., & Kim, E. J. (2018). Effects of relaxation therapy on anxiety disorders: A systematic review and meta-analysis. *Archives of Psychiatric Nursing, 32*(2), 278-284.

Montero-Marin, J., Garcia-Campayo, J., López-Montoyo, A., Zabaleta-del-Olmo, E., & Cuijpers, P. (2018). Is cognitive-behavioural therapy more effective than relaxation therapy in the treatment of anxiety disorders? A meta-analysis. *Psychological Medicine, 48*(9), 1427-1436.

11  Banks, K., Newman, E., & Saleem, J. (2015). An overview of the research on mindfulness-based interventions for treating symptoms of posttraumatic stress disorder: A systematic review. *Journal of Clinical Psychology, 71*(10), 935-963.

Hale, L., Strauss, C., & Taylor, B. L. (2013). The effectiveness and acceptability of mindfulness-based therapy for obsessive compulsive disorder: A review of the literature. *Mindfulness, 4*(4), 375-382.

Hofmann, S. G., Sawyer, A. T., Witt, A. A., & Oh, D. (2010). The effect of mindfulness-based therapy on anxiety and depression: A meta-analytic review. *Journal of Consulting and Clinical Psychology, 78*(2), 169-183.

Norton, A. R., Abbott, M. J., Norberg, M. M., & Hunt, C. (2015). A systematic review of mindfulness and acceptance-based treatments for social anxiety disorder. *Journal of Clinical Psychology, 71*(4), 283–301.

Piet, J., Würtzen, H., & Zachariae, R. (2012). The effect of mindfulness-based therapy on symptoms of anxiety and depression in adult cancer patients and survivors: A systematic review and meta-analysis. *Journal of Consulting and Clinical Psychology, 80*(6), 1007–1020.

Vøllestad, J., Nielsen, M. B., & Nielsen, G. H. (2012). Mindfulness- and acceptance-based interventions for anxiety disorders: A systematic review and meta-analysis. *British Journal of Clinical Psychology, 51*(3), 239–260.

12   Clark, D., & Beck, A. (2010). *Cognitive therapy of anxiety disorders: Science and practice.* New York, NY: Guilford.

13   Byrne, M., Carr, A., & Clarke, M. (2004b). The efficacy of couples-based interventions for panic disorder with agoraphobia. *Journal of Family Therapy, 26*, 105–125.

Macdonald, A., Pukay-Martin, N., Wagner, A. C., Fredman, S. J., & Monson, C. M. (2016). Cognitive-behavioural conjoint therapy for PTSD improves various PTSD symptoms and trauma-related cognitions: Results from a randomized controlled trial. *Journal of Family Psychology, 30*(1), 157–162.

Monson, C., Fredman, S., Macdonald, A., Pukay-Martin, N., Resick, P. A., & Schnurr, P. (2012). Effect of cognitive-behavioural couple therapy for PTSD: A randomized controlled trial. *JAMA: Journal of the American Medical Association, 308*, 700–709.

Thompson-Hollands, J., Edson, A., Tompson, M. C., & Comer, J. S. (2014). Family involvement in the psychological treatment of obsessive-compulsive disorder: A meta-analysis. *Journal of Family Psychology, 28*(3), 287–298.

Calhoun, L. G., & Tedeschi, R. G. (2013). *Posttraumatic growth in clinical practice.* London, UK: Routledge.

Wagner, A. C., Torbit, L., Jenzer, T., Landy, M. S. H., Pukay-Martin, N. D., Macdonald, A., . . . Monson, C. M. (2016). The role of posttraumatic growth in a randomized controlled trial of cognitive-behavioural conjoint therapy for PTSD. *Journal of Traumatic Stress, 29*(4), 379–383.

14   Blakey, S. M., & Abramowitz, J. S. (2016). The effects of safety behaviours during exposure therapy for anxiety: Critical analysis from an inhibitory learning perspective. *Clinical Psychology Review, 49*, 1–15.

15   Calhoun, L. G., & Tedeschi, R. G. (1999). *Facilitating posttraumatic growth: A clinician's guide.* Mahwah, NJ: Lawrence Erlbaum.

Calhoun, L. G., & Tedeschi, R. G. (2006). *Handbook of posttraumatic growth: Research and practice.* Mahwah, NJ: Lawrence Erlbaum.

Calhoun, L. G., & Tedeschi, R. G. (2013). *Posttraumatic growth in clinical practice.* New York, NY: Routledge.

Tedeschi, R. G., & Calhoun, L. G. (2004). Posttraumatic growth: Conceptual foundations and empirical evidence. *Psychological Inquiry, 15*(1), 1–18.

Tedeschi, R. G., Cann, A., Taku, K., Senol-Durak, E., & Calhoun, L. G. (2017). The posttraumatic growth inventory: A revision integrating existential and spiritual change. *Journal of Traumatic Stress, 30*(1), 11–18.

Tedeschi, R. G., & Calhoun, L.G. (1996). The posttraumatic growth inventory: Measuring the positive legacy of trauma, *Journal of Traumatic Stress, 9*, 455–471.

16   Casellas-Grau, A., Ochoa, C., & Ruini, C. (2017). Psychological and clinical correlates of posttraumatic growth in cancer: A systematic and critical review. *Psycho-Oncology, 26*(12), 2007–2018.

Elderton, A., Berry, A., & Chan, C. (2017). A systematic review of posttraumatic growth in survivors of interpersonal violence in adulthood. *Trauma, Violence, & Abuse, 18*(2), 223–236.

Koutrouli, N., Anagnostopoulos, F., & Potamianos, G. (2012). Posttraumatic stress disorder and post-traumatic growth in breast cancer patients: A systematic review. *Women & Health, 52*(5), 503–516.

Michael, C., & Cooper, M. (2013). Post-traumatic growth following bereavement: A systematic review of the literature. *Counselling Psychology Review, 28*(4), 18–33.

Sawyer, A., Ayers, S., & Field, A. P. (2010). Posttraumatic growth and adjustment among individuals with cancer or HIV/AIDS: A meta-analysis. *Clinical Psychology Review, 30*(4), 436–447.

Sherr, L., Nagra, N., Kulubya, G., Catalan, J., Clucas, C., & Harding, R. (2011). HIV infection associated post-traumatic stress disorder and post-traumatic growth: A systematic review. *Psychology, Health & Medicine, 16*(5), 612–629.

17   Casellas-Grau, A., Ochoa, C., & Ruini, C. (2017). Psychological and clinical correlates of posttraumatic growth in cancer: A systematic and critical review. *Psycho-Oncology, 26*(12), 2007-2018.

Kolokotroni, P., Anagnostopoulos, F., & Tsikkinis, A. (2014). Psychosocial factors related to posttraumatic growth in breast cancer survivors: A review. *Women & Health, 54*(6), 569-592.

Prati, G., & Pietrantoni, L. (2009). Optimism, social support, and coping strategies as factors contributing to posttraumatic growth: A meta-analysis. *Journal of Loss and Trauma, 14*(5), 364-388.

Shand, L. K., Cowlishaw, S., Brooker, J. E., Burney, S., & Ricciardelli, L. A. (2015). Correlates of posttraumatic stress symptoms and growth in cancer patients: A systematic review and meta-analysis. *Psycho-Oncology, 24*(6), 624-634.

Shaw, A., Joseph, S., & Linley, P. A. (2005). Religion, spirituality, and posttraumatic growth: A systematic review. *Mental Health, Religion & Culture, 8*(1), 1-11.

Turner, J. K., Hutchinson, A., & Wilson, C. (2018). Correlates of post-traumatic growth following childhood and adolescent cancer: A systematic review and meta-analysis. *Psycho-Oncology, 27*(4), 1100-1109.

18   Roepke, A. M. (2015). Psychosocial interventions and posttraumatic growth: A meta-analysis. *Journal of Consulting and Clinical Psychology, 83*(1), 129-142.

Roepke, A. M., Tsukayama, E., Forgeard, M., Blackie, L., & Jayawickreme, E. (2018). Randomized controlled trial of SecondStory, an intervention targeting posttraumatic growth, with bereaved adults. *Journal of Consulting and Clinical Psychology, 86*(6), 518-532.

Shiyko, M. P., Hallinan, S., & Naito, T. (2017). Effects of mindfulness training on posttraumatic growth: A systematic review and meta-analysis. *Mindfulness, 8*(4), 848-858.

## Chapter 16. Assertiveness and anger

1   Blanchard, R., Blanchard, C., Griebel, G., & Nutt, D. (Eds.) (2008). *Handbook of anxiety and fear.* Oxford, UK: Academic Press.

Potegal, M., Stemmler, G., & Spielberger, C. (Eds.) (2010). *International handbook of anger: Constituent and concomitant biological, psychological, and social processes.* New York, NY: Springer.

2   Buss, D. (2015). *Evolutionary psychology: The new science of the mind* (Fifth Edition). New York, NY: Routledge.

3   Alberti, R., & Emmons, M. (2017). *Your perfect right: Assertiveness and equality in your life and relationships* (Tenth Edition). Atascadero, CA: Impact Publishers.

Speed, B. C., Goldstein, B. L., & Goldfried, M. R. (2017). Assertiveness training: A forgotten evidence-based treatment. *Clinical Psychology: Science and Practice,* https://doi.org/10.1111/cpsp.12216.

4   Jones, S. M., & Bodie, G. D. (2014). Supportive communication. In C. R. Berger (Ed.), *Handbook of communication science: Interpersonal communication* (pp. 371-394). Berlin, Germany: De Gruyter Mouton.

MacGeorge, E. L., Feng, B., & Burleson, B. R. (2011). Supportive communication. In M. L. Knapp & J. A. Daly (Eds.), *Handbook of interpersonal communication* (Fourth Edition, pp. 317-354). Los Angeles, CA: Sage.

Rogers, C. R., & Farson, R. E. (2007). Active listening. In S. D. Ferguson & S. Ferguson (Eds.)., *Organizational communication* (Second Edition, pp. 319-334). Piscataway, NJ: Transaction.

5   D'Zurilla, T. J., & Nezu, A. M. (2007). *Problem-solving therapy: A positive approach to clinical intervention* (Third Edition). New York, NY: Springer.

Nezu, A., Nezu, M., & D'Zurilla, T. (2013). *Problem-solving therapy: A treatment manual.* New York, NY: Springer.

6   Potegal, M., Stemmler, G., & Spielberger, C. (Eds.) (2010). *International handbook of anger: Constituent and concomitant biological, psychological, and social processes.* New York, NY: Springer.

7   Beck, R., & Fernandez, E. (1998). Cognitive-behavioural therapy in the treatment of anger: A meta-analysis. *Cognitive Therapy and Research, 22*, 63-74.

Del Vecchio, T., & K. D. O'Leary (2004). Effectiveness of anger treatments for specific anger problems: A meta-analytic review. *Clinical Psychology Review, 24*, 15-34.

DiGuiseppe, R., & Tafrate, R. C. (2003). Anger treatments for adults: A meta-analytic review. *Clinical Psychology: Science and Practice, 10*, 70-84.

Edmonson, C. B., & Conger, J. C. (1996). A review of treatment efficacy for individuals with anger problems: Conceptual, assessment, and methodological issues. *Clinical Psychology Review, 16*, 251-275.

Gansle, K. A. (2005). The effectiveness of school-based anger interventions and programs: A meta-analysis. *Journal of School Psychology, 43*, 321-341.

Henwood, K. S., Chou, S., & Browne, K. D. (2015). A systematic review and meta-analysis on the effectiveness of CBT informed anger management. *Aggression and Violent Behaviour, 25*, 280-292.

Ho, B. P. V., Carter, M., & Stephenson, J. (2010). Anger management using a cognitive-behavioural approach for children with special education needs: A literature review and meta-analysis. *International Journal of Disability, Development and Education, 57*, 245-265.

Saini, M. (2009). A meta-analysis of the psychological treatment of anger: Developing guidelines for evidence-based practice. *Journal of the American Academy of Psychiatry and the Law, 34*, 473-488.

Sukhodolsky, D. G., Kassinove, H., & Gorman, B. S. (2004). Cognitive-behaviour therapy for anger in children and adolescents: A meta-analysis. *Aggression and Violent Behaviour, 9*, 247-269.

Tafrate, R. C. (1995). Evaluation of treatment strategies for adult anger disorders. In H. Kassinove (Ed.), *Anger disorders: Definition, diagnosis, and treatment* (pp. 109-129). Washington, DC: Taylor and Francis.

8   Beck, A. (1999). *Prisoners of hate: The cognitive basis of anger hostility and violence.* New York, NY: Harper/Collins.

Novaco, R., & Taylor, J. (2016). Anger. In A Carr & M. McNulty (Eds.), *Handbook of adult clinical psychology* (Second Edition, pp. 380-404). London, UK: Routledge.

Tafrate, R. C., & Kassinove, H. (2009). *Anger management for everyone.* Atascadero, CA: Impact Publishers.

## Chapter 17. Forgiveness

1   Blanchard, R., Blanchard, C., Griebel, G., & Nutt, D. (2008). *Handbook of anxiety and fear.* Oxford, UK: Academic Press.

LeDoux, J. E., & Pine, D. S. (2016). Using neuroscience to help understand fear and anxiety: A two-system framework. *The American Journal of Psychiatry, 173*(11), 1083-1093.

2.  Akhtar, S., & Parens, H. (2014). *Revenge: Narcissistic injury, rage, and retaliation.* Lanham, MD: Jason Aronson.

3   Exline, J., & Baumeister, R. (2000). Expression forgiveness and repentance: Benefits and barriers. In M. McCullough, K. Pargament, & C. Thoresen (Eds.), *Forgiveness: Theory, research and practice* (pp. 133-155). New York, NY: Guilford.

Fu, W., Zhang, S., Li, X., & Han, Y. (2016). A meta-analysis of relationship between forgiveness and mental health. *Chinese Mental Health Journal, 30*(5), 395-400.

Lovelock, C. R., Griffin, B. J., & Worthington, E. L., Jr. (2013). Forgiveness, religiousness, spirituality, and health in people with physical challenges: A review and a model. *Research in the Social Scientific Study of Religion, 24*, 53-92.

Worthington, E. L., Jr., Witvliet, C. V. O., Pietrini, P., & Miller, A. J. (2007). Forgiveness, health, and well-being: A review of evidence for emotional versus decisional forgiveness, dispositional forgivingness, and reduced unforgiveness. *Journal of Behavioural Medicine, 30*(4), 291-302.

4   McCullough, M. E., Kurzban, R., & Tabak, B. A. (2013). Cognitive systems for revenge and forgiveness. *Behavioural and Brain Sciences, 36*(1), 1-15.

McCullough, M. E., Kurzban, R., & Tabak, B. A. (2013). Putting revenge and forgiveness in an evolutionary context. *Behavioural and Brain Sciences, 36*(1), 41-58.

5   McCullough, M., Root, L. Tabak, B. & van Oyen Witvliet, C. (2009). Forgiveness. In S. Lopez & C.R. Snyder (Eds.), *Oxford handbook of positive psychology* (Second Edition, pp. 427-436). New York, NY: Oxford University Press.

Worthington, E. L., Jr. (2005). *Handbook of forgiveness.* New York, NY: Routledge.

6   Exline, J., & Baumeister, R. (2000). Expressing forgiveness and repentance: Benefits and barriers. In M. McCullough, K. Pargament, & C. Thoresen (Eds.), *Forgiveness: Theory, research and practice* (pp. 133-155). New York, NY: Guilford.

7   McCullough, M., Root, L. Tabak, B., & van Oyen Witvliet, C. (2009). Forgiveness. In S. Lopez & C. R. Snyder (Eds.), *Oxford handbook of positive psychology* (Second Edition, pp. 427-436). New York, NY: Oxford University Press.

8   McCullough, M., Pargament, K., & Thoresen, C. (2000). *Forgiveness: Theory, research and practice* (pp. 133–155). New York, NY: Guilford.
    Worthington, E. L., Jr. (2006). *Forgiveness and reconciliation: Theory and application*. New York, NY: Routledge.
9   Akhtar, S., & Barlow, J. (2018). Forgiveness therapy for the promotion of mental well-being: A systematic review and meta-analysis. *Trauma, Violence, & Abuse, 19*(1), 107-122.
    Baskin, T. W., & Enright, R. D. (2004). Intervention studies on forgiveness: A meta-analysis. *Journal of Counselling & Development, 82*(1), 79–90.
    Lundahl, B. W., Taylor, M. J., Stevenson, R., & Roberts, K. D. (2008). Process-based forgiveness interventions: A meta-analytic review. *Research on Social Work Practice, 18*(5), 465-478.
    Recine, A. (2015). Designing forgiveness interventions. Guidance from five meta-analyses. *Journal of Holistic Nursing, 33*(2), 161-167.
    Rainey, C. A., Readdick, C. A., & Thyer, B. A. (2012). Forgiveness-based group therapy: A meta-analysis of outcome studies published from 1993-2006. *Best Practices in Mental Health: An International Journal, 8*(1), 29-51.
    Wade, N. G., Hoyt, W. T., Kidwell, J. E. M., & Worthington, E. L., Jr. (2014). Efficacy of psychotherapeutic interventions to promote forgiveness: A meta-analysis. *Journal of Consulting and Clinical Psychology, 82*(1), 154-170.
    Worthington, E. L., Jr., Griffin, B. J., Lavelock, C. R., Hughes, C. M., Greeer, C. L., Sandage, S. J., & Rye, M. S. (2016). Interventions to promote forgiveness are exemplars of positive clinical psychology. In A. Parks & S. Schueller (Eds.), *The Wiley Blackwell handbook of positive psychological interventions* (pp. 20–41). Chichester: Wiley.
    Worthington, E. L., Jr., Wade, N. G., & Hoyt, W. T. (2014). Positive psychological interventions for promoting forgiveness: History, present status, and future prospects. In A. Wood & J. Johnson (Eds.), *The Wiley handbook of positive clinical psychology* (pp. 364-380) Chichester: Wiley.
10  Worthington, E. L., Jr., Witvliet, C. V. O., Pietrini, P., & Miller, A. J. (2007). Forgiveness, health, and well-being: A review of evidence for emotional versus decisional forgiveness, dispositional forgivingness, and reduced unforgiveness. *Journal of Behavioural Medicine, 30*(4), 291-302.
11  Worthington, E. L., Jr. (2016). *The path to REACH forgiveness: Less than two hours to becoming a more forgiving person self-directed learning workbook*. Virginia Commonwealth University, USA. www.evworthington-forgiveness.com/diy-workbooks.
    Worthington, E. L., Jr. (2001). *Five steps to forgiveness: The art and science of forgiving*. New York, NY: Crown.
    Worthington, E. L., Jr., Griffin, B. J., Lavelock, C. R., Hughes, C. M., Greeer, C. L., Sandage, S. J., & Rye, M. S. (2016). Interventions to promote forgiveness are exemplars of positive clinical psychology. In A. Parks & S. Schueller (Eds.), *The Wiley Blackwell handbook of positive psychological interventions* (pp. 20–41). Chichester: Wiley.
12  The practice of acting out imagined conversations using two chairs, often referred to as 'chair work', has been most extensively developed and researched within the context of emotion-focused therapy, by Robert Elliott and Les Greenberg: Elliott, R., Watson, J. C., Goldman, R. N., & Greenberg, L. S. (2004). *Learning emotion-focused therapy: The process-experiential approach to change*. Washington, DC: American Psychological Association. Chapter 11. Two-chair work for conflict splits. Chapter 12. Empty chair work for unfinished interpersonal issues.
13  Jeter, W. K., & Brannon, L. A. (2017). The effect of mindfulness and implementation planning on the process of granting and seeking forgiveness among young adults. *Mindfulness, 8*(5), 1304-1318.
    Oman, D., Shapiro, S. L., Thoresen, C. E., Plante, T. G., & Flinders, T. (2008). Meditation lowers stress and supports forgiveness among college students: A randomized controlled trial. *Journal of American College Health, 56*(5), 569-578.

## Chapter 18. Managing your life

1   Schueller, S. M. (2014). Person-activity fit in positive psychological interventions. In A. Parks & S. Schueller (Eds.), *The Wiley Blackwell handbook of positive psychological interventions* (pp. 385–402). Chichester: Wiley.
    Lyubomirsky, S., Dickerhoof, R., Boehm, J. K., & Sheldon, K. M. (2011). Becoming happier takes both a will and a proper way: An experimental longitudinal intervention to boost well-being. *Emotion, 11*(2), 391-402.

2   Lyubomirsky, S., & Layous, K. (2013). How do simple positive activities increase well-being? *Current Directions in Psychological Science, 22*(1), 57-62.
    Lyubomirsky, S., Dickerhoof, R., Boehm, J. K., & Sheldon, K. M. (2011). Becoming happier takes both a will and a proper way: An experimental longitudinal intervention to boost well-being. *Emotion, 11*(2), 391-402.
3   Weber, B., & Hertel, G. (2007). Motivation gains of inferior group members: A meta-analytical review. *Journal of Personality and Social Psychology, 93*(6), 973-993.
4   Bao, K. J., & Lyubomirsky, S. (2014). Making happiness last: Using the hedonic adaptation prevention model to extend the success of positive interventions. In A. Parks & S. Schueller (Eds.), *The Wiley Blackwell handbook of positive psychological interventions* (pp. 373-384). Chichester: Wiley.
5   Witkietvitz, K., & Kirouac, M. (2016). Relapse prevention. In C. M. Nezu & A. M. Nezu (Eds.), *The Oxford handbook of cognitive and behavioural therapies* (pp. 215-228). New York, NY: Oxford University Press.
    Witkiewitz, K., & Marlatt, G. A. (2007). *Therapist's guide to evidence-based relapse prevention.* San Diego, CA: Elsevier Academic Press.

# Index